A Lector's Guide & Commentary

To the Revised Common Lectionary

Year B

J. Ted Blakley

St. Mark's Press
www.stmarkspress.net

A Lector's Guide and Commentary to the Revised Common Lectionary, Year B.

St. Mark's Press
A Ministry of Good Shepherd Episcopal Church
8021 West 21st Street North
Wichita, KS 67205-1743

Phone: 1-800-365-0439
Email: stmarkspress@gmail.com
For orders and information: www.stmarkspress.net

Cover Image: Ian Britton
Cover and Interior Design: J. Ted Blakley

ISBN-10: 0-9839-8990-7
ISBN-13: 978-0-9839-8990-5

I dedicate my third book to my third child,
whose biblical namesake just happens appear
in Year B and only in Year B (Esther 7, Prop 21).

to Esther

You shine like a star with the courage,
strength and independence of Queen Esther;
may God's Word and Spirit bless you with the same
grace and laughter that you have blessed us with.

Εἰρήνη τοῦ Χριστοῦ σοι,
θύγατερ.

Peace of Christ to you,
Daughter.

Praise the Lord, praise the Lord,
Let the earth hear His voice!
Praise the Lord, praise the Lord,
Let the people rejoice!
O come to the Father, through Jesus the Son,
And give Him the glory, great things He hath done.

— *To God Be the Glory* by Fanny Crosby

TABLE OF CONTENTS

AUTHOR'S PREFACE

He said to me, "Mortal, can these bones live?"
I answered, "O Lord GOD, you know."

Ezekiel 37:3

Some people came from Jairus' house to say,
"Your daughter is dead. Why trouble the teacher any further?"
But overhearing what they said, Jesus said to the leader of the synagogue,
"Do not fear, only believe."

Mark 5:35–36

This book has a story… a death and resurrection story.

Three years ago, I was approached by St. Mark's Press to revise *A Lector's Guide to the Episcopal Eucharistic Lectionary* by Frank Mulligan, which unfortunately had been rendered obsolete by the adoption of the Revised Common Lectionary (RCL) by The Episcopal Church in 2006. St. Mark's Press commissioned me to update Mulligan's work by bringing it into conformity with the RCL. At least, that was the plan, but plans have a way of changing.

As I started working on the revised edition, a new vision for the guide began to emerge. What if the guide were designed not only for those who *read* the Scriptures aloud in worship, but also for those who *hear* the Scriptures being read. In short, what if we produced a combination *lector's* guide and *listener's* guide? Might this be a way of helping people engage the Scriptures? Might this transform the lectionary from just a convenient list of readings to a tool of community spiritual formation. Imagine what could happen, if not only lectors and lay readers, but all those in the pews developed a habit of reading, studying, and praying the lectionary readings in preparation for worship. What if, while lectors are practicing and preparing themselves to proclaim the Word of God through the public reading of Holy Scripture, the rest of the Christian community is preparing itself to receive the Word of God by engaging the readings in advance? This new vision could be achieved if we expanded the commentary portion of the guide. In *A Lector's Guide*, Mulligan offered a very brief "General Sense" of each reading (30 to 70 words). My thought was to offer a much longer, yet still brief "Commentary" (400 to 800 words) that would illuminate a reading by explaining it and by situating it within its historical, cultural, and literary contexts.

I presented this new vision to St. Mark's Press. They offered their enthusiastic support, and *A Lector's Guide and Commentary to the Revised Common Lectionary* (LGC) was born. Thus, within a few months, the project that began as a single-volume revision of an earlier work soon became a completely new, three-volume series. Since I began the project in a Year B, Year C was the first volume to be published. Year C came out in June 2009, and Year A appeared the following year in October 2010. So, while Year B is the second volume in the LGC series, it is the final volume to be published.

Friends of Year B

But Year B almost wasn't.

Earlier this year, before the manuscript was a third complete, I received the sudden and unexpected news that I had lost my job; my position had been eliminated due to a lack of funds. Losing a job is never easy, and my concern about the future was compounded by the fact that there are many fewer jobs in a depressed economy and my wife, Rebekah, was pregnant with our fourth child. Furthermore, I did not know what would happen to Year B. Without an income and needing to find a new job, I wondered where would I get the time and energy to finish the book. While other types of writing projects might be able to be put on hold, Year B could not; it needed to be ready by Advent. If Year B did not get published this year, then the chances were that it would never get published. That was a dark thought.

But, into this darkness, God shone a ray of light: the Friends of Year B. The Friends of Year B is an ad hoc group made up of some two dozen parishioners from Good Shepherd Episcopal Church in Wichita, Kansas, which is the parish that operates St. Mark's Press. When Year B looked dead, the Friends of Year B suddenly sprung up and sprang into action. They were inspired and united by a shared vision for the ministries of St. Mark's Press and the LGC series, convinced that God raised them up in order to find a way to make Year B a reality. The Friends of Year B composed letters, wrote proposals, and secured funding for the writing, printing, and initial marketing of the book. They prayed with one another and for one another. They shared their hopes and their dreams, their faith and their doubts. Members will tell you that they did not always see how God would bring Year B about, but they remained committed to what they discerned as their calling. They even organized a rota of babysitters so that I could write and Rebekah could edit. As the Friends of Year B sought to make Year B a reality, they faced many challenges, and they met those challenges with wisdom, grace, and trust. Needless to say, the final volume of *A Lector's Guide and Commentary* would not have become a reality save for the toil and vision of the Friends of Year B and all the others, both inside and outside Good Shepherd parish, who supported this endeavor with their time, talent, and treasure. As it takes a village to raise a child, so it took a village to resurrect Year B.

The Friends of Year B and those who offered their financial support have requested to remain anonymous as testimony to the fact that the successful completion of Year B was a community effort and that it is God who deserves all the praise and glory. Nevertheless, I have told their story here to honor them, to thank them, and to thank God for inspiring and working through them. Rebekah and I are grateful for the spiritual, emotional, and financial support that you have showered upon us.

Acknowledgements
In addition, I would like to thank the clergy and vestry of Good Shepherd Episcopal Church for all the time and energy they devoted this past year to matters related to St. Mark's Press and the publishing of Year B. In particular, I would like to thank Fr. Andrew O'Connor for supporting this process and Deacon Robert Hirst for his prophetic voice and encouragement.

As always, a very special thanks goes to the host of editors and proofreaders who helped bring this manuscript into its final form: Jo Auchterlonie, Rebekah Blakley, Mike Buchanan, Linda Dixon, Diane Grubb, Doug Lipperd, Meg Rice, and Robert Seaton. You will never know how much better this book is because of your work. (Well, maybe you do know.)

Lastly, I wish to extend my sincerest love and affection to my family: to my wife, Rebekah, and to our three children—Emma (10), Thaddaeus (7), and Esther (2½)—and our soon-to-be fourth child. I wish I could write faster so that I would have less time away from you. Thank you for the sacrifices you have made.

My continued hope and prayer is that *A Lector's Guide and Commentary* will contribute to what God is doing to transform the world through his beloved Son, our Lord and Saviour Jesus Christ. May God draw so close to us and may we be drawn so close to God that we come to know and experience God as love and come to know and accept ourselves, our neighbors, and our enemies as God's beloved children.

Blessings.

J. Ted Blakley
Twelfth Sunday after Pentecost, A.D. 2011

jtedblakley@gmail.com

To report any errors or to make suggestions for improvement, please contact St. Mark's Press at stmarkspress@gmail.com

INTRODUCTION

For as the rain and the snow come down from heaven,
and do not return there until they have watered the earth,
making it bring forth and sprout,
giving seed to the sower and bread to the eater,
so shall my word be that goes out from my mouth;
it shall not return to me empty,
but it shall accomplish that which I purpose,
and succeed in the thing for which I sent it.

Isaiah 55:10–11

The Word that God speaks and the Word that God is is a dynamic, powerful and effective word. In Isaiah 55, the Word that proceeds from the mouth of the LORD is characterized as life-producing and life-sustaining, qualities manifest throughout the biblical narrative. By his eternal Word, God spoke creation into being. Where before there had been nothing but the nothingness of chaos, God, through his Word, fashioned fertile and habitable spaces, where the life God created might take root and flourish. By his eternal Word made manifest in the Law, the LORD sustained his chosen people, Israel, that they might become a nation of priests, who would mediate the presence, knowledge, and forgiveness of God to all peoples everywhere. Then, in the fullness of time, God's eternal Word became a human being, Jesus of Nazareth, the one Israelite who perfectly and obediently fulfilled Israel's vocation to be the light of the world. Through the life, death, resurrection, and ascension of his forever incarnate Word, God has redeemed the world and inaugurated the New Creation, to be consummated when the incarnate Word of God returns.

When, as Christians, we profess the Bible to be the Word of God, whatever else we might mean by this, we are claiming that the Bible possesses the qualities of God's eternal Word: it is dynamic, powerful, effectual, life-giving, and life-sustaining. In addition, we are claiming that the Story of the Word is of central importance for the whole world. This Story is the good news of how the God of creation became a creature so that the old creation, which had become subject to sin, violence, and death might give way to the New Creation, where human beings would finally fulfill their original calling to be faithful stewards and the bearers of God's image in the world.

From the very first days of the Church until now, Holy Scripture has played a vital role in the life and worship of Christian communities. In the Scriptures, we discover our true identity as God's chosen and beloved people. When we enter into the biblical Story, we are encountered by the God who created us and sustains us, the God who loves, rescues, and restores us, and the God who equips and empowers us to participate in the New Creation, enabling us to love God, to love our neighbors, and even to love our enemies. Thus, the ongoing proclamation of the Word of God through preaching, teaching, *and* the public reading of Holy Scripture continues to be a central and vital ministry of the Church.

When the Bible is read aloud in a setting of communal worship, the Word of God is activated and sent forth. Therefore, those who read the Bible publicly are a principal means by which the Word of God accomplishes God's purposes. This is why the Church needs not only gifted preachers and teachers, but gifted lectors and lay readers. *A Lector's Guide and Commentary to the Revised Common Lectionary* is designed to equip and prepare those who are called and privileged with the responsibility of proclaiming the Word of God through the public reading of Holy Scripture. The Guide does this by providing a brief, reliable commentary for each lectionary reading, and then by offering suggestions for how the text can be delivered aloud so that the Story of the Word might have its full impact on the Christian community gathered for worship.

Although the Guide is designed first and foremost for lectors and lay readers, it has also been written with other groups and uses in mind. For example, the Guide can be used to trigger discussions in a Sunday school class or small group Bible study, or it could serve as a resource for personal study, reflection, and devotion. The Guide can assist lay Eucharistic ministers who deliver the Word and Sacrament to shut-ins, and even function as a first stop for preachers and teachers.

BASIC FEATURES OF THE GUIDE

A Lector's Guide and Commentary is for use by any Christian congregation or tradition that follows the Revised Common Lectionary (RCL). It also includes the adaptations authorized for use in The Episcopal Church; these are described below. The following describes the basic features of the Guide.

Notes

Some of the lectionary readings include brief notes, which are of two kinds: Suggested Reading and Sequence.

Suggested Reading. According to the RCL, when it is appropriate, readings may be lengthened at discretion. The RCL includes suggested lengthenings, which are cited in parentheses. For example, the OT reading for Epiphany 2 is cited as 1 Samuel 3:1–10, (11–20). The person responsible for selecting the readings must decide whether 1 Samuel 3:1–10 or 3:1–20 is to be read.

Occasionally, the Guide offers its own suggestions for lengthening a reading; these suggestions are found in the Notes. For example, in the RCL, the OT reading for Epiphany 3 is Jonah 3:1–5, 10. However, I think it the story is much more powerful when we read about what the Ninevites did to show the extent of their repentance, so I suggest that Jonah 3:1–10 be read in its entirety.

In most congregations, a pastor, priest, or preacher determines whether a reading will be lengthened. However, if you as a lector think that your assigned reading would benefit from being lengthened, discuss this with the person responsible for making those decisions.

Sequence. One of the benefits of the RCL is that it provides many opportunities for continuous or semi-continuous reading of biblical texts. For example, in Year B, the Gospel of Mark is read almost every Sunday in the Season after Pentecost. Since one of the chief goals of the Commentary is to situate a reading within its larger literary context, the Notes will indicate when a lectionary reading occurs in a sequence of readings from the same biblical book. With this information, a reader who wants to understand more about their assigned text has the opportunity to explore the Commentary for the previous or subsequent weeks' readings.

For example, in Proper 15, the Notes for Ephesians 5:15–20 reads: *Sequence.* 6 of 7. This indicates that Ephesians 5:15–20 is the sixth of seven sequential NT readings from The Letter of Paul to the Ephesians.

Commentary

When we are unclear about the purpose and meaning of a biblical text, our uncertainty and confusion can be conveyed to our listeners in our reading of the text. The converse is equally true. Even when we possess just a basic understanding of a text, we are able to communicate that understanding to our listeners, often intuitively in subtle, yet very significant ways (for example, through our tone of voice, our tempo and pace, our overall demeanor, and so on). To assist lectors in communicating meaning, the Guide provides a Commentary for every lectionary reading (except for the Psalms and other scriptures that serve as The Response to the first reading).

The purpose of the Commentary is to help lectors gain a better understanding and feel for their assigned passage so that they can read it with confidence and understanding. To do this, the Commentary sometimes provides background information in order to situate a reading within its broader historical and cultural contexts. Sometimes references are made to other biblical events and passages of Scripture in order to locate a reading within the wider biblical context and to show what role it plays within the larger Christian Story. When this occurs, these other biblical passages are cited so that readers can consult them. If the cited passage happens to be a lectionary reading in Year B, then the day on which that reading occurs is also cited. For example, in the Commentary for the Wisdom of Solomon reading for Proper 8, reference is made to Solomon's prayer for wisdom at the beginning of his reign, and so the following parenthetical cross-reference is included: *1 Kings 3:6–9, Prop 15.* Armed with this information, a reader can look up the story in 1 Kings and also consult its Commentary in Proper 15.

Most of all, readings are interpreted within their own literary contexts. For example, when addressing a reading from one of the gospels, the Commentary generally includes comments about what has happened in the narrative prior to the assigned reading. In addition, if the reading exhibits any of the gospel writer's trademark motifs or themes, these are discussed as well. Here, the goal of the Commentary is to help readers see that their assigned texts are not individual, isolated units that stand on their own, but that they belong to larger narratives, teachings, arguments, and stories. Inevitably, this broadening of the horizons will have a positive effect on one's understanding and delivery of Scripture.

Suggestions for Lectors

Understanding the meaning and purpose of a biblical text is just the first step in fulfilling our role as lectors and lay readers. The second step involves learning how to convey that understanding to our listeners through our reading of the text. To assist in this task, the Guide provides Suggestions for Lectors, which offers specific advice and practical suggestions, not absolute rules, for how the text can be delivered so that it might have its intended rhetorical impact upon its listeners.

As with the Commentary, the Suggestions for Lectors does not seek to be exhaustive; it does not comment on every aspect of a text but merely draws attention to its more prominent features. The Suggestions for Lectors does not presume to offer the only, or even the best, way to read a given text aloud. After all, biblical texts are not dead or inert, rather they are dynamic, alive, and rich with meaning. A single passage of Scripture often lends itself to multiple interpretations and thus to multiple ways of being read that are faithful to its meaning and intent. This is not to say that every interpretation of a text is a faithful interpretation; only that a single reading can never capture or convey everything within a given biblical text. One of the benefits of following a lectionary cycle of readings is that it gives us the opportunity to revisit the same text again and again. This allows texts to unfold and reveal more of their meaning over time. In short, the Suggestions for Lectors should be taken as just that, suggestions. They are not designed to replace, but to complement, a lector's own engagement with the biblical text and their own experience as a reader.

Pronunciation Guide

If a reading contains names or words that are potentially unfamiliar or difficult to pronounce, phonetic pronunciations are included in the Pronunciation Guide that immediately follows the Suggestions for Lectors. For names that occur frequently, pronunciations are not generally included with the reading; instead, these can be found in the Comprehensive Pronunciation Guide at the end of the book, which offers pronunciations for all the biblical names that occur in the Year B readings. There you will also find the Pronunciation Key.

✠ Adaptations to the RCL for use in The Episcopal Church

Recently, The Episcopal Church adopted the RCL as its official lectionary, albeit in a slightly adapted form. In the Guide, the adaptations for use in The Episcopal Church have been marked with the symbol, ✠. The following discussion provides a few more details regarding these adaptations.

In 2000, the 73rd General Convention of The Episcopal Church approved the continued trial use of the RCL, and at the same time, authorized a number of adaptations. Three years later, the 74th General Convention approved the continued trial use of the adapted RCL. Then, in 2006, the 75th General Convention directed that the RCL, along with the authorized adaptations, become the official lectionary of The Episcopal Church beginning in Advent 2007.

Most of the adaptations are minor. For example, many concern the Response to the first reading, where a Canticle from the BCP replaces a Psalm or other biblical text serving as the Response. For example, for Easter Vigil, Canticle 9 replaces Isaiah 12:2–6 as the Response for Isaiah 55:1–11. This is certainly a minor change as Canticle 9 is the First Song of Isaiah (*Ecce, Deus*) and is taken directly from Isaiah 12:2–6. Other minor adaptations include the omission of certain alternative readings. So, for the gospel reading in Lent 2, the RCL offers both Mark 8:31–38 and Mark 9:2–9 as possible readings; however, the Episcopal adaptations omit Mark 9:2–9.

In addition, the Episcopal adaptations include readings for days and services that the RCL makes no provision for, including weekday readings for Easter week and readings for the Vigil of Pentecost. The most significant adaptations occur in the Christmas season, where the readings authorized for Christmas 1 and 2 are entirely different from those provided in the RCL.

THE PUBLIC READING OF HOLY SCRIPTURE

As we have seen, the Suggestions for Lectors offers guidance for reading a given biblical text. What follows below is more general advice on the public reading of Holy Scripture, which applies to all biblical texts. No attempt has been made to be comprehensive; these are just a few things to keep in mind as you seek to develop and hone your skills as a lector. For more detailed guidance consult the following:

Clayton J. Schmit. *Public Reading of Scripture: A Handbook*. Nashville, Tenn.: Abingdon Press, 2002.

Virginia Meagher and Paul Turner. *The Liturgical Ministry Series: Guide for Lectors*. Chicago, Ill.: Liturgy Training Publications, 2007.

Prepare! Prepare! Prepare!

As a lector charged with proclaiming the Word of God through the public reading of Holy Scripture, nothing is as important as spending quality time in preparation. Preachers, teachers, musicians, soloists, and choirs need preparation, and so do readers. So always *Prepare! Prepare! Prepare!* How much time one will need for preparation depends upon a variety of factors and will vary from person to person and from text to text. The goal of preparation is to become so familiar with your assigned passage and with your plan of delivery that you can read it before others with relative ease and confidence. Preparation includes the following basic elements.

Get to know your text. Getting to know your text involves reading it through multiple times until you no longer stumble over words or phrases or lose your place. Getting to know your text also involves understanding its meaning. Reading is an act of interpretation, so when you read a biblical text in worship, you are offering an interpretation of Scripture, *your* interpretation. So study the text, seeking to discern its meaning and purpose; the Commentary will assist you. In addition, make the text personal by identifying with someone or something in the text or by incorporating the text into your devotional life in the week leading up to your reading.

Practice reading your text aloud. In the same way singers practice their songs aloud, it makes sense for readers to practice their readings aloud. As Clay Schmit notes, reading aloud helps you identify any potential problems with pronunciation, pauses, and pacing in a way that reading silently to yourself cannot. Look up any words whose pronunciations you are unsure about. Then read and re-read those words along with any other tricky phrases, sentences, or sections until you can read everything smoothly and easily. Vary the tempo and the stresses until the reading feels right to you. Rehearse your text aloud before others and elicit their feedback. Consider taping yourself and listening to your reading, even if only occasionally.

Loud and Clear

As you read, control the volume of your voice so that you can speak each word loudly and clearly. It is easy to read too quietly, but almost impossible to read too loudly. There is no need to shout, but simply read with more intensity, letting the strength of your voice come from your gut (your diaphragm) and not your throat.

Pace and Tempo

Pace and tempo has to do with the speed at which one reads a text. While it is possible to read too slowly, the more common problem is reading too quickly. Reading too quickly is often a symptom of nervousness, which can be addressed by adequate preparation and which will decrease with experience. So, force yourself to read at a slow and deliberate pace, never hurried.

Pauses

Knowing when to pause and for how long is perhaps the finest skill a reader can develop. Pauses in reading are like rests in music. A well-placed pause can transform a poor reading into a great reading. A slight pause after each sentence, and sometimes additional pauses within a sentence, helps the thought sink in and gives your listeners time to reflect on it, which enables them to follow the passage more intelligently. Pauses also mark major transitions—between scenes, between movements, etc.

Reading vs. Dramatic Reading

While it is important that lectors read with emotion and with variations of tone and mood in their voice, it is also important that their reading not become a dramatic reading. Remember that your listeners know that you are reading, so they do not expect you to employ hand gestures, facial expressions, or the expressiveness of voice associated with a dramatic reading or play.

In our capacity as lectors, we are readers not actors, so we only provide hints of the joy, anger, or frustration of the characters in the stories we read. This can be accomplished by putting ourselves in a particular frame of mind—awe, for instance—and then letting that awe express itself in and through our reading in subtle yet significant ways. As lectors, we allow the text to provide the primary emotional and tonal input, while we serve only to support the text through the subtle modifications of our voice.

Eye Contact

When it comes to making eye contact with your listeners, there are two schools of thought: one says that eye contact is absolutely essential, and the other says it is not necessary. I have witnessed both approaches and found them both to work equally well. In the end, the effectiveness of either depends primarily upon the personality, demeanor, and comfort level of the individual reader. My advice to lectors is that they experiment and decide upon an approach that works for them. If a lector possesses good reading skills, then eye contact or the lack thereof makes little difference.

That being said, if you are a reader who prefers not to look up or make eye contact with your listeners during your reading, then be sure to make eye contact before you begin reading and after you have finished. This helps create and maintain a connection with your listeners.

On the other hand, if you are a reader who likes to make eye contact with your listeners, avoid bobbing your head up and down. Looking up for the sake of looking up can be quite distracting. Instead, only look up to reinforce a message that is being conveyed at a particular point in the reading. Suggestions for when to look up are included in the Suggestions for Lectors.

Handling Mistakes Gracefully

While we certainly wish to avoid mistakes, as readers our focus and energy is not on producing a flawless reading free of all mistakes but on conveying a text's meaning to our listeners. No matter how well one prepares for a reading, mistakes can and will occur. Thus, you will want to think through how you intend to handle mistakes with poise and grace so as to minimize further distraction.

When we stumble over a word or phrase, our listeners' attention is momentarily drawn to our mistake, which may cause them to miss the next few seconds of the reading. If the mistake is minor, it is appropriate to continue without attempting to correct it. If, however, you think the meaning of the text has been compromised or lost, do not be afraid to pause, take a short breath, and start the whole sentence over; this will help your listeners get back into the flow of the reading. Do not attempt to make up for your mistake by simply repeating the missed word or phrase. Also, avoid the temptation to say *Excuse me* or *I'm sorry*, which only creates further distraction for your listeners.

If you make a number of errors within the opening sentences of your reading, instead of trying to continue on and plow through the reading as if nothing happened, simply stop and start over from the beginning. On this occasion, it would be appropriate to say something simple like, *Let's try this again.*

ABBREVIATIONS

OLD TESTAMENT

Gen	*Genesis*
Exod	*Exodus*
Lev	*Leviticus*
Num	*Numbers*
Deut	*Deuteronomy*
Josh	*Joshua*
Judg	*Judges*
Ruth	*Ruth*
1–2 Sam	*1–2 Samuel*
1–2 Kgs	*1–2 Kings*
1–2 Chr	*1–2 Chronicles*
Ezra	*Ezra*
Neh	*Nehemiah*
Esth	*Esther*
Job	*Job*
Ps, Pss	*Psalm, Psalms*
Prov	*Proverbs*
Eccl	*Ecclesiastes*
Song	*Song of Solomon (a.k.a., Song of Songs)*
Isa	*Isaiah*
Jer	*Jeremiah*
Lam	*Lamentations*
Ezek	*Ezekiel*
Dan	*Daniel*
Hos	*Hosea*
Joel	*Joel*
Amos	*Amos*
Obad	*Obadiah*
Jonah	*Jonah*
Mic	*Micah*
Nah	*Nahum*
Hab	*Habakkuk*
Zeph	*Zephaniah*
Hag	*Haggai*
Zech	*Zechariah*
Mal	*Malachi*

APOCRYPHA/ DEUTEROCANONICAL

Tob	*Tobit*
Jdt	*Judith*
Wis	*Wisdom of Solomon*
Sir	*Sirach (Ecclesiasticus)*
Bar	*Baruch*
Let Jer	*Letter of Jeremiah*
Sus	*Susanna*
Bel	*Bel and the Dragon*
1–2 Macc	*1–2 Maccabees*
1 Esd	*1 Esdras*
Pr Man	*Prayer of Manasseh*
Psalm 151	*Ps 151*
3 Macc	*3 Maccabees*
2 Esd	*2 Esdras*
4 Macc	*4 Maccabees*

NEW TESTAMENT

Matt	*Matthew*
Mark	*Mark*
Luke	*Luke*
John	*John*
Acts	*Acts of the Apostles*
Rom	*Romans*
1–2 Cor	*1–2 Corinthians*
Gal	*Galatians*
Eph	*Ephesians*
Phil	*Philippians*
Col	*Colossians*
1–2 Thess	*1–2 Thessalonians*
1–2 Tim	*1–2 Timothy*
Titus	*Titus*
Phlm	*Philemon*
Heb	*Hebrews*
Jas	*James*
1–2 Pet	*1–2 Peter*
1–2–3 John	*1–2–3 John*
Jude	*Jude*
Rev	*Revelation*

CHURCH SEASONS AND HOLY DAYS

Adv	*Advent*
Asc	*Ascension*
AshW	*Ash Wednesday*
Chr	*Christmas*
East	*Easter*
EastEv	*Easter Evening*
EastVig	*Easter Vigil*
Epi	*Epiphany*
GFri	*Good Friday*
Lent	*Lent*
MThu	*Maundy Thursday*
Name	*The Holy Name of Jesus*
Palm	*Palm Sunday*
Pent	*Pentecost*
PentVig	*Pentecost Vigil*
Prop	*Proper*
Tri	*Trinity Sunday*

BIBLE TRANSLATIONS

KJV	*King James Version*
NET	*New English Translation*
NIV	*New International Version*
NLT	*New Living Translation*
NRSV	*New Revised Standard Version*
RSV	*Revised Standard Version*

MISCELLANEOUS

a.k.a.	*also known as*
A.D.	*Anno Domini*
B.C.	*Before Christ*
BCP	*Book of Common Prayer*
c.	*about*
cf.	*compare*
ch.	*chapter*
chs.	*chapters*
e.g.	*for example*
esp.	*especially*
et al.	*and others*
Gr.	*Greek*
i.e.	*that is*
JW	*The Jewish Wars*
NT	*New Testament*
OT	*Old Testament*
RCL	*Revised Common Lectionary*
v.	*verse*
vv.	*verses*

SEASON OF ADVENT

FIRST SUNDAY OF ADVENT

Isaiah 64:1–9
Psalm 80:1–7, 17–19 (= 80:1–7, 16–18 BCP)
1 Corinthians 1:3–9
Mark 13:24–37

Overview of Readings
The first season of the Christian year is the season of Advent, which is a season of eager anticipation and expectant waiting. The word *advent* derives from the Latin *adventus*, which means *coming*. Thus, during the four Sundays of Advent, we—both individually and as the worshipping Christian community—are preparing ourselves for the coming of God in Jesus, the Christ (that is, the Messiah).

While we might associate Advent primarily with Christ's first coming as God incarnate, the readings for Advent 1 concern Christ's second coming at the end of history when he will complete God's work of redemption begun during his earthly life, nothing less than the restoration of all of creation. Therefore, today's readings prepare us to remember and celebrate Christ's birth even, as they help us reorient our lives in the light of Christ's return.

ISAIAH 64:1–9

Notes
Sequence. 1 of 3

Commentary
Isaiah 63:7–64:12 is a psalm of lament (or complaint), which is a common form of psalm found in the Psalter. Psalms of lament can be offered by an individual or a whole community. They normally begin with a recounting of the LORD's past deeds of deliverance in the hope that the LORD will respond in like manner and deliver the petitioner from the present crisis. This litany of the LORD's past deeds occurs in 63:7–14. Then, in 63:15, the community begins to offer up its petitions. They ask the LORD to "Look down from heaven and see" the trouble that they are in. The Promised Land has been taken away from them, and their enemies have destroyed God's house, the temple.

64:1–4. In today's reading, the people's petitions intensify. They do not simply want the LORD to see what is happening, they want him to do something about it, something decisive and radical. They want the LORD to rip open the curtain that separates the heavenly and earthly realms and to come down and perform mighty deeds just like he has done in ages past. They want all the nations of the world, especially those who have oppressed them, to see the glory and power of their God.

64:5–7. The community then offers a corporate confession of sin, of sorts. They acknowledge that their own sins have made them unclean, so unclean that even their righteous deeds are like filthy rags, rags that a woman uses during her menstrual period. Yet, with the same breath they use to confess their sin, they argue that their waywardness is the LORD's fault. "*You were angry*, and we sinned; *because you hid yourself* we transgressed" (64:5b).

What sort of confession is this? Even though it was the people's ongoing unfaithfulness that triggered the LORD's anger, they reverse the order of cause and effect in a desperate attempt to get the LORD to act on their behalf. Essentially, they are saying, "If you, O LORD, would stop being angry with us and would cease hiding your face from us, if you would just turn and save us, then we would be able to worship and serve you once again."

64:8–9. In their final petition, the people back away from this accusatory approach and appeal to the LORD's mercy as their Father. They acknowledge that the LORD has every right to deal with them as he sees fit, to shape them in whatever way he desires. They would ask, though, that he remember that they are his people.

Suggestions for Lectors

As reflected in the Commentary, today's reading occurs in three movements, each of which has a different tenor. In the first movement (64:1–4), the people are desperate for the LORD to act, *O that you would tear open the heavens and come down* (64:1). Read these verses with the pleading intensity that they require.

In the second movement (64:5–7), there is a mixture of penitence and accusation; your voice should convey these qualities at the appropriate time.

Finally, in the third movement (64:8–9), the people express unadulterated, unqualified remorse. You are the people's representative, so soften your voice as you acknowledge your sin and ask for the LORD's mercy.

Pronunciation Guide

Isaiah (ī-ZAY-uh)

1 CORINTHIANS 1:3–9

Commentary

The First Letter of Paul to the Corinthians is the second longest of Paul's letters in the NT; only Romans is longer. In this lengthy epistle, Paul addresses a number of problems besetting the Christian community in Corinth. Many of the problems relate to the question of how the Corinthian Christians, both individually and as a community, are to live out their Christian faith within a culture whose values are often so different and antithetical to those of the gospel.

The church in Corinth was established by the Apostle Paul during his second missionary journey (Acts 18:1–17). Corinth was clearly an important mission, for Paul remained there eighteen months preaching the gospel, all the while supporting himself by making tents. In today's reading, Paul writes from Ephesus (1 Cor 16:8) and sends his greetings.

1:3. In keeping with ancient Greco-Roman conventions of letter writing in the ancient world, 1 Corinthians begins by identifying the sender and the recipient (1:1–2). In this case, the senders are identified as Paul and Sosthenes, and the recipient is the "church of God that is in Corinth" (1:2). Instead of the standard, "Greetings!" of the Greco-Roman world, Paul employs the distinctly Jewish-Christian salutation of "Grace to you and peace..." (1:3).

1:4–9. In ancient letters, the salutation was often followed by a short prayer of thanksgiving. Here Paul gives thanks for the grace, knowledge, and spiritual gifts that God has showered upon the Corinthians. All these things demonstrate that God is committed to the Corinthians' ongoing transformation, growth, and maturity. God has not only called them (and us) into relationship with him, God has also provided what they (and we) need to remain faithful until the Lord Jesus Christ returns.

Suggestions for Lectors

Deliver the salutation with warmth in your voice: *Grace to you and peace from God our Father and the Lord Jesus Christ* (1:3). As you continue with the prayer of thanksgiving (1:4–9), be conscious of what you are saying and to whom you are saying it. For example, as you read *I give thanks to my God always for you* (1:4) and *He will also strengthen you to the end* (1:8), think of yourself as the apostle Paul, and direct your heartfelt prayer to those who have gathered for worship. Remember, as lectors, we are not simply passing on information; our voices are the vehicle for the living Word of God.

Pronunciation Guide

Corinthians (kuh-RIN-thee-uhnz)

MARK 13:24–37

Notes

Sequence. 1 of 2

Commentary

Today's reading is set in Jerusalem near the end of the last week of Jesus' life. At the beginning of this week, Jesus performed two symbolic actions. On Palm Sunday, he rode into Jerusalem as Israel's king (11:1–11). Afterward, he entered the temple and disrupted commercial activities (11:15–19). Citing the prophets, Jesus argued that the temple, which God had intended to be "a house of prayer for all the nations" (Isa 56:7), had been turned into "a den of robbers" (Jer 7:11). By temporarily disrupting such activities in the temple, Jesus was dramatizing the fact that temple operations would one day cease altogether.

The next day, Jesus returned to the temple where he was questioned about his authority to engage in these prophetic actions (11:27–12:44). As Jesus leaves the temple for the last time, his disciples express amazement about the grandeur of the temple complex with its massive stones and buildings. Jesus is not impressed. Since the temple is not fulfilling its God-ordained purpose, it will be destroyed. Its destruction will be thorough for "not one stone will be left hereupon another, all will be thrown down" (13:2). Within a generation, his predictions come true. In A.D. 70, the armies of Rome raze the temple as punishment for the First Jewish Revolt in A.D. 66.

When questioned by his disciples about the coming destruction, Jesus begins a lengthy discourse of which today's reading is a part. He talks about wars, rumors of wars, and the upheavals of creation (13:5–8, Prop 28); he talks about his followers being persecuted (13:9–13); and he talks about false messiahs and false prophets coming in his name (13:14–23). Then, in today's reading, Jesus talks about his own coming (13:24–37). He will arrive at an unexpected hour, so his followers will need to remain vigilant.

13:24–27. After all the political upheavals and persecutions, Jesus will come with the glory and power of a king, and he will gather all the citizens of his kingdom who have, by the grace of God, persevered. The image of the Son of Man coming in the clouds is taken from Daniel 7:13 (Prop 29). In Daniel, one like a son of man comes to the Ancient of Days (that is, God) and receives a kingdom after having endured great suffering and persecutions. This is the perfect image for Jesus, who suffered the humiliation and pain of the cross and yet one day will receive a kingdom.

13:28–31. Unlike evergreens, which are so prominent in the land of Israel, fig trees can be used to interpret the seasons. When a fig tree goes into leaf, one knows that summer is just around the corner. Everything that Jesus has been telling his disciples functions like the fig tree's leaves. When his disciples see all these things taking place, then they will know that the Son of Man—Jesus himself—is at the gates.

13:32–37. However, he wants to make clear that these signs will not be as precise as we might like. The signs might indicate that the end is near, but they cannot tell us the day or the hour of Jesus' coming. In fact, Jesus himself does not even know when he is coming; only the Father knows. The Son of Man is coming at an unexpected hour, so constant vigilance is required. Jesus has called and equipped his disciples to proclaim the kingdom of God by word and by deed (3:13–15). Instead of wasting their time with fruitless speculations, wondering when their master will return, his disciples ought to devote themselves to their apostolic mission. That is what it means to keep alert and awake.

Suggestions for Lectors

In today's reading, Jesus discloses things that will happen in the future, so read with a hint of mystery in your voice, especially in the opening section (13:24–27).

Emphasize the commands and instructions Jesus issues by elevating your voice and reading slowly and deliberately: *From the fig tree learn its lesson* (13:28); *Beware, keep alert* (13:33); *Therefore, keep awake* (13:35), and *Keep awake* (13:37).

In 13:32, do not pause at the comma after *heaven*, but do pause after *Son*; this will better emphasize the contrast between *neither the angels of heaven nor the Son*, on the one hand, and *but only the Father*, on the other. In 13:35–36, the word *or* occurs four times. The first three belong together because they link different times in the night watch: *evening*, *midnight*, *cockcrow*, and *dawn*. Initially, the fourth *or* looks like it belongs to this sequence but does not, so it is important to distinguish it from the previous *ors*.

Therefore, treat the last comma in 13:35 as a period, and the *or* in 13:36 as though it begins a new sentence, as in: ...*or a dawn. Or else he may find*....

SECOND SUNDAY OF ADVENT

Isaiah 40:1–11
Psalm 85:1–2, 8–13
2 Peter 3:8–15a
Mark 1:1–8

Overview of Readings
While the readings for Advent 1 concern Jesus' *second* coming, the readings for Advent 2 focus upon his *first* coming. In all three years of the lectionary cycle, the OT readings express the expectations of a future messianic age, an age of restoration, reconciliation, and peace (*shalom*) to be inaugurated with the arrival of God's anointed agent. The word for *anointed one* is *Messiah* in Hebrew and *Christ* in Greek.

Similarly, in all three years, the gospel readings introduce us to John the Baptist, whose vocation was to prepare the people of Israel for the coming of God's Messiah. Texts like Malachi 4:5 led people to believe that the prophet Elijah would return to prepare the way for the coming of God and God's anointed agent (cf. Mark 9:11). The gospels present John the Baptist as fulfilling this role (Matt 11:7–15; Mark 9:13; Luke 1:13–17). As Jesus once said of John, "if you are willing to accept it, he is Elijah who is to come. Let anyone with ears listen" (Matt 11:14–15).

ISAIAH 40:1–11

Notes
Sequence. 2 of 3

Commentary
In Isaiah 1–39, the prophet announces the LORD's judgment upon the people of Judah for their centuries of idolatry and injustice, that is, for their ongoing refusal to love God with their whole heart (Deut 6:5, Prop 26; Exod 20:1–7, Lent 3) and their failure to love their neighbors as themselves (Lev 19:18; Exod 20:8–17). Isaiah 39 ends ominously as the predicted destruction and exile of Judah at the hands of the Babylonian empire becomes imminent. Isaiah 40 skips ahead many years and introduces a new movement in the prophetic drama. Beginning in Isaiah 40, the ominous note of judgment gives way to a joyful tune of hope, forgiveness, and restoration for God's people as the prophet announces a *new thing* that the LORD is about to do (42:9; 43:19; 48:6).

40:1–2. Isaiah 40 presupposes that God's people have been in exile for some time. After years of silence, the word of the LORD is sent forth to offer solace to these exiles in Babylon. "Comfort, O comfort my people, says your God. Speak tenderly to Jerusalem, and cry to her that she has served her term, that her penalty is paid, that she has received from the LORD's hand double for all her sins" (40:1–2). In other words, the exile is officially over. The LORD has forgiven his people and is soon coming to bring them back home to Zion.

40:3–5. In Isaiah 6, the prophet Isaiah is granted a vision of the LORD of hosts. The hosts are the heavenly beings who serve as royal attendants and who belong to the LORD's divine council (cf. Ps 82:1; Job 1:6). When the LORD asks, "Whom shall I send, and who will go for *us*?" (6:8), those whom the LORD is addressing, and who constitute the *us*, are members of the divine council.

In today's reading, the divine council is addressed again, this time by the voice that cries out, "In the wilderness prepare the way of the LORD, make straight in the desert a highway for our God" (40:3). The divine council is called up to construct a highway right through the wilderness that stretches between Judah and Babylon, a highway that will facilitate the return of the exiles. As if in a royal procession, the LORD himself will gather his people from Babylon and lead them swiftly and safely home. This wilderness highway will stand as a monument showing the whole world that the LORD has taken his people back. In this way, the LORD's glory will be seen by all peoples everywhere.

40:6–8. In 40:6, another angelic voice is heard. Unlike in 40:3, this voice does not itself cry out, but issues the command to cry out. The prophet responds, "What shall I cry?," and then proceeds to speak of grasses withering and flowers fading. Initially, it seems as though the prophet is talking about the transitory nature of human life in general, but with further reflection, it appears that something more specific is in view.

At this point, the prophet has not yet heard the new message of "Comfort, O comfort my people" (40:1). He is only familiar with the old message of judgment, which has dominated chapters 1–39. Therefore, when he hears the command to "Cry out," he wonders aloud, "What's the point? The LORD has breathed his word of judgment upon his people, and they have withered. The predicted exile has come about, so what more needs to be said?" (40:6b–7). In reply, the angelic voice affirms what the prophet has said, "The grass withers, the flower fades," but then adds, "*but* the word of our God will stand forever" (40:8). This *but* is important because it points to a new word of the LORD, the good tidings of forgiveness and return from exile that the prophet is to announce to the exiles.

Nevertheless, this word is not entirely new, because alongside the declarations of imminent judgment in Isaiah 1–39, we also find declarations of restoration. For example, in Isaiah 28, the prophet first proclaims the word of judgment by referring to "the proud garland" of God's people and "the fading flower of its glorious beauty" (28:1, 4). Right after, the prophet proclaims the word of restoration: "In that day the LORD of hosts will be a garland of glory, and a diadem of beauty, to the remnant of his people" (28:5).

Therefore, while the word of the LORD in Isaiah begins with judgment, it ends with mercy and forgiveness. With God, judgment never seems to be the last word. In today's reading, the prophet is commissioned to cry out the good news to the exiles: "The LORD has forgiven you; your God is bringing you home."

40:9–11. Even Jerusalem and Mt. Zion are enlisted as heralds of the good news. "Get you up to a high mountain, O Zion, herald of good tidings; lift up your voice with strength, O Jerusalem, herald of good tidings, lift it up, do not fear; say to the cities of Judah, '*Here is your God!*'" (40:9).

When God comes, he will come with power and might to free his people from their foreign captors. And then afterwards, God will become the shepherd of his people, gathering his scattered flock, feeding them, and guiding them.

Suggestions for Lectors

There are four movements in today's reading (40:1–2, 3–5, 6–8, 9–11). Between movements, pause for a full second and conclude each by reading the last line of the movement slowly and deliberately.

Deliver the opening line of the first movement slowly and with feeling: *Comfort, O comfort my people* (40:1). When you come to the three lines beginning with *that*, increase your intensity and tempo as you read each successive line. Your intensity should climax with *hand*. After *hand*, pause and emphasize *double*. Then, read the final line slowly and calmly with pauses after almost every word, as in: *<u>double</u>... for all... her... sins* (40:2).

The whole of the second movement is the proclamation of the voice, so read it with a raised voice as if you are delivering this message to a large crowd.

The third movement is dynamic and features the back-and-forth exchange between the angelic voice and the prophet. Raise your voice for the angelic command, *Cry out!*, then respond in the uncertain voice of the prophet, *What shall I cry?* As suggested in the Commentary, 40:6b–7 constitutes the prophet's own musings, and in 40:8, the angelic voice responds to those musings. Since this change of speaker is not signaled in the text, your voice will need to make the distinction for your listeners. Read *All people... surely the people are grass* (40:6b–7) in a reflective tone of voice almost as though you are talking to yourself. Then pause for a second before proceeding with 40:8. Begin the angelic voice repeating the prophet's words in a straightforward manner, *The grass withers, the flower fades* (40:8a). Then say *but* and pause for a second. Resume the angelic voice with strength and conviction as it proclaims, *the world of our God will stand forever* (40:8b).

In the fourth movement, the angelic voice continues with even more energy and intensity as it announces the arrival of God. Finally, in 40:11, replace the intensity with tenderness and compassion as you deliver the final line. In fact, you should use the same calming tone of voice here as you did at the opening of today's reading.

Pronunciation Guide

Isaiah (ī-ZAY-uh), *Jerusalem* (juh-ROO-suh-luhm), *Judah* (JOO-duh), *Zion* (ZĪ-uhn)

2 PETER 3:8–15A

Commentary

The Second Letter of Peter presents itself as having been written by Simon Peter, one of Jesus' twelve disciples. In the opening chapter, Peter confides in his readers that the Lord Jesus Christ has informed him that he will not live much longer (1:14). Therefore, with the time he has remaining, Peter intends to devote himself to the task of reminding his Christian readers about the grace, power, and truth of the gospel of Jesus Christ, whose "divine power has given us everything needed for life and godliness" (1:3) and who has made it possible for us to "escape from the corruption that is in the world" (1:4a) so as to "become participants in the divine nature" (1:4b). In today's reading, Peter concludes his epistle by talking about the day of the Lord's return at the end of the present evil age.

In chapter 3, Peter begins by saying that, in the last days, there will be those who scoff at the idea of the Lord's return, saying, "Where is the promise of his coming? For ever since our ancestors died, all things continue as they were from the beginning of creation!" (3:4).

3:8–9. Some of this scoffing may be due to the fact that the Lord has not returned as quickly as some had been expecting or teaching. For Peter, this "delay" is no cause for concern because, as he reminds his readers, God's timing is different from ours. "With the Lord one day is like a thousand years, and a thousand years are like one day" (3:8). Consequently, we really have no basis for saying that the Lord is slow in returning. In fact, what we regard as slowness is better understood as an example of the Lord's love and patience because his desire is that all people have the opportunity to repent and receive the gift of eternal life. This is what Peter is talking about at the end of today's reading when he writes that we should "regard the patience of the Lord as salvation" (3:15a).

3:10–13. That being said, Peter warns that the Lord's patience in coming is not endless; one should not treat his delay as an opportunity to become lax in matters of holiness and godliness. The Lord's arrival will still be as sudden and unexpected as a nighttime burglar. As Jesus himself said, "Keep awake therefore, for you do not know on what day your Lord is coming,… for the Son of Man is coming at an unexpected hour" (Matt 24:42, 44).

When he comes, all of creation will experience the effects. The old heavens and the old earth, which have become subject to decay and death, will dematerialize in order to be replaced by a new heavens and a new earth. And everything that people have done upon the earth will be disclosed and made known to all.

3:14–15a. This should give Peter's readers an extra incentive to lead lives of holiness and righteousness in the here and now as they await their Lord's return with patient trust.

Suggestions for Lectors

As reflected in the Commentary, today's reading falls into three sections: 3:8–9, 10–13, 14–15a. Lectors should draw each section to a close by slowing down at the end and then pausing for a second before moving on.

Each section has something worth emphasizing. In the first and third sections, emphasize the patience of God, which keeps the door to salvation open: *but is <u>patient</u> with you, not wanting any to perish, but <u>all</u> to come to repentance* (3:9) and *regard the <u>patience</u> of our Lord as salvation* (3:15). In the second section, emphasize the question, *what sort of persons ought you to be in leading lives of holiness and godliness…?* (3:11).

Throughout the reading, Peter expresses a sense of urgency. At the same time, he conveys a real concern for those whom he addresses as beloved (3:8). Let both of these qualities come through in your reading.

MARK 1:1–8

Notes

Sequence. 2 of 2

Commentary

Unlike the gospels of Matthew and Luke, the Gospel of Mark does not begin with stories of Jesus' birth and childhood. Instead, Mark begins with Jesus as an adult at the beginning of his public ministry. In today's reading, we are introduced to John the Baptist who introduces Jesus to the people of Judea and Jerusalem and to the readers of Mark as well.

1:1. The question that Mark is primarily concerned with is the question of Jesus' identity, which resurfaces throughout the gospel narrative. For example, in response to the first healing Jesus performs, an exorcism, the witnesses exclaim, "*What is this?* A new teaching—with authority! He commands even the unclean spirits, and they obey him" (1:27, Epi 4). Likewise, when Jesus stills a storm at sea, his awestruck disciples wonder aloud, "*Who then is this*, that even the wind and the sea obey him?" (4:41, Prop 7). Even Jesus poses the question of his identity. At the midpoint of the narrative, he asks his disciples, "*Who* do people say that I am?," and then, "But who do you say that I am?" (8:27, 29, Prop 19). These questions keep the matter of Jesus' identity at the forefront of the reader's mind. Of course, as readers, we already know who Jesus is because this information is provided in the opening line of the gospel; Jesus is the Messiah and the Son of God. Thus, the reader knows from the very beginning what characters in the gospel, especially the disciples, are at pains to understand. This is part of Mark's dramatic irony, and what makes the gospel so interesting.

Yet, just knowing these titles for Jesus is not enough because we all have our own ideas of what these titles connote. Thus, Mark's story about Jesus is designed to provide us with a more complete and accurate picture of what it means for Jesus to be Messiah and Son of God. As the reader will discover, being the Messiah and the Son of God does not just entail great deeds of power but profound acts of suffering as well.

In addition to revealing Jesus' identity, the twin titles in Mark 1:1 are reflective of the gospel's overall two-part structure. The body of Mark's narrative is framed by a brief prologue (1:1–8) and epilogue (16:1–8). The body itself can be divided into two, slightly overlapping parts (1:9–8:30; 8:27–15:47). Each part concludes with a climactic recognition scene in which a character identifies Jesus with one of the titles from the opening line. Part I concludes with Peter's confession, "You are the Messiah" (8:29), and Part II concludes with the centurion's declaration, "Truly this man was God's Son!" (15:39). What is so striking about these two scenes is how unique they are within the gospel. Peter is the only human character in the entire narrative to identify Jesus as the Messiah, and the centurion is the only human character to recognize Jesus' divine identity as the Son of God. Demons know who Jesus is (1:24; 3:11; 5:7), and God himself identifies Jesus as his Son (1:11, Lent 1; 9:7, Lent 2), but Peter and the Gentile centurion are the only *human* characters to declare Jesus to be "the Messiah, the Son of God" (1:1).

1:2–3. For Mark, the beginning of the good news about Jesus does not begin with Jesus. It begins with the promises God made to his people that predate Jesus, promises that speak of one who will come and prepare the way for God's Messiah. Although Mark writes, "as it was written in the prophet *Isaiah*" (1:2a), the citation that follows is a conflation of at least two OT texts—Malachi 3:1 and Isaiah 40:3, and perhaps Exodus 23:20 as well.

The prophet Malachi is concerned with "the great and terrible day of the LORD" (4:5), the day when Israel's God will come in judgment to restore his people. In Malachi, the LORD says to his people, "See, I am sending my messenger to prepare the way before *me*" (3:1). When Mark appropriates this prophecy, he changes the last pronoun from first person to second person. "See, I am sending my messenger ahead of *you*, who will prepare *your* way" (1:2). In Malachi, the messenger was to prepare for *God's* arrival, but in Mark, this messenger prepares for *Jesus'* arrival. This modification of Malachi's prophecy is Mark's way of underscoring the unique connection between Jesus and God.

Mark does something similar with Isaiah 40:3. He does not alter the text itself but alters the context within which the text is read.[1] In Isaiah, preparations are to be made for the arrival of the Lord God, but in Mark, it is clearly the arrival of the Lord Jesus that is in view. Once again, Mark employs a subtle strategy in an effort to bring into sharper relief the mysterious link between God and Jesus. The prophets spoke of God's coming to restore his wayward people; Mark sees these prophecies as having been fulfilled in the coming of Jesus of Nazareth.

1:4–8. The messenger of Malachi and the voice of Isaiah turn out to be John the Baptist. In Malachi, the messenger is specifically identified as the prophet Elijah (Mal 4:5), and the description of the Baptist's clothing matches that of Elijah (2 Kgs 1:8; cf. Zech 13:4). In Isaiah, the voice is located in the wilderness, so the Baptist carries out his ministry in the wilderness. John enjoins the people to get ready to meet their Lord and King. His message must have been powerful and effective, for crowds of people traipsed out into the wilderness to confess their sins and be baptized as a sign of their repentance.

Yet, the Baptist knows his ministry is merely preparatory in nature. He knows that someone more powerful is coming. His ritual washings with water are nothing compared to the one who will wash people on the inside with God's cleansing Spirit.

Suggestions for Lectors

Read 1:1 as though it were the title of a book, then pause for a second or two afterwards before proceeding in a storytelling voice.

---

[1] Mark 1:3 differs from Isaiah 40:3 in most English bibles. This is not because Mark has altered the text of Isaiah but because he is drawing upon a Greek version of Isaiah 40:3 that differs from the Hebrew version upon which most English translations are based. In the Hebrew text of Isaiah 40:3, the voice cries out, "In the wilderness prepare the way of the LORD, make straight in the desert a highway for our God." In the Greek version, the voice is in the wilderness, proclaiming the message, "Prepare the way of the Lord, make straight the paths of our God."

At the end of 1:3, increase the volume and pitch of your voice as you proclaim: *Prepare the way of the Lord, make his paths straight.* Direct these words to your listeners as though they were the intended audience—which, of course, they are.

Use this same elevated voice when delivering the words of the Baptist. In 1:8, emphasize the points of contrast between the ministries of John and Jesus, as in: *I have baptized you with water; but he will baptize you with the Holy Spirit.*

Pronunciation Guide
Isaiah (ī-ZAY-uh), *Jerusalem* (juh-ROO-suh-luhm), *Judean* (joo-DEE-uhn; -DAY-)

THIRD SUNDAY OF ADVENT

Isaiah 61:1–4, 8–11
Psalm 126 *or* Luke 1:46b–55; ✠ Canticle 3 *or* 15
1 Thessalonians 5:16–24
John 1:6–8, 19–28

ISAIAH 61:1–4, 8–11

Notes
Sequence. 3 of 3

Commentary
Isaiah 61–62 offers a poetic, prophetic description of the restoration of God's exiled people and of a rebuilt Jerusalem (= Zion) following the Babylonian exile. In today's reading, an unnamed figure is introduced. His description brings to mind the servant figure(s) in the four Servant Songs of Isaiah (42:1–4; 49:1–6; 50:4–9, Palm; 52:13–53:12, GFri). Whether this figure represents a single individual or God's people as a whole, he has been called to execute the LORD's plans of restoration and transformation.

61:1–4, The Servant. In the OT, the LORD equips those whom he calls to perform particular tasks. For example, when David was still a boy, the prophet Samuel was sent to anoint him as king over Israel. When Samuel "took the horn of oil, and anointed [David] in the presence of his brothers,... the Spirit of the LORD came mightily upon [him] from that day forward" (1 Sam 16:13, Prop 6). The Spirit would be David's constant companion, giving him the authority and ability to rule over God's people on God's behalf.

The same has happened here. The Lord GOD has anointed the speaker with the Spirit so that he can carry out all of the assigned tasks identified in 61:1b–3a. These include the actions of bringing, binding up, proclaiming, releasing, comforting, providing, and giving. The beneficiaries of these activities are the poor, the powerless, the oppressed, and the marginalized. The year of the LORD's favor refers to the Year of Jubilee (Lev 25:10ff), which occurred every 50 years. In the Year of Jubilee debts were cancelled, slaves were freed, and all land that had been sold reverted to its original ancestral line of ownership.

Those who mourn in Zion will be given a festival wreath instead of ashes of sorrow because the city and its walls will be rebuilt, as will the other cities devastated by invading armies. In fact, those who are restored and transformed by the servant's work will themselves rebuild the ancient ruins.

61:8–9, The LORD. At this point, the LORD steps in and speaks for himself. The LORD loves what is equitable and just. His people who have been oppressed and deprived of their land and freedom will be compensated. Moreover, the LORD will establish an everlasting covenant with them so that they, and their descendants after them, will inherit these blessings. Then, all the peoples and all the nations of the world will know that these are God's chosen people. In this, we hear echoes of the LORD's original promise to Abraham and Sarah.

> I will make of you a great nation, and I will bless you, and make your name great, so that you will be a blessing. I will bless those who bless you, and the one who curses you I will curse; and in you all the families of the earth shall be blessed (Gen 12:2–3; cf. 17:1–8, Lent 2).

61:10–11, The Servant. The reading concludes with the servant offering a song of thanksgiving for what the LORD has and will accomplish.

Suggestions for Lectors

Today's reading uses first person pronouns throughout (*I, me, my*), yet as we saw in the Commentary, the speaker actually alternates between the Servant and the LORD. This shift is quite subtle and could easily be missed by your listeners. Be sure to pause for a full second both before and after 61:8–9 to signal this change in speakers.

Also, adopt a different tone of voice for the Servant and the LORD. Read the Servant's parts with an elevated voice and a slightly accelerated tempo as though you are announcing something wonderful and joyous to your listeners. In contrast, read the LORD's part slowly and deliberately, though not subdued, in order to convey his majesty and the grandeur of his vision.

Isaiah 61:1b–3a comprises one long, complex sentence. Practice it until you can read it easily and naturally and with the right intonation. Sometimes it can be helpful to reformat complex sentences so that its logic and flow can be visualized.

1b he has sent me
to bring good news to the oppressed,
to bind up the brokenhearted,
to proclaim liberty to the captives,
and release to the prisoners;
2 to proclaim the year of the LORD's favor,
and the day of vengeance of our God;
to comfort all who mourn;
3a to provide for those who mourn in Zion—
to give them a garland instead of ashes,
the oil of gladness instead of mourning,
the mantle of praise instead of a faint spirit.

As we can see, the most striking feature is the sequence of infinitive clauses—*to bring*, *to bind*, *to proclaim*, etc. The second and third of these infinitive clauses take up two lines, so make sure to sustain your intonation through to the end of the second line. You can do this more easily by not pausing at the commas after *captives* and *favor*.

Pronunciation Guide
Isaiah (ī-ZAY-uh), *Jerusalem* (juh-ROO-suh-luhm), *Zion* (ZĪ-uhn)

1 THESSALONIANS 5:16–24

Commentary
The First Letter of Paul to the Thessalonians is one of two NT letters addressed to Christians in Thessalonica, the capital city of the Roman province of Macedonia. Paul founded the church in Thessalonica during his second missionary journey (Acts 17:1–9). Written from Corinth a few months after he left Thessalonica, 1 Thessalonians is our oldest surviving Christian writing. It is the first of Paul's extant letters and predates all other writings within the NT.

In the second half of the letter (4:1–5:22), Paul instructs these new Christians in matters of belief and practice. He reminds them that they live at the end of the ages and that the Lord Jesus Christ will return suddenly like a thief in the night (5:2, 4). Consequently, they should remain awake and take care not become spiritually complacent as they await Christ's return.

5:16–22. In today's reading, Paul draws his letter to a close by offering a litany of parting exhortations. These are designed to offer some direction and support for what it means for us to lead intentional, attentive Christian lives.

5:23–24. The reading concludes with a benediction in which Paul expresses his hope that God will sanctify his readers entirely. In other words, Paul prays that God will heal, renew, and transform every dimension of their human person and personality—spirit, soul, and body—so that they will be ready to receive their Lord when he comes. Of course, Paul's prayer is not mere wishful thinking. He is confident that the one who has called the Thessalonians is committed to their transformation. "He will do this" (5:24). Paul writes the same thing to the Christians in Philippi: "I am confident of this, that the one who began a good work in you will bring it to completion by the day of Jesus Christ" (Phil 1:6).

Paul wants us to know two things. First, we must be intentional about leading lives of holiness and goodness. Second, we have not been left to ourselves to lead such lives. We participate with God in our transformation by developing such spiritual habits as rejoicing always, praying without ceasing, and giving thanks in all circumstances, but it is the work of the Holy Spirit at the core of our being that produces the fruits of "love, joy, peace, patience, kindness, generosity, faithfulness, gentleness, and self-control" (Gal 5:22).

Suggestions for Lectors
There is a qualitative difference in both form and content between 5:16–22 and 5:23–24. In 5:16–22, Paul issues a series of short commands, but in 5:23–24, he offers a

relatively longer blessing. When you read, make sure that the tone and tempo of your voice reflects these differences.

When you read the commands in 5:16–22, seek a balance. On the one hand, each of these commands stands on its own, so you want to give each its due by reading slowly and pausing between each command. On the other hand, some of the commands are related to one another. Those should be read with an intonation that conveys that they belong together. Let the punctuation be your guide. For example, in 5:16–18, there are three separate commands: *Rejoice always, pray without ceasing,* and *give thanks in all circumstances.* Yet, they all belong under the same rubric, *for this is the will of God in Christ Jesus for you*, which is why they are separated by commas instead of semicolons or periods.

Pronunciation Guide
Thessalonians (thes'-uh-LOH-nee-uhnz)

JOHN 1:6–8, 19–28

Commentary
In all four gospels, John the Baptist serves as the forerunner to Jesus. John's preaching and practice of baptism prepares the people of Israel for Jesus' arrival. And John's baptism of Jesus is the starting point of the Jesus' ministry, for it is only when John baptizes Jesus that the latter is anointed by the Holy Spirit and equipped for his messianic task.

While the supporting role of John the Baptist is emphasized in each gospel, only in the Gospel of John is there such a concerted effort to clarify the Baptist's identity and secondary status. But why? Like Jesus, John the Baptist had a following, and there is evidence that a John the Baptist movement continued to exist after his death (cf. Acts 18:24–19:5), even into the second century. It is likely, then, that these disciples of the Baptist regarded him as the Messiah. If so, then the author of John is attempting to defend Jesus' messianic identity against rival messianic claims for the Baptist. That is the focus of today's passage.

1:6–8. Today's reading begins in the famous prologue to the gospel. Only three people are specifically mentioned by name in the prologue—John the Baptist, Moses, and Jesus—and only the Baptist is mentioned by name more than once (1:6, 15). Up to this point, the prologue has been focused upon the eternal Word of God as the agent of creation and as the source of light for all people. Then, in 1:6, John the Baptist is suddenly introduced as one who was called by God to direct people's attention to the light that was coming into the world. John played a critical role as a witness to the light, but he himself was not the light (1:7–8; cf. 1:15, 29–36; 3:25–30).

1:19–23. During the Baptist's public ministry, he is questioned by a delegation of priests and Levites from the Jerusalem temple: "Who are you?" Without hesitation, he clearly and unambiguously states that he is not the Messiah. When pressed further, he also denies being any of the other messianic-type figures that many of his contemporaries have been expecting. He is not Elijah (Mal 4:5), nor is he the prophet like Moses (Deut 18:18; cf. John 6:14; 7:40).

The Baptist's interrogators demand an answer to their question that goes beyond mere denials, so he offers them a cryptic response by citing Isaiah 40:3 (Adv 2). In Isaiah, the announcement, "make straight the way of the Lord," belonged to the good news that the exile was over. The LORD had forgiven his people, and he was coming to collect them from Babylon and to lead them back home. The Baptist makes clear that he is just a voice; he is simply calling people to prepare for the arrival of God.

1:24–28. The Pharisees ask a follow-up question. If he is not anyone special, then why is he engaged in a ministry of ritual cleansing. The Baptist does not answer their question, at least not directly. Instead, he takes it as an opportunity to point away from himself to the one who is coming after him. Thus, he fulfills his role as one who was sent "as a witness to testify to the light" (1:7a).

Suggestions for Lectors

Rely upon your skill as a storyteller as you present today's episode to your listeners. The episode comes with its own introduction (1:6–8), so read it in a different manner than you read the rest. Read it as though you are reading a prologue.

The episode is driven by dialogue, so focus your attention there. The Baptist is asked a series of questions by priests and Levites who have come down from Jerusalem. The first three questions are fairly straightforward; they appear to be simple, fact-finding questions: *Who are you?... Are you Elijah?... Are you the prophet?* However, the responses the Baptist offers are not satisfying, so his interviewers become a bit animated: *Who are you? Let us have an answer for those who sent us. What do you say about yourself?* (1:22). Finally, they become almost agitated, and they begin to challenge his activities, *Why then are you baptizing if you are neither the Messiah, nor Elijah, nor the prophet?* (1:25). Just as the tenor of the Baptist's questioners change, you need to change the tenor and intensity of your voice as you repeat their questions.

At each stage of the story, the Baptist responds with the same level of intensity as his questioners. Initially, his answers are straightforward and without emotion, but they become increasingly more energetic as the episode unfolds. Again, convey this in your reading. The Baptist's last response should receive the most emphasis. Raise your voice as though you are making an announcement to a large group of people: *I baptize with water.... his sandal* (1:26–27).

Pronunciation Guide

Bethany (BETH-uh-nee), *Elijah* (ee-LĪ-juh; ih-), *Isaiah* (ī-ZAY-uh), *Jerusalem* (juh-ROO-suh-luhm), *Jews* (JOOZ), *Jordan* (JOR-duhn), *Levites* (LEE-vīts), *Messiah* (muh-SĪ-uh), *Pharisees* (FAIR-uh-seez)

FOURTH SUNDAY OF ADVENT

2 Samuel 7:1–11, 16
Luke 1:46b–55 *or* Psalm 89:1–4, 19–26
✠ Canticle 3 *or* 15 *or* Psalm 89:1–4, 19–26
Romans 16:25–27
Luke 1:26–38

2 SAMUEL 7:1–11, 16

Commentary

In last week's reading from 2 Samuel, we read the story of how David brought the ark of the covenant into his new capital, Jerusalem. When the ark was first constructed in the wilderness years, it was housed in the tabernacle, which was a portable shrine. So, when David brings the ark into Jerusalem, it seems entirely appropriate that he should install it in a tent.

7:1–3. Yet, when things have settled down and the kingdom is at peace, David begins to wonder about the disparity between his own palace of cedar and the LORD's tent. His prophetic advisor Nathan does not need a special word from the LORD. He has seen how the LORD has been with David and how he has blessed everything David has put his hand to, so he simply encourages David to do as he sees fit.

7:4–7. Still the LORD does have an opinion on the matter; after all it is his house they are talking about. The LORD sends a message to David through Nathan. He begins by stating that in all the time he has been with his people, he has never once asked anyone to construct a permanent place of residence for him. In any case, it would be impossible, for he is not a god made of wood or stone but the Creator of all that is, seen and unseen. As he says in Isaiah, "Heaven is my throne and the earth is my footstool; what is the house that you would build for me, and what is my resting place?" (Isa 66:1). In short, the LORD is content with what he has; he is not interested in a new house.

7:8–11. What the LORD *is* interested in are his people and those whom he calls to shepherd them. The LORD has not forgotten his promise to Abraham and Sarah to make them into a great nation so that they may become the means by which God's blessing comes to all peoples (Gen 12:3). The LORD intends to protect and preserve his chosen people. He intends to shape them with his character so that they may live out their priestly vocation to mediate the presence, knowledge, and forgiveness of God to all peoples everywhere.

God's people need good leaders if they are going to live out their vocation as God's people. One way the LORD will accomplish this purpose is by making a house for David. Despite David's many faults, the LORD sees in him a faithful follower, a man after his own heart (1 Sam 13:14). The LORD will not only bless David, he will bless David's offspring as well.

7:16. In short, the LORD is committing himself to the Davidic line and is establishing a royal dynasty. From now on and for forever, one of David's descendants will rule as king over the people of God. The first will be David's son Solomon; the last will be David's descendant and Lord, Jesus the Messiah.

Suggestions for Lectors

Read the opening verses in your normal narrating voice (7:1–3). Then, at the beginning of 7:4, drop your voice slightly and read with a different overall tone as you deliver the LORD's words to David through Nathan. In 7:4–7, the LORD asks two rhetorical questions, both of which expect a negative response: *Are you the one to build me a house to live in?* (7:4) and *did I ever speak a word…?* (7:7). Increase the pitch of your voice when asking these questions.

The most important part of today's reading is the covenant that the LORD establishes with David and his offspring, so do what you can to highlight it. Since the covenant the LORD is making with David is a unilateral covenant, one established and maintained by the LORD himself, highlight the commitments the LORD is making to David, by emphasizing each of the *I will*'s:

7:9 *I will make…*
7:10 *I will appoint…*
7:11 *I will give…*

Then, when you reach the final verse, slow down and intensify your voice as say, *Your house and your kingdom shall be made sure forever before me;…* (7:16a). Do not let a syllable be lost here, especially in the final clause, *your throne shall be established forever* (7:16b).

Pronunciation Guide
David (DAY-vid), *Egypt* (EE-jipt), *Israel* (IZ-ree-uhl; -ray-), *Nathan* (NAY-thuhn)

ROMANS 16:25–27

Commentary
In the last chapter of Romans, Paul begins to draw his letter to a close. In 16:1–16, he extends his greetings to various Christians, and then in 16:17–23 he offers some final instructions. In today's reading, Paul concludes his letter with a doxology.

16:25–27. A doxology is an offering of praise to God, and in this doxology Paul praises God for "the revelation of the mystery that was kept secret for long ages but is now disclosed… and made known to all the Gentiles… to bring about the obedience of faith" (16:25b–26). This language recalls the opening lines of Romans (1:1–7), especially where Paul speaks of bringing about "the obedience of faith among all the Gentiles" (1:5).

In Paul's usage, a mystery did not refer to something mysterious but simply to something that remains undisclosed and, therefore, unknown. What is this mystery that has been kept secret for so long, but has now finally been revealed on account of Jesus? Simply this, all people come into a right-relationship with God on the basis of the faithfulness of Jesus and not on the basis of obedience to the law. Since this righteousness is rooted in faith instead of the law, it is open to all who come to trust in Jesus, be they Jew or Gentile. Moreover, because this righteousness is rooted in the faithfulness of Jesus versus the workings of the law, it is able to produce a truer, more lasting obedience than the law ever could. This is what Paul means by the obedience of faith, obedience that is enlivened, motivated, and sustained by faith versus the dead works of the law. For Paul, this is truly grounds for praise.

Suggestions for Lectors
Today's reading is quite short so make sure your listeners are ready and attentive before you begin. Since a doxology is praise directed toward God, direct your words to God instead of to your listeners.

Today's reading is also complex, with three verses constituting a single sentence. The basic thought is quite simple, *Now to God be the glory forever.* But Paul wants to identify this God and offer reasons why this God deserves our praise and adoration, so he describes God with reference to Jesus Christ and the gospel.

One way to tackle a complex sentence is to reformat it so that you can see its logic and flow more easily. Identify the central thought and then build your intonation around that. The following is just one way to visualize the structure of this sentence. The italicized portions are the main thought, and these should be emphasized in your reading. Read them slowly in a raised voice full of praise.

Now to God
    who is able to strengthen you
        according to my gospel and the proclamation of Jesus Christ,
        according to the revelation of the mystery
            that was kept secret for long ages but
            is now disclosed, and
                through the prophetic writings
            is made known to all the Gentiles,
                    according to the command of the eternal God,
                to bring about the obedience of faith—
to the only wise God,
    through Jesus Christ,
        to whom be the glory forever! Amen.

Pronunciation Guide
Gentile (JEN-tīl), *Romans* (ROH-muhnz)

Luke 1:26–38

Notes
Sequence. 1 of 3

Commentary
The Gospel of Luke begins with two annunciations, that is, two angelic announcements of coming births. In the first annunciation, the angel Gabriel appears to the priest Zechariah and announces that his wife Elizabeth will bear him a son named John, whom we know as the Baptist (1:5–25). In the second annunciation, Gabriel is sent to a teenage girl, Mary of Nazareth, to inform her that she will conceive and give birth to a son, whom she is to name Jesus (1:26–38). Each of these births is remarkable in its own way. Elizabeth is barren and beyond normal child-bearing years, while Mary will conceive without the aid of a human partner. As the angel says to Mary in today's reading, nothing is impossible with God.

1:26–29. In today's reading, the angel Gabriel is sent to Nazareth, a small backwater village located on the outskirts of Jewish society and on the fringes of the great Roman Empire. In other words, Nazareth is a most unlikely place for the beginning of God's empire. Gabriel arrives "in the sixth month" (1:26), that is, the sixth month of Elizabeth's pregnancy. He is sent to Mary, who is described as a betrothed virgin. Mary is likely young, and she has never engaged in sexual relations with a man. This information makes Gabriel's announcement all the more remarkable.

1:30–33. Gabriel's greeting says a lot about Mary for he greets her as one who is favored by God. The reader is never told why Mary should be so honored. Whatever the reason, she has been chosen to play a special part in God's plans to restore Israel and to redeem the world. Mary will conceive and bear the Messiah, the anointed king who will rule over God's people throughout all eternity.

1:34–38. Mary is understandably perplexed by Gabriel's words. Not only is she speaking with an angel, but this angel is talking about matters that seem quite impossible to her. How could she possibly become mother to the Messiah, the Son of God, when she is still a virgin? After all, even though God has performed some amazing deeds in the biblical record, nothing like this has ever happened. God has made it possible for barren women to conceive, but always with the aid of their husbands. Yet, on this occasion, Joseph will play no role in the conception.

Instead, much as the Spirit of God brooded over the chaotic waters at the beginning of creation (Gen 1:2), so now the Spirit will brood over Mary, and the power of God will bring into being the child who will be called the Son of God. As evidence of God's ability to bring about the seemingly impossible, Gabriel informs Mary of the pregnancy of her cousin Elizabeth. (In the scene following today's reading, Mary confirms this by visiting Elizabeth (1:39–45).) With all humility and without concern for what this will mean for her, this young village girl gives her consent and agrees to participate in what God wishes to accomplish through her. "Here am I, the servant of the Lord; let it be with me according to your word" (1:38).

Suggestions for Lectors

Today's story is not a fairytale, but it begins like one. Begin by reading *In the sixth month* with the same intonation you would use for *Once upon a time*, then continue in your best storytelling voice as you narrate this story to your listeners.

The angel gives two brief speeches. Draw each speech to a close by slowing down and reading the concluding clause with purposefulness. At the end of the first speech, pause after *kingdom*, *be*, and *no* and emphasize *no*, as in: *and of his kingdom… there will be… <u>no</u>… end* (1:33). At the end of the second speech, accent and pause after *nothing* and pause again after *impossible*, as in: *For <u>nothing</u>… will be impossible… with God* (1:37).

The line that deserves the most attention is Mary's willing consent to her role as the bearer of God's Son. Deliver her words of acceptance with a quiet confidence and a strong quietude.

Pronunciation Guide

David (DAY-vid), *Galilee* (GAL-uh-lee),
Gabriel (GAY-bree-uhl; *not* GAB-ree-el'),
Jacob (JAY-kuhb), *Joseph* (JOH-sif; -suhf),
Mary (MAIR-ee), *Nazareth* (NAZ-uh-reth; *not* -rus)

SEASON OF CHRISTMAS

CHRISTMAS DAY — PROPER I

Isaiah 9:2–7
Psalm 96
Titus 2:11–14
Luke 2:1–14, (15–20)

ISAIAH 9:2–7

Commentary

In Isaiah 7, King Ahaz and the leading citizens of Jerusalem are in a state of panic because King Pekah of the northern kingdom of Israel has forged an alliance with King Rezin of Aram against the southern kingdom of Judah. To alleviate the people's concerns regarding the safety and security of Jerusalem and Judah, Isaiah is sent to Ahaz with a word from the LORD saying that the plans hatched by Israel and Aram will fail. In fact, within a relatively short time, these two kingdoms will fall to the Assyrian empire and will pose no further threat. Consequently, Ahaz should not attempt to make any alliances of his own but trust Isaiah's counsel regarding the LORD's plans. "If you do not stand firm in faith, you shall not stand at all" (7:9b). To confirm that these things shall happen as Isaiah has said, the LORD gives Ahaz a sign that concerns a young woman giving birth to a child whose name will be Immanuel, that is, *God with us*. Specifically, the sign is this: The child "shall eat curds and honey by the time he knows how to refuse the evil and choose the good. For before the child knows how to refuse the evil and choose the good, the land before whose two kings you are in dread will be deserted" (7:15–16). In other words, by the time the child reaches two years of age, Assyria will have destroyed Israel and Aram. This sign is reconfirmed in 8:1–4, using slightly different metaphors.

In the end, Ahaz and the people of Judah do not trust the LORD to deliver them (8:6), which is not particularly surprising since the message Isaiah was given for Judah was destined to fail (6:9–10). Since the people remained fearful, Isaiah announced that Assyria would not stop with Aram and Israel but would also move against Judah as well, reaching "up to its neck" (8:8). Judah would experience a measure of judgment but not enough to destroy it completely. This hope for the continued existence of Judah finds expression in today's reading, which seems to anticipate Judah's exile to Babylon and its subsequent restoration.

9:2–5. In the interpretation being followed here, "the people who walked in darkness" and "lived in a land of deep darkness" refers to God's chosen people who have been sent into exile for their sins of idolatry and injustice. In that land of darkness, a light has dawned, which refers to the coming of the LORD to rescue his people from the land of their exile. When the people see their salvation, they will rejoice and all the instruments of their oppression—yoke, bar, and rod—will be destroyed "as on the day of Midian" (9:4).

The day of Midian recalls an incident from Judges where Gideon led a small band of Israelites armed with torches, jars, and trumpets in a successful campaign against the more numerous, better equipped Midianites (Judg 7:15–25), whom the LORD had sent to oppress the Israelites for seven years as punishment for their unfaithfulness (Judg 6:1–10). In today's reading, the allusion to *the day of Midian* supports the assertion that the scenario being depicted is the restoration of God's people after they have served time in judgment for unfaithfulness (cf. Isa 40:1–3, Adv 2). Though the Midianites had been God's instrument of judgment, they were defeated in order to procure Israel's deliverance. Likewise, the restoration of God's exiled people will be accomplished in part by executing judgment against the nation whom the LORD will appoint to execute judgment upon Judah (9:5; cf. 14:2).

9:6–7. Because one of the key factors contributing to the people's unfaithfulness was poor leadership (3:12b–15; 56:10–12), Isaiah envisions the LORD raising up a Davidic king who will possess all of the qualities necessary to rule and guide God's people into leading lives characterized by righteousness and justice (5:7).

Suggestions for Lectors

In this reading, you are the prophet Isaiah announcing a message of hope, joy, and peace to a people who have lived for years in the darkness and gloom of despair. Since it can be difficult to sustain such an exuberant mood throughout a reading, start out slowly and build to a crescendo in the last verse. You may wish to adopt a slower tempo for this reading, giving you and your listeners a chance to exult in all of the wonderful things to occur.

In 9:2–3, lean strongly on *great light*, *light*, *joy*, *rejoice*, and *exult*. Notice that verses 4, 5, and 6 all begin with *For*, which introduces the three reasons why *they rejoice before you* (9:3b). That is, the people rejoice because they have been released from captivity (9:4), their enemies have been destroyed (9:5), and they have been given a new and glorious leader (9:6–7). So, as you read the *For* statements, in your mind and in your reading, connect them back to *they rejoice before you* in 9:3b.

In 9:6, *For* introduces the climactic grounds for rejoicing, so you might pause a full second before reading 9:6–7. As you announce the good news of this ideal ruler, speak slowly and carefully. Drop your voice after *child*; the notion of *born* is not important here since it is a routine part of any birth announcement. Instead of reading the four titles as though they belong to a list, enunciate each of them one by one. As you conclude, pause before *The zeal of the LORD of hosts will do this* (9:7). Then read this line slowly with a sense of awe in your voice. You might also try adding an *And* before this concluding line, which will help set it apart from the rest of the reading.

Pronunciation Guide

Isaiah (ī-ZAY-uh), *Midian* (MID-ee-uhn)

Titus 2:11–14

Notes
Sequence. 1 of 2

Commentary
Titus was a Gentile Christian (Gal 2:3) whom Paul had assigned certain responsibilities to within the churches on Crete (1:5). In this letter, Paul gives Titus advice on a variety of matters. In 2:1–10, he outlines the types of behavior that should characterize the lives of Christian men, women, and slaves.

2:11–14. Then, in today's reading, Paul supplies the rationale that underlies and undergirds Christian morality. In short, salvation entails God rescuing us from our indebtedness to sin and from slavery to our own worldly passions and ungodly tendencies (cf. 3:4, Chr II). Jesus Christ, who is our God and Savior, gave himself for us that we might be free to love through the doing of good works.

Suggestions for Lectors
This is a brief passage, so read it more deliberately and slowly than you might read a much longer passage. The passage starts quickly; so after introducing the reading, make sure your listeners are ready and attentive before you begin. There is no particular emphasis. The whole passage can be read with the same tone of voice, confident and strong.

Notice that 2:11–13 comprises one single, complex sentence. There is plenty of punctuation throughout these verses, giving you sufficient opportunity to pause. Your challenge, then, will be to develop such a feel for the flow of this sentence that you are able, through the intonation of your voice, to draw all of these phrases and clauses together into a single, coherent thought for your listeners. This is not particularly difficult, though it may take some practice until you discover an intonation that you think works.

Pronunciation Guide
blessed (adj., two syllables; BLES-id), *Titus* (TĪ-tuhs)

Luke 2:1–14, (15–20)

Notes
Sequence. 2 of 3

Commentary
Matthew and Luke are the only two canonical gospels that narrate the events surrounding the birth of Jesus. In our Christmas nativities and plays, these two accounts are woven into a single account. For example, in Matthew, it is Magi from the east who follow a star and come to visit Jesus sometime after he is born; in Luke, it is local shepherds visited by angels who come to the manger on the night of his birth.

2:1–2. Today's reading begins with a decree by Emperor Augustus that all the world should be registered. Interestingly, whereas Matthew associates Jesus' birth with the reign of the local Jewish ruler, King Herod (Matt 2:1, ✠ Chr 2), Luke associates his birth with the reign of Rome's first emperor, Caesar Augustus (Luke 2:1), thereby situating Jesus' birth within the larger context of world history, specifically within the political context of the Roman Empire. Luke, however, is doing more than simply dating these events or providing a bit of historical background. He is setting up a contrast between the wealthy and powerful Augustus, emperor of the great Roman Empire, and the Jewish infant Jesus, born in a stable in a tiny village of Bethlehem.

2:3–7. On account of the registration, or the census, Mary and Joseph travel from Nazareth in Galilee to Bethlehem in Judea, the hometown of Israel's most celebrated king, King David. Like his ancestor, Jesus will also be a king, though his kingship and kingdom will look quite different. Furthermore, just as the emperor Augustus had inscriptions extolling his reign, so also Jesus will have an inscription extolling his reign; when he is executed by Rome, the inscription above him will read, "The King of the Jews" (23:38). When Jesus is born, Mary wraps him in strips of cloth and places him in a feeding trough for domestic animals—just one of the clues that Mary and Joseph are poor. Another indication of their economic status occurs after today's reading, when they present a sacrifice for Mary's purification after childbirth. They offer "a pair of turtledoves or two young pigeons" (2:24), which is what the law prescribed for those who could not afford a sheep (Lev 12:6–8).

2:8–14. Before he became king over Israel, David had been a shepherd, and so it is appropriate that shepherds were the first to hear about and see Israel's long-awaited Messiah King. Also, in the first-century world, shepherds generally belonged to the peasant class at the bottom of the scale of power and privilege and so stand in marked contrast to the power and privilege of those mentioned at the beginning of the episode: Emperor Augustus and Governor Quirinius. This is just one more example among many reflecting the theme of reversal found throughout Luke's gospel. As Mary proclaims in the Magnificat, the Lord "has brought down the powerful from their thrones, and lifted up the lowly" (1:52).

Caesar Augustus was born Gaius Octavian; the grandnephew and later the adopted son and heir of Julius Caesar. Ruling from 27 B.C. to 14 A.D., Augustus ushered in an era of relative peace known as the *Pax Romana*, or Roman peace. Consequently, Augustus was accorded great honor throughout the empire. What is so striking and significant for our understanding of the angels' announcement is that most of the descriptions and designations applied to Jesus are those that were applied to Augustus. For example, compare the italicized words and phrases in the following inscriptions with what the angels announce to the shepherds.

> "Decree of the Greek Assembly in the province of Asia… Augustus, whom Providence has filled with virtue for the benefit of *humanity*, and has in her beneficence granted us and those who will come after us a *Savior* who has made *war to cease* and who shall put everything in *peaceful order*… with the result that the *birthday of our God* signaled the beginning of *good news* for *the world* because of his coming" (Priene Inscription, 9 B.C.).

> "Divine Augustus Caesar, *son of a god*, imperator of land and sea, the benefactor and *savior* of the *whole world*" (Myrian Inscription).

This demonstrates that in the first-century Mediterranean world, *good news*, *savior*, and *son of God* were not simply religious terms, they were inherently political as well. Consequently, when Luke and other early Christians spoke of Jesus as Savior and Son of God, they were making religious as well as political claims. When they confessed that Jesus is Lord, they were also saying that the Roman emperor was not.

2:15–20. When the angels leave, the shepherds make their way to the stable and find the baby just as the angels told them, wrapped in bands of cloth and lying in a manger. All were amazed at the shepherds' tale of angels, but "Mary treasured all these words and pondered them in her heart" (2:19), something she will do again when her son is twelve years old (2:51b).

Suggestions for Lectors

Today's episode occurs in two or three movements (1–7, 8–14, (15–20)), depending upon whether your reading stops at 2:14 or 2:20. Whatever the case may be, make sure to pause for a full second between movements to mark the transition from one to the next. In addition, decide from whose perspective you wish to narrate each movement. For example, the first movement could be intoned from Mary's point of view, the second from the shepherds' point of view, and then, the third could begin from the shepherds' point of view before shifting to Mary's at the midway point.

The first movement presents a very simple narrative about a census, a journey, and a birth, which can all be read very simply in the voice of a narrator. This simple narrative continues on into the second movement with the setting of the scene in 2:8. Yet, this ordinary narrative suddenly becomes extraordinary with the unexpected appearance of the angel of the Lord; so pause for a second before 2:9, then read 2:9–14 in an elevated and animated tone, perhaps slowly increasing your intensity until it climaxes in the angelic song of praise in 2:14.

If you conclude with the third movement (2:15–20), return to your normal narrative voice and season it with awe as the shepherds recount and Mary ponders these extraordinary events. Pause before 2:19, and then proceed in a slow, introspective manner, as though you have just turned, amidst all the excitement, and noticed Mary's face. Pausing again before 2:20, conclude your reading by trying to convey some measure of the shepherds' joy and excitement.

Pronunciation Guide

Augustus (uh-GUHS-tuhs; aw-)
Bethlehem (BETH-luh-hem')
Galilee (GAL-uh-lee)
Judea (joo-DEE-uh; -DAY-)
Messiah (muh-SĪ-uh)
Nazareth (NAZ-uh-reth; *not* -rus)
Quirinius (kwih-RIN-ee-uhs; kwuh-)
Syria (SIHR-ee-uh)

CHRISTMAS DAY — PROPER II

Isaiah 62:6–12
Psalm 97
Titus 3:4–7
Luke 2:(1–7), 8–20

Isaiah 62:6–12

Commentary

Throughout Isaiah, but especially after chapter 40, the prophet envisions a time when the Babylonian exile will be over and Jerusalem (= Zion), "the City of the LORD" (60:14b), will be rebuilt and will once again serve as the center of instruction and worship for God's chosen people as well as for all the peoples of the world (cf. 60:1–6, Epi). Isaiah 62 offers a poetic, prophetic description of the vindication and salvation of Jerusalem brought about by the LORD.

While granting the possibility that the speaker in today's reading is the LORD, here we will take the position that the speaker is the prophet-servant introduced in 61:1. This servant describes himself as having been anointed with the Spirit of the Lord GOD in order "to provide for those who mourn in Zion—to give them a garland instead of ashes, the oil of gladness instead of mourning, the mantle of praise instead of a faint spirit" (61:3, Adv 3).

62:6–9. Consequently, the servant takes personal responsibility for making sure that the LORD follows through with what he has promised. In 62:1–2 (✠ Chr 1), the servant declares that he will not keep silent or rest until Zion has been restored and all the nations and kings of the world behold her glory. Likewise, in today's reading, the servant posts sentinels on Jerusalem's walls. Their job is not to remain silent or to rest but to pester the LORD "until he establishes Jerusalem and makes it renowned throughout the earth" (62:7). They are to remind the LORD of his promises, some of which the servant lays out in 62:8–9.

62:10–12. In Isaiah 6 (Tri), Isaiah is granted a vision of the LORD of hosts. The hosts are the heavenly beings who serve as royal attendants and who belong to the LORD's divine council (cf. Ps 82:1; Job 1:6). So, when the LORD asks, "Whom shall I send, and who will go for *us*?" (6:8), those whom the LORD is addressing and who constitute the *us* are members of the divine council. In Isaiah 40:3 (Adv 2), the divine council is addressed when a voice cries out, "In the wilderness prepare the way of the LORD, make straight in the desert a highway for our God." In the underlying Hebrew text, it is clear that the LORD is addressing the divine council, but not in most English translations. One exception is the KJV, which uses *ye*, the plural for you: "Prepare *ye* the way of the LORD." Likewise, in Isaiah 57:14, the divine council is called upon to "Build up, build up, prepare the way, remove every obstruction from my people's way." Consequently, in today's reading, it is members of the divine council who are being instructed to clear a highway for the exiles' return to Jerusalem and to announce to Zion that her LORD and husband is coming to restore her grandeur. When this occurs, the people will be called "The Holy People, The

Redeemed of the LORD" (cf. Hosea 1:9–10), and Jerusalem will be called "Sought Out, A City Not Forsaken" (cf. 62:4).

Suggestions for Lectors
As you read today, imagine that you are the servant, and speak directly to your listeners as though they are Jerusalem personified. Be joyful as you attempt to give hope and encouragement to a people tired and worn down by their own failures and the constant pressures of this world.

The reading can be divided into three sections (62:6–7, 8–9, 10–12) by pausing and looking up before each section. Read 62:10–12 in an elevated voice, making sure to grant special emphasis to *See, your salvation comes; his reward is with him, and his recompense before him* (62:11b), which serves as the climax. The resolution then follows in 62:12, so drop your voice and slow down as you conclude your reading.

Pronunciation Guide
Isaiah (Ī-ZAY-uh), *Jerusalem* (juh-ROO-suh-luhm), *Zion* (ZĪ-uhn)

TITUS 3:4–7

Notes
Sequence. 2 of 2

Commentary
In this reading, Paul instructs his apprentice Titus to remind the Christians under his care that their salvation is solely due to God's "goodness and loving kindness" (3:4).

3:4–7. God our Savior did not come to us, justify us, and grant us eternal life because we had somehow made ourselves worthy. Instead, it was through God's grace and mercy alone that we have been saved and renewed through the power of the Holy Spirit that has been given to us through Jesus Christ our Savior.

Suggestions for Lectors
On this Christmas Day, proclaim these words loud and clear with a sense of awe-filled joy and gratitude for what God has made possible through Jesus Christ our Lord and Savior. Read this brief passage slowly and carefully, enunciating every clause and phrase according to its role within the sentence structure.

Pronunciation Guide
Titus (TĪ-tuhs)

LUKE 2:(1–7), 8–20

Notes
Sequence. 2 of 3

Commentary
Matthew and Luke are the only two canonical gospels that narrate the events surrounding the birth of Jesus. In our Christmas nativities and plays, these two accounts are woven into a single account. For example, in Matthew, it is Magi from the

east who follow a star and come to visit Jesus sometime after he is born; in Luke, it is local shepherds visited by angels who come to the manger on the night of his birth.

2:1–2. Today's reading begins with a decree by Emperor Augustus that all the world should be registered. Interestingly, whereas Matthew associates Jesus' birth with the reign of the local Jewish ruler, King Herod (Matt 2:1, ✠ Chr 2), Luke associates his birth with the reign of Rome's first emperor, Caesar Augustus (Luke 2:1), thereby situating Jesus' birth within the larger context of world history, specifically within the political context of the Roman Empire. Luke, however, is doing more than simply dating these events or providing a bit of historical background. He is setting up a contrast between the wealthy and powerful Augustus, emperor of the great Roman Empire, and the Jewish infant Jesus, born in a stable in a tiny village of Bethlehem.

2:3–7. On account of the registration, or the census, Mary and Joseph travel from Nazareth in Galilee to Bethlehem in Judea, the hometown of Israel's most celebrated king, King David. Like his ancestor, Jesus will also be a king, though his kingship and kingdom will look quite different. Furthermore, just as the emperor Augustus had inscriptions extolling his reign, so also Jesus will have an inscription extolling his reign; when he is executed by Rome, the inscription above him will read, "The King of the Jews" (23:38). When Jesus is born, Mary wraps him in strips of cloth and places him in a feeding trough for domestic animals—just one of the clues that Mary and Joseph are poor. Another indication of their economic status occurs after today's reading, when they present a sacrifice for Mary's purification after childbirth. They offer "a pair of turtledoves or two young pigeons" (2:24), which is what the law prescribed for those who could not afford a sheep (Lev 12:6–8).

2:8–14. Before he became king over Israel, David had been a shepherd, and so it is appropriate that shepherds were the first to hear about and see Israel's long-awaited Messiah King. Also, in the first-century world, shepherds generally belonged to the peasant class at the bottom of the scale of power and privilege and so stand in marked contrast to the power and privilege of those mentioned at the beginning of the episode: Emperor Augustus and Governor Quirinius. This is just one more example among many reflecting the theme of reversal found throughout Luke's gospel. As Mary proclaims in the Magnificat, the Lord "has brought down the powerful from their thrones, and lifted up the lowly" (1:52).

Caesar Augustus was born Gaius Octavian; the grandnephew and later the adopted son and heir of Julius Caesar. Ruling from 27 B.C. to 14 A.D., Augustus ushered in an era of relative peace known as the *Pax Romana*, or Roman peace. Consequently, Augustus was accorded great honor throughout the empire. What is so striking and significant for our understanding of the angels' announcement is that most of the descriptions and designations applied to Jesus are those that were applied to Augustus. For example, compare the italicized words and phrases in the following inscriptions with what the angels announce to the shepherds.

> "Divine Augustus Caesar, *son of a god*, imperator of land and sea, the benefactor and *savior* of the *whole world*" (Myrian Inscription).

"Decree of the Greek Assembly in the province of Asia… Augustus, whom Providence has filled with virtue for the benefit of *humanity*, and has in her beneficence granted us and those who will come after us a *Savior* who has made *war to cease* and who shall put everything in *peaceful order*… with the result that the *birthday of our God* signaled the beginning of *good news* for *the world* because of his coming" (Priene Inscription, 9 B.C.).

This demonstrates that in the first-century Mediterranean world, *good news*, *savior*, and *son of God* were not simply religious terms, they were inherently political as well. Consequently, when Luke and other early Christians spoke of Jesus as Savior and Son of God, they were making religious as well as political claims. When they confessed that Jesus is Lord, they were also saying that the Roman emperor was not.

2:15–20. When the angels leave, the shepherds make their way to the stable and find the baby just as the angels told them, wrapped in bands of cloth and lying in a manger. All were amazed at the shepherds' tale of angels, but "Mary treasured all these words and pondered them in her heart" (2:19), something she will do again when her son is twelve years old (2:51b).

Suggestions for Lectors

Today's episode occurs in two or three movements ((1–7), 8–14, 15–20), depending upon whether your reading begins with 2:1 or 2:8. Whatever the case may be, make sure to pause for a full second between movements to mark the transition from one to the next. In addition, decide from whose perspective you wish to narrate each movement. For example, the first movement could be intoned from Mary's point of view, the second from the shepherds' point of view, and then, the third could begin from the shepherds' point of view before shifting to Mary's at the midway point.

The first movement presents a very simple narrative about a census, a journey, and a birth, which can all be read very simply in the voice of a narrator. This simple narrative continues on into the second movement with the setting of the scene in 2:8. Yet, this ordinary narrative suddenly becomes extraordinary with the unexpected appearance of the angel of the Lord; so pause for a second before 2:9, then read 2:9–14 in an elevated and animated tone, perhaps slowly increasing your intensity until it climaxes in the angelic song of praise in 2:14.

In the final movement (2:15–20), return to your normal narrative voice and season it with awe as the shepherds recount and Mary ponders these extraordinary events. Pause before 2:19, and then proceed in a slow, introspective manner, as though you have just turned, amidst all the excitement, and noticed Mary's face. Pausing again before 2:20, conclude your reading by trying to convey some measure of the shepherds' joy and excitement.

Pronunciation Guide

Augustus (uh-GUHS-tuhs; aw-), *Bethlehem* (BETH-luh-hem'),
Galilee (GAL-uh-lee), *Judea* (joo-DEE-uh; -DAY-),
Messiah (muh-SĪ-uh), *Nazareth* (NAZ-uh-reth; *not* -rus),
Quirinius (kwih-RIN-ee-uhs; kwuh-), *Syria* (SIHR-ee-uh)

CHRISTMAS DAY — PROPER III

Isaiah 52:7–10
Psalm 98
Hebrews 1:1–4, (5–12)
John 1:1–14

Isaiah 52:7–10

Commentary

In Isaiah 1–39, the prophet announces the LORD's judgment upon the people of Judah and Jerusalem for their centuries of idolatry and injustice, that is, for their ongoing refusal to love God with their whole heart (Deut 6:5, Prop 26; Exod 20:1–7, Lent 3) and their failure to love their neighbors as themselves (Lev 19:18; Exod 20:8–17). Isaiah 39 ends ominously as the predicted destruction and exile of Judah and Jerusalem by the Babylonian empire becomes imminent.

Isaiah 40 skips ahead many years, introducing a new movement in the prophetic drama. It begins on a completely different note than that with which Isaiah 39 concludes. Isaiah 40 presupposes that God's people have been in exile for some time and opens with a message of hope for these exiles in Babylon: "Comfort, O comfort my people, says your God. Speak tenderly to Jerusalem, and cry to her that she has served her term, that her penalty is paid, that she has received from the LORD's hand double for all her sins" (40:1–2, Adv 2). In other words, the exile is over. The LORD has forgiven his people and is coming soon to bring them back home. Therefore, the members of the LORD's divine council (cf. 6:8; Ps 82:1; Job 1:6) are told to "prepare the way of the LORD" (40:3a). Even Jerusalem situated on Mount Zion is called to make preparations: "Get you up to a high mountain, O Zion, herald of good tidings; lift up your voice with strength, O Jerusalem, herald of good tidings, lift it up, do not fear; say to the cities of Judah, '*Here is your God!*'" (40:9). This same basic message of hope, forgiveness, and restoration is repeated in today's reading.

52:7–10. The vehicle for this message is the scenario of a messenger who runs long distances to bring news and updates regarding the progress of a distant battle. Sentinels are posted on the city walls not only to protect the city but also to keep watch for messengers. The battle in question is between the LORD and Babylon. Although Babylon was the LORD's chosen instrument for executing judgment upon his own people, Babylon itself is also in need of judgment (13:1–22; 14:3–23). In turn, Babylon's judgment would mean salvation for the exiles. Babylon's judgment would be executed by Cyrus, the king of the Persians, through whom the LORD would simultaneously bring about the downfall of Babylon and the restoration of Judah. "The LORD, your Redeemer… says of Cyrus, 'He is my shepherd, and he shall carry out all my purpose.… I have aroused Cyrus in righteousness, and I will make all his paths straight; he shall build my city and set my exiles free'" (44:24a, 28a; 45:13a; cf. 2 Chr 36:22–23; Ezra 1:1–4).

Thus, in today's reading, the messenger has come from Babylon with good news: the LORD has won; Babylon has been defeated; the exile is finally over. The sentinels announce this message of victory and salvation throughout the city. With singing and shouts of joy, they run about proclaiming, "Your God reigns! Your God reigns!" (52:7). With this news comes the realization that in a very short while the exiles themselves will come over those mountains led by none other than the LORD. Thus, in the arrival of the good news, the sentinels anticipate as though "in plain sight... the return of the LORD to Zion" (52:10; cf. 40:10–11, Adv 2). Moreover, the people rejoice, for in rolling up his sleeves to redeem them and to restore Jerusalem, the LORD has revealed to all people everywhere his mighty power and commitment to his chosen people.

Suggestions for Lectors

One of the most difficult lessons for us to learn as lectors and lay readers is that it is okay to raise our voices when a reading demands it. People can be so overwhelmed and distracted by worldly troubles of all kinds that we must call out the Good News to attract their attention, not only at Christmas but all the year round.

In today's reading, read 52:7 in your normal reading voice, giving your listeners a chance to settle into the reading. Beginning with *Listen!* in 52:8, raise your voice and read the remainder of the passage with an increasingly joyful intensity. When you come to the last sentence, *and all the ends...*, read slowly and deliberately, pausing for a second after *see* before delivering the final phrase *the salvation of our God* (52:10b).

Pronunciation Guide

Isaiah (ī-ZAY-uh), *Jerusalem* (juh-ROO-suh-luhm), *Zion* (ZĪ-uhn)

HEBREWS 1:1–4, (5–12)

Commentary

The Letter to the Hebrews begins with a description of Jesus as the one uniquely identified with God and, therefore, uniquely qualified to reveal God and to implement God's purposes for humanity and all of creation.

1:1–4. Throughout Hebrews, the author highlights the superiority of Jesus and his vocation over all of God's other servants, past, present and future. In the opening lines, these later themes are anticipated. In the past, God communicated God's purposes through the prophets whom God called and equipped to speak his word. But now, in these climactic days, God speaks to us through one who knows God intimately—God's very own Son. Jesus does not simply *tell* us about God, he actually *reveals* God, which goes well beyond what any prophet could do. He is able to do this because, as God's Son, Jesus bears the family resemblance, or as Hebrews says, "He is the reflection of God's glory and the exact imprint of God's very being" (1:3). This description of Jesus' unique, divine identity is consistent with what we find elsewhere in the New Testament (cf. John 1:1, 18, 14:9; Col 1:15) and is expressed in the Nicene Creed ("Light of Light, very God of very God,... of one substance with the Father"). Consequently, Jesus exercises God's authority and power. Jesus has been appointed as God's heir over all things. All things were created through him, and everything is sustained by his word.

Moreover, Jesus not only revealed God to us, he made *us* presentable to God by cleansing us from all our sins (1:3). Unlike other high priests who had to offer sacrifices year after year because their sacrifices were provisional at best (10:11), as our Great High Priest (4:14–5:10, GFri), Jesus purified us once and for all through his single, once-for-all-time sacrifice of himself (10:10, 12). Jesus then sat down at the right hand of God because his work was complete (1:3; 10:12). His name and his ministry are far superior to all others, even to that of the angels (cf. Phil 2:6–11, Name).

1:5–12. The author then provides a litany of OT texts that highlight Jesus' superiority to the angels: 1:5a (Ps 2:7); 1:5b (2 Sam 7:14, Prop 11); 1:6 (Deut 32:43); 1:7 (Ps 104:4); 1:8–9 (Ps 45:6–7); 1:10–12 (Ps 102:25–27); 1:13 (Ps 110:1).

Suggestions for Lectors

Today's reading begins in a story-like fashion with the words *Long ago*, so adopt a storytelling voice for the first two verses. Pause before verse 3, and then read 1:3–4 in a more explanatory manner with a hint of proclamation in your voice.

Pause again before verse 5 as you begin reading the masterful chain of OT quotations attesting to the pre-eminence of Jesus. Make sure your voice separates the quotations with the words and phrases that introduce each one—for example, *or again* (1:5), *and again* (1:6), *of the angels he says* (1:7), *but of the Son he says*, (1:8), and even the single word *and* introducing the quotation in 1:10. Avoid any temptation to rush through these quotations. Instead let each one be heard in a voice both solemn and triumphant.

JOHN 1:1–14

Commentary

The Gospel according to John begins with a prologue that introduces themes that are woven throughout John's narrative about Jesus (1:1–18). Of particular importance is the question of Jesus' identity and specifically his relation to God. This is the focus of today's reading.

1:1–5. The *in the beginning* of John 1:1 recalls the *in the beginning* of Genesis 1:1 (Epi 1). With this simple phrase, John connects the story of Jesus with the story of creation. The Word, whom we later discover becomes a particular human being at a particular point in time (1:14), existed before time began; for even at the beginning of creation itself, the Word already was. This Word was not only *with* God in the beginning, this Word *was* God. In other words, while the Word has its own distinct identity as the Word, it belongs to the unique identity of the One God. This is but the first of many of John's mysteries. Then, in language that recalls the role of God's Wisdom in creation (Prov 8:22–31), John presents the Word as having played a decisive role in bringing creation into existence "for all things came into being through [the Word], and without [the Word] not one thing came into being" (1:3). Here, one is reminded of how God brought order and structure out of chaos and nothingness simply by *speaking* things into existence, that is, through *the Word.* Whereas Wisdom seems to have had a beginning (Prov 8:22), the Word is presented here as coeternal with God.

1:6–9. At this point, the author wishes to make clear that this Word of God, which is the light and life of all people (1:5), was not John the Baptist. It appears that some of John the Baptist's followers regarded him as God's anointed Messiah, but here and elsewhere in the gospel, the author of John seeks to clarify the Baptist's status and role: the Baptist was sent from God to be a witness to the light, but he himself was not the light (1:7–8; cf. 1:15, 29–36; 3:25–30).

1:10–13. In 1:10, the Prologue returns to the Word and reveals the drama surrounding the Word's coming. The Word was in the world and the whole world came into being through the Word, yet ironically, the world did not know him nor did the Word's own people accept him, and this is the nature of judgment (cf. 3:19, Tri). Nevertheless, the situation is not dire because anyone and everyone who accepted and believed in the Word was given the power (i.e., the Holy Spirit) to become a child of God.

1:14. Today's reading ends with arguably the greatest mystery within human history: this Word which was with God in the beginning and is God, this very Word "became flesh and lived among us" (1:14). Thus, the mystery of the Incarnation is that God became a full and complete human being, Jesus of Nazareth, even while remaining fully and completely God.

Suggestions for Lectors

As reflected in the Commentary, today's reading falls into three movements plus a climactic conclusion, so include major pauses before verses 6, 10, and 14.

The reading starts quickly with the well-known first verse of John, so make sure that your listeners are completely settled and attuned before you begin reading. Read 1:1 slowly and deliberately. The first sentence, *in the beginning was the Word*, can be read as a simple statement. In the second and third sentences of 1:1, accent the words *with* and *was* respectively. Increase your tempo slightly as you complete the rest of the first movement. The second and third movements are somewhat like narratives and so can be read in your normal storytelling voice.

The reading reaches its climax with 1:14, which describes the incarnation of the Word and the revelation of God's glory. While the first part, *And the Word became flesh and lived among us*, rightfully receives emphasis in readings, the conclusion of the verse deserves equal regard, for the Word's purpose in becoming a human being was so that the fullness of God's glory might be revealed to human beings, as 1:18 reaffirms.

FIRST SUNDAY AFTER CHRISTMAS

Isaiah 61:10–62:3
Psalm 148
Galatians 4:4–7
Luke 2:22–40

Isaiah 61:10–62:3

Commentary

Isaiah 61 and 62 offer poetic, prophetic descriptions of the restoration of God's exiled people and of the rebuilt Jerusalem (= Zion) following the Babylonian exile. In 61:1, an unidentified servant figure is introduced. The description of this figure brings to mind the servant figure(s) in the four so-called Servant Songs of Isaiah (42:1–4; 49:1–6; 50:4–9, Palm; 52:13–53:12, GFri). The servant describes himself as having been anointed with the Spirit of the Lord GOD and sent "to bring good news to the oppressed, to bind up the brokenhearted, to proclaim liberty to the captives, and release to the prisoners;… [and] to provide for those who mourn in Zion—to give them a garland instead of ashes, the oil of gladness instead of mourning, the mantle of praise instead of a faint spirit" (61:1–2a, 3, Adv 3; cf. Luke 4:18–19).

In today's reading, the servant offers a song of thanksgiving (61:10–11) before turning his attention to the vindication and salvation of Jerusalem and its people (62:1–3).

Suggestions for Lectors

This is one of those occasions when you must discipline yourself to speak loudly to reflect the joy of the Christmas season and the joy in today's reading. The printed punctuation lends itself admirably to the theme of the reading, so the only challenge to you remains the raising of your voice to the tone of a proclamation. Do not strain yourself by shouting; instead, let the power come from your midsection up through your vocal passages. After some practice with this at home, you will find that this works quite well.

None of the verses require special emphasis; it will be sufficient to pause for a second between 61:11 and 62:1 in order to signal the slight shift in topic and tone.

Pronunciation Guide

Isaiah (ī-ZAY-uh), *Jerusalem* (juh-ROO-suh-luhm), *Zion* (ZĪ-uhn)

Galatians 4:4–7

Commentary

In his letter to the Galatians, and against the views of some Jewish Christians, Paul argues that Gentiles do not have to be circumcised in order to become Christian, for no one is justified through the law (3:11). Instead, all people—be they Jew or Greek, slave or free, male or female (3:28)—are made right with God and receive the Holy Spirit on the basis of faith. However, if no one is or has ever been justified through the law, then why did God give the law? What was its purpose (3:19)?

In 3:23–26 (✠ Chr 1), Paul begins to answer this question by likening the law to a disciplinarian, what might better be called a guardian or a custodian (Gk., *paidagōgos*). In the ancient Greco-Roman world, a *paidagōgos* was a man, usually a slave, whose duty it was to conduct those under his charge to and from school, overseeing their conduct until they came of age, at which point the *paidagōgos* no longer served in this capacity. Likewise, the law served as our *paidagōgos*, protecting us from the ravaging chaos of sin until the appointed time when the law would be replaced by the Holy Spirit, who would be given to all believers and would accomplish what the law never could do, namely, make sinful, dead human beings alive, holy, and righteous (2:21).

4:4–7. In today's reading, Paul continues by noting that this new age of the Spirit was inaugurated and made possible by God's own Son. The Son became a human being, not just any human being, but one born under the law in order that, through his life, death, resurrection, and ascension, we may become the adopted children and heirs of God, free from the law and filled with the very Spirit that indwelt and guided God's Son, Jesus.

Suggestions for Lectors

Today's reading proceeds in a somewhat narrative tone as Paul explains how the law functioned as a safeguard until the age of faith in Christ arrived. When you come to 4:4 and read, *But when the fullness of time had come…*, try to convey the magnitude of this moment in salvation history when God's Son was sent that *we might receive adoption as children.* Highlight the difference between the former age and the new age by emphasizing the words *born*, *slaves*, and *the law*, on the one hand, and *adoption*, *children*, and *the Spirit*, on the other.

In 4:6b, *Abba! Father!* could be delivered in an emotionally dramatic fashion, but it does not have to be. However, at a minimum, your voice should become elevated as you direct these words to God. Verse 7 not only serves as the reading's conclusion, it also provides a succinct summary of Paul's argument. Consequently, pause for a full second before 4:7, and then read it slowly with frequent pauses and in a tone that suggests you are summing up an argument.

Pronunciation Guide

Abba (AH-buh), *Galatians* (guh-LAY-shuhnz)

LUKE 2:22–40

Notes

Sequence. 3 of 3

Commentary

The Jerusalem temple plays an important role in the Gospel of Luke. The temple is a principal meeting place for the God of Israel and human beings. The temple's centrality is reflected in the fact that the gospel begins and ends in the temple; that is, activities in the temple form an *inclusio* (or bookends) around Luke's story of Jesus. In the opening scene, Zechariah is visited by the angel Gabriel while he is carrying out his priestly duties in the temple (1:5–25). Then, in the final scene, after Jesus' ascension into heaven, his disciples "returned to Jerusalem with great joy, and they were continually in the temple blessing God" (24:52b–53). Moreover, in the birth narratives of John the Baptist and Jesus (1:5–2:52), as related by Luke, nearly forty percent of the story takes place within the temple (1:5–23; 2:22–38; 2:41–51, ✠ Chr 2). Today's reading is one of these stories.

2:22–24. In accordance with Jewish custom, Jesus was circumcised on the eighth day after his birth (2:21; cf. Lev 12:3; Gen 17:12, Lent 2). Once Mary's thirty-three days of ceremonial impurity are complete (Lev 12:4), she and Joseph travel to Jerusalem in order to perform two liturgical acts.

First, a pair of turtledoves or pigeons are sacrificed to effectuate Mary's purification after childbirth. The fact that two birds are used is significant for it reveals that Mary and Joseph were poor. According to Leviticus legislation, this sacrifice for purification was to consist of a lamb for a burnt offering and a pigeon or turtledove for a sin offering (Lev 12:6). If the mother could not afford a sheep, a second pigeon or turtledove could be substituted (12:8). This hint of Mary and Joseph's low economic status is in keeping with descriptions of Jesus' birth, where he is wrapped in bands of cloth and placed in a feeding trough (Luke 2:7, 12, 16).

Second, Jesus is presented to the Lord. According to the OT, all firstborn belonged to the LORD, and so they were to be set apart and dedicated to the LORD (Exod 13:11–16; 34:19–20; Num 3:44–51). Firstborn of livestock were to be sacrificed. Since Israelites did not engage in human sacrifice, firstborn human males were placed in the LORD's service or redeemed from priestly service through the payment of five shekels of silver (Num 18:15–17). In the OT, Hannah dedicated her firstborn, Samuel, by leaving him at the temple in Shiloh to be raised by Eli the priest. As she said, "For this child I prayed; and the LORD has granted me the petition that I made to him. Therefore, I have lent him to the LORD; as long as he lives, he is given to the LORD" (1 Sam 1:27–28a).

The text does not explicitly state that Jesus was redeemed, though this is perhaps implied. Instead, the focus is upon his being dedicated and being designated as holy to the Lord, set apart for service to the Lord. Jesus will not grow up in the temple precincts like Samuel, but he will certainly enter into the Lord's service. This fact is recognized by the next two characters we encounter in today's episode—Simeon and Anna.

2:25–35. Though we meet Simeon in the temple, he is not a priest. Instead, he is characterized as deeply devout lay person, and he is distinguished by the fact that he is quite attuned to the promptings of the Holy Spirit. The narrator describes Simeon as "looking forward to the consolation of Israel" (2:25), a reference to Israel's political situation. At this time, the Jewish people are under Roman occupation. Like many of his fellow Jews, Simeon is eagerly awaiting for the time when God will send an anointed king to restore and rule over their nation. On this day, the Spirit directs Simeon to the temple, and he, like the shepherds on the night of Jesus' birth, recognize this infant boy to be the long-awaited Messiah.

Yet, in contrast to most of his Jewish contemporaries, Simeon sees in this Messiah a salvation that is not reserved for the Jews alone, but for all people, Jews and Gentiles alike. This implies that Jesus' mission as the Lord's Messiah will exceed and perhaps even challenge the expectations of many of God's people. This latter possibility is confirmed by Simeon's comment to Mary that "This child is destined for the falling and rising of many *in Israel*, and to be a sign that will be opposed" (2:34). Of course, Simeon's words come to pass. At the end of his life, Jesus challenges the

Jewish leadership on their own turf, the Jerusalem temple (19:45–48). Within a week, Jesus is declared to be a false prophet by the Jewish leaders and delivered over to be executed as an enemy of the Roman state. No doubt this is the sword that will pierce his mother's heart.

2:36–38. Just like Simeon, Anna is also not officially connected with the temple; she is simply a very devout lay person, a prophet endowed with the Spirit and called to speak the word of the Lord. On this day, the word she speaks concerns Jesus and his role in the redemption of Jerusalem. Many of her listeners are probably thinking of political freedom from Roman authority, but given what has transpired thus far in the gospel, the reader understands this redemption to be primarily spiritual in nature.

2:39–40. Today's reading concludes with Mary and Joseph returning with their new son to their home in Nazareth of Galilee. It has been over six weeks since they left Nazareth in order to register for the census (2:1–5). As for Jesus, his next twelve years of growth and development are summarized in a single sentence: "The child grew and became strong, filled with wisdom; and the favor of God was upon him" (2:40; cf. 2:52).

Suggestions for Lectors

Today's narrative should be read in your best storytelling style and voice. In 2:23, drop your voice as you read the parenthetical expression.

Read Simeon's song of praise with a smile on your face and with hints of joy and excitement on your lips. Read 2:30 slowly, emphasizing *eyes*. In 2:31–32, emphasize *all* and *light.* The words Simeon directs at Mary are serious and grave, so set aside your exuberance as you deliver Simeon's prophetic word regarding her child's future. Read 3:34b–35 somberly, yet firmly and strong. The final line can be delivered with evident emotion: *and a sword will pierce your own soul too.*

As you draw the episode to a close, read the final statement slowly and deliberately. Emphasize *favor* and pause briefly after *God*, as in: *and the favor of God… was upon him* (2:40).

Pronunciation Guide

Anna (AN-uh)
Asher (ASH-uhr)
Galilee (GAL-uh-lee)
Gentiles (JEN-tīlz)
Israel (IZ-ree-uhl; -ray-)
Jerusalem (juh-ROO-suh-luhm)
Messiah (muh-SĪ-uh)
Moses (MOH-zuhs)
Nazareth (NAZ-uh-reth; *not* -rus)
Phanuel (FAN-yoo-uhl; fuh-NOO-uhl)
Simeon (SIM-ee-uhn)

✠ FIRST SUNDAY AFTER CHRISTMAS

✠ Isaiah 61:10–62:3
✠ Psalm 147 *or* 147:13–20 (= 147:13–21 BCP)
✠ Galatians 3:23–25; 4:4–7
✠ John 1:1–18

✠ ISAIAH 61:10–62:3

Commentary

Isaiah 61 and 62 offer poetic, prophetic descriptions of the restoration of God's exiled people and of the rebuilt Jerusalem (= Zion) following the Babylonian exile. In 61:1, an unidentified servant figure is introduced. The description of this figure brings to mind the servant figure(s) in the four so-called Servant Songs of Isaiah (42:1–4; 49:1–6; 50:4–9, Palm; 52:13–53:12, GFri). The servant describes himself as having been anointed with the Spirit of the Lord GOD and sent "to bring good news to the oppressed, to bind up the brokenhearted, to proclaim liberty to the captives, and release to the prisoners;… [and] to provide for those who mourn in Zion—to give them a garland instead of ashes, the oil of gladness instead of mourning, the mantle of praise instead of a faint spirit" (61:1–2a, 3, Adv 3; cf. Luke 4:18–19).

In today's reading, the servant offers a song of thanksgiving (61:10–11) before turning his attention to the vindication and salvation of Jerusalem and its people (62:1–3).

Suggestions for Lectors

This is one of those occasions when you must discipline yourself to speak loudly in order to reflect the joy of the Christmas season and the joy in today's reading. The printed punctuation lends itself admirably to the theme of the reading, so that the only challenge to you remains the raising of your voice to the tone of a proclamation. Do not strain yourself by shouting; instead, let the power come from your midsection up through your vocal passages. After some practice with this at home, you will find that this works quite well.

None of the verses require special emphasis; it will be sufficient to pause for a second between 61:11 and 62:1 in order to signal the slight shift in topic and tone.

Pronunciation Guide

Isaiah (ī-ZAY-uh), *Jerusalem* (juh-ROO-suh-luhm), *Zion* (ZĪ-uhn)

✠ GALATIANS 3:23–25; 4:4–7

Notes

Suggested Reading. Galatians 3:23–26; 4:4–7

Commentary

In his letter to the Galatians, and against the views of some Jewish Christians, Paul argues that Gentiles do not have to be circumcised in order to become Christian, for no one is justified through the law (3:11). Instead, all people—be they Jew or Greek, slave or free, male or female (3:28)—are made right with God and receive the Holy Spirit on the basis of faith. However, if no one is or has ever been justified through the law, then why did God give the law? What was its purpose (3:19)?

3:23–26. Today, Paul begins to answer this question by likening the law to a disciplinarian, what might better be called a guardian or a custodian (Gk., *paidagōgos*). In the ancient Greco-Roman world, a *paidagōgos* was a man, usually a slave, whose duty it was to conduct those under his charge to and from school, overseeing their conduct until they came of age, at which point the *paidagōgos* no longer served in this capacity. Likewise, the law served as our *paidagōgos*, protecting us from the ravaging chaos of sin until the appointed time when the law would be replaced by the Holy Spirit, who would be given to all believers and would accomplish what the law never could do, namely, make sinful, dead human beings alive, holy, and righteous (2:21).

4:4–7. Paul notes that this new age of the Spirit was inaugurated and made possible by God's own Son. The Son became a human being, not just any human being, but one born under the law in order that, through his life, death, resurrection, and ascension, we may become the adopted children and heirs of God, free from the law and filled with the very Spirit that indwelt and guided God's Son, Jesus.

Suggestions for Lectors

Today's reading proceeds in a somewhat narrative tone as Paul explains how the law functioned as a safeguard until the age of faith in Christ arrived. When you come to 4:4 and read, *But when the fullness of time had come…*, try to convey the magnitude of this moment in salvation history when God's Son was sent that *we might receive adoption as children*. Highlight the difference between the former age and the new age by emphasizing the words *born*, *slaves*, and *the law*, on the one hand, and *adoption*, *children*, and *the Spirit*, on the other.

In 4:6b, *Abba! Father!* could be delivered in an emotionally dramatic fashion, but it does not have to be. However, at a minimum, your voice should become elevated as you direct these words to God. Verse 7 not only serves as the reading's conclusion, it also provides a succinct summary of Paul's argument. Consequently, pause for a full second before 4:7, and then read it slowly with frequent pauses and in a tone that suggests you are summing up an argument.

Pronunciation Guide

Abba (AH-buh), *Galatians* (guh-LAY-shuhnz)

✠ JOHN 1:1–18

Commentary

The Gospel according to John begins with a prologue that introduces themes that are woven throughout John's narrative about Jesus (1:1–18). Of particular importance is the question of Jesus' identity and specifically his relation to God. This is the focus of today's reading.

1:1–5. The *in the beginning* of John 1:1 recalls the *in the beginning* of Genesis 1:1 (Epi 1). With this simple phrase, John connects the story of Jesus with the story of creation. The Word, whom we later discover becomes a particular human being at a particular point in time (1:14), existed before time began; for even at the beginning of creation itself, the Word already was. This Word was not only *with* God in the beginning, this Word *was* God. In other words, while the Word has its own distinct identity as the Word, it belongs to the unique identity of the One God. This is but the first of many of John's mysteries. Then, in language that recalls the role of God's Wisdom in creation (Prov 8:22–31), John presents the Word as having played a decisive role in bringing creation into existence "for all things came into being through [the Word], and without [the Word] not one thing came into being" (1:3). Here, one is reminded of how God brought order and structure out of chaos and nothingness simply through *speaking* things into existence, that is, through *the Word.* Whereas Wisdom seems to have had a beginning (Prov 8:22), the Word is presented here as coeternal with God.

1:6–9. At this point, the author wishes to make clear that this Word of God, which is the light and life of all people (1:5), was not John the Baptist. It appears that some of John the Baptist's followers regarded him as God's anointed Messiah, but here and elsewhere in the gospel, the author of John seeks to clarify the Baptist's status and role: the Baptist was sent from God to be a witness to the light, but he himself was not the light (1:7–8; cf. 1:15, 29–36; 3:25–30).

1:10–13. In 1:10, the Prologue returns to the Word and reveals the drama surrounding the Word's coming. The Word was in the world and the whole world came into being through the Word, yet the world did not know him nor did the Word's own people accept him, and this is the nature of judgment (cf. 3:19, Tri). Nevertheless, the situation is not dire because anyone and everyone who accepted and believed in the Word was given the power (i.e., the Holy Spirit) to become a child of God.

1:14–18. The final section of the Prologue begins with the greatest mystery within human history: this Word which was with God in the beginning and is God, this very Word "became flesh and lived among us" (1:14). The mystery of the Incarnation is that God became a full and complete human being even while remaining completely and fully God. Now, while the reader of John has probably by this point guessed the human identity of the incarnate Word, it is not until the Prologue nears its conclusion that the author reveals the incarnate Word to be Jesus Christ. Thus, it is only through Jesus of Nazareth that we glimpse God's glory and gracious nature; for it is only the incarnate Son of God—who has seen God and who bears the family resemblance—who is able to reflect God's image and make God known.

Suggestions for Lectors

As reflected in the Commentary, today's reading falls into four movements, so include major pauses before verses 6, 10, and 14.

The reading starts quickly with the well-known first verse of John, so make sure that your listeners are completely settled and attuned before you begin reading. Read 1:1 slowly and deliberately. The first sentence, *in the beginning was the Word,* can be read as a simple statement. In the second and third sentences of 1:1, accent the words *with* and *was* respectively. Increase your tempo slightly as you complete the rest of the first movement. The second and third movements are somewhat like narratives and so can be read in your normal storytelling voice.

The reading reaches its climax with the opening verse of the fourth movement (1:14), which describes the incarnation of the Word and the revelation of God's glory. While the first part, *And the Word became flesh and lived among us*, rightfully receives emphasis in readings, the conclusion of the verse deserves equal regard, for the Word's purpose in becoming a human being was so that the fullness of God's glory might be revealed to human beings, as 1:18 reaffirms.

The NRSV places 1:15 within parentheses, treating the re-introduction of John the Baptist as a narrative aside. You may wish to drop your voice a bit as you present your listeners with this information. Verse 17 makes a strong contrast, so a full pause after *Moses* will help make that evident to your listeners. Verse 18 presents another contrast between *no one*, on the one hand, and *God the only Son*, on the other hand; accent these words as well as the two *who*'s.

THE HOLY NAME OF JESUS

January 1

Numbers 6:22–27
Psalm 8
Galatians 4:4–7 *or* Philippians 2:5–11
Luke 2:15–21

NUMBERS 6:22–27

Commentary
Aaron was Moses' elder brother and the one who generally spoke for Moses when Moses addressed the elders of Israel and Pharaoh (Exod 4:14, 29–30). Aaron was a descendant of Levi, and the Levites were set apart by God to be priests. As priests, they were responsible for maintaining the tabernacle and its furnishings, including the ark of the covenant (Num 1:48–54), for slaughtering the people's sacrifices (8:14–19), and for collecting tithes (18:23–32). More particularly, Aaron and his descendants were set apart to serve as the high priests, the priests to the priests (18:1–7).

One of the priestly duties was to bless the people when the people came to offer sacrifices and offerings (Deut 21:5). In today's OT reading, the LORD through Moses gives Aaron and his descendants a specific blessing with which they are to bless the people; it is a blessing that has been used throughout the centuries in both Jewish and Christian contexts.

Suggestions for Lectors
This is a short but important reading, so make the most of your time. The emphasis lies with the blessing itself (6:24–26), so highlight it by shifting into a different tone and by pausing for a full second both before and after the blessing. Moreover, as you say these words, do not imagine that you are Moses relaying the blessing to Aaron; instead, imagine you are Aaron blessing your listeners.

Pronunciation Guide
Aaron (AIR-uhn), *Moses* (MOH-zuhs), *Israelites* (IZ-ree-līts)

GALATIANS 4:4–7

Commentary
In his letter to the Galatians, and against the views of some Jewish Christians, Paul argues that Gentiles do not have to be circumcised in order to become Christian, for no one is justified through the law (3:11). Instead, all people—be they Jew or Greek, slave or free, male or female (3:28)—are made right with God and receive the Holy Spirit on the basis of faith. However, if no one is or has ever been justified through the law, then why did God give the law? What was its purpose (3:19)?

In 3:23–26 (✠ Chr 1), Paul begins to answer this question by likening the law to a disciplinarian, what might better be called a guardian or a custodian (Gk., *paidagōgos*). In the ancient Greco-Roman world, a *paidagōgos* was a man, usually a slave, whose duty it was to conduct those under his charge to and from school, overseeing their conduct until they came of age, at which point the *paidagōgos* no longer served in this capacity. Likewise, the law served as our *paidagōgos*, protecting us from the ravaging chaos of sin until the appointed time when the law would be replaced by the Holy Spirit, who would be given to all believers and would accomplish what the law never could do, namely, make sinful, dead human beings alive, holy, and righteous (2:21).

4:4–7. In today's reading, Paul continues by noting that this new age of the Spirit was inaugurated and made possible by God's own Son. The Son became a human being, not just any human being, but one born under the law in order that, through his life, death, resurrection, and ascension, we may become the adopted children and heirs of God, free from the law and filled with the very Spirit that indwelt and guided God's Son, Jesus.

Suggestions for Lectors
Today's reading proceeds in a somewhat narrative tone as Paul explains how the law functioned as a safeguard until the age of faith in Christ arrived. When you come to 4:4 and read, *But when the fullness of time had come…*, try to convey the magnitude of this moment in salvation history when God's Son was sent that *we might receive adoption as children*. Highlight the difference between the former age and the new age by emphasizing the words *born*, *slaves*, and *the law*, on the one hand, and *adoption*, *children*, and *the Spirit*, on the other.

In 4:6b, *Abba! Father!* could be delivered in an emotionally dramatic fashion, but it does not have to be. However, at a minimum, your voice should become elevated as you direct these words to God. Verse 7 not only serves as the reading's conclusion, it also provides a succinct summary of Paul's argument. Consequently, pause for a full second before 4:7, and then read it slowly with frequent pauses and in a tone that suggests you are summing up an argument.

Pronunciation Guide
Abba (AH-buh), *Galatians* (guh-LAY-shuhnz)

PHILIPPIANS 2:5–11

Commentary

In this reading, Paul offers up Jesus as the one who fully embodies the self-emptying, self-sacrificing humility that Paul is calling the Philippians to adopt in 2:1–4.

2:5–8. Philippians 2:6–11 is thought to be an ancient Christian hymn that poetically recounts the story of the humiliation and exaltation of Jesus. It does not stand on its own but offers a narrative portrait of the humility and regard for others that Paul is encouraging the Philippians to practice. Even though Jesus, as the eternal Son of God, had every right to use his divine status to achieve his own interests and ambitions, he did not. Instead Jesus disregarded his divine prerogatives, electing to become a human being, subject to all human limitations (2:7). Jesus' regard for others went so far as to embrace death, even the shameful and painful death of crucifixion (2:8).

2:9–11. Such a demonstration of selfless ambition is rewarded. God raised Jesus from the dead *and* appointed him to the highest position in the universe, making him Lord over the whole cosmos. As Jesus says following his resurrection, "All authority in heaven and on earth has been given to me" (Matt 28:18). Consequently, all allegiances are owed to Jesus. When his name is announced, every knee in creation should bend in thankful reverence and every tongue in creation should confess that Jesus is indeed the one and only Lord of all.

Suggestions for Lectors

In today's reading, you are presenting a biography like no other; so read it with a tone befitting its awesome dignity and grandeur. Imagine yourself reading for the coronation of a monarch, as you invite your listeners to consider the life and accomplishments of this incomparable individual.

Philippians 2:6–8 describes the descent of Jesus in humility, so read these verses with increasing solemnity, slowing your tempo as you proceed and making sure to enunciate each phrase with great care and precision. In contrast, 2:9–11 describes the ascent and exaltation of Jesus; so after a lengthy pause following 2:8, read these verses with increasing intensity, seasoned with awe and joy, which should reach a climax with the confession that *Jesus Christ is Lord* (2:11).

Pronunciation Guide

Philippians (fih-LIH-pee-uhnz)

LUKE 2:15–21

Commentary

When the angel Gabriel visits Mary and tells her that she has found favor with God, he says, "And now, you will conceive in your womb and bear a son, and you will name him Jesus" (1:31, Adv 4). In today's reading, the child is circumcised and finally given his name.

2:15–20. In 2:8–14 (Chr I), the shepherds are visited by a host of angels who announce that the Messiah, who is the Lord, has been born in Bethlehem. When the angels depart, the shepherds make their way to Bethlehem and find the child just as the angel has said, "wrapped in bands of cloth and lying in a manger" (2:12). Thus, the shepherds, who belong to the lower classes, find the Messiah in lowly estate at the bottom of the ranks of power and privilege, much like themselves. All are amazed at the shepherds' tale of the angels, and "Mary treasured all these words and pondered them in her heart" (2:19), something she will do again when Jesus is twelve (2:51b, ✠ Chr 2).

2:21. In the opening chapters of Luke, Mary and Joseph are portrayed as faithful adherents to the Mosaic Law. As it is written, "If a woman conceives and bears a male child, she shall be ceremonially unclean seven days; as at the time of her menstruation, she shall be unclean. On the eighth day the flesh of his foreskin shall be circumcised" (Lev 12:2b–3). Mary and Joseph circumcise their son on the eighth day in strict accordance with the law. Consequently, Jesus belongs to God's covenant people as a descendant of Abraham through Isaac, with whom the covenant of circumcision was made (Gen 17:9–14). In addition, the child finally receives his name, Jesus, which in Hebrew is Yeshua (that is, Joshua) and means *Yahweh saves* (cf. Matt 1:21).

Suggestions for Lectors

On this celebration of the Holy Name, the focus of the reading is the circumcision and the naming of Mary's child, so 2:21 should receive the greatest emphasis. Begin 2:15–20 in your normal narrative voice, though seasoned with awe as the shepherds recount and Mary ponders these extraordinary events. Pause before 2:19, and then proceed in a slow, introspective manner, as though you have just turned, amidst all the excitement, and noticed Mary's face. Pausing again before 2:20, conclude this section by trying to convey some measure of the shepherds' joy and excitement.

After pausing again, begin reading 2:21 up to *child* in your normal narrating voice. Then, let your pace slacken so you can enunciate every word in *and he was called Jesus.* Pause briefly between each word and slightly longer before *and* and after *called.*

Pronunciation Guide

Bethlehem (BETH-luh-hem')
Joseph (JOH-sif; -suhf)
Mary (MAIR-ee)

SECOND SUNDAY AFTER CHRISTMAS

Jeremiah 31:7–14 *or* Sirach 24:1–12
Psalm 147:12–20 *or* Wisdom of Solomon 10:15–21
Ephesians 1:3–14
John 1:(1–9), 10–18

JEREMIAH 31:7–14

Commentary

When Jeremiah was called to be a "prophet to the nations" (Jer 1:5), his prophetic vocation was described with six actions: "See, today I appoint you over nations and over kingdoms, to pluck up and to pull down, to destroy and to overthrow, to build and to plant" (1:10). The first four actions denote judgment, and it is with the judgment and exile of Judah that the first twenty-nine chapters of Jeremiah is concerned. Yet, in Jeremiah 30–33, the actions *to build* and *to plant* hold precedence. These chapters are often designated *The Book of Consolation*, for in them the LORD speaks to his exiled people and promises to restore them (30:2–3; cf. 33:26):

> Thus says the LORD, the God of Israel: Write in a book all the words that I have spoken to you. For the days are surely coming, says the LORD, when I will restore the fortunes of my people, Israel and Judah, says the LORD, and I will bring them back to the land that I gave to their ancestors and they shall take possession of it.

In today's reading, the prophet paints a picture of reconciliation between the LORD and his people. This reconciliation is manifest in the ending of the exile, the gathering of the exiles, and their return to the Promised Land.

31:7–9. In 722 B.C., the northern kingdom of Israel was defeated by the Assyrian empire and its citizens dispersed throughout the world. Then, in 597 and 586 B.C., the southern kingdom of Judah was twice defeated by the Babylonian empire and its citizens exiled to Babylon. These are the exiles whom the LORD intends to bring "from the land of the north, and gather… from the farthest parts of the earth" (31:8a). Moreover, the LORD will not just bring back the unblemished and the able-bodied, for among them will be "the blind and the lame, those with child and those in labor, together; a great company, they shall return here" (31:8b). The return journey may be a long one, but it will not be difficult, for like a good shepherd, the LORD will lead them back along "brooks of water" and guide them along "a straight path in which they shall not stumble" (31:9a).

31:10–14. At times, when the LORD becomes angry with Israel's idolatries and injustices and decides to abandon or destroy them, someone intercedes on behalf of the people by appealing to God's sense of honor. For example, following the golden calf incident, the LORD tells Moses to step aside so that his wrath might burn white hot and consume his idolatrous people, to which Moses responds, "Why should the Egyptians say, 'It was with evil intent that he brought them out to kill them in the mountains, and to consume them from the face of the earth'? Turn from your fierce wrath; change your mind and do not bring disaster on your people" (Exod 32:12). Likewise, when the people refuse to enter into the Promised Land because they do not trust in the LORD's ability to protect them against the land's inhabitants, the LORD decides "to strike them with pestilence and disinherit them" (Num 14:12). Once again, Moses intercedes for the people saying, "Now if you kill this people all at one time, then the nations who have heard about you will say, 'It is because the LORD was not able to bring this people into the land he swore to give them that he has slaughtered them in the wilderness'" (14:15–16).

Incidents such as these seem to stand behind the announcement to the nations that "He who scattered Israel will gather him, and will keep him as a shepherd [keeps] a flock" (31:10). The LORD may have pawned Jacob, yet he has also returned to redeem him. Consequently, the people will rejoice and sing as they return to Jerusalem on Mount Zion. The land will once again produce, flowing with milk and honey, and people's lives "shall become like a watered garden, and they shall never languish again" (31:12). The years of mourning while in exile will be turned into joy as the LORD comforts his people and replaces their sorrow with gladness.

Suggestions for Lectors

Today's reading falls into two sections, the first beginning with *For thus says the LORD* (31:7a) and the second with *Hear the word of the LORD, O nations* (31:10a). So conclude the first section as though it were the end of a reading by slowing your tempo and dropping your voice as you read the last lines of 31:9, and then pause for a full second before proceeding with 31:10.

There are no mood changes in this passage and no verses that require special attention or emphasis. Read with your voice raised in gladness as though you are leading the company of returning exiles as they march through the wilderness toward the Holy City (31:8).

Your principal effort will be to keep a positive, happy tone throughout. Notice how many groups you are addressing: the blind, the lame, the pregnant, the farmers, the young men and women, and even the priests. Accent each group as they are named for this good news, as Jeremiah insists repeatedly, is for all the people.

Pronunciation Guide

Ephraim (EE-free-uhm), *Israel* (IZ-ree-uhl; -ray-),
Jacob (JAY-kuhb), *Jeremiah* (jair'-uh-MĪ-uh), *Zion* (ZĪ-uhn)

SIRACH 24:1–12

Commentary

The Book of Sirach—also known by the titles The Wisdom of Jesus, Son of Sirach and Ecclesiasticus (not to be confused with the OT book of Ecclesiastes)—belongs to the collection of biblical books known within Protestant traditions as the Apocrypha and within Roman Catholicism as Deuterocanonical (that is, Second Canon). In Eastern Orthodoxy, Sirach simply belongs to the OT. Written by Ben Sira in Jerusalem, prior to 180 B.C. and so before the Maccabean revolt, Sirach is a book of wisdom comparable to the book of Proverbs.

In Proverbs, God's Wisdom (or understanding, prudence, intelligence, etc.) is personified as a woman. The sage writes, "Does not wisdom call, and does not understanding raise *her* voice" (8:1, EastVig; cf. 8:2–3; 9:1–3). Likewise, Wisdom is personified as a woman in Sirach, as reflected in the opening verses of today's reading. Proverbs credits Wisdom with playing a critical role in bringing creation into being (Prov 8:22–31). In today's reading, Sirach focuses upon God's giving of Wisdom to creation, especially to his chosen people.

24:1–2. Since Wisdom is personified, it is fitting that today's reading begins with Wisdom being introduced to the reader. The sage presents Wisdom as neither shy nor reserved, for she is one who "praises herself and tells of her glory in the midst of her people" (24:1). Wisdom speaks candidly; she even opens her mouth when the heavenly beings are assembled before God (24:2). Once introduced, Wisdom takes center stage, providing us with an autobiographical account of her life.

24:3–7. Wisdom begins by speaking of her origins. She proceeded "from the mouth of the Most High" (24:3), and so is the very Word of God. The description that follows reveals that there is no place in all of creation that Wisdom has not visited and where Wisdom is not present. Implicit in this description is the idea that if God created everything by means of Wisdom, then Wisdom resides in everything that God created.

24:8–12. Even though Wisdom is present throughout creation, Wisdom is not known by creation's inhabitants. God instructs Wisdom to take up residence in the midst of a particular people, God's chosen people, Israel (= Jacob). Wisdom did as instructed; she pitched her tent and began to dwell in the midst of God's people and in the holy city of Jerusalem.

Following today's reading, Wisdom continues to praise herself (24:13–17), ending with a call for all people to come and partake of her (24:19–22). Then, the sage reveals Wisdom's particular identity within Israel; she is none other than the Law that was given to the people on Mount Sinai following the Exodus from Egypt.

> All this [i.e., Wisdom] is the book of the covenant of the Most High God,
> the law that Moses commanded us
> as an inheritance for the congregations of Jacob (24:23).

Suggestions for Lectors

As with all poetic texts, pay particular attention to the punctuation—the commas, semicolons, and periods. The punctuation will assist you in creating the proper pace and flow of phrases and thoughts.

In 24:1–2, the sage introduces Wisdom, who then speaks for herself in the remainder of the reading. For the sage, you might proceed with your basic reading voice without much expression. But when you read as Wisdom, read with increased intensity and with the dynamics of expression demanded by the text. Imagine that Wisdom is excited and honored by the role that she has been given; after all, she is unique among all God's creatures.

As you near the end of your reading, slow down, reading 24:11–12 more deliberately, taking care to enunciate each word, especially in 24:12.

Pronunciation Guide
Israel (IZ-ree-uhl; -ray-)
Jacob (JAY-kuhb)
Jerusalem (juh-ROO-suh-luhm)
Sirach (SĪ-rak), *Zion* (ZĪ-uhn)

EPHESIANS 1:3–14

Commentary
Throughout his Letter to the Ephesians, Paul celebrates the grace of God, bestowed upon us in the Lord Jesus Christ, the Beloved, and made effective through the promised Holy Spirit. In today's reading, Paul's letter begins with a veritable litany of praises and thanksgivings for the salvation and spiritual blessings that have been made available through the gospel of Christ.

1:3–6. Paul begins by blessing "the God and Father of our Lord Jesus Christ" for all of the blessings of salvation that were wrought for us through the life, death, resurrection, and ascension of Jesus. Even before the world was created, God's plan was to adopt us as his children, not on the basis of who we are and what we do, but on the basis of who Jesus is and what he would do. In short, our salvation in Christ is a gift freely given, a manifestation of God's grace. In the three sections that follow, Paul identifies the spiritual blessings that are found *in the Beloved* (1:6). Note how each section begins with a reference to the Beloved: "*In him* we have…" (1:7); "*In Christ* we have also…" (1:11); and "*In him* you also… (1:13).

1:7–10. First, we have been redeemed by the blood of Christ. That is, through Christ's death, our trespasses have been forgiven, and we have been set free from the power of sin that enslaves us. All of this contributes to God's vision of reconciling all things to himself in Christ, as Paul says, "to gather up all things in him [that is, Christ], things in heaven and things on earth" (1:10). As Paul says elsewhere,

> So if anyone is in Christ, there is a new creation: everything old has passed away; see, everything has become new! All this is from God, who reconciled us to himself through Christ;… that is, in Christ God was reconciling the world to himself, not counting their trespasses against them (2 Cor 5:17–19a, Prop 6).

1:11–12. Second, having become God's adopted children in Christ, it stands to reason that we have also been granted an inheritance. Though Paul does not explicitly state it here, the inheritance to which he refers likely concerns the future hope of resurrection from the dead. For example, when Paul speaks of the future resurrection of the dead in 1 Corinthians 15, he uses the language of inheritance (15:50ff.). Moreover, the word *hope*, which occurs in 1:12, is often used by Paul as shorthand for resurrection from the dead (Rom 8:19–24, ✠ PentVig; 1 Cor 15:19; Col 1:27). Thus, when Paul speaks of "we, who were the first to set our *hope* on Christ," he is referring to those who first believed in Jesus and so first received the promised inheritance of eternal life, which Paul always understood to be a resurrected, embodied life in a restored creation (1 Cor 15:12–58).

Paul believes that, through Christ, God was not only rescuing humanity but was rescuing *the whole* of the created order from its subjugation to the chaotic, corrupting forces of sin and death. Consider the following from Romans 8:19–25 (✠ PentVig):

> For the creation waits with eager longing for the revealing of the children of God; for the creation was subjected to futility, not of its own will but by the will of the one who subjected it, in hope that the creation itself will be set free from its bondage to decay and will obtain the freedom of the glory of the children of God. We know that the whole creation has been groaning in labor pains until now; and not only the creation, but we ourselves, who have the first fruits of the Spirit, groan inwardly *while we wait for adoption, the redemption of our bodies. For in hope we were saved.* Now hope that is seen is not hope. For who hopes for what is seen? But if we hope for what we do not see, we wait for it with patience.

So, for Paul, the inheritance that awaits us as God's children is eternal life in God's restored creation, and the means by which we will come into our inheritance is through the restoration of our bodies, that is, through resurrection from the dead.

1:13–14. Of course, all of this is a future hope, a hope that we do not yet see, so we must be patient until God brings it about. Yet thankfully, God has left us with a guarantee that the inheritance of which Paul speaks really does await those of us who believe. When we come to faith in Christ Jesus, we are graciously granted the indwelling of the Holy Spirit. The Holy Spirit serves as God's pledge that one day we will in fact receive our inheritance, resurrection from the dead into God's new world. Furthermore, the Holy Spirit marks us as Christ's own forever and seals us to preserve and protect us until the time when we come into our inheritance (2 Cor 1:22, Epi 7).

Suggestions for Lectors

Read this passage so as to convey some measure of Paul's excitement and gratitude for the salvation that has been so graciously wrought for us in Christ.

This passage is filled with one theological truth after another, so it is important not to rush. Pay particular attention to the punctuation, and in keeping with the structure outlined above in the Commentary, pause for full a second prior to verses 7, 11, and 13.

Pronunciation Guide

Beloved (n., buh-LUV-uhd), *Ephesians* (eh-FEE-zhuhnz; ih-),
blessed in 1:3a (adj., two syllables; BLES-id),
blessed in 1:3b (vb., one syllable; BLEST)

John 1:(1–9), 10–18

Commentary

The Gospel according to John begins with a prologue that introduces themes that are woven throughout John's narrative about Jesus (1:1–18). Of particular importance is the question of Jesus' identity and specifically his relation to God. This is the focus of today's reading.

1:1–5. The *in the beginning* of John 1:1 recalls the *in the beginning* of Genesis 1:1 (Epi 1). With this simple phrase, John connects the story of Jesus with the story of creation. The Word, whom we later discover becomes a particular human being at a particular point in time (1:14), existed before time began; for even at the beginning of creation itself, the Word already was. This Word was not only *with* God in the beginning, this Word *was* God. In other words, while the Word has its own distinct identity as the Word, it belongs to the unique identity of the One God. This is but the first of many of John's mysteries. Then, in language that recalls the role of God's Wisdom in creation (Prov 8:22–31), John presents the Word as having played a decisive role in bringing creation into existence "for all things came into being through [the Word], and without [the Word] not one thing came into being" (1:3). Here, one is reminded of how God brought order and structure out of chaos and nothingness simply through *speaking* things into existence, that is, through *the Word.* Whereas Wisdom seems to have had a beginning (Prov 8:22), the Word is presented here as coeternal with God.

1:6–9. At this point, the author wishes to make clear that this Word of God, which is the light and life of all people (1:5), was not John the Baptist. It appears that some of John the Baptist's followers regarded him as God's anointed Messiah, but here and elsewhere in the gospel, the author of John seeks to clarify the Baptist's status and role: the Baptist was sent from God to be a witness to the light, but he himself was not the light (1:7–8; cf. 1:15, 29–36; 3:25–30).

1:10–13. In 1:10, the Prologue returns to the Word and reveals the drama surrounding the Word's coming. The Word was in the world and the whole world came into being through the Word, yet ironically, the world did not know him nor did the Word's own people accept him, and this is the nature of judgment (cf. 3:19, Tri). Nevertheless, the situation is not dire because anyone and everyone who accepted and believed in the Word was given the power (i.e., the Holy Spirit) to become a child of God.

1:14–18. The final section of the Prologue begins with arguably the greatest mystery within human history: this Word which was with God in the beginning and is God, this very Word "became flesh and lived among us" (1:14). The mystery of the Incarnation is that God became a full and complete human being even while remaining completely and fully God. Now, while the reader of John has probably by this point guessed the human identity of the incarnate Word, it is not until the Prologue nears its conclusion that the author reveals the incarnate Word to be Jesus Christ. Thus, it is only through Jesus of Nazareth that we glimpse God's glory and gracious nature; for it is only the incarnate Son of God—who has seen God and who bears the family resemblance—who is able to reflect God's image and make God known.

Suggestions for Lectors

As reflected in the Commentary, today's reading falls into four movements, so include major pauses before verses 6, 10, and 14.

The reading starts quickly with the well-known first verse of John, so make sure that your listeners are completely settled and attuned before you begin reading. Read 1:1 slowly and deliberately. The first sentence, *in the beginning was the Word*, can be read as a simple statement. In the second and third sentences of 1:1, accent the words *with* and *was* respectively. Increase your tempo slightly as you complete the rest of the first movement. The second and third movements are somewhat like narratives and so can be read in your normal storytelling voice.

The reading reaches its climax with the opening verse of the fourth movement (1:14), which describes the incarnation of the Word and the revelation of God's glory. While the first part, *And the Word became flesh and lived among us*, rightfully receives emphasis in readings, the conclusion of the verse deserves equal regard, for the Word's purpose in becoming a human being was so that the fullness of God's glory might be revealed to human beings, as 1:18 reaffirms.

The NRSV places 1:15 within parentheses, treating the re-introduction of John the Baptist as a narrative aside. You may wish to drop your voice a bit as you present your listeners with this information. Verse 17 makes a strong contrast, so a full pause after *Moses* will help make that evident to your listeners. Verse 18 presents another contrast between *no one*, on the one hand, and *God the only Son*, on the other hand; accent these words as well as the two *who*'s.

✠ SECOND SUNDAY AFTER CHRISTMAS

✠ Jeremiah 31:7–14
✠ Psalm 84 *or* 84:1–9 (= 84:1–8 BCP)
✠ Ephesians 1:3–6, 15–19a
✠ Matthew 2:13–15, 19–23 *or* Luke 2:41–52 *or* Matthew 2:1–12

✠ JEREMIAH 31:7–14

Commentary

When Jeremiah was called to be a "prophet to the nations" (Jer 1:5), his prophetic vocation was described with six actions: "See, today I appoint you over nations and over kingdoms, to pluck up and to pull down, to destroy and to overthrow, to build and to plant" (1:10). The first four actions denote judgment, and it is with the judgment and exile of Judah that the first twenty-nine chapters of Jeremiah is concerned. Yet, in Jeremiah 30–33, the actions *to build* and *to plant* hold precedence. These chapters are often designated *The Book of Consolation*, for in them the LORD speaks to his exiled people and promises to restore them (30:2–3; cf. 33:26):

> Thus says the LORD, the God of Israel: Write in a book all the words that I have spoken to you. For the days are surely coming, says the LORD, when I will restore the fortunes of my people, Israel and Judah, says the LORD, and I will bring them back to the land that I gave to their ancestors and they shall take possession of it.

In today's reading, the prophet paints a picture of reconciliation between the LORD and his people. This reconciliation is manifest in the ending of the exile, the gathering of the exiles, and their return to the Promised Land.

31:7–9. In 722 B.C., the northern kingdom of Israel was defeated by the Assyrian empire and its citizens dispersed throughout the world. Then, in 597 and 586 B.C., the southern kingdom of Judah was twice defeated by the Babylonian empire and its citizens exiled to Babylon. These are the exiles whom the LORD intends to bring "from the land of the north, and gather... from the farthest parts of the earth" (31:8a). Moreover, the LORD will not just bring back the unblemished and the able-bodied, for among them will be "the blind and the lame, those with child and those in labor, together; a great company, they shall return here" (31:8b). The return journey may be a long one, but it will not be difficult, for like a good shepherd, the LORD will lead them back along "brooks of water" and guide them along "a straight path in which they shall not stumble" (31:9a).

31:10–14. At times, when the LORD becomes angry with Israel's idolatries and injustices and decides to abandon or destroy them, someone intercedes on behalf of the people by appealing to God's sense of honor. For example, following the golden calf incident, the LORD tells Moses to step aside so that his wrath might burn white hot and consume his idolatrous people, to which Moses responds, "Why should the Egyptians say, 'It was with evil intent that he brought them out to kill them in the mountains, and to consume them from the face of the earth'? Turn from your fierce wrath; change your mind and do not bring disaster on your people" (Exod 32:12). Likewise, when the people refuse to enter into the Promised Land because they do not trust in the LORD's ability to protect them against the land's inhabitants, the LORD decides "to strike them with pestilence and disinherit them" (Num 14:12). Once again, Moses intercedes for the people saying, "Now if you kill this people all at one time, then the nations who have heard about you will say, 'It is because the LORD was not able to bring this people into the land he swore to give them that he has slaughtered them in the wilderness'" (14:15–16).

Incidents such as these seem to stand behind the announcement to the nations that "He who scattered Israel will gather him, and will keep him as a shepherd [keeps] a flock" (31:10). The LORD may have pawned Jacob, yet he has also returned to redeem him. Consequently, the people will rejoice and sing as they return to Jerusalem on Mount Zion. The land will once again produce, flowing with milk and honey, and people's lives "shall become like a watered garden, and they shall never languish again" (31:12). The years of mourning while in exile will be turned into joy as the LORD comforts his people and replaces their sorrow with gladness.

Suggestions for Lectors

Today's reading falls into two sections, the first beginning with *For thus says the LORD* (31:7a) and the second with *Hear the word of the LORD, O nations* (31:10a). So conclude the first section as though it were the end of a reading by slowing your tempo and dropping your voice as you read the last lines of 31:9, and then pause for a full second before proceeding with 31:10.

There are no mood changes in this passage and no verses that require special attention or emphasis. Read with your voice raised in gladness as though you are leading the company of returning exiles as they march through the wilderness toward the Holy City (31:8).

Your principal effort will be to keep a positive, happy tone throughout. Notice how many groups you are addressing: the blind, the lame, the pregnant, the farmers, the young men and women, and even the priests. Accent each group as they are named for this good news, as Jeremiah insists repeatedly, is for all the people.

Pronunciation Guide

Ephraim (EE-free-uhm), *Israel* (IZ-ree-uhl; -ray-),
Jacob (JAY-kuhb), *Jeremiah* (jair'-uh-MĪ-uh), *Zion* (ZĪ-uhn)

✠ Ephesians 1:3–6; 15–19a

Commentary

Throughout his Letter to the Ephesians, Paul celebrates the grace of God, bestowed upon us in the Lord Jesus Christ, the Beloved, and made effective through the promised Holy Spirit.

1:3–6. In today's reading, Paul begins by blessing "the God and Father of our Lord Jesus Christ" for all of the blessings of salvation that we receive through the life, death, resurrection, and ascension of Jesus. Even before the world was created, God's plan was to adopt us as his children, not on the basis of who we are and what we do, but on the basis of who Jesus is and what he would do. In short, our salvation in Christ is a gift freely given, a manifestation of God's grace.

1:15–19a. In the second portion of the reading, Paul acknowledges the faith and love of the Ephesian Christians. This faith and love has occasioned many of Paul's prayers of thanksgiving to God. Paul specifically prays that the Ephesian Christians might be granted the wisdom to know and fully understand the hope, the inheritance, and the power of God into which they have been called and in which they even now participate. As the letter continues, the reader will discover that Paul is writing about the new life Christians receive by faith in Jesus, a life made available to all people, Jews and Gentiles alike.

Suggestions for Lectors

Begin strongly with Paul's invocation of praise in 1:3–4. Speak these lines with a hint of thanksgiving and gratitude in your voice and continue in this vein into 1:5–6, which announces our adoption as God's sons and daughters. Let your voice soften a bit as you describe this amazing change in the status of the believer.

In these opening verses, Paul directs his gratitude toward God, but this changes in 1:15. Pause, then, for a full second before continuing with 1:15; for here Paul takes a breath, as it were, and turns his full attention toward his readers. Read these last five verses more carefully, being conscious of making eye contact with your listeners. Throughout these verses, Paul uses the second person pronouns *you* and *your* until the last verse, where he uses the first-person pronoun *us*. When you conclude today's reading, emphasize Paul's identification of his faith with the faith of his recipients by leaning heavily on *us* in *the immeasurable greatness of his power for us who believe* (1:19a).

Pronunciation Guide

Beloved (n., buh-LUV-uhd), *Ephesians* (eh-FEE-zhuhnz; ih-),
blessed in 1:3a (adj., two syllables; BLES-id),
blessed in 1:3b (vb., one syllable; BLEST)

✠ MATTHEW 2:13–15, 19–23

Notes

Suggested Reading. Matthew 2:13–23

Commentary

In today's reading, the relocation of the Holy Family to Egypt and their eventual return to the Promised Land evokes key events from Israel's ancient past, most notably, the relocation of Jacob's (that is, Israel's) entire family to Egypt, the rescue of the infant Moses from infanticide, the Exodus from Egypt, and Israel's settlement in the Promised Land.

2:13–15. Just as the magi were warned in a dream not to return to Herod with the news of the child king's whereabouts, so Joseph is warned in a dream to flee to Egypt, where they are all to remain until Herod dies. Matthew sees in these events a typological fulfillment of Hosea 11:1, "Out of Egypt I called my son" (2:15). In Hosea, *my son* denotes the nation of Israel as a whole, while in Matthew, *my son* refers specifically to Jesus. Thus, in representing these events as a fulfillment of Hosea 11:1, Matthew is not only presenting Jesus as God's unique son, he is also presenting Jesus as the embodiment of God's special covenant people.

2:16–18. In this middle scene, the reader sees why it was necessary for Jesus to be taken to Egypt. When King Herod discovers that the magi have left the country without disclosing the whereabouts of "the child who has been born king of the Jews" (2:2; cf. 2:8, 12), he issues an order that all male children in and around Bethlehem, two years of age and younger, are to be slaughtered. Here, Herod's desperate attempt to secure his authority and power through the slaughtering of innocents recalls the equally desperate attempts of the Egyptian Pharaoh who issued orders that all Jewish males were to be killed at birth (Exod 1:16). Of course, Moses is spared this fate, and he ultimately becomes Pharaoh's downfall. Likewise, Jesus escapes Herod's decree of death. Ironically though, at the end of the gospel, it is Jesus' death that becomes the means through which Jesus becomes Lord and is granted "*all* authority in heaven and earth" (28:18).

2:19–23. When Herod the Great died in 4 B.C., his kingdom was divided among three of his sons. Herod Philip II became tetrarch of Iturea and Traconitis; Herod Antipas the tetrarch of Galilee and Perea; and Herod Archelaus the ethnarch of Judea, Idumea, and Samaria. From the Jewish historian Josephus, we learn that Archelaus was even more violent than his father Herod and as a result was dismissed by Rome in A.D. 6. This stands in stark contrast to the reigns of Philip and Antipas, which lasted until A.D. 34 and 39, respectively. After Archelaus' dismissal, Judea was placed under direct Roman rule, which is why Jesus' execution was overseen by the Roman governor Pilate.

Archelaus' violent character leads to the holy family's decision to settle in Nazareth. Joseph is told in a dream to return to Israel because "those who were seeking the child's life are dead" (2:20). Upon arriving back at their home in Bethlehem, Joseph discovers that Archelaus is ruling Judea in his father's place. Joseph is afraid to resettle in Judea. After being warned in another dream, the family relocates to Nazareth in Galilee, which is under the more amiable rule of Antipas.

Suggestions for Lectors

Today's reading is a straightforward narrative account that requires basic storytelling techniques. Just let the story tell itself as you read. Pause for a full second between 2:15 and 2:19 to indicate the passage of time. When reading the words of the angel in 2:13 and 2:20, adopt a somewhat lower, less animated voice. Read *He will be called a Nazorean* in a slower, more deliberate manner, which befits the statement and helps conclude the reading.

When reading of Herod's massacre of the children in 2:16–18, adopt a tone that conveys the evil of this deed. In addition, read the quotation from Jeremiah with evident emotion, with hints of anguish and despair in your voice.

Pronunciation Guide

Archelaus (ahr'-kuh-LAY-uhs), *Bethlehem* (BETH-luh-hem'), *Galilee* (GAL-uh-lee), *Herod* (HAIR-uhd), *Israel* (IZ-ree-uhl; -ray-), *Jeremiah* (jair'-uh-MĪ-uh), *Judea* (joo-DEE-uh; -DAY-), *Nazareth* (NAZ-uh-reth; *not* -rus), *Nazorean* (NAZ-or-ee-uhn), *Rachel* (RAY-chuhl), *Ramah* (RAY-muh)

✠ Luke 2:41–52

Commentary

While Luke and Matthew are the only canonical gospels that tell a story of Jesus' birth, Luke is the only canonical gospel that narrates an event from Jesus' childhood. In one sense, this is quite remarkable for we might expect, given his extraordinary birth and his extraordinary adult life, that Jesus would also have had an extraordinary childhood. Yet this is not the picture of Jesus we find in the NT. Not only are there no miraculous stories of Jesus as a youth, but when Jesus begins his ministry, his family, friends, and neighbors are utterly astounded at his mighty words and deeds. Apparently, they had never seen, nor did they expect anything like this from Jesus (Matt 13:54–58; Luke 4:22; Mark 6:1–6, Prop 9). In fact, according to the Gospel of Mark, when Jesus goes about Capernaum exorcising demons, his family comes to take him home because they think he is out of his mind (3:20–21, Prop 5).

We do know that by the second century A.D. stories circulated about Jesus' "miraculous" childhood. We have a collection of such stories in a second century work entitled, *The Infancy Gospel of Thomas* (not to be confused with *The Gospel of Thomas*, a sayings gospel). *Infancy Thomas* narrates all manner of miracles performed by Jesus between the ages of five and twelve, including raising people from the dead, striking people blind, lengthening boards that his father cut too short, and turning mud sparrows into real sparrows. It seems likely that such stories would have been known by the authors of our NT gospels, yet they were not included in their gospels. This may tell us something about their understanding of Jesus and his childhood.

Of course, Luke knew of at least one remarkable story from Jesus' youth, for it forms today's reading. It relates an event that occurs when the twelve-year-old Jesus accompanies his parents on a trip to Jerusalem for Passover. The story is as remarkable for what it does *not* say about Jesus as much for what it *does* say. Certainly, we learn that Jesus is not your typical twelve year old. Yet, it is striking that the story highlights, not some supernatural ability, but Jesus' understanding of the law and his sense of connection with God. This emphasis is further reflected in the concluding statement that as he grew in years, "Jesus increased in *wisdom*" (2:52).

2:41–51. Although Jesus and his parents made the annual trip to celebrate Passover, it is when Jesus is twelve years old that this incident takes place. Jesus' age may be significant since, according to the Jewish historian Josephus, the prophet Samuel was twelve years old when the LORD called to him in the tabernacle (Ant. 5:348; cf. 1 Sam 3:1–14). In any case, when Passover ends, Mary and Joseph begin the return trip to Nazareth. They assume that Jesus is somewhere among their caravan of friends and family, but he is not. When they go back to Jerusalem to search for Jesus, it takes them three days to find him. In their parental fear, they question him, "Child, why have you treated us like this?" (2:49). Jesus puzzles them with his response, "Did you not know that I must be in my Father's house?" (2:50). Just as Mary treasured and pondered in her heart the story about the angels that the shepherds told on the night of her son's birth (2:19), so now she treasures in her heart the words and actions of her son as he approaches the age of accountability and nears adulthood. At this point, the narrator notes that Jesus returns to Nazareth with his parents and "was obedient to them" (2:51). Jesus has learned his lesson, and this sort of behavior never happens again.

2:52. Another unique feature of Luke's gospel is that it narrates events surrounding the conception and birth of John the Baptist (1:5–25, 57–80). At the conclusion of his account of John's birth, Luke provides a single-sentence summary of John's growth and development into adulthood. "The child grew and became strong in spirit, and he was in the wilderness until the day he appeared publicly to Israel" (1:80). Today's reading concludes with a similar summary for Jesus, "And Jesus increased in wisdom and in years, and in divine and human favor" (2:52). Both summaries evoke that of the boy Samuel from today's OT reading: "Now the boy Samuel continued to grow both in stature and in favor with the LORD and with the people" (1 Sam 2:26).

Suggestions for Lectors

There are two groups of people that are in the best position to read this incident with the emotion it demands. The first group consists of parents who have searched for a missing child, who when found is oblivious to the fact that they were lost, that they were not where they were supposed to be, and that their parents have been frantically searching for them. The second group consists of the children themselves who have been found in the manner described above. Many of us fit into both groups, providing us with the life experiences that will help us convey the anxiety, anger, and annoyance that Mary and Joseph must have felt as well as the innocent incredulity that Jesus expresses.

Begin reading with your typical narrating voice and at your normal pace until Jesus' parents discover that he is not with them. Then, pick up your pace as you read 2:45–46a. When you hit the phrase *in the temple*, read slowly with longer pauses and with increasing astonishment as this unimaginable scene unfolds before them: their son… *is in the temple,… sitting among the teachers,… listening to them and asking them questions.* You might then imagine Mary, both embarrassed and angry, pulling Jesus aside and saying to him in hushed tones, *Child, why have you treated us like this?* (2:48). Then, you might imagine that Jesus is completely oblivious to the anxiety and trouble he has caused or perhaps only partially aware. Whatever you decide, adopt a suitable voice. While you are not engaged in a dramatic reading, your voice should have hints of all of the emotions discussed above.

Pronunciation Guide

Jerusalem (juh-ROO-suh-luhm), *Nazareth* (NAZ-uh-reth; *not* -rus)

✠ Matthew 2:1–12

Commentary

In the concluding scene of Matthew's gospel, the resurrected Jesus instructs his Jewish apostles to proclaim the good news of Jesus' lordship throughout the world and to make disciples of *all* nations, that is, disciples of both Jews *and* Gentiles (28:18–19). In today's reading, which occurs at the beginning of Matthew, this future inclusion of Gentiles within the people of God is foreshadowed by the arrival of Gentiles who have made a long and arduous journey to pay homage to the child who will one day receive "all authority in heaven and on earth" (28:19).

2:1–2. From 37 B.C. until his death in 4 B.C., Herod the Great ruled Judea as the appointed client king of Rome. Today's reading opens with the arrival in Jerusalem of men who are looking for "the child who has been born king of the Jews" (2:8). These magi (generally referred to as *wise men* or *kings*) appear to be astrologers from the Far East who have witnessed the rising of a star that they interpret as a sign that a new Jewish king has been born. Naturally, they travel to the capital city to make inquiries.

2:3–8. Upon hearing news of the birth of a rival king, King Herod becomes frightened and calls together those in official religious leadership in an effort to ascertain where the Messiah was expected to be born. Surprisingly, or perhaps not so surprisingly, the prophet Micah identifies the little Judean village of Bethlehem (Micah 5:2), the hometown of Israel's most revered king, King David. Herod convenes with the magi secretly, finding out exactly when the king's star first appeared. Later, Herod will use this information when giving the order to slaughter all of the children in and around Bethlehem who are two years of age and under (2:16). Herod then provides the magi with the name of the town, requesting that they send word once they locate the child so that he too might come and offer homage.

2:9–12. The magi set out for Bethlehem and are overjoyed when the star they have been following for so long stops over the place where the child resides. Entering the structure, they see the child with his mother; they kneel and pay him homage. From their treasure chests, they bring out three gifts worthy of any king—gold and frankincense and myrrh (cf. Isa 60:6, Epi). In Matthew, dreams are one of the ways God communicates with people (1:20; 2:13, 19, 22; 27:19); so in a dream, the magi are warned not to return to Herod.

Suggestions for Lectors

Few passages in the Bible are as well suited to storytelling than this smoothly flowing narration in which not a word is wasted. Drop your voice after *Jerusalem* in 2:1. In 2:2, glide through *asking* since you want the emphasis to fall upon the question itself. Pause for a full second before and after the scripture citation in 2:6; read it in an elevated, yet solemn tone. While still speaking loudly enough for your listeners to hear you, read 2:7 in a somewhat hushed tone to convey Herod's secrecy. In 2:8, Herod instructs the magi. Here, he is trying to appear aboveboard, so return to your normal narrating voice.

As you reach the part where the wise men near their destination, reduce your speed. Without losing the intonation for the whole sentence, pause for a full second after *stopped* in 2:10. Then, proceed with *they were overwhelmed with joy*, enunciating each word in a voice tinged with the awe, excitement, joy, and thanksgiving over having found what they have been looking for. Pause for a second or two after *paid him homage* (12:11) to create a moment of reverence as the Jewish and Gentile worlds meet. Then return to your default narrative voice and tempo for the remainder of the reading.

Pronunciation Guide

Bethlehem (BETH-luh-hem')
frankincense (FRANG-kin-sens)
Herod (HAIR-uhd)
Israel (IZ-ree-uhl; -ray-)
Jews (JOOZ)
Judah (JOO-duh)
Judea (joo-DEE-uh; -DAY-)
Mary (MAIR-ee)
Messiah (muh-SĪ-uh)
myrrh (MER)

SEASON OF EPIPHANY
ORDINARY TIME

EPIPHANY OF THE LORD

January 6

Isaiah 60:1–6
Psalm 72:1–7, 10–14
Ephesians 3:1–12
Matthew 2:1–12

Overview of Readings
The word epiphany means *manifestation* or *revelation.* The day of The Epiphany signals the beginning of a new season in the church year (much as Ash Wednesday signals the beginning of Lent). On this day, we remember and celebrate the revelation of who Jesus is as Son of God, Christ/Messiah, and Lord. The theme that runs through all of today's readings concerns the revelation of Israel's God to the people of all nations.

ISAIAH 60:1–6

Commentary
Throughout Isaiah, we see that the restoration of God's people after the exile involves the rebuilding of Jerusalem (= Zion), and vice-versa. That is, the rebuilding of Jerusalem is a key element in the restoration of God's exiled people. In today's reading, the prophet envisions the reversal of fortunes for Jerusalem, "the City of the LORD" (60:14), which not only brings about the salvation of God's chosen people, but people from every nation.

In 51:17–20, the prophet describes the aftermath of Jerusalem's destruction by the Babylonian armies. Jerusalem is personified as a woman in distress who has become drunk, having been forced to consume the full cup of the LORD's wrath, even the dregs. In her drunken state, Jerusalem is unstable and so unable to support herself. Her children (that is, the city's inhabitants) are likewise inebriated, and so, "There is no one to guide her among all the children she has borne; there is no one to take her by the hand among all the children she has brought up" (51:18).

60:1–6. Likewise, in today's reading, Jerusalem is personified and addressed as a woman, which is less obvious in English translations than in the Hebrew text. The prophet speaks to her saying, "Arise, shine; for your light has come" (60:1). Since her judgment, Jerusalem has resided in darkness, but now a thick darkness will descend upon the world even as her own light reignites and flickers into life. Consequently, the rest of the world will be drawn to Jerusalem, and thus she shall finally fulfill her vocation to be "a light to the nations" (42:6). Mother Jerusalem will have reason to rejoice, for when the nations come, they will bring their wealth into Jerusalem in tribute to the LORD. Moreover, they will bring back her sons and daughters, the exiles of Israel and Judah.

Suggestions for Lectors

In today's reading, you are the voice of the prophet describing a glorious vision of future restoration for all of God's people. Read these poetic lines like a proclamation in an upbeat and triumphant mode. None of the verses stand out over any of the others, so maintain essentially the same tone throughout. If you would like to emphasize something in this reading, the two commands would be quite appropriate: *Arise, shine; for your light has come* (60:1a) and *Lift up your eyes and look around* (60:4a). The last clause in 60:6, *and shall proclaim the praise of the LORD*, affords an excellent conclusion to this reading.

Pronunciation Guide

Ephah (EE-fah), *frankincense* (FRANG-kin-sens),
Isaiah (ī-ZAY-uh), *Midian* (MID-ee-uhn), *Sheba* (SHE-buh)

EPHESIANS 3:1–12

Commentary

Paul addresses the Ephesian Christians, speaking of his vocation to proclaim the gospel of Jesus Christ to the Gentiles. Previously, in 2:11–22 (Prop 11), Paul gave an account of how Christ made it possible for Gentiles to become members of God's household. By abolishing, through his death, "the law with its commands and ordinances" (2:15), many of which served to set Israel apart from all other nations, Jesus broke down the wall that separated Jews and Gentiles, creating one new humanity where previously there had been two.

3:1–12. In today's reading, Paul continues this theme by speaking of the mystery of Christ. This mystery had not been made known in ages past, but has now been revealed to those apostles and prophets who have been entrusted with proclaiming the gospel. This mystery, which Paul "wrote above in a few words" (3:3; cf. 1:9–10; 2:11–22), concerns God's plan "to gather up all things in him" (1:10, Chr 2). More specifically, the mystery is that Gentiles can now share in Israel's inheritance. The people of God no longer consist of people from a single nation, but people from all nations. Paul's mission, therefore, is not only to call Gentiles to faith in Christ, but also to make sure everyone knows that this has been God's plan all along. This last part is an important piece in Paul's argument, for many of his fellow Jews, including many Jewish-Christians, neither understand nor accept this newly-revealed mystery. Consequently, they oppose Paul's offering of salvation to Gentiles solely on the basis of faith in Christ rather than on the basis of performing the works of the law.

Suggestions for Lectors

It is typical for Paul's letters to contain lengthy sentences that are logically and theologically compact, as in today's reading, where 3:1–4 comprises a single sentence, as do 3:5–6 and 3:8–10. When confronted with such complex sentences, it is important for the lector to become familiar with their grammar and logic by reading the sentences through multiple times. Your challenge is to gain such a feel for the flow of the sentence that you are able, through strategically placed pauses and the intonation of your voice, to draw all of its phrases and clauses together into a single, coherent thought for your listeners.

The heart of today's reading is 3:6 where Paul discloses the content of the mystery he has been alluding to. This mystery is that *the Gentiles have become fellow heirs, members of the same body, and sharers in the promise in Christ Jesus through the gospel.* Everything prior to 3:6 anticipates this revelation, while everything after 3:6 draws out the implications of this mystery. So in 3:1–5, use your voice to create a sense of mounting suspense in your listeners, which is then satisfied when you disclose the mystery in 3:6 in a voice that assumes your listeners have never heard or even guessed at what this hitherto undisclosed mystery might be.

After reading 3:6, pause for a second or two before commencing with the second half of the reading, in which Paul explains how this mystery relates to his calling to be an apostle. This portion of the reading can be read in your basic reader's voice, as there are no points requiring particular emphasis other than the concluding clause.

Pronunciation Guide

Ephesians (eh-FEE-zhuhnz; ih-), *Gentiles* (JEN-tīlz)

MATTHEW 2:1–12

Commentary

In the concluding scene of Matthew's gospel, the resurrected Jesus instructs his Jewish apostles to proclaim the good news of Jesus' lordship throughout the world and to make disciples of *all* nations, that is, disciples of both Jews *and* Gentiles (28:18–19). In today's reading, which occurs at the beginning of Matthew, this future inclusion of Gentiles within the people of God is foreshadowed by the arrival of Gentiles who have made a long and arduous journey to pay homage to the child who will one day receive "all authority in heaven and on earth" (28:19).

2:1–2. From 37 B.C. until his death in 4 B.C., Herod the Great ruled Judea as the appointed client king of Rome. Today's reading opens with the arrival in Jerusalem of men who are looking for "the child who has been born king of the Jews" (2:8). These magi (generally referred to as *wise men* or *kings*) appear to be astrologers from the Far East who have witnessed the rising of a star that they interpret as a sign that a new Jewish king has been born. Naturally, they travel to the capital city to make inquiries.

2:3–8. Upon hearing news of the birth of a rival king, King Herod becomes frightened and calls together those in official religious leadership in an effort to ascertain where the Messiah was expected to be born. Surprisingly, or perhaps not so surprisingly, the prophet Micah identifies the little Judean village of Bethlehem (Micah 5:2), the hometown of Israel's most revered king, King David. Herod convenes with the magi secretly, finding out exactly when the king's star first appeared. Later, Herod will use this information when giving the order to slaughter all of the children in and around Bethlehem who are two years of age and under (2:16). Herod then provides the magi with the name of the town, requesting that they send word once they locate the child so that he too might come and offer homage.

2:9–12. The magi set out for Bethlehem and are overjoyed when the star they have been following for so long stops over the place where the child resides. Entering the structure, they see the child with his mother; they kneel and pay him homage. From their treasure chests, they bring out three gifts worthy of any king—gold and frankincense and myrrh (cf. Isa 60:6, Epi). In Matthew, dreams are one of the ways God communicates with people (1:20; 2:13, 19, 22; 27:19); so in a dream, the magi are warned not to return to Herod.

Suggestions for Lectors

Few passages in the Bible are as well suited to storytelling than this smoothly flowing narration in which not a word is wasted. Drop your voice after *Jerusalem* in 2:1. In 2:2, glide through *asking* since you want the emphasis to fall upon the question itself. Pause for a full second before and after the scripture citation in 2:6; read it in an elevated, yet solemn tone. While still speaking loudly enough for your listeners to hear you, read 2:7 in a somewhat hushed tone to convey Herod's secrecy. In 2:8, Herod instructs the magi. Here, he is trying to appear aboveboard, so return to your normal narrating voice.

As you reach the part where the wise men near their destination, reduce your speed. Without losing the intonation for the whole sentence, pause for a full second after *stopped* in 2:10. Then, proceed with *they were overwhelmed with joy*, enunciating each word in a voice tinged with the awe, excitement, joy, and thanksgiving over having found what they have been looking for. Pause for a second or two after *paid him homage* (12:11) to create a moment of reverence as the Jewish and Gentile worlds meet. Then return to your default narrative voice and tempo for the remainder of the reading.

Pronunciation Guide

Bethlehem (BETH-luh-hem')
frankincense (FRANG-kin-sens)
Herod (HAIR-uhd)
Israel (IZ-ree-uhl; -ray-)
Jews (JOOZ)
Judah (JOO-duh)
Judea (joo-DEE-uh; -DAY-)
Mary (MAIR-ee)
Messiah (muh-SĪ-uh)
myrrh (MER)

FIRST SUNDAY AFTER EPIPHANY

Baptism of the Lord

Genesis 1:1–5
Psalm 29
Acts 19:1–7
Mark 1:4–11

GENESIS 1:1–5

Commentary

In today's gospel reading, we are transported back to "the *beginning* of the good news of Jesus Christ, the Son of God" (Mark 1:1). In today's OT reading, we are transported even further back to the beginning of all things. The book of Genesis begins at the very beginning with an orderly account of God's creation of the world that reflects the orderliness of creation itself (see EastVig for a more detailed commentary that covers the whole of the first creation account).

1:1–2. Christians rightly speak of God having created the world *ex nihilo*, that is, out of nothing (cf. Rom 4:17, Lent 2; 1 Cor 1:28; Heb 11:3; 2 Macc 7:28). Genesis 1, however, offers a slightly different story. The story is not so much of creation out of *nothing* as it is creation out of *chaos*. In the Bible, chaos is that which opposes God and attempts to frustrate God's purposes. Here, chaos finds representation in the impenetrable darkness and the unbounded waters of the primordial deep.

1:3–5. On the first day of creation, the first of these chaotic forces is dealt with. God speaks into the darkness, and immediately, light flickers into being. That God is able to overcome the darkness simply by speaking (vs. a cosmic showdown) demonstrates that the forces of chaos offer no real challenge to God and God's purposes. Interestingly enough, the darkness is not entirely vanquished. Instead, God separates the light from the darkness. God gathers the darkness together into a region called Night, while the light is collected into a separate region called Day. Creation, then, is not so much a matter of obliterating the forces of chaos as it is of establishing order in the midst of chaos. In fact, the forces of chaos will remain a part of Creation until their ultimate destruction in the New Creation (cf. Rev 21:1, 25). In the meantime, the story of Genesis calls us to recognize the inherent goodness of creation and of God, as evidenced in the orderliness of Day and Night.

Suggestions for Lectors

As reflected in the Commentary, today's reading falls into two sections. The first two verses provide the setting and background for the first act of creation, which occurs in the last three verses. Therefore, pause for a full second between verses 2 and 3.

Genesis 1:1–2 comprises a single, complex sentence. Make sure you have sufficient breath to deliver the whole sentence smoothly and with the proper intonation. When faced with long sentences, it is always important to identify the central message and build your reading and intonation around that. In this case, the message is *the earth was a formless void and darkness covered the face of the deep*, and it is flanked by two dependent clauses.

In 1:3–5, the style is much diffcrent from the style in 1:1–2, as these verses are filled with relatively short sentences. As you read, attend to the punctuation by pausing at the commas, semicolons, and periods. However, make sure that your reading is smooth and does not become choppy. Use the intonation of your voice to tie everything together.

It has become increasingly common for lectors to emphasize words like *said* or *saying* when introducing direct speech or a quotation, but this often puts the emphasis in the wrong place. The emphasis should be on the quote itself. So in 1:3, drop your voice when reading *said*, and then emphasize *Let*. It is also common to pause slightly longer after *said* and *saying* in an attempt to draw attention to what is being said, but these pauses tend to make the reading choppy. So, in 1:3, only introduce the slightest of pauses after *said*. To get a feel for the difference these two suggestions make, read the following sentences aloud. Notice how the second example draws attention to *what* God is saying instead of to the mere fact that God is saying it.

> Then God *said*,… "Let there be light."
>
> Then God said, "*Let* there be light."

In 1:5, pause ever so slightly before *Day* and *Night*, and emphasize both words. Pause slightly longer at the period after *Night* and then again at the comma after *morning*. Then, reading at a slower pace, enunciate the final three words very deliberately, *the first day*, as you draw the reading to a close.

ACTS 19:1–7

Commentary

Like Jesus, John the Baptist had his own disciples (Mark 2:18; Luke 5:33; John 1:35, 3:25, 4:1). Clearly, he had quite a following, for in today's reading, we encounter disciples of John in Ephesus, which is far from Galilee. Moreover, evidence outside the NT indicates that a John the Baptist movement continued well into the fourth century. As we see in today's reading, not all of the Baptist's disciples were aware of his role as forerunner to Jesus. This may explain why Luke repeatedly clarifies the relationship of John to Jesus in the narrative of Acts (1:5; 11:16; 13:24–25; 18:25; 19:1–7). The last of these clarifications comprises today's reading.

At the end of his second missionary journey (Acts 15:36–18:22), Paul is making his way back to Antioch when he stays over in Ephesus. He visits the Jewish synagogue and enters into discussions with Jews. They ask Paul to stay, but he declines, saying, "I will return to you, if God wills" (18:21). God did will it, for on his Third Missionary Journey (Acts 18:23–21:17), Paul does return to the Ephesian synagogue.

19:1–7. When Paul arrives, he finds some Jews who appear to him to be Christians since he addresses them using the language of *believer*. Yet, their complete lack of knowledge about the Holy Spirit indicates that they have not yet become Christian because, in Acts and in the writings of Paul, a person is only a Christian if they have received the gift of the indwelling Holy Spirit. Perhaps these Ephesians had heard the gospel and had come to believe that Jesus was the Messiah, but the only baptism they were familiar with was John's.

Paul explains that John's baptism was a baptism of repentance. Certainly, there was nothing wrong with it, but like John himself, his baptism was preparatory. As John says in today's gospel (Mark 1:8) and as Acts repeatedly reminds us (Acts 1:5; 11:16), John baptized with water but Jesus baptizes with the Holy Spirit. Moreover, John told the crowds that he was not the Messiah (Acts 13:24; John 1:20), but that there was a more powerful one coming after him, the thong of whose sandals he was not even worthy to stoop down and untie (Mark 1:7). Paul explains all of this to these twelve men, and they respond by submitting to baptism in Jesus' name. Immediately, the Holy Spirit comes upon them, and they begin to speak in other languages and prophecy, just like the first believers did on the day of Pentecost (Acts 2:4, Pent) and just like the Gentiles of Cornelius household (Acts 10:44–46, East 6).

Afterwards, Paul spends the next two years in Ephesus proclaiming the kingdom of God in both religious and civic venues.

Suggestions for Lectors

In the interactions between Paul and the Ephesian disciples, adopt a different tone of voice for each. You will be aided by the fact that, in their first two interactions, Paul asks questions and they respond with answers, and by nature questions and statements require a different intonation. Invest Paul's voice with curiosity, and their voices with hints of confusion.

When Paul talks about John's baptism and about Jesus (19:4), intensify your voice and speak with confidence. Do not read these words, proclaim them.

Pronunciation Guide

Apollos (uh-POL-uhs; -ohs), *Corinth* (KOR-inth; KAHR-; *not* koh-RINTH), *Ephesus* (EF-uh-suhs; EH-fuh-suhs)

MARK 1:4–11

Commentary

In Hebrew, *messiah* means *anointed one.* A messiah is someone who is anointed with oil as a sign of having been commissioned by God to carry out a specific vocation or task. In the OT, it was principally kings and high priests, but sometimes prophets, who were anointed. In today's reading, Jesus is anointed for his messianic vocation, not with oil, but with the Holy Spirit in the waters of baptism.

1:4–8. For Mark, the beginning of the good news about Jesus Christ begins in the OT Scriptures with the promises God made through the prophets, like Malachi and Isaiah:

> See, I am sending my *messenger* ahead of you,
>   who will prepare your way (Mal 3:1);
> the *voice* of one crying out in the wilderness:
>   "Prepare the way of the Lord, make his paths straight" (Isa 40:3)

The *messenger* of Malachi and the *voice* of Isaiah are John the Baptist. In Malachi, the messenger is identified as the prophet Elijah (Mal 4:5), and the description of the Baptist's clothing matches that of Elijah (2 Kgs 1:8; cf. Zech 13:4). In Isaiah, the voice cries out in the wilderness, so the Baptist conducts his ministry of preaching and preparation in the wilderness of Judea. John entreats the people to get ready to meet their Lord and King. His preaching is powerful and effective. Crowds of people traipse out into the wilderness in order to confess their sins and be baptized as a sign of their repentance. Yet, the Baptist fully understands the preparatory and provisional nature of his ministry of ritual cleansing. He announces, "I have baptized you with water; but he will baptize you with the Holy Spirit."

In Mark, the Spirit is called the *Holy* Spirit because it has the power to make things holy and pure, to cleanse what Satan and his minions have infected and defiled. In Mark, there is a cosmic conflict between God's *Holy* Spirit and Satan's legions of *unclean* spirits. Unclean spirits communicate impurity, sin, and sickness, whereas the Holy Spirit communicates purity, holiness, and wholeness. Consequently, the spiritual conflict in Mark is not only manifest in Jesus' exorcisms, but in everything he does. When the Baptist says of Jesus, "he will baptize you with the Holy Spirit" (1:8), he is not referring to some specific event that Mark never narrates (like the coming of the Spirit at Pentecost); instead the Baptist is characterizing Jesus' entire ministry. To baptize is to cleanse, and everything Jesus does—his exorcisms and healings, his authoritative teachings, his pronouncements of forgiveness, his table-fellowship with tax-collectors and sinners, etc.—amounts to a cleansing of the world by the power of the Holy Spirit.

1:9–11. Jesus joins the crowds of people who have journeyed out into the Judean wilderness to be baptized by John. When Jesus comes up out of the river, he sees the heavens being torn apart. In Matthew and Luke, the heavens simply *open* (Matt 3:16; Luke 3:21), but here they are *torn apart*, which is a much more dramatic descriptor. The only other occurrence of this verb in Mark is at Jesus' crucifixion. The moment Jesus breathes his last, the temple curtain is *torn* in two from top to bottom (15:38). The Gentile centurion then declares, "Truly this man was God's Son" (15:39).

The parallels between the Jesus' crucifixion and his baptism are striking, for when the heavens are torn apart, a voice declares Jesus to be God's beloved Son. In apocalyptic literature (like the book of Revelation), the rending of the sky indicates that a revelation is forthcoming. In Mark, these rendings of sky and curtain are preludes to the revelation of Jesus' divine identity. Of course, the scenes are quite different; one is glorious and the other tragic. But together they reveal what it means for Jesus to be the Son of God; it entails both glory and suffering.

The heavens are also rent so that the Holy Spirit might descend upon Jesus and anoint him for his messianic vocation. In the OT, Israel's king was often referred to as God's son (2 Sam 7:8–16, esp. 14). Psalm 2, which employs this language, is a royal psalm and is generally thought to have been used in the coronation ceremony of Israel's king. In it, the LORD says to the king, "You are my son; today I have begotten you. Ask of me, and I will make the nations your heritage, and the ends of the earth your possession" (2:7b–8). Likewise, Jesus' baptism serves as his coronation ceremony. He is anointed as the Messiah, the long-awaited king who will execute God's heavenly rule over the whole earth on God's behalf. Jesus is equipped for this messianic task by the Holy Spirit, and he is crowned with the dove of peace, a symbol reflecting the nature of kingdom that he rules—a peaceable kingdom in which a peaceful state of affairs is achieved by peaceful means.

Suggestions for Lectors

Today's episode is composed of two scenes: the first focuses upon John the Baptist (1:4–8) and the second upon Jesus of Nazareth (1:9–11). Pause for a full second when you transition from one scene to the next.

In 1:7–8, John the Baptist is speaking to a large crowd, so increase the volume and pitch of your voice as you deliver his proclamation. In 1:8, emphasize the points of contrast between the ministries of John and Jesus, as in: *I have baptized you with water; but he will baptize you with the Holy Spirit.*

The account of Jesus' baptism is quite brief, so you may want to decrease your tempo in order to give the scene more time to play out. Despite the paucity of description in Mark's account of Jesus' baptism, the scene is quite breathtaking, so read 1:10 with a sense of awe in order to convey the sheer wonder and majesty of it all. Read 1:11 slowly and deliberately, enunciating each word with care. Read it with a smile on your face as though you are a proud parent.

As lectors, when we emphasize something in a reading by changing the tone, pitch, or volume of our voice, we are bringing that element to the foreground while resigning other elements to the background, which affects how our listeners understand and experience the text. That is why it is so important to make conscious decisions regarding what to and what not to emphasize, though there is rarely only one way of reading a text that is faithful to its meaning. Consider the following.

When the heavenly Voice declares, *You are my Son, the Beloved*, there is more than one way to add emphasis:

> *You* are my Son, the Beloved;
> You are *my Son*, the Beloved;
> You are my Son, *the Beloved*;

Each of these renderings faithfully represents the text, but they are all slightly different. So, as you prepare for this and other readings, take the time to think through the question of emphasis. What might I emphasize, how shall I emphasize it, and what will be its impact upon my listeners?

Pronunciation Guide

Beloved (n., buh-LUV-uhd)
Galilee (GAL-uh-lee)
Jerusalem (juh-ROO-suh-luhm)
Jordan (JOR-duhn)
Judean (joo-DEE-uhn; -DAY-)
Nazareth (NAZ-uh-reth; *not* -rus)

SECOND SUNDAY AFTER EPIPHANY

1 Samuel 3:1–10, (11–20)
Psalm 139:1–6, 13–18 (= 139:1–5, 12–17 BCP)
1 Corinthians 6:12–20
John 1:43–51

1 SAMUEL 3:1–10, (11–20)

Commentary

Samuel is the beloved firstborn son of Hannah. In 1 Samuel 1:1–20 (Prop 28), we learn that Hannah lives with the disgrace of barrenness. On one of her annual pilgrimages to the central sanctuary in Shiloh, she pleads with the LORD for a child. If only the LORD would but look upon her and grant her a male child, she would return the LORD's favor by devoting that child to the LORD's service. The LORD did indeed look upon Hannah, and she kept her promise. When Samuel was weaned, Hannah brought him to Shiloh and left him to be raised at the sanctuary by the priest Eli (1:27–28). Once a year, Hannah would return to visit her son and provide him with a new robe. Thus, the boy Samuel "ministered to the LORD, in the presence of the priest Eli" (2:11). And it became said of him that as he "grew up in the presence of the LORD" (2:21), he grew "both in statue and in favor with the LORD and with the people" (2:26; compare this with what is said of Jesus in Luke 2:40, 52).

These descriptions of Samuel's character stand in sharp relief to those of Eli's own sons, Hophni and Phinehas, who are portrayed as scoundrels (2:11). In fact, just prior to today's reading, an unnamed man of God comes to Shiloh and announces judgment upon the house of Eli. So, in today's reading, the LORD's calling of Samuel simultaneously serves as the LORD's rejection of Eli and his line.

3:1. Today's episode begins with the words: "the word of the LORD was rare in those days; visions were not widespread" (3:1). This statement serves two purposes. First, it is a sign that things have become corrupt in Israel. The LORD has stopped speaking and appearing because there are precious few with eyes willing to see and ears willing to hear. Second, it helps explain why Samuel thinks the voice he hears is that of Eli and why Eli does not pick up on the fact that the LORD is calling the boy.

3:2–10. The lamp of God was lit from evening to morning (Lev 24:2), so the LORD calls to Samuel in the middle of the night, perhaps in early morning hours just before dawn. The text is ambiguous, but it appears that Samuel does not merely sleep in the temple but in the inner sanctuary where the ark of the covenant is housed. If so, then this is quite extraordinary since the inner sanctuary was off limits to everyone except the high priest. It reveals Samuel's purity and innocence and his devotion to the LORD.

3:11–18. The LORD informs Samuel of the judgment that will befall Eli and his sons. Though Eli seems to have been a good priest, he was not a good father for he allowed his sons to act shamefully in their priestly duties. How hard it must have been for Samuel to disclose the LORD's plans to this man who had been like a father to him! Eli, however, tries to lighten Samuel's burden by saying, "It is the LORD, let him do what seems good to him" (3:18).

3:19–20. Samuel is singularly devoted to the LORD, and everything that Samuel says comes to pass for "the LORD was with him and let none of his words fall to the ground" (3:20). For your information, Dan and Beer-sheba were the traditional northern and southern limits of Israel.

Suggestions for Lectors

Today's reading comes with its own introduction, so read 3:1 and then pause for a full second before continuing on. Also, introduce full-second pauses prior to verses 10, 15, and 19 as these are the beginning of new paragraphs.

The whole narrative is driven by dialogue, which tends to be the most challenging type of a narrative for the lector. Focus your preparations on the dialogues, practicing the speaking parts until you are comfortable and pleased with your delivery. In today's reading, three characters speak: the LORD, Samuel, and Eli.

On two occasions, the LORD repeats Samuel's name when he calls him: *Samuel! Samuel!* (3:4, 3:10). Instead of saying both names the same way, increase the volume on the second one as though you are trying to get his attention.

Samuel is clearly a devoted and obedient boy. Even though he is awakened three different times, every time he comes to Eli with the same simple words: *Here I am, for you called me* (3:4, 6, 8). In other words, there is no suggestion that Samuel is even the slightest bit annoyed. So deliver all three responses in the exact same way, with a respectful innocence. Then, use this same tone of voice when Samuel answers the LORD in 3:10, only increase your volume and deliver the line slowly for this is the high point of the story: *Speak, for your servant is listening.* One other line that deserves emphasis is Eli's response to Samuel's vision (3:18). Deliver this line without any bitterness, but with a sense of understanding and resignation: *It is the LORD; let him do what seems good to him* (3:18).

Between the second and third calls, the narrator stops the story to offer the reader some information to help explain why Samuel does not know that it is the LORD who is calling him. So lower your voice when reading 3:7, using the same voice you would use for a parenthetical expression. Also, it would be appropriate to make eye contact with your listeners as you begin your explanation.

The tone of the whole narrative drastically changes in 3:11 as the LORD reveals his intentions to punish the house of Eli. Let your voice be strong and determined, and invest it with hints of anger and especially disappointment.

Pronunciation Guide

Beer-sheba (beer'-SHEE-buh; bihr'-)
Dan (DAN)
Eli (EE-lī)
Israel (IZ-ree-uhl; -ray-)
Samuel (SAM-yoo-uhl; SAM-yuhl)

1 Corinthians 6:12–20

Notes

Sequence. 1 of 5

Commentary

The church in Corinth was established by the Apostle Paul during his second missionary journey (Acts 18:1–17). Corinth was clearly an important mission, for Paul remained there eighteen months preaching the gospel, all the while supporting himself by making tents. In 1 Corinthians, Paul addresses a number of problems besetting this fledgling Christian community. Many of the problems relate to the question of how the Corinthians, as individuals and as a community, are to live out their faith within a culture whose values are so different and antithetical to those of the gospel.

In today's reading, Paul stresses the vital role our physical bodies play in our spiritual (trans)formation. Apparently, there were those in Corinth who did not see any direct connection between the physical and spiritual dimensions of the human person. This idea fits well with the ancient Greco-Roman worldview that maintained a radical dualism between the temporal, ever-changing physical world and the eternal, unchanging world of spirit. Since the physical and spiritual worlds were utterly distinct, some in Corinth lived as though bodily activities and behavior had little if any moral or spiritual consequences. Paul challenges the Corinthians on this point and argues that what we do in the body has everything to do with our spiritual condition.

6:12–13a. The opening verses of today's reading can be confusing until one recognizes that Paul is actually responding to statements that the Corinthians have made in support of their body-spirit dualism. Notice the use of quotation marks in the NRSV and in many other recent English translations.

> "All things are lawful for me," *but not all things are beneficial.*
> "All things are lawful for me," *but I will not be dominated by anything.*
> "Food is meant for the stomach and the stomach for food," *and God will destroy both one and the other. The body is meant not for fornication but for the Lord, and the Lord for the body* (6:12–13 NRSV).

The quotation marks identify the arguments that the Corinthians are putting forward to justify their behavior. Everything in *italics* represents Paul's response. What we see, then, is that Paul agrees with the Corinthians in principal, but disagrees with the conclusions that they have drawn. The New Living Translation brings this out:

> *You say,* "I am allowed to do anything"—but not everything is good for you. *And even though* "I am allowed to do anything," I must not become a slave to anything. *You say,* "Food was made for the stomach, and the stomach for food." (This is true, though someday God will do away with both of them.) But you can't say that our bodies were made for sexual immorality. They were made for the Lord, and the Lord cares about our bodies (6:12–13 NLT).

Some scholars even argue that these quotations represent statements that Paul himself made, that Paul taught, "All things are lawful for me." The problem, then, is that the Corinthians have taken these statements out of context and misapplied them in support of behaviors and practices that Paul regards as highly immoral and unchristian.

Because of Christ, Christians have been set free from the law, and so in a very real sense, all things *are* lawful for Christians. Yet, Paul reminds the Corinthians that actions still have consequences, be they lawful or not. Not everything that might be construed as lawful is actually good for us. Moreover, Christian freedom can be taken to such an extreme that it becomes just another form of slavery. For example, eating whatever we want—like food sacrificed to idols (see 1 Cor 8, Epi 4)—may be permissible for the Christian, but there is so much more to the Christian life than getting to eat whatever we want.

6:13b–14. Moreover, freedom with regard to food does not translate into freedom with regard to sexual intimacy, eating whatever we want is not remotely akin to having sex with anyone we want. Here, Paul states a principle that offers a foundation and context for everything else that he wants to say about our physical bodies: "The body is meant… for the Lord, and the Lord for the body" (6:13b). For Paul, the body is indispensable because human beings are not just souls by nature. A human being is not just a spiritual soul trapped in a physical body (as many in Corinth would have maintained). Instead, human beings are physical-spiritual wholes, what some have termed "enfleshed souls" or "ensouled bodies."

For Paul, the body is of inestimable value. Not only did God create human beings with physical bodies, human beings will continue to have physical bodies in the new creation. That is the meaning of resurrection, which stands in stark contrast to the idea of the immortality of the soul, where only the soul survives for eternity. Jesus' resurrection was the beginning of the new creation. In raising Jesus bodily from the dead, God demonstrated his commitment to restoring every dimension of fallen humanity, the material as well as the nonmaterial. According to Paul, we know that God will resurrect us because God resurrected Jesus. And because God intends to resurrect us, we know that the body is important to God. "The body is meant… for the Lord, and the Lord for the body" (6:13b). Therefore, what we do with our bodies is very important. In the remainder the reading, Paul both argues for and draws out the implications of what it means that our bodies are meant for the Lord.

6:15. First, Paul reminds his readers that Christians are not just individuals. Believers are members of a community, and their bodies are members of Christ's body. To engage in sexual immorality, therefore, is to involve the whole of the Christian community in sexual immorality.

6:16–17. Second, because our bodies are integral to who we are as human persons, sex is not merely a physical act; it involves our whole being. Therefore, we cannot engage in acts of sexual immorality and still think our spiritual nature remains unaffected. To have sex with a prostitute is to become one with a prostitute. Our bodies are meant for the Lord, and so we should engage in practices that make us one with Christ.

6:18–20. Third, Paul reminds his readers that their bodies are temples in which the Holy Spirit resides (cf. 3:16–17). Therefore, the Corinthians should avoid sexual immorality at all costs because it destroys God's temple. They need to remember that they have been redeemed. That is, God paid a high price for them, so they do not belong to themselves but to God. In gratitude, they should bring glory to God by everything they do, not least by what they do with their bodies.

Suggestions for Lectors

Today's reading falls into two sections. In the first (6:12–14), Paul recites some talking points of the Corinthians and then responds to them. Find a way to distinguish the quotations from Paul's responses. As you present this back and forth, think of yourself as two different people on opposite sides of a debate. Read the talking points with some intensity as though you were interjecting these into an argument. Pause afterwards, then respond in a lower, calmer, more measured voice. In short, deliver the talking points with emotion and Paul's responses without emotion.

In the second section (6:15-20), Paul moves on from responding to the Corinthians' arguments and addresses the them directly, "Do *you* not know…?" In this section, it is Paul's turn to show some intensity. Beginning in 6:15, let your voice become increasingly energetic and animated until it reaches a climax in the final question: *Or do you not know that your body is a temple of the Holy Spirit within you, which you have from God, and that you are not your own?* (6:19). Pause after this question, and then in a calm, compassionate, and sincere voice deliver the final line. Read slowly, with slight pauses after *bought*, *price*, and *therefore*, as in: *For <u>you</u> were bought… with a price;… therefore… glorify God in your <u>body</u>* (6:20). Also, emphasize *you* and *body*.

Pronunciation Guide

Corinthians (kuh-RIN-thee-uhnz)

JOHN 1:43–51

Commentary

In all four gospels, one of the first things Jesus does following his baptism is to call disciples. In the Gospel of John, we discover that some of Jesus' first disciples were originally disciples of John the Baptist. In the episode prior to today's reading (1:35–40), the Baptist is standing with two of his disciples when Jesus happens to walk by. John points Jesus out and exclaims, "Look, here is the Lamb of God!" (1:36). Here we have another example of the Baptist deferring to Jesus. These two disciples follow Jesus and end up spending the rest of the day with him. One of these disciples turns out to be Andrew, who then finds his brother Simon Peter and brings him to Jesus. In today's reading, Jesus himself takes the initiative to recruit disciples.

1:43–46. Today's episode begins with Jesus making his way back to Galilee after having left the region of the Transjordan, where John the Baptist had been preaching and baptizing (1:28). When Jesus arrives, he finds Philip and calls him to become his disciple. This is unusual behavior for a first-century Jewish rabbi. Rabbis did not generally recruit followers. Instead, would-be disciples sought out rabbis to study with.

The little we know about Philip comes from the Gospel of John, where he appears in a handful of episodes (1:43–51; 6:5–6; 12:21–22; 14:8–9). Philip's encounter with Jesus convinces him that Jesus is indeed the Messiah so he immediately shares the news with his friend Nathanael. When Nathanael is informed that this long-awaited anointed figure—referred to by Moses and the prophets in the pages of the Jewish scriptures—comes from Nazareth, he is skeptical. Nazareth is a small, insignificant Galilean village on the outskirts of Jewish society. How could someone so important come from someplace so inconsequential? Philip offers no argument or defense, just an invitation, "Come and see" (1:46).

1:47–51. When Nathanael meets Jesus, he is duly impressed. Jesus greets Nathanael by declaring him to be a true Israelite in whom there is no deceit or guile. This is likely an allusion to the patriarch Jacob, whose name was changed to Israel and who was known for his deceit and trickery (Gen 27:35–36; cf. Ps 32:2). Clearly, Jesus knows something of Nathanael's character. When pressed about this, Jesus answers that he saw Nathanael before Philip ever called him. Scholars have long speculated about the meaning and significance of the phrase "under the fig tree" (1:48). Is it to be taken literally or metaphorically? Does it imply natural sight or supernatural insight? Whatever the case, Jesus' insights regarding Nathanael prompt Nathanael's insights regarding Jesus. Nathanael is now convinced: Jesus is the Messiah—the Son of God, the King of Israel!

Here it is important to recognize that for Nathanael these three titles are essentially synonymous. In first-century Judaism, the Messiah was not understood to be a divine figure but a human being (albeit a special one) who would be appointed and anointed by God. In many cases, it was believed that God's Messiah would be a royal figure, a king in the line of David who would lead Israel against her enemies. Moreover, in the OT, Israel's king was often described as God's son (cf. 2 Sam 7:14 and Ps 2:7, which is generally thought to be a coronation hymn). Jesus identifies Nathanael as a true Israelite, and Nathanael responds by declaring Jesus to be the King of Israel. By acknowledging Jesus as *his* king, Nathanael is implicitly pledging his full allegiance to Jesus.

Jesus is the *son of God* in this political, human sense, but he is also *the Son of God* in a divine sense. The reader already knows this from the prologue to the gospel, but characters in the story do not discover this until much later in the narrative. Nathanael is correct regarding Jesus' identity; he simply does not understand the full significance of his words. The full reality of who Jesus is as the divine Son of God will be revealed later on, and his disciples will "see heaven opened and the angels of God ascending and descending upon the Son of Man" (1:51).

This last image evokes the story of Jacob's ladder in Genesis 28. One night, Jacob dreams that "there was a ladder set up on the earth, the top of it reaching to heaven; and the angels of God were ascending and descending on it" (28:12). The ladder connects heaven and earth and is used by God's messengers. It is the means by which God and his purposes are made known. This is why, when Jacob awakes he declares, "Surely the LORD is in this place—and I did not know it!… This is none other than the house of God, and this is the gate of heaven" (28:16–17). When Jesus invokes this image, he puts himself in the place of the ladder; God's messengers are ascending and descending upon *him*. Thus, as the incarnate Son of God and the suffering Son of Man, *Jesus* is the link between heaven and earth; *Jesus* is the means by which God makes himself and his purposes known; *Jesus* is humanity's doorway to heaven.

Suggestions for Lectors

Today's episode is driven by dialogue, so in your preparations, focus upon how to deliver the lines of each of the characters. Ask yourself these questions: What are Philip, Nathanael, and Jesus thinking and feeling at each point in the episode? What tone of voice would best convey those thoughts and feelings? The following offers one possible interpretation of this scene.

When Philip first approaches Nathanael, he is clearly very excited, so deliver his lines with enthusiasm and energy. Nathanael, however, is skeptical and dismissive, so respond sarcastically with, *Can anything <u>good</u> come out of <u>Nazareth</u>?* (1:45). Not to be deterred, Philip energetically responds, *Come and see* (1:46).

Next, raise your voice as you proclaim Jesus' evaluation of Nathanael's character (1:47). Jesus praises Nathanael's candor, and he may even be amused by the comment about anything good coming from Nazareth. So, you might deliver Jesus' line with a smile on your face and a hint of good-natured amusement in your voice.

In a confused voice, Nathanael asks, *Where did you get to know me?* (1:48a). Then, as though the answer is obvious, Jesus responds, *I saw you under the fig tree before Philip called you* (1:48b). Finally, adopting Philip's perspective and excitement, Nathanael declares Jesus to be *the Son of God* and *the King of Israel* (1:49). Again, Jesus may be amused, this time by how quickly Nathanael has moved from disparaging Nazareth to declaring a Nazarene to be God's Son and Israel's king, especially since Nathanael's grand proclamation is based upon something quite unremarkable, at least as far as Jesus is concerned (1:50). Finally, Jesus becomes serious as he concludes with, *Very truly, I tell you,…* (1:51).

Pronunciation Guide

Andrew (AN-droo)
Bethsaida (beth-SAY-uh-duh)
Galilee (GAL-uh-lee),
Israel (IZ-ree-uhl; -ray-)
Israelite (IZ-ree-līt)
Joseph (JOH-sif; -suhf)
Moses (MOH-zuhs)
Nazareth (NAZ-uh-reth; *not* -rus)
Peter (PEE-ter)
Philip (FIL-ip)
Rabbi (RAB-bī)

THIRD SUNDAY AFTER EPIPHANY

Jonah 3:1–5, 10
Psalm 62:5–12 (= 62:6–14 BCP)
1 Corinthians 7:29–31
Mark 1:14–20

JONAH 3:1–5, 10

Notes

Suggested Reading. Jonah 3:1–10

Commentary

The book of Jonah belongs to a collection of OT writings called the Book of the Twelve, which comprises the twelve Minor Prophets from Hosea to Malachi. Jonah stands out among the prophetic books of the OT because it narrates a sustained story that is centered upon the actions, versus the words, of the prophet himself.

The book begins, as many prophetic books do, with the calling of the prophet. The word of the LORD comes to Jonah, saying, "Go at once to Nineveh, that great city, and cry out against it; for their wickedness has come up before me" (1:2). Nineveh's significance lies in the fact that it was the capital city of the Assyrian Empire, the same empire that wiped out the northern kingdom of Israel in 722 B.C. Thus, Jonah's prophetic task is to preach judgment to Israel's archenemy. Like other prophets, Jonah responds to the LORD's call immediately, albeit in an atypical fashion. He quickly sets out in the *opposite* direction. At the time of Jonah's departure, the reader is given no explanation for his actions. As is the case with a good novel, it is not until the final chapter that the mystery is solved. What the reader eventually discovers is that Jonah did not want to announce judgment upon Israel's enemies because he was afraid that the Ninevites would repent of their wickedness and that the LORD would in turn repent of the destruction he had planned for them (4:2).

As it turns out, Jonah was correct on both accounts, and he becomes enraged.

> He prayed to the LORD and said, "O LORD! Is not this what I said while I was still in my own country? That is why I fled to Tarshish at the beginning; for I knew that you are a gracious God and merciful, slow to anger, and abounding in steadfast love, and ready to relent from punishing. And now, O LORD, please take my life from me, for it is better for me to die than to live" (4:2–3).

In today's reading, we hear of Jonah's preaching in Nineveh that led to their repentance and God's forgiveness.

3:1–5. The second half of the book begins just like the first half, with the word of the LORD coming to Jonah. The word is the same, but Jonah's response is different. Instead of trying to escape his calling, Jonah obediently travels to Nineveh. Once there, he preaches a message of hellfire and brimstone to the city's inhabitants. The response to Jonah's message is both immediate and unexpected; the people repent in fine fashion.

3:6–9. In the unassigned portion of today's reading, the king of Nineveh issues a decree, and all the Ninevites from the smallest to the greatest repent with fasting, with sackcloth and ashes, and with turning from their evil ways. Even the domestic animals participate (3:7–8). The king issues the decree in the off chance that God would change his mind. "Who knows? God may relent and change his mind; he may turn from his fierce anger, so that we do not perish" (3:9).

3:10. The king guesses correctly for when God sees the Ninevites' transformation, he does exercise mercy, and he does not follow through with his original plan of destruction. The reader gets the impression that this had been the LORD's plan all along.

Suggestions for Lectors

As you read today's narrative, employ all of your storytelling skills. Pay attention to the punctuation and to the pace of the narrative. Also, practice delivering the lines of the various characters. The LORD's command to Jonah in 3:2 is fairly straightforward. However, in 3:4, increase the intensity and volume of your voice as you deliver Jonah's message: *Forty days more, and Nineveh shall be overthrown!* As he made his way through the city, Jonah would have said this line more than once, so it would be appropriate to repeat this line twice. When delivering the king's proclamation, increase your volume as though you are speaking to a large crowd. When your reach 3:9, you can continue in the same manner as you have been, or you might drop your voice a bit as though you are talking to yourself.

The reading occurs in two or three movements, depending upon whether 3:6–9 is read. As you draw each movement to a close, slow down and deliberately enunciate each word of the concluding clause or phrase. Pause slightly after each of the words, as seems appropriate. Consider the following:

3:5 put. . on. . sackcloth.
3:9 do. . not. . perish.
3:10 and he. . . did. . . not. . . do it.

Longer pauses are employed in 3:10 since it draws the whole reading to a close. After 3:5 and 3:9, pause for a second before proceeding with the next movement.

Pronunciation Guide

Jonah (JOH-nuh), *Nineveh* (NIN-uh-vuh)

1 CORINTHIANS 7:29–31

Notes

Sequence. 2 of 5

Commentary

First Corinthians is interesting because it gives us a glimpse into how Paul stayed in contact with the church in Corinth. In 1:10–11, Paul references some reports he has received regarding divisions that have arisen within the church. Then, in chapter seven, we discover that the Corinthians had written to Paul, for he begins: "Now concerning the matters about which you wrote" (7:1).

The first matter Paul addresses concerns the related questions of marriage, remarriage, singleness, divorce, and sexual intimacy within the Christian community. He directs his remarks to married couples, to widows, and to virgins. He talks about conjugal relationships within marriage and about couples contemplating divorce, especially in cases where one spouse is a Christian and one is not. At times, he issues commands, and at other times he offers friendly advice. Through it all, the principle he keeps returning to is, "let each of you lead the life that the Lord has assigned, to which God called you" (7:17). In short, he is encouraging the Corinthians not to make any radical changes to their lives. "Let each of your remain in the condition in which you were called" (7:20).

In today's reading, Paul is addressing virgins, those who have never been married and who are trying to determine whether they should marry. Here Paul's advice is more pragmatic than theological. Based upon his conviction that Jesus is returning soon, Paul thinks it would be better for such persons to remain single, not least because it affords them the opportunity to devote more time and energy to "the affairs of the Lord" (7:32). This is the context in which today's reading should be heard.

7:29–31. Paul tells the Corinthians that, since the world as they know it is disappearing, they should reorder their lives so as to free themselves from the anxieties of everyday affairs. They can then participate more fully in what the Lord is doing in the world. Even married Christians would do well to live as though they were not married. Following today's reading, Paul does qualify his advice. He says that he is not wanting to place restraints upon people. He is simply trying "to promote good order and unhindered devotion to the Lord" (7:35).

Suggestions for Lectors

Today's reading is quite short so make sure your listeners are settled in and ready before you begin. Also, in order to extend the reading a bit, read at a slightly slower pace than you normally would. The bulk of the reading is taken up with a single sentence in which Paul uses the same structure over and over again: *those who… as though they….* When faced with a repeated element that recurs more than two or three times, it is important to vary one's tempo and intonation. In short, do not read each line the exact same way; otherwise, your reading will become monotonous.

The following is just one example of how to make a reading more dynamic by introducing minor variations in how the lines are delivered. In lines 2 and 3, the verb in the relative clause is accented (*mourn, rejoice*) and followed by a pause. Another pause occurs at the end of these lines. In lines 1 and 4, the negatives are emphasized (*none, no*), and the lines are read more quickly with no pauses. Finally, line 5 combines features of the above. The verb *deal* is emphasized as well as the negative *no.* In addition, a pause is introduced prior to *as.*

1 from now on, let even those who have wives be as though they had *none,*
2 and those who *mourn…* as though they were not mourning,…
3 and those who *rejoice…* as though they were not rejoicing,…
4 and those who buy as though they had *no* possessions,
5 and those who *deal* with the world… as though they had *no* dealings with it.

Pronunciation Guide
Corinthians (kuh-RIN-thee-uhnz)

MARK 1:14–20

Notes
Sequence. 1 of 8

Commentary
In Mark, Jesus first appears in the Judean wilderness where he is baptized by John the Baptist (1:9–11, Lent 1). When Jesus comes up out of the water onto the banks of the Jordan river, the Holy Spirit comes upon him and immediately drives him further out into the wilderness, where he is tested by Satan for a period of forty days (1:12–13, Lent 1).

1:14–15. Jesus emerges from the wilderness only to discover that John the Baptist has been arrested. At this point in the narrative, the circumstances surrounding the Baptist's arrest are not given; that story will be told later (6:14–29, Prop 10). Instead, the reader is told that Jesus returns to Galilee, where he begins a ministry of proclaiming the gospel, of announcing the good news that the kingdom of God had arrived. In the gospels, *the kingdom of God* refers to God's rule or reign or, one might even say, God's government. Given that Jesus heralds the arrival of God's kingdom in a country that has been ruled by foreign empires for the better part of six hundred years, it would also make sense to speak in terms of *the <u>empire</u> of God.*

As with any new administration or government, the advent of God's empire means that things will change. God's way of conducting business in the world is radically different from the way the world conducts its business. Therefore, those who wish to participate in God's new world must repent. They must let go of the world's values, its ways of being and doing. Instead, they must put their trust in God and practice God's way of being and doing in the world.

1:16–20. The first task Jesus undertakes is to recruit others to join him in ushering in God's new world. Walking along the Sea of Galilee, Jesus finds four men who are willing to forsake their livelihoods and families to follow him. Up to this point, they have led a life of fishing for fish, but now he will teach them to cast their nets for people. Three of the four—Peter, James, and John—will constitute Jesus' innermost circle. They will accompany him on errands that the other disciples do not (5:37; 9:2; 14:33; cf. 13:3).

Suggestions for Lectors
Today's episode is composed of two distinct scenes (1:14–15, 16–20), so pause for a second or two between scenes and take the opportunity to look up at your audience.

In each scene, emphasize Jesus' statements by increasing the volume and intensity of your voice. In 1:15, pause after *fulfilled*, *near*, and *repent* and also underscore the two commands, as in: *The time is fulfilled,… and the kingdom of God has come near;… <u>repent</u>… and <u>believe</u> in the good news.* In 1:17, emphasize *people*, *I*, and the command to follow, and also introduce a pause after *me*, as in: *<u>Follow me</u>… and <u>I</u> will make you fish for <u>people</u>* (1:17).

Pronunciation Guide
Andrew (AN-droo), *Galilee* (GAL-uh-lee), *James* (JAYMZ), *John* (JAHN; JON), *Simon* (SĪ-muhn), *Zebedee* (ZEB-uh-dee)

FOURTH SUNDAY AFTER EPIPHANY

Deuteronomy 18:15–20
Psalm 111
1 Corinthians 8:1–13
Mark 1:21–28

DEUTERONOMY 18:15–20

Commentary
Deuteronomy is the fifth book of the Bible and the last of the Five Books of Moses (a.k.a., the Pentateuch or the Torah). Deuteronomy is presented as a speech that Moses delivers to the Israelites just prior to his death and just prior to Israel's entrance into the Promised Land of Canaan under the leadership of Joshua (Josh 3:1–17). In this speech (Deut 1:6–30:20), Moses reviews Israel's forty-year sojourn in the wilderness and instructs the people in the laws of the covenant that are to govern their personal and corporate lives once they are settled in Canaan. In today's reading and in anticipation of his death, Moses discloses the LORD's intentions to raise up a prophet to take his place.

18:15–20. Originally, Moses became a prophet—one who conveys God's words to God's people—because the Israelites were too afraid to approach the LORD without a mediator. After the LORD gave his people the Ten Commandments at a spectacular covenant ceremony on Mt. Sinai, the people came to Moses, trembling and saying, "You speak to us, and we will listen; but do not let God speak to us, or we will die" (Exod 20:19; cf. Deut 5:24–27):

Like Moses, the prophet the LORD will raise up after him will not declare his own words, he will only declare the words the Lord gives him to speak. Heeding the words of such a prophet is the same as heeding the LORD. Moreover, the death penalty is reserved for any prophet who speaks in the name of a false god or who falsely claims to speak the name of the LORD. The severity of this punishment illustrates just how important it is to God that people are able to hear and receive his word.

Suggestions for Lectors
Today's reading is fairly straightforward. The one thing to pay attention to is the complexity and length of some of the sentences. You do not want to run out of breath or run out of intonation, so practice today's reading until you are able to read it smoothly and effortlessly.

There are a couple of places where emphasis would be appropriate. First, in 18:15, the command *you shall heed such a prophet* can be read with greater intensity and deliberateness and at a slightly slower tempo. You might also wish to memorize this line so that you can deliver it while looking at your listeners. In order to let the command sink in, pause for a second afterwards before continuing. The final clause of today's reading also deserves some emphasis. Read it slowly and solemnly with a slight pause after *prophet*, as in: *that prophet... shall die* (18:20). Again, it would be worth delivering this line while looking at your listeners.

Pronunciation Guide
Deuteronomy (doo'-tuh-RON-uh-mee), *Horeb* (HOR-uhb; HOH-reb)

1 CORINTHIANS 8:1–13

Notes
Sequence. 3 of 5

Commentary
Paul penned 1 Corinthians, in part, to respond to issues that were raised in a letter he had received from the church in Corinth. Paul begins to address these matters in chapter seven: "Now concerning the matters about which you wrote" (7:1a). The first matter Paul takes up had to do with the issues of sex, marriage, and singleness within the Christian community (7:1–40).

In today's reading, Paul takes up the question of whether it is permissible for Christians to eat food that has been sacrificed to idols. In first-century Corinth, a person might consume sacrificial meat in one of two ways. They could purchase it at the local market and prepare it at home. Paul addresses this in 10:23–30. Or, a person could attend a ritual meal or banquet at a temple and partake of the sacrifice. Paul addresses this in today's reading (8:10; cf. 10:14, 21). As you read, take care to note the places where Paul is quoting what the Corinthians wrote him. In the NRSV, quotation marks have been placed around this material (8:1, 4a, 4b, 8).

8:1–6. Although we do not possess the letter the Corinthians wrote, their arguments can be reconstructed from Paul's response. There were those in Corinth who argued that Christians could, in all good conscience, eat meat sacrificed to idols. They justified their position by arguing that, as enlightened Christians, they possessed knowledge about such spiritual matters. They wrote, "All of us possess knowledge" (8:1). In particular, they knew that "no idol in the world really exists" and that "there is no God but one" (8:4). They argued, therefore, that there is no real difference between eating meat that originated as part of a pagan sacrifice and eating meat that did not; meat is meat.

Paul agrees in principal with everything they say, but he challenges their application of these truths. While knowledge is to be desired (1 Cor 1:5), it cannot compare with love. Knowledge too easily and too often produces arrogance. Love, on the other hand, is always edifying. Knowledge tears down, but love builds up. Knowing something *about* God is not near as valuable as being known *by* God; and it is the one who *loves* God who is known by God.

And, as Paul will argue below, we love God when we sacrifice our own rights for the sake of fellow Christians who might not be as spiritually mature as we are. After all, we belong to the same family. We all have the same God, "the Father... for whom we exist" (8:6a), and we all have the same Lord, "Jesus Christ... through whom we exist" (8:6b). Since we all belong to the same family, we ought to treat one another with sacrificial love.

8:7–13. At this point, Paul returns to the original premise. The Corinthians claim, "*all* of us possess knowledge" (8:1), but Paul begs to differ. Not everyone in the Corinthian church has reached the same level of knowledge and maturity in the Christian faith. Most of the Corinthian Christians were Gentiles (not Jews) and so had previously participated in the world of pagan cults and idolatry. Many of these ex-pagans still operated under the assumption that meat sacrificed to idols was different from other meat and was to be avoided. If they were to eat idol meat, then they would be doing something wrong, not because of what they ate, but because they were going against their own consciences.

Paul agrees that what we eat makes us neither spiritual nor defiled, but that is not the issue. The issue is whether our actions become an occasion for fellow Christians to experience temptation and fall into sin. Yet, there were those in Corinth who defended their right to eat sacrificial meat. Why should their rights be restricted on account of those whose faith had not yet matured? When viewed from the perspective of knowledge, such restrictions did not make any sense.

Paul, however, challenges these Corinthians to reexamine the situation with the eyes of love. Christ died for these so-called weak Christians, and so those who are mature in their Christian faith should exhibit the same quality of self-sacrifice. Instead of simply defending their right to do what is permissible, they should act in ways that honor and preserve the faith of their brothers and sisters in Christ, even if that means foregoing certain freedoms and privileges. As for Paul, not only would he give up eating meat sacrificed to idols; but he would give up eating meat altogether if he thought it would help fellow believers in their Christian faith.

Suggestions for Lectors

Your listeners do not have the benefit of seeing the quotation marks in the text so they will not be able to distinguish Paul's quoting of the Corinthians from his responding to the Corinthians, unless you make a distinguish between them with your voice. One approach would be to read the whole letter in a calm, straightforward manner, except for the quotations. When Paul quotes the Corinthians, increase the volume and pitch of your voice and read with greater intensity. In order to facilitate this change in voice, pause for a second before and after each quotation.

8:1 we know that… "*all of us possess knowledge.*"…

8:4 we know that… "*no idol in the world really exists,*"
and that… "*there is no God but one.*"…

8:8 …"*Food will not bring us close to God.*"…

In the middle of the reading, Paul makes a creedal statement, which has a poetic quality to it (8:6). Paul's confession about the *one God* and the *one Lord* is offered as a contrast to the *many*, so-called *gods and lords* of the ancient world; so emphasize *one.* Within the confession itself, subtle distinctions are made between the Father and Jesus Christ, so highlight these by stressing the prepositions *from*, *for*, and *through.*

8:6 yet for us there is <u>one</u> God,… the Father,
from whom are all things and for whom we exist,
and one Lord,… Jesus Christ,
through whom are all things and through whom we exist.

In addition, pause after *God* and *Lord.* Paul is not saying there is one God the Father, but one God, who is the Father. Likewise, it is not that there is just one Lord Jesus Christ, but that there is one Lord, who, it turns out, is Jesus Christ.

Pronunciation Guide
Corinthians (kuh-RIN-thee-uhnz)

MARK 1:21–28

Notes
Sequence. 2 of 8

Commentary
It is not accidental that the first miracle Jesus performs in Mark is an exorcism. Exorcisms are extremely important to Mark's presentation of Jesus, as is demonstrated by the number of exorcisms narrated (1:21–28; 5:1–20; 7:24–30; 9:14–29), by the summaries of Jesus' exorcisms (1:32–34; 39; 3:11–12), by the controversies occasioned by his exorcisms (3:21–30; 9:38–40), and by the fact that having authority over unclean spirits is a principal function of the Twelve (3:15; 6:7, 13; cf. 9:38). Exorcisms are so pronounced because Jesus' proclamation regarding the arrival of God's kingdom takes place within an apocalyptic arena in which the two opposing kingdoms—God's and Satan's—are engaged in a winner-takes-all eschatological conflict. Jesus' exorcisms are, therefore, a primary means by which human beings are set free from subjugation to Satan, sin, and evil and God's reign made effectual.

In Mark, demons are often called unclean spirits because they are understood to defile those whom they afflict and possess. Referring to demons as unclean spirits makes the inherent difference between *unclean* spirits and the *Holy* Spirit much more explicit. In Mark, God's Spirit is called the *Holy* Spirit because it has the power to make things holy and pure, to cleanse what Satan has defiled. Thus, the Holy Spirit is a cleansing Agent. And because Jesus possesses this Holy Spirit (or perhaps, because he is possessed *by* the Holy Spirit), he has the power to cleanse people from anything and everything that may defile them, be it unclean spirits, leprosy, sin, or even death itself.

1:21–22. Jesus grew up in Nazareth, but when he began his public ministry he relocated to Capernaum, a small fishing village located on the western shore of the Sea of Galilee (cf. 2:1; 9:33). In today's reading, Jesus enters the synagogue in Capernaum with his first four followers—Simon, Andrew, James, and John—and he teaches. Mark does not provide the content of Jesus' teaching, but presumably it had to do with the good news of the kingdom (cf. 1:14–15; 1:39). Mark does provide us with the reaction to his teaching. The people are amazed because Jesus teaches with an authority that they have never witnessed before, not even from the scribes, who unlike Jesus, are formally trained in reading and interpretation of the Scriptures.

1:23–24. The sudden appearance of a man with an *unholy* spirit in a *holy* place (the synagogue) on a *holy* day (the sabbath) is both striking and ironic. We are not told how the man got there, only that he knows who Jesus is. By naming him, the unclean spirit hopes to gain power over Jesus but to no avail. Jesus has already overcome forty days of being tested by Satan in the wilderness, so one of Satan's minions poses no real threat. In fact, the spirit is anxious because it knows that, as the Holy One of God, Jesus is uniquely endowed with the Holy Spirit and so possesses the authority and power to destroy everything within Satan's realm.

1:25–28. In Mark, Jesus never lets unclean spirits reveal his divine identity (1:34; 3:12), so he orders the spirit to be quiet and come out of the man. The spirit does so immediately. At the beginning of the episode, the people were astounded by Jesus' teaching; now they are beside themselves with amazement. Not only is Jesus able to exorcise a demon, he does it with relative ease. Unlike other exorcists, Jesus employs no elaborate spells, incantations, or rituals. He speaks, and the unclean spirits obey.

Here, one is reminded of the beginnings of creation, how things came into being with just a word. God spoke into the chaos of darkness, and said, "'Let there be light,' and there was light" (Gen 1:3, EastVig). As with the first creation, so it is with the new creation. Jesus speaks, and order is brought out of chaos.

Suggestions for Lectors

Begin today's reading in your normal narrating voice. In 1:22, emphasize *astounded*, then pause for a second at the end of the verse. When you resume in 1:23 with *Just then*, speak slowly, yet with animation as you note the sudden appearance of a man in the synagogue, not just any man, but one possessed by an unclean spirit. Convey the surprise and curiosity of this unusual occurrence; after all, it is not every day that a demon-possessed person walks into a synagogue, not even in Jesus' day.

When the unclean spirit addresses Jesus, raise your voice and speak more quickly. For Jesus' rebuke, slow your delivery and speak loudly and firmly, perhaps even investing your voice with a hint of anger. The unclean spirit vacates the man so suddenly that the people are beside themselves. The narrator says, *they kept on asking one another* (1:27), so deliver their response in an excited voice. You might even imagine that more than one person is speaking, for example:

Person 1: What is this?
Person 2: A new teaching
Person 3: —with authority!
Person 4: He even commands the unclean spirits,
Person 5: and they obey him!

Return to your normal narrating voice for the final verse.

Pronunciation Guide

Capernaum (kuh-PER-nay-uhm, -nuh-),
Nazareth (NAZ-uh-reth; *not* -rus), *Galilee* (GAL-uh-lee)

FIFTH SUNDAY AFTER EPIPHANY

Isaiah 40:21–31
Psalm 147:1–11, 20c (= 147:1–12, 21c BCP)
1 Corinthians 9:16–23
Mark 1:29–39

ISAIAH 40:21–31

Commentary
In Isaiah 1–39, the prophet announces the LORD's judgment upon the people of Judah for their centuries of idolatry and injustice, that is, for their ongoing refusal to love God with their whole heart (Deut 6:5, Prop 26; Exod 20:1–7, Lent 3) and their failure to love their neighbors as themselves (Lev 19:18; Exod 20:8–17). Isaiah 39 ends ominously as the predicted destruction and exile of Judah at the hands of the Babylonian empire becomes imminent.

Isaiah 40 skips ahead many years and introduces a new movement in the prophetic drama, which strikes a completely different note than that with which Isaiah 39 concluded. Isaiah 40 presupposes that God's people have been in exile for some time and opens with a message of hope for these exiles in Babylon (40:1–2):

> Comfort, O comfort my people,
> says your God.
> Speak tenderly to Jerusalem,
> and cry to her
> that she has served her term,
> that her penalty is paid,
> that she has received from the LORD's hand
> double for all her sins.

In other words, the exile is over. The LORD has forgiven his people and is coming soon to bring them back home. The prophet, along with Jerusalem and Mt. Zion, is commissioned to announce these glad tidings to the exiles (40:6–11, Adv 2).

But the exile has been hard on God's people. They feel beaten, bruised, and bedraggled; they are emotionally and spiritually spent. The good news seems too good to be true, and they have no more energy for hope and faith. And so, in today's reading, the prophet offers encouragement and support, arguing that the LORD will make good on his promise. Not only does the LORD have the power to free his exiled people from their captivity, but he has the desire to do so.

40:21–26. The exiles can take comfort in the fact that the LORD their God is not just any god, but *the* God, the *only* God who created the heavens and the earth and everything in them. Though the rulers of the mighty Babylonian empire may be like gods to the downtrodden exiles, these rulers are merely grasshoppers in the LORD's eyes. No one, absolutely no one, compares to the LORD.

40:27–31. The LORD's exiled people feel abandoned by their God, believing that the LORD no longer cares about them or is concerned with their fate. The words they speak are reminiscent of the psalmist who asks, "Why do you hide your face? Why do you forget our affliction and oppression?" (Ps 44:24).

In response, the prophet once again declares that the LORD is the eternal Creator. The LORD's ways are unsearchable; they do not follow human logic. The LORD does not grant power to the powerful but to the weak. There is a special place in his heart for those who are oppressed, demoralized, and spent. If God's people will just wait upon the LORD in trusting faith, they will find the resources of strength they need to patiently endure their present circumstances until the LORD comes to heal them and bring them home.

Suggestions for Lectors

Today's reading is a rhetorical delight, and it deserves to be read with great feeling and energy. It is rich with rhetorical questions that should be read with an increased volume and pitch:

> Have you not known? Have you not heard?
> Has it not been told you from the beginning?
> Have you not understood from the foundations of the earth? (40:21)

It is also rich with repetition, which should be emphasized in your reading.

> *Scarcely* are they planted, *scarcely* sown,
> *scarcely* has their stem taken root in the earth,... (40:24).

Today's text is also very dynamic so give yourself plenty of time to practice your timing and tempo. Explore the poetic structure and notice what goes with what. For example, in 40:26, the last strophe begins with *because he is great in strength, mighty in power.* Note that this dependent clause goes with what follows, not with what precedes. It goes with *not one is missing,* rather than with *calling them all by name.* Without adequate preparation and attentiveness, a lector might easily use an intonation that connects the *because*-clause with the preceding clause, leaving the final line, *not one is missing,* dangling and disconnected.

In 40:22–23, three relative clauses are used to describe *he.* Each clause is formed by two poetic lines, and because these clauses are lengthy, the lector must ensure that the second and third clauses connect back to *he.* There are two simple strategies for doing this. First, emphasize *who* in each clause.

> 22 It is he *who* sits above the circle of the earth,
> and its inhabitants are like grasshoppers;
> *who* stretches out the heavens like a curtain,
> and spreads them like a tent to live in;
> 23 *who* brings princes to naught,
> and makes the rulers of the earth as nothing.

Alternatively, the lector could add *he* at the beginning of the second and third clauses, and then emphasize *he* each time. This alternative approach makes the text much clearer.

22 It is *he* who sits above the circle of the earth,
and its inhabitants are like grasshoppers;
he who stretches out the heavens like a curtain,
and spreads them like a tent to live in;
23 *he* who brings princes to naught,
and makes the rulers of the earth as nothing.

Pronunciation Guide
Isaiah (ī-ZAY-uh), *Israel* (IZ-ree-uhl; -ray-), *Jacob* (JAY-kuhb)

1 Corinthians 9:16–23

Notes
Sequence. 4 of 5

Commentary
Today's and next week's readings from 1 Corinthians belong to a larger discussion regarding the question of food that originates from pagan sacrifices (8:1–11:1). Was it permissible for Christians to eat meat sacrificed to idols? There were those in Corinth who said *Yes.* They argued that since there is only one God and idols do not actually exist (8:4), then eating idol meat was no different from eating any other type of meat. Paul seems to agree with them, but only partly. While it seems that Christians are permitted to eat meat sacrificed to idols, the question of whether they *should* is more complicated. Paul notes that there are Christians in Corinth whose faith and knowledge has not matured to the point where they can eat sacrificial meat without doing serious damage to their conscience and faith. Consequently, Paul counsels the strong: "Take care that this liberty of yours does not somehow become a stumbling block to the weak" (8:11). Christ died for these so-called weak Christians, and those who are mature in their Christian faith should exhibit the same quality of self-sacrifice. Instead of defending their right to do what is permissible, they should act in ways that honor and preserve the faith of their brothers and sisters in Christ, even if that means foregoing certain freedoms and privileges. As for Paul, not only would he give up eating sacrificial meat, but he would give up eating meat altogether so that he might not cause one of the least of these to stumble and fall (8:13; cf. Matt 18:6).

In 1 Corinthians 9, Paul continues this discussion by talking about how he has not made use of certain rights as an apostle. At first, he appears to have changed the subject since there are no references to meat sacrificed to idols. But in actuality, Paul is continuing the discussion by using himself as an example of one who sacrifices his rights and privileges for the sake of the gospel. For example, while some apostles receive financial support and so make their living by the gospel (9:14), Paul has chosen to work for a living (9:6). Now Paul makes it clear that he is not writing these things so that the Corinthians will start supporting him; after all, if he started accepting a stipend, then he would lose his ground for boasting (9:15).

9:16–18. This last statement is made somewhat tongue-in-cheek because Paul is really not in a position to boast. As he himself says, he did not choose this way of life; it was chosen for him. Had he decided on his own to proclaim the gospel, it would make sense for him to be compensated. As it is, the Lord called him, and he has had no power to resist. Like Jeremiah, the gospel has become for Paul, "something like a burning fire shut up in [his] bones" (Jer 20:9), and he cannot help but proclaim it. Though he has every right to receive financial support as an apostle, he has chosen not to exercise these rights fully. This allows Paul to proclaim the gospel free of charge, which is its own reward.

9:19–23. This *modus operandi* grants Paul a great deal of freedom. Because he has no benefactors other than God, he is free to "become all things to all people" so that he might save at least some of them (9:22). Paul sees himself as being under no obligation to live like a Jew under the law or to live like a Gentile outside the law. He is free. And yet, he has freely chosen to submit himself "in various ways to the cultural structures and limitations of the people he hopes to reach with the gospel."[2] No doubt, when Paul is trying to reach Jews, he observes Jewish dietary regulations. Yet, when he proclaims the gospel to the Gentiles, he transgresses his Jewish sensibilities and dines with them as though he himself were a Gentile.

Exactly how does Paul become weak to win the weak? He does not actually say, but he may have left us a clue at the end of chapter eight, where he writes: "Therefore, if food is a cause of their falling, I will never eat meat, so that I may not cause one of [the weak] to fall" (8:13). Paul's reference to becoming weak reminds us of his larger discussion regarding meat sacrificed to idols, in which he argues that loving God often entails setting aside our rights and privileges so that we might reach out to those God has called us to serve. For Paul, Christian *freedom* is absolutely essential, but Christian *love* is supreme.

Suggestions for Lectors

Today's reading falls into two movements (9:16–18, 19–23). Read the first movement in a straightforward manner until you reach the last sentence. Pause after *Just this*, then read the last sentence slowly and deliberately, emphasizing the phrase *free of charge.*

Read the second movement with more energy as you make your way through the various categories of people that Paul became like. Emphasize the first instance of a new group when it is mentioned:

9:20a	To the *Jews* I became…
9:20b	To those *under the law* I became …
9:21	To those *outside the law* I became …
9:22	To the *weak* I became…

The second half of 9:22 should receive the most emphasis. Slow down and read it more deliberately, emphasizing the three *alls.* Slow down even more for the final clause, pausing before and after *by all means*, as in: *I have become <u>all</u> things to <u>all</u> people, that I might… by <u>all</u> means… save some.*

Pronunciation Guide

Corinthians (kuh-RIN-thee-uhnz)

---

[2] Richard B. Hays, *First Corinthians* (Interpretation. Louisville, Ky.: John Knox, 1989), 153.

Mark 1:29–39

Notes

Sequence. 3 of 8

Commentary

In last week's reading, Jesus performed his first public act in Mark, the exorcism of an unclean spirit in the synagogue in Capernaum. Those who witnessed this mighty deed were amazed, "and they kept on asking one another, 'What is this? A new teaching—with authority! He commands even the unclean spirits, and they obey him'" (1:27). In this week's reading, the reverberations from that one exorcism are felt as Jesus' "fame [begins] to spread throughout the surrounding region of Galilee" (1:28).

1:29–31. In 1:16–20 (Epi 3), Jesus called his first disciples—Simon and Andrew, James and John. These four accompanied Jesus to the synagogue in Capernaum, and today they all make their way from the synagogue to the house of Simon and Andrew. Having witnessed Jesus' authority as an exorcist, they immediately draw his attention to Simon's mother-in-law, who lay sick in bed with a fever. Without hesitation and unconcerned about his own well-being, Jesus takes the sick woman by the hand. Immediately, the fever *leaves* her just as the unclean spirit *left* the man.

Here we see that this simple healing has an exorcistic quality to it, just like some of Jesus' other healings and miracles in Mark (4:39, Prop 7). We see this, for example, in next week's cleansing of a leper. Jesus issues a command, and immediately the leprosy *leaves* the man (1:41–42). In Mark, Jesus' exorcisms and exorcistic healings disclose a world that is under Satan's dominion. When Jesus announces that the kingdom of God is at hand, he is also saying that the kingdom of Satan has come to an end. Jesus demonstrates the reality of this new state of affairs by freeing people from the spiritual forces—whether in the form of demonic possession, fever, leprosy, or sin (2:9, Epi 7)—that subjugate human beings.

1:32–34. By evening, the whole city has heard of Jesus' exorcism of the unclean spirit, so anyone who is sick or demon possessed is brought to Jesus, and he heals them. The people waited until sunset because sunset signaled the end of the sabbath, meaning that the people were free to move about again.

1:35–39. With so many people clamoring to see him, Jesus wakes up well before dawn and withdraws to a deserted place in order to spend some time in solitude and prayer. Clearly, being filled with the Holy Spirit does not override a person's need for physical rest and spiritual refreshment. When Jesus' disciples eventually find him, they inform him that he is in great demand. Yet, Jesus' commission is to establish the kingdom of God wherever the kingdom of Satan has a foothold, so he is not content to stay in one place. Instead of returning to Capernaum, Jesus leads his disciples on a missionary tour of duty throughout the synagogues of Galilee. He announces the arrival of God's empire and demonstrates its presence and power by casting out demons.

Suggestions for Lectors

Today's episode is straightforward; it requires nothing more and nothing less than the voice and approach of a storyteller.

As reflected in the Commentary, the episode consists of three short scenes (1:29–31, 32–34, 35–39). The second and third scenes begin with a change in the time of day: *That evening, at sunset* (1:32) and *In the morning, while it was still very dark* (1:35). Notice that these temporal statements both have two parts. Notice also that the second part is more specific than the first. This is known as a two-step progression, and the Gospel of Mark is filled with them. Some of the progressions are temporal, some are spatial, and some are thematic. In Mark 5, we have an example of a spatial two-step progression. The episode begins, "They came to the other side of the sea, to the country of the Gerasenes" (5:1). Here again, the second element, "the country of the Gerasenes," adds greater specificity to the first element, "the other side of the sea." In a two-step progression, the emphasis is on the second part, so slightly emphasize the second phrase or clause in each of the temporal statements above.

Pronunciation Guide
Andrew (AN-droo), *Galilee* (GAL-uh-lee),
James (JAYMZ), *John* (JAHN; JON), *Simon* (SĪ-muhn)

SIXTH SUNDAY AFTER EPIPHANY

Same Readings as Proper 1

2 Kings 5:1–14
Psalm 30
1 Corinthians 9:24–27
Mark 1:40–45

2 Kings 5:1–14

Notes
Suggested Reading. 2 Kings 5:1–15c (ending with the word *Israel*)

Commentary
Elisha son of Shaphat was a prophet who was active in the northern kingdom of Israel in the mid- to late-ninth century B.C. Elisha's name means *my God is salvation*, and his stories are found in 1 Kings 19:19–21 and 2 Kings 2–9, 13:14–21. Elisha and his predecessor, Elijah, are sometimes referred to as *signs* prophets since they are remembered primarily for the signs and wonders they perform, in contrast to the *writing* prophets—figures like Isaiah, Jeremiah, Micah, Amos, etc.—who are primarily remembered for their words.

In today's reading, Elisha becomes instrumental in the healing of a non-Israelite, a foreigner named Naaman. In Luke 4:27, Jesus recalls this incident when defending his ministry in his hometown synagogue. While Elisha's cleansing of Naaman's contagious skin disease contributes to the dramatic quality of this story, the drama is heightened by the fact that Naaman is not just any foreigner, but the commander of the army of Aram, a nation who was often at war with Israel (1 Kgs 20).

5:1–5. The story begins with a description of its central character, Naaman, who is a commander and a great soldier, yet who suffers from leprosy, a contagious skin disease. His wife's maid servant happens to be from Israel, having been taken as booty on a previous campaign. She informs her mistress that there is a prophet in Israel who has the power to cure her master's leprosy. This information is communicated to Naaman, who then seeks the king's permission to travel to Israel.

5:6–7. Since prophets were generally in the king's service, when the king of Aram writes to the king of Israel requesting healing for Naaman, he is most likely not asking the king to heal Naaman personally, but rather asking him to permit his prophet to heal Naaman. As a token of his gratitude, the king sends along a very generous offering of gold, silver, and garments. The king of Israel, however, seems to interpret the request personally. Or perhaps, he knows that none of his prophets have the ability to heal. In any case, the king of Israel regards this impossible request as some sort of pretense by the king of Aram to wage war against Israel, so he tears his royal garments in anguish and grief.

5:8–10. Elisha, however, receives word of the request. He sends the king of Israel a message, admonishing him for overlooking the fact that there is a genuine prophet in Israel, a prophet who serves the LORD and would easily be able to fulfill the request, given the LORD's ability to perform wonders and deeds of power. This reveals how disconnected Israel's king is from the LORD and his prophet. Naaman is referred to Elisha, so he makes his way to the prophet's house.

5:11–14. In a surprising move, Elisha does not meet with Naaman personally but instead provides instructions to Naaman through his servant. Naaman becomes angry because he interprets Elisha's refusal to meet with him as a sign of disrespect and a challenge to his honor. His anger also stems from the fact that he had assumed Elisha would have to perform a series of rituals and prayers to heal him. He is, therefore, unable to see how such a simple act as immersing himself in Israel's river could cleanse him of leprosy. Perhaps he thinks Elisha is trying to get rid of him.

Fortunately for Naaman, he is surrounded by wise servants, and he has the humility to listen to their wise counsel. At the reasoned behest of his servant, Naaman washes in the Jordan. The reading ends with the announcement that Naaman's skin has been restored, and he is now clean.

5:15. The suggested reading ends with Naaman's confession, "Now I know that there is no God in all the earth except in Israel" (5:15c).

In 2 Kings 5:15–19, Naaman's story continues with his returning to Elisha and offering him gold, silver, and garments, which Elisha refuses. Naaman then requests that he be permitted to return to Aram with two mule loads of soil from the land of Israel, proclaiming that he "will no longer offer burnt offering or sacrifice to any god except the LORD" (5:17). His request is granted, and he is told to go in peace.

Suggestions for Lectors

This is such a smoothly-told tale that it should lend itself quite logically to your hearers' understanding. Your own experience with human interactions should take you through the variations in tone and emphasis without trouble. As the climax of the story comes in 5:14, your voice should slow down and become a bit lower. Alternatively you could read in your normal narrating voice through 5:14a, which ends with *according to the word of the man of God.* Then, after pausing for a full second (and perhaps looking up), proceed slowly with a hint of joyful awe in your voice as you read 5:14b.

If you continue with 5:15, pause between 5:14 and 5:15 and then again before Naaman's confession. As you speak Naaman's part, imagine that you are Naaman and your listeners are Elisha, and proclaim with a confident, grateful, and awe-filled voice, *Now I know that there is no God in all the earth except in Israel.*

Pronunciation Guide

Abana (uh-BAY-nuh; AB-uh-nuh), *Aram* (AIR-uhm), *Arameans* (air'-uh-MEE-uhnz), *Damascus* (duh-MAS-kuhs), *Elisha* (ee-LĪ-shuh; ih-), *Naaman* (NAY-uh-muhn), *Pharpar* (FAHR-pahr), *Samaria* (suh-MAIR-ee-uh), *shekels* (SHEK-uhlz)

1 Corinthians 9:24–27

Notes

Sequence. 5 of 5

Commentary

Today's reading could be read on its own as a general call to become more intentional about one's Christian formation, yet these verses actually belong to a much larger discussion in 1 Corinthians 8:1–11:1.

In these chapters, Paul takes up the issue of whether it is permissible for Christians to eat meat that has been sacrificed to idols. This question, in turn, serves as a vehicle for exploring the relationship between Christian freedom and love. On the one hand, Paul grants that Christians are free to eat meat sacrificed to idols, yet he cautions the Corinthians: "Take care that this liberty of yours does not somehow become a stumbling block to the weak" (8:11). Here, *the weak* denotes Christians whose faith had not matured to the point where they could eat idol meat without doing serious damage to their conscience and their faith. Having come out of a pagan context, they still regarded the consumption of idol meat to be incompatible with their newly-acquired faith in Christ. Yet, in Corinth, there were those who wanted to exercise their right to eat whatever they wanted. Their consciences were clear, so why should their freedom be restricted?

Paul's response is to say that Christ died for these weak Christians; therefore, those who are mature in their faith should exhibit the same quality of self-sacrifice. Instead of just defending their right to do what is permissible, they should act in ways that honor and preserve the faith of their brothers and sisters in Christ, even if that means foregoing certain freedoms and privileges. As for Paul, he would give up eating meat altogether if that would keep even one of the least of these from stumbling and falling (8:13; cf. Matt 18:6).

As evidence for this claim, Paul offers up his apostolic career as an example of the type of sacrifice for others he is calling the Corinthians to make. Whereas other apostles are paid to preach the gospel, Paul has refrained from exercising this apostolic right. Instead, he provides for himself by working for a living so that he might "make the gospel free of charge" (9:18). He would endure anything "rather than put an obstacle in the way of the gospel" (9:12). In fact, Paul has gone so far as to "become all things to all people" just so that he might save *some* of them (9:22).

9:24–27. This is the sort of self-control Paul has in mind when he employs the athletic metaphor in today's reading. While Christians have all sorts of freedoms and rights because of Christ, they should become like athletes who are singularly focused upon winning the prize. "Athletes exercise self-control in all things" in order to win a wreath that withers away (9:25). How much more, then, should Christians exercise self-control given that they are seeking a prize that lasts forever? Paul has disciplined himself so that he might bring as many people as possible to Christ. And yet, some of the Corinthian Christians are willing to sacrifice the faith of their weaker brothers and sisters so that they might eat a little meat. They need to put things into perspective, and live their lives as though they are competing for an imperishable crown, and not for one that perishes. In short, they need to live lives of self-emptying, self-sacrificing love.

Suggestions for Lectors
Today's reading is brief so make sure your listeners are settled in before you begin. As you read, speak directly to your listeners as though you are Paul speaking to the Corinthians. In 9:25, highlight the contrast Paul is making by emphasizing the final line, *but we an imperishable one.*

Pronunciation Guide
Corinthians (kuh-RIN-thee-uhnz)

Mark 1:40–45

Notes
Sequence. 4 of 8

Commentary
In Jesus' day, *leprosy* was a general term referring to any number of contagious skin maladies, and in this context is not to be equated with modern day leprosy known as Hansen's disease. Lepers were socially and religiously quarantined from the community. As long as their symptoms persisted, they were required to separate themselves from the rest of society, even living apart from their families. Since lepers were regarded as being in a perpetual state of ritual impurity, they were not allowed to participate in any synagogue or temple activities. Lepers were not to touch or be touched by others, lest through physical contact they infect and defile others. If they found themselves in the vicinity of other people, they were to warn them of their condition by shouting, "Unclean! Unclean!" (Lev 13:45). In short, leprosy was a most dreaded disease in Jesus' day; it was a "living death." According to the rabbis, curing leprosy was akin to raising the dead, namely, it was something only God could do.

1:40–42. In today's reading, both the leper and Jesus transgress social and religious regulations. Instead of keeping his distance and shouting, "Unclean, unclean," the leper boldly approaches Jesus and kneels before him. He shows remarkable faith in Jesus' ability to cure him. "If you choose, you can make me clean" (1:40).

Jesus responds with unconventional compassion. Before speaking a word of healing, Jesus reaches out and touches the leper. But why? Previously, Jesus demonstrated his ability to exorcise an unclean spirit through speech alone (1:25, Epi 4), and here, he ultimately renders the man clean with just a word. So why does Jesus risk physical and ritual defilement by touching the man when it is not necessary? As we have seen, leprosy is not just a physical disorder but a social disorder. By touching the leper, Jesus is already drawing him back into community. By touching him, Jesus demonstrates that his state of uncleanness does not pose any obstacle to relationship with God. Jesus' touch heals the stigma of leprosy before his word heals the leprosy itself.

As with all of his exorcisms and healings thus far, Jesus' words have an immediate effect. Jesus says, "Be made clean," and the man is made clean. The leprosy *leaves* the man just like the unclean spirits *leave* their victims (1:27).

1:43–45. Throughout Mark, Jesus tries to keep his identity a secret. When Peter declares, "You are the Messiah," Jesus sternly warns the disciples not to tell anyone about him (8:33–34, Prop 19). When unclean spirits speak his name, Jesus commands them to be silent (1:25). As the narrator notes, Jesus does not allow demons to speak because they know who he is (1:34). In today's reading, we have another injunction to silence. Jesus sternly orders the man to say nothing about how he has been made clean. Instead, he simply needs to be examined by a priest so that he can be officially declared clean and thus return to Jewish society. He then needs to offer the appropriate sacrifice for his cleansing. The man, however, does none of these things. Instead, he tells everyone what Jesus has done for him causing Jesus to keep to the countryside, away from public places.

It is ironic; Jesus cleanses a leper with a simple word, but not even a stern warning can keep the leper quiet about his cleansing. This is an interesting feature of Mark's narrative. Jesus exercises absolute authority over demonic forces and nature but never over human agents. For example, after exorcising the Gerasene demoniac, Jesus says to the man, "Go home to your friends, and tell them how much *the Lord* has done for you, and what mercy he has shown you" (5:19). Instead of going home, the man travels throughout the Decapolis, proclaiming how much *Jesus* has done for him (5:20). So, later in the gospel, when Jesus arrives in the Decapolis, he is met by a crowd of thousands (7:31; 8:1–10). The kingdom of God simply cannot be hidden (cf. 4:21–22).

Suggestions for Lectors

In today's simple and straightforward narrative, focus your attention on the speaking parts. As you prepare, take time to imagine what each character is thinking and feeling at each moment in the narrative, then convey their mood through the intonation and inflection of your voice.

As was noted in the Commentary, the leper is quite bold to approach Jesus. At the same time, he is quite vulnerable because he is breaking social customs and cannot be sure how Jesus will respond. Deliver the leper's statement with an intonation that conveys his uncertainty. Of course, he is only unsure about Jesus' *willingness* to heal, not his *ability* to heal. Consequently, only the first clause should be read with uncertainty, *If you choose*; the second clause should be read with the conviction of faith, *you can make me clean.*

Jesus is moved with pity, so he answers the leper's uncertain, *If you chose*, with a compassionate, *I do choose.* In the NRSV, the subsequent command is punctuated with an exclamation point. You can treat this in a couple of ways. You could proclaim, *Be made clean!*, loudly and firmly, using the same tone that Jesus employs when rebuking demons, *Be silent!* (cf. 1:25). Or, you could invest your voice with more emotion and empathy. Imagine looking deep into the leper's uncertain eyes and saying calmly and compassionately, *I do choose. Be made clean!*

In 1:44, Jesus' tone becomes serious, though not harsh, as he instructs the leper to *say nothing to anyone.*

Pronunciation Guide
Moses (MOH-zuhs)

SEVENTH SUNDAY AFTER EPIPHANY

Same Readings as Proper 2

Isaiah 43:18–25
Psalm 41
2 Corinthians 1:18–22
Mark 2:1–12

Isaiah 43:18–25

Commentary
In Isaiah 1–39, the prophet announces the LORD's judgment upon the people of Judah and Jerusalem for their persistent sins of idolatry and injustice, that is, for their ongoing refusal to love God with their whole heart (Deut 6:5; Exod 20:1–7) and their refusal to love their neighbors as themselves (Lev 19:18; Exod 20:8–17). Isaiah 39 ends ominously as the predicted destruction and exile of Judah and Jerusalem by the Babylonian empire becomes imminent.

Then, in Isaiah 40, a new movement in the prophetic drama is introduced. It begins on a completely different note than that with which Isaiah 39 concluded. Isaiah 40 presupposes that God's people have been in exile for some time and opens with a message of hope for these exiles in Babylon: "Comfort, O comfort my people, says your God. Speak tenderly to Jerusalem, and cry to her that she has served her term, that her penalty is paid, that she has received from the LORD's hand double for all her sins" (40:1–2). The exile is over, and the LORD has forgiven his wayward people.

When the text continues with, "In the wilderness prepare the way of the LORD, make straight in the desert a highway for our God" (40:3), the members of the

LORD's divine council (cf. 6:8; Ps 82:1; Job 1:6) are being called upon to cut a trail through the wilderness from Babylon to Jerusalem so that the LORD himself might go and gather his exiled people and lead them back home swiftly and safely.

A very similar scene is depicted in today's reading as the prophet describes Israel's return from exile using imagery and language that recall Israel's exodus from Egypt. In 43:16–17, the references to *a way in the sea* and to *chariots* and *horses* being extinguished recalls Israel's passing through the Red Sea on dry ground, which culminated in the destruction of Pharaoh's armies (Exod 14:1–15:21, EastVig). Just as the LORD rescued Israel from its slavery in Egypt, so now the LORD promises to rescue his people from their captivity in Babylon.

43:18–21. The language of *a way in the wilderness* and *rivers in the desert* evokes memories of Israel's forty year sojourn in the wilderness. During this period, the LORD protected Israel from wilderness beasts and sustained the people by providing them with daily bread from heaven (Exod 16:1–36, Prop 13) and water from a rock (Exod 17:1–7; cf. 15:22–27). Therefore, just as the LORD led his people through the wilderness from Egypt to the Promised Land, so now the LORD will lead his people through another wilderness from Babylon to Judah. This wilderness, however, will be a fruitful and abundant wilderness. There will be plenty of water and, therefore, no need for grumbling as was the case during the Exodus from Egypt.

The phrase, *the former things*, occurs seven times within the latter half of Isaiah (41:22; 42:9; 43:9, 18; 46:9; 48:3; 65:17) and could refer to the Exodus event or to God's original act of creation; however, there is another possibility. When the LORD declares in 42:9, "See the former things have come to pass and new things I now declare," *the former things* could be a reference to the judgment Isaiah announced in chapters 1–39 that came about through the Babylonian exile. If so, then *new things* refers to the end of exile and to the promise of restoration that Isaiah has been announcing since chapter 40. This interpretation makes sense of today's reading as well. When the LORD says, "Do not remember the former things" (43:18), he is calling upon his people to forget their years of exile and to look ahead to the new things he is about to do, namely, to come and gather them together and to lead them through the wilderness back to the Promised Land.

43:22–24. The tone of the passage takes a sudden turn. Up to this point, the LORD has been talking about forgiveness and the return of his people from exile, but now he accuses them. The LORD's chosen people were sent into exile because they had become weary of serving their God and had stopped calling upon him and offering the appropriate sacrifices and offerings. But, according to the prophet, the LORD was not demanding so much that his people should have become weary and lax in their devotion; he did not burden them with excessive ritual. However, *they* have burdened *him* with the weight of their manifold sin and wickedness.

By accusing his people at this point, the LORD is reminding them why they were sent into exile in the first place. This is important because their returning home is not simply a physical return from Babylon to Jerusalem, but also a spiritual return to the LORD. If they forget the cause of the exile, they might fall back into their old ways.

43:25. With that point being made, the LORD shifts gears once again, and he returns to the motif of forgiveness. It is in the LORD's nature to forgive. Moreover, the LORD's forgiveness is offered as a gift not a reward. The LORD has not forgiven his people because they repented; he forgives them solely out of his own interest. Such unconditional forgiveness becomes the foundation of true repentance, for only in the grace and power of unconditional forgiveness are we able to experience and express true remorse. If repentance is offered in an effort to gain forgiveness, then our remorse can too easily be contaminated and spoiled by self-interest and our need for self-preservation.

Suggestions for Lectors

In today's reading, the LORD is the speaker, so deliver his message with a strong, clear voice. The tone of the reading shifts back and forth. In the beginning (43:18–21) and at the end (43:25), the LORD speaks of the things that he will do to restore his people. In the middle (43:22–24), however, he reminds the people of their sins. Therefore, read the middle section in a more subdued, serious tone, even with a hint of anger and frustration. Pause for a second both before and after the middle section to help signal the shift in tone.

Also, notice the poetic structure of the middle section. As is common in biblical poetry, all the lines occur in pairs, called strophes, such that the second line restates and reinforces the first line, often through synonymous parallelism. Consider 43:22:

22	a	Yet you did not call upon me, O Jacob;
	a'	but you have been weary of me, O Israel!

Verses 23 and 24 both contain two strophes (a-a', b-b'), and each strophe exhibits synonymous parallelism. Moreover, the whole of verse 23 is paralleled by the whole of verse 24. Notice the repetition of the words *brought*, *sacrifices*, *burdened*, and *wearied*. Also, notice how 23a parallels 24a, and 23a' // 24a', and 23b // 24b, and 23b' // 24b'.

23	a	You have not *brought* me your sheep for burnt offerings,
23	a'	or honored me with your *sacrifices*.
23	b	I have not *burdened* you with offerings,
23	b'	or *wearied* you with frankincense.
24	a	You have not *bought* me sweet cane with money,
24	a'	or satisfied me with the fat of your *sacrifices*.
24	b	But you have *burdened* me with your sins;
24	b'	you have *wearied* me with your iniquities.

By developing an appreciation and a feel for how a poetic passage is structured, you will be able to read it with a cadence and intonation that will enhance your ability to communicate the meaning of the passage to your listeners.

Pronunciation Guide

Isaiah (ī-ZAY-uh)

2 CORINTHIANS 1:18–22

Notes

Sequence. 1 of 4

Commentary

Between the time Paul had written the letters of 1 and 2 Corinthians, Paul's relationship with the church in Corinth had gone through a rough period. In today's reading, Paul responds to charges that he is unreliable and ineffective as an apostle.

After writing 1 Corinthians, Paul received a report from his co-worker Timothy that a situation was brewing in Corinth. Paul immediately left Ephesus and made what he would later describe as a painful visit to the church in Corinth (2 Cor 2:1). During that visit, Paul was apparently confronted by a member of the church and his authority was undermined. In some people's minds, Paul did not handle the situation with the leadership and strength that they expected from an apostle (2:5–9; 10:1, 10). Paul left Corinth with the intention of returning soon. He had planned to visit them on his trips both to and from Macedonia (1:16), but later he thought better of it. He writes, "I call on God as witness against me; it was to spare you that I did not come again to Corinth.... So I made up my mind not to make you another painful visit" (1:23; 2:1).

1:18–22. So, Paul defends his integrity. He does not operate according to human standards; he is not one to say "Yes" and "No" at the same time. They may regard Paul as unreliable, but he is simply following God's leading, and God is reliable and faithful. As has been demonstrated through the gospel message that he and his coworkers proclaim, God has spoken a resounding "Yes" to the Corinthians. It was God who brought Paul and the Corinthians together, for it was God who anointed Paul for his apostolic mission. Moreover, God has imprinted his seal of ownership upon them. The Holy Spirit marks them as Christ's own forever and serves as a first installment, that is, a down payment or deposit that serves as God's guarantee that they will receive the fullness of salvation when it comes.

Suggestions for Lectors

Today's reading is short so make sure that your listeners are ready before you begin. Pause slightly longer than normal after you introduce the reading. Up to this point in 2 Corinthians, Paul has been defending himself. He is quite animated so read with great energy. Given the brevity of the passage, read slowly and deliberately, but again with energy. If there is a verse worth highlighting, it is 1:20a: *For in him every one of God's promises is a "Yes."*

Pronunciation Guide

Corinthians (kuh-RIN-thee-uhnz)
Silvanus (sil-VAY-nuhs)
Timothy (TIM-uh-thee, -oh-)

Mark 2:1–12

Notes

Sequence. 5 of 8

Commentary

Up to this point in Mark's narrative, Jesus has been traveling about the region of Galilee announcing the arrival of God's kingdom. His authority and power has been evident not only in the numerous exorcisms and healings he has performed but also in his teaching. So far, the response to Jesus and his message has been overwhelmingly positive, but that all changes in today's episode, which is the first in a series of five conflict stories in which Jesus' identity and authority are debated (2:1–3:6).

2:1–5. Jesus carried out an itinerate ministry, so the gospels present him as always on the move. Yet, here in Mark, we discover that Jesus has a residence in Capernaum, so the roof that the four men dig through is actually the roof of Jesus' house.

Following his Galilean missionary tour (1:39, 45), Jesus gets only a few days rest before the people descend upon him en mass. While he is teaching the people, four men bring their paralyzed friend to be healed by Jesus. Unable to gain access through the front door, they dig through Jesus' roof and lower the man down. Their persistence demonstrates their faith in Jesus' ability to set their friend free from his disability, and their faith does not go unnoticed.

In Mark, faith is important. When Jesus heralds the arrival of God's kingdom, he announces, "repent, and *believe* in the good news" (1:15, Epi 3). Thus, faith (also belief and trust) is how people participate in what God is doing in the world. Not surprisingly, then, faith plays an important role in the healings in Mark. When the woman with a twelve-year flow of blood touches Jesus and is immediately cured, Jesus says to her, "Daughter, your *faith* has made you well; go in peace, and be healed of your disease" (5:34, Prop 8). When Jairus receives the dreaded news that his daughter has just died, Jesus says to him, "Do not fear, only *believe*" (5:36, Prop 8). On the other hand, when Jesus is confronted by *unbelief* in his hometown synagogue, his ability to heal is severely inhibited (6:5–6, Prop 9).

Now, with all of this being said, we must be careful not to oversimplify matters. Too many people have been traumatized by the claim that if they only had enough faith they would be healed of whatever ails them. Things are more complicated than that, for there is still a mystery regarding the relationship between faith and healing, both in Mark and our lives. We must remember that, strictly speaking, it is not faith, but God that heals people. When the hemorrhaging woman touched Jesus, power went forth from him (5:30). The woman's faith may have initiated her healing, but it was the cleansing power of the Holy Spirit that healed her. Finally, we must remember that faith and anything that comes by faith is first and foremost a gift from God. Faith is not something we can or must generate on our own; it comes from God who is gracious. Later in Mark, when a distraught father brings his demon-afflicted son to Jesus, he says, "if you are able to do anything, have pity on us and help us." Jesus responds with, "If you are able!—All things can be done for the one who believes," to which the man replies, "I believe, help my unbelief!" (9:22b–24). Though the man's faith is filled with doubt, Jesus does not hesitate to heal his son. Returning to today's episode, the faith that inspires Jesus' response is not the paralytic's own faith, but that of his friends.

When Jesus sees the friends' faith, he says to the paralytic, "Son, your sins are forgiven" (1:5). The reader is surprised by Jesus' response. Instead of healing the man with an authoritative word, as the reader has come to expect, Jesus absolves him of his sins.

2:6–12. The scribes are surprised as well. In fact, they are shocked and offended. "Why does this fellow speak in this way? It is blasphemy! Who can forgive sins but God alone?" (2:7).

Here, we must take time to understand the nature of the scribes' objections. Too often, readers of the gospels treat Jesus' opponents as though they are just being petty or legalistic. But if we fail to appreciate the reasons why the scribes are so offended, then we may miss the significance of what Jesus has done to prompt such a reaction. It must be said that the scribes are not against forgiveness or even an attitude of forgiveness. What they oppose is Jesus' presumption in declaring this man's sins forgiven. Sins are debts owed to God, and in the Law, God established a system whereby those debts could be forgiven. Who is this Jesus to step in and forgive a debt that is owed to God, a debt that only God, or his authorized agents (i.e., the temple priests), has the right to forgive?

Of course, the reader of Mark already knows the answer to this question. Jesus is the Son of God, the Messiah who has been anointed with the Holy Spirit and so is authorized to act on God's behalf (1:1, 9–11). However, as characters in the story, the scribes do not have access to the same information as the reader, so Jesus demonstrates his authority to forgive sins with just a word by healing the paralytic with just a word. Logically, if Jesus has the authority to eradicate the consequences of sin—the scribes likely regarded the man's paralysis a consequence of sin—then Jesus clearly has the authority to declare the man's sins forgiven.

The people are amazed, but the reader suspects that the scribes are not so impressed. They know that there are two powers at work in the world, God and Satan, and they are not yet convinced that God is behind Jesus' authority and power. In next week's episode, they question Jesus' practice of eating with tax-collectors (2:16), and later on they will claim that his ability to exorcise demons comes from Beelzebul, the ruler of demons (3:22, Prop 5).

Suggestions for Lectors

As reflected in the Commentary, today's episode occurs in two movements (2:1–5, 6–12). It begins like any other story of healing, but midway through, it turns into a story of controversy.

Begin reading in your normal narrating voice. Draw the first movement to an end by slowing down as you deliver Jesus' pronouncement: *Son, your sins are forgiven* (2:5b). Since Jesus addresses the paralytic as *Son,* let there be a hint of compassion in your voice. Pause for a second or two before commencing with the second movement.

The second movement begins with a description of what the scribes are thinking. This is an internal dialogue, so drop your voice as you deliver 2:6–7 as though you are speaking to yourself. Then, when Jesus responds to the scribes, elevate your voice by increasing your volume and pitch. In 2:10, Jesus suddenly changes addressees. At the beginning of the verse, Jesus is talking to the scribes, then he breaks off mid-sentence in order to address the paralytic. As you read the line, *he said to the paralytic*, make a mental shift. Imagine that you are turning away from the scribes and directing all of your attention to this poor paralyzed man. In the same calm and compassionate voice you used for *Son, your sins are forgiven*, say to the paralytic, *I say to you, stand up,… take your mat… and go to your home* (2:10b). Pause after each command.

Conclude the reading with a sense of awe and amazement in your voice, as the crowd exclaims, *We have never seen anything like this!* (2:12).

Pronunciation Guide
Capernaum (kuh-PER-nay-uhm, -nuh-)

EIGHTH SUNDAY AFTER EPIPHANY

Same Readings as Proper 3

Hosea 2:14–20
Psalm 103:1–13, 22
2 Corinthians 3:1–6
Mark 2:13–22

HOSEA 2:14–20

Commentary
The book of Hosea is the first book in the collection of OT writings known as the Book of the Twelve, which comprises the twelve Minor Prophets from Hosea to Malachi. Hosea was a prophet in the northern kingdom of Israel in the latter half of the eighth century, in the decades leading up to the destruction of Israel by the Assyrians in 722 B.C. Like many prophets, Hosea was sent to confront God's people and their leaders over their practices of idolatry and social injustice. But, alongside these prophetic chastisements, Hosea paints a picture of the LORD's great love and commitment to his chosen people.

Throughout Hosea, the imagery and language of marriage is used to depict the covenant relationship between God and Israel. Consequently, when people commit idolatry, it is characterized in terms of adultery. In this drama, the LORD is the ever-faithful husband, Israel is the unfaithful wife of whoredom, and the idols and false gods she worships are her lovers.

In this period, the cult of Baal played a significant role in the northern kingdom's national life. Baal was the storm and fertility god of Canaanite religion, and so it was believed that Baal was the god primarily responsible for the productivity of the land. In an arid, agricultural society so highly dependent upon rain, devotion to

Baal was just a normal part of Canaanite agricultural practice. If you wanted a good harvest, offering sacrifices and burning incense to Baal was just as important as plowing and planting. When the Israelites entered the Promised Land, they began to be influenced by these Baalistic practices. Israelites began to worship Baal alongside their own god, Yahweh. Not only was this in direct violation of the first commandment, "You shall have no other gods before me." (Exod 20:3, Lent 3; Deut 5:7), but it fostered the mistaken belief that it was Baal, and not Yahweh, who was responsible for the Promised Land's productivity. As the LORD says in Hosea, Israel "did not know that it was I who gave her the grain, the wine, and the oil and who lavished upon her silver and gold that they used for Baal" (2:8). Thus, the LORD decrees that all of these things will be taken away, and his people will be punished for their unfaithfulness (2:9–13).

2:14–20. Yet once these words are spoken, the LORD begins to speak about alluring his people back to him. The LORD is not simply going to forgive his adulterous wife and take her back, he is going to woo her. Israel has not even repented of her adulteries, yet the LORD is going to go after her. Such is the steadfast love and mercy of God. The LORD is going to lure Israel into the wilderness because that is where they first met and that is where their covenant relationship was first established. God is going to recreate their first date. He is going to make his people fall in love with him all over again; such is the extravagant, prodigal love of God for his people.

In the end, Israel will truly become the faithful wife, and she will know her husband as intimately as any husband and wife know one another (2:20).

Suggestions for Lectors

In today's reading, the LORD speaks like a man who is envisioning a wonderful future with the woman of his dreams, so throughout your reading, convey with your voice a sense of joyful hope and excitement.

The reading falls into two sections (14–15, 16–20). Hosea 2:14–15 is written in poetic verse, while 2:16–20 is in prose. Moreover, in 2:14–15, the LORD employs third person as he talks *about* Israel, but in 2:16–20, the LORD shifts into second person and begins talking *to* Israel. Bring these differences out in your reading by adopting a slightly different tempo and tone for each section.

As you read 2:14–15, imagine that you are telling your friends of your plans to woo your beloved. Speak slowly, reveling in the dreams and plans you have. Afterwards, pause for a second or two before turning your attention to your beloved.

As you read 2:16–20, direct these words to your listeners as though you are the LORD and they are your beloved. Increase the intensity and pitch of your voice to convey your excitement. You might also increase your tempo, so long as you do not rush. Verse 17 briefly shifts back into third person. Treat it like a narrative aside by lowering your voice. In your mind, imagine yourself turning away from your beloved in order to offer your friends a brief explanation. Afterwards, return to the voice you have adopted for the rest of 2:16–20.

Finally, as you draw the reading to a close, emphasize the final clause by slowing down and enunciating each word clearly with slight pauses after every pair of words, as in: *and you. . shall know. . the* LORD (2:20b).

Pronunciation Guide
Achor (AY-kohr), *Baal* (BAY-uhl), *Baals* (BAY-uhlz), *Egypt* (EE-jipt)

2 CORINTHIANS 3:1–6

Notes
Sequence. 2 of 4

Commentary
In 2 Corinthians, Paul responds to those who question his apostolic authority. Apparently, there were those in Corinth who did not think that he had the necessary credentials to carry out an apostolic ministry. Paul must, therefore, defend himself and his calling to be an apostle. He regrets doing this because it gives the impression that he is extolling himself when what he really wants to be doing is commending and extolling the gospel of Christ.

3:1–3. In the ancient world, it was common for people to carry with them letters of introduction or recommendation when they travelled abroad. Written by a third party, letters of recommendation introduced its bearer and included requests for hospitality, lodging, employment, or financial support. Apparently, some travelling apostles had made their way to Corinth bearing letters of recommendation. These "super-apostles," as Paul calls them (11:5; 12:11), are proclaiming a different gospel than the one Paul proclaimed to the Corinthians, and they are calling Paul's apostolic credentials into question.

Through the use of a rhetorical question, Paul argues that he and his coworkers should not need letters of recommendation either *to* or *from* them. They should not need letters *to them* because Paul founded the church in Corinth in the first place, and he is already well-known by them. Neither should they need any written endorsements from the Corinthian church. The only letter needed is the Corinthians themselves. They are a living letter that speaks more eloquently than any written letter ever could. Anyone reading this Spirit-composed letter would recognize and acknowledge Paul's calling to be an apostle.

3:4–6. Though the relationship between Paul and the Corinthians is strained, he still maintains that the Christian community in Corinth is better than any written letter of recommendation. This is not because Paul has confidence in his own abilities, but because he is confident that God's Spirit is at work in him and his gospel coworkers, as they serve as the spokespersons and ministers of a new covenant that is able to impart life.

Suggestions for Lectors
In today's passage, the apostle Paul is once again defending himself, so read with an elevated voice, with increased volume and pitch. As you read, imagine that you are Paul and that you are delivering your letter in person. Look up at your listeners as

you say, *<u>You yourselves</u> are our letter* (3:2). In the last line, emphasize *kills* and *Spirit*, as in: *for the <u>letter</u> kills, but the <u>Spirit</u> gives life* (3:6).

Pronunciation Guide
Corinthians (kuh-RIN-thee-uhnz)

MARK 2:13–22

Notes
Sequence. 6 of 8

Commentary
In last week's reading, Jesus made enemies of the scribes—those who studied the law of Moses—by presuming to have the authority to forgive sins, an authority that belongs to God alone. In this week's reading, Jesus' practice of eating with tax-collectors and sinners is questioned as is the absence of a regular habit of fasting amongst his disciples. Behind both of these issues is the question of Jesus' identity and authority.

2:13–14. In the first century, the typical practice was for would-be disciples to seek out a rabbi with whom to study. Jesus, however, is the one who takes the initiative to seek out and call disciples to join him in announcing the arrival of God's kingdom in word and deed. In 1:16–20 (Epi 3), Jesus was passing along the sea of Galilee when he called four fishermen: Peter and Andrew, James and John. In today's scene, Jesus is once again walking along the Galilean shore when he calls a man named Levi to follow him. Levi is not a fisherman but a tax-collector. Given that his tax office is located beside the sea, Levi probably participated in the tax-fishing system, wherein fishing rights were leased from the government and then sold to local fishermen. Levi would have collected taxes from the Galilean fisher folk, and perhaps from Peter, Andrew, James and John. Like the four fisherman before him, Levi immediately abandons his fish-related livelihood to follow Jesus.

2:15–17. Later, Jesus and his disciples are eating with Levi along with many tax collectors and other sinners who had become followers of Jesus. This practice of table fellowship raises the ire of the Pharisees. The Pharisees were a first-century Jewish sect concerned with the spiritual renewal of the Jewish nation. They attempted to live their daily lives with the same level of ritual purity that priests observed when carrying out their priestly duties in the temple. As much as possible, the Pharisees avoided situations that might render them ritually impure, so they were hyper-vigilant when it came to dietary matters. What you ate, how you prepared your food, and the company you kept were all matters of utmost importance. So, when the Pharisees observe Jesus eating with non-observant Jews, that is, those who are in a perpetual state of ritual impurity, they question his disciples.

In Mark, Jesus responds to opponents with parables and other figures of speech because these have a way of smuggling the truth in behind their defenses. Instead of listing the reasons why he engages in table fellowship with the likes of tax-collectors and sinners, he makes a pronouncement that no one can argue with: "Those who are well have no need of a physician, but those who are sick" (2:17).

2:18–20. The Pharisee and John the Baptist movements were both concerned with the spiritual renewal of Israel. An ascetical practice like fasting was associated with repentance and, therefore, was a part of their program to prepare God's people for the arrival of God's kingdom. The Jesus movement was also concerned with the renewal of God's people. In fact, Jesus probably appointed *twelve* apostles to symbolize the restoration of the Twelve Tribes of Israel. Yet, fasting did not have a place within his movement because the kingdom of God had already arrived. What was called for, then, was *feasting*, not fasting.

When Jesus is asked why his disciples do not fast, he once again responds with a parable. The coming kingdom was often envisioned as a great banquet (Matt 8:11; Luke 13:29, 14:15), and here, Jesus portrays it as a wedding banquet. According to Jesus, it would be inappropriate for wedding guests to fast because wedding feasts are a time for celebration, not mourning. Jesus' listeners would readily agree. But then, Jesus takes the parable one step further and subtly identifies himself as the bridegroom. His disciples do not fast because he is the bridegroom of the kingdom; he is the Messiah, and as long as he is with them, his disciples shall feast. But there will come a day when he is taken away from them; that day will be a day for fasting.

2:21–22. Finally, Jesus employs two parabolic wisdom sayings that highlight the impossibility of combining something new with something old. In both cases, mixing old with new destroys both. The renewal that Jesus is announcing with the coming of the kingdom cannot be contained by the old practices, forms, and traditions of his contemporaries. Once again, the reality of the kingdom cannot be expressed through fasting nor through the practice of avoiding unclean people. The arrival of the kingdom is a time of celebration, a time to invite *everyone* to participate in what God is doing in the world.

Suggestions for Lectors

Today's episode comprises three scenes: 2:13–14, 15–17, 18–22. Pause for a second or two between each scene. At the end of the first scene (2:13–14), raise your voice as Jesus says, *Follow me.* Then, read the last sentence slowly and in a matter-of-fact tone, as though there was nothing strange about Levi abandoning his livelihood to follow Jesus. Also, pause after *got up*, as in: *And he got up… and followed him* (2:14b).

In the second scene (2:15–17), ask the Pharisees' question in a dismissive tone, perhaps with a hint of disgust in your voice as though eating with tax collectors and sinners is the last thing anybody should or would want to do. When Jesus responds, he appeals to their common sense; it is sick people who need doctors. So deliver Jesus' words in a tone that says, "Eating with such people—that is, those who most need spiritual guidance—is the most natural and obvious thing in the world to do be doing. So why aren't you doing it?"

In the third scene (2:18–22), employ this same tone of voice when delivering Jesus' parables of the bridegroom and wineskins, because once again he is appealing to their common sense.

Pronunciation Guide

Alphaeus (al-FEE-uhs), *Levi* (LEE-vī), *Pharisees* (FAIR-uh-seez)

NINTH SUNDAY AFTER EPIPHANY*

Same Readings as Proper 4

**These readings are for churches whose calendar requires a Ninth Sunday after Epiphany and who do not observe the Last Sunday after the Epiphany as Transfiguration Sunday. These are the same readings as Proper 4 except that 1 Samuel 3:1–10, (11–20) is not offered as an option for the first reading.*

Deuteronomy 5:12–15
Psalm 81:1–10
2 Corinthians 4:5–12
Mark 2:23–3:6

DEUTERONOMY 5:12–15

Commentary

Deuteronomy is the fifth book of the Bible and the last of the Five Books of Moses (a.k.a., the Pentateuch or the Torah). Deuteronomy is presented as a speech that Moses delivers to the Israelites just prior to his death and just prior to Israel's entrance into the Promised Land of Canaan under the leadership of Joshua (Josh 3:1–17). In this speech (Deut 1:6–30:20), Moses reviews Israel's forty-year sojourn in the wilderness and instructs the people in the laws of the covenant that are to govern their personal and corporate lives once they are settled in Canaan. One might regard Deuteronomy, then, as a prolonged exposition on the Ten Commandments, a detailing of the many varied and specific ways one goes about loving the LORD with all of one's life and possessions and loving one's neighbor as oneself.

The Ten Commandments first appear in Exodus 20 (Lent 3) and then reappear in Deuteronomy 5 as Moses recounts the story of the giving of the law at Mt. Sinai. Today's reading focuses upon the fourth commandment regarding the sabbath.

5:12–14a. In the Bible, *holy* is a term generally used to denote someone or something that is set apart for special use. In this usage, the opposite of holy is not sinful or bad but *common* and *ordinary*. For example, we might say that a set of fine china is holy because it is only brought out and used on special occasions. In contrast, our common, everyday dishes are not bad, simply ordinary.

According to the fourth commandment, the seventh day of the week is to be set apart for special purposes. Whereas the people of God have been provided six good, ordinary days on which to do all their work, the seventh day is to be a sabbath, a day of rest. The seventh day is distinguished from all the other days because no ordinary work is done on this day. Sabbath observance is rooted in the created order itself. God completed his work of creation in six days. On the seventh day, God rested from all the work he had done in creation. In so doing, God blessed the sabbath and made it holy so that it could in turn be a blessing (Gen 2:2–3). As Jesus says in today's gospel, the sabbath was made for human beings (Mark 2:27).

For the Israelites, observing the sabbath day and keeping it holy was an exercise in trust. After all, in the subsistent economies of nomadic and agrarian societies, one did not eat if one did not work. By abstaining from work every seventh day, the Israelites were putting their faith in God's goodness and trusting that God would provide for them. Moreover, observing the sabbath can foster faith. If a person abstains from work on the sabbath and then finds that they still have everything they need, their trust in God is justified and their faith increases.

5:14b–15. Keeping the sabbath not only affects our relationship with God, it also affects our relationships with other people and even with creation itself. Not only are the Israelites not to do any work, but their children, their household slaves, and even their domesticated animals are not allowed to do any work. Even resident aliens are not allowed to do any work on the sabbath. The sabbath is not only a day of rest, it is a day of remembrance. In particular, it is a day to remember what their lives were like when they lived as slaves in Egypt and to remember how God rescued them. They, in turn, should treat their slaves and workers with the same regard and respect. Thus, sabbath observance is not only a matter of personal spirituality, it is also a matter of social justice.

Suggestions for Lectors

In today's reading, remember that you are Moses speaking to the Israelites, a people that you have led these past forty years. Like a father speaking to his adult children, let your voice be earnest, affectionate, and firm.

Moses begins by issuing the commandment to keep the sabbath holy; then, he devotes the rest of the reading to explaining the commandment and explicating its implications. This means that the opening verse is the most important and, therefore, should receive the most emphasis. So before you begin reading, make sure that your listeners are settled in, attentive, and ready. Then, deliver the opening line with a strong, firm voice, reading the first half of the verse at a slightly slower pace with a few additional pauses. For example, *<u>Observe</u> the sabbath day… and <u>keep</u> it… holy* (5:12).

In 5:12, emphasize the imperatives, *observe* and *keep* as well as the imperative, *remember* in 5:15. Further, in 5:13–14, emphasize *six days* and *seventh day* to bring out the contrast.

Pronunciation Guide

Deuteronomy (doo'-tuh-RON-uh-mee), *Egypt* (EE-jipt)

2 Corinthians 4:5–12

Notes

Sequence. 3 of 4

Commentary

In the intervening time between the writing of 1 and 2 Corinthians, false apostles had infiltrated the church in Corinth. These "super-apostles," as Paul calls them pejoratively (11:5; 12:11), spend much of their time in self-aggrandizement as they seek to discredit Paul's apostolic authority and credentials. Paul must defend himself and his ministry so that the gospel might not be undermined. He hates doing it, not only because it gives the impression that he is engaging in a campaign of self-promotion much as the super-apostles, but more importantly because it takes the focus off of Christ.

4:5–6. And so, today's reading begins with a reminder from Paul that he and his coworkers do not proclaim themselves, they proclaim the gospel, the good news that Jesus Christ is Lord of all. Paul may be an apostle, but he does not regard his apostleship to be a position of privilege. Compared to Jesus, Paul is just a slave, serving the Corinthians for the sake of Jesus. Paul did not choose to be an apostle; he simply responded to God's call. The God who began creation with the words, "Let there be light," is the same God who revealed Jesus to Paul so that Paul might reveal Jesus as the face of God to the world.

4:7–12. Paul has suffered many hardships in his work as an apostle. In 2 Corinthians 11, he speaks of imprisonments, floggings and beatings, shipwrecks, hunger and thirst, sleepless nights, and all manner of other dangers. For Paul, these hardships constitute his apostolic credentials; they demonstrate that he and his coworkers are not in it for the money. "For we are not peddlers of God's word like so many; but in Christ we speak as persons of sincerity, as persons sent from God and standing in his presence" (2:17). In contrast, Paul's opponents point to these same hardships as evidence that he is not a true apostle and that his gospel is defective.

Paul argues, however, that despite appearances, they have been entrusted with a treasure, the gospel concerning Jesus Christ who is the image-bearer and face of God (4:4, 6). Unlike the false apostles, Paul and his coworkers do not carry this treasure around in an ornate treasure chest. Instead, they keep it, as it were, in simple clay jars so that nothing might take away from the glory of the treasure itself. If Paul were eloquent, charismatic, and untouched by the shame of persecution, then those who came to believe through his preaching might mistakenly attribute the power they experience through the gospel to Paul and not to God.

For many, Jesus' crucifixion was a clear indication that he was not the Messiah. Yet, just as Paul is not ashamed of the cross of Christ (1 Cor 2:2), neither is he ashamed of his own persecutions. Christ's painful and humiliating death was the clay vessel that housed the glory of God. Likewise, the glory of the gospel is transported in the humiliations and hardships of its messengers. Far from disqualifying him as an apostle, Paul's persecutions are a sign that he is following in the way of his Lord.

Suggestions for Lectors

The first part of the reading contains a lengthy verse (4:6). As always, it is important to practice reading and rereading long verses until your timing, breathing, and intonation have been worked out. Verse 6 is complicated by the fact that it ends with a string of five prepositional phrases. Group the first three into one intonational unit, and the last two into a unit. An intonational unit is a phrase or clause that should be read in one breath without any internal pauses. The following shows the intonational units in verse 6:

1 For it is the God who said, ...
2 "Let light shine out of darkness, ...
3 who has shone in our hearts. .
4 to give the light of the knowledge of the glory of God. .
5 in the face of Jesus Christ.

Pause longer at the end of units 1 and 2 and more briefly at the end of units 3 and 4.

In 4:8–9, Paul repeats a grammatical structure four times. Whenever you are confronted by a repeated element or feature that occurs more than three times, it is important to vary your delivery so that the repetition becomes dynamic instead of monotonous. Read the first two lines in the same way; read them at a normal pace, with longer pauses after the commas and semicolons. Then, read lines 3 and 4 more quickly, almost as though they are a single line. Afterwards, return to your normal tempo.

1 We are afflicted in every way,... but not crushed;...
2 perplexed, ... but not driven to despair;...
3 persecuted, but not forsaken;
4 struck down, but not destroyed;

In the last three verses, emphasize the words *life* and *live*; there are four occurrences. In the final verse, slow down and read more deliberately. Emphasize *death* as well as *life* to bring out the contrast (4:12).

Pronunciation Guide
Corinthians (kuh-RIN-thee-uhnz)

Mark 2:23–3:6

Notes
Sequence. 7 of 8

Commentary
Prior to Mark 2:1, the response to Jesus' message about the kingdom and to his deeds of power has been overwhelmingly positive. But in 2:1, the first signs of opposition begin to surface. From 2:1 to 3:6, Jesus participates in a series of five public debates with the scribes and the Pharisees over matters related to Jewish law and practice. These debates are energized by the underlying, unanswered question of Jesus' identity and authority. Who is Jesus? Where does his power to do such amazing deeds come from? From God, or from Satan? Of course, the reader has known the answer to these questions since the opening line of the gospel; Jesus is "the Messiah, the Son of the God" (1:1, Adv 2). However, the characters in the gospel are not given this information in such a straightforward, unambiguous manner. They must weigh the evidence and decide for themselves who this Jesus is. The seriousness of these questions is reflected in the fact that following the last debate, two groups combine forces to bring about Jesus' death.

As God's anointed Messiah, Jesus has been called and equipped to inaugurate the kingdom of God by word and by deed. Jesus' *modus operandi* is to make an authoritative pronouncement about the kingdom and then perform a miracle that demonstrates the truth of the pronouncement. So Jesus proclaims, "Repent, for the kingdom of God has come near" (cf. 1:15), and then he exorcizes an unclean spirit (1:21–28, Epi 4). The exorcism not only proves that God's kingdom is overthrowing Satan's, it is also the means by which God's kingdom is being established.

Likewise, in the first public debate, Jesus tells a paralytic, "Son, your sins are forgiven" (2:5, Epi 7). When Jesus is questioned about this pronouncement, he heals the paralytic with a word. According to Jesus, his ability to set a person free from a debilitating physical condition is proof that he has been granted the authority by God to set a person free from the debt and power of sin. As he says to the scribes, "'So that you may know that the Son of Man has authority on earth to forgive sins'—he said to the paralytic—'I say to you, stand up, take your mat and go to your home'" (2:10). The same pattern is present in today's episodes. Jesus proclaims himself lord of the sabbath, and then he performs a healing on the sabbath to substantiate his claim.

2:23–28. The Pharisees were a lay renewal movement that promoted strict observance of the law of Moses and the tradition of the elders, especially with regard to matters of Jewish identity (circumcision, the reading of Torah, kosher regulations, sabbath observance, etc.). In this scene, the Pharisees object to the disciples plucking grain on the sabbath, likely because they regard it as a form of work, which is not permitted on the sabbath (see today's OT reading). Instead of questioning the disciples about their actions, the Pharisees question Jesus, even though he himself was not plucking grain. This suggests that the real question being asked of Jesus is not, "Why are *they* doing what is not lawful on the sabbath?" but "Why are *you* allowing *your* disciples to do what is not lawful on the sabbath?" In short, the Pharisees are once again questioning Jesus' authority, his prerogative in sanctioning such actions on the sabbath. Jesus responds accordingly.

Jesus recalls an incident from the life of David, Israel's most celebrated king (1 Sam 21:1–9). He appeals to David's actions not only to defend his disciples' behavior but also to defend his authorizing their behavior. In short, Jesus' appeal to David serves two purposes. First, Jesus notes that David's *eating* of the loaves of the Presence was motivated by hunger and need. With this, Jesus is justifying his disciples' sabbath transgression on the presumption that they too were hungry and in need. This answers the Pharisees' *stated* question, "Why are *they* doing what is not lawful on the sabbath?" And it also provides justification for Jesus' first pronouncement: "The sabbath was made for humankind, and not humankind for the sabbath" (2:27). In their attempt to honor the sabbath and keep it holy, the Pharisees have obscured the original intent and purpose of the sabbath. Second, by highlighting David's *giving* of the loaves to his companions, Jesus defends his own authority to authorize his disciples' actions. This answers the Pharisees' *unstated* question, "Why are *you* allowing *your* disciples to do what is not lawful on the sabbath?" Moreover, it also provides justification for Jesus' second pronouncement: "the Son of Man is lord even of the sabbath." (2:28).

"Son of Man" is how Jesus refers to himself, especially when he is talking about matters related to his authority and vocation as the Messiah (cf. 2:10; 8:31; 13:26; 14:62). As Lord of the sabbath, Jesus claims the authority—the same authority as God—to make pronouncements about what is and is not lawful on the sabbath. In the next scene, Jesus justifies this provocative claim by healing a man on the sabbath.

3:1–6. Presumably, the Pharisees regarded healing as a form of work, and therefore, something that was not permitted on the sabbath. We have evidence for such a belief in Luke. In Luke 13, the leader of a synagogue became indignant when Jesus healed a woman on the sabbath. He kept saying to the crowd, "There are six days on which work ought to be done; come on those days and be cured, and not on the sabbath day" (13:14).

Jesus is aware of those who are seeking to entrap him, so he behaves very shrewdly. Instead of asking whether healing on the sabbath constitutes work, Jesus asks a broader question, one that gets at the heart of the matter and one that exposes the hard-heartedness of his opponents: "Is it lawful to do good or to do harm on the sabbath, to save life or to kill?" (3:4). The answer is obvious, yet the Pharisees refuse to respond because they know what the next question will be, something along the lines of, "Is not healing the equivalent of doing good and saving a life?" Their failure to respond discloses their unwillingness to open themselves and their views to criticism or debate. Their stubborn silence shows them to be fundamentally opposed to Jesus and his kingdom-of-God mission. Though the kingdom of God is right there in front of them, they refuse to repent and believe in the good news. Grieved at their hardness of heart, Jesus heals the man anyway. In turn, the Pharisees begin to conspire with the Herodians against Jesus (cf. 12:13). The Herodians were political supporters of Herod Antipas, the tetrarch of Galilee who himself had arrested and killed Jesus' forerunner, John the Baptist, (6:14–29, Prop 10). From this point on, Jesus is a marked man.

Suggestions for Lectors

Today's episode comprises two related, yet distinct scenes (2:23–28; 3:1–6), so pause for a few seconds between the scenes.

By this point in the gospel, the Pharisees have already been in a few debates with Jesus, and by the end of the second scene, they are ready to kill him. Tensions are running high, so in the first scene, ask the Pharisees' question in a challenging, versus merely inquiring, tone of voice (2:24). Jesus is becoming frustrated with these debates as well, so respond with hints of exasperation and irritation in your voice. Intensify your voice as you read Jesus' final declaration. Emphasize *not*, *even*, and the first *humankind*, and pause briefly after *lord*, as in: *The sabbath was made for <u>humankind</u>, and <u>not</u> humankind for the sabbath; so the Son of Man is lord… <u>even</u> of the sabbath* (2:28).

In the second scene (3:1–6), return to your normal narrating voice until Jesus begins speaking in 3:4. Given the history between Jesus and the Pharisees, Jesus' question is already laced with frustration and anger, so convey this by intensifying your voice. When you ask Jesus' question, emphasize the positive options as though Jesus is helping the Pharisees by giving them clues to the correct answers. *Is it lawful <u>to do good</u> or to do harm on the sabbath, <u>to save life</u> or to kill?* (3:4). To emphasize their stubborn silence, pause for a second after the question, then read the next statement very slowly and deliberately with a slight pause after *they* and/or *were*, as in: *But they… were… silent* (3:4b). Pause again for a full second afterwards as Jesus looks around and his anger boils. You might even choose this moment to look up at your listeners. The narrator says that Jesus was both angry and grieved at their hardness of heart. So when you say to the man, *Stretch out your hand* (3:5), try to convey a sense of grief, resignation, and tiredness, knowing that even the restoration of the man's hand will not prompt a change of heart.

Pronunciation Guide
Abiathar (uh-BĪ-uh-thahr; ab-i-AY-thahr; *not* uh-BEE-), *David* (DAY-vid), *Herodians* (hih-ROH-dee-uhnz), *Pharisees* (FAIR-uh-seez), *sabbath* (SAB-uhth)

LAST SUNDAY AFTER THE EPIPHANY

Transfiguration Sunday

2 Kings 2:1–12
Psalm 50:1–6
2 Corinthians 4:3–6
Mark 9:2–9

2 Kings 2:1–12

Commentary
In 1 Kings 19, the LORD instructs Elijah to anoint Elisha, a farmer, to be his successor (19:16). When Elijah finds Elisha, he performs a symbolic act; Elijah takes his mantle (that is, his cloak) and throws it over Elisha. Elijah's mantel symbolizes his prophetic office and power. By placing it upon Elisha, Elijah is calling Elisha to follow in his footsteps. After a brief exchange, Elisha burns the bridges to his former way of life and begins to accompany Elijah as his servant (19:19–21).

In today's reading, Elijah is taken up into heaven in a chariot of fire, making way for Elisha to take up his master's prophetic vocation.

2:1–3. Today's episode begins with Elijah and Elisha traveling from Gilgal. When Elijah tries to go on to Bethel alone, Elisha, who suspects that his master is about to be taken away from him, insists on accompanying him. When they arrive at Bethel, the guild of prophets stationed there ask Elisha if he knows what is about to happen. Elisha assures them that he does know.

2:3–5. Once there, Elijah attempts to go to Jericho by himself, yet once again Elisha accompanies him. When they arrive, the prophets in Jericho also ask Elisha if he knows what is going to happen. Yes, he certainly does.

2:6–8. Elijah then attempts to go to the Jordan river alone, and for the third time, Elisha states, "As the LORD lives, and as you yourself live, I will not leave you" (2:7). When they reach the Jordan, Elijah rolls up his cloak and strikes the water with it. The waters of the Jordan part, just as the waters of the Red Sea did during Israel's

Exodus from Egypt (Exod 14:21–25, EastVig) and just as the waters of the Jordan did during Israel's entrance into the Promised Land (Josh 3:14–17). Elijah and Elisha cross over to the other side on dry ground.

2:9–12. Once they cross, Elijah grants Elisha one last request. Elisha wishes to receive a double portion of the spirit that Elijah possesses. When the chariot of fire comes and takes Elijah away, Elisha can be heard calling out "Father, father!" His tone is one of anguish and grief at the loss of his master, as is indicated by the rending of his clothes.

Following today's reading, Elisha takes up Elijah's mantle and returns to the Jordan. When he strikes the Jordan with the mantle, the waters part, signifying that the prophetic spirit and power of Elijah has indeed been passed on to Elisha.

Suggestions for Lectors

Generally speaking, funerals are more about those who have been left behind than about the one who has gone on, and this is the perspective from which today's story is told. Although the story relates the wondrous account of Elijah's being taken up to heaven by a whirlwind, the story itself centers upon Elisha as he prepares himself for his master's departure. Consequently, the story's climax comes not with Elijah's miraculous departure, but with Elisha's heartfelt and repeated cry of anguish, *Father, father!* (2:12). As a reader, your goal will be to tell the story from Elisha's perspective, doing what you can to communicate his mounting anxiety and his attempt to hold back his grief as the time for his master's departure nears. In 2:12, Elisha's mounting anxiety suddenly breaks forth in anguish as his master is, without warning, taken from him and disappears from view.

Normally, one would slow down and soften one's voice as the story reaches its end, but here you may want to depart from this normal practice for dramatic effect. Experiment with just ending abruptly after *and tore them in two pieces* (2:12); this may help you convey Elisha's intense sense of loss. If you take this route, make sure to wait at least two to three seconds before concluding with, *The Word of the Lord* (or whatever phrase your church uses).

Pronunciation Guide

Bethel (BETH-uhl), *Elijah* (ee-LĪ-juh; ih-), *Elisha* (ee-LĪ-shuh; ih-), *Gilgal* (GIL-gal), *Jericho* (JAIR-ih-koh; -uh-), *Jordan* (JOR-duhn)

2 Corinthians 4:3–6

Notes

Sequence. 4 of 4

Commentary

In 2 Corinthians, Paul devotes significant space to defending himself and the gospel. Between the writing of 1 and 2 Corinthians, false apostles had infiltrated the church in Corinth. They were proclaiming a different gospel than the one Paul had preached to the Corinthians, and their message was gaining adherents (2 Cor 11:1–6). These "super-apostles," as Paul calls them pejoratively (11:5; 12:11), spend much of their time promoting themselves as they seek to discredit Paul's apostolic authority and credentials. Thus, Paul is forced to defend himself and his ministry so that the gospel of glory might not be undermined.

4:3–4. Leading into today's reading, Paul argues that he and his coworkers "refuse to practice cunning or to falsify God's word" (4:2). Here, Paul is either accusing his opponents of these practices or defending himself against such accusations, or perhaps both.

Another charge leveled against Paul concerns the effectiveness of his ministry. Not everyone who has heard Paul preach has been converted, and their unbelief is offered up as evidence that the gospel he proclaims is defective. For the sake of argument, Paul grants that the gospel has not always been understood and accepted, that at times its truth appears to be hidden from view. Even if the gospel is veiled, Paul maintains that it is only veiled to some, for many have come to faith in Christ. Only those who have allowed themselves to be blinded by Satan (and here Paul would include the false apostles) have failed to see the glory of the gospel, which is Jesus Christ, who is the spitting image of God himself.

4:5–6. Throughout the letter, Paul registers his frustration at having to defend his apostolic calling and qualifications. Instead of allowing themselves to be taken in by these false apostles, the Corinthians should have been defending Paul and the gospel he proclaimed. After all, he founded the church in Corinth. So, he chastises them: "I have been a fool! You forced me to it. Indeed you should have been the ones commending me, for I am not at all inferior to these super-apostles, even though I am nothing" (12:11).

Paul hates defending himself, not only because it gives the impression that he is engaging in a campaign of self-promotion just like the false apostles, but more importantly, because it takes people's attention away from the gospel and from Christ. So, in the midst of his defense, Paul reminds his readers that he is not proclaiming himself, but the good news that Jesus Christ is Lord of all. Paul is an apostle, but he does not regard this as a position of privilege. Compared to Jesus, Paul is just a slave, serving the Corinthians for the sake of Jesus. Paul did not choose to be an apostle; he simply responded to God's call. The God who began creation with the words, "Let there be light," is the same God who revealed Jesus to Paul in order that Paul might reveal Jesus as the face of God to the world.

Suggestions for Lectors

In today's reading, Paul strings prepositional phrases together. In 4:4, three phrases are strung together: *of the gospel of the glory of Christ.* And in 4:6, five are strung together: *of the knowledge of the glory of God in the face of Jesus Christ.* In normal, everyday speech, we usually only encounter two prepositional phrases in sequence, not three and certainly not five. In your preparations, practice reading and rereading these in context until your delivery—your timing, breathing, and intonation—become smooth and natural.

Below, the verses in which these prepositional phrases occur have been divided into intonational units. An intonational unit is a phrase or clause that should be read in one breath without any internal pauses. In 4:4, the three prepositional phrases are read as a single unit. Pause longer at the end of units 1 and 4 and more briefly at the end of units 2 and 3.

1 In their case . . . .
2 the god of this world has blinded the minds of the unbelievers, . .
[take a quick breath]
3 to keep them from seeing . .
4 the light of the gospel of the glory of Christ, ...
5 who is the image of God.

In 4:6, group the first three prepositional phrases into an intonational unit, and the last two into another unit. Pause longer at the end of units 1 and 2 and more briefly at the end of units 3 and 4.

1 For it is the God who said, ...
2 "Let light shine out of darkness, ...
3 who has shone in our hearts. . *[take a quick breath]*
4 to give the light of the knowledge of the glory of God. .
5 in the face of Jesus Christ.

If you decide that the intonational units or the length of pauses should be different from those presented above, then by all means change them. As lectors, we need to read texts in the way that feels most comfortable and right to us. Generally, there is more than one way to deliver a reading effectively; we simply need to be intentional about what we are doing.

Pronunciation Guide
Corinthians (kuh-RIN-thee-uhnz)

MARK 9:2–9

Notes
Sequence. 8 of 8

Commentary
One of the questions each of our NT gospels seeks to answer is, "Who is Jesus?" Ironically, the reader often has more insight into Jesus' identity than do the characters in the gospels, especially the disciples. For example, in Mark, the reader knows from the outset that Jesus is the Messiah, for the gospel begins: "The beginning of the good news of Jesus, *the Messiah*, the Son of God" (1:1, Adv 2). Yet, it is not until the midpoint of the gospel that the disciples finally recognize Jesus as the Messiah. After much prompting by Jesus, Peter declares, "You are the Messiah" (8:30, Prop 19).

Once his disciples know who he is, Jesus begins to tell them about his impending death and resurrection (8:31). He calls on them to take up their cross and follow him down that road of suffering and vindication (8:34–38). In other words, once the disciples know him to be the Messiah, Jesus reveals what being Messiah truly entails, for himself *and* for any who would follow him. Being the Messiah is not only about working miracles, it is also about redeeming and transforming a violent, sinful world

God's way, which often entails being on the receiving end of the world's sin and violence.

Immediately prior to today's episode, Jesus says to his disciples, "Truly I tell you, there are some standing here who will not taste death until they see that the kingdom of God has come with power." (9:1). In today's reading, three of Jesus' disciples are granted a preview of the kingdom coming in power when they see Jesus transfigured on the mountain.

The similarities between today's story and a story from Exodus are quite interesting. In Exodus 24:12–18, Moses ascends a mountain with his disciple and future successor, Joshua. In Matthew, Jesus ascends a mountain with his inner circle of disciples. After six days, Moses enters the cloud, and after six days, Jesus begins his ascent. In both readings, a cloud representing God's glory envelops the mountain.

9:2–8. When they ascend the mountain, Peter, James, and John see their master transfigured before their eyes. Jesus' clothes become dazzling white, and his face shines with the brilliance of the sun. Without warning, Moses and Elijah appear and converse with Jesus. Moses and Elijah represent the Law and the Prophets, yet their presence is also due to their having beheld God's glory on Mount Sinai (a.k.a., Mount Horeb; Exod 33:17–34:9; 1 Kgs 19:11–13).

When Peter suggests that three tabernacles be constructed—one for Jesus, one for Moses, and one for Elijah—he seems to assume that Moses and Elijah are in the same category as Jesus. Peter clearly does not understand. Suddenly a cloud envelopes them, and they hear a heavenly voice declaring, "This is my Son, the Beloved; with him I am well pleased; listen to him!" (9:7). This is the same pronouncement made by the heavenly voice at Jesus' baptism (1:11, Lent 2). It also foreshadows the declaration offered by the centurion at Jesus' crucifixion, "Truly this man was God's son" (15:39, Palm). Jesus is not only the Messiah, the one chosen to fulfill God's purposes in the world, he is also God's very own Son, making him far superior to Moses and Elijah.

9:9. Prior to today's episode, when Peter declared Jesus to be the Messiah, Jesus ordered the disciples not to reveal this to anyone (8:30, Prop 19). Similarly, Jesus instructs Peter, James, and John not to tell anyone about what they have seen on the mountain until after his resurrection. On neither of these occasions does Jesus give any reason for wanting his identity to remain a secret. Perhaps, he does not want to get diverted from his mission. Perhaps, he does not want people to misunderstand what he is about, especially since he understands his messianic vocation to be different from the popular notions of what the Messiah would be and do. Or, perhaps, it is simply not the right time.

Suggestions for Lectors

In today's reading, vary your tone with the changing narrative to help dramatize this episode and so attract your listeners' attention. After setting the scene with 9:2a, read 9:2b–4 with mounting intensity as the transfiguration takes place. Return to your basic storytelling voice for 9:5 as you draw the disciples back into the scene. In 9:6, drop your voice as the narrator interrupts the story to explain Peter's suggestion. In 9:7, slow your pace as the cloud descends and overshadows them. Increase your volume, but not your pitch, as you deliver the words of the unseen Voice. For dramatic effect, pause briefly after *This*, *Son*, and *Beloved* and emphasize *listen*, as in: *This… is my Son,… the Beloved;… listen to him!* (9:7). Pause afterwards, then read 9:8 with hints of confusion and bewilderment in your voice as you relay the sudden disappearance of Moses, Elijah, and the cloud. In 9:9, return to your normal narrative voice and speed as you close out the episode.

Pronunciation Guide

Beloved (n., buh-LUV-uhd)
Elijah (ee-LĪ-juh; ih-)
James (JAYMZ)
John (JAHN; JON)
Moses (MOH-zuhs)
Peter (PEE-ter)
Rabbi (RAB-bī)

SEASON OF LENT

ASH WEDNESDAY

Joel 2:1–2, 12–17 *or* Isaiah 58:1–12
Psalm 51:1–17; ✠ Psalm 103 *or* 103:8–14
2 Corinthians 5:20b–6:10
Matthew 6:1–6, 16–21

JOEL 2:1–2, 12–17

Commentary

The book of Joel belongs to a collection of OT writings known as the Book of the Twelve, which comprises the twelve Minor Prophets from Hosea to Malachi. Beyond the fact that Joel was a prophet and the son of Pethuel (Joel 1:1), we know nothing about him. The book of Joel can be divided into two major sections: the first concerns a devastating plague of locusts (1:1–2:17), and the second concerns the Day of the LORD (2:18–3:21, ✠ PentVig). Today's reading comes from the first section.

2:1–2. In 2:2–11, the prophet describes in vivid detail the devastation wrought by a plague of locusts throughout the land, which he likens to an invading army (1:6). So pervasive is the destruction that no one in living memory can recall witnessing or hearing anything like this ever happening before (1:2).

> What the cutting locust left,
>   the swarming locust has eaten.
> What the swarming locust left,
>   the hopping locust has eaten, and
> what the hopping locust left,
>   the destroying locust has eaten (1:4).

With these and other such descriptions, the reader glimpses the prophet's anguish and disbelief.

2:12–17. The prophet sees in the land's destruction a sign that the Day of the LORD's coming is drawing near. This day will be "a great and terrible day" (2:11) and "a day of darkness and gloom" (2:2) for it will be a day of judgment for the persistent sins of the people and their leaders. It is this day that the swarming locusts portend. Yet into this darkness, the LORD himself shines a ray of light. If the people would only return to the LORD with fasting, weeping, and mourning, rending their hearts instead of their clothing, then the Day of the LORD could be a day of forgiveness and restoration. For the LORD is "gracious and merciful, slow to anger, and abounding in steadfast love, and relents from punishing" (2:12–13). Here, in the second portion of today's reading, the prophet calls the priests to mourn in sackcloth and calls the elders and the people to fast as a sign of their repentance and their pledge to return to the LORD with their whole heart.

Suggestions for Lectors

Today's reading comprises two distinct sections, and you will want to adopt an appropriate voice and mood for each. In 2:1–2, with a loud prophetic voice full of foreboding, announce the coming day of judgment, the devastation of which is beyond all imagination. Read the final phrase, *in ages to come* (2:2), slowly, and then pause for a full second afterwards, looking up at your listeners giving this dark and gloomy vision a chance to sink in.

Beginning with 2:12, the mood changes completely as the message becomes one of hope and possibility. The LORD does not desire the destruction of his people, but merely their repentance and return, much as the prodigal father longed for the return of his prodigal son (Luke 15:11–32). Here, the prophet is not just engaging in wishful thinking, rather he knows the LORD to be a God who is *gracious and merciful, slow to anger, and abounding in steadfast love, and relents from punishing* (2:13b). This description of the LORD's identity and character recurs throughout the OT and is of central importance here. Thus, it should be given special attention in your reading. You might pause before and after it, reading it in a calmer, more deliberate fashion. Another phrase worthy of emphasis is *rend your hearts and not your clothing* (2:13a) as this gets at the heart of true repentance and connects with Jesus' teaching in today's gospel reading.

Pronunciation Guide

Joel (JOH-uhl; JOHL), *Zion* (ZĪ-uhn)

ISAIAH 58:1–12

Commentary

The prophetic speeches of Isaiah 40–66 presuppose that the people have been taken into exile in fulfillment of the judgment that was announced in Isaiah 1–39. Beginning with Isaiah 40, the message sent to the exiles in Babylon becomes one of reconciliation and forgiveness: "cry to her that she has served her term, that her penalty is paid, that she has received from the LORD's hand double for all her sins" (40:2, Adv 2). Isaiah's message also communicates the LORD's intention to gather his lost sheep and lead them back home (40:9–11, Adv 2).

Despite these promises, by the time of today's reading, the awaited return from exile has still not occurred. Isaiah 58 addresses the reasons for the delay. A few chapters earlier the prophet wrote, "Thus says the LORD: Maintain justice, and do what is right, for soon my salvation will come, and my deliverance be revealed" (56:1). At first, this sounds as though the LORD's promise of deliverance from exile is conditional, but that is not quite what is going on here. Instead, the people are being called to be active participants in the salvation that the LORD is bringing, for salvation and justice belong together. It must be remembered that the exiles of Israel and of Judah were due in large part to their long histories of injustice. "For the vineyard of the LORD of hosts is the house of Israel, and the people of Judah are his pleasant planting; he expected *justice*, but saw bloodshed; *righteousness*, but heard a cry!" (5:7). So, when the LORD announces that he has forgiven his people for their idolatry and injustice and he is bringing the exile to an end, he expects them to *respond* to his grace and mercy by repenting and recommitting themselves to their covenant obligations: to love the LORD with everything they are and have (Deut 6:5, Prop 26; Exod 20:1–7, Lent 3) and to love their neighbors as themselves (Lev 19:18; Exod 20:8–17).

This has not happened. So, in Isaiah 58, the prophet reminds the people of the sins that led to their exile and specifies what it is that the LORD is wanting from them. In today's reading, the prophet focuses on what it means to fast for God. Immediately after today's reading, he focuses on what it means to keep the sabbath (58:13–14). In short, fasting and sabbath keeping are about pursuing the LORD's interests, not our own (58:3, 13).

58:1–5. In the opening portion of today's reading, the people of God are frustrated at what appears to them to be a lack of responsiveness on the LORD's part. "Why," they ask, "do we fast, but you do not see? Why humble ourselves, but you do not notice?" (58:3). In other words, "We're doing our part, why aren't You?" The LORD responds by telling them that while they appear to be very religious, they are not particularly righteous. This is the same complaint the LORD hurled at them in Isaiah's opening chapter (1:11–15). The people's fasting has become self-serving. They think that they can practice injustice and then make up for it by performing religious rituals, but this is not the essence of the fasting in which the LORD delights and finds acceptable.

58:6–9a. Instead, God's chosen fast is about working for social justice—fighting oppression, feeding the hungry, clothing the naked, caring for the homeless poor, and embracing familial obligations. If the people would only commit themselves to serving the LORD by doing these things and maintaining justice (56:1), they would see the day of their salvation dawn, and they would find the LORD more responsive to their cries for assistance.

58:9b–12. This message is so important it is reiterated with different words and images. If the people would only provide for those in need, then they would find their own needs taken care of and soon find themselves back in a restored and rebuilt homeland.

Suggestions for Lectors

In today's reading, there is one speaker—the LORD—and two addressees. In 58:1–3a, the LORD addresses the prophet, telling him what to speak to the people. Then, beginning with *Look* in 58:3b, the LORD turns toward his people, as it were. Pause for a full second before *Look* to indicate this change in addressees. You might also wish to look up at this point as you begin to direct Isaiah's words to your listeners. Two additional full-second pauses could be inserted before 58:6 and 58:9b, *If you remove*, as these introduce new stanzas. Note where the LORD's tone is accusatory and intense and where it is gentle and inviting, and adjust your own voice accordingly.

Also pay attention to the imagery and especially to the poetic structure of the reading, where many of the lines occur in pairs. For example, 58:10 comprises two pairs of poetic lines (a-a', b-b'). Notice how the thoughts in a and b are restated in a' and b' using different words.

a if you offer your food to the hungry
a' and satisfy the needs of the afflicted,

In b-b', the sequence of the parallelism is reversed, where *your light* comes first in b, but the equivalent phrase *the noonday* comes second in b'. This is called a chiasm.

b then your light shall rise in the darkness
b' and your gloom be like the noonday.

By attending to such parallelism, your voice will fall into a cadence and an intonation that is well-suited for reading poetic texts and that will help your listeners to better experience, appreciate, and understand the reading.

Pronunciation Guide
bulrush (BOOL-ruhsh), *Isaiah* (ī-ZAY-uh)

2 Corinthians 5:20b–6:10

Commentary
In today's reading, Paul recounts the hardships that "we," Paul and Timothy, have endured as ministers of the gospel, as "ambassadors of Christ" (5:20a) who have been entrusted with "the message of reconciliation" (5:19). This message of reconciliation reveals that, through the life, death, resurrection, and ascension of Jesus Christ, God "was reconciling the world to himself, not counting their sins against them" (5:19). God has removed any obstacles between the world and himself, and he has called people like Paul and Timothy to announce to the world what God has accomplished in Christ for humanity.

5:20b–6:10. Today's reading begins with the appeal that God is making to all of humanity through his chosen ambassadors, "Be reconciled to God" (5:20b). For our sakes (not for God's), Jesus, who never sinned, became an offering for sin on our behalf so that any barriers that keep us from God (*not* God from us) might be removed so that we would be able to enter into a right-relationship with God. As Paul says, "All of this is from God, who reconciled us to himself through Christ" (5:18). So again, since God has already reconciled us to himself, God entreats us to respond to his gracious love, mercy, and forgiveness by being reconciled to God in return.

On this Ash Wednesday, we enter into the season of Lent, a season of preparation, self-examination and repentance. We enter Lent knowing that it is God who took the initiative to restore the broken relationship between humanity and himself and who "demonstrated his love for us in that, *while we were still sinners*, Christ died for us" (Rom 5:8). In this, God has given us the freedom we need to examine ourselves, to identify and confront our own sin and brokenness, and to turn everything over to God. We know that God's love and forgiveness are unconditional; they depend not upon who we are or what we have done, but solely upon who God is as revealed through what he has done in and through Christ.

Suggestions for Lectors

Today's reading begins quickly with the call to be reconciled to God, so open your reading somewhat slowly, yet with firmness. After reading *We entreat you on behalf of Christ*, pause for a second to create a sense of anticipation. Then read *be reconciled to God*, enunciating each word as you make eye contact with your listeners. In 5:21, accent the first *him* and the *we* to emphasize what Christ has done for us.

After the quotation from Isaiah, read its implications in an elevated animated voice: *See, now is the acceptable time; see, now is the day of salvation!* (6:2b); then, pause before continuing.

Reading lists, like the one contained in 6:4b–7a, can be a tricky business. One wants to avoid the extremes of monotonous recitation, on the one hand, and "punching" or over-emphasizing each item, on the other hand. To avoid these extremes, group the individual items of a list into intonational units, or phrases. These phrases should be of varying lengths, ranging from one to three, or even four items each. Do not group an entire list into phrases of the same length because this can produce a cadence with a sing-song quality. The following is just one example of how the items in 6:4b–7a could be grouped; you may wish to adopt different groupings:

> through great endurance,… in afflictions, hardships, calamities,…
> beatings, imprisonments,… riots, labors,… sleepless nights, hunger;…
> by purity, knowledge, patience, kindness,… holiness of spirit,…
> genuine love, truthful speech,… and the power of God;

The concluding verses (6:7b–10) have a rhetorically-rich repetitiveness to them that can be quite a joy to read aloud. Pay particular attention to the punctuation and vary the intonation of your voice to bring out the text's dynamics. Again, you do not want to fall into a sing-song cadence as you read, so vary your tempo as you make your way through these verses. For 6:8b–10, mark the contrasts clearly by the tones of your voice, concluding on a strong and positive note.

Pronunciation Guide

Corinthians (kuh-RIN-thee-uhnz)

MATTHEW 6:1–6, 16–21

Commentary

In the Sermon on the Mount, Jesus states that "unless your righteousness exceeds that of the scribes and Pharisees, you will never enter the kingdom of heaven" (Matt 5:20). In today's reading, Jesus gives us some insight into what he means by *the righteousness of the scribes and Pharisees*, and how we can surpass it.

6:1, Introduction. The righteousness of the scribes and Pharisees involved engaging in spiritual practices and habits—like almsgiving, prayer, and fasting—in such a way as to draw attention to themselves in an attempt to impress others with their piety, holiness, and religiosity. The practices themselves were not the problem, only the manner in which they were carried out. Jesus assumes that his followers will give alms, pray, and fast, but he calls them to carry out these actions covertly so that their energy and focus will be directed toward pleasing God and not toward impressing others, toward glorifying God and not themselves (cf. 5:16).

6:2–4, On Almsgiving. When Jesus' followers give to the poor, they should not announce it to the world by bringing along musical accompaniment. Instead, the one giving alms should give in so secretive a manner that they themselves do not even know they are giving alms. Here, of course, Jesus is engaging in a bit of hyperbole, but the point is not lost; for if our left hand does not know what our right hand is doing, then certainly no one else other than God will know.

Jesus labels those who draw attention to their own good deeds as hypocrites. In Greek, *hypocrite* was a word for *actor*, and so referred to a person who put on a mask, as was typical in Greek theater, and pretended to be someone they were not. For Jesus, hypocrites are those who present themselves as pious, that is, as honoring God, when in fact they are simply seeking their own glory through attempts to capture the attention and admiration of others. Interestingly, Jesus notes that hypocrites are indeed rewarded for their public display of piety; however, it is an earthly reward not a heavenly one.

6:5–6, On Prayer. When Jesus' followers pray, their focus should be upon God and not themselves. Consequently, they should not seek to draw attention to themselves by standing and praying in public, be it on the street corners or in the synagogue. Instead, when they wish to pray, they should go home and shut themselves in their room (or their closet), and pray to their heavenly Father who is himself in secret and so cannot be seen, and yet sees everything.

6:16–18, On Fasting. When Jesus' followers fast, they should not walk around with a sullen, gloomy and downcast countenance, but should anoint their heads with oil, a sign of celebration and joy. Likewise, Jesus' followers should not disfigure their faces as the hypocrites do, by pouring ashes on their head; instead they should wash their faces, which is not something ancient Jews did as a normal part of daily hygiene. Once again, Jesus offers practical advice for how we can engage in spiritual practices so that our focus is upon pleasing God and not upon courting the admiration and praise of others.

6:19–21, Conclusion. Today's reading concludes with Jesus calling on his followers to store up treasures in heaven instead of treasures on earth. One can certainly hear in these words a warning about the dangers of amassing material possessions. Yet given its present context, Jesus' warning entails more than just material wealth; it also includes one's efforts to amass personal glory and honor. For Jesus, to practice our piety so as to be seen and praised by others is in effect to store up for ourselves earthly treasures of human honor and prestige. These treasures are transitory; they can be eaten up and stolen by others just as any material possession can. If we practice our piety before God alone and solely for God's glory, our heavenly Father will reward us, and we shall indeed be storing up for ourselves treasures in heaven.

Suggestions for Lectors
In today's reading, Jesus is teaching, so adopt an instructional tone and manner of presentation. With the introduction, the reading can be read in five sections as indicated in the Commentary. Pause for a full second or two between sections. In 6:1, Jesus announces the basic principles that he will then explicate throughout the reading, so begin your reading with a loud, clear voice.

The three central sections follow the same basic pattern: (1) *whenever you...*, (2) *do not... hypocrites...*, (3) *Truly I tell you...*, (4) *but when...*, and (5) *your Father... will reward you.* So, when you work out how to read the first section in terms of tone, pace, pauses, and what words and phrases to emphasize, you can apply this to the second and third sections.

As was mentioned above, 6:19–21 is not so much another teaching as it is a summary of everything Jesus has taught since 6:1, so read it as the conclusion it is. Finish the reading by proclaiming 6:21 in a clear, strong voice so that your listeners are left with these powerful words ringing in their ears.

FIRST SUNDAY IN LENT

Genesis 9:8–17
Psalm 25:1–10 (= 25:1–9 BCP)
1 Peter 3:18–22
Mark 1:9–15

GENESIS 9:8–17

Notes
Sequence. 1 of 2

Commentary
From the time of Adam and Eve's expulsion from the garden of Eden until the time of Noah, sin and violence increase exponentially within the world so much so that God is sorry that he ever made human beings.

> The LORD saw that the wickedness of humankind was great in the earth, and that every inclination of the thoughts of their hearts was only evil continually. And the Lord was sorry that he had made humankind on the earth, and it grieved him to his heart (Gen 6:5–6).

Thus, the LORD decides to wipe out the human race along with all the other animals and creatures that live on land. Fortunately, the LORD finds in Noah someone he can work with. He instructs Noah to construct an ark that will preserve him, his family, and representatives of the animal kingdom.

In today's reading, the flood has already come and gone; the flood waters have abated, and the dry land has appeared. Noah and his family and all the living creatures with them have come out of the ark, the seeds of a new creation and a new humanity.

9:8–17. Though Noah is described as "a righteous man, blameless in his generation" (6:9), he is not perfect; and his sons are far from perfect (cf. 9:18–28). So, what will keep this from happening again? How can we be sure that God won't resort to another deluge to protect his good creation from the havoc wreaked by human sin and violence? This uncertainty regarding the future of the human race and creation is resolved when God makes a personal commitment to all who come out of the ark, human and animal alike. God's covenant with them and their offspring is that he will *never* again destroy the world and its inhabitants with a flood. As a sign of this eternal covenant, God will place a bow in the clouds that will serve two purposes. First, when human beings see the rainbow, they will be reminded of God's commitment to them. Second, when God himself sees the rainbow, he will be reminded of his covenant with creation and will act accordingly.

The fact that God, immediately after the flood, resolves never again to resort to a flood is significant. It suggests that the flood was at best a stopgap measure; that it was certainly not God's ultimate answer to the problem of human sin. For God, the world will not and cannot be redeemed through violence, but only through redemptive suffering which transforms sin, death, and violence into love, life, and peace. This is why the cross of Jesus serves as the most appropriate symbol of the Christian faith.

Suggestions for Lectors

In today's reading, God delivers a monologue that is fairly straightforward from beginning to end. You will not need to greatly modify the dynamics of your voice as you read, although, of course, you will want to avoid delivering the monologue in a monotone. God makes a personal promise to Noah and his sons, so you might invest your voice with a tone that conveys dependability and engenders trust.

Notice the interruptions that occur in 9:12 and 9:17. Although God remains the speaker and his audience does not change, the narrator inserts *God said* and *God said to Noah* into the speech. This technique is quite common in biblical narratives. Here it serves to highlight what is most important in God's speech. On both occasions, these interruptions are followed by, *This is the sign of the covenant*.... So when you deliver 9:12 and 9:17, decrease your tempo, and read these lines in a more deliberate fashion so that the references to *the sign of the covenant* stand out.

Pronunciation Guide

Genesis (JEN-uh-sis), *Noah* (NOH-uh)

1 PETER 3:18–22

Commentary

The First Letter of Peter identifies its author as the apostle Peter and its recipients as "the exiles of the Dispersion in Pontus, Galatia, Cappadocia, Asia, and Bithynia," which are all regions in Asia Minor, or present-day Turkey. "The Dispersion" (a.k.a., the Diaspora) was a term that collectively referred to Jews who resided outside the Jewish homeland. In the first century, significant Jewish populations pocketed the ancient world. This dispersion originated with the destructions of Israel (722 B.C.)

and Judah (586 B.C.), in which the people of God were exiled from their homeland and dispersed throughout the known world. In 1 Peter, the author uses "the Dispersion" metaphorically to designate Christians living in the world of the Roman Empire, a world whose values and way of life stand in stark contrast to those of God's Empire (cf. James 1:1). These first-century Christians have suffered and continue to suffer persecution for being followers of Jesus (cf. 4:16; 5:9). They live as exiles and aliens in a hostile world, and they are finding it difficult to live life between the time of God's promises and the fulfillment of those promises.

Prior to today's reading, Peter encourages his readers by saying they are blessed if they suffer for doing what is right (3:13). That being said, Peter does not advocate suffering for suffering's sake; in and of itself, suffering is not redemptive. Nor is it redemptive to respond to injustice with violence. If Christians repay "evil for evil or abuse for abuse" (3:9), then the cycle of sin and violence is neither broken nor transformed. Christians are called to repay evil and abuse with a blessing (3:9).

3:18–22. The followers of Christ are to follow his example. Christ demonstrated his righteousness by suffering for the sake of the unrighteous, so also Christians demonstrate their righteousness when they suffer injustice for the sake of the unjust. Clearly God has a burning desire to rescue sinners. Not only did Christ die for the sins of the world, he also proclaimed the gospel to the spirits of sinners from as far back as the time of Noah.

Suggestions for Lectors

Today's reading is compose of long, complex sentences. There are just three sentences in five verses. When confronted with such complex sentences, it is important for the lector to become familiar with their grammar and logic by reading the sentences through multiple times. Your challenge is to gain such a feel for the flow of the sentence that you are able, through strategically placed pauses and the intonation of your voice, to draw all of its phrases and clauses together into a single, coherent thought for your listeners. As always, your goal is to read in such a way that your listeners, with minimal effort, can follow the author's train of thought and understand what he is saying.

One way to get a handle on complex sentences is to reformat them so that you can more easily see their logic and flow. The following is just one way of visualizing a sentence's structure. The independent clauses have been underlined. These should stand out in your delivery.

18 For Christ also suffered for sins once for all,
the righteous for the unrighteous,
in order to bring you to God.
He was put to death in the flesh,
but made alive in the spirit,
19 in which also he went and made a proclamation to the spirits in prison,
20 who in former times did not obey,
when God waited patiently in the days of Noah,
during the building of the ark,
in which a few, that is, eight persons, were saved through water.

21 And baptism, which this prefigured, now saves you—
not as a removal of dirt from the body,
but as an appeal to God for a good conscience,
through the resurrection of Jesus Christ,
22 who has gone into heaven
and is at the right hand of God,
with angels, authorities, and powers made subject to him.

Pronunciation Guide

Noah (NOH-uh)

Mark 1:9–15

Notes

Sequence. 1 of 2

Commentary

In Hebrew, *messiah* means *anointed one.* A messiah is someone who is anointed with oil as a sign of having been commissioned by God to carry out a specific vocation or task. In the OT, it was principally kings and high priests, but sometimes prophets, who were anointed. In today's reading, Jesus is anointed for his messianic vocation, not with oil, but with the Holy Spirit in the waters of baptism. His anointing is then tested in the wilderness for a period of forty days, from which he emerges triumphant and victorious, ready to begin his ministry of proclaiming the arrival of God's kingdom.

1:9–11. Jesus joins the crowds of people who have journeyed out into the Judean wilderness to be baptized by John. When Jesus comes up out of the river, he sees the heavens being torn apart. In Matthew and Luke, the heavens simply *open* (Matt 3:16; Luke 3:21), but here they are *torn apart*, which is a much more dramatic descriptor. The only other occurrence of this verb in Mark is at Jesus' crucifixion. The moment Jesus breathes his last, the temple curtain is *torn* in two from top to bottom (15:38). The Gentile centurion then declares, "Truly this man was God's Son" (15:39).

The parallels between the Jesus' crucifixion and his baptism are striking, for when the heavens are torn apart, a voice declares Jesus to be God's beloved Son. In apocalyptic literature (like the book of Revelation), the rending of the sky indicates that a revelation is forthcoming. In Mark, these rendings of sky and curtain are preludes to the revelation of Jesus' divine identity. Of course, the scenes are quite different; one is glorious and the other tragic. But together they reveal what it means for Jesus to be the Son of God; it entails both glory and suffering.

The heavens are also rent so that the Holy Spirit might descend upon Jesus and anoint him for his messianic vocation. In the OT, Israel's king was often referred to as God's son (2 Sam 7:8–16, esp. 14). Psalm 2, which employs this language, is a royal psalm and is generally thought to have been used in the coronation ceremony of Israel's king. In it, the LORD says to the king, "You are my son; today I have begotten you. Ask of me, and I will make the nations your heritage, and the ends of the earth your possession" (2:7b–8). Likewise, Jesus' baptism serves as his coronation ceremony. He is anointed as the Messiah, the long-awaited king who will execute God's heavenly rule over the whole earth on God's behalf. Jesus is equipped for this messianic task by the Holy Spirit, and he is crowned with the dove of peace, a symbol reflecting the nature of kingdom that he rules—a peaceable kingdom in which a peaceful state of affairs is achieved by peaceful means.

1:12–13. In Matthew and Luke, the Spirit *leads* Jesus into the wilderness (Matt 4:1; Luke 4:1), but in Mark, the Spirit *drives* him into the wilderness. It is almost as if Jesus is possessed by the Spirit. In the OT, the Israelites' forty-year sojourn in the wilderness prepares them for life in the Promised Land. As Moses says, "Remember the long way that the LORD your God has led you these forty years in the wilderness, in order to humble you, testing you to know what was in your heart, whether or not you would keep his commandments" (Deut 8:2). Similarly, Jesus is tested for a period of forty days in the wilderness to prepare him for his messianic vocation.

As the Messiah, Jesus has been anointed to establish the kingdom of God in a world that is under the dominion of Satan. In order to do that, Jesus must first defeat Satan. As he says in a parable, "No one can enter a strong man's house and plunder his property without first tying up the strong man; then indeed the house can be plundered" (3:27). When Jesus emerges from the wilderness, he begins to proclaim the good news that the kingdom of God has arrived (1:15), and his first public act is to exorcise a demon (1:21–28, Epi 4). It appears, then, that Jesus did more than pass a test in the wilderness; he won a decisive victory over Satan. He bound the strong man, Satan, and then began plundering his property by setting people free from unclean spirits, sickness, and sin, thereby redeeming and transforming the world by the power of the kingdom.

1:14–15. Jesus emerges from the wilderness only to discover that John the Baptist has been arrested. At this point in the narrative, the circumstances surrounding the Baptist's arrest are not given; that story will be told later (6:14–29, Prop 10). Instead, the reader is told that Jesus returns to Galilee, where he begins a ministry of proclaiming the gospel, of announcing the good news that the kingdom of God had arrived. The term *gospel* was often used in connection with military victories, so when we hear Jesus announce the good news of God's kingdom, we should also hear him announcing the defeat and downfall of Satan.

In the gospels, *the kingdom of God* refers to God's rule or reign or, one might even say, God's government. Given that Jesus heralds the arrival of God's kingdom in a country that has been ruled by foreign empires for the better part of six hundred years, it would also make sense to speak in terms of *the empire of God.*

As with any new administration or government, the advent of God's empire means that things will change. God's way of conducting business in the world is radically different from the way the world conducts its business. Therefore, those who wish to participate in God's new world must repent. They must let go of the world's values, its ways of being and doing. Instead, they must put their trust in God and practice God's way of being and doing in the world.

Suggestions for Lectors

Today's episode consists of three scenes, all of which are quite brief. So read at a slightly-reduced tempo in order to give each scene more time to play out.

Despite the paucity of description in Mark's account of Jesus' baptism, the scene is quite breathtaking, so read 1:10 with a sense of awe in order to convey the sheer wonder and majesty of it all. Read 1:11 slowly and deliberately, enunciating each word with care. Read it with a smile on your face as though you are a proud parent.

As lectors, when we emphasize something in a reading by changing the tone, pitch, or volume of our voice, we are bringing that element to the foreground while resigning other elements to the background, which affects how our listeners understand and experience the text. That is why it is so important to make conscious decisions regarding what to and what not to emphasize, though there is rarely only one way of reading a text that is faithful to its meaning. Consider the following.

When the heavenly Voice declares, *You are my Son, the Beloved*, there is more than one way to add emphasis:

> *You* are my Son, the Beloved;
> You are *my Son*, the Beloved;
> You are my Son, *the Beloved*;

Each of these renderings faithfully represents the text, but they are all slightly different. So, as you prepare for this and other readings, take the time to think through the question of emphasis. What might I emphasize, how shall I emphasize it, and what will be its impact upon my listeners?

In the final scene, emphasize Jesus' proclamation by increasing the volume and intensity of your voice. In 1:15, pause after *fulfilled*, *near*, and *repent* and also underscore the two commands, as in: *The time is fulfilled,… and the kingdom of God has come near;… repent… and believe in the good news.*

Pronunciation Guide

Beloved (n., buh-LUV-uhd)
Galilee (GAL-uh-lee)
Jordan (JOR-duhn)
Nazareth (NAZ-uh-reth; *not* -rus)
Satan (SAY-tuhn)

SECOND SUNDAY IN LENT

Genesis 17:1–7, 15–16
Psalm 22:23–31 (= 22:22–30 BCP)
Romans 4:13–25
Mark 8:31–38 *or* Mark 9:2–9; ✠ *omit* Mark 9:2–9

GENESIS 17:1–7, 15–16

Notes
Sequence. 2 of 2

Commentary
In last week's OT reading, we read of God's covenant with Noah and his offspring, a covenant in which God promises never again to send a flood to destroy the world. In today's reading, we read of God's covenant with Abram, a descendant of Noah through his son Shem (Gen 11:10–26).

When the LORD first called Abram and Sarai in Genesis 12, he promised to make them into a great nation by blessing them with children and generation upon generation of descendants (12:2–3). Abram and Sarai were a most unlikely choice, for at the time they were seventy-five and sixty-five years old respectively; and more to the point, Sarai was barren and childless (11:30). Nevertheless, they demonstrated their trust by relocating to the land of Canaan as the LORD had directed.

Today's reading takes place nearly twenty-five years later, and much has transpired. They have endured famine and war and more years of barrenness. After having lived in the Promised Land for an entire decade without conceiving, they took matters into their own hands. Sarai offered up her Egyptian slave-girl, Hagar, as a surrogate (16:1–3). Hagar conceived and gave birth to Ishmael, whom Abram and Sarai have treated as the promised offspring.

17:1–7. In today's reading, Ishmael is thirteen years old when the LORD appears to Abram to reaffirm his original promise to make Abram "exceedingly numerous" and "the ancestor of a multitude of nations" (17:3–4). To indicate that these things are about to come to pass, the LORD changes Abram's name. No longer will he be called *Abram*, that is, *exalted father*; rather, from now on, he shall be called *Abraham*, that is, *the father of a multitude.*

17:15–16. For her part, Sarai will no longer be *Sarai*, but *Sarah*. Etymologically, both names mean *princess*, but *Sarah* represents her new identity as the mother of nations and kings.

Incidentally, this is the first time in the narrative that a child has been specifically promised to Sarah. Up to this point, it would appear that both Abram and Sarai have been operating out of a patriarchal worldview, assuming that the promised heir need only be of Abraham's issue. In fact, right after the LORD's pronouncement, Abraham laughs at the thought that his ninety-year-old barren Sarai could bear a child and asks God to regard Ishmael as the promised heir: "O that Ishmael might live in your sight!" (17:18). The LORD, however, objects. "No, but your wife Sarah shall bear you a son" (17:19).

A change of names means a change of identity, purpose, and destiny. This unlikely elderly couple has been chosen and blessed by God to be the matriarch and patriarch of God's special covenant people, a people that God will fashion in his own image in order that they might be the vehicle through which God will bless all peoples everywhere. Through Abraham and Sarah, "*all* the families of the earth shall be blessed" (12:3).

Suggestions for Lectors

Learning to handle repetition is an important part of becoming a good lector. Repetition is a characteristic feature of biblical literature, especially in the narratives of the OT. There are many different types of repetition in the Bible, some of which present a challenge to modern listeners who experience it as superfluous and monotonous. For example, in today's reading, the phrase, "your offspring after you," occurs three times within a span of two verses (17:7–8):

> I will establish my covenant between me and you, *and your offspring after you* throughout their generations, for an everlasting covenant, to be God to you *and to your offspring after you.* And I will give to you, *and to your offspring after you*, the land where you are now an alien, all the land of Canaan, for a perpetual holding; and I will be their God.

When faced with this type of repetition, lectors sometimes unconsciously adopt a tone of voice that is essentially apologetic, as if to say, "I know this seems a bit repetitious and is hard to listen to, but bear with me while I get through it." Sometimes a lector will quickly read through the repetitive elements in order to get past them to what seems more important and interesting.

Yet, in today's reading, the repeated phrase, *your offspring after you*, serves an important rhetorical function. Note that God is promising to make Abraham the ancestor of a multitude of nations, which means that the covenant being established is not simply between God and Abraham but between God and all of Abraham's offspring. In fact, one might reasonably argue that the covenant is more about Abraham's offspring than about Abraham himself because it is an *eternal* covenant and Abraham's life is short by comparison. In any case, the repetition of *your offspring after you* is not accidental or inconsequential; rather it highlights what God is really promising, and it shows the extent of God's commitment to Abraham and Sarah. Repetition such as this often indicates what is important in a text, and so it affords the lector insight into what should be highlighted in their delivery.

In addition to repetition, it is important for lectors to learn to handle complex sentences, and today's reading is filled with them. A prime example is 17:7–8 with all of its phrases, clauses, and punctuation. The best approach to learning to read complex sentences is to prepare, prepare, prepare and practice, practice, practice. As you prepare, read the sentences over and over again until you are able to read them smoothly and naturally with minimal effort. Work out the best places to pause, the best places to take breaths, and the intonation for each element.

Pronunciation Guide

Abram (AY-bruhm)
Abraham (AY-bruh-ham)
Canaan (KAY-nuhn)
Sarah (SAIR-uh)
Sarai (SAIR-ī)

Romans 4:13–25

Commentary

Prior to Romans 4, Paul makes the argument that all people—both Jews and Gentiles—enter into a right-relationship with God on the basis of faith, quite apart from performing the works of the law (3:28). As the prophet Habakkuk said, "The one who is righteous will live by faith" (Hab 2:4; Rom 1:17). This raises some questions. If it is true that a person is made righteous by faith alone, what is the purpose of circumcision and the law? What has become of God's promises to Israel, promises that are linked with the covenant of circumcision given through Abraham and the covenant of the law given through Moses? These questions are of critical importance because God's trustworthiness is at stake. If the righteousness that comes by faith displaces the righteousness that comes through the law, then hasn't God broken his covenant with his chosen people? And if that is the case, how can those who base their salvation on faith in Jesus be assured that this new covenant will not be broken in the future? In other words, if God has changed the rules once, what is to keep him from changing them again?

These are the questions that Paul wrestles with in Romans 4, and he will make two points. First, faith takes precedence because it was in play before circumcision or the law came along. Second, neither circumcision nor the law were introduced to replace faith, but rather to support faith as the basis of a right-relationship with God. When Paul writes, "But *now*, apart from the law, the righteousness of God has been disclosed,… the righteousness of God through the faith of Jesus Christ for all who believe" (3:21–22), he is not saying that righteousness by faith alone is a new thing, for faith has always been the basis of a covenant relationship with God. Instead, what is new is that this righteousness by faith is now received not by simply trusting in God, but by trusting in God's Son, Jesus the Christ, whose own faithfulness to God even unto death has become the basis of justification by faith alone.

4:13–25. Paul begins his defense of God's covenant faithfulness and of the righteousness that comes by faith by recalling the story of the patriarch Abraham. Paul appeals to Abraham for two reasons. First of all, Abraham is an example of someone God regarded as righteous solely because he trusted God. Had Abraham been declared righteous because he obeyed the law, his righteousness would have been payment for a job well done and, therefore, something he could have been proud of (4:3–5). As it is, Abraham was reckoned righteous because he believed God's promise that his descendants would be as numerous as the stars of heaven, despite the fact that he was an old man and his beloved Sarah was barren (Gen 15:5–6). Abraham's righteousness was not earned as a wage but received as a gift. Having no basis for boasting in his accomplishments, all that remained for Abraham was to give thanks to God for his gracious gift of righteousness.

More importantly, Paul appeals to Abraham because he sees in God's calling of Abraham the beginning of the story of God's chosen people, a story that reaches its climax in the life, death, resurrection, and ascension of Jesus of Nazareth. God's vision was to rescue creation from its subjugation to sin, violence, and death. Central to creation's renewal was the return of human beings to their vocation as God's image-bearers. God chose Abraham and Sarah to be the patriarch and matriarch of a special, covenant people who would perform a key role in God's plan to reverse the effects of Adam and Eve's disobedience, thereby bringing all of humanity back into a right-relationship with God. As we read in today's OT lesson, the LORD said to Abraham (Gen 12:1–3):

> Go from your country and your kindred and your father's house to the land that I will show you. I will make of you a great nation, and I will bless you, and make your name great, *so that you will be a blessing*. I will bless those who bless you, and the one who curses you I will curse; and in you all the families of the earth shall be blessed.

Here, we see that God's choosing of Abraham and Sarah had a broader purpose. God intends to bless them so that they and their offspring might be a blessing. For Paul, the Jews were not merely the recipients of God's blessing but the means by which God's blessing would come to the Gentiles. As a Jewish apostle to the Gentiles, Paul sees himself as having been entrusted with this blessing for the Gentiles, which he offers by proclaiming the good news that salvation is a gift received by faith in Jesus Christ, the offspring of Abraham and Sarah.

When the LORD changed Abram's name to Abraham, he said, "No longer shall your name be Abram, but your name shall be Abraham; for I have made you the ancestor of a multitude of nations" (Gen 17:5, see OT reading above). Little did he know at the time that he would one day become a spiritual father, whose children would include all who, like himself, were made righteous by faith and not by the law. When Christians read of Abraham, "that it was reckoned to him as righteousness" (Rom 4:22), they can hear a description of themselves. For they belong to Abraham's family by virtue of having come to believe in Jesus, who died to free us from our transgressions of the law and who was raised that we, who were spiritually dead, might live in a new right-relationship with God by faith.

Suggestions for Lectors

Nothing helps us in our role as lectors as much as understanding what we are reading. When we study, work with, and come to understand the passage we have been entrusted with, we are better able to convey that understanding through our delivery. When we understand what we are reading, we intuitively adopt speech patterns that help us communicate the meaning of what we are reading to our listeners. The Commentary has been designed to support lectors in their understanding of the text, but nothing can replace situating a reading within its biblical context by reading the passages surrounding the assigned reading. This is particularly true when dealing with a complex argument like Paul's treatise on faith, righteousness, and the law. So, as part of your preparation for today's reading, read Romans 4:1–5:11.

Throughout Romans, Paul explains and defends his understanding of the gospel, so read with conviction and confidence. Imagine that you are the apostle and that you are responding to your listeners' questions and doubts as you attempt to persuade them of your position.

The reading is relatively straightforward except for 4:16–17, which is convoluted. The primary difficulty concerns the parenthetical expression that interrupts the flow of Paul's thought.

> For this reason it depends on faith,
> in order that the promise may rest on grace
> and be guaranteed to all his descendants,
> not only to the adherents of the law
> but also to those who share the faith of Abraham
> *(for he is the father of all of us,*
> *as it is written, "I have made you the father of many nations")—*
> in the presence of the God in whom he believed,
> who gives life to the dead
> and calls into existence the things that do not exist.

Maintain your intonation as you read, *but also to those who share the faith of Abraham... in the presence of the God in whom he believed*, and drop your voice as you interrupt this statement with the parenthetical aside *(for he is the father of all of us, as it is written, "I have made you the father of many nations")*. In other words, read *in the presence of the God in whom he believed*, not as though it were a new thought, but as though it continues a previous thought. This is not the easiest sentence to deliver, so spend time working on it, and do your best to make it smooth.

Pronunciation Guide
Abraham (AY-bruh-ham), *Sarah* (SAIR-uh)

MARK 8:31–38

Notes
Sequence. 2 of 2

Commentary
Prior to today's reading, Jesus and his disciples traveled north to Caesarea Philippi, deep in Gentile territory. On the way, Jesus asked his disciples about people's speculations regarding his identity, "Who do people say that I am?" (8:27, Prop 19). After they responded, Jesus then turned the question on them, "But who do *you* say that I am?" Peter, speaking for the disciples, declared, "You are the Messiah" (8:29).

Peter's confession is a watershed moment. The exorcisms, healings, and mighty deeds that are so prominent in the first half of the gospel all but come to an end in the second half. In their place, Jesus begins to prepare his disciples for the fate that awaits him in Jerusalem.

8:31–33. Now that his disciples know he is the Messiah, Jesus begins to reveal what his messianic vocation entails. "He began to teach them that the Son of Man must undergo great suffering, and be rejected by the elders, the chief priests, and the scribes, and be killed, and after three days rise again" (8:31). Here, we see that Jesus is no longer speaking in metaphor and in parable; rather, he is speaking quite openly and unambiguously about his death.

Jesus predicts his suffering, death, and resurrection three times in Mark (8:31; 9:30–32; 10:32–34), and each of these passion predictions follows the same pattern. After each prediction, the disciples do or say something that indicates they have not fully understood the implications of what Jesus has told them. In today's episode, Peter plays this part. He rebukes Jesus for talking about suffering and death, and he thereby exposes a deficiency in his and the other disciples' understanding of who Jesus is. Just a few moments previous, Peter correctly identified Jesus as the Messiah, but clearly he does not understand what messiahship entails.

Here, Peter is like the blind man Jesus had to touch twice in order to restore him to full sight (8:22–26). When the blind man is brought for healing, Jesus spits in his eyes and touches him. Jesus then asks him, "Can you see anything?," to which he replies, "I can see people, but they look like trees, walking" (8:24). Jesus then touches the blind man a second time, and finally "he can see everything clearly" (8:25). Like the blind man after Jesus' first touch, Peter sees who Jesus is, but his vision is blurred. The disciples have seen Jesus say and do some powerful and amazing things, and on this basis, they rightly recognize that Jesus is the Messiah. Yet, again their sight is only partial. If they (and we as Mark's readers) are to gain full sight of who Jesus is as Messiah and Son of God, a second touch is required.

In Mark, second touch that brings full sight is the crucifixion itself, which constitutes a second climactic recognition scene. When the Gentile centurion sees the way in which Jesus dies, he declares, "Truly this man was God's Son!" (15:39, Palm). The centurion stands out as the only human character in Mark to recognize Jesus as the Son of God. Demons know it (1:24, 34; 3:11; 5:7), and God declares it (1:11; 9:7), but again, the centurion is the only *human* character to recognize and acknowledge Jesus as God's Son. Ironically, it is not one of Jesus' miracles, but rather his death that generates the centurion's insight. Jesus' death on the cross is not only a sacrifice for sins (cf. 10:45; 14:24), it is also the means by which his divine identity is fully and finally made known. In short, the crucifixion is an act of divine revelation.

The authoritative words and deeds of Jesus reveal him to be the Messiah (the first touch), but it is only his suffering and death that reveal him to be the divine Son of God (the second touch). Together, these two confessions—Messiah and Son of God—paint the full picture of who Jesus is (cf. 1:1). In today's episode, the disciples are halfway there. From Jesus' exorcisms and healings, they have rightly discerned that he is the Messiah who has come to usher in the kingdom of God. But, only when the disciples are finally able to incorporate suffering and death into their understanding of who Jesus is as the Messiah will they have full insight, not only into who Jesus is, but also into who they are as his followers.

Unfortunately, the disciples never come to full recognition of who Jesus is, at least not within the narrative of Mark's gospel. In the end, they abandon Jesus to his fate, and he dies alone, forsaken by his closest companions and seemingly forsaken by God. Thus, it is up to a Gentile centurion—a non-Jew and a non-disciple—to receive the revelation of who Jesus is as the suffering Son of God.

8:34–38. If the way of the Messiah entails suffering and death, then the way of the Messiah's disciples will also entail suffering and death. Paradoxically, only those who give up their lives for Jesus and the gospel will save their lives. When Jesus says, "Those who are ashamed of me and my words..." (8:38), Peter's rebuke of Jesus is in the background. In this context, to be ashamed of the Messiah is to reject the way of the Messiah and so refuse to walk the way of the cross. Those who are ashamed of Jesus will find that he is ashamed of them when he appears in all his kingly glory. Persons cannot share in Jesus' messianic glory unless they are also willing to share in his messianic suffering.

Without diminishing the severity of these words or the importance of taking up one's cross, it is of some comfort to recall that every one of Jesus' disciples abandoned him, yet he did not abandon them. On the eve of his crucifixion, Jesus predicts that his disciples will all desert him, yet he promises to meet them again in Galilee after his resurrection (14:27–28). Peter denies Jesus, and the rest run away, but Jesus still forgives them. Anyone who wants to follow Jesus must travel the way of suffering and death; there are no exceptions. Fortunately, however, there are signposts and rest stops of grace all along the way.

Suggestions for Lectors

Although Jesus speaks in the third person (the Son of Man), he is talking about his own fate, so read with evident emotion in your voice. Read slowly and adopt a tone of voice that conveys the gravity of what Jesus is trying to communicate to his disciples. Raise and harden your voice when rebuking Peter. Emphasize *Satan*, *not*, *divine*, and *human*, and also introduce slight pauses after *mind* and *things*, as in: *Get behind me, Satan! For you are setting your mind... not on divine things... but on human things* (8:33).

Pause for a full second as the scene shifts from the disciples to the crowds. Then, raise your voice and proclaim Jesus' words to your listeners as though they are meant for them—which, of course, they are. Highlight Jesus' first two statements by reading them slowly and deliberately. In the first statement, emphasize all of the imperatives: *deny*, *take up*, and *follow* (8:34). In the second statement, emphasize *save* and *lose*, both of which occur twice (8:35). In 8:36–37, shift to a slightly higher tempo, then reduce the tempo for 8:38. In this final declaration, emphasize both occurrences of *ashamed* (8:38).

MARK 9:2–9

Notes

Sequence. 2 of 2

Commentary

One of the questions each of our NT gospels seeks to answer is, "Who is Jesus?" Ironically, the reader often has more insight into Jesus' identity than do the characters in the gospels, especially the disciples. For example, in Mark, the reader knows from the outset that Jesus is the Messiah, for the gospel begins: "The beginning of the good news of Jesus, *the Messiah*, the Son of God" (1:1, Adv 2). Yet, it is not until the midpoint of the gospel that the disciples finally recognize Jesus as the Messiah. After much prompting by Jesus, Peter declares, "You are the Messiah" (8:30, Prop 19).

Once his disciples know who he is, Jesus begins to tell them about his impending death and resurrection (8:31). He calls on them to take up their cross and follow him down that road of suffering and vindication (8:34–38). In other words, once the disciples know him to be the Messiah, Jesus reveals what being Messiah truly entails, for himself *and* for any who would follow him. Being the Messiah is not only about working miracles, it is also about redeeming and transforming a violent, sinful world God's way, which often entails being on the receiving end of the world's sin and violence.

Immediately prior to today's episode, Jesus says to his disciples, "Truly I tell you, there are some standing here who will not taste death until they see that the kingdom of God has come with power." (9:1). In today's reading, three of Jesus' disciples are granted a preview of the kingdom coming in power when they see Jesus transfigured on the mountain.

The similarities between today's story and a story from Exodus are quite interesting. In Exodus 24:12–18, Moses ascends a mountain with his disciple and future successor, Joshua. In Matthew, Jesus ascends a mountain with his inner circle of disciples. After six days, Moses enters the cloud, and after six days, Jesus begins his ascent. In both readings, a cloud representing God's glory envelops the mountain.

9:2–8. When they ascend the mountain, Peter, James, and John see their master transfigured before their eyes. Jesus' clothes become dazzling white, and his face shines with the brilliance of the sun. Without warning, Moses and Elijah appear and converse with Jesus. Moses and Elijah represent the Law and the Prophets, yet their presence is also due to their having beheld God's glory on Mount Sinai (a.k.a., Mount Horeb; Exod 33:17–34:9; 1 Kgs 19:11–13).

When Peter suggests that three tabernacles be constructed—one for Jesus, one for Moses, and one for Elijah—he seems to assume that Moses and Elijah are in the same category as Jesus. Peter clearly not does understand. Suddenly a cloud envelopes them, and they hear a heavenly voice declaring, "This is my Son, the Beloved; with him I am well pleased; listen to him!" (9:7). This is the same pronouncement made by the heavenly voice at Jesus' baptism (1:11, Lent 2). It also foreshadows the declaration offered by the centurion at Jesus' crucifixion, "Truly this man was God's son" (15:39, Palm). Jesus is not only the Messiah, the one chosen to fulfill God's purposes in the world, he is also God's very own Son, making him far superior to Moses and Elijah.

9:9. Prior to today's episode, when Peter declared Jesus to be the Messiah, Jesus ordered the disciples not to reveal this to anyone (8:30, Prop 19). Similarly, Jesus instructs Peter, James, and John not to tell anyone about what they have seen on the mountain until after his resurrection. On neither of these occasions does Jesus give any reason for wanting his identity to remain a secret. Perhaps, he does not want to get diverted from his mission. Perhaps, he does not want people to misunderstand what he is about, especially since he understands his messianic vocation to be different from the popular notions of what the Messiah would be and do. Or, perhaps, it is simply not the right time.

Suggestions for Lectors

In today's reading, vary your tone with the changing narrative to help dramatize this episode and so attract your listeners' attention. After setting the scene with 9:2a, read 9:2b–4 with mounting intensity as the transfiguration takes place. Return to your basic storytelling voice for 9:5 as you draw the disciples back into the scene. In 9:6, drop your voice as the narrator interrupts the story to explain Peter's suggestion. In 9:7, slow your pace as the cloud descends and overshadows them. Increase your volume, but not your pitch, as you deliver the words of the unseen Voice. For dramatic effect, pause briefly after *This*, *Son*, and *Beloved* and emphasize *listen*, as in: *This… is my Son,… the Beloved;… listen to him!* (9:7). Pause afterwards, then read 9:8 with hints of confusion and bewilderment in your voice as you relay the sudden disappearance of Moses, Elijah, and the cloud. In 9:9, return to your normal narrative voice and speed as you close out the episode.

Pronunciation Guide

Beloved (n., buh-LUV-uhd), *Elijah* (ee-LĪ-juh; ih-), *James* (JAYMZ),
John (JAHN; JON), *Moses* (MOH-zuhs), *Peter* (PEE-ter), *Rabbi* (RAB-bī)

THIRD SUNDAY IN LENT

Exodus 20:1–17
Psalm 19
1 Corinthians 1:18–25
John 2:13–22

Exodus 20:1–17

Commentary

After their dramatic escape from Egypt, the Israelites are led by stages through the wildernesses to Mount Sinai (= Mount Horeb), where Moses first encountered the LORD in the burning bush (3:1–6). In that encounter Moses asks God, "Who am I that I should go to Pharaoh and bring the Israelites out of Egypt?" (3:11), to which God replies, "I will be with you; and this shall be the sign for you that it is I who sent you: when you have brought the people out of Egypt, you shall worship God on this mountain" (3:12). In Exodus 19, that sign is fulfilled.

When they arrive at the mountain, the LORD begins to define the terms of the covenant that will govern the relationship between him and the Israelites. If the Israelites obediently keep their side of the covenant, then the LORD will make them his "treasured possession out of all the peoples" of the earth (19:5), and Israel will become for God "a priestly kingdom and a holy nation" (19:6a). In other words, as Israel lives in covenant relationship with the LORD, Israel will begin to acquire, embody, and reflect the very character of God. This will equip the chosen people to serve as God's priests to the world, mediating the presence, knowledge, and forgiveness of God to all peoples everywhere. Being God's treasured people does not so much characterize Israel's *status* as it defines Israel's *vocation*; being the chosen people of God signifies obligation not privilege. When Moses lays out the terms of the covenant before the people, they readily assent saying, "Everything that the LORD has spoken we will do" (19:8).

The covenant is officially ratified with a ceremony. The people are instructed to gather at the foot of the mountain, but they are not to attempt to go up the mountain or even touch it under penalty of death (19:12–13). Moses alone ascends the shaking, smoking mountain amidst sounds of loud trumpets and thunder and lighting. Out of the cloud, the LORD's voice is heard proclaiming the Ten Commandments, or the Decalogue (literally, "the Ten Words" in Hebrew (Exod 34:28; Deut 4:13; 10:4)).

The Ten Commandments are to govern and shape the lives of the Israelites as they seek to live out their vocation as a light and blessing unto the nations. The commandments fall into two principal groupings. The first four specify how the Israelites are to honor and respect their God (20:3–11), while the remaining six specify how the people are to respect and honor one another (20:12–17). This is why Jesus can condense the entire law and prophets into just two commandments: love of God and love of neighbor (Matt 22:37–40).

20:1–2. In the various debates in the United States over whether the Ten Commandments can or should be posted in government buildings or public school classrooms, there is one element that is often overlooked or underappreciated. Namely, the Ten Commandments is not a statement of general morality that all members of a secular society could easily agree to. Certainly the commandments governing relations between human beings, such as the prohibitions against murder and theft, fit the category of general morality, but the commandments governing the relationship between human beings and God do not. Why? Because the Ten Commandments were not intended to serve as a timeless treatise on how all people everywhere should live and act. In their original biblical and historical context, the Ten Commandments served to govern the special covenant relationship between the LORD, Yahweh, and his chosen people, the Israelites.

This is clearly seen in the fact that the Ten Commandments does not begin with a commandment but with a narrative. "I am the LORD your God, who brought you out of the land of Egypt, out of the house of slavery" (20:2). Here, the LORD lays claim to Israel. The LORD acted on Israel's behalf, so the people owe him their complete allegiance and obedience. "The law expresses the will of God for Israel. It spells out what God requires from a covenant people whom he delivered without demanding a prior commitment."[3] In short, the Ten Commandments cannot be divorced from the particular historical narrative of which it is a part. Only when that setting is fully appreciated, can we begin to discern how the Commandments might apply to our contemporary context, both inside and outside the church.

20:3–11, Love of God. One would think that *the belief* in the existence of only one god (monotheism) would naturally precede *the worship* of only one god (monolatry), yet that is not how we find it presented here. At the time of the giving of the Ten

---

[3] Brevard S. Childs, *The Book of Exodus: A Critical, Theological Commentary* (Old Testament Library; Louisville, Ky.: Westminster, 1974), 402.

Commandments, the Israelites did not yet believe that the LORD was the only god there was, nor did the LORD require them to. Instead, the LORD demanded that they worship him alone. "I am the LORD your God, who brought you out of the land of Egypt, out of the house of slavery; [therefore] *you shall have no other gods before me*" (20:2–3). This is followed by a ban on all idol production and worship, the reason being, "for I the LORD your God am a jealous God" (20:5). Interestingly, the LORD does not demand Israel's undivided loyalty because he is the only god on the market. The people's loyalty to the LORD is not rooted in monotheism, at least not in this stage of their relationship with God. Instead, Israel's call to monolatry is in recognition of the fact that the LORD alone, and no other god, was responsible for safely leading Israel out of Egypt. It is not until one gets to prophets like Isaiah that one encounters unambiguous statements that the other so-called gods do not actually exist (cf. Isa 44:6–20).

Refraining from work every seventh day is a significant act of trust, especially for a people who live in a subsistence economy. Beyond providing the obvious benefits of rest, observing the sabbath serves as a constant reminder that it is the LORD who provides, even if it is we who do the work.

20:12–17, Love of neighbor. The first commandment governing human relationships stands out among the rest on two accounts. First, it is stated positively, "Honor your father and your mother," whereas all the others begin with, "You shall not...." In addition, this is the only commandment of the six that offers a rationale. Or, in the words of Paul, "this is the first commandment with a promise" (Eph 6:2).

The final commandment prohibits coveting. It stands out among the other prohibitions in both length and detail. It is by far the longest of the five and, in fact, longer than the other four combined. Perhaps this signifies its importance. If people successfully curbed their covetous impulses, then perhaps the other prohibitions would not present a significant problem. If people did not covet their neighbors' possessions, then perhaps they would never feel compelled to steal, murder, or misrepresent their neighbors in court. Likewise, if a person did not covet their neighbor's spouse, then perhaps they would never find themselves tempted to commit adultery.

Suggestions for Lectors

Today's reading comes with its own introduction: *Then God spoke all these words* (20:1). Read this statement, and then pause for a second afterwards before continuing.

While there is a tendency to regard OT laws as restrictive and oppressive, the Ten Commandments were intended to be good news for Israel because they outlined the way of life with God. Read them as the good news that they are. Since they address important matters, your voice can be serious but do not let it come across as depressed; let your reading be serious yet vigorous and energetic.

Each of the commandments deserves to be heard on its own, so do not speed through the reading or rush from one commandment to the next. This is more of an issue with the sixth through ninth commandments, given that they are all very short and succinct (20:13–16). Give them their due by reading them slowly and deliberately and by pausing after each one has been delivered.

In the second commandment, bring out the contrast between *the third and fourth generation* and *the thousandth generation*, by elevating your voice when you say *but* and *thousandth* (20:6).

Pronunciation Guide
Egypt (EE-jipt), *Moses* (MOH-zuhs), *sabbath* (SAB-uhth)

1 Corinthians 1:18–25

Commentary
In 1 Corinthians 1:10–17, Paul registers his concern over cliques that have arisen and are causing discord and division within the Corinthian church. Paul begins to address these divisions by refocusing the Corinthian Christians' attention on Jesus, specifically, upon his crucifixion. This emphasis continues in today's reading where Paul characterizes the crucified Christ as both the wisdom and the power of God.

1:18–25. Crucifixion was an indescribably shameful and tortuous affair, the goal of which was to completely dehumanize its victim in the eyes of others. It is no small wonder then that the world would regard as ludicrous the claim that God's solution to what ails humanity rests upon the shoulders of a crucified criminal. Yet for Paul, Christ crucified reflects both the wisdom and power of God. Such logic is incomprehensible because it does not align with any human definition or experience of what constitutes wisdom and power.

For example, Israel's history is filled with stories of how God rescues and sustains his people by performing signs and wonders and other deeds of power, such as the parting of the Red Sea and the daily provision of manna in the wilderness. According to Jewish experience and logic, this is how God operates in the world. Therefore, Jews demand such deeds of power as proof that God is at work. Within this framework, the cross becomes an obstacle to faith because it connotes weakness, not power. The cross is indeed a sign, but it a sign of God's judgment and rejection. More than anything, Jesus' crucifixion argues against his being God's messiah.

The Greeks, on the other hand, have a rich tradition in philosophy, logic, and rhetoric. Consequently, they value wisdom above all else. Yet, there is nothing in the crucifixion of Jesus that would appeal to anyone's intellectual sensibilities. In such a tradition, the message of the cross is ridiculous, even offensive. Despite these obstacles, Paul continues to preach to both Jews and Gentiles that Christ is the power and the wisdom of God. Certainly, the cross is foolishness, yet God's folly is wiser than any and all human wisdom. Likewise, the cross is a sign of weakness, yet God's weakness outstrips all human strength combined.

Suggestions for Lectors
Today's reading begins quickly; the opening line about the foolishness of the cross states the main thesis that Paul defends throughout the rest of the reading. You do not want your listeners to miss this opening line, so make sure they are seated and attentive before you begin the reading.

In 1:20, Paul uses rhetorical questions to great effect. Increase your tempo and intensity as you deliver each succeeding question. Your goal is to generate enough energy and momentum to sustain yourself through the end of the reading. When you come to 1:25, slow down and read it more deliberately as you draw the reading to a close.

Pronunciation Guide
Corinthians (kuh-RIN-thee-uhnz), *Gentiles* (JEN-tīlz)

John 2:13–22

Notes
Sequence. 1 of 3

Commentary
All four gospels record Jesus' demonstration in the Jerusalem temple during the festival of Passover. In the Synoptic Gospels (Matthew, Mark, and Luke), this event is narrated at the end of Jesus' life. In fact, it is the temple demonstration that prompts the authorities to plot Jesus' arrest and execution (Mark 11:18). Moreover, when Jesus is questioned before the Jewish high council, the charges that are brought against him have to do with comments he supposedly made about his plans to destroy the temple (Mark 14:58). Here, we say *supposedly* because, in the Synoptics, Jesus never talks about destroying and rebuilding the temple. It is clear that these are false charges that have been manufactured.

In John, however, Jesus' demonstration in the temple occurs at the beginning of his public ministry, and while Jesus explicitly talks about destroying the temple, this is never brought up at any of his trials. Instead, the event in John that galvanizes Jesus' opponents is his resuscitation of Lazarus (11:45–53). In today's reading, we shall look at John's account.

2:13–17. Jesus' demonstration in the Jerusalem temple occurred during Passover, one of three annual pilgrimage festivals. In the Synoptics, Jesus is only ever presented as attending one Passover. In John, he attends three Passovers (2:13; 6:4; 11:55), which is why we generally think of Jesus as having had a three-year public ministry. When Jesus enters the temple precincts, he becomes incensed at what had become of his Father's house. The temple was to be the place where God met those who sought him through sacrifice, offering, and prayer, but now it had devolved into a marketplace. Covenant relationship between God and God's people had been coopted economics. Jesus drove everybody out, all the merchants and moneychangers. Later on, when his disciples read Psalm 69:9, "Zeal for your house will consume me," they would recall this incident.

2:18–22. The Jews question Jesus' authority for engaging in such behavior in the temple. Their request for a sign suggests that they believe him to be playing the role of a prophet. After all, the OT contains stories of prophets who performed symbolic actions. For example, Jeremiah was once instructed by God to take an earthenware jug into the temple courts and smash it to pieces in order to symbolize the destruction that God had decreed for Judah and Jerusalem (Jer 19). Jesus responds to their request for a sign with a cryptic saying about his death and resurrection. Understandably, his questioners have no idea what he is talking about. Even his own disciples will not understand until after his resurrection.

Suggestions for Lectors

Start out the reading in your normal narrating voice. Then, in 2:15, when Jesus begins driving people from the temple with a whip, increase the volume and pitch of your voice, and relate these events in a more serious tone. When Jesus speaks, endow your voice with hints of righteous anger and indignation. Use this same tone when Jesus responds to questions in 2:19.

In 2:17 and 2:21–22, the narrator interrupts the narrative to offer additional information and interpretive comments. Read these verses in a lower, less animated voice almost as though you are letting your listeners in on a secret.

Pronunciation Guide

Jerusalem (juh-ROO-suh-luhm), *Jews* (JOOZ)

FOURTH SUNDAY IN LENT

Numbers 21:4–9
Psalm 107:1–3, 17–22
Ephesians 2:1–10
John 3:14–21

NUMBERS 21:4–9

Commentary

Numbers is the fourth book of the Bible and the fourth book of the Pentateuch (a.k.a., The Five Books of Moses). Its English title, Numbers, is a translation of its title in ancient Greek editions, *Arithmoi*. These titles emphasize the two military censuses that take place in chapters 1 and 26. However, its Hebrew title offers a more accurate description of the book's contents. In Hebrew, the book is called *Bemidbar*, that is, *In the Wilderness*, because it recounts the story of Israel's forty-year sojourn in the wilderness as they make their way from Mt. Sinai to the borders of the Promised Land on the plains of Moab.

As today's reading illustrates, an even more accurate title might be *Grumblings in the Wilderness*. Earlier in Numbers, the Israelites grumble about their misfortunes (11:1), then about wanting meat instead of manna (11:4–6), and then about their desire to return to Egypt (14:1–4).

21:4–6. In todays' reading, the Israelites grumble once again about the lack of real food and water and how they are tired of manna. They not only speak against Moses but they speak against the LORD. The LORD responds to their ongoing complaints by sending a plague of venomous serpents upon his people with the result that many Israelites die.

21:7–9. Unlike the plagues that hardened Pharaoh's heart, this plague triggers repentance. The people acknowledge their sin and ask that the serpents be taken away.

The LORD responds to their petition, but in a manner different than requested. The serpents are not taken away, but a means of deliverance is provided. Though the Ten Commandments expressly forbids the making of any graven image (Exod 20:4), on this occasion, the LORD directs Moses to make such an image. Of course, the bronze serpent is not designed to be an idol, an object of worship. Instead, it is something of an icon, an image that serves to remind the people of their sin and its consequences while simultaneously reminding the people of God's mercy. Had the serpents simply been taken away, one expects that the people would have simply found something else to grumble about. As it is, this is the last incident of grumbling in the book of Numbers, and perhaps even in the Pentateuch.

Incidentally, the bronze serpent reappears in the biblical narrative. Centuries later, as part of a comprehensive program of reforming Judah's worship, King Hezekiah destroys "the bronze serpent that Moses had made, for until those days the people of Israel had made offerings to it" (2 Kgs 18:4). Unfortunately, the icon had become an idol.

Suggestions for Lectors

In today's reading, the emphasis lies in the speaking parts, so read the non-speaking portions in your normal storytelling voice. But when you deliver the speaking parts, adopt an intensity and tone of voice that matches the tone and intensity of what is being said. In 21:5, the people are grumbling, so elevate your voice and invest it with a hint of anger born of fear. In 21:7, convey the people's fear with a hint of sorrow in your voice. Finally, deliver the LORD's instructions to Moses in a straightforward manner.

The reading falls into three parts—an introduction that sets the scene (21:4), the principal action of the episode (21:5–8), and a conclusion (21:9). Pause for a full second between each part.

Pronunciation Guide

Edom (EE-duhm), *Egypt* (EE-jipt)
Hor (HOR), *Moses* (MOH-zuhs)

EPHESIANS 2:1–10

Commentary

In today's gospel, we encounter those famous words, "For God so loved the world that he gave his only Son, so that everyone who believes in him may not perish but may have eternal life" (John 3:16). In today's epistle, this same sentiment is expressed in Pauline language and terms, as Paul highlights the new life Christians possess by virtue of God's gracious actions in Jesus Christ.

2:1–3. Paul begins by reminding his readers that when God first lay hold of them, they were dead—completely dead spiritually and in the process of dying physically. Before Christ rescued them, their spiritual deadness was evidenced by the fact that they were not following God and his ways. Instead, the course of their lives was dictated by the values and practices of human culture, and they were subject to demonic forces. Moreover, they lived as slaves to their own bodily passions and desires.

2:4–7. In contrast, the abundant grace and mercy of God is evidenced by the fact that God rescued humanity while it was still in the cesspool of its sins and trespasses. In keeping with his great love for fallen humanity, God did not wait for us to extricate ourselves from the quagmire of sin, death, and violence. Instead, stepped into our human situation and "made us alive together with Christ" (2:5). Jesus was *physically* raised from the dead and seated in the heavenly places above all cosmic powers and forces. Believers have been spiritually raised from the dead and brought into the heavenly kingdom.

2:8–10. All of this is a sheer act of God's grace. People are not saved on the basis of their own good works; after all, dead people cannot do anything. Instead, people are saved through faith, and even this faith is a gift from God. Good works do have an important place in the Christian life, but only as a response to the rich grace and mercy of God.

Suggestions for Lectors

In keeping with the Commentary, deliver today's passage in three movements (2:1–3, 4–7, 8–10). Slow down as you draw a movement to a close, and pause for a second or two at the end of each.

The reading is filled with wonderful truths about God's love and mercy and about salvation, grace, and faith. Unfortunately, it is not possible to emphasize everything, so as you make your preparations, identify those items that you think deserve special treatment.

Paul seems to enjoy packing everything he wants to say on a subject into a single sentence. For example, the second movement is four verses (2:4–7), yet it comprises a single, complex sentence. When faced with such sentences, begin by identifying the main, unadorned thought that weaves its way through the complex tapestry of embellishments. Once you have isolated the main thread of thought, build your reading and intonation around that. In 2:4–7, the main thought is: *But God made us alive together with Christ and raised us up with him and seated us with him in the heavenly places in Christ Jesus*; it has been <u>underlined</u> below.

4 <u>But God,</u>
    who is rich in mercy,
    out of the great love with which he loved us
5   even when we were dead through our trespasses,
<u>made us alive together with Christ</u>
    —by grace you have been saved—
6 <u>and raised us up with him</u>
<u>and seated us with him in the heavenly places in Christ Jesus,</u>
7   so that in the ages to come he might show
    the immeasurable riches of his grace
        in kindness toward us in Christ Jesus.

Pronunciation Guide

Ephesians (eh-FEE-zhuhnz; ih-)

John 3:14–21

Notes

Sequence. 2 of 3

Commentary

In last week's reading, Jesus drove out all the merchants and money changers from the temple in Jerusalem. When his opponents request him to produce a sign that would demonstrate his authority for engaging in such a demonstration, Jesus makes a cryptic allusion to his death and resurrection. His resurrection on the third day will establish his authority. Clearly, they do not understand what he is talking about; it is not a sign that leads to belief.

On the other hand, Jesus perform signs that do lead to belief. "When he was in Jerusalem during the Passover festival, many believed in his name because they saw the signs that he was doing" (2:23). These signs motivate a Pharisee named Nicodemus to meet with Jesus secretly (3:1). Nicodemus comes to Jesus by night, and says, "Rabbi, we know that you are a teacher who has come from God; for no one can do these signs that you do apart from the presence of God" (3:2). This comment starts a discussion that ranges over such topics as spiritual rebirth, the kingdom of God, and the activity of the Spirit. In today's reading, Jesus continues his discussion with Nicodemus by talking about love and judgment.

3:14–16. Jesus recalls an incident that took place during Israel's forty-year sojourn in the wilderness following the Exodus from Egypt and which is recounted in today's reading from Numbers. Tired of trekking through the wilderness with little water and only manna to eat, the Israelites once again grumble against God and Moses. God responds by unleashing poisonous serpents upon the people, which produces many casualties. When the people repent, the LORD instructs Moses to make a bronze serpent and attach it to a pole so that it is visible. Whenever a fiery serpent bit someone, if they looked to the bronze serpent, they would live. Just as Moses lifted up the serpent in the wilderness, so God intends to lift up his one and only Son on a cross so that all who look to him might live. Such is the breadth and depth of God's love for the world.

3:17–21. After all, God does not desire the world's destruction. Jesus was not sent to condemn the world but to be the agent of its transformation and renewal. That being said, condemnation still remains as an unintended, natural consequence of Jesus being the light of the world. In John, there is no middle ground. There are no shadows, only light and darkness, and a person belongs to one or the other. Those who believe in Jesus have come into the light, while those who do not yet believe remain in the darkness. This is not predestination, only natural consequence for the choice to believe remains open to all (cf. 1:11–12). Yet, those who live in darkness must be willing to expose themselves to the light. Unfortunately, some people prefer the darkness and choose to remain blind rather than trust themselves to the one whom God sent to rescue them (cf. 9:39–41).

Suggestions for Lectors

John 3:16 is perhaps the most quoted verse in all of Scripture. Yet, we are not used to hearing this verse in context; we generally only hear it by itself. One of your goals, then, will be to deliver today's reading so that 3:16 is heard within its larger context. As was hinted at in the Commentary, the clause, *For God so loved the world*, connects God's giving of his Son with Moses' lifting up of the serpent. That is, the *so* refers not so much to how much God loves us as it points to the way in which God loves us. A translation that brings this out is, "For God loved the world *in this way* that he gave…," which refers back to the lifting up of the Son of Man in 3:15.

Consequently, when you read 3:16, do not pause beforehand; proceed from 3:15 to 3:16 as you normally would so that the relationship between these two verses is maintained. Also, deliver both verses in the same manner; do not emphasize 3:16. Its familiarity will provide it with all the emphasis it needs. Instead, take the opportunity to highlight 3:17, by reading it slowly and deliberately. Emphasize *Indeed*, *condemn*, and *saved*, and also pause after *Indeed*, as in: *Indeed,… God did not send the Son into the world to condemn the world, but in order that the world might be saved through him.* Then, finish out the reading in your normal narrating voice.

Pronunciation Guide

Moses (MOH-zuhs)

FIFTH SUNDAY IN LENT

Jeremiah 31:31–34
Psalm 51:1–12 (= 51:1–13 BCP) *or* Psalm 119:9–16
Hebrews 5:5–10
John 12:20–33

JEREMIAH 31:31–34

Commentary

When Jeremiah was called to be a "prophet to the nations" (1:5), his prophetic vocation was described with six actions: "See, today I appoint you over nations and over kingdoms, to pluck up and to pull down, to destroy and to overthrow, to build and to plant" (1:10). The first four actions denote judgment, and it is with the judgment and exile of Judah that the first twenty-nine chapters of Jeremiah is concerned. Yet, in Jeremiah 30–33, *to build* and *to plant* hold precedence. These chapters are often designated *The Book of Consolation*, for in them the LORD speaks to his exiled people and promises to restore them (30:2–3; cf. 33:26):

> Thus says the LORD, the God of Israel: Write in a book all the words that I have spoken to you. For the days are surely coming, says the LORD, when I will restore the fortunes of my people, Israel and Judah, says the LORD, and I will bring them back to the land that I gave to their ancestors and they shall take possession of it.

In today's passage, the LORD speaks of a *new covenant* with Israel and Judah, which is the only time this phrase occurs in the OT. In the NT, *new covenant* occurs in a number of places (Luke 22:20; 1 Cor 11:25, MThu; 2 Cor 3:6, Prop 3; Heb 8:8, 13; 9:15; 12:24), and the author of Hebrews cites Jeremiah 31:31–34 in its entirety (Heb 8:8–12).

The northern kingdom of Israel was conquered by the Assyrian Empire in 722 B.C. and its citizens dispersed throughout the world. Similarly, in 586 B.C., the Babylonian Empire overthrew the southern kingdom of Judah and exiled its citizens to Babylon. So when the LORD declares, just prior to today's reading, that "the days are surely coming" when he "will sow the house of Israel and the house of Judah" (31:27), the LORD is in effect declaring the end of exile for both kingdoms. It was the LORD who oversaw their destruction, and now the LORD will oversee their restoration.

Yet, the covenant relationship between God and his reconciled people will not simply revert back to the way it had been before; there will be a few changes. For example, when the LORD established his covenant with Israel, the second commandment disavowed the making or worshipping of idols, for "I the LORD your God am a jealous God, punishing children for the iniquity of parents, to the third and the fourth generation of those who reject me, but showing steadfast love to the thousandth generation of those who love me and keep my commandments" (Exod 20:5–6; cf. Deut 5:9–10; Exod 34:7; Num 14:18). Under this original covenant, God's blessings to the thousandth generation far outweighs his punishments to the fourth generation. The new covenant takes this one step further for under the new covenant, persons will only be punished for their own sins and no longer for those of their parents, grandparents, etc.

31:31–34. This is just one of the differences with the new covenant that the LORD will make with Israel and Judah. Another difference concerns the law. Under the new covenant, the LORD will not abolish the law that his covenant people were unable to obey; instead the LORD will put his law within them, he will write it on their hearts. In other words, the law will not be an external motivating force, but an internal force, one that resides at the core of their being to guide and direct their wills, thoughts, and actions. When this occurs, then the LORD will truly be their God, and Israel and Judah will truly be his people. This same situation is described by the prophet Ezekiel in very similar terms. When the LORD gathers his exiled people, he declares, "I will give them one heart, and put a new spirit within them; I will remove the heart of stone from their flesh and give them a heart of flesh, so that they may follow my statutes and keep my ordinances and obey them. Then they shall be my people, and I will be their God" (Ezek 11:19–20).

Finally, before Judah went into exile, the LORD said he would "remember their iniquity and punish their sins" (14:10), but now he says, "I will forgive their iniquity, and remember their sin no more" (31:34).

Suggestions for Lectors

Today's reading is relatively short so make sure your listeners are settled in before you begin reading. Begin by reading 31:31–32 at a normal tempo. Adopt a tone of voice that creates a sense of anticipation about this new covenant.

Pause a full second before 31:33, and then slow your voice down as you begin to reveal the details of this new and glorious covenant between God and his people. When you come to the two places where the LORD announces what he himself will do, then elevate your voice and read more deliberately: *I will put my law within them, and I will write it on their hearts; and I will be their God, and they shall be my people* (31:33b), and *for I will forgive their iniquity, and remember their sin no more* (31:34b).

Pronunciation Guide
Jeremiah (jair'-uh-MĪ-uh)

HEBREWS 5:5–10

Commentary
In Jewish tradition, the high priest was responsible for what took place in the temple. While the other priests carried out their priestly duties in the inner court (a.k.a., the Holy Place), only the high priest was ever allowed to enter the Most Holy Place (a.k.a., the Holy of Holies), the inner sanctuary where the ark of the covenant resided. Even then, the high priest only entered the Holy of Holies once a year on the Day of Atonement (a.k.a., Yom Kippur; Lev 16; Heb 9:3–7).

Because high priests were fallible, sinful human beings like everybody else, they should not take it upon themselves to seek the office of high priest. Instead, this honor was reserved for those whom God had especially chosen. This is how it was when God appointed Moses' brother Aaron to be the first high priest (Num 16:5; 17:5; 18:1–7).

5:5–6. Even Jesus, who was "without sin" (4:15, Prop 23), did not presume to take this honor. Instead, he was appointed by God as the psalms testify: "You are my Son, today I have begotten you" (Ps 2:7), and "You are a priest forever, according to the order of Melchizedek" (110:4). Thus, humility is the first qualification for being chosen to be high priest.

5:7–10. One might naturally assume that a high priest is too important and too holy to suffer, but suffering is what qualified Jesus to be our great high priest. One might also assume that because Jesus was the Son of God obedience was automatic. Yet, the author of Hebrews writes that, "Although he was a Son, he *learned* obedience through what he suffered" (5:8). Jesus achieved perfection by living a life of obedience even in the midst of suffering. Therefore, Jesus became the source of eternal life and salvation for any who would follow after him and live a life of humble obedience even in the face of suffering and death.

Generally speaking, in the OT, priests were taken from the tribe of Levi, and they made up the Levitical priesthood (Num 3:5–10). Moses' brother, Aaron, was a Levite and a priest. He and his sons were appointed by God to be responsible for the priestly duties that took place in relation to the tabernacle (Exod 28). In addition, Aaron was anointed as the first high priest, and all other high priests were to be descendants of Aaron. So within the Levitical priesthood, there was the Aaronic priesthood, which included the office of high priest. As a descendant of Judah (vs. Levi), Jesus belonged to neither of these priestly orders. Instead, in keeping with Psalm

110, the author of Hebrews sees Jesus as belonging to the priestly order of Melchizedek (5:6, 10; 6:20; 7:11, 17). Melchizedek is a mysterious figure who briefly appears in Genesis, where he is identified as the *king* of Salem and the *priest* of God Most High (14:18–20; Heb 7:1–10). These twin roles make Melchizedek—whose name means *king of righteousness*—the ideal candidate to prefigure the coming of the kingly high priest, Jesus.

Because Jesus is alive forevermore, he remains in the office of high priest indefinitely, and so is able to offer a salvation that never ends. As we read later in Hebrews: Jesus "holds his priesthood permanently, because he continues forever. Consequently he is able for all time to save those who approach God through him, since he always lives to make intercession for them" (Heb 7:24–25, Prop 25).

Suggestions for Lectors

In today's reading, the author of Hebrews is like an instructor lecturing on the topic of high priests, the services they perform and how they are appointed to office. So deliver this reading as though you are giving a lecture, not a dry, boring lecture, but a stimulating one. Speak with enthusiasm and evident interest in your subject.

The concluding quotation from the OT should receive the most emphasis. Raise your voice, and read it more deliberately. Emphasize *You*, and pause slightly after each of the first five words, as in: *You… are… my… Son,… today… I have begotten you* (5:5).

Pronunciation Guide

Aaron (AIR-uhn), *Christ* (KRĪST)

JOHN 12:20–33

Notes

Sequence. 3 of 3

Commentary

Today's episode occurs on the heels of Jesus' triumphal entry. Passover is fast approaching, thousands of pilgrims are arriving in Jerusalem, and reports of Jesus' raising of Lazarus have been spreading. In fact, it was on account of these reports that crowds of people came out to meet him, waving palm branches and shouting, "Hosanna! (that is, "Save us!"). Blessed is the one who comes in the name of the Lord—the King of Israel!" (12:13). The Pharisees are dismayed at the crowd's joyous reception of Jesus. They remark to one another, "You see, you can do nothing. Look, the world has gone after him!" (12:19). And for once they are correct, after a fashion, for today's reading begins with some Greeks asking to see Jesus.

12:20–22. Though the Passover was a Jewish festival, it was not uncommon for Gentiles to make the pilgrimage to Jerusalem in order to participate in the festivities. Instead of approaching Jesus directly, the Greeks approach Philip with their request, "Sir, we wish to see Jesus" (12:22). Why they choose Philip is not stated; perhaps it is because he has a Greek name. Whatever the reason, he is an interesting choice. In John, Philip is the first disciple Jesus recruits (1:43, Epi 2). After Philip is called, the first thing he does is to approach Nathanael with the news that the messiah is Jesus of Nazareth. When Nathanael questions the possibility of anything good coming out of Nazareth, Philip responds with a simple, "Come and see" (1:46). And now, people are approaching Philip with the request to come and see Jesus.

12:23–26. Why their request prompts Jesus to talk about his upcoming death is not readily apparent. Perhaps he does not want people to misunderstand the significance of his raising of Lazarus or of his triumphal procession into Jerusalem. Perhaps he wants to clarify what his mission entails, not only for himself but for those would come after him. Certainly, the hour has come for him to be glorified, but the road to glory leads through Golgotha.

12:27–33. Jesus has come to draw *all people* to himself in order to bring *all people* into relationship with the Father. Perhaps, then, it is the fact that *Gentiles* are seeking Jesus that explains why he talks about his death. For if his being lifted up on a Gentile cross is the means by which all people—Jews and Gentiles alike—are drawn to him; and if some Gentiles are already being drawn to him, then their request to see him might serve as a sign that his death is close at hand.

Suggestions for Lectors

Begin today's reading in your normal narrative style. When the Greeks approach Philip, read their request in a very polite voice.

In 12:23, when Jesus begins talking about his death, there is no suggestion of anxiety or sorrow, rather he uses positive images. He describes his death as being *glorified* and of it *bearing much fruit.* If he is anxious, it has not surfaced yet, so deliver this initial discourse as you would any of his teachings.

However, in 12:27, Jesus' tone takes a decided downward turn. Jesus rarely describes his emotional state, but here he says quite plainly that he is struggling, *Now my soul is troubled.* Pause for a second before 12:27, then read these words with hints of anxiety and despair in your voice. Pause again before delivering the rest of 12:27 as though you are speaking aloud to yourself, as though you are carrying on an internal debate. Then, look up toward the sky as you pray in a loud voice, *Father, glorify your name!* (12:28). While the heavenly voice is not first and foremost for Jesus, it must surely have encouraged him and strengthened his resolve, so return to your normal narrating voice for the remainder of the narrative.

Highlight Jesus' final statement, by reading it with more intensity. Pause after *I* and *earth*, and emphasize *all*, as in: *And I,... when I am lifted up from the earth,... will draw all people to myself* (12:32).

Pronunciation Guide

Andrew (AN-droo)
Bethsaida (beth-SAY-uh-duh)
Galilee (GAL-uh-lee)
Greek (GREEK)
Philip (FIL-ip)

HOLY WEEK

PALM SUNDAY — LITURGY OF THE PALMS

also known as Passion Sunday

Mark 11:1–11 *or* John 12:12–16
Psalm 118:1–2, 19–29

Mark 11:1–11

Commentary
In Mark 10:32, Jesus is making his way up to Jerusalem with the twelve for Passover. As they travel, Jesus once again reminds his disciples about the fate that awaits him. "See, we are going up to Jerusalem, and the Son of Man will be handed over to the chief priests and the scribes, and they will condemn him to death; then they will hand him over to the Gentiles; they will mock him, and spit upon him, and flog him, and kill him; and after three days he will rise again." (10:33–34; cf. 8:31–33, Prop 19; 9:30–32, Prop 20). In today's reading, Jesus finally arrives in the holy city, and it is just a few more short steps to the cross.

11:1–6. As they near their destination, Jesus sends two of his disciples into a small village to secure a colt for his entry into the city. Jesus has traveled all the way from Galilee on foot, so why does he now secure transportation? In the OT, prophets performed symbolic actions. For example, Jeremiah was once instructed by God to purchase a potter's vessel, take it to Jerusalem, and then to smash it to pieces in front of witnesses, thereby announcing God's plans to bring destruction upon the city of Jerusalem and its temple (Jer 19).

Here in Mark, Jesus is performing a symbolic action by entering Jerusalem on the back of a colt. He is mimicking the actions of a king or general who, after having vanquished his foes, rides into the city in a triumphal procession. Jesus processes into Jerusalem as her victorious king. He has established the kingdom of God by conquering the enemies of God through teaching, healing, exorcising unclean spirits, pronouncing forgiveness, eating with tax collectors and sinners, etc. Of course, one would normally expect a king to enter his capital on a mighty steed, a symbol of power and authority. Jesus, however, is a different sort of king with a different understanding of authority and power. He rides astride a donkey, symbolizing strength through humility. As it is written in the prophet Zechariah: "Rejoice greatly, O daughter Zion! Shout aloud, O daughter Jerusalem! Lo, your king comes to you; triumphant and victorious is he, humble and riding on a donkey, on a colt, the foal of a donkey"

(9:9; cf. Matt 21:5). Ironically, by week's end, Jesus will be hailed as King of the Jews by his enemies as they enthrone and exalt him on the hard wood of a cross.

11:7–11. When the prophet Elisha anointed Jehu as king over Israel, Jehu's companions "took their cloaks and spread them for him on the bare steps; and they blew the trumpet, and proclaimed, 'Jehu is king'" (2 Kgs 9:13). Likewise, Jesus' followers throw their cloaks on the back of the colt, while others spread their cloaks on the road. As Jesus approaches Jerusalem, the crowds around him shout, "Hosanna to the Son of David! Blessed is the one who comes in the name of the Lord! Hosanna in the highest" (21:9). The scene is a royal procession. *Son of David* is a common description for Israel's king, and *hosanna* is a Hebrew word meaning "Save us." The crowds are made up of Jewish pilgrims who have come to celebrate Passover—a festival for remembering and celebrating Jewish independence from the oppression of imperial Egypt. It is not surprising, then, that these pilgrims would have the words of Psalm 118 on their lips. What *is* surprising is that they apply these words to Jesus:

> This is the gate of the LORD;
> the righteous shall enter through it.
> I thank you that you have answered me
> and have become my salvation.
> The stone that the builders rejected
> has become the chief cornerstone.
> This is the LORD's doing;
> it is marvelous in our eyes (cf. Mark 12:10–11).
> This is the day that the LORD has made;
> let us rejoice and be glad in it.
> *Save us* (Hosanna), we beseech you, O LORD!
> O LORD, we beseech you, give us success!
> *Blessed is the one who comes in the name of the* LORD.
> We bless you from the house of the LORD.
> The LORD is God,
> and he has given us light.
> Bind the festal procession with branches,
> up to the horns of the altar.
> You are my God,
> and I will give thanks to you;
> you are my God,
> I will extol you.
> O give thanks to the LORD, for he is good,
> for his steadfast love endures forever (Psalm 118:20–29).

Suggestions for Lectors

Today's reading offers a straightforward and simple narrative. The highpoint comes with the crowd's chorus in 11:9b–10; these lines warrant an elevated, jubilant delivery. Emphasize the two *Hosannas* and the two *Blesseds*:

Hosanna!
Blessed is the one who comes in the name of the Lord!
Blessed is the coming kingdom of our ancestor David!
Hosanna in the highest heaven!

Pronunciation Guide
Bethany (BETH-uh-nee), *Bethphage* (BETH-fuh-jee; BETH-fayj), *blessed* (adj., two syllables; BLES-id), *Hosanna* (hoh-ZAN-nuh; -ZAHN-), *Jerusalem* (juh-ROO-suh-luhm)

JOHN 12:12–16

Commentary
Throughout the Gospel of John, Jesus refuses to entrust himself to other people's timetables or expectations because he understands people and what motivates them (cf. 2:24–25). For example, at the wedding in Cana, when Jesus' mother informs him that the wine has run out, he responds, "Woman, what concern is that to you and to me? *My hour has not yet come*" (2:4). Later, when his brothers try to harass him into attending a festival in Jerusalem, Jesus replies, "Go to the festival yourselves. I am not going to this festival, for *my time has not yet fully come*" (7:8). However, after his brothers leave for the festival, Jesus follows and attends the festival in secret. Then, there is the time when Jesus feeds a crowd of thousands with just a few loaves and fish. The people are enthralled, and when Jesus realizes that they intend "to come and take him by force to make him king," he immediately withdraws (6:15, Prop 12). Jesus *is* a king, but he is going to be king on his own terms and according to his own schedule.

In today's reading, with the hour of his death fast approaching (12:23, Lent 5), Jesus participates in a symbolic, public act whereby he subtly, yet unmistakably, presents himself as the king of the Jews.

12:12–13. The scene takes place in Jerusalem just five days before Passover, the great annual festival that celebrated the Exodus when the Israelites were set free from the oppression of imperial Egypt. Crowds of people have gone up to Jerusalem, many of whom have heard the reports about Jesus' raising Lazarus from the dead (12:9–11, 17–19). When they learn that Jesus is making his way to Jerusalem, they rush out to meet him with palm branches in their hands and shouts of "Hosanna" on their lips. Palm branches were symbols of victory, a sign of homage to a conquering hero (1 Macc 13:51), and *hosanna* is a Hebrew word meaning "Save us" (Ps 118:25). The people are looking for a savior. Surely a man who can raise the dead can free them from the occupational forces of imperial Rome.

12:14–16. Surprisingly, Jesus does not withdraw. On this occasion, he joins in by riding through the crowd on the back of a donkey. This has now become a triumphal entry in the tradition of Zechariah. Zechariah was a post-exilic prophet who was active in Judea after the exiles had returned from their seventy-year captivity in Babylon. Although the Persians had granted the Jews a measure of political and religious autonomy, they were not allowed a king, only a provincial governor. Consequently, many Jews thought of themselves as still in exile. For them, the exile would not be over until a descendant of David reigned as king over the people of God (2 Sam 7:13). In Zechariah 9, the prophet offers the returned exiles hope as he envisions the day when a king of the Jews would once again be enthroned in Jerusalem.

> Rejoice greatly, O daughter Zion!
>   Shout aloud, O daughter Jerusalem!
> Lo, your king comes to you;
>   triumphant and victorious is he,
> humble and riding on a donkey,
>   on a colt, the foal of a donkey (9:9).

It is significant that Zechariah's king processes into the city astride a donkey instead of a war horse. It reveals that this king is the epitome of humility and that his kingdom will be a kingdom of peace where there will be no need for weapons of war (9:10). Jesus participates in the crowd's celebration, even as he subverts their expectations. As Israel's king, Jesus has no intention of lifting up a sword against Rome. In fact, by week's end, it will be Rome lifting up Jesus on a cross.

In John, the cross is Jesus' throne, and his crucifixion is his enthronement. From there he will reign as Lord over all peoples everywhere. As he says in the very next episode:

> "The hour has come for the Son of Man to be glorified.... And I, when I am lifted up from the earth, will draw all people to myself." He said this to indicate the kind of death he was to die (12:23, 32–33, Lent 5).

Suggestions for Lectors

In John's account of the triumphal entry, the focus is upon the OT scriptures that offer an interpretation of Jesus' symbolic action, scriptures that affirm his identity as Israel's King. Highlight the Scriptures in your reading, emphasizing *King* within each of them. Increase the volume and pitch of your voice and proclaim them as though you are addressing a large crowd.

In 12:16, the narrator interrupts the story to offer some information about what is going on in the minds of Jesus' disciples. Relay this information to your readers by dropping your voice, much as you would when reading a parenthetical expression.

Pronunciation Guide

blessed (adj., two syllables; BLES-id)
Hosanna (hoh-ZAN-nuh; -ZAHN-)
Israel (IZ-ree-uhl; -ray-)
Jerusalem (juh-ROO-suh-luhm)
Zion (ZĪ-uhn)

PALM SUNDAY — LITURGY OF THE PASSION

also known as Passion Sunday

Isaiah 50:4–9a
Psalm 31:9–16
Philippians 2:5–11
Mark 14:1–15:47 *or* Mark 15:1–39, (40–47)

ISAIAH 50:4–9A

Commentary

Through its rich poetry and prose, the book of Isaiah narrates a dramatic story of rebellion and judgment that gives way to forgiveness and redemption. The plot begins with God's chosen people, but then broadens to encompass all the nations of the world and even creation itself. In Isaiah 1–39, the drama focuses upon rebellion as humanity serves the gods of its own making and orders society through unjust practices and power structures. The prophet Isaiah is sent to announce the various judgments that will be executed by the LORD, the Holy One of Israel and the creator of the heavens and the earth. Judgment begins with the LORD's own people who have forsaken the covenant (Isa 1–12, 28–35) through their willful and persistent failure to love God with their whole heart (Deut 6:5, Prop 26; Exod 20:1–7, Lent 3) and to love their neighbors as themselves (Lev 19:18; Exod 20:8–17). Judgment then extends to the nations and empires of the world who oppose the sovereign rule of the LORD through their prideful and unjust exercise of power (Isa 13–23). Even the forces of chaos and evil that threaten God's good creation will be judged, not least death itself (25:7–8, East).

Yet beginning in Isaiah 40, the ominous tone of judgment gives way to a joyful note of hope as the prophet announces a *new thing* that the LORD is about to do (42:9; 43:19; 48:6). This new thing, which will eventually result in the restoration of all creation, will begin with the LORD forgiving and redeeming his chosen people. Through his chosen people, God will bring about the redemption and reconciliation of all peoples everywhere, in keeping with his covenant promises to Abraham and Sarah (Gen 12:2–3; Gen 17:16; 22:17–18, EastVig). Within this redemptive drama of Isaiah 40–55, we find four passages concerning an unidentified servant of the LORD (42:1–4; 49:1–6; 50:4–9; 52:13–53:12, GFri). These passages are often referred to as the Servant Songs. The servant appears sometimes as a corporate personality and sometimes as a single individual. There is a broad, general movement from the servant as *Israel* to the servant as *a single Israelite* who takes on Israel's vocation to be both the restorer of God's chosen people and the light to the nations (cf. 49:5–6).

Early Christians saw many similarities between Jesus and Isaiah's servant, especially with regard to Jesus' suffering and death. Their understanding of what God had done through Jesus' suffering and death was informed by the description of what the LORD did through the suffering of the servant in Isaiah, and vice versa. The importance of Isaiah's servant for understanding Jesus is reflected in the fact that each of the Servant Songs is read during Holy Week. In today's reading of the third Servant Song, we see that the servant's living out of his vocation was not without significant personal risk.

50:4–6. The servant begins by noting that the LORD has equipped him for his prophetic vocation by giving him "the tongue of a teacher, that I may know how to sustain the weary with a word" (50:4). In this context, the weary are those of God's chosen people who are living in Babylon waiting for the LORD to lead them back to the Promised Land, as the prophet announced God was about to do (cf. 40:1–11, Adv 2). Yet, the words that the servant has been given to speak are not welcomed by everyone. Perhaps the Babylonian authorities fear that the servant is inciting rebellion among the exiles. Much more likely, however, is the possibility that the servant is opposed by his own people. Among the exiles were those who had made good lives for themselves in Babylon; they were not disposed to re-immigrate to Judah and Jerusalem. They were not ready to take up their vocation as God's chosen people, a vocation that they found oppressive. Whatever the cause, the servant suffers humiliation and abuse as a direct result of his being obedient to his calling to be the servant of the LORD. The servant does not back down in the face of such persecution; he neither retaliates violently nor passively submits.

50:7–9a. Moreover, despite such persecution, the servant does not abandon his trust in God. The servant faithfully lives out his calling with firm resolve, knowing that in the end no one will be able to question the legitimacy of what he has done. Here, one is reminded of Jesus' predictions of his own suffering and death and his conviction that God would vindicate him by raising him from the dead (Mark 8:31–33, Lent 2; 9:30–32, Prop 20; 10:32–34).

Suggestions for Lectors

As a lector, it is helpful to break a reading up into smaller sections that are easier for aural consumption. Today's reading falls naturally into three sections, each of which begins with *The Lord GOD* (50:4, 5–6, 7–9a). Alternatively, since the reading is relatively short and the first two sections fit well together, you could think in terms of two sections (50:4–6; 50:7–9a). Whatever option you choose, pause for a full second before proceeding with each section, and slow your tempo as you conclude each section. Raise your voice in 50:7, as the servant uses courtroom terminology to state his case and express his hope. The reading ends firmly on this positive note.

Pronunciation Guide

Isaiah (ī-ZAY-uh)

PHILIPPIANS 2:5–11

Commentary

In this reading, Paul offers up Jesus as the one who fully embodies the self-emptying, self-sacrificing humility that Paul is calling the Philippians to adopt in 2:1–4.

2:5–8. Philippians 2:6–11 is thought to be an ancient Christian hymn that poetically recounts the story of the humiliation and exaltation of Jesus. It does not stand on its own but offers a narrative portrait of the humility and regard for others that

Paul is encouraging the Philippians to practice. Even though Jesus, as the eternal Son of God, had every right to use his divine status to achieve his own interests and ambitions, he did not. Instead Jesus disregarded his divine prerogatives, electing to become a human being, subject to all human limitations (2:7). Jesus' regard for others went so far as to embrace death, even the shameful and painful death of crucifixion (2:8).

2:9–11. Such a demonstration of selfless ambition is rewarded. God raised Jesus from the dead *and* appointed him to the highest position in the universe, making him Lord over the whole cosmos. As Jesus says following his resurrection, "All authority in heaven and on earth has been given to me" (Matt 28:18). Consequently, all allegiances are owed to Jesus. When his name is announced, every knee in creation should bend in thankful reverence and every tongue in creation should confess that Jesus is indeed the one and only Lord of all.

Suggestions for Lectors

In today's reading, you are presenting a biography like no other; so read it with a tone befitting its awesome dignity and grandeur. Imagine yourself reading for the coronation of a monarch, as you invite your listeners to consider the life and accomplishments of this incomparable individual.

Philippians 2:6–8 describes the descent of Jesus in humility, so read these verses with increasing solemnity, slowing your tempo as you proceed and making sure to enunciate each phrase with great care and precision. In contrast, 2:9–11 describes the ascent and exaltation of Jesus; so after a lengthy pause following 2:8, read these verses with increasing intensity, seasoned with awe and joy, which should reach a climax with the confession that *Jesus Christ is Lord* (2:11).

Pronunciation Guide

Philippians (fih-LIH-pee-uhnz)

Mark 14:1–15:47

The Gospel of Mark comprises five narrative movements, a five-act drama, if you will. Today's reading constitutes its fifth and final act, which ends in tragedy. The act opens with the enemies of Jesus conspiring to bring about his death. In the end, the conspiracy succeeds. This final act concludes as the curtain closes on Jesus' lifeless body, which has been taken down from the cross and placed in a tomb.

Jesus knew that this was the fate that awaited him. Three times he predicted what would happen to him once he and his disciples arrived in Jerusalem (8:31; 9:30–32; 10:32–34). *Everything* in this final movement anticipates that fateful end. The fifth movement opens with the chief priests and scribes conspiring against Jesus. Immediately, the scene shifts to Bethany, where an unnamed woman enters the house where Jesus is dining, and anoints his head with a costly ointment. The woman's extravagant act of generosity has royal connotations, for the heads of kings were anointed in ancient Israel. Jesus, however, interprets her actions as anointing his body beforehand for its burial. Thus, this opening episode foreshadows Jesus' death as the King of the Jews.

Anticipations of Jesus' death continue as Judas Iscariot joins the conspiracy against his master. During the last supper, Jesus predicts that one of the Twelve will betray him, that Peter will deny any association with him, and that the rest will desert him. As they eat the Passover meal, Jesus interprets his death as the ratification of the covenant between God and his people, a covenant in which many, including Gentiles, will participate. At Gethsemane, Jesus becomes distressed about the suffering and death that looms ahead, and prays that another way might be found. His prayer ends as two of his predictions come to pass: Judas betrays him and everybody else abandons him.

That night, Jesus is brought before the Jewish council, where he is interrogated, charged with blasphemy, and condemned as a false prophet. Meanwhile, Peter is outside in the courtyard below, vehemently denying any knowledge of Jesus. In the morning, Jesus is brought before the Roman governor, Pontius Pilate. Though Pilate does not perceive Jesus to be a threat, he gives into political pressure and hands him over to be executed as a royal pretender, an enemy of the empire. Jesus is tortured and sexually humiliated by the Roman cohort, then taken outside the city where he is crucified. The inscription of the charge against him read, "The King of the Jews." To complete the picture, two other subversives are crucified alongside Jesus. They flank Jesus, one on his right and one on his left, as though they belong to his royal entourage (cf. 10:37, 40).

Jesus is on the cross for six hours, and on three separate occasions, comments are made about him coming down from the cross. One of these comments is made by the chief priests and scribes—the chief conspirators—who mockingly shout, "Let the Messiah, the King of Israel, come down from the cross now, so that we may see and believe" (15:32). Jesus' opponents have it all backwards, for it is Jesus' death *on the cross*, not his coming down *from the cross* that reveals who he is as Messiah and Son of God. This realization becomes the foundation of genuine insight and faith. In Mark, then, the crucifixion of Jesus is more than a sacrifice for sin, it is the means by which Jesus' divine identity and vocation is fully and finally made known. Ironically, it is the centurion, a Gentile, who gets it right. When the centurion sees the way in which Jesus dies—suffering, all alone, and with a cry of God-forsakenness on his lips—in that moment, he recognizes who Jesus is and declares, "Truly this man was God's Son!" (15:39). This scene has been influenced by the conventions of Greek tragedy where the identity of the central character is not known until it is too late, for the centurion speaks in past tense, "Truly this man *was* God's Son!"

In Mark, the centurion is the only human character in the entire gospel to recognize that Jesus is the Son of God. Demons know it and God declares it, but again the centurion is the only human character to recognize and acknowledge Jesus as God's Son. This reinforces the fact that Jesus' death on the cross is an act of divine revelation. Jesus cannot be recognized as the Son of God unless he is first recognized as the suffering Son of Man, the crucified Messiah.

Suggestions for Lectors

In today's reading, draw upon your skill as a storyteller in keeping with the dictates of the narrative. It has become quite common for the Passion narrative to be read, or even acted out, by several people in a dramatic fashion. When participating in a dramatic reading, you are not only allowed, but expected, to convey more feeling and emotion than you would in a typical reading, so the normal cautions against being overdramatic do not apply here. If you are not reading alone, make sure that your level of dramatic expression matches that of the other participants.

Pronunciation Guide

Abba (AH-buh), *Alexander* (al'-ig-ZAN-duhr; -ZAHN-), *Arimathea* (air'-uh-muh-THEE-uh), *Barabbas* (bah-RA-buhs; bahr-AB-uhs), *Bethany* (BETH-uh-nee), *blessed* in 14:61 (adj., two syllables; BLES-id), *centurion* (sen-CHUR-ee-uhn), *Cyrene* (sī-REE-nee; *not* sī-REEN), *Elijah* (ee-LĪ-juh; ih-LĪ-juh), *Eloi, Eloi, lema sabachthani* (EE-loi EE-loi LAY-muh sah-bahk-TAH-nee *or* suh-BAK-thuh-nī), *Galilean* (gal'-uh-LEE-uhn), *Galilee* (GAL-uh-lee), *Gethsemane* (geth-SEM-uh-nee, -SEH-muh-), *Golgotha* (GOL-guh-thuh; gol-GOTH-uh), *Iscariot* (is-KAIR-ee-uht), *Jeremiah* (jair'-uh-MĪ-uh), *Joses* (JOH-seez; JOH-zehz), *Judas* (JOO-duhs), *Magdalene* (MAG-duh-leen; -lee-nuh), *Messiah* (muh-SĪ-uh), *myrrh* (MER), *Nazareth* (NAZ-uh-reth; *not* -rus), *Pilate* (PĪ-luht), *prophesy* in 14:65 (vb., PRAH-fuh-sī) [*not* prophecy], *Rabbi* (RAB-bī), *Rufus* (ROO-fuhs), *Salome* (suh-LOH-mee), *Simon* (SĪ-muhn)

MARK 15:1–39, (40–47)

Commentary

In the Gospel of Mark, Jesus undergoes two baptisms, one at the very beginning of his ministry and one at the very end. The first baptism takes place in the Judean wilderness in the waters of the Jordan River (1:9–11), while the second takes place just outside Jerusalem on a wooden cross at Golgotha (15:25–39). To refer to Jesus' crucifixion as a baptism is not to be fanciful, for Jesus himself describes his suffering and death in such terms. Earlier, when James and John requested seats of honor in Jesus' kingdom, Jesus responded with the question, "Are you able to drink the cup that I drink, or be baptized with the baptism that I am baptized with?" (10:38, Prop 24). Without any doubt, Jesus is referring to his upcoming death. Furthermore, the scenes of Jesus' baptism and crucifixion share some striking parallels.

In Mark's account of Jesus' baptism, when Jesus comes up out of the water, he looks up and sees the heavens being *torn apart*.[4] The only other occurrence of this verb in Mark is at Jesus' crucifixion. When Jesus expels his last breath, the temple curtain is *torn* in two from top to bottom (15:38). In Jesus' day, there were two temple curtains (or veils), an outer curtain which hung at the entrance to the temple and an inner curtain separating the Holy of Holies from the rest of the temple. Mark never explicitly tells his readers which curtain was torn, and commentators have long debated this question. We will not resolve this debate here, but it is interesting to recall the description of the outer curtain by the first-century Jewish historian, Josephus. The outer curtain was a massive Babylonian tapestry, beautifully woven with many colors, and the image portrayed on this tapestry was a panorama of the heav-

[4] This is a much more graphic description than we find in Matthew's and Luke's account of Jesus' baptism where the heavens are simply described as *opening* (Matt 3:16; Luke 3:21).

ens (JW 5.5.4 §§ 212–14). If this is the curtain that Mark has in view, then we have a second occurrence of the heavens being torn apart. In apocalyptic literature (e.g., the books of Daniel and Revelation), the rending of the sky signals that a revelation is forthcoming, and that is exactly what we find at Jesus' baptism and crucifixion. In Mark, these rendings of sky and curtain are both preludes to the revelation of Jesus' divine identity. At Jesus' baptism, the voice of God declares Jesus to be his beloved Son (1:11). Then, at Jesus' death, the centurion declares, "Truly this man was God's Son!" (15:39). These two scenes could not be more different from one another; one is glorious and the other tragic. Nevertheless, they belong together, for only together can they reveal what it means for Jesus to be the Son of God; being the Son of God involves both glory and suffering.

Jesus is on the cross for six long hours, and on three separate occasions, a group of bystanders makes comments about Jesus coming down from the cross (15:29–30, 32, 36). One of these groups is the chief priests and scribes—the chief conspirators—who mockingly shout, "Let the Messiah, the King of Israel, *come down from the cross* now, so that we may see and believe" (15:32). They regard Jesus' crucifixion as a sure sign that Jesus is a false prophet and a royal pretender; for God would never allow his Anointed One to die on a Roman cross, forsaken and humiliated. Of course, Jesus' opponents have it all backwards, for it is in *remaining* on the cross that Jesus reveals himself to be God's.

Ironically, it is a Roman official, the man in charge of the executions, who receives the revelation of Jesus' divine identity. And the revelation comes through seeing the way in which Jesus dies: "Now, when the centurion, who stood facing him, saw that in this way he breathed his last, he said, 'Truly this man was God's Son!'" (15:39). This Gentile centurion is the only human character in the entire gospel to recognize Jesus as the Son of God. Demons know it (1:24, 34; 3:11; 5:7), and God declares it (1:11; 9:7), but again, the centurion is the only *human* character to recognize Jesus as God's Son. Moreover, it is not one of Jesus' miracles that generates this insight, but Jesus' death.

This demonstrates that, for the author of Mark, Jesus' death is not only a sacrifice for sins (cf. 10:45; 14:24), it is also the means by which his divine identity is fully and finally made known. Jesus' death serves as the climactic event in the drama of God's self-revelation to humanity. As the incarnate Son of God, Jesus makes God known *and* makes it possible for us to know God. Jesus not only brings God close to us, he also gives us the eyes to see, the ears to hear, and the hearts to believe. The mystery of it all is that he accomplishes these things, not in spite of, but through suffering and death.

Suggestions for Lectors

Today's reading is quite dramatic and powerful, so while it is a long and familiar reading, there is no need to rush. Begin reading in your normal storytelling voice and proceed at a regular pace until you come to the moment of crucifixion. At 15:24, slow down as you read very solemnly, *and they crucified him.* Pause briefly afterwards before completing the sentence. Then, from this point forward, read more slowly and deliberately with increased feeling and emotion.

When the darkness descends in 15:33, slow down even more. Then, pause for a second after *afternoon* as you prepare for Jesus' final words from the cross. Deliver Jesus' cry of forsakenness in an elevated voice and in a tone that conveys his confusion and despair. Use the same voice for the translation, *My God, my God, why have you forsaken me?*, as you do for the original Aramaic words, *Eloi, Eloi, lema sabachthani?* (15:34). Jesus' cry could be read slowly, or it could be read somewhat quickly, especially when Jesus addresses God: *Eloi, Eloi,* and *My God, my God.*

In 15:35–36, quicken your pace as people talk excitedly and scurry about to secure some sour wine for Jesus. Then, slow back down as you relate Jesus' death.

The centurion's confession should receive the primary emphasis. Pause after *Truly* and *man*, and stress *this man*, as in: *Truly,… this man… was God's Son!* (15:39). After the confession, maintain a reverential silence for at least three to five seconds. Do this whether the reading continues with 15:40–47 or concludes with 15:39. In other words, if the reading ends at 15:39, let the centurion's pronouncement hang in the air for three to five seconds before saying *The Word of the Lord* (or whatever conclusion your community employs). If your reading continues with 15:40–47, then return to the same storytelling voice and tempo you used at the outset of the reading.

Pronunciation Guide
Alexander (al'-ig-ZAN-duhr; -ZAHN-), *Arimathea* (air'-uh-muh-THEE-uh), *Barabbas* (bah-RA-buhs; bahr-AB-uhs), *centurion* (sen-CHUR-ee-uhn), *Cyrene* (sī-REE-nee; *not* sī-REEN), *Elijah* (ee-LĪ-juh; ih-LĪ-juh), *Eloi, Eloi, lema sabachthani* (EE-loi EE-loi LAY-muh sah-bahk-TAH-nee *or* suh-BAK-thuh-nī), *Galilee* (GAL-uh-lee), *Golgotha* (GOL-guh-thuh; gol-GOTH-uh), *Israel* (IZ-ree-uhl; -ray-), *Joses* (JOH-seez; JOH-zehz), *Magdalene* (MAG-duh-leen; -lee-nuh), *Messiah* (muh-SĪ-uh), *myrrh* (MER), *Pilate* (PĪ-luht), *Rufus* (ROO-fuhs), *Salome* (suh-LOH-mee), *Simon* (SĪ-muhn)

MAUNDY THURSDAY

Exodus 12:1–4, (5–10), 11–14
Psalm 116:1–2, 12–19 (= 116:1, 10–17 BCP)
1 Corinthians 11:23–26
John 13:1–17, 31b–35

Exodus 12:1–4, (5–10), 11–14

Commentary
The tenth and final plague to strike the land of Egypt is the death of all the firstborn, including livestock and people, both royal and slave. In today's reading, Moses gives the Israelites instructions for how to prepare for this plague so that the angel of the Lord will pass over the firstborn of Israel and assail only the firstborn of Egypt. Today's episode offers something of a reversal to what took place at the beginning of the book when Pharaoh ordered the death of every male infant born to the Israelites (1:15–22).

12:1–4. This last plague will finally result in Israel's being set free from its four hundred years of slavery. Freedom for Israel means a new beginning for a new people. The month in which the first Passover is observed will become the first month of Israel's year. This demonstrates just how central the Exodus, and the Passover in particular, becomes to the national identity and life of God's people. The central symbol around which the Passover observance is oriented is a lamb.

12:5–10. Moses provides detailed instructions regarding what kind of lamb is acceptable and how it is to be prepared. A lamb is to be secured on the tenth of the month (12:3) and is to remain with the family until it is to be slaughtered at twilight on the fourteenth of the month (12:6). The lamb's blood is to be smeared upon the door frames and lintel of every Israelite house so that the LORD will see the blood and not visit the plague of the firstborn on its inhabitants (12:13).

12:11–14. Finally, Moses offers instructions regarding the manner in which the lamb, called "the passover of the LORD," is to be eaten (12:11). The people are to eat the Passover hurriedly and dressed in travel gear, for the moment that Pharaoh gives the word, they are to be on their way. Today's reading concludes with the instructions that this Passover observance is to become an annually-celebrated festival.

Suggestions for Lectors

Since today's reading consists of the LORD instructing Moses and Aaron on how the people are to protect themselves against the plague of the firstborn, read in an instructional manner, yet without reverting to a monotone.

An important shift in tone occurs between 12:11 and 12:12. As you near the end of 12:11 begin to slow down a bit. Read the final sentence, *It is the passover of the LORD*, slowly, making sure to enunciate each word clearly; then, pause for a full second before continuing. Read 12:12 slowly and in a very serious tone as you describe the LORD's plans to pass through the land, striking down the firstborn of Egypt. Again, read the final sentence, *I am the LORD*, slowly and deliberately, enunciating each word and pausing for a full second afterwards.

Verses 13 and 14 can be read at a normal speed without the seriousness required by the previous verses, for here the LORD speaks of Israel's salvation and of the annual festival that will commemorate it.

Pronunciation Guide

Aaron (AIR-uhn), *lintel* (LIN-t^{uh}l), *Moses* (MOH-zuhs), *Pharaoh* (FAY-roh; FAIR-oh)

1 CORINTHIANS 11:23–26

Commentary

In 1 Corinthians 11:17–34, Paul addresses some abuses he has heard of in connection with the Corinthians' celebration of the Lord's Supper. Here, it is important to recognize that, for the early Christian communities, the Lord's Supper did not denote a separate liturgical ritual, such as our modern day communion or Holy Eucharist. The Lord's Supper was a full-fledged communal meal, part of which was devoted to the symbolic sharing of Christ's body and blood. Since the early Christians gathered for worship in homes, the Lord's Supper would most likely have been celebrated in the home of one of the wealthier Corinthian Christians, who would have had a house large enough to host such a communal meal.

Paul has received news that when the Corinthians gather to celebrate the Lord's Supper, there are divisions among them. Most likely distinctions are being made between members of different social ranks and classes. Such distinctions were a reflection of the social mores of the wider Roman culture, of which the city of Corinth was a part. For example, in accordance with accepted social conventions, wealthier persons and persons of higher social rank would be given the better seats and the better food at a communal meal. This practice, however, does not accord with the view of the Christian community as the body of Christ where every member is to be given equal regard. It is not acceptable for wealthier members to get drunk while poorer members go hungry (11:21). Practices that perpetuate such social and economic inequality have no place at Christian gatherings, not least at the Lord's Supper where Christians come together to celebrate Christ's death for *all* people, be they Jew or Greek, slave or free, male or female, rich or poor (1 Cor 12:13; Gal 3:28).

These are the distinctions and practices Paul has in mind when he writes about their eating the bread and drinking the cup of the Lord in an unworthy manner (11:27), that is, without discerning the body (11:29). Here, *the body* refers not to the symbolic loaf of bread, but to the body of Christ comprising people from every social class (cf. 1 Cor 12:12–31). Consequently, Paul instructs the Corinthians to examine themselves before partaking of the bread and cup of Christ to see if they have been discerning the body, that is, to see if they have acted with equal regard for *all* the members of Christ's body (11:28–29). At the conclusion of this discussion, Paul writes, "So then, my brothers and sisters, when you come together to eat, wait for one another. If you are hungry, eat at home, so that when you come together, it will not be for your condemnation" (11:33–34a).

11:23–26. Today's reading stands at the heart of this larger discussion. In it, Paul reminds the Corinthians of the tradition that he handed down to them regarding Christ's words and actions at the Last Supper. But, what exactly does the *Last Supper* have to do with the particular problems the Corinthians are manifesting when they gather to celebrate the *Lord's Supper*? Just this: Paul is reminding the Corinthians that Jesus sacrificed himself for *others.* Whenever they celebrate the Lord's Supper, they are proclaiming Jesus' death until he returns (11:26). Yet how can the Corinthians proclaim Jesus' self-sacrificial death for *others*, when, in the meal that celebrates his death, the Corinthians actions are self-serving and disregard *the others* in their midst. In today's reading, Paul is not engaged in mere historical reminiscence but is engaged in profound theological reflection.

Suggestions for Lectors

As you read today's brief passage, imagine that you are the apostle Paul addressing a congregation that you founded. Were you reading these words from one of the gospels, you might read them with some feeling, since Jesus himself would be speaking them. Here, however, Paul is passing on a tradition that he received, so an informative tone might be more fitting.

Verse 26 is Paul's own theological interpretation of the tradition related in 11:23–25, so pause for a full second before reading 11:26 in order to distinguish them from one another. In addition, you might read this line with some feeling and intensity, as this line contributes to the larger argument Paul is making in the chapter.

Pronunciation Guide
Corinthians (kuh-RIN-thee-uhnz)

JOHN 13:1–17, 31B–35

Commentary
All four gospels present accounts of Jesus' last meal with his disciples. The Synoptic gospels (Matthew, Mark, and Luke) present the Last Supper as a Passover meal in which Jesus interprets the bread and the cup in relation to his death, providing the foundation for a (new) covenant (Matt 26:26–30; Mark 14:22–26; Luke 22:15–20; cf. 1 Cor 11:23–25, see above). In contrast, John does not include this scene in his account of the Last Supper, although earlier in the gospel, Jesus is presented as talking about eating his flesh and drinking his blood in connection with the feeding of the five thousand (6:25–59, esp. 53–58, Prop 15). Instead, John presents Jesus as engaged in lengthy conversations with his disciples about his going away and what will become of them. Moreover, John includes the account of Jesus washing his disciples' feet, which is the focus of today's reading.

13:1–11. Today's reading opens after the evening meal on the eve of Jesus' crucifixion. Up to this point in the gospel, numerous references have been made to Jesus' *hour*, a veiled reference to his hour of glory, that is, his death. In chapter two, for example, when Jesus' mother informs her son that the wine at the wedding feast has given out, Jesus responds, "Woman, what concern is that to you and to me? *My hour* has not yet come" (2:4). Similarly, in 7:30 and 8:20, the authorities are unable to arrest Jesus because "*his hour* had not yet come." But now Jesus' hour has come, so he strips down to his undergarments, dons a servant's towel, and begins washing his disciples' feet. Among those whose feet are washed is Judas Iscariot, whom Jesus already knows will betray him.

Following his exchange with Peter, Jesus says, "One who has bathed does not need to wash, except for the feet, but is entirely clean. And you are clean" (13:10a). Jesus says something similar later on in the evening, "You have already been cleansed by the word that I have spoken to you" (15:3, East 5). Those who belong to Jesus have been made clean through their association with Jesus, although not everyone who follows Jesus truly belongs to him, as in the case of Judas (13:10b–11).

13:12–17. After washing his disciples' feet, Jesus dresses and then explains the meaning of this symbolic action. As their Teacher and Lord, Jesus has taken on the role of a servant; so they too should serve one another as he has served them. Serving one another is what it means to love one another as Jesus has loved them (13:34). Given the theology of John's gospel, Jesus' example is quite profound in its implications. According to John, Jesus is the incarnate Word of God (1:14) and the eternal Son of God. He is the spitting image of his heavenly Father, and he is so close to the Father's heart that he can make the Father known (1:18, ✠ Chr 1). So when Jesus is washing his disciples' feet, he is manifesting God's glory. His simple act of service reveals a God who is humble and self-emptying by nature, qualities that we are expected to acquire and embody as God's children.

13:31b–35. When Judas Iscariot, who intends to betray Jesus, heads out into the night, Jesus remarks, "Now the Son of Man has been glorified, and God has been glorified in him" (13:31). In John, Jesus' glory is described as "the glory as of a father's only son" (1:14, ✠ Chr 1), which means that to see Jesus is to see God. As the incarnate Son of God, what Jesus does and says reflects the very image and nature of God. Jesus' glory is manifest not only in the wondrous signs he performs, but most supremely in his obedient death on the cross, which has now been set in motion with the withdrawal of Judas.

Jesus then tells the disciples that the time has drawn near for him to go away and that they will not be able to follow him. Jesus gives them a new commandment to follow in his absence, namely, that they love one another as Jesus has loved them. In other places in the gospels, Jesus teaches that the whole of the Law and the Prophets hangs on two commandments: the commandment to love God with all we are and have and the commandment to love our neighbors as ourselves. Thus, it is perhaps a bit surprising that this new commandment that Jesus gives his disciples focuses upon their love for one another, and not their love for the world or for those outside their circle. Of course, these different love commands are not mutually exclusive. Moreover, given its present context, the commandment to love one another serves a particular function. For if Jesus' disciples show love for one another, then the world "will know that [they] are [his] disciples" (13:35). In other words, how can the community of God show the world God's love if members of that community do not love one another? Jesus' followers are ambassadors of God's love, and they show God's love to the world first and foremost by loving one another.

Suggestions for Lectors

As reflected in the Commentary, today's reading occurs in three movements and combines both narration and teaching. Make sure to pause for a full second between movements, that is, before 13:12 and 13:31. As this is Jesus' last meal with his disciples, read with a sense of the occasion in mind. This will contribute to your presentation in subtle, yet profound ways.

The first movement (13:1–11) consists of narration mixed with dialogue. Employ your storytelling skills to set the tempo for the narrative and to express the feelings of each of the characters. In 13:1, a sentence that deserves special emphasis is, *Having loved his own who were in the world, he loved them to the end.* This sentence helps set the mood for what follows, so read it slowly and deliberately, clearly enunciating each word of *he loved them to the end.* Then, pause for a second before continuing with 13:2. Verse 11 can be read in a somewhat lower tone, as it functions like a narrative aside.

The second movement (13:12–17) consists mainly of Jesus' teaching, so adopt an instructional tone, yet one with some feeling and intensity to it. This portion is filled with punctuation, so use it to your advantage; there is no need to rush.

In the final movement (13:31b–35), force yourself to pause after each verse to heighten the impact. Pause slightly longer before verses 33 and 34, which will divide this movement into three smaller units: 31–32, 33, 34–35. Again, remember that Jesus is bidding farewell to his beloved disciples, so let your voice be tinged with affection. Emphasize 13:34–35 as Jesus gives his followers the new commandment of love and mutual regard. Deliver these words as you imagine Jesus to have done.

Pronunciation Guide
blessed (vb., one syllable; BLEST), *Iscariot* (is-KAIR-ee-uht), *Judas* (JOO-duhs

GOOD FRIDAY

Isaiah 52:13–53:12
Psalm 22
Hebrews 10:16–25 *or* 4:14–16; 5:7–9
John 18:1–19:42

ISAIAH 52:13–53:12

Commentary
Through its rich poetry and prose, the book of Isaiah narrates a dramatic story of rebellion and judgment that gives way to forgiveness and redemption. The plot begins with God's chosen people, but then broadens to encompass all the nations of the world and even creation itself. In Isaiah 1–39, the drama focuses upon rebellion as humanity serves the gods of its own making and orders society through unjust practices and power structures. The prophet Isaiah is sent to announce the various judgments that will be executed by the LORD, the Holy One of Israel and the creator of the heavens and the earth. Judgment begins with the LORD's own people who have forsaken the covenant (Isa 1–12, 28–35) through their willful and persistent failure to love God with their whole heart (Deut 6:5, Prop 26; Exod 20:1–7, Lent 3) and to love their neighbors as themselves (Lev 19:18; Exod 20:8–17). Judgment then extends to the nations and empires of the world who oppose the sovereign rule of the LORD through their prideful and unjust exercise of power (Isa 13–23). Even the forces of chaos and evil that threaten God's good creation will be judged, not least death itself (25:7–8, East).

Yet beginning in Isaiah 40, the ominous tone of judgment gives way to a joyful note of hope as the prophet announces a *new thing* that the LORD is about to do (42:9; 43:19; 48:6). This new thing, which will eventually result in the restoration of all creation, will begin with the LORD forgiving and redeeming his chosen people. Through his chosen people, God will bring about the redemption and reconciliation of all peoples everywhere in keeping with his covenant promises to Abraham and Sarah (Gen 12:2–3; 17:16; 22:17–18). Within this redemptive drama of Isaiah 40–55, we find four passages concerning an unidentified servant of the LORD (42:1–4; 49:1–6; 50:4–9, Palm; 52:13–53:12). These passages are called the Servant Songs. The servant appears sometimes as a corporate personality and sometimes as a single individual. There is a broad, general movement from the servant as *Israel* to the servant as *a single Israelite* who takes on Israel's vocation to be both the restorer of God's chosen people and the light to the nations (cf. 49:5–6).

Early Christians saw many similarities between Jesus and Isaiah's servant, especially with regard to Jesus' suffering and death. Their understanding of what God had done through Jesus' suffering and death was informed by the description of what the LORD did through the suffering of the servant in Isaiah, and vice versa. The importance of Isaiah's servant for understanding Jesus is reflected in the fact that each of the Servant Songs is read during Holy Week.

In today's reading of the fourth and final Servant Song, we see an intensification of the abuse and humiliation that the servant underwent in the third Servant Song (50:4–9a), culminating in the death of the servant (53:8–9). The fourth Servant Song goes beyond the third, seeing the suffering servant's death and vindication as the means by which the LORD enacts the forgiveness, healing, and restoration of his chosen people and all the peoples of the world.

52:13–15. Today's reading begins as it ends with a description of the vindication of the servant. The LORD declares, "See, my servant shall prosper; he shall be *exalted* and *lifted up*, and shall be very *high*," which employs terms used elsewhere to describe the LORD himself. For example, in 6:1, the prophet sees the LORD "sitting on a throne, *high* and *lofty*." After the servant has suffered, he will be given rank over all other rulers and authorities, and they will be in awe of him, "so he shall startle many nations; [and] kings shall shut their mouths because of him" (52:15a).

53:1–6. In this section, the change in pronouns from first person singular (*my*) to first person plural (*we*, *us*, *our*) indicates that the speaker has changed from the LORD to Israel. Here, God's chosen people make a public confession of sin. They bear witness to the unspeakable things that the servant endured as a direct result of their own rebellion and disobedience. They are responsible for the servant's suffering and death. The people acknowledge that when the servant was alive, they completely disregarded him because he was "despised and rejected by others" (53:3). Like Job's friends, they assumed that his chronic sickness and suffering were a sure sign that the LORD had forsaken him, so they too took no account of him. But now they recognize that they were completely mistaken about the servant and that they themselves are to blame. They see that the servant bore the humiliation and abuse that they should have borne had they not abandoned their vocation as God's chosen people.

53:7–11a. The people continue by bearing witness to the fact that the servant himself was innocent of any wrongdoing and that he endured the unjust abuse, humiliation, and death willingly. Moreover, they have come to see that the servant's life of suffering, far from being a sign of God-forsakenness, actually served God's purposes, for the LORD vindicated his servant by accepting and making "his life an offering for [the people's] sin" (53:10a).

53:11b–12. In the last section of today's reading, the speaker is the LORD, and he bears witness to the life and accomplishments of "my servant" (53:11b). The servant's life, though cut short (53:8), was not without significance. Because the servant remained obedient to God and carried out his calling faithfully even unto death, the LORD will raise him up and "allot him a portion with the great" (53:12), for he gave his life for others less righteous than he.

Suggestions for Lectors

Today's reading is somewhat lengthy, so it will be important not to simply read it from beginning to end, but to read it in sections, or in this case, stanzas. According to the NRSV, this suffering Servant Song comprises five stanzas of three verses each: 52:13–15; 53:1–3, 4–6, 7–9, 10–12. Pause for a full second at the beginning of each stanza, and conclude each stanza by slowing down during the last line.

In this reading, the phrases and sentences are simple ones. The punctuation is all there and need not be changed. What is of paramount importance, then, is the tone of voice you adopt. To convey the atmosphere of these somber enumerations of suffering, you must read slower than usual. Frequent pauses, at least after every sentence, will help set the scene and will serve to accent, by isolation, the importance of each trial the Servant endures. Though the whole passage possesses a somber tone, a few rays of light break through in the last stanza (53:10–12) as the prophet speaks of the servant's vindication and the community's gratitude for what the servant has endured on account of its sins.

Pronunciation Guide

Isaiah (ī-ZAY-uh)

HEBREWS 10:16–25

Commentary

During his ministry in the gospels, Jesus of Nazareth is portrayed primarily as a prophet. Even Jesus refers to himself as a prophet (Mark 6:4, Prop 9; Luke 4:24; 13:33–34) and compares himself to other prophets (Luke 4:25–27; 11:32; Matt 12:41). Acts 3:22–23 also describes Jesus as a prophet. Near the end of his earthly life, Jesus begins to be characterized as a king (Matt 21:5; John 18:37, Prop 29), and Jesus is even crucified as "The King of the Jews" (Mark 15:26). Throughout the rest of the NT, Jesus' kingship is expressed through such designations as Messiah, Christ, and Lord. Jesus is also depicted as a priest in the Letter to the Hebrews.

More specifically, Hebrews depicts Jesus as a high priest. Within Jewish tradition, the high priest was responsible for what took place at the temple. In particular, the high priest was the only person allowed to enter the Holy of Holies where the ark of the covenant resided, and then only once a year on the Day of Atonement to offer sacrifices that would atone for the sins of the whole nation (Lev 16; Heb 9:3–7). According to Hebrews, Jesus served as our great high priest by removing our sin by sacrificing *himself* (9:26, Prop 27) and by taking his *own blood*, not the blood of bulls and goats (9:12, Prop 26), into the *heavenly sanctuary*, not the earthly sanctuary (9:24).

Moreover, Jesus' self-sacrifice accomplished what all other sacrifices could never accomplish, the complete removal of sin (10:12, Prop 28). The blood of bulls and goats might *cover* sins, thereby offering worshippers temporary respite from their conscience, yet such sacrifices could never *take away* sins (10:4); otherwise "would they not have ceased being offered since the worshippers, cleansed once for all [time], would no longer have any consciousness of sin?" (10:2). When Christ came, his self-sacrifice served as a single, once-for-all-time removal of sins (10:12) that "perfected for all time those who are sanctified" (10:1). Jesus stands in marked contrast to those who served as high priests up until the time of Jesus. These priests never ran out of work; instead, they stood performing their high priestly duties day after day and year after year, "offering again and again the same sacrifices that [could] never take away sins" (10:11). With sin finally being taken care of once and for all, Jesus' work was finished, and so he sits down at the right hand of God. Today's reading picks up here in Hebrews.

10:16–18. Today's reading begins with scriptural citations from the prophet Jeremiah, which concern the new covenant that the LORD intended to establish with the houses of Israel and Judah after they had served their time in exile (Jer 31:31–34, Lent 5). Earlier in Hebrews 8:8–12, the author cited Jeremiah's new covenant prophecy in its entirety in order to demonstrate that a new and better covenant had already been envisioned in the OT. Here, the author returns to Jeremiah in order to highlight two features of the new covenant that Jesus as high priest fulfilled through his sacrificial death.

First, under the new covenant, the LORD says, "I will put my laws in their hearts, and I will write them on their minds" (10:16; Jer 31:33). Through his death, Jesus has "made perfect those who approach" to worship God (10:1; cf. 10:14), by cleansing them so thoroughly that they "no longer have any consciousness of sin" (10:2). With no consciousness of sin, they can worship God with their whole heart, which is the essence of the whole law. Thus, to have the law of God written on one's heart and mind corresponds to having one's heart emptied of any consciousness of sin.

Second, under the new covenant, the LORD says, "I will remember their sins and their lawless deeds no more" (10:17; Jer 31:34). This suggests a complete removal of sin, which as we have already seen, was accomplished through Christ's once-for-all-time, self-sacrifice. Thus, the author concludes, "Where there is forgiveness of these, there is no longer any offering for sin" (10:18).

10:19–25. The implications of our sins having been completely forgiven and of our consciences thoroughly cleansed of sin is that now there is nothing standing between us and God. We can now approach God without fear and with "a true heart in full assurance of faith" (10:22), confident of the fact that the death of our great high priest, Jesus, has opened for us a "new and living way" into the heavenly Holy of Holies where God and Jesus sit enthroned. When we have confidence in what Jesus has accomplished on our behalf, we no longer have to be preoccupied with the business of making ourselves right before God. Instead, we can focus our life and energies on loving and serving others, provoking "one another to love and good deeds,... meeting together,... and encouraging one another" (10:24–25).

Suggestions for Lectors

Today's reading is fairly straightforward without any verse standing apart or above the others, so read with an even voice throughout, though not in a monotone. Also, watch out for the two lengthy sentences (19–22, 24–25) that comprise most of the reading. Practice reading them so that with pauses and intonation of voice, you are able to hold these sentences together and convey them as a single thought.

Given that the reading is filled with the first person pronouns *we* and *us*, adopt a tone and expression that indicates that you belong to and identify with the people to whom you are speaking.

Hebrews 4:14–16; 5:7–9

Commentary

During his ministry in the gospels, Jesus of Nazareth is portrayed primarily as a prophet. Even Jesus refers to himself as a prophet (Mark 6:4, Prop 9; Luke 4:24; 13:33–34) and compares himself to other prophets (Luke 4:25–27; 11:32; Matt 12:41). Acts 3:22–23 also describes Jesus as a prophet. Near the end of his earthly life, Jesus begins to be characterized as a king (Matt 21:5; John 18:37, Prop 29), and Jesus is even crucified as "The King of the Jews" (Mark 15:26). Throughout the rest of the NT, Jesus' kingship is expressed through designations like Messiah, Christ, and Lord. In addition to prophet and king, Jesus is also depicted as a high priest, especially in the Letter to the Hebrews. In today's reading, we discover that our great high priest is able to sympathize with our weaknesses as human beings because he himself endured suffering as a human being.

4:14–16. The Letter to the Hebrews opens with a creed-like description of Jesus' exalted status as the Son of God:

> He is the reflection of God's glory and the exact imprint of God's very being, and he sustains all things by his powerful word. When he had made purification for sins, he sat down at the right hand of the Majesty on high, having become as much superior to angels as the name he has inherited is more excellent than theirs (1:3–4, Chr III).

In today's reading, this same Jesus who has passed into the heavens as our great high priest is also able to sympathize with our human predicament. Although Jesus passed through life committing no sin, as a human being, he experienced every category of temptation and test known to humankind. Consequently, he is able to sympathize with us in our struggles, and we are able to approach his throne with boldness knowing that he will receive us with mercy. On the other hand, precisely because he remained without sin, despite being tested in every respect as we are, we are able to approach him with confidence knowing that he will supply us with the grace, that is, the power and strength, to remain obedient in our time of need.

5:7–9. Being the Son of God by nature did not mean that Jesus obeyed the will of God automatically, as though it were impossible for him to sin. For as the author of Hebrews writes, "Although he was a Son, he *learned* obedience through what he suffered" (5:8). Since Jesus achieved perfection by living a life of obedience even in the midst of suffering, he has become the source of eternal life and salvation for those who follow him in living a life of obedience.

Suggestions for Lectors

Today's reading falls into two distinct, albeit related, sections, so make sure to pause for a second or two between 4:16 and 5:7 to signal the change.

In 4:14–16, the reading is filled with the first person plural pronouns *we* and *us*, so adopt a tone and an expression that indicates that you belong to and identify with the people to whom you are speaking. In other words, imagine the different tone you might adopt if *we* and *us* had simply been *you* throughout. In 1:15, pause after *as we are*, before you add the exception *yet without sin*.

In 5:7–9, there are no more first person pronouns as the focus has shifted entirely to Jesus *in the days of his flesh*. Read verses 7 and 8 more solemnly. Then, let your solemnity turn to joy and hope when reading verse 9.

JOHN 18:1–19:42

Commentary

This lengthy reading begins with Judas' betrayal of Jesus in the garden and concludes less than twenty-four hours later when Jesus' lifeless body is taken down from the cross and placed in the tomb. It includes Peter's threefold denial of Jesus, the accounts of Jesus before the Jewish high priest, Caiaphas, and before the Roman governor, Pilate, and of course Jesus' crucifixion.

Some of the unique features of John's account are the exchange between Pilate and Jesus that ends with Pilate's famous line, "What is truth?" (18:38); Jesus' placing his mother in the beloved disciples' care (19:26–27); Jesus' last words on the cross, "It is finished" (19:30); and Jesus' side being pierced with a sword in fulfillment of scripture (19:31–37).

Suggestions for Lectors

In today's reading, draw upon your skill as a storyteller in keeping with the dictates of the narrative. It has become quite common for the Passion narrative to be read, or even acted out, by several people in a dramatic fashion. When participating in a dramatic reading, you are not only allowed, but expected, to convey more feeling and emotion than you would in a typical reading, so the normal cautions against being overdramatic do not apply here. If you are not reading alone, make sure that your level of dramatic expression matches that of the other participants.

Pronunciation Guide

Annas (AN-uhs), *Arimathea* (air'-uh-muh-THEE-uh),
Barabbas (bah-RA-buhs; bahr-AB-uhs),
Caiaphas (KĪ-uh-fuhs; KAY-uh-fuhs),
Clopas (KLOH-puhs), *Gabbatha* (GAB-uh-thuh),
Golgotha (GOL-guh-thuh; gol-GOTH-uh),
Kidron (KID-rahn; KID-ruhn), *Malchus* (MAL-kuhs),
Magdalene (MAG-duh-leen; -lee-nuh), *myrrh* (MER),
Nazareth (NAZ-uh-reth; *not* -rus), *Nicodemus* (nik'-uh-DEE-muhs),
Pharisees (FAIR-uh-seez), *Pilate* (PĪ-luht)

SEASON OF EASTER

EASTER VIGIL

Resurrection of the Lord

Genesis 1:1–2:4a	Psalm 136:1–9, 23–26
Genesis 7:1–5, 11–18; 8:6–18; 9:8–13	Psalm 46
Genesis 22:1–18	Psalm 16
Exodus 14:10–31; 15:20–21	Exodus 15:1b–13, 17–18; ✠ Canticle 8
Isaiah 55:1–11	Isaiah 12:2–6; ✠ Canticle 9
Baruch 3:9–15; 3:32–4:4 *or* Proverbs 8:1–8, 19–21; 9:4b–6	Psalm 19
Ezekiel 36:24–28	Psalm 42 and 43
Ezekiel 37:1–14	Psalm 143
Zephaniah 3:14–20	Psalm 98
Romans 6:3–11	Psalm 114
Mark 16:1–8	

GENESIS 1:1–2:4A

Commentary

The book of Genesis begins with an orderly account of the creation of the world that reflects the orderliness of creation itself. As we shall see, the six days of God's creative activity can be divided into two parallel groups. The first three days are related to one another as are the second three days. In addition, God's creative activity on Days 1, 2, and 3 correspond to his creative activity on Days 4, 5, and 6, respectively.

Day 1. Light; Separation of Day and Night	**Day 4.** Lights; Day Light and Night Lights
Day 2. Sky; Separation of the Waters	**Day 5.** Sky and Water Creatures
Day 3. Land Masses and Vegetation	**Day 6.** Land Animals and Human Beings
Day 7. The Sabbath: God Rested from All the Work That He Had Done	

1:1–2, In the Beginning. Christianity generally speaks of God's creating the world *ex nihilo*, that is, out of nothing. Support for this view can be found in such texts as Romans 4:17 (Lent 2), 1 Corinthians 1:28, Hebrews 11:3, and 2 Maccabees 7:28. Genesis 1:1 is also used to support this view. Strictly speaking, however, Genesis 1 is not so much a creation out of *nothing* as it is a creation out of *chaos*, here represented by the impenetrable darkness and the unbounded waters of the primordial deep. Of course, one could well argue that from a theological standpoint, the notions of chaos and nothingness are essentially synonymous, such that Genesis 1 could be read in support for the doctrine of *creatio ex nihilo*. Be that as it may, it nevertheless remains critical to our understanding of this text, as well as many other biblical texts, that Genesis 1 presents God as creating by bringing order out of chaos. For example, in other Ancient Near Eastern literature (e.g., the Babylonian epic, Enuma Elish), creation was depicted as a cosmic struggle between the gods and the forces of chaos. Yet the picture Genesis 1 paints, which refutes and subverts such pagan accounts of creation, is one in which the forces of chaos offer no challenge for God. God does not struggle or war against chaos; instead God overcomes chaos simply by speaking things into being. In addition, it is significant that, in creating the world, God does not destroy the forces of chaos but delimits them. This is the story of the first three days of creation.

1:3–13, The First Three Days. On each of the first three days, God's creative activity results in an inhabitable region where life can take root and flourish. God achieves this by delimiting the forces of chaos, that is, by creating boundaries that establish limits and restricts the darkness and the deep. So on Day One, God creates light and then separates the light from the darkness by relegating each to their own respective spheres of influence, here called Day and Night. Similarly, on Day Two, God creates a dome called Sky (a.k.a., the firmament), which is designed to divide the waters of the deep. By separating the waters under the dome from the waters above the dome, God reduces the havoc they might wreak if they were allowed to join forces against creation. This is, in fact, what happens during the great flood, "on that day all the fountains of the great deep burst forth, and the windows of the heavens were opened" (Gen 7:11; see the following reading). Then, on Day Three, two distinct but related acts of creation are performed. First, the waters under the sky are gathered together into Seas, thus allowing the dry land called Earth to appear. Second, the earth brings forth every type of vegetation. Thus, after just three days, everything necessary to support and sustain life has been established.

Interestingly, the next to the last chapter of the Bible offers a glimpse of the new heavens and the new earth, in which *the sea* (Rev 21:1) and *the night* (Rev 21:25; 22:5) are expressly absent. In the original creation, the night and the sea are restricted, yet their ongoing presence in creation still threatens to undo creation. In the new creation, the forces of chaos have no place, no sphere of influence. Consequently, the new creation will never experience a fall because chaos itself—violence, sin, and evil—will no longer be able to threaten creation or God's purposes in creation.

1:14–31, The Second Three Days. On the second three days, God populates each of the inhabitable regions with creatures who are called to exercise dominion within their region. On Day Four (≈ Day One), God creates two great lights, the greater to rule the Day and the lesser to rule the Night. Here, these lights are not named Sun and Moon since they would have been the names of pagan deities. On Day Five (≈ Day Two), God populates the Sky and the Seas with birds and sea creatures who are to exercise dominion by reproducing and filling their respective spheres. On Day Six (≈ Day Three), two related acts of creation are performed as was the case on Day 3. God first created all of the living creatures for whom the land would be their home. Last of all, God created human beings and gave them dominion over all the living creatures God had made. Together and side by side as male and female, human beings were to be the image-bearers of God in creation; that is, they were to care for and rule over creation as God's vice-regents. That this role is granted to humanity as a whole stands in marked contrast to the stories and practices of other ancient peoples in which only rulers were regarded as the image-bearers of a god or gods.

2:1–4a, The Seventh Day. Having completed his work of creation in six days, God rests on the seventh day, thereby blessing it and setting it apart as a holy day of rest. Eventually, this will provide the model for how God's image-bearers are to go about their work as stewards of creation. As God says in the fourth commandment, "Six days you shall labor and do all your work. But the seventh day is a sabbath to the LORD your God; you shall not do any work.... For in six days the LORD made heaven and earth, the sea, and all that is in them, but rested the seventh day; therefore the LORD blessed the sabbath day and consecrated it" (Exod 20:9–11, Lent 3).

Suggestions for Lectors

The orderliness and stateliness of this creation account should be expressed through an orderly, majestic reading. This can be achieved by decreasing the tempo at key points and by employing a number of well-placed pauses, many of which are already provided in the punctuation of the text. The account's overall structure is ordered through the repeated, *And there was evening and there was morning, the _____ day*; so you will want to pause for a full second at the end of each day and perhaps take an opportunity to look at your listeners before continuing.

Since this creation account emphasizes how God ordered the chaos and brought things into being with a simple word, you may wish to draw attention to God's speaking in the following ways. First, when you read *Then* or *And God said*, drop your voice slightly on *said*, and then pause briefly to create a sense of expectation. Pause again after the speaking part has concluded. You may wish to pause even longer before 1:26 and after 1:31 since the creation of humankind serves as the climax of God's creative activity. Conclude by reading 2:1–4 in a somewhat lower tone.

Though this reading is both familiar and long, avoid the temptation to rush or to feel like you have to apologize to your audience with your voice. Instead, imagine that your audience is eager to hear the story again.

Pronunciation Guide

blessed (vb., one syllable; BLEST)

GENESIS 7:1–5, 11–18; 8:6–18; 9:8–13

Commentary

From the time of Adam and Eve's expulsion from the garden of Eden until the time of Noah, sin and violence increased exponentially within the world so much so that, when the LORD saw that "every inclination of the thoughts of [people's] hearts was only evil continually,… [he] was sorry that he had made humankind on the earth, and it grieved him to his heart" (Gen 6:5b–6). Thus, the LORD decides to wipe out the human race along with all the other animals and creatures that live on the land because he is sorry that he ever made them. "But Noah found favor in the sight of the LORD" (6:8), and so the LORD instructs Noah to build an ark that will preserve him and his immediate family as well as representatives of each of God's creatures from the flood that the LORD is bringing upon the whole earth (6:9–22).

7:1–5. When today's reading begins, the ark has been built, and the time for the flood is drawing near. The LORD instructs Noah to enter the ark with his household and to take along seven pairs of birds and seven pairs of clean animals but only one pair of unclean animals. These numbers differ from those presented in 6:19–20 where two of every kind of living thing are to be brought into the ark (cf. 7:8–9). This points to the fact that, as it now stands, the story of the flood in Genesis 6:1–9:17 is composed of two separate, though similar, flood stories that have been woven together to form a single narrative. This also helps explain the repetition that one finds throughout these chapters. In any case, Noah faithfully executes all that the LORD commands him to do.

7:11–18. On the second day of creation (1:6–8; see prior reading), God created the sky dome in order to separate "the waters that were under the dome from the waters that were above the dome" (1:7), which is a strategy of divide and conquer. Instead of ridding creation of these chaotic waters of the deep, God divides them and relegates them to their own respective regions, thereby reducing significantly the threat they pose to creation. Yet in this scene, much of God's original creation is undone as these waters are once again allowed to join forces to wreak havoc upon the earth for "on that day all the fountains of the great deep burst forth, and the windows of the heavens were opened" (7:11). While the flood destroyed every living thing that lived upon the face of the earth (7:21–22), Noah and all those with him were preserved on the ark. The rains lasted for forty days and forty nights, and the waters swelled for a total of one hundred and fifty days (7:24).

8:6–18. Then God remembered Noah and all those upon the ark and began to reduce the flood waters by sending a wind to blow upon the earth and by closing up the fountains of the deep and the windows of heaven. From this point, it took seven months before the waters had abated and the earth had dried sufficiently. Thus, Noah, his family, and the animals come out of the ark one full year and ten days after they entered the ark (cf. 7:11, 8:14). In keeping with their original creation mandate (1:22, 28), they are all instructed to "be fruitful and multiply on the earth" (8:17; cf. 9:1, 7).

9:8–13. Before the flood, God had been sorry that he had ever made humankind (6:7), but now after the flood, God decides that he will never again send a flood to destroy the earth. In keeping with this intention, God establishes a covenant between himself and Noah, his descendants, and every living creature upon the earth, an eternal covenant of which the rainbow becomes the sign.

Suggestions for Lectors

Though this is another long story, following the even longer story of creation, there is still no need to rush. In recounting these familiar narratives, we are remembering, reconfirming, and reinforcing our identity as the people of God.

Genesis 9:12–13 serves as the climax for the story. Pause after 9:12; then, as though you were inviting everyone to glance skyward with you, reduce your speed as God sets the rainbow in the clouds as an eternal sign of the covenant that God has established between himself and all creation.

Pronunciation Guide

Ham (HAM), *Japheth* (JAY-fuhth), *Noah* (NOH-uh), *Shem* (SHEM)

GENESIS 22:1–18

Commentary

The book of Genesis is replete with drama as human beings attempt to come to terms with what it means to live life in trust and faithful obedience before God. One of the narrative threads woven throughout Genesis is the dramatic tension between promise and threat. This tension arises when the promises God makes to human beings are juxtaposed with situations that appear to threaten the fulfillment of those promises. This often initiates a crisis of faith. God's people are faced with a decision. Will they trust God to bring about what he has promised to do? Or, will they attempt to bring about the fulfillment of the promise themselves?

This motif is particularly prominent in the narratives concerning Abraham and Sarah (11:30–25:18). For example, when the LORD first calls Abram, he promises to make him into a great nation by blessing him with *land* and *offspring* (12:1–9). Yet no sooner are Abram and Sarai in the land that the LORD is giving them than a situation arises that threatens both promises (12:10–20). First, the promise of land is threatened by a severe famine that forces Abram and Sarai to become resident aliens in Egypt. As they are about to enter Egypt, Abram becomes afraid, thinking that, when the Egyptians see Sarai's beauty, they will kill Abram. Instead of trusting in God's provision and protection, Abram convinces Sarai to pretend that she is his sister, but his plan backfires. Though Abram is not killed, Sarai is taken into Pharaoh's harem, thus threatening the LORD's promise of offspring. Despite Abram's lack of trust, the LORD rescues Sarai from Pharaoh's house, and both return to the Promised Land (13:1).

When the LORD first makes his promise of children, Abram is seventy-five years old and Sarai is sixty-five. Ten years later, they are prospering in the Promised Land, but they have not yet conceived the promised offspring. Convinced that the LORD has prevented her from bearing any children, Sarai offers up Hagar, her Egyptian slave-girl, as a surrogate (16:1–3). Hagar conceives and gives birth to Ishmael, whom Abram and Sarai treat as the promised heir. Once again, they have taken matters into their own hands. Thirteen years later, when Abram and Sarai are ninety-nine and eighty-nine respectively, the LORD visits Abram and gives him the name Abraham and informs him that Sarai, who is now to be known as Sarah, will bear Abraham a son. When Abraham objects asking if thirteen-year-old Ishmael might be his promised heir, the LORD says, "No, but your wife Sarah shall bear you a son, and you shall name him Isaac. I will establish my covenant with him as an everlasting covenant for his offspring after him" (17:19). So, again despite Abraham and Sarah's lack of trust, the LORD fulfills his promises in his own way and in his own time.

These are just two of many examples illustrating Abraham and Sarah's tendency to orchestrate the fulfillment of God's promises in response to perceived threats. The reader who has closely followed the story from Genesis 12 is therefore surprised when, in today's reading, Abraham offers no resistance to the LORD's command that he sacrifice his beloved son Isaac.

22:1–8. The episode begins by informing the reader that what the LORD is about to request of Abraham is part of a test. Of course, Abraham is not privy to this information, so when he responds without hesitation, it speaks to his obedience as well as his trust in God. Abraham's trust is also revealed in the response he gives to Isaac's question: "God himself will provide the lamb for a burnt offering, my son" (22:8).

22:9–14. When they arrive at the place God directed them to, Abraham methodically makes all of the necessary preparations for a whole burnt offering—building an altar, laying the wood in order, binding his own son, and placing him upon the altar. The reader can only imagine what Abraham must be feeling and thinking as he takes the knife to kill his own son. Even if he fully trusted in God's wisdom and goodness, he surely must have felt relief when the angel of the LORD called out to him and stayed his hand. In the end, Abraham's trust in God is vindicated. As he had told Isaac, the LORD did provide the lamb for the offering.

22:15–18. For the first time in the narrative, Abraham demonstrates complete trust and obedience in God, so it is fitting that the LORD chooses this opportunity to reconfirm the original promise of land and offspring that he first made to Abraham and Sarah some thirty years ago (12:1–3).

It is little wonder that Christians throughout the centuries have seen in the binding of Isaac a prefiguring of Jesus. Just as Abraham offered up his only beloved son, so God offered up his only beloved Son. Isaac's ascending the mountain bearing the wood on which he is to be sacrificed finds parallel in Jesus' march to Golgotha bearing his own cross. Moreover, just as all the nations of the earth will be blessed through Isaac, so all the nations of the world are blessed through Jesus who, according to Paul, is ultimately the offspring referred to here in Genesis 22:18 (Gal 3:16, 19).

Suggestions for Lectors

In this story, whatever might be going on inside Abraham, he acts as though he has complete faith in the LORD's ability to provide. So you might tell this story with a quiet, simple confidence in your voice. Likewise, Isaac trusts his father completely, so when he asks, *Father,... where is the lamb for a burnt offering?* (22:7), he is not afraid, merely curious. Of course, Abraham's quiet confidence may begin to break down as he goes through the process of binding his son, placing him on the altar, taking his knife, and raising it over him (22:9b–10); so let this be reflected in your voice. Pause before *He bound his son* (22:9b) and decelerate your tempo up until *to kill his son* (22:10)—as though you are slowing down in a countdown: 5, 4, 3, 2, 1½, 1¼, 1, etc. Then, pause for a full second to let the dramatic tension develop before you say, *But the angel* (22:11). When the LORD calls out, *Abraham! Abraham!* (22:11) there is no need to shout; instead, just say Abraham's name with more intensity.

Pause before 22:13 to let the LORD's words sink in. Imagine the relief and joy Abraham must have felt upon hearing these words and upon seeing the ram. Then read 22:13–14 with these emotions reflected in your voice.

Though 22:15–18 is spoken by the angel of the LORD, read this blessing with the same tone you imagine Abraham is feeling as he is listening to these words, as though you have just passed the biggest test in your life and you are so relieved, joyful, and happy to be alive.

Pronunciation Guide
Abraham (AY-bruh-ham), *Isaac* (Ī-zik), *Moriah* (moh-RĪ-uh)

EXODUS 14:10–31; 15:20–21

Commentary
Arguably, no other single event so formed and informed ancient Israel's developing sense of ethnic, religious, and national identity like their Exodus from Egypt. Of course, many centuries prior to the Exodus, the LORD had aligned himself with an unlikely couple, Abraham and Sarah, in order that he might fashion for himself a chosen people, through whom all the peoples of the world would be blessed and come to know the one true God of all creation (Gen 12:1–3). Nevertheless, it was through the events of the Exodus, wherein the LORD freed Israel from its four-hundred-year captivity, that Israel understood itself as having been constituted as a people. This is reflected in the opening line of the Ten Commandments, where the LORD says, "I am the LORD your God, who brought you out of the land of Egypt, out of the house of slavery; you shall have no other gods before me" (Exod 20:2–3, Lent 3). In other words, because of the Exodus, the people of Israel began to recognize themselves as God's chosen people. Thus, before the Exodus, the LORD instructed Moses to say to the Israelites:

> I am the LORD, and I will free you from the burdens of the Egyptians and deliver you from slavery to them. I will redeem you with an outstretched arm and with mighty acts of judgment. *I will take you as my people, and I will be your God.* You shall know that I am the LORD your God, who has freed you from the burdens of the Egyptians (Exod 6:6b–7).

In addition, although many events conspired to bring about Israel's escape and exodus from Egypt, two events in particular played a more prominent role in Israel's national memory. The first was Passover in which the firstborn of the Egyptians died while the firstborn of the Israelites were spared. The second was Israel's passing through the waters of the Red Sea on dry ground, where once again the people of Israel were spared while their enemies were destroyed. This is the story found in today's reading. The importance of the crossing of the Red Sea for Jewish and Christian self-understanding and identity cannot be overestimated for it is recounted, evoked, and alluded to throughout the Old and New Testaments.

Leading up to today's story, the death of the Egyptian firstborn at Passover had been the last straw for Pharaoh who then commanded Moses and Aaron to take the Israelites away from his people (12:31–32). Yet when the Israelites exited Egypt, they did not take the shortest route to the Promised Land, which passed through the land of the Philistines, for God thought, "If the people face war, they may change their minds and return to Egypt" (13:17b), which in fact occurs in today's reading. Instead, God chose to "lead the people by the roundabout way of the wilderness toward the Red Sea" (13:18). This strategy also served another purpose, for it would appear that the Israelites were wandering aimlessly in the wilderness, prompting Pharaoh to pursue them with his armies and thereby leading them to their destruction.

14:10–14. Today's reading begins with Pharaoh and his armies drawing near to the Israelites who are backed up against the Red Sea with no escape route. Filled with fear, the Israelites lash out at Moses, blaming him for their predicament and asking that they might return to Egypt. This is a recurring motif during Israel's forty-year wilderness sojourn (cf. Num 14:1–4).

14:15–20. The LORD instructs Moses to take the staff that had performed so many wonders in Egypt and stretch it out over the Red Sea in order to divide it so that the Israelites might pass through the waters on dry ground. In the meantime, the angel of the LORD, who had been going ahead of the people as a pillar of cloud by day and a pillar of fire by night (13:21–22), takes up a position between the people and the armies of Pharaoh.

14:21–29. Moses does as the LORD instructed, and the Israelites begin to pass through the Red Sea on dry ground. The Egyptians pursue, but the angel of the LORD inhibits their progress. When the Israelites arrive safely on the other side, Moses stretches his hand over the sea causing it to return to its normal level and so drowning Pharaoh's entire army in the process.

14:30–31. In this way, the LORD both rescued his people and exercised his judgment over Pharaoh and the Egyptians for their treatment of the Israelites. Moreover, having witnessed all of these things, the Israelites began to revere the LORD, trusting in the LORD and in his servant Moses.

15:20–21. After these events, Moses and the Israelite men sing a song of victory and praise to the LORD (15:1–18). Following this, Moses and Aaron's sister, Miriam, leads the Israelite women in a chorus taken from the first line of Moses' song (15:1): "Sing to the LORD, for he has triumphed gloriously; horse and rider he has thrown into the sea" (15:21).

Suggestions for Lectors

This well-known episode from Israel's history is filled with drama and excitement as the well-equipped Egyptian armies close in on the ill-equipped, helpless Israelites and then as the LORD executes a dramatic rescue that leaves Israel safe while simultaneously vanquishing its pursuers. As with any drama, this story is filled with a wide range of emotions: anger, fear, panic, resentment, desperation, frustration, awe, relief, joy, etc. Consequently, you will want to become very familiar with this story, practicing the speaking parts until you are comfortable with how your voice expresses the various feelings of the different characters and groups.

Though we never want to rush through a reading, you may want to slowly increase your tempo as the story progresses to match the drama. As the story reaches its climax in 14:28, pause briefly before reading *not one of them remained* slowly and without emotion. Pause again before 14:29, reading it slowly and more matter-of-factly now that the danger has passed. As you read 14:30–31, return to your normal narrating voice. As you read the epilogue (15:20–21), try to imagine and then convey the joy, hope, and happiness of a people who have just been delivered from centuries of slavery.

Pronunciation Guide
Egyptians (ih-JIP-shuhnz; ee-), *Israelites* (IZ-ree-līts), *Miriam* (MIR-ee-uhm), *Moses* (MOH-zuhs), *Pharaoh* (FAY-roh; FAIR-oh)

Isaiah 55:1–11

Commentary
In Isaiah 1–39, Isaiah announces the LORD's judgment upon the people of Judah and Jerusalem for their centuries of idolatry and injustice, that is, for their ongoing refusal to love God with their whole heart (Deut 6:5, Prop 26; Exod 20:1–7, Lent 3) and their failure to love their neighbors as themselves (Lev 19:18; Exod 20:8–17). Isaiah 39 concludes on an ominous note as the predicted destruction and exile of Judah and Jerusalem by the Babylonian empire becomes imminent.

Isaiah 40 skips ahead many years and introduces a new movement in the prophetic drama. This strikes a completely different note than that with which Isaiah 39 concluded. Isaiah 40 presupposes that God's people have been in exile for some time and opens with a message of hope for these exiles in Babylon (40:1–2):

> Comfort, O comfort my people,
> says your God.
> Speak tenderly to Jerusalem,
> and cry to her
> that she has served her term,
> that her penalty is paid,
> that she has received from the LORD's hand
> double for all her sins.

In other words, the exile is over. The LORD has forgiven his people and is coming soon to bring them back home. This is a recurrent motif throughout Isaiah 40–55.

In Isaiah 54, which leads up to today's reading, the LORD instructs the exiles not to become fearful or discouraged; he is going to redeem them, and they shall soon forget the shame of their past unfaithfulness and the humiliation of their exile. The LORD swears that he will not be angry with his people or rebuke them (54:9); as he says, "For a brief moment I abandoned you, but with great compassion I will gather you. In overflowing wrath for a moment I hid my face from you, but with everlasting love I will have compassion on you" (54:7–8a). The LORD'S "steadfast love shall not depart from [his people], and [his] covenant of peace shall not be removed" (54:10). In today's reading, the LORD continues with his words of reconciliation and forgiveness as he seeks to alleviate the exiles' fear of being punished.

55:1–5. The reading begins with the LORD calling out to his exiled people like a street vendor: "Ho, everyone who thirsts, come to the waters; and you that have no money, come, buy and eat! Come, buy wine and milk without money and without price" (55:1). The exile is over, and the LORD is once again providing for the physical and spiritual needs of his chosen people. He calls upon his people to gather round and listen to his counsel that they might live and experience life as it was meant to be. In keeping with his promise to David (2 Sam 7:11b–16, Adv 4; 1 Kgs 8:25, Prop 16), the LORD will enter into a covenant relationship with the people that will last forever (cf. 54:10). When that happens, Israel will function as God's image-bearers in the world, reflecting the glory of the LORD and so drawing all the nations to them and to the Holy One of Israel. Thus, as servants of the LORD (54:17), God's people will finally fulfill their covenant vocation to be "a light to the nations" (42:6).

55:6–9. In this section, the people are instructed to repent and return to the LORD so that he might have the opportunity to demonstrate his love and mercy by forgiving them their sins. Here repentance is described in terms of the people forsaking their ways and thoughts for the LORD's ways and thoughts—that is, his plans for Israel and for the nations—are so much higher and grander than those of human beings. For example, no human being would ever have envisioned that the redemption of Israel, humanity, and all of creation could be brought about through suffering and death, and more specifically, through the suffering and death of the LORD's chosen servant, which occurs in 52:13–53:12 (GFri).

55:10–11. Though the LORD's thoughts and ways may be incomprehensible to human beings, appearing foolish and impractical, it remains the case that whatever the LORD sets in motion comes out as planned. For example, at creation, everything the LORD spoke into being came into being; when he said, "Let there be light," there was light (Gen 1:3, Epi 1). Thus, like the rain and the snow from heaven, when the word of the LORD goes forth from his mouth, it does not return until it has brought about all that the LORD intended, namely, life.

Suggestions for Lectors

This is a lengthy enough reading that you will want to read it in more than one section. The NRSV organizes it into three stanzas: 1–5, 6–9, 10–11. Whenever you come to the last phrase or clause of a stanza, drop your voice and read slowly and deliberately, then pause for a full second before beginning the next stanza.

The whole reading is an invitation to the life that God has to offer, so read this passage with intensity. As always, remember that there is no need to be shrill. The voice is raised, of course, but the secret here is the intensity of conviction which, through your preparation, should seize you and transform your voice.

As you practice and as you read, be particularly attentive to the various images that are being offered. Note as well the repetition in grammar and language that recurs throughout. Attentiveness to these elements will allow you to read with a cadence and an intonation that is well suited for the reading of a poetic text.

Pronunciation Guide
Ho (HOH), *Isaiah* (ī-ZAY-uh)

BARUCH 3:9–15, 32–4:4

Commentary
The book of Baruch exists only in Greek and so is not part of the Hebrew canon. As such, it belongs neither to the OT nor the NT, but to a collection of books known within Protestant traditions as the Apocrypha and within Roman Catholicism as Deuterocanonical (that is, Second Canon). In Eastern Orthodoxy, Baruch is simply part of the OT scriptures. The book is attributed to Baruch, son of Nariah, who served as a secretary and amanuensis for the prophet Jeremiah (Jer 36:4) and who is said to have composed this book in Babylon during the Babylonian exile (1:1–2). In it, Baruch presents vignettes from the history of the Exile and reflections on that history.

3:9–14. In today's reading, the author calls upon Israel to give an ear to the Wisdom of God, who is here personified as a woman, as in the book of Proverbs (see Proverbs below). Baruch attributes Israel's exile to the fact that the people forsook "the fountain of wisdom" (3:12). Thus, Israel would do well to discover where Wisdom stores her treasures, to learn where wisdom, strength, and understanding are to be found; for where Wisdom is, there is life, light, and peace.

3:15, 32–35. Yet "Who has found her place? And who has entered her storehouses?" (3:9), for only the one who has found Wisdom can lead others to her. Likewise, "Who has gone up into heaven, and taken her, and brought her down from the clouds? Who has gone over the sea, and found her, and will buy her for pure gold?" (3:29–30). Only God has done these things and "found her by his understanding" (3:32). Only the God, who created the heavens and the earth, knows all things and so knows Wisdom, and the God who has done all these things is the God of Israel, to whom no other gods can be compared.

3:36–4:4. Moreover, when God discovered Wisdom, he did not keep her to himself but gave her to his beloved, chosen people. Though Wisdom resided in heaven and beyond the sea (3:29–30), she now dwells upon earth for she is the Law, the Torah, the commandments that God bestowed on his covenant people. Thus, Jacob (that is, Israel) should return to the Wisdom of the Law and cling to her; for she is life, and she shows God's people what is pleasing to God.

Suggestions for Lectors
This reading is wonderfully long, giving your listeners a chance to really settle into it; so there is no need to rush. Because the reading is as long as it is, it will be important to break it up into smaller sections, at least into the three sections identified above, by pausing for a full second between the sections and perhaps looking up at your listeners. You might adopt a slightly different tone of voice for each section.

In 3:9–15, Baruch highlights Israel's forsaking the commandments of God, the fountain of wisdom. Baruch's questions and indictments could easily be read in a harsh, critical, and accusatory tone of voice. Alternatively, they could be read in a compassionate, gentle manner as an expression of genuine concern and love even in the midst of frustration. Remember that you are not simply a third party passing on Baruch's words to your listeners; instead, you are Baruch speaking directly to those with whom you most identify. In the latter two sections, your voice should be filled with a sense of awe as you express your amazement and wonder with regard to God and God's law.

Pronunciation Guide
Baruch (bah-ROOK), *Hades* (HAY-deez)

PROVERBS 8:1–8, 19–21; 9:4B–6

Commentary
When Solomon succeeded his father David as king over Israel and Judah, the LORD asked him in a dream, "Ask what I should give you" (1 Kgs 3:5, Prop 15). Solomon asked for understanding in order to govern God's people wisely (3:9). God was so pleased with Solomon's request that he gave him such a wise and discerning a mind (3:12) that he became famous and his wisdom legendary (4:29–34). The book of Proverbs is just one testament to that wisdom. Proverbs bears the superscription, "The proverbs of Solomon son of David, king of Israel" (1:1). This should not be read as indicating that Solomon himself composed all of the proverbs in the book; for not only does Proverbs contain much traditional wisdom known from elsewhere in the Ancient Near East, but the book itself attributes proverbs to other sources (1:6; 22:17; 24:23; 30:1; 31:1). Therefore, the book of Proverbs is better understood as an anthology of wisdom sayings, containing proverbs Solomon composed as well as those he and others collected.

8:1–8. In Proverbs, God's Wisdom (or understanding, prudence, intelligence, etc.) is personified as a woman; as in: "Does not wisdom call, and does not understanding raise *her* voice (8:1; cf. 8:2–3; 9:1–3). In today's reading, Wisdom travels about calling out to all people everywhere and inviting them to listen to her and heed her counsel. Wisdom can be trusted for she speaks only what is noble, she only utters the truth.

8:19–21. Because Wisdom walks "in the way of righteousness" and "along the paths of justice," the fruit she bears is priceless. Consequently, those who love God's Wisdom and eat her fruit will find themselves rich beyond measure.

9:4b–6. Today's reading ends with the image of Wisdom hosting a feast to which the simple are invited. She builds her house, butchers the meat, prepares the wine, and sets the table (9:1–2). Then, when everything is ready, Wisdom sends her servant-girls with an invitation to all and sundry (9:3), "You that are simple, turn in here!… Come, eat of my bread and drink of the wine I have mixed" (9:4a, 5). Those who accept the invitation to lay aside their foolishness and immaturity and to feast at the house of Wisdom will find life.

Suggestions for Lectors

In today's reading, you will need two voices: one for the sage who introduces Wisdom (8:1–3; 9:4b) and one for Wisdom herself (8:4–8, 19–21; 9:5–6). Also make sure to pause for a full second at the end of 8:3 and 9:4b in order to signal the change in speakers. As always, read these words to your listeners as though you yourself are the sage speaking, as though you yourself are Wisdom addressing a tired and disillusioned people and inviting them to *walk in the way of insight* (9:6b), that is, the way of life.

As you practice and when you read, be attentive to the poetic structure of these verses, the medium through which their meaning is conveyed. In most cases, you will find that a verse is composed of two lines that reinforce, parallel, or relate to one another in some fashion. For example, consider the following:

> 8:5a. O simple ones, learn prudence;
> 8:5b. acquire intelligence, you who lack it.

Notice that each line expresses the same thought with different words. Notice also how each line can be further divided into two parts—a direct address and a command—and how, on this occasion, the two parts occur in a different sequence, forming an a–b–b'–a' pattern. This is a common rhetorical feature called a chiasm. You will also find instances where two or three verses oriented around the same image are grouped together (e.g. 8:6–7 and 8:20–21); let the punctuation be your guide to these groupings, especially the period.

In short, have fun exploring and playing around with the variety of rhetorical structures and devices in Hebrew poetry. The more you cultivate an awareness, an appreciation, and an enjoyment of these features, the more you will be able to develop the ability to communicate the meaning of poetic texts to your listeners.

EZEKIEL 36:24–28

Commentary

In 598 B.C., the Babylonian empire under the leadership of King Nebuchadnezzar (a.k.a., Nebuchadrezzar) moved against Jerusalem and quashed a rebellion led by King Jehoiakim of Judah (2 Kgs 24:1–7). A few months later, in 597 B.C., the Babylonians returned to ransack the palace and temple, taking everything of value back to Babylon. In addition, in what is known as the First Deportation, a select group of Jerusalem's leading officials and citizens were taken as exiles to Babylon (2 Kgs 24:8–17). Among this group of Judean exiles was a young priest by the name of Ezekiel who, in the fifth year of the exile (Ezek 1:1–3), received a heavenly vision of God enthroned on a chariot-like throne (1:4–28). In this vision, Ezekiel is commissioned as a prophet and called to speak the word of the LORD to the people of Israel (2:4, Prop 9; 3:11, 27), to those who now live as exiles in Babylon as well as those who still reside back in Judah. Like Isaiah and Jeremiah, Ezekiel's message was initially one of imminent judgment and exile, but after these came to pass, his message became one of forgiveness and restoration. A summary of Ezekiel's double message can be found in 39:23–29.

In today's reading, Ezekiel announces the end of exile. This will entail not only the physical return of Israel to the homeland but also the spiritual transformation of the people.

36:24–28. One of the principal reasons for the LORD's judging and sending of his own people into exile had to do with their centuries of idolatry and injustice, that is, their willful and persistent failure to love God with their whole heart (Deut 6:5, Prop 26; Exod 20:1–7, Lent 3) and to love their neighbors as themselves (Lev 19:18; Exod 20:8–17). So in today's reading, when the LORD announces the end of exile, he speaks of cleansing his people "from all [their] uncleannesses, and from all their idols" (36:25). Yet the LORD has more in mind for his people than forgiving and healing them of their past sins, however significant that is in and of itself. In addition, the LORD intends to address the root problem of his people's persistent sin and unfaithfulness, exchanging their hearts of stone for hearts of flesh. The LORD will accomplish this by placing a new spirit within them, his very own Spirit, which will enable and equip them to live faithfully and obediently in their covenant partnership with God. When the people possess the Spirit of the LORD, then they shall truly and finally be the people of God even as the LORD will truly and finally be their God. This is essentially what the LORD says in Jeremiah when he speaks of making a new covenant with the houses of Israel and Judah: "This is the covenant that I will make with the house of Israel after those days, says the LORD: I will put my law within them, and I will write it on their hearts; and I will be their God, and they shall be my people" (Jer 31:33).

In the following reading (see below), Ezekiel is granted a glimpse of this spiritual transformation of God's people as a vision of the resurrection from the dead.

Suggestions for Lectors

In today's reading, Ezekiel is speaking to the people on behalf of the LORD (36:22). Yet when you read these words, imagine that you are the LORD and your listeners are your exiled people. Announce the good news of your plans to restore and renew them spiritually. Your voice should reflect the LORD's love for his people as well as the grandeur of his vision for their future.

Pronunciation Guide

Ezekiel (ee-ZEE-kee-uhl; ee-ZEE-kyuhl)

EZEKIEL 37:1–14

Commentary

As was mentioned in the Commentary for the previous reading, Ezekiel was a young priest who was taken as a captive from Jerusalem to Babylon in 597 B.C. in what is known as the First Deportation (2 Kgs 24:8–17). In the fifth year of the exile (Ezek 1:1–3), Ezekiel received a heavenly vision of God in which he was called to speak the word of the LORD to the people of Israel (2:4, Prop 9; 3:11, 27). Like Isaiah and Jeremiah, Ezekiel's message was initially one of imminent judgment and exile, but after these came to pass, his message became one of forgiveness and restoration. A summary of this double message can be found in 39:23–29.

In today's reading, Ezekiel is granted a vision of the restoration of the exiled people of God, represented here as resurrection from the dead. Some ninety-five times, the LORD addresses the prophet as *Son of Man*, which is rendered *Mortal* in the NRSV.

37:1–6. The reading begins with the Spirit of the LORD transporting the prophet to a valley filled with dry bones. As the LORD guides Ezekiel around the valley, he asks him whether he thinks these dry dusty bones can live again, to which Ezekiel replies, "O Lord GOD, you know" (37:3). The LORD commands Ezekiel to prophesy to the bones, communicating the LORD's intention to restore their bodies—sinew, flesh and skin—and then to put his breath into them that they might live again. Here, one is reminded of the creation of Adam where, like a sculptor, the LORD fashioned a man out of the dry dust of the ground and then breathed into his nostrils the breath of life with the result that "the man became a living being" (Gen 2:7).

37:7–10. Ezekiel prophesies as commanded, and everything comes about in two dramatic stages. In the first stage, the bones are reconnected and reformed into fully physical human bodies, yet the breath of life has not yet entered them. Then, at the LORD's animated behest, Ezekiel prophesies a second time, and a breath from the four winds sweeps through the valley and fills these bodies with life. When all is complete, the reconstituted and reanimated bodies stand forming as "a vast multitude" (37:10).

37:11–14. After this occurs, the LORD then explains to Ezekiel the meaning and significance of this vision. The exiles are in despair, believing that the LORD has abandoned them forever. They lament, "Our bones are dried up, and our hope is lost; we are cut off completely" (37:11). In response, the LORD gives Ezekiel this vision so that he might give the people hope by announcing that the end of exile is near. Yet the end of exile entails not only the physical return of Israel to the land, but also the spiritual transformation of the people (36:24–28, see previous reading). For the breath that Ezekiel prophesies to is the very Spirit of God, who will give the people new life by enabling them to live faithfully and obediently in their covenant partnership with the LORD their God.

Suggestions for Lectors

Ezekiel's visionary experience easily lends itself to a dramatic reading, so your preparation will involve making sure that your reading is not overly dramatic. Of course, you still want to read it with feeling and intensity, but you may find it necessary to reign these in a bit in order to allow the text to have a more active role.

Begin 37:1 in your normal narrating voice until you come to *it was full of bones*, which you will want to read slowly and with a hint of surprised curiosity in your voice. Also, pause for a full second before you deliver this line. Then, as you read 37:2–3, imagine the silence as the prophet wanders through this spectacle, stricken mute with wonder. Let your voice be hushed, intense, and filled with awe.

In 37:4–6, the story gathers momentum as the Lord GOD utters the life-giving words of prophecy. In 37:9, when the Lord GOD says, *Prophesy to the breath, prophesy, mortal*, one gets the impression that God himself is eager to see these bones live again, perhaps even a bit impatient like an enthusiastic child; add some excitement into your voice as you say these words.

Ezekiel 37:7–10 demands your greatest effort as the vision surges into action. Read 37:10 slowly, phrase by phrase, as the miracle happens. In 37:11–14, when the meaning of the vision is finally revealed—the restoration of the exiled nation by its God—speak more quietly, but with intensity, to the end.

Pronunciation Guide
Note the difference in pronunciation between the verbs, prophesy and prophesied, and the noun, prophecy: *prophesy* (vb., PRAH-fuh-sī), *prophesied* (vb., PRAH-fuh-sīd), *prophecy* (n., PRAH-fuh-see), *Ezekiel* (ee-ZEE-kee-uhl; ee-ZEE-kyuhl)

ZEPHANIAH 3:14–20

Commentary
The book of Zephaniah belongs to the collection of OT writings called the Book of the Twelve, which comprises the twelve Minor Prophets from Hosea to Malachi. A contemporary of the prophet Jeremiah, Zephaniah carried out his prophetic ministry in the southern kingdom of Judah in the mid seventh century B.C. (c. 630–620 B.C.), about a generation or two before the Babylonian exile.

Like Amos a century earlier, Zephaniah's proclamations are centered around the approaching day of the LORD (Zeph 1:7, 14). This will be a day of judgment for Judah (1:4–18), for its capital Jerusalem (3:1–8), and for its pagan neighbors (2:4–15).

3:14–20. Yet in the latter part of the book, including today's reading, Zephaniah's prophetic message becomes one of hope in the promise of a future restoration for all of Israel (3:9–20). While the day of the LORD may dawn in deep darkness, the darkness will give way to the light of day, for the LORD—the king of Israel and Jerusalem's most important citizen—will release God's people from their punishments and liberate them from their oppressors. With God, then, judgment never seems to be the last word.

Suggestions for Lectors
This reading involves two speakers—the prophet Zephaniah (3:14–18a) and the LORD (3:18b–20)—so adopt a tone and a manner appropriate to each. Zephaniah is attempting to instill hope in the people of Israel; therefore, read his words with strength and confidence in an attempt to inspire your listeners to rejoice in hope. You may need to practice 3:14, as it can sometimes be difficult to start a reading on such a strong note. After *on a day of festival* (3:18a), pause for a moment glancing up at your listeners in order to signal a change in speakers from Zephaniah to the LORD.

When you continue with *I will remove disaster from you* (3:18b), speak as though you are the LORD addressing his people directly. With the repeated use of the first person pronoun, *I*, the LORD has come close to his listeners, so speak these lines with a hint of intimacy in your voice.

Pronunciation Guide
Zephaniah (zef'-uh-NĪ-uh)
Zion (ZĪ-uhn)

Romans 6:3–11

Notes
Suggested Reading. Romans 6:1–11

Commentary
Up to this point in Romans, Paul has emphasized that God's righteousness has now been revealed and made available through the *faith* of Jesus Christ received solely as a *gift* of God's grace (3:22). Thus, Paul argues that a person is made righteous and put in a right-relationship with God "by *faith* apart from works prescribed by the law" (3:28). This results in "peace with God through our Lord Jesus Christ" (5:1). In Christ, God's righteousness is made available as a free gift to the one who believes, which demonstrates the overflowing abundance of God's grace (5:17). In fact, God's grace is so abundant that wherever sin increases, grace abounds all the more (5:20). This raises an important question, which introduces today's suggested reading.

6:1–4. Today's reading begins with a question that Paul anticipates from his audience. If, as Paul has argued, "where sin increased, [God's] grace abounded all the more" (5:20), then "Should we continue in sin in order that grace may abound?" (6:2). From this question, it would appear that Paul's audience may be looking to use the gospel of grace, which announces God's unconditional love and forgiveness in Jesus Christ, as a license to sin. On the other hand, it is possible that the question intends to demonstrate the absurdity of Paul's argument that we are saved by faith through grace independent of works of the law. That is, perhaps there are those who object to Paul's argument precisely because it would offer people an excuse to sin and lead to moral chaos and anarchy. Whatever the motivation behind the question, Paul strongly disagrees with the inference being made. As he says, "How can we who died to sin go on living in it?" (6:2). For Paul, when persons are baptized into Christ Jesus, they become so united with Christ that they participate in the life Jesus lived and continues to live. Thus, in baptism a person undergoes burial, death, and resurrection, leading to newness of life in the here and now.

6:5–11. Paul then spells this out in greater detail. By his death and resurrection, Jesus defeated the powers of sin and death. Consequently, a person who has been united with Christ Jesus through baptism has been united with him in his death and so set free from captivity to sin, "For whoever has died is freed from sin" (6:7). Then, having participated in Jesus' death, this same person is united with Jesus in his resurrection and so participates in Jesus' new life, for "if we have died with Christ, we believe that we will also live with him" (6:8). Moreover, this eternal kind of life, which we share with Jesus, is indestructible for he has defeated death truly and finally once for all time. Those who have been united with Christ Jesus have already died to their old life of sin and are already experiencing the eternal kind of life in the here and now. Thus, to think that one could continue fostering a life of sin, *which is death* (cf. 6:23), in order that grace, *which is life*, might abound is, for Paul, patently absurd. Consequently, instead of wondering whether it might be a good idea to sin so that grace might abound, one should continually, repeatedly, and actively consider themselves "dead to sin and alive to God in Christ Jesus" (6:11).

Suggestions for Lectors

In Romans, Paul writes with an insistent quality that you want to convey to your listeners; so read with a confidence in your voice that expresses the conviction that everything you read today is of utmost importance and absolutely true. If you can invest your delivery of these lines with the urgent tone of a defense attorney, you will strike the mood in which they were written.

As is so often the case, the final verse summarizes the argument, transforming it into a rhetorically-rich, easy-to-remember aphorism. So, pause for a second after 6:10, and then read 6:11 slowly and deliberately, leaning hard on the words *dead* and *alive*.

MARK 16:1–8

Commentary

The gospel readings for Palm Sunday and Good Friday ended in tragedy. When the Gentile centurion sees the way in which Jesus died—suffering, alone, and with a cry of God-forsakenness—he declares, "Truly this man *was* God's Son!" (15:39). Notice the past tense. The centurion is the only human character in Mark to recognize Jesus as the Son of God, but unfortunately, the recognition comes too late. Jesus is dead, all that remains is to take him down from the cross and give him a proper burial. The curtain closes.... The story is over.... At least, that is how Greek tragedy normally worked in the ancient world. But, in the case of Jesus, the story isn't over. Three days later, something unexpected happens that transforms the tragedy of Jesus' death into a triumph over death.

A note regarding the ending of Mark. As we shall discuss below, the Gospel of Mark ends rather abruptly and on a rather strange note. Having been instructed by an angel to tell Jesus' disciples about his resurrection, the women who had come to the tomb fled in terror "and they said nothing to anyone, for they were afraid" (16:8). Our earliest and best Greek manuscripts of Mark conclude the gospel at this point. Yet, early readers of Mark were clearly dissatisfied because, at least by the second century A.D., alternative endings had been composed and were attached to the end of the gospel. These endings were attempts to complete the story by including resurrection appearances, Jesus' commissioning of the disciples, and his ascension into heaven. The so-called Shorter and Longer Endings of Mark are included in most English bibles after 16:8. Few, if any, scholars would argue that either of these endings were penned by the author of Mark, although there continue to be debates as to whether the gospel ended at 16:8 or the original ending has been lost. The interpretation followed here assumes that the Gospel of Mark originally ended with 16:8.

16:1–2. None of Jesus' male disciples were present at the crucifixion, all but Peter having abandoned him at his arrest. There were, however, three female disciples who watched the proceedings from a distance: Mary Magdalene, Mary the mother of James and Joses, and Salome (15:40). When Joseph of Arimathea took Jesus' body down from the cross and placed it in his own tomb, the two Marys were present and saw where he laid the body. It was a quick burial because twilight was approaching, and the sabbath was about to begin.

After the sabbath, the three women return to the tomb to properly prepare the body for burial. Of course, this is unnecessary. Not only did Jesus predict his resurrection on the third day (8:31; 9:31; 10:34), but two days before his death, an unnamed woman anointed Jesus with very expensive ointment, and Jesus said, "She has done what she could; she has anointed my body beforehand for its burial" (14:8). So, from the perspective of the narrative, Jesus has already received a proper burial. Thus, the actions of these three women, however well-intentioned, suggest that they, just like Jesus' male disciples, have not fully understood what Jesus has been teaching them about his death and resurrection.

16:3–7. When they arrive at the tomb, they are alarmed to see the tomb open, the body gone, and a young man sitting inside. Though the young man is not explicitly identified as such, his white robe and the information he possesses, suggest that he is an angel. The young man tells them exactly what Jesus did on the night of his arrest (14:28), namely, that he has been raised from the dead and will meet them in Galilee where it all began. The young man then instructs them to pass this news on to the rest of the disciples.

16:8. Fear, of course, is a natural reaction to an encounter with an angel. This is why the first words out of an angel's mouth are so often, "Do not be afraid" (Luke 1:13, 30; 2:10), or as the young man says today, "Do not be alarmed." But to remain silent and not inform anyone about the resurrection and Jesus' plans to meet them in Galilee is much harder to understand, let alone explain. One thing is for certain, their silence is highly ironic. Throughout the gospel, Jesus has instructed people not to reveal who he is or what he has done, but generally to no avail. For example, at the beginning of the gospel, Jesus sternly ordered the leper to *say nothing to anyone* about his cleansing, but he went out and proclaimed it freely (1:44–45, Epi 6; cf. 5:19–20; 7:36–37). But now, when the women are told to make an announcement they, *say nothing to anyone*. Of course, as the reader knows, their silence will not inhibit the good news of Jesus' resurrection from spreading. If it had, then the Gospel of Mark itself would never have been written.

In recent years, narrative critics have suggested that the open-ended ending of Mark may serve as a rhetorical device designed to invite a response from the reader. On the night of his arrest, Jesus' male disciples fled in fear (14:50). And now, on the morning of his resurrection, Jesus' female disciples run away in fear. Who then is left to believe the good news of the kingdom of God (1:15) and to proclaim the good news about Jesus the Messiah, the Son of God (1:1)?

> The story that began with the trumpet call announcement of the dawning of God's kingdom ends not with a bang but a whimper, trailing off in midsentence. After all, no one in the story who has been with Jesus is willing to carry the message and continue his mission. Is there anyone else who might after all be a faithful disciple? Throughout the story, there has been a nonparticipant observer who has been with Jesus in every scene. The narrator has permitted the reader to be "with Jesus" the whole time, from beginning to end. The reader heard the voice of God declaring Jesus to be his Son,

> when no one else heard; the reader was present with Jesus in the wilderness, tested by Satan, when no one else was there. When family rejected him, the reader persisted. When religious leaders, crowds, and disciples misunderstood and abandoned Jesus, the reader stood by him. When the inner circle went to sleep in Gethsemane, oblivious to Jesus' plea to watch with him one hour, the reader stayed awake and heard Jesus' anguished prayer. When the disciples fled and were absent at the cross, the reader was present. When Jesus cried out to God in abandonment, the reader was still there. Now, the readers stand at the brink of the incomplete narrative in which all have failed, and, with terrible restraint, the narrator breaks off the story and leaves the readers, who may have thought the story was about somebody else, with a decision to make....[5]

Suggestions for Lectors

Today's episode is both climactic and anticlimactic, and so should prove to be an interesting assignment. Begin reading in your normal narrating voice. In 16:3, endow you voice with a measure of concern as the women wonder aloud who will roll the heavy stone away for them. In 16:4–5, the women are both confused and curious as they enter the tomb. These feelings give way to alarm when they behold a young man clad all in white sitting on the shelf where Jesus' body had been placed.

When the "angel" speaks, his voice is calm initially as he seeks to alleviate the their fear. But the moment he begins talking about Jesus' resurrection, he becomes animated. So raise your voice and proclaim the good news in a voice filled with joy, wonder, and excitement. Be generous with exclamation points, and also be generous with pauses, making sure not to lose any energy so that the proclamation does not drag. Along with emphasizing the initial proclamation, emphasize those elements that directly relate to your listeners. For example:

> *He has been raised!*... He is not here!.... *Look!*... There is the place they laid him. But *go*,... tell his disciples and Peter that he is going ahead of you to Galilee; there... *you* will see him,... just as he told you (16:6–7).

In 16:8, the story takes a sudden turn, and this should be reflected in your delivery. The excitement over the resurrection is replaced by the women's terror. Increase your tempo as you read of their flight from the tomb, but slow down for the final line, which should receive the most emphasis. Stress both *nothing* and *anyone*, and pause at the comma and also briefly after *they*, as in: *and they said nothing to anyone,... for they... were afraid.*

Alternatively, you could read the whole of 16:8 at a quickened pace, without slowing down at the end and without introducing the pauses suggested above. In which case, the reading would conclude suddenly after *afraid.* This abrupt ending would leave your listeners hanging much in the same way that generations of Markan read-

---

[5] M. Eugene Boring, *Mark* (New Testament Library; Louisville, Ky.: John Knox, 2006), 449.

ers have been left hanging. If you choose this route, then pause for at least three to five seconds before concluding the reading with *The Word of the Lord* (or whatever conclusion your community employs).

Pronunciation Guide
Galilee (GAL-uh-lee), *Nazareth* (NAZ-uh-reth; *not* -rus),
Magdalene (MAG-duh-leen; -lee-nuh), *sabbath* (SAB-uhth), *Salome* (suh-LOH-mee)

EASTER DAY

Resurrection of the Lord

Acts 10:34–43 *or* Isaiah 25:6–9
Psalm 118:1–2, 14–24
1 Corinthians 15:1–11 *or* Acts 10:34–43
John 20:1–18 *or* Mark 16:1–8

ACTS 10:34–43

Notes
Sequence. 1 of 8

Commentary
Before ascending into heaven, the resurrected Jesus instructed his disciples to remain in Jerusalem until they received the empowering presence of the promised Holy Spirit, who would equip them for their vocation to be Jesus' witnesses "in Jerusalem, in all Judea and Samaria, and to the ends of the earth" (Acts 1:8, Asc). Interestingly, the Acts of the Apostles follows this geographic and social trajectory as it tells the story of how the members of Jesus' Spirit-filled and Spirit-equipped community work to spread the good news of God's kingdom and of Jesus' lordship throughout the world, from Jerusalem to the ends of the earth. Up to this point in Acts, the good news has spread from Jerusalem to Judea and Samaria and beyond, yet it has still only spread among Jews. In today's reading, the gospel is proclaimed to Gentiles for the first time.

We are first introduced to Cornelius, a centurion of the Italian Cohort, in 10:1. Cornelius is described as "a devout man who feared God" (10:2). This description is technical language indicating that Cornelius was a Gentile who worshipped the Jewish God and adhered to Jewish customs but had not yet officially converted to Judaism, which would have required him to be circumcised. Cornelius is instructed by God to send for a man named Peter who is staying in Joppa. Meanwhile, Peter is in Joppa praying when he receives a vision in which he is commanded three times to kill and eat animals that are unclean according to Jewish kosher regulations. Each time when he refuses, a voice says to him, "What God has made clean, you must not call profane" (10:15). Still puzzled as to the meaning of his vision, Peter is instructed to go with the men that Cornelius has sent. Peter goes and enters Cornelius' house, and in today's reading, we hear the gospel that he preaches to Gentiles, the same gospel he has proclaimed to Jews.

10:34–36. Today's reading begins with Peter standing before Cornelius and his entire household, having just now understood the meaning of his vision of unclean animals, namely, that "God shows no partiality, but in every nation *anyone* who fears him and does what is right is acceptable to him" (10:34b–35). He gains new insight into the broader implications of the gospel message that he has been preaching to his fellow Jews. When he proclaims "[Jesus] is Lord of all" (10:36), he now understands the *all* to include Gentiles as well as Jews.

10:37–43. With these things in mind, Peter proceeds to present the gospel to Gentiles for the first time, highlighting Jesus' baptism and anointing with the Spirit, his good deeds and healings, and his execution and resurrection. He concludes with an invitation, noting that, as the prophets have testified, "*everyone* who believes in him receives forgiveness of sins through his name" (10:43).

Today's reading ends at this point, yet the story of Cornelius continues in 10:44–48 (East 6). "While Peter was still speaking, the Holy Spirit fell upon all who heard the word" (10:44), and they, like the Jewish disciples in Acts 2, began speaking in other languages. Thus, this scene is often referred to as the Gentile Pentecost, and it comes quite unexpectedly and without precedence. Not only is this the first time the Spirit has been poured out upon Gentiles, it is also the first time the giving of the Spirit has preceded baptism. For example, see Acts 8:14–16 where the Samaritans who had come to believe in Jesus were baptized but did not receive the Spirit until later through the laying on of hands.

Suggestions for Lectors

Today's reading provides a succinct summary of the narrative and message of the gospel. As you read, imagine that you are Peter standing before the Jerusalem church, and invest your voice with a measure of the awe, wonder, excitement, and sheer gratitude that Peter and those listening to him must have experienced.

The reading can be divided into two movements (34–36, 37–43), as reflected in the Commentary. As you near the end of each movement, slow down, and read the concluding lines more deliberately: *he is Lord of all* (10:36) and *everyone who believes in him receives forgiveness of sins through his name* (10:43). These two proclamations stand at the heart of the Christian faith, so proclaim them with conviction and joy.

Pronunciation Guide

Galilee (GAL-uh-lee), *Israel* (IZ-ree-uhl; -ray-),
Judea (joo-DEE-uh; -DAY-), *Nazareth* (NAZ-uh-reth; *not* -rus)

Isaiah 25:6–9

Commentary

The first half of Isaiah is primarily given over to condemning the prevalence of idolatry and injustice in the world, though it is not without glimpses of forgiveness, reconciliation, and restoration in the future. The first twenty-seven chapters form something of a concentric framework. In Isaiah 1–12, Isaiah's prophecies detail the

LORD's indictment of his chosen people. In Isaiah 13–23, the horizon of judgment broadens to include the nations of the world. Then, in Isaiah 24–27, the horizon broadens still further to include the LORD's condemnation of the forces of chaos and evil that threaten the goodness of creation. Today's reading belongs to this last section; in it, we witness the judgment and destruction of death itself.

25:6–9. The scene is of a grand, eschatological banquet hosted by the LORD on Mount Zion, where Jerusalem and the temple are situated. The banquet has been prepared for *all* peoples, not just God's chosen people. Like a predator swallowing its prey, so the LORD of hosts will one day swallow up death itself, depicted here as "the shroud that is cast over all peoples, the sheet that is spread over all nations" (25:7). Thus, it is this passage that Paul cites, when speaking of the general resurrection. "When this perishable body puts on imperishability, and this mortal body puts on immortality, then the saying that is written will be fulfilled: 'Death has been swallowed up in victory'" (1 Cor 15:54).

When death is no more, the Lord GOD will wipe away his people's tears and restore their honor. On that day, they and the whole world with them will recognize and celebrate the One who created everything and has now restored everything. Here, one is reminded of the description of the new heavens and the new earth in Revelation, which draws upon Isaiah for much of its imagery:

> See, the home of God is among mortals.
> He will dwell with them; they will be his peoples,
>   and God himself will be with them;
>   he will wipe every tear from their eyes.
> Death will be no more;
>   mourning and crying and pain will be no more,
>   for the first things have passed away (21:3–4).

Suggestions for Lectors

Ideally, this passage is read with a raised, energetic voice throughout. It expresses, in language relevant to its time and culture, the same hope of future salvation we all seek today. The first line in 25:8, *he will swallow up death forever*, should be emphasized as it climactically concludes the previous section. Read it deliberately, dropping your voice slightly as you say *death* and pausing ever so slightly before concluding with *forever* (25:8a). Then, pause for a full second before continuing with *Then, the Lord GOD will wipe. . . .*

Remember that you are not just reciting a passage of scripture; you are the prophet Isaiah announcing to your listeners the good news of God's salvation. This attitude will be particularly important as you deliver the concluding line, *let us be glad and rejoice in his salvation* (25:9).

Pronunciation Guide

Isaiah (ī-ZAY-uh)

1 Corinthians 15:1–11

Commentary

In today's reading, Paul begins a chapter-long discussion of the resurrection because there were some within the Corinthian church who were teaching that there was no such thing as the resurrection of the dead (15:12). Those in Corinth who denied resurrection of the dead certainly believed in some form of post-mortem existence. They did not deny the idea of life after death in general only the particular form of life after death that is known as resurrection, the idea that those die in this age will be reconstituted as fully physical human beings in the age to come. This denial of resurrection reflected currents of ancient Greco-Roman thought that operated with a radical dualism between the temporal, ever-changing physical world and the eternal, unchanging world of spirit. Matter was regarded as inherently base and evil, and only the spiritual was good. Within this worldview, salvation was often conceived of as an escape from the physical world. Upon death, salvation occurred when the immortal soul was finally be set free from the prison of the human body.

For Paul, the denial of resurrection amounts to a denial of the original goodness of the created, material world. Moreover, such a denial also challenges the truth of the Christian gospel and its message of salvation. In today's reading, Paul begins his defense of the doctrine of the resurrection of the dead by arguing for the historicity of Jesus' own resurrection.

15:1–2. Paul reminds the Corinthians that the gospel message he first proclaimed to them, the message that led them to faith, concerned Christ's death for sins, his burial, *and* his resurrection on the third day, all of which happened in accordance with God's plans as laid out in the OT scriptures. Thus, Jesus' resurrection is a central feature of the gospel and of God's plans to restore humanity and all of creation.

15:3–7. Moreover, says Paul, there exists substantial eye-witness testimony corroborating Jesus' resurrection. After his crucifixion and death, the resurrected Jesus appeared to a variety of people on a number of different occasions.

15:8–11. These eyewitnesses to Christ's resurrection include Paul himself, who, when en route to Damascus to persecute Christians, encountered the risen Jesus.

Suggestions for Lectors

Today's reading provides its own introduction in 15:1–2. The reading, then, falls into two main sections (3–7, 8–11), so pause for a full second before each. Remember that, as a reader, you are not simply reporting what Paul wrote to the Corinthians two millennia ago; instead, you are addressing your listeners using Paul's words.

Therefore, read 15:3–7 with confidence as you certify the bodily resurrection of Jesus by listing his many appearances. Then, as Paul reflects upon his own unworthiness in the concluding section, your voice should descend a bit as you read 15:8–9 slowly and deliberately. In 15:10–11, let the confidence in your voice return as you convey Paul's confidence in God and his gratitude for God's grace.

Pronunciation Guide

Cephas (SEE-phus)
Corinthians (kuh-RIN-thee-uhnz)

John 20:1–18

Notes

Sequence. 1 of 2

Commentary

In John, Jesus' execution took place the day before Passover, on the day of Preparation when preparations for celebrating the Passover were made, including the slaughtering of the Passover lambs (19:14). Since the Passover was a special sabbath, the Jewish leaders did not want the bodies of crucified victims to remain on display, as was the normal procedure (19:31). So the body of Jesus was taken down, prepared for burial, and placed in a tomb on the Jewish day of Preparation (19:42), which on this occasion would have been a Friday afternoon.

In today's reading, two days have passed since Jesus' crucifixion and burial. It is Sunday, the first day of the week; the sabbath is over, and the disciples are now free to visit the tomb where Jesus was laid. Today's episode falls into two scenes: the first concerns the discovery of the empty tomb and the second relates the risen Jesus' appearance to Mary Magdalene.

20:1–10. Mary Magdalene is one of the women who witnessed Jesus' crucifixion (19:25). Early on Sunday morning, Mary makes her way to the tomb. When she sees that the stone covering the entrance has been rolled away, she immediately goes back and informs Simon Peter and the beloved disciple. When they arrive at the tomb, they discover only the linen cloths that Jesus' body had been wrapped in. When the beloved disciple enters the tomb, the narrator states, "he saw and believed; for as yet they did not understand the scripture, that [Jesus] must rise from the dead" (20:8–9). So when Mary and the disciples had arrived at the tomb that morning, they had not been expecting to find it empty because they had not yet understood from the Scriptures that the Messiah must be killed, let alone raised from the dead.

This would be one of the truths that the Holy Spirit would guide them into after Jesus went away (16:12). Jesus had said that the Spirit would remind his disciples of all that he had told them (14:26). In fact, earlier in the gospel, when he had carried out a demonstration in the temple and said, "Destroy this temple, and in three days I will raise it up" (2:20), his words were misunderstood by his audience who assumed that he was talking about the grand and magnificent Jerusalem temple. Yet as the narrator says, Jesus was actually "speaking about the temple of his body. After he was raised from the dead, his disciples remembered that he had said this; and they believed the scripture and the word that Jesus had spoken" (2:21–22).

Here, the beloved disciple is presented as a model of faith for those who have never and will never see the risen Jesus yet nevertheless believe in him. Such faith anticipates next week's reading, when Jesus says to Thomas, "Have you believed because you have seen me? Blessed are those who have not seen and yet have come to believe" (20:29).

20:11–18. Simon Peter and the beloved disciple return home, while Mary Magdalene remains at the tomb weeping. As her reply to the angels' question indicates, she still thinks that someone has removed the body. Even when she turns around and sees Jesus standing behind her, she thinks that he is the gardener. It is not until Jesus calls her by name that Mary recognizes him. Here, one may remember Jesus' words earlier in the gospel when he says, "I am the good shepherd. I know my own and my own know me" (10:14), and "the sheep hear his voice. He calls his own sheep by name and leads them out" (10:3). In her excitement, Mary turns and cries out, "Rabbouni!," yet Jesus prohibits her from grabbing and holding onto him. Though he has been raised from the dead, make no mistake, things have not simply returned to normal; things are not back to the way they were before his arrest and execution. Jesus' resurrection marks the beginning of a new era, an entirely new way of life. As he said before he died, Jesus is ascending and returning to his Father, and his relationship with his followers will take a different form. For now, Mary is to return to the disciples to tell them what she has seen and heard. Though she may not have been the first to believe, Mary is the first disciple to be a witness of and a witness for the risen Jesus.

Suggestions for Lectors

The resurrection appearances of Jesus on the first day of the week are so familiar that the suspension inherent in the gospel accounts is no longer available. You might choose to try to recreate that suspense, by telling the story as if your listeners are hearing it for the first time. Or, you might assume that this story is an old favorite and that your listeners' interest and enjoyment comes from how different people tell the story. In short, tell the story in a way that appeals to you, and it will appeal to your listeners, for your telling will likely draw upon your personal strengths in storytelling.

That being said, your presentation of this incident will receive its dramatic force from the gradual increase in the action. Read 20:2–7 with some urgency, as Mary passes on the shocking news to the two disciples who run to the tomb. At 20:8, let your voice soften and slow as the beloved disciple sees and believes.

Pause for a full second before 20:11 as it introduces a new scene with Mary alone. Whereas urgency was the characteristic of the first half, depth of feeling will be the dimension you want to capitalize on here in the second half. Though the narrative is in third person, it is told from the perspective of Mary, so be very attentive to how she feels at each moment and adjust your voice accordingly.

Pronunciation Guide

Magdalene (MAG-duh-leen; -lee-nuh), *Rabbouni* (rab-BOH-nī; -nee)

Mark 16:1–8

Commentary

The gospel readings for Palm Sunday and Good Friday ended in tragedy. When the Gentile centurion sees the way in which Jesus died—suffering, alone, and with a cry of God-forsakenness—he declares, "Truly this man *was* God's Son!" (15:39). Notice the past tense. The centurion is the only human character in Mark to recognize Jesus as the Son of God, but unfortunately, the recognition comes too late. Jesus is dead, all that remains is to take him down from the cross and give him a proper burial.

The curtain closes.... The story is over.... At least, that is how Greek tragedy normally worked in the ancient world. But, in the case of Jesus, the story isn't over. Three days later, something unexpected happens that transforms the tragedy of Jesus' death into a triumph over death.

A note regarding the ending of Mark. As we shall discuss below, the Gospel of Mark ends rather abruptly and on a rather strange note. Having been instructed by an angel to tell Jesus' disciples about his resurrection, the women who had come to the tomb fled in terror "and they said nothing to anyone, for they were afraid" (16:8). Our earliest and best Greek manuscripts of Mark conclude the gospel at this point. Yet, early readers of Mark were clearly dissatisfied because, at least by the second century A.D., alternative endings had been composed and were attached to the end of the gospel. These endings were attempts to complete the story by including resurrection appearances, Jesus' commissioning of the disciples, and his ascension into heaven. The so-called Shorter and Longer Endings of Mark are included in most English bibles after 16:8. Few, if any, scholars would argue that either of these endings were penned by the author of Mark, although there continue to be debates as to whether the gospel ended at 16:8 or the original ending has been lost. The interpretation followed here assumes that the Gospel of Mark originally ended with 16:8.

16:1–2. None of Jesus' male disciples were present at the crucifixion, all but Peter having abandoned him at his arrest. There were, however, three female disciples who watched the proceedings from a distance: Mary Magdalene, Mary the mother of James and Joses, and Salome (15:40). When Joseph of Arimathea took Jesus' body down from the cross and placed it in his own tomb, the two Marys were present and saw where he laid the body. It was a quick burial because twilight was approaching, and the sabbath was about to begin.

After the sabbath, the three women return to the tomb to properly prepare the body for burial. Of course, this is unnecessary. Not only did Jesus predict his resurrection on the third day (8:31; 9:31; 10:34), but two days before his death, an unnamed woman anointed Jesus with very expensive ointment, and Jesus said, "She has done what she could; she has anointed my body beforehand for its burial" (14:8). So, from the perspective of the narrative, Jesus has already received a proper burial. Thus, the actions of these three women, however well-intentioned, suggest that they, just like Jesus' male disciples, have not fully understood what Jesus has been teaching them about his death and resurrection.

16:3–7. When they arrive at the tomb, they are alarmed to see the tomb open, the body gone, and a young man sitting inside. Though the young man is not explicitly identified as such, his white robe and the information he possesses, suggest that he is an angel. The young man tells them exactly what Jesus did on the night of his arrest (14:28), namely, that he has been raised from the dead and will meet them in Galilee where it all began. The young man then instructs them to pass this news on to the rest of the disciples.

16:8. Fear, of course, is a natural reaction to an encounter with an angel. This is why the first words out of an angel's mouth are so often, "Do not be afraid" (Luke 1:13, 30; 2:10), or as the young man says today, "Do not be alarmed." But to remain silent and not inform anyone about the resurrection and Jesus' plans to meet them in Galilee is much harder to understand, let alone explain. One thing is for certain, their silence is highly ironic. Throughout the gospel, Jesus has instructed people not to reveal who he is or what he has done, but generally to no avail. For example, at the beginning of the gospel, Jesus sternly ordered the leper to *say nothing to anyone* about his cleansing, but he went out and proclaimed it freely (1:44–45, Epi 6; cf. 5:19–20; 7:36–37). But now, when the women are told to make an announcement they, *say nothing to anyone.* Of course, as the reader knows, their silence will not inhibit the good news of Jesus' resurrection from spreading. If it had, then the Gospel of Mark itself would never have been written.

In recent years, narrative critics have suggested that the open-ended ending of Mark may serve as a rhetorical device designed to invite a response from the reader. On the night of his arrest, Jesus' male disciples fled in fear (14:50). And now, on the morning of his resurrection, Jesus' female disciples run away in fear. Who then is left to believe the good news of the kingdom of God (1:15) and to proclaim the good news about Jesus the Messiah, the Son of God (1:1)?

> The story that began with the trumpet call announcement of the dawning of God's kingdom ends not with a bang but a whimper, trailing off in midsentence. After all, no one in the story who has been with Jesus is willing to carry the message and continue his mission. Is there anyone else who might after all be a faithful disciple? Throughout the story, there has been a nonparticipant observer who has been with Jesus in every scene. The narrator has permitted the reader to be "with Jesus" the whole time, from beginning to end. The reader heard the voice of God declaring Jesus to be his Son, when no one else heard; the reader was present with Jesus in the wilderness, tested by Satan, when no one else was there. When family rejected him, the reader persisted. When religious leaders, crowds, and disciples misunderstood and abandoned Jesus, the reader stood by him. When the inner circle went to sleep in Gethsemane, oblivious to Jesus' plea to watch with him one hour, the reader stayed awake and heard Jesus' anguished prayer. When the disciples fled and were absent at the cross, the reader was present. When Jesus cried out to God in abandonment, the reader was still there. Now, the readers stand at the brink of the incomplete narrative in which all have failed, and, with terrible restraint, the narrator breaks off the story and leaves the readers, who may have thought the story was about somebody else, with a decision to make....[6]

Suggestions for Lectors

Today's episode is both climactic and anticlimactic, and so should prove to be an interesting assignment. Begin reading in your normal narrating voice. In 16:3, endow

---

[6] M. Eugene Boring, *Mark* (New Testament Library; Louisville, Ky.: John Knox, 2006), 449.

you voice with a measure of concern as the women wonder aloud who will roll the heavy stone away for them. In 16:4–5, the women are both confused and curious as they enter the tomb. These feelings give way to alarm when they behold a young man clad all in white sitting on the shelf where Jesus' body had been placed.

When the "angel" speaks, his voice is calm initially as he seeks to alleviate the their fear. But the moment he begins talking about Jesus' resurrection, he becomes animated. So raise your voice and proclaim the good news in a voice filled with joy, wonder, and excitement. Be generous with exclamation points, and also be generous with pauses, making sure not to lose any energy so that the proclamation does not drag. Along with emphasizing the initial proclamation, emphasize those elements that directly relate to your listeners. For example:

> *He has been raised!*… He is not here!…. *Look!*… There is the place they laid him. But *go*,… tell his disciples and Peter that he is going ahead of you to Galilee; there… *you* will see him,… just as he told you (16:6–7).

In 16:8, the story takes a sudden turn, and this should be reflected in your delivery. The excitement over the resurrection is replaced by the women's terror. Increase your tempo as you read of their flight from the tomb, but slow down for the final line, which should receive the most emphasis. Stress both *nothing* and *anyone*, and pause at the comma and also briefly after *they*, as in: *and they said <u>nothing</u> to <u>anyone</u>,… for they… were afraid.*

Alternatively, you could read the whole of 16:8 at a quickened pace, without slowing down at the end and without introducing the pauses suggested above. In which case, the reading would conclude suddenly after *afraid.* This abrupt ending would leave your listeners hanging much in the same way that generations of Markan readers have been left hanging. If you choose this route, then pause for at least three to five seconds before concluding the reading with *The Word of the Lord* (or whatever conclusion your community employs).

Pronunciation Guide

Galilee (GAL-uh-lee)
Nazareth (NAZ-uh-reth; *not* -rus)
Magdalene (MAG-duh-leen; -lee-nuh)
sabbath (SAB-uhth)
Salome (suh-LOH-mee)

EASTER EVENING

Isaiah 25:6–9
Psalm 114
1 Corinthians 5:6b–8
Luke 24:13–49

Isaiah 25:6–9

Commentary

The first half of Isaiah is primarily given over to condemning the prevalence of idolatry and injustice in the world, though it is not without glimpses of forgiveness, reconciliation, and restoration in the future. The first twenty-seven chapters form something of a concentric framework. In Isaiah 1–12, Isaiah's prophecies detail the LORD's indictment of his chosen people. In Isaiah 13–23, the horizon of judgment broadens to include the nations of the world. Then, in Isaiah 24–27, the horizon broadens still further to include the LORD's condemnation of the forces of chaos and evil that threaten the goodness of creation. Today's reading belongs to this last section; in it, we witness the judgment and destruction of death itself.

25:6–9. The scene is of a grand, eschatological banquet hosted by the LORD on Mount Zion, where Jerusalem and the temple are situated. The banquet has been prepared for *all* peoples, not just God's chosen people. Like a predator swallowing its prey, so the LORD of hosts will one day swallow up death itself, depicted here as "the shroud that is cast over all peoples, the sheet that is spread over all nations" (25:7). Thus, it is this passage that Paul cites, when speaking of the general resurrection. "When this perishable body puts on imperishability, and this mortal body puts on immortality, then the saying that is written will be fulfilled: 'Death has been swallowed up in victory'" (1 Cor 15:54).

When death is no more, the Lord GOD will wipe away his people's tears and restore their honor. On that day, they and the whole world with them will recognize and celebrate the One who created everything and has now restored everything. Here, one is reminded of the description of the new heavens and the new earth in Revelation, which draws upon Isaiah for much of its imagery:

> See, the home of God is among mortals.
> He will dwell with them; they will be his peoples,
>   and God himself will be with them;
>   he will wipe every tear from their eyes.
> Death will be no more;
>   mourning and crying and pain will be no more,
>   for the first things have passed away (21:3–4).

Suggestions for Lectors

Ideally, this passage is read with a raised, energetic voice throughout. It expresses, in language relevant to its time and culture, the same hope of future salvation we all seek today. The first line in 25:8, *he will swallow up death forever*, should be emphasized as it climactically concludes the previous section. Read it deliberately, dropping your voice slightly as you say *death* and pausing ever so slightly before concluding with *forever* (25:8a). Then, pause for a full second before continuing with *Then, the Lord GOD will wipe....*

Remember that you are not just reciting a passage of scripture; you are the prophet Isaiah announcing to your listeners the good news of God's salvation. This attitude will be particularly important as you deliver the concluding line, *let us be glad and rejoice in his salvation* (25:9).

Pronunciation Guide
Isaiah (ī-ZAY-uh)

1 CORINTHIANS 5:6B–8

Commentary
The First Letter of Paul to the Corinthians is the second longest of Paul's letters in the NT. In it, Paul addresses a number of problems besetting the Christian community in Corinth, many of which relate to the question of how the Corinthian Christians, both individually and as a community, are to live out their Christian faith within a culture whose values are often so different and antithetical to those of the gospel.

In 1 Corinthians 5, Paul takes up the matter of sexual immorality, prompted by a report he had received about a member of the church who is cohabitating with his stepmother (5:1a). Paul is astounded that the Corinthian Christians have permitted such a practice as this, one "that is not found even among the pagans" (5:1b). The Corinthians appear to be proud about the fact that they have shown such tolerance (5:6). Yet as Paul warns the church in today's reading, sexual immorality is not something to be tolerated, for its corrupting influence can affect the whole community.

5:6b–8. In today's reading, there are two related images that stand behind Paul's comments. First, in Jewish tradition, yeast (or rather, leaven) served as a metaphor for a corrupting influence or force. So, for example, Jesus warns his disciples to "beware of the leaven of the Pharisees, that is, their hypocrisy" (Luke 12:1; cf. Matt 16:11–12). Paul, therefore, regards sexual immorality as having the ability to spread throughout the whole community, just as "a little yeast leavens the whole batch of dough" (5:6b). If Paul had known about viruses, he might have described sexual immorality as a little virus that can infect the whole body.

The second image concerns the Feast of Unleavened Bread, which was a seven-day festival beginning with Passover that celebrated Israel's Exodus from Egypt. In preparation for the festival, all leaven was to be discarded: "Unleavened bread shall be eaten for seven days; no leavened bread shall be seen in your possession, and no leaven shall be seen among you in all your territory" (Exod 13:7; Deut 16:3–4). Paul is drawing upon this practice when he instructs the Corinthians to "clean out the old yeast so that you may be a new batch, as you really are unleavened" (5:7a). Thus, Paul wants the Corinthians to confront the man who is sleeping with his stepmother so as to clean out the old yeast of sexual immorality (5:4–5). Paul continues the metaphor by saying, "For Christ, our Passover lamb, has been sacrificed" (5:7b). That is, since the Feast of Unleavened Bread began with Passover, Christ's death as the Passover lamb indicates that the Feast of Unleavened Bread has already begun; therefore, only unleavened bread should be eaten. Metaphorically speaking, these instructions refer to the Christian church, the community brought into existence through the cross of Christ in which individual members are united through the Spirit of Christ. The church, therefore, is the community of "the unleavened bread of sincerity and truth" where "the leaven of malice and evil" has no place.

Suggestions for Lectors

Given that today's reading is brief and starts quickly, pause for a few seconds after introducing the reading before you begin. This will ensure that your listeners are attuned and ready. Read slowly, deliberately, and with a strong, confident voice. If there is a line worth special emphasis, it would be *For our paschal lamb, Christ, has been sacrificed* (5:7b).

Pronunciation Guide

Corinthians (kuh-RIN-thee-uhnz), *paschal* (PAS-kuhl)

LUKE 24:13–49

Commentary

In Luke 24:1–12, Luke narrates the discovery of Jesus' empty tomb. On the Sunday morning following his execution and burial, some of his faithful female disciples arrived at the tomb with spices for Jesus' body, which had been hastily entombed on Friday evening just prior to the beginning of the sabbath. To their amazement, they do not find Jesus' body; instead, they are encountered by two brightly-attired men who announce that Jesus has been raised from the dead. When the women return to report these events to the male apostles, their "words seemed to them like an idle tale, and they did not believe them" (24:11). Thus, prior to this evening's reading, though reports about Jesus' resurrection have circulated, none of his male disciples have yet seen Jesus alive again.

24:13–27. This episode begins with two of Jesus' followers traveling west on the road from Jerusalem to Emmaus. As they are traveling and talking about the strange events of the day, they are joined by another traveler, whom they do not recognize but whom the reader is told is Jesus. Upon his request, the two disciples tell the stranger about their master, Jesus of Nazareth, whom they characterize as "a prophet mighty in deed and word before God and all the people" (24:19) yet who had been condemned as a false prophet by the Jewish leadership and handed over to be executed by the Roman authorities. They express their once-held hope that Jesus was the Messiah who had been sent by God to redeem Israel, that is, to restore Israel's independence by ridding their land of the occupational forces of the Roman empire. In Acts, the disciples express this same hope when they ask the risen Jesus, "Lord, is this the time when you will restore the kingdom to Israel?" (1:6, Asc). In addition, these two disciples express their astonishment regarding the women's story of the empty tomb, angels, and Jesus' resurrection. At this point, Jesus breaks in and admonishes them for being foolish and slow of heart. On numerous occasions during his life, Jesus himself spoke to his disciples about the necessity of his impending death *and* resurrection (9:21–22; 9:43b–45; 18:31–34). Yet interestingly, he does not chastise them for not believing what *he* had declared before his death but for not believing what the *prophets* had declared, namely, that it belonged to God's purposes that the Messiah should suffer and die before he was vindicated as Lord. Jesus then walks them through the OT Scriptures that concerned him and his messianic vocation and mission.

24:28–32. When they arrive at Emmaus, they convince Jesus to dine with them. At table, Jesus plays the role of host by taking the bread and blessing it, breaking it, and giving it to them. These are the same actions he performed when feeding the five thousand (9:10–17) and when hosting his final Passover meal with his disciples (22:14–23). Thus, it is when, and only when, Jesus breaks the bread that their eyes, which had been kept from recognizing him (24:16), "were opened, and they recognized him" (22:31). Then, Jesus disappears, and they are left to recall how their hearts burned when he was opening the Scriptures to them on the road to Emmaus.

24:33–35. Though it was already evening, these two make the seven-mile journey back to Jerusalem that very night where they hear from the apostles and the other disciples that Jesus had appeared to Simon Peter. They then relate their own experience, focusing upon "how he had been made known to them in the breaking of the bread" (24:35). This points to the manner in which the resurrected Jesus will be known to his disciples after he ascends into heaven and his resurrection appearances cease.

24:36–43. As they are talking, Jesus suddenly appears in their midst, and his followers are frightened because they think they are seeing a ghost. Now, this might seem to be a strange response given that three of their number have just reported seeing Jesus alive again, not of seeing his ghost or spirit. This shows that what had happened to Jesus was so unexpected that his followers were still trying to make sense of it all. After all, in first-century Jewish thought, resurrection was a belief concerned with what would happen to a large group of people at the end of history, when all of the righteous who had died would be fully reanimated as physical human beings in order to enjoy and participate in the new creation. In other words, resurrection never concerned the reanimation of *one* individual in the *middle* of history. This helps explain why Jesus' disciples did not understand what he was talking about when he told them that he would rise from the dead after three days (Mark 9:10). When early Christians spoke of Jesus as having been resurrected, they were not simply stating that Jesus was in some general sense still alive after his death, enjoying some sort of disembodied existence. Instead, they were claiming that Jesus had been resurrected to and so enjoyed a full-fledged human existence complete with a physical body, albeit one that possessed some unique properties. In other words, Jesus did not simply return to his former life and body but was raised to the life of the age to come with a new resurrection body, a physical body possessing both continuity and discontinuity with his old body (cf. 1 Cor 15). This is brought out in today's reading. On the one hand, the resurrected Jesus has flesh and bones and is able to consume food (continuity); on the other hand, he can also appear and disappear (discontinuity).

24:44–49. Having demonstrated that he is not a ghost but has in fact been raised from the dead, Jesus then opens their minds to understanding everything written about him in every major division of the Jewish Scriptures—the Law of Moses, the Prophets, and the Writings. With their eyes now opened, Jesus' followers are able to see that his death was not a tragedy but part of God's plan. Far from disqualifying Jesus from being the Messiah, his suffering and death are the means by which he fulfilled his messianic vocation. Moreover, they are also led to see that the deliverance the Messiah was to bring, is not for Israel alone, but for all people everywhere and that they are to play a key role in exporting that salvation to the whole world. This will be accomplished through the power of the indwelling Holy Spirit, which the Father has promised and which Jesus will send upon them (cf. Acts 1:1–11, Asc; Acts 2:1–21, Pent).

Suggestions for Lectors

This is such a wonderfully dramatic, powerful, and compelling story that you need only attend to the narrative; let it be your guide. As always, the best way to the heart and meaning of this story will be through your own thorough preparation. For example, meditation on this passage will show you how to pace it, how to vary the tone from the disciples' original discouragement (24:19–24) to Jesus' somewhat edgy impatience (24:25–26) then to his calm exposition of the Scriptures (24:27).

Major pauses are warranted in three places: after 24:27, to indicate a passage of time; prior to 24:36, to prepare for the appearance of Jesus; and prior to 24:44, to mark a shift in topics.

As the conclusion of today's reading nears, read with increasing intensity and solemnity in order to convey the magnitude not only of who Jesus is and what he has accomplished (24:44–46), but also of what will be proclaimed and accomplished in his name following his ascension (24:47–49). Jesus has literally transformed the world through his life, death, and resurrection His followers are now commissioned by Jesus for the roles they shall play in God's plan to redeem humanity and renew all creation.

Pronunciation Guide

Cleopas (KLEE-oh-puhs)
Emmaus (eh-MAY-uhs; ih-)
Messiah (muh-SĪ-uh)
Nazareth (NAZ-uh-reth; *not* -rus)

SECOND SUNDAY OF EASTER

Acts 4:32–35
Psalm 133
1 John 1:1–2:2
John 20:19–31

ACTS 4:32–35

Notes

Sequence. 2 of 8

Commentary

One of the most remarkable things about the early Jewish-Christian movement was the fellowship and community that developed among them. Early in Acts, following the day of Pentecost when thousands of new converts were brought into the fold of Jesus' followers, the author of Acts offers the following summary of this fledgling movement.

> They devoted themselves to the apostles' teaching and fellowship, to the breaking of bread and the prayers.
>
> Awe came upon everyone, because many wonders and signs were being done by the apostles. All who believed were together and had all things in common; they would sell their possessions and goods and distribute the proceeds to all, as any had need. Day by day, as they spent much time together in the temple, they broke bread at home and ate their food with glad and generous hearts, praising God and having the goodwill of all the people. And day by day the Lord added to their number those who were being saved (2:42–47).

4:32–35. In today's reading, a similar summary statement is offered. This one focuses upon the sharing of goods and resources among the first Christians. From this description, it does not appear that membership in the community required persons to sell their possessions. Instead, people simply did not think in terms of private ownership. Further support for this view appears in the following episode when Peter confronts a couple who sold a piece of property, kept some of the money back, and presented the rest to the apostles *as if* it were the entire purchase price.

> "Ananias," Peter asked, "why has Satan filled your heart to lie to the Holy Spirit and to keep back part of the proceeds of the land? While it remained unsold, did it not remain your own? And after it was sold, were not the proceeds at your disposal? How is it that you have contrived this deed in your heart? You did not lie to us but to God!" (5:3–4).

In contrast to the behavior of Ananias and his wife is the behavior of Joseph in today's reading. Joseph belonged to the tribe of Levi, and he was a Jew of the Diaspora (a.k.a., the Dispersion), just one of the multitude of Jews in the ancient world who lived outside the Promised Land. Perhaps he was among those who had come to celebrate Pentecost in Jerusalem and heard Peter's spirit-filled witness to the life, death, and resurrection of Jesus. In any case, this Joseph sold a field and brought the proceeds to the apostles without reservation. He became known among the apostles as Barnabas, that is, *son of encouragement*, suggesting that he was a very generous and supportive member of the community of Christ's followers.

Barnabas reappears later in Acts. He helps Paul (a.k.a., Saul) enter the community he once persecuted (9:27), and he also accompanies Paul his first two missionary journeys.

Suggestions for Lectors
Today's reading is straightforward. If anything deserves emphasis it is the statement in the middle of the reading: *There was not a* *<u>needy</u>* *person among them…* (4:34). Pause for a second beforehand, then deliver this line with a raised voice, at a slightly slower pace, and with an accent on the word *needy*. It would also make sense to emphasize the concluding clause, *as any had* *<u>need</u>* (4:35).

1 JOHN 1:1–2:2

Notes
Sequence. 1 of 6

Commentary
Today's reading from the First Letter of John begins a sequence of six readings from that letter, which extends through the Easter season. Although 1 John is generally referred to as a letter, it does not actually bear any of the marks of an ancient letter. Unlike 2 and 3 John and the letters of Paul, 1 John does not open with a salutation that identifies its author and its recipients, nor does it conclude with a farewell. Consequently, 1 John is probably best understood as a homily written to address a particular situation.

According to church tradition, the three Letters of John were written by the author of the Gospel of John, which seems likely given the thematic and stylistic similarities among the four works. Traditionally, their author was identified as John the Apostle, one of the original twelve disciples. The Johannine writings were composed around the turn of the first century A.D., so they are some of the latest writings in the NT. By this time, the Christian movement had been around for a few generations, enough time for alternative, unorthodox movements to arise. First John seems to have been written to combat certain heretical teachings and teachers, whom he labels antichrists (2:18).

For example, in 1 John 4:2, the author writes, "By this you know the Spirit of God: every spirit that confesses that Jesus Christ has come *in the flesh* is from God." It appears, then, that there were those within the Christian ranks who denied the full humanity of Jesus. Perhaps they were influenced by a Greek philosophical thought that maintained a radical dualism between spiritual and material realities, where the spiritual world was regarded as wholly pure and good while anything belonging to the material world was deemed innately base and corrupt. Within such a worldview, the Incarnation—the belief that God had become the human being—had no place and was highly offensive. Consequently, an early Christian heresy arose called docetism, which maintained that Jesus Christ was not really a human being but that he only seemed to be human.

1:1–4. Utilizing language reminiscent of the prologue to John's gospel (1:1–18), the author begins his homily by responding to the docetic heresy. What he and the other apostles have declared is "what was from the beginning" namely, "the word of life" (1:1). Here, *the word of life*, refers both to the eternal Word of God who became Jesus of Nazareth as well as to the gospel message about this Jesus. The Word that has always been with God and is God truly became a flesh and blood human being. Not only did the apostles hear and see Jesus, but they touched him and handled him with their hands, and they are simply passing on what they experienced firsthand. All those who come to believe in their apostolic witness belong to their fellowship, which is not only fellowship with other believers but with God himself.

1:5–10. In this section, the author addresses his opponents' views regarding sin. Apparently, there were those who claimed to be without sin. Why they thought this is unclear. Perhaps, they believed that sin only touched their material nature and not their spiritual nature and so believed sin to be of no real consequence. Whatever the case, John argues that we deceive ourselves if we claim to be without sin. Moreover, if we are without sin, Christ's sacrifice for sin does not apply to us, which adversely affects our relationship with one another and with God. Instead of walking in darkness and denying our sin, the Christian response to sin is to trust God enough to confess our sins. When we bring our sins out of the darkness and into the light of God's grace, we experience the power of God's love and forgiveness, which cleanses us from all guilt and shame.

2:1–2. Of course, John does not want any of his listeners to commit sin, but when we do sin all is not lost, for Jesus serves as our advocate. His death on the cross served as an atoning sacrifice with far-reaching implications. Not only did his death atone for the sins of those who would come to believe in him, his death atoned for the sins of the whole world. In other words, God not only loves unconditionally, God also forgives unconditionally.

Suggestions for Lectors

Today's passage is rhetorically rich, putting repetition to good use. For example, in the first section (1:1–4), the author offers a litany of relative clauses beginning with *what* (1:1).

We declare to you *what* was from the beginning,
what we have heard,
what we have seen with our eyes,
what we have looked at and touched with our hands,
concerning the word of life—

As you read through these, emphasize *what* and increase your intensity and tempo with each successive relative clause. Let your energy climax with *life*. Then pause for a second before resuming with 1:2 in your default reading voice.

In the second section (1:5–10), the author offers a litany of conditional clauses beginning with *if we*. The verses alternate between *if we say* and *if we* plus another verb. Again, as you read through these, accent *if we* and the verb.

1:6	*If we say....*	1:9	*If we confess...*
1:7	*If we walk...*	1:10	*If we say...*
1:8	*If we say...*		

In the second section, the message that the author refers to should receive the most emphasis, namely, *God is light and in him there is no darkness at all* (1:5b).

In the third section (2:1–2), notice the change in style and tone. Up to this point, the author has primarily used first person plural pronouns (*we, us, our*), but in 2:1, first person singular pronouns begin to predominate (*I, my*). This change is also accompanied by a shift in the overall tone. The author begins to address his readers as *my little children* (2:1; cf. 2:12, 14, 18, 28, et al.) or as *beloved* (2:7; 3:2, 21; et al.). The author still proclaims and teaches, but the tone has become more personal, more compassionate and filled with concern. Convey this with your voice.

As you draw the reading to a close, highlight the final line by reading it slowly and with well-placed pauses: *and not for ours only… but also… for the sins… of the whole… world* (2:2b).

John 20:19–31

Notes

Sequence. 2 of 2

Commentary

Today's reading follows on from last week's, wherein Jesus' disciples discovered the empty tomb and Mary Magdalene was the first disciple to encounter the risen Jesus. In today's reading, Jesus makes two more resurrection appearances to his disciples, and the question regarding the nature of Christian faith is explored.

20:19–23. The first scene takes place in the evening on the same day that the empty tomb was discovered. The disciples are hiding out for fear that they might meet the same fate as their master. The doors are locked; nevertheless, Jesus appears in their midst with the words, "Peace be with you" (20:21). Jesus shows them his hands and his side which still bear the nail marks and the hole from the spear. This demonstration convinces them that it is indeed Jesus. Jesus then repeats the words, "Peace be with you" as he breathes the Holy Spirit upon them.

Here, Jesus' blessing of peace and his giving of the Holy Spirit recalls his words on the night before his death when he spoke of his going away. He told his disciples not to be afraid or let their hearts be troubled (14:27b) because, when Jesus goes away, he will not abandon them and leave them orphaned (14:18). Instead, he will leave *his peace* with them; he will give them *his peace* (14:27a), which will come in the form of the *Holy Spirit,* whom the Father will send in his name and who will teach them everything they need to know (14:26).

20:24–25. At this point, the narrator informs the reader that Thomas, though one of the Twelve, was absent and missed seeing the resurrected Jesus. When the other disciples say that they have seen the Lord Jesus and describe the encounter, Thomas responds with, "Unless I see the mark of the nails in his hands, and put my finger in the mark of the nails and my hand in his side, I will not believe" (20:25). Though he will forever be known as "Doubting Thomas" on account of Jesus' words in 20:27, it is worth noting that Thomas is not asking for anything more or different from what the other disciples had already received. Nevertheless, Christian faith must be able to rest upon something other than a personal encounter with the risen Jesus for he is about to return to his Father. This matter, for which Thomas is the foil, is addressed in the following scene.

20:26–29. The third scene takes place exactly a week later. The disciples are again in hiding and the doors are locked, but on this occasion Thomas is present. Once again, the risen Jesus appears with the words, "Peace be with you." Then, in an act of grace, Jesus grants Thomas' request to see and touch the scars of his wounds. Whether Thomas takes up Jesus' offer is unclear; what is clear is that Thomas believes, and he expresses his belief in Jesus with a staggering confession, "My Lord and my God" (20:28). Though Jesus has been presented as God's Son throughout the gospel, ironically, it is only here on the lips of *doubting* Thomas that Jesus is addressed in the absolute sense as "my God." Moreover, this confession at the end of the gospel recalls the beginning of the gospel where the eternal Word, who becomes Jesus of Nazareth, is with God and is God (1:1, ✠ Chr 1). Nevertheless, Christian faith must be able to rest upon something other than a personal encounter with the risen Jesus, for he is scheduled to return to his Father. So while Jesus acknowledges Thomas' confession, he regards as blessed "those who have not seen and yet have come to believe" (20:29). Thus, it is the beloved disciple who serves as the model for Christian faith, for before he had encountered the risen Jesus, the beloved disciple had entered the tomb, and upon finding it empty believed (20:8).

20:30–31. Thus, faith in the risen Jesus does not depend upon seeing the risen Jesus with our own eyes, for faith involves being able to rely upon the testimony of others who experienced these things. In other words, Christian faith is not a blind faith, for it does rest upon evidence, yet that evidence is only accessible to us through the testimony of others. Christian faith is more a matter of *hearing* and believing rather than of *seeing* and believing; faith requires that we trust the testimony of others, the testimony of those who, like John, tell the story of Jesus in order that we "may come to believe that Jesus is the Messiah, the Son of God, and that through believing [we] may have life in his name" (20:31) and also the testimony of the Holy Spirit who has been sent to "guide [us] into all truth" (16:13).

Suggestions for Lectors

In today's reading, the dialogue and not the action drives the plot, so place particular emphasis upon each character's words. In 20:19–23, focus upon Jesus' twice-repeated *Peace be with you* and his *Receive the Holy Spirit.* In 20:24–25, highlight Thomas' demand.

In 20:26–28, the words of both Thomas and Jesus should receive attention. When Jesus turns to Thomas and says, *Put your finger here…* and *Reach out your hand…* (20:27a), let there be a measure of affection in your voice that even extends to *Do not doubt but believe* (20:27b). When Thomas declares, *My Lord and my God!* (20:28), fill your voice with excitement, wonder, and gratitude. In addition, you may decide to treat this confession as the story's climax. On the other hand, a case could be made for treating Jesus' concluding words as the climax, *Blessed are those who have not seen and yet have come to believe* (20:29b).

Pause before reading the narrating conclusion in 20:30–31. Read 20:30 in your default storytelling voice and pace, but then slow down as you read 20:31 more deliberately and with deep conviction in your voice.

Pronunciation Guide
blessed (adj., two syllables; BLES-id), *Messiah* (muh-SĪ-uh)

THIRD SUNDAY OF EASTER

Acts 3:12–19
Psalm 4
1 John 3:1–7
Luke 24:36b–48

Acts 3:12–19

Notes
Sequence. 3 of 8

Commentary
On the night of his arrest, Jesus spoke with his disciples about his going away. In the Gospel of John, he makes an extraordinary statement:

> Very truly, I tell you, the one who believes in me will also do the works that I do and, in fact, will do greater works than these, because I am going to the Father. I will do whatever you ask in my name, so that the Father may be glorified in the Son (14:12–13).

How is it that Jesus' followers will do the same works that he did and even greater works than he did? The answer is the Holy Spirit.

Although Jesus was the incarnate Son of God, his ability to perform miracles did not derive from his identity as God's Son but from his being empowered by the Holy Spirit that he received at his baptism. As Jesus himself says, "If it is by the Spirit of God that I cast out demons, then the kingdom of God has come to you" (Matt 12:28). So when Jesus goes away, he does not leave his disciples orphaned (John 14:18), for he sends the Holy Spirit upon them at Pentecost. The Holy Spirit not only comforts them in the absence of Jesus, the Holy Spirit empowers and equips them to say and do the same things that Jesus said and did. This is why the community of Jesus' followers are called the body of Christ because the Spirit dwells within them in order that they might be the hands and feet of Jesus in this world.

As its name indicates, the Acts of the Apostles is the story of the things that Jesus' earliest followers did following Pentecost. Time and again we read of their doing the very sorts of things Jesus did. They heal the sick, cast out demons, raise the dead, and in the story leading up to today's reading, Peter and John restore the legs of a crippled beggar as they make their way to the temple (Acts 3:1–10). Such an amazing work in such a public place draws a lot of attention, and in today's reading, Peter explains to the awestruck crowd the nature of this man's miraculous restoration.

3:12–16. Peter begins by stating very clearly that this man's healing had nothing to do with them; they possess neither the power nor the piety to bring about such a miracle. Instead, this man was made whole because of the name of Jesus, the man who was rejected by God's people and crucified at Passover but whom God raised from the dead.

3:17–19. Peter continues in a different tone. He understands that his people and their rulers acted in ignorance. Moreover, he has come to understand from the Scriptures that it was necessary for God's Messiah to endure rejection, humiliation, and death. All of that is in the past. All that remains is for people to repent and turn toward God. If they do, they will find their sins wiped away.

Suggestions for Lectors

In today's reading, Peter is addressing a crowd of people in the temple precincts, so when you deliver his words, elevate your voice as though you are speaking to a large group of people without the aid of modern technology.

Peter's address has two parts. The first part begins with *You Israelites* (3:12–16), while the second part begins with *And now, friends* (3:17–19). Notice the difference in tone between these two parts. In the first part, Peter is accusatory, but in the second, he becomes empathetic and understanding. Thus, these two parts should be read differently. In the first part, increase the volume and intensity of your voice, and read at a slightly faster pace. Then, in the second part, slow down and soften your voice and read at a normal speed.

As you bring the reading to a close, emphasize Peter's parting command: *Repent therefore, and turn to God so that your sins may be wiped out* (3:19). While the word "repent" often carries a negative connotation, in this context it is offered as a gift, a lifeline. It is a blessing, not a curse, as is confirmed by the very next line: "Repent therefore, and turn to God so that your sins may be wiped out, *so that times of refreshing may come from the presence of the Lord*" (3:19–20a). Therefore, deliver this call to repentance with the same tone of voice that you used when you said, *And now, friends.*

Pronunciation Guide

Abraham (AY-bruh-ham), *Isaac* (Ī-zik), *Israelites* (IZ-ree-līts),
Jacob (JAY-kuhb), *Messiah* (muh-SĪ-uh), *Peter* (PEE-ter), *Pilate* (PĪ-luht)

1 John 3:1–7

Notes

Sequence. 2 of 6

Commentary

Today's reading is the second in a series of six from 1 John. As was noted in last week's Commentary, although we generally describe first 1 John as a letter or an epistle, it does not bear the marks of an ancient letter but fits more the genre of a homily. Two motifs that recur throughout this homily are the nature of love and the nature of sin, both of which are addressed in today's reading.

3:1–3. The nature of love. Acorns become oaks, and eggs become chickens, and the love of God is the seed that transforms people into the children of God (cf. 3:9). John expresses how remarkable it is "that we should be called the children of God" (3:1b). But why is this so remarkable? Simply because we do not deserve such an honor. We were sinners when God encountered us, yet he chose to adopt us and make us his children anyway. Of course, as adopted children, it takes time for us to become fully acclimated to our new home and to acquire the virtues and habits of our new family. Nevertheless, we are already the children of God by virtue of our adoption in Christ. Over time as we participate in our new life, we will begin to bear the family resemblance more fully. This already and not yet quality of our identity as children of God is what John is referring to when he writes, "Beloved, we are God's children now; what we will be has not yet been revealed" (3:2a). As the beloved children of God, we are in the process of becoming what we already are, and this process of becoming will be brought to completion when Christ returns.

3:4–7. The nature of sin. At this point, the author seems to shift gears when he begins to talk about sin and lawlessness but that is not the case. As God's beloved children, we are to take sin and its consequences quite seriously. Jesus did not come simply to take away the penalty of sin but to take away sin itself. That is, we were not just sinners in need of forgiveness but dead people in need of life. In sending Jesus, God intended to do more than free us from the guilt of our sins. His plan was to deliver us from the impulse to sin.

In last week's reading, John criticized those who claimed that they have not sinned (1:8, 10). Now he claims that those who abide in God do not sin. Moreover, in 3:9, he goes a step further and claims that such a person *cannot* sin. How are we to understand this seeming contradiction? The answer lies in the fact that the verb tenses employed in most English translations do not adequately convey the sense of the underlying Greek tenses. There is not space here for a technical discussion. Suffice it to say, when John writes, "Everyone who commits sin is guilty of lawlessness" (3:4a) and "No one who abides in him sins" (3:6a), he does not have in mind individual sins but a life oriented around sin. In short, he is describing a state of being rather than single acts. Paraphrases that bring this emphasis out might be, "Everyone who persists in sinning is guilty of lawlessness" and "No one who abides in him will continue in a life of sin." A righteous person may sin, but their life as a whole is oriented to abiding in God and performing acts of righteousness.

Suggestions for Lectors

Whether John is talking about the nature of love or the nature of sin, his concern for the spiritual well-being of his readers remains consistent and evident. So deliver today's reading with evident concern for the well-being of your listeners. Speak to them as though these words were written by you for their benefit.

In the first half of the reading (3:1–3), emphasize the references to our present identity as God's children: *and that is what we are* (3:1b) and *we are God's children now*

(3:2a). In the second half (3:4–7), stress the concluding line: *Everyone who does what is right is righteous, just as he is righteous* (3:7b).

Pronunciation Guide
Beloved (n., buh-LUV-uhd)

LUKE 24:36B–48

Commentary
In Luke 24:1–12, Luke narrates the discovery of Jesus' empty tomb. On the Sunday morning following his execution and burial, some of his faithful female disciples arrived at the tomb with spices for Jesus' body, which had been hastily entombed on Friday evening just prior to the beginning of the sabbath. To their amazement, they do not find Jesus' body; instead, they are encountered by two brightly-attired men who announce that Jesus has been raised from the dead. When the women return to report these events to the male apostles, their "words seemed to them like an idle tale, and they did not believe them" (24:11).

Later that day, two of Jesus' followers encounter the risen Jesus on the road from Jerusalem to Emmaus (24:13–32, EastEv). Though Jesus speaks with them, his identity remains unknown to them until the moment he blesses and breaks bread with them at the evening meal. As soon as they recognize him, he disappears. Though it is already evening, these two make the seven-mile journey back to Jerusalem that very night where they hear from the apostles and the other disciples that Jesus has appeared to Simon Peter. They relate their own experience, focusing upon "how he had been made known to them in the breaking of the bread" (24:35). This points to the manner in which the resurrected Jesus will be known to his disciples after he ascends into heaven and his resurrection appearances cease.

24:36b–43. As they are discussing these things, Jesus suddenly appears in their midst, and his followers are frightened because they think they are seeing a ghost. Now, this might seem to be a strange response given that three of their number have just reported seeing Jesus alive again. This demonstrates, however, that what had happened to Jesus was so unexpected that his followers were still trying to make sense of it all.

In first-century Jewish thought, resurrection was a belief concerned with what would happen to a large group of people at the end of history, when all of the righteous who had died would be fully reanimated as physical human beings in order to enjoy and participate in the new creation. In other words, resurrection never concerned the reanimation of *one* individual in the *middle* of history. This helps explain why Jesus' disciples did not understand what he was talking about when he told them that he would rise from the dead after three days (Mark 9:10). When early Christians spoke of Jesus as having been resurrected, they were not simply stating that Jesus was in some general sense still alive after his death, enjoying some sort of disembodied existence. Instead, they were claiming that Jesus had been resurrected to a full-fledged human existence complete with a physical body, albeit one that possessed some unique properties. In other words, Jesus did not simply return to his former life and body but was raised into the new life of the age to come with a new resurrection body, a physical body possessing both continuity and discontinuity with his old body (cf. 1 Cor 15). This is brought out in today's reading. On the one hand, the resurrected Jesus has flesh and bones and is able to consume food (continuity); on the other hand, he can also appear and disappear (discontinuity).

24:44–48. Having demonstrated that he is not a ghost but has in fact been raised from the dead, Jesus then opens their minds to understanding everything written about him in every major division of the Jewish Scriptures—the Law of Moses, the Prophets, and the Writings. With their eyes now opened, Jesus' followers are able to see that his death was not a tragedy but part of God's plan. Far from disqualifying Jesus from being the Messiah, his suffering and death are the means by which he fulfilled his messianic vocation. Moreover, Jesus leads them to see that the deliverance the Messiah was to bring is not for Israel alone, but for all people everywhere. His followers are to play a key role in exporting that salvation to the whole world; that is what it means to be "witnesses of these things" (24:48).

All of this will be accomplished through the power of the indwelling Holy Spirit, which the Father has promised and which Jesus will send upon them after his ascension into heaven (Luke 24:49; cf. Acts 1:1–11, Asc; Acts 2:1–21, Pent).

Suggestions for Lectors

Today's episode requires nothing more than the basic skills and techniques of a storyteller. As you prepare, spend some time meditating on what the disciples must have experienced, what must have been going through their minds and hearts as they beheld their crucified Master standing before them alive again, the same yet different.

Deliver Jesus' opening words in a strong, yet calming voice. Emphasize *Peace*, and then pause for a second or so after Jesus' statement in order to give the words a chance to have their intended effect. When you continue with the description of the disciples' fears and doubts, invest your voice with traces of fear and incredulity. Increase the pitch and volume of your voice, as Jesus responds to the reactions of his disciples.

As the conclusion of today's episode nears, read with increasing intensity and solemnity in order to convey the magnitude not only of who Jesus is and what he has accomplished (24:44–46), but also of what will be accomplished in his name following his ascension (24:47–48). In 2:47, emphasize *all* in the phrase *to all nations*, and in 2:48, emphasize *You.*

Pronunciation Guide

Messiah (muh-SĪ-uh), *Moses* (MOH-zuhs)

FOURTH SUNDAY OF EASTER

Acts 4:5–12
Psalm 23
1 John 3:16–24
John 10:11–18

ACTS 4:5–12

Notes
Sequence. 4 of 8

Commentary
In last week's reading from the Acts of the Apostles, Peter and John were addressing a large, excited crowd that had gathered around them within the precincts of the Jerusalem temple. All the commotion was due to an extraordinary event. Earlier, Peter and John had been making their way to the temple for the afternoon hour of prayer when they encountered a crippled beggar. Peter said to the man, "I have no silver or gold, but what I have I give you; in the name of Jesus Christ of Nazareth, stand up and walk" (3:6). Peter took the man by the hand and raised him up, and immediately the man began to walk around leaping and praising God. Peter explained to the crowd that he and John were not the reason for this man's healing. Instead all the credit goes to Jesus of Nazareth, whose name restored this man to perfect health. They went on to argue that this Jesus, who was unjustly executed, was in fact God's Messiah. They know this because God raised him from the dead. So, all that remains is for the people to repent and to turn to God by believing in his servant Jesus.

While Peter was speaking to the crowd, he and John were arrested by the temple authorities, many of whom no doubt would have participated in Jesus' arrest and conviction on the charge of blasphemy. No doubt they were concerned to maintain order within the temple precincts. But they were also annoyed and angry because Peter and John were "proclaiming that in Jesus there is the resurrection of the dead" (4:2).

There were at least two reasons for their reaction. First, the Sadducees did not believe in the idea of resurrection from the dead. They did not believe that at the end of the age God would physically raise and reanimate his people so that they might enjoy the kingdom of God in the new age. But more to the point, even if they had believed in resurrection, they certainly would not have believed that a man who was convicted of blasphemy, declared a false prophet, and executed upon a Roman cross could be God's Messiah, let alone the harbinger of the resurrection of the dead.

4:5–7. In today's reading, after having spent the night in prison, Peter and John are brought before the ruling elite in Jerusalem and questioned about the healing of the crippled beggar. They ask, "By what power or by what name did you do this?" This is a significant question. Today, if we were to witness a miraculous healing, we would most likely assume that it must be of God, but that is not the assumption being made here. After all, Deuteronomy 13 issues clear warnings about false prophets who have been sent to deceive God's people by performing signs and wonders. In the minds of the scribes and elders, it could very well be that a power other than God is behind this man's healing, especially if the miracle is being performed by one of the followers of the false prophet Jesus.

4:8–12. Up to this point in Acts, Peter has been the primary spokesman for the Jewish-Christian community, and once again he seizes the opportunity to serve as a witness to the resurrection of Jesus. When Peter spoke, he was filled with the Holy

Spirit. This statement recalls something Jesus said to his disciples during the last week of his life:

> As for yourselves, beware; for they will hand you over to councils; and you will be beaten in synagogues; and you will stand before governors and kings because of me, as a testimony to them. And the good news must first be proclaimed to all nations. When they bring you to trial and hand you over, do not worry beforehand about what you are to say; but say whatever is given you at that time, for it is not you who speak, but the Holy Spirit (Mark 13:9–11).

Peter begins subtly chastising the leaders for the assumptions underlying their question when he speaks of the healing as a *good* deed versus a miraculous one. After all, who but God can perform good deeds. Jesus took this same approach on numerous occasions (cf. Mark 3:4, Epi 9, Prop 4).

Peter then becomes more pointed in his criticism when he cites Psalm 118:22 and inserts the pronoun "you" into the text. With this little addition, Peter identifies his interrogators as the builders who rejected the stone. The temple leadership regarded Jesus as a false prophet and conspired to bring about his death. By raising Jesus from the dead, God reveals that he had been his anointed servant all along. And now, there is no other name by which people must be saved because Jesus and Jesus alone has been chosen by God to be the cornerstone of his new temple, the foundation of a new people of God comprising both Jews and Gentiles.

Suggestions for Lectors

As you deliver Peter's address, raise your voice as though you were talking to a large crowd. Speak with confidence and conviction. Do not simply relay Peter's words to your listeners, but proclaim them.

Begin the address in a more reserved manner, but begin to become animated in 4:10 when you talk about Jesus. As you proceed, become increasingly more animated until you reach a crescendo in Peter's final statement: *There is salvation in no one else, for there is no other name under heaven given among mortals by which we must be saved.* As you deliver this concluding line, emphasize the phrases *no one else* and *no other name.*

In 4:11, adopt an accusatory tone, especially when delivering the following lines, *whom you crucified* and *the stone that was rejected by you, the builders*.

Pronunciation Guide

Alexander (al'-ig-ZAN-duhr; -ZAHN-)
Annas (AN-uhs)
Caiaphas (KĪ-uh-fuhs; KAY-uh-fuhs)
Jerusalem (juh-ROO-suh-luhm)
Israel (IZ-ree-uhl; -ray-)
Nazareth (NAZ-uh-reth; *not* -rus)

1 JOHN 3:16–24

Notes

Sequence. 3 of 6

Commentary

Throughout the whole witness of Scripture, love of God and love of neighbor are inexorably intertwined; one does not exist apart from the other. Our love and devotion toward God is expressed primarily through loving our neighbor. This is the focus of today's reading.

3:16–17. For John and other biblical writers, love is not a sentiment or a feeling but an action that benefits another. For love to be love, it must be concrete. How do we know this to be true? Because the God whose divine essence is love sent his only Son into the world and that Son laid down his life for us. If God expresses his love in concrete ways, then we, as the adopted children of God, are called to do the same.

3:18–22. When we love others, not with our mouths but with our hands and feet, we become increasingly aware of our relationship with God and assured of his presence with us. Too often we operate with the mistaken assumption that God is absent, and our hearts condemn us through feelings of guilt and shame. Yet, when we find ourselves increasingly able to love our neighbor as ourselves, we can take that as evidence that God is abiding in us and working through us. This, in turn, gives us the confidence and the faith we need to approach God with our requests.

3:23–24. Of course, the love we show others is not of our own making; it does not originate with us but comes as a byproduct of our abiding with God. When we place our trust in Christ, we are drawn more deeply into God and we begin to experience the love that eternally exists between the Father and the Son and the Spirit. As we participate in this love, we find ourselves increasingly able to act with love toward others. This is why John makes a connection between believing in Jesus and loving one another, and why he regards these two things as a single commandment.

Suggestions for Lectors

Throughout 1 John, the author's concern for the spiritual well-being of his listeners is evident, regardless of the topic. Today's passage is no exception, so convey concern for your listeners as you deliver the reading.

As reflected in the Commentary, the reading falls into three sections. Each section begins, as it were, with a thesis that is then explored. Consequently, emphasize the first statement of each section by reading it slowly and deliberately: *he laid down his life for us—and we ought to lay down our lives for one another* (3:16); *let us love, not in word or speech, but in truth and action* (3:18), and *we should believe in the name of his Son Jesus Christ and love one another* (3:23). All of these concern loving others in concrete ways.

Pronunciation Guide

Beloved (n., buh-LUV-uhd)

John 10:11–18

Notes
Sequence. 1 of 6

Commentary
In John 9, Jesus heals a man suffering from congenital blindness. Because the healing is performed on the sabbath, controversy ensues. The Pharisees claim that Jesus could not be from God, and Jesus accuses the Pharisees of being blind (9:41). Jesus then launches into a subtle diatribe in which he depicts himself as the true shepherd and gate for God's people, vis-à-vis the Pharisees who are thieves and bandits (10:1–5). Unfortunately, his audience does not catch the meaning of this figure of speech (10:6), so he clarifies it with two of his famous *I am* statements: I am the sheep gate (10:7–10) and I am the good shepherd (10:11–18). The second of these constitutes today's reading.

In the OT, and indeed in the wider ancient world, the language and imagery of a shepherd were employed as metaphors for leadership. Not only were Moses and David, Israel's most celebrated leaders, shepherds when God pressed them into service (Exod 3:1–6; 2 Sam 16:11–13), but their roles are described using shepherding imagery (Num 27:13–14; 2 Sam 5:1–5). In prophetic literature, Israel's kings are depicted as shepherds of God's people. Some were good; most were not (Ezek 34; Zech 11). Even the LORD himself is characterized as the shepherd of his people (Pss 23; 95:7; Ezek 34:11–31). So when Jesus identifies himself as "the good shepherd," he is applying to himself a metaphor that is particularly associated with God and God's anointed leaders.

10:11–13. For Jesus, the principal hallmark of the good shepherd is the care and concern he shows for his sheep, even to the point of risking his own life to protect and preserve the lives of his sheep. The self-appointed leaders of God's people (e.g., the Pharisees) do not act like shepherds but hirelings. Unlike the shepherd, their primary concern is themselves. When danger arises, they are unwilling to risk their lives for sheep.

10:14–16. Jesus repeats the assertion, "I am the good shepherd," which affords him the opportunity to introduce a second hallmark of good shepherding and leadership. The good shepherd is the one who participates in an intimate relationship with his sheep; he knows them, and they know him. This mutuality of knowing between the good shepherd and his flock is a reflection of the mutuality of knowing that exists between Jesus and the Father. Moreover, it is this close relationship that inspires and motivates the good shepherd's willingness to lay down his life for the sheep.

When Jesus speaks of "other sheep," he is referring to Gentiles—those, who up to this point, do not officially belong to the chosen people of God. Yet God's vision has always been for a single flock, gathered together under a single shepherd. God's desire is for all people everywhere to be in relationship with one another even as they come know him as the one, true, and living God.

10:17–18. Mysteriously, it will be the death (and resurrection) of the good shepherd that will bring about the restoration and reconciliation of humanity (cf. 11:49–52).

Suggestions for Lectors

As reflected in the Commentary, today's reading can be divided into three sections (10:11–13, 14–16, 17–18), so pause for a full second between sections. The first two sections begin with *I am* statements and assert something about Jesus in his role as the Good Shepherd. The last section serves as a conclusion by recapitulating the motif of self-sacrifice that appears in the other sections.

Since the first two sections begin with the same *I am* statement, emphasize the second statement of each section: *The good shepherd lays down his life for the sheep* (10:11), and *I know my own and my own know me* (10:14). In 10:16, stress both *ones*, as in: *one* flock, *one* shepherd. In the concluding section, emphasize the second clause: *because I lay down my life* (10:17).

FIFTH SUNDAY OF EASTER

Acts 8:26–40
Psalm 22:25–31 (= 22:24–30 BCP)
1 John 4:7–21
John 15:1–8

Acts 8:26–40

Notes

Sequence. 5 of 8

Commentary

Following his resurrection, Jesus appeared to his followers for a period of forty days, offering proof of his resurrection and speaking about the kingdom of God (Acts 1:1; Asc). At the end of those forty days, Jesus ascended into heaven, and the resurrection appearances essentially ceased. Before his ascension, Jesus commanded his disciples, many of whom were from Galilee, to wait in Jerusalem until they received the gift of the indwelling Holy Spirit. He said, "But you will receive power when the Holy Spirit has come upon you; and you will be my witnesses in Jerusalem, in all Judea and Samaria, and to the ends of the earth" (Acts 1:8). In many respects, the narrative of Acts is organized along these lines.

In the early chapters, we read of how the gospel is proclaimed in Jerusalem and Judea. Then in Acts 8:4–25, we read of how a certain Philip first took the gospel to Samaria. In today's reading, this same Philip brings an Ethiopian into the faith, perhaps making him the first Christian convert that fits under the rubric, "to the ends of the earth." This Philip is not the apostle Philip, one of the Twelve. Instead, he is one of the group of seven deacons who were first appointed in Acts 6.

8:26–31. In today's reading, an angel of the LORD instructs Philip to travel along the wilderness road that leads southwest from Jerusalem to Gaza. There he encounters a foreigner, a eunuch who serves in the court of the queen of Ethiopia. (Candace is a title rather than the name of a particular queen). Jews and converts to Judaism were not the only people who made pilgrimage to the temple in Jerusalem.

There were Gentiles who attended Jewish synagogues and offered worship in Jerusalem who, nevertheless, did not go through the steps to officially convert to Judaism. They were called God-fearers, and this Ethiopian may have been one. Clearly, he is a high ranking official of some means. Not only is he in charge of the queen's entire treasury, but he has made a very long trip on his own. He is educated and so can read, and he possesses a scroll, an item that only the elite could afford.

In those days, to read was to read aloud; persons read aloud even when reading to themselves. Philip is therefore able to hear what the man is reading and immediately recognizes it as coming from the prophet Isaiah.

8:32–35. The passage in question comes from Isaiah 53:7–8 and belongs to what is known as the fourth Servant Song. Within the redemptive drama of Isaiah, we find four passages concerning an unidentified servant of the LORD (Isa 42:1–4; 49:1–6; 50:4–9, Palm; 52:13–53:12, GFri). In these Servant Songs, the servant appears sometimes as a corporate personality and sometimes as a single individual. There is a broad, general movement from the servant as *Israel* to the servant as *a single Israelite* who takes on Israel's vocation to be both the restorer of God's chosen people and the light to the nations (cf. Isa 49:5–6). Early Christians saw many similarities between Isaiah's servant and Jesus, especially with regard to Jesus' suffering and death. Their understanding of what God had done through Jesus' suffering was informed by their understanding of the suffering servant of Isaiah, and vice versa. The importance of Isaiah's servant for understanding Jesus' suffering and death is reflected in the fact that each of the Servant Songs is read during Holy Week.

The ambiguity surrounding this figure in Isaiah prompts the Ethiopian to ask after his identity. Is Isaiah writing about himself or about someone else? Philip then does what all of the first Christians did, including the early church Fathers, he proclaims the gospel using the Scriptures, what we know as the Old Testament.

8:36–40. In Acts, all who come to faith in Jesus are initiated into the Christian community through baptism (2:41; 8:12–13; 9:18, etc.). So when the chariot carrying Philip and the eunuch comes across some water, Philip baptizes him then and there. When they are making their way up onto the bank, the Spirit of the Lord whisks Philip away. The Ethiopian joyfully continues on his way home. Presumably, he becomes the first Christian missionary to the Nubian kingdom. As for his part, Philip finds himself in the coastal town of Azotus (a.k.a., Ashdod). From there he travels northward along the coast to Caesarea, all the while carry out his evangelistic mission.

Suggestions for Lectors

In today's reading, use the same voice for the Spirit and for the angel of the Lord. Since Philip is the only one who hears these voices, drop your voice as though he is hearing them in his head.

When the episode begins, the focus is upon Philip. Then, at 8:27b, the focus shifts to the Ethiopian eunuch, so pause for a second or two between *went* and *Now* to signal this shift.

When reading the passage from Isaiah, slow down and read it more deliberately, with a firm, strong voice.

Pronunciation Guide
Azotus (uh-ZOH-tuhs), *Caesarea* (ses'-uh-REE-uh, sez'-, seez'-), *Candace* (KAN-duh-see; kan-DAY-see; *not* KAN-duhs), *Ethiopian* (ee'-thee-OH-pee-uhn), *Ethiopians* (ee'-thee-OH-pee-uhnz), *eunuch* (YOO-nuhk; YOO-nik), *Gaza* (GAH-zuh; GAY-zuh), *Isaiah* (ī-ZAY-uh), *Jerusalem* (juh-ROO-suh-luhm), *Philip* (FIL-ip)

1 John 4:7–21

Notes
Sequence. 4 of 6

Commentary
In last week's reading, the author of 1 John addressed the importance of loving one another, not with words and feelings but with concrete actions. In today's reading, John offers us a theological treatise on the nature of love in which our love of neighbor is rooted and grounded in the concrete love God has shown us in Christ Jesus.

4:7–12. Today's reading begins with a gentle exhortation: "let us love one another" (4:7). John addresses readers as "Beloved" as a way to remind them that they are God's beloved children. They have already experienced the gracious, unconditional love of God; this puts them in the perfect position to share and demonstrate that love to others. We can love only to the extent that we have been loved. Consequently, John is not asking his readers to do anything that is beyond their ability. As in the covenant of marriage, the love of one's neighbor is not a condition but a calling and a response. God does not say, "If you love others, I will love you." Instead, God says, "I have loved you, therefore love one another" (cf. 4:21). Before we ever did anything to deserve it, God sent his Son to deliver us from death and to restore us to new life. In other words, love does not begin with us but with God's gracious giving of himself. John writes, "In this is love, not that we loved God but that he loved us" (4:10) Followers of Jesus follow Jesus in everything, including love. Love of neighbor is a response to love of God; we are not manufacturers of love, but distributors. As John writes below, "We love because he first loved us" (4:19). Moreover, when we find ourselves increasingly able to love our neighbor in concrete ways, this is evidence that God's love is alive with in us—growing, maturing, and bearing fruit.

4:13–16a. Furthermore, bearing the fruit of love and charity is also evidence that God's Spirit resides within us. The Holy Spirit is the Christian's constant companion, and the Spirit continually witnesses to the fact that God sent his Son to save the world and that this act of self-giving sacrifice is the ground and being of all genuine love.

4:16b–21. In the third and final movement of today's reading, John reasserts the need for Christians to express their love for God and God's love for them by loving one another. While John no doubt believes that Christians are called to love all people, in this particular context, he is talking about our loving others within the Christian community. How can we claim to love God if we hate our brothers and sisters in Christ? Moreover, how can we offer God's love to the world if we cannot even practice it within the church? Here, we are reminded of Jesus' words during the Last Supper: "I give you a new commandment, that you love one another. Just as I have loved you, you also should love one another. By this everyone will know that you are my disciples, if you have love for one another" (John 13:34-35). When God's children love one another, their love serves as a witness to the whole world that God is by nature love.

To say that "love has been perfected" is to say that love has achieved its goal. A principal goal of God's love is to transform us into people who can love like God. To be in relationship with God is to have the transforming power of God's love working within us. Many people, even Christians, live with the fear that God will punish them on the day of judgment. Yet, as God's love matures and ripens within us, it drives out this fear by reminding us whose and who we are—we are God's, and we are God's beloved. God's love transforms how we see God and how we see ourselves in relation to God. We will know that God's love has achieved its goal when our fear of punishment has been replaced by a boldness and confidence in God's presence.

Suggestions for Lectors

In the Commentary, we detected a certain logic in today's reading, a certain progression of thought—God is love; God has loved us; and we ought to love others. Yet, many of the statements John makes about love could stand on their own. In fact, at times, today's reading has the feel of the book of Proverbs, as though it were not so much a treatise on love as a collection of aphorisms and maxims on the topic of love.

For example, in the final section of today's reading, the first four verses can easily be read as four individual statements on love. If we were to rearranged their order, there would be little if any discernible difference in how we understood them.

4:16b God is love, and those who abide in love abide in God, and God abides in them.

4:17 Love has been perfected among us in this: that we may have boldness on the day of judgment, because as he is, so are we in this world.

4:18 There is no fear in love, but perfect love casts out fear; for fear has to do with punishment, and whoever fears has not reached perfection in love.

4:19 We love because he first loved us.

Recognizing the proverbial quality of the reading affects how we approach it as lectors. Instead of trying to make smooth transitions between sentences as though they were logically connected, it would be better to pause for a full second or so at the end of each statement that stands on its own. Of course, there are portions of the reading where two or more sentences belong together and so should be read as one normally would with smooth transitions (e.g., 4:7–8; 4:13–16a; 4:20–21). As you prepare, decide what goes with what and what stands on its own.

JOHN 15:1–8

Notes

Sequence. 2 of 6

Commentary

In this and next week's gospel readings, Jesus calls upon his disciples to remain connected to him just as he has remained connected to the Father. The setting is the night before his death. The evening begins with Jesus stripping down, donning a towel, and then washing his disciples' feet as though he were a household servant. He says: "If I, your Lord and Teacher, have washed your feet, you also ought to wash one another's feet. For I have set you an example, that you also should do as I have done to you" (13:14–15). Soon afterward Jesus issues a new commandment: "Love one another. Just as I have loved you, you also should love one another. *By this everyone will know that you are my disciples, if you have love for one another*" (13:34–35). These scenes offer important information as we seek to understand what Jesus means when he says in today's reading, "Abide in me as I abide in you" (15:4).

In the Gospel of John, Jesus does not teach in parables per se. Instead, he uses extended metaphors, many of which take the form of his famous *I am* sayings. The vehicle for today's teaching is an image taken from the world of ancient viticulture.

15:1–4. Jesus begins saying, "I am the true vine, and my Father is the vinegrower" (15:1). The vinedresser is responsible for the health and productivity of the vine. To ensure fruitfulness, the vinedresser cuts off barren branches, while he prunes productive branches so that they might be even more fruitful. Pruning involves clearing away dead wood and useless growth so that more of the vine's energy can go toward bearing fruit.

Aspects of this image have the potential to produce unnecessary anxiety, so Jesus lets his disciples know that they need not worry because they have already been cleansed (that is, pruned) by virtue of the word he has spoken to them. In a general sense, this word denotes everything Jesus has done and taught in order to draw them into relationship with him and thus with his Father. Having already been cleansed, the disciples' responsibility is nothing more and nothing less than abiding in Jesus. Jesus abides in them through the love and service he has shown them, which will find ultimate expression in his death for them. His disciples are to follow his example by loving and serving one another in all humility. Such love and service is what it means to abide in Jesus.

15:5–6. Moreover, such abiding is the key to fruitfulness. Branches do not generate fruit, vines do. This is because branches do not have life in and of themselves, only vines do. If a branch is to bear fruit, it must remain in the vine. Jesus will eventually command his disciples to bear fruit (15:16, East 6), but here he repeatedly emphasizes abiding because one does not produce fruit directly. That is, fruit is a natural byproduct of abiding. Focusing our attention upon producing fruit will not in and of itself produce fruit. Instead, our energies should be dedicated to abiding in Jesus. As Jesus says, "Those who abide in me and I in them bear much fruit" (15:5a).

15:7–8. One of the fruits of such mutual abiding is that when Jesus' disciples pray to God, they will have the assurance of being heard. The Father will not only listen to their requests but grant them as well (cf. 14:12–14).

Suggestions for Lectors

Today's reading divides easily into two movements, each of which begins with an *I am* statement (15:1–4, 5–8). Pause for a second between the two movements. Begin each movement by highlighting the first sentence. Raise your voice as you read the sentences, and emphasize the predicate nouns, as in: *I am the true vine, and my Father is the vinegrower* (15:1); and *I am the vine, you are the branches* (15:5).

Read 15:3 in a positive, affirming tone as Jesus tells his disciples that they have already been cleansed. Conversely, read 15:6 with a somewhat grave and serious tone as you describe what happens to those who choose not to abide in Jesus.

SIXTH SUNDAY OF EASTER

Acts 10:44–48
Psalm 98
1 John 5:1–6
John 15:9–17

ACTS 10:44–48

Notes

Sequence. 6 of 8

Commentary

On Easter Day, the story is told of how the apostle Peter, a Jew, was sent to proclaim the gospel to the household of Cornelius, a Gentile. The Lord prepared Peter for his encounter with this "unclean" Gentile by giving him a vision in which the statement is repeatedly made, "What God has made clean, you must not call profane" (10:15). By the time Peter arrives at Cornelius' house, he has come to realize that "God shows no partiality, but in every nation *anyone* who fears him and does what is right is acceptable to him" (10:34b–35). Peter has gained new insight into the broader implications of the gospel message that he has been preaching to his fellow Jews. So when he proclaims "[Jesus] is Lord of all" (10:36), he now understands the *all* to include Gentiles just as much as Jews. With these things in mind, Peter proceeds to present the gospel to Gentiles for the first time, highlighting Jesus' baptism and anointing with the Spirit, his good deeds and healings, and his execution and resurrection. He concludes with an invitation, noting that, as the prophets have testified, "*everyone* who believes in him receives forgiveness of sins through his name" (10:43).

This is where the Easter Day reading concludes, but in today's reading we hear the rest of the story.

10:44–48. Even before Peter finishes his speech, the Holy Spirit falls upon all who had heard the word. And they, like the Jewish disciples in Acts 2, began speaking in other languages. Consequently, this scene is often referred to as the Gentile Pentecost, and it comes quite unexpectedly and without precedence. Not only is this the first time the Spirit has been poured out upon Gentiles, it is also the first time the giving of the Spirit has preceded baptism. For example, see Acts 8:14–16 where the Samaritans who had come to believe in Jesus were baptized but did not receive the Spirit until later through the laying on of hands.

The implications of the coming of the Spirit upon Gentiles is far reaching, and it takes the early Jewish-Christians some time to fully appreciate the meaning and significance of this event. In Acts 11, Peter must defend his preaching of the gospel to the Gentiles, and later on in Acts 15, Paul must do the same. But over time, the Jewish-Christians came to understand that at the heart of God's vision for the new creation is a united people of God, constituted of both Jews and Gentiles (cf. Eph 2:11–22, Prop 11; Gal 3:28; Col 3:11; Rev 5:9).

Suggestions for Lectors
The coming of the Holy Spirit on Gentiles is a watershed moment in the history of the church and even in the history of God's dealings with humanity. So present today's episode with great energy and enthusiasm, but without rushing. Try to convey the awe and amazement that Peter and his companions are feeling.

Pronunciation Guide
Gentiles (JEN-tīlz)

1 JOHN 5:1–6

Notes
Sequence. 5 of 6

Commentary
In 1 John 3:23 (East 4), we read, "This is his commandment, that we should believe in the name of his Son Jesus Christ and love one another, just as he has commanded us." What is interesting about this statement is that this one commandment has two imperatives, believe and love. In today's reading, the author returns to this idea and further explores the relationship between orthodoxy (right belief) and orthopraxy (right action), specifically, the relationship between believing in Jesus and loving one's neighbor.

5:1–5. In the prologue to John's gospel, the author writes that "to all who received [Jesus], who believed in his name, he gave the power to become children of God, who were born . . . of God" (1:12–13). This same point is reiterated in today's reading. Believing that Jesus is the only-begotten Son of God is the means by which persons are themselves begotten of God. But that is just the beginning. To love God is also to love the children of God; this is what is meant by "everyone who loves the parent loves the child" (5:1). Said another way, to love God is to obey God's commandments, and the sign that we are obeying God's commandments is when we are loving God's children. It is all interconnected.

Moreover, it is all possible. Loving God, loving God's people, and obeying God's commandments are not burdensome, for to be born of God is to have all the resources we need at our disposal. In particular, we who are born of God have received the indwelling Holy Spirit, who equips us to live and love as children of God. Faith in Jesus is ultimately what gives us access to the Holy Spirit, and so faith is the weapon with which we conquer the world.

5:6. Today's reading ends with a somewhat cryptic statement, which actually begins a new section in 1 John that extends through 5:12. Many views have been put forward in an attempt to understand what the author intends by his references to water and blood. The view taken here is that the water signifies Jesus' baptism while the blood signifies his crucifixion. At his baptism, Jesus was declared to be the beloved Son of God, and no one in John's community disputes Jesus' divinity. Yet, as we saw in 1 John 1 (East 2), there were heretical Christians who claimed that Jesus was not human but only seemed to be. This is why John writes in 4:2, "By this you know the Spirit of God: every spirit that confesses that Jesus Christ has come *in the flesh* is from God." There was no room in their dualistic worldview for the Incarnation, for the belief that God could and did become a flesh-and-blood human being. They would have denied that the Christ really died a human death. John counters this heretical position by asserting the full divinity and full humanity of Jesus. He argues that Jesus Christ did not merely come by means of water but by means of the water (his baptism which demonstrated his divinity) and the blood (his death which demonstrated his humanity). Of course, the mystery of the Incarnation is spiritually discerned, so the Spirit serves to testify to the truth of Jesus' identity as the incarnate Son of God.

Suggestions for Lectors

Today's reading is fairly straightforward. The only issue needing attention is the cryptic final verse. Read it in as clear and as confident a manner as possible; it will be up to the preacher to explain it.

JOHN 15:9–17

Notes

Sequence. 3 of 6

Commentary

In last week's gospel, Jesus spoke privately with his disciples on the eve of his execution. Drawing upon imagery from the world of viticulture, Jesus presents himself as the true vine. Jesus develops this metaphor by casting his Father as the vinedresser and his disciples as the branches. Through this metaphor, Jesus highlights the importance of abiding in him, which has to do with loving and serving one another. When we love one another, we demonstrate that we belong to Jesus (13:34–35); that is, we reveal ourselves as branches of the true vine.

15:9–17. Today's reading picks up where last week's left off. The call to abide in Jesus remains, but now there is an emphasis upon the priority of God's initiative.

Abiding is presented as a faithful, obedient *response* to things God has already done. In other words, abiding is not a *condition* that we need to meet before God will act.

This fits well with our role as branches. Branches do not produce fruit, only vines do. Apart from the vine, branches are dead and useless. When branches are properly connected to the vine, the vine is able to generate fruit through them. Likewise, as disciples, we do not generate love, we simply share with others the love that has been showered upon us. Consequently, the accent is upon what *Jesus* has done to generate our faithful response.

> As the Father has loved me,
> so *I have loved you*; abide in my love (15:10).
>
> This is my commandment,
> that you love one another *as I have loved you* (15:12).
>
> You did not choose me but *I chose you* (15:16).

Moreover, as the first of these statements reveals, God's love for humanity is rooted and grounded in the Father's love for the Son. In other words, Jesus' love for his disciples is itself a reflection and a sharing of the love he has received from the Father. Thus, when we experience the love of Jesus, we are drawn into the very being of God, and we participate in the love that the Father has for his one and only Son. We see this truth reflected in Jesus' final prayer for his disciples:

> The glory that you have given me I have given them, so that they may be one, as we are one, I in them and you in me, that they may become completely one, so that the world may know that you have sent me and *have loved them even as you have loved me*.... I made your name known to them, and I will make it known, *so that the love with which you have loved me may be in them*, and I in them (17:22–23, 26).

Suggestions for Lectors

Read John 15:1–8 as background as you make preparations for today's passage.

Today's reading is filled with complex sentences, sentences with many commas and places without commas that would benefit from pauses, so read at a slower tempo. This will not only help you read complex sentences more naturally and smoothly, it will also help you read with more depth of emotion. This reading you have been entrusted with is a part of Jesus' last conversation with his disciples before his death and calls for emotion. Keep this in mind, especially when delivering a line like, *No one has greater love than this; to lay down one's life for one's friends* (15:13). This is no mere academic assertion, for Jesus will do this very thing in less than twenty-four hours. Surely, he does not deliver this statement without emotion, so make sure you deliver it with emotion.

There are a lot of elements in today's reading worthy of emphasis, but we cannot emphasize everything. So as you work with the text, decide which phrases or ideas you would most like to highlight, then work out how you will do this.

ASCENSION DAY

Acts 1:1–11
Psalm 47 *or* 93
Ephesians 1:15–23
Luke 24:44–53

ACTS 1:1–11

Commentary

The Acts of the Apostles is the second volume of a two-volume work, as the opening line indicates "In the first book, Theophilus, I wrote…" (1:1). The first book mentioned here refers to the Gospel according to Luke. Consequently, these two books are sometimes referred to collectively as Luke-Acts.

Since Acts is a continuation of Luke's story about Jesus, when we read of Jesus' ascending into heaven in the opening chapter of Acts, we should not think of it as the beginning of a new story. Nor should we regard it as the end of a story even though Jesus' ascension is how Luke's gospel ends (24:50–53, see below). Instead, Jesus' ascension into heaven is *the beginning of the second half of the story*, a story that gets underway at the end of Jesus' *earthly* ministry but at the beginning of his *heavenly* ministry.

1:1–5. Today's reading begins with the author's summary of what he wrote in his gospel. Luke's comments are addressed to a certain individual, Theophilus (1:1), whom he also addresses in the introduction to his gospel (Luke 1:1–4). Theophilus, whose Greek name means a *friend* or *lover of God*, is nowhere else mentioned in the NT or in other early Christian writings. It is likely that he was Luke's patron, a wealthy, first-century Christian who supported Luke financially as Luke researched and wrote Luke-Acts. In summarizing his gospel, Luke mentions Jesus' death, resurrection, and ascension, and in so doing draws special attention to the presence and role of the Holy Spirit. In Luke, the Holy Spirit is presented as playing a significant role in the life of Jesus as he carried out his messianic vocation. Likewise, the Holy Spirit will play a significant role in the lives of Jesus' disciples as they continue Jesus' vocation to seek and save the lost by announcing to the whole world the good news of God's kingdom.

1:6–8. Throughout his ministry and during the forty-day period between his resurrection and ascension, Jesus spoke to his disciples about the kingdom of God. On this occasion, the disciples ask Jesus, "Lord, is this the time when you will restore the kingdom to Israel?" (1:6). Jesus treats their question as legitimate for not only does he not rebuke his disciples but many of the OT prophets speak of the day when God would return to restore the fortunes of his covenant people. In any case, Jesus says that whatever comes it is not for the disciples to know "the times or periods" (1:6). He then redirects their attention to something his Father does want them to prepare for, namely, the coming of the Holy Spirit who will empower them to be Jesus' witnesses not only in Jewish lands but throughout the world for God's purposes include the salvation of all peoples and nations.

1:9–11. With this said, Jesus is taken up into heaven. This marks the end of his earthly ministry. After this, Jesus makes no more resurrection appearances, save one to Paul. Instead Jesus conducts his messianic vocation from heaven at the right hand of God, working through his followers by means of "the promise of the Father" (1:4), the indwelling Holy Spirit, who will be sent to them at Pentecost.

Suggestions for Lectors

After the initial run-through of what has transpired, pause after 1:5 to take a breath and make the transition to the words of the risen Jesus. Speak the Lord's words with strength and authority. While 1:7 could be read as a chastisement, it need not be. Instead it could be intoned as a genuine response to a legitimate question. Read 1:8 with particular emphasis as this statement not only summarizes the plot for the whole book of Acts, but also provides the basis for Christian life and mission.

In 1:9, we are suddenly into "live action." Slow down as you read about the Lord's ascension, which we are celebrating today. Read these last three verses as if everything that went before was their prelude. The key phrase is the promise in 1:11, that *he will come again in the same way*, namely, in glory. This is your strongest and most direct statement. Conclude your reading on this high, joyful, and hopeful note.

Pronunciation Guide

Galilee (GAL-uh-lee), *Judea* (joo-DEE-uh; -DAY-),
Samaria (suh-MAIR-ee-uh), *Theophilus* (thee-OFF-ih-luhs)

EPHESIANS 1:15–23

Commentary

1:15–19. In today's reading, Paul acknowledges the faith and love of the Ephesian Christians, which has occasioned many of Paul's own prayers of thanksgiving to God. Paul specifically prays that they might be granted the wisdom to know and fully understand the hope, the inheritance, and the power of God into which they have been called and in which they even now participate. As the letter continues, the reader will discover that these things all have to do with the new life Christians receive by faith in Jesus and which is open to Jews and Gentiles alike.

1:20–23. Paul continues stating that God's great power was handed over to Jesus to wield when Jesus was resurrected from the dead and ascended to heaven, where he shares God's heavenly throne. And so, Jesus' name and authority are greater than all other authorities, earthly and heavenly, and not just for a time but for all time (1:21). As Jesus says after his resurrection in Matthew, "All authority in heaven and on earth has been given to me" (28:18). Therefore, Jesus is owed complete allegiance, by all peoples and powers, not least the church which is his body and through which he rules and exercises his lordship over all creation.

Suggestions for Lectors

Today's reading can be read in two movements as indicated in the Commentary. In 1:15–19, let your voice convey Paul's gratitude for the faith and love of his addressees. Pause for a full second at the end of 1:19 in order to prepare your listeners for the second movement, in which Paul paints a picture of the exalted majesty of the Lord Jesus Christ. As you read these verses, phrase by phrase, slowly invest your voice with excitement and awe that reaches a climactic crescendo with the concluding phrase *the fullness of him who fills all in all* (1:23).

As is so often the case with Paul's writings, you will want to spend extra time practicing his longer sentences until they can be read smoothly and without any loss of meaning. In today's reading, 17–19 and 20–21 each comprises a single, complex sentence.

Pronunciation Guide
Ephesians (eh-FEE-zhuhnz; ih-)

LUKE 24:44–53

Commentary
As was noted in the Commentary for today's reading from Acts (see above), the Gospel of Luke and the Acts of the Apostles are the first and second volumes of a single work written by the same author, Luke, and addressed to the same recipient, Theophilus (Luke 1:3; Acts 1:1). Interestingly, the end of Luke and the beginning of Acts overlap as they both relate the story of Jesus' ascension into heaven. None of the other gospels narrate this event, but Jesus' ascension seems to be of particular importance for Luke, not only because he tells the story twice but because he makes an earlier reference to it at a critical turning point in his gospel. In Luke 9:51, the narrator says of Jesus, "When the days drew near for him to be *taken up*, he set his face to go to Jerusalem." Here, the reference to Jesus' being *taken up* is not a reference to his crucifixion but to his ascension into heaven. But, why does the narrator highlight the ascension? Why does the text not say, "When the days drew near for him *to be killed* or for him *to be raised*"?

For Luke, more than any other event, Jesus' ascension into heaven is a watershed moment, marking the transition from the *Acts of Jesus*, who proclaimed the good news of the kingdom through the power of the Holy Spirit, to the *Acts of the Apostles*, who proclaim the good news of God's reign by means of the same Holy Spirit. Jesus began his earthly ministry when the Holy Spirit came upon him at his baptism (Luke 3:21–22; cf. 4:14; 18). Likewise, Jesus' disciples begin their earthly ministries after the promised Holy Spirit comes upon them at Pentecost (Acts 2:1–21, Pent). In this regard, the ascension of Jesus resembles the ascension of Elijah into heaven. In 2 Kings 2:1–12 (Epi L), the prophet Elijah does not die. Instead, Elijah is taken up into heaven in a chariot of fire. Upon Elijah's departure, his disciple Elisha receives a double-portion of his master's spirit and so takes up his master's vocation as the LORD's prophet in Israel.

Thus, Jesus' ascension is not the end of the gospel story, only the end of the first half. Jesus' ascension is not an epilogue; it is the beginning of the second half of the story, a story in which Jesus continues his work of saving the lost by working through his followers by means of the Holy Spirit who will come upon them at Pentecost.

12:44–49. Today's reading begins with the resurrected Jesus opening the minds of his followers to what was written about him in the Scriptures, our Old Testament. This includes the suffering, death, and resurrection of the Messiah, as well as the gifts of repentance and forgiveness that are to be proclaimed in his name to all nations. By *all nations*, Jesus does not mean that these gifts are only for other Jews who live elsewhere in the world; they are for *all* people of *all* nations, Jews and Gentiles alike. Jesus' followers are to serve as witnesses to these things, and they shall be empowered and equipped with the same Holy Spirit that empowered and equipped Jesus to carry out his vocation. The Holy Spirit, however, will not come until after Jesus has departed, and so they need to wait in Jerusalem until they "have been clothed with power from on high" (24:49).

12:50–53. At the conclusion of these words, Jesus takes them out to Bethany, which is situated on the Mount of Olives. Then, as Jesus is blessing them, he is taken up into heaven. His disciples remain for a while worshipping him, which is unprecedented in Luke. Interestingly, Luke's gospel begins and ends in the Jerusalem temple. In the first episode, Zechariah is going about his priestly duties in the temple when the angel of the Lord appears to him (1:5–23). And then, in the last episode, the disciples return to Jerusalem with great joy where they are "continually in the temple blessing God" (24:53; cf. 2:37).

Suggestions for Lectors

As reflected in the Commentary, today's reading occurs in two movements, so pause for a full second between verses 49 and 50.

Read the first movement with increasing intensity and solemnity in order to convey the magnitude not only of who Jesus is and what he has accomplished (24:44–46) but also of what will be proclaimed and accomplished in his name following his ascension (24:47–49). Jesus has literally transformed the world through his life, death, and resurrection, and his followers are now commissioned for the roles they shall play in God's plan to redeem humanity and renew creation.

Read the second movement slowly as it narrates Jesus' ascension, which is what we are celebrating today. Though Jesus is leaving his disciples, his disciples do not experience any gloom or sadness, only joy. Consequently, read these final verses in an upbeat manner with a hint of reverence and joy in your voice.

Pronunciation Guide

Bethany (BETH-uh-nee)
Messiah (muh-SĪ-uh)
Moses (MOH-zuhs)

SEVENTH SUNDAY OF EASTER

Acts 1:15–17, 21–26
Psalm 1
1 John 5:9–13
John 17:6–19

ACTS 1:15–17, 21–26

Notes

Sequence. 7 of 8

Commentary

Following his resurrection, Jesus appeared to his followers for a period of forty days, offering proof of his resurrection and speaking about the kingdom of God (Acts 1:1; Asc). At the end of those forty days, Jesus ascended into heaven. Before his ascension, he commanded his disciples, many of whom were from Galilee, to wait in Jerusalem until they received the gift of the indwelling Holy Spirit, who would empower them to be Jesus' witnesses throughout the world.

1:15–17. While they are waiting in Jerusalem, Peter stands up and addresses the community of Jesus' followers. He broaches the subject of Judas Iscariot, one of the Twelve who had, in the end, betrayed Jesus to the authorities. In response to the unstated question of *Why?*, which had surely plagued the disciples, Peter argues that Judas' role in the drama of Jesus' death was so that the Scriptures might be fulfilled.

1:21–22. Peter then continues by stating that a replacement should be found, for as the Scriptures say, "Let another take his position of overseer" (Acts 1:20; cf. Psalm 109:8). The principal qualification is that the replacement should be a disciple from the earliest days, from the days of Jesus' baptism by John, which is the event that inaugurated Jesus' public ministry. Two qualified candidates are put forward. Then after prayer, they cast lots, and Matthias is selected.

1:23–26. That lots were employed to make such an important decision may seem strange to us, especially since this is not a common practice among Christians today. But it should be recognized that both candidates were qualified to serve as witnesses of Jesus' resurrection. In other words, lots were not cast for the whole group indiscriminately, but only for those who met the qualifications.

Suggestions for Lectors

In the opening verse, drop your voice as you read the parenthetical expression, *(together the crowd numbered about one hundred twenty persons)* (1:15).

In today's reading, Peter is speaking to a large group of people so when you deliver his address, elevate your voice to give the impression that you are speaking to a crowd, without the aid of modern technology. After Peter's speech concludes in 1:22, pause for a second before continuing on.

When you pray the prayer in 1:24–25, do not direct your words to your listeners but to God. If you are a reader who likes to look up during the reading, then do not make eye contact with your listeners at this point. If you want to look up, glance skyward, again because your words are directed to God.

Pronunciation Guide

Barsabbas (BAHR-suh-buhs; *not* bahr-SAB-buhs)
Justus (JUS-tuhs)
Matthias (muh-THĪ-uhs)

1 JOHN 5:9–13

Notes

Sequence. 6 of 6

Commentary

In 1 John, the author often presents spiritual matters in black and white terms with no middle ground. Consider the following examples:

> Everyone who does what is right is righteous, just as he is righteous. Everyone who commits sin is a child of the devil; for the devil has been sinning from the beginning (3:7b–8).

> By this you know the Spirit of God: every spirit that confesses that Jesus Christ has come in the flesh is from God, and every spirit that does not confess Jesus is not from God (4:2–3)

5:9–13. In today's reading, the author remains true to form. For John, there are just two type of people in the world—those with eternal life and those without it, and the difference between these two types of people turns on one and only one matter. Those who believe in Jesus, the Son of God, have eternal life, while those who do not believe in him don't. Why? Because the eternal kind of life that God has given to us is only available in his Son.

Not only did God send his Son into the world to give us life, God has offered testimony to this fact. To disregard God's testimony about his Son is to treat God as a liar. Yet, when a person places their trust in the Son, they will discover that this testimony has been written on their hearts. They will have an internal witness that offers them assurance of their faith and salvation. In fact, that is exactly why 1 John was written. As the author says, "I write these things to you who believe in the name of the Son of God, so that you may *know* that you have eternal life" (5:13). Here, one is reminded of the purpose for John's gospel: "Now Jesus did many other signs in the presence of his disciples, which are not written in this book. But these are written so that you may come to believe that Jesus is the Messiah, the Son of God, and that through believing you may have life in his name" (20:30–31).

Suggestions for Lectors

The first two verses make repeated reference to the *testimony* that God has given, but it is not until 5:11 that the content of that testimony is revealed. So when you come to 5:11, pause for a second after *testimony*, and then raise your voice as you proclaim, *God gave us eternal life, and this life is in his Son* (5:11b). Pause again afterwards before continuing.

In 5:9–12, John speaks in third person, talking about *those* and about *whoever*, but in the final verse, he addresses his readers directly, *I write these things to you* (5:13). So when you come to 5:13, take a moment to look up at your listeners before you read the final verse.

JOHN 17:6–19

Notes

Sequence. 4 of 6

Commentary

In John, on the eve of his execution, Jesus shares a final meal with his disciples, which is narrated over the course of five chapters (13:1–17:26). The evening begins with Jesus washing his disciples' feet (13:1–20) and concludes with Jesus praying for them (17:1–26). In between these two scenes, Jesus bids his farewells as he offers a series of parting instructions. He speaks of his going away and of the coming of the Spirit (14:1–31); he commands his followers to love and serve one another (13:12–20, 31–35); and he encourages them to abide in him as they confront a hostile world (15:1–27).

In today's reading, our attention is directed to the central portion of Jesus' final prayer. Jesus delivers this prayer aloud in the presence of his disciples, for what he asks the Father concerns them. He begins by saying that he has completed the work the Father sent him to do, so he asks that he be restored to the glory he formally had in the Father's presence (17:1–5). He concludes by praying for the unity of all his followers, present and future. He wants them to share and experience the same oneness of spirit, purpose, and glory that he and the Father have shared for all time (17:20–26).

17:6–10. Jesus came *to make God known.* In John's gospel, this idea is expressed as early as the prologue. The Word of God became a flesh-and-blood human being so that the glory of God—that is, God's essential character and identity—might become known by all human beings (1:14). The Word was in a position to reveal God's glory because the Word has always been with God and is God (1:1). This same truth is expressed through the metaphor of sonship. As the incarnate Son of God, Jesus is the spitting image of his Father. Therefore, he is able to embody and reveal God's character and purposes. "No one has ever seen God. It is God the only Son, who is close to the Father's heart, who *has made him known*" (1:18).

Moreover, to know God is to have eternal life, for knowing God and possessing eternal life are one and the same. As Jesus says at the beginning of his prayer, "This is eternal life, that *they may know you*, the only true God, and Jesus Christ whom you have sent" (17:3). Of course, Jesus' death plays an essential role in our coming to know God. Not only does his death remove any obstacles to our entering into an intimate relationship with God, his death also reveals the shape of God's character. In offering up his one and only Son for us, God reveals his nature to be that of self-sacrificing, self-emptying love. Thus, Jesus' death is not simply a sacrifice for sin (even though we Christians often present it as such). Even more fundamentally, Jesus' death serves as the climactic event in the drama of God's self-revelation to humanity that began when the Word became flesh. As the incarnate Son of God, Jesus came to make God known and to render us capable of knowing God. This, Jesus says, he has done.

17:11–19. Jesus asks the Father to protect all those who have come to know him. Jesus has guarded and protected his disciples, but now he must go away and entrust them into his Father's care. Specifically, Jesus asks his Father to preserve the community and unity of his followers (17:11) and to protect them from the evil one (17:15). Jesus also asks the Father "to sanctify them in the truth" (17:17). Here, he is requesting that his Holy Father make his followers holy by separating them from the world and the world's ways through the truth of his word. In this way, they can be sent into the world to carry out the same mission that Jesus himself has had, namely, to make God known through his beloved Son. After Jesus departs, the Father will grant all these requests by sending the Holy Spirit upon the disciples (14:15–31; 15:26–27; 16:4b–15, Pent).

Suggestions for Lectors

As lectors, we generally direct our readings to those who have gathered for worship. If we are reading a narrative, we become a storyteller and tell the story to our listeners. If we are reading an epistle, we become the author and speak to our listeners. Today's episode is different, however, because Jesus is praying to the Father. So, as you read, direct your words and thoughts to God, and allow your listeners, as it were, to overhear your prayer.

Emphasize the verbs in the petitions that Jesus makes. The first occurs in 17:11, where Jesus addresses God for the first time, *Holy Father,… protect them in your name that you have given me, so that they may be one, as we are one.* The other petitions are as follows: *I am not asking you to take them out of the world, but I ask you to protect them from the evil one* (17:15); and *Sanctify them in the truth* (17:17).

✠ PENTECOST VIGIL

✠ Genesis 11:1–9	✠ Psalm 33:12–22
or ✠ Exodus 19:1–9a, 16–20a; 20:18–20	✠ Canticle 2 *or* 13
or ✠ Ezekiel 37:1–14	✠ Psalm 130
or ✠ Joel 2:28–32	✠ Canticle 9
✠ Acts 2:1–11	
or ✠ Romans 8:14–17, 22–27	✠ Psalm 104:24–31 (= 104:25–32 BCP)
✠ John 7:37–39a	

✠ GENESIS 11:1–9

Commentary

Our NT reading from Acts 2 tells the story of Pentecost, of how the Holy Spirit comes upon Jesus' followers after his ascension into heaven. When this happened, they found themselves speaking other languages, with the result that all the Jews who had made pilgrimage to Jerusalem from different parts of the world were able to hear the good news of Jesus Christ in their own native languages. So, we see in Acts that the proclamation of the gospel by the power of the Holy Spirit is able to bring people together, by overcoming the barriers of language and culture that separate people from one another. This fulfills God's vision for a restored humanity, where human beings are reconciled to one another in service to God. The story of Pentecost offers a reversal of what happens in today's reading from Genesis, in which millennia earlier God confuses the language of humanity to introduce barriers between people who are united in service to their own self-interest.

The Tower of Babel is the concluding story in what is known as the Primeval History (Genesis 1–11), which recounts events from world history, the history of humanity in general—like the Creation, the Fall, and the Flood—as distinct from the particular history of Israel, which begins in Genesis 12 with the calling of Abraham and Sarah. Beginning with Adam and Eve's disobedience, which introduced sin, shame, and death into God's good creation (Gen 3, Prop 5), things have progressively worsened. Cain murders his brother Abel, and violence increases exponentially. God sends a flood to provide a temporary check on the spread of human sin and violence, but it is now many years later. Noah's descendants have multiplied, and once again humanity's propensity toward sin and violence threatens God's purposes for creation.

11:1–9. On this occasion, the people of the earth have gathered together to make a name for themselves by building a tower to reach the heavens, presumably as a monument to their own glory and power. This activity, however, goes against their creation mandate to bear God's image in such a way as to give glory to God and to God's name. Humanity is able to make rapid progress in their self-glorification because at this point "the whole earth had one language and the same words" (11:1). In 11:5, God comes down to see what humanity has been up to, and seeing their city and tower, God takes counsel with his heavenly court to discuss the matter. Anticipating more of the same from humanity, God decides to inhibit their rebellious progress by confusing their language and spreading them abroad. Thus, God protects creation and protects humanity from its own devices until there comes that time in the future when humanity will be granted a new Spirit, the Holy Spirit of God himself, so that they can once again be united, not to make a name for themselves but to make a name for God.

Suggestions for Lectors

Ever since Adam and Eve's disobedience, the LORD has been increasingly frustrated with the spread of wickedness and violence and with the way humanity has conducted itself in the world. Thus, in today's reading, there is a contrast in tone between the people's pride over their ingenuous plans and the LORD's ongoing frustration, which you can reflect in your voice. There is no particular emphasis within the narrative; only remember that, as you read, you yourself are the narrator telling this story to an attentive audience.

Pronunciation Guide

Babel (BA-buhl; BAY-)
bitumen (bih-TOO-muhn; -tyoo-)
Shinar (SHĪ-nahr)

✠ Exodus 19:1–9a, 16–20a; 20:18–20

Commentary

After escaping from Egypt and passing through the Red Sea, Moses led the Israelites through the wilderness to Mount Horeb (a.k.a., Mount Sinai), where Moses was first encountered by the LORD in the burning bush (3:1–6). During that encounter Moses asks God, "Who am I that I should go to Pharaoh and bring the Israelites out of Egypt?" (3:11). God replies, "I will be with you; and this shall be the sign for you that it is I who sent you: when you have brought the people out of Egypt, you shall worship God on this mountain" (3:12). And so, it comes to pass in today's reading. The Israelites finally arrive at the base of Mount Sinai, where their covenant with God will be ratified, and they will receive the Ten Commandments (20:1–17, Lent 3).

19:1–8. It takes Israel a few months to travel from Egypt to Mount Sinai (19:1). When they arrive, the LORD begins to define the terms of the covenant that will govern the relationship between him and the Israelites. The LORD promises that, if the Israelites obediently keep their side of the covenant, then the LORD will make them his special people, his "treasured possession out of all the peoples" of the earth (19:5), such that Israel will become for God "a priestly kingdom and a holy nation" (19:6a). In other words, as Israel lives in covenant relationship with God, Israel will begin to acquire, embody, and reflect the very character of God, as individuals and as a community. This will enable the chosen people to serve as God's priests to the world, who mediate the presence, knowledge, and forgiveness of God to all peoples everywhere. Thus, being God's treasured people does not so much characterize Israel's *status* as it defines Israel's *vocation*; being the chosen people of God signifies obligation not privilege. When Moses lays out the terms of the covenant before the people, they readily assent saying, "Everything that the LORD has spoken we will do" (19:8).

19:9a, 16–20a. In this scene, the LORD speaks to Moses in the form of a dense cloud that engulfs Mount Sinai so that the people will learn to trust Moses as God's prophet and spokesperson. The people are instructed to gather at the foot of the mountain, yet any who attempt to go up the mountain or even touch it will be subject to death (19:12–13). Moses alone ascends the smoking, shaking mountain where he receives the Ten Commandments amidst sounds of trumpets and thunder and lighting.

20:18–20. Having witnessed all of this, the people are so utterly terrified that they stand away from the mountain. Moreover, when Moses descends, the Israelites beg him saying, "You speak to us, and we will listen; but do not let God speak to us, or we will die" (20:19). So, while the Israelites have been called to mediate God's presence to the world, for now Moses will mediate God's presence to the Israelites.

Suggestions for Lectors

Today's reading recounts a momentous event in Israel's relationship with the LORD. Having dramatically rescued the people and brought them through the wilderness to his mountain, the LORD intends to enter into a binding covenant with the children of Israel. Read the words of the LORD with dignity and deep conviction, conveying the magnitude of the event and pausing at their conclusion in 19:6. The principal stress comes when you mark the people's enthusiastic response in 19:8a, which should be read very deliberately and at a reduced tempo. Pause after *spoken* and then deliver the last three words, *we will do*, with quiet confidence. You may wish to pause slightly after each of these monosyllabic words, enunciating them with a bit of staccato: *we… will… do….*

Read 19:16–20a and 20:18 a bit slower with hints of awe, reverence, and fear in your voice to convey the people's apprehension and terror. Then, increase the intensity of your voice when you read their entreaty to Moses, *You speak to us… or we will die* (20:19). In response, Moses attempts to calm the people's fears even as he stresses the importance of their obedience and commitment. Consequently, you might speak Moses' words strongly with a hint of compassion in your voice.

Pronunciation Guide
Egypt (EE-jipt), *Egyptians* (ih-JIP-shuhnz; ee-), *Israel* (IZ-ree-uhl; -ray-),
Israelites (IZ-ree-līts), *Jacob* (JAY-kuhb), *Moses* (MOH-zuhs),
Rephidim (REF-uh-dim), *Sinai* (SĪ-nī; SĪ-nee-ī)

✠ EZEKIEL 37:1–14

Commentary
In 598 B.C., the Babylonian empire under the leadership of King Nebuchadnezzar (a.k.a., Nebuchadrezzar) moved against Jerusalem and quashed a rebellion led by King Jehoiakim of Judah (2 Kgs 24:1–7). A few months later, in 597 B.C., the Babylonians returned to ransack the palace and temple, taking everything of value back to Babylon. Then, in what is known as the First Deportation, a select group of Jerusalem's leading officials and citizens were taken as exiles to Babylon (2 Kgs 24:8–17). Among this group of Judean exiles was a young priest by the name of Ezekiel who, in the fifth year of the exile (Ezek 1:1–3), received a heavenly vision of God enthroned on a chariot-like throne (1:4–28). In this vision, Ezekiel is commissioned as a prophet and called to speak the word of the LORD to God's people (2:4; 3:11, 27), to those who live as exiles in Babylon and to those who still reside back in Judah. Like Isaiah and Jeremiah, Ezekiel's message was initially one of imminent judgment and exile, but after these came to pass, his message became one of forgiveness and restoration. A summary of Ezekiel's double message can be found in 39:23–29.

In today's reading, Ezekiel is granted a vision of the restoration of the exiled people of God, depicted as resurrection from the dead. Some ninety-five times, the LORD addresses the prophet as *Son of Man*, which is rendered *Mortal* in the NRSV.

37:1–6. The reading begins with the Spirit of the LORD transporting the prophet to a valley filled with dry bones. As the LORD guides Ezekiel around the valley, he asks him whether he thinks these dry dusty bones can live again, to which Ezekiel replies, "O Lord GOD, you know" (37:3). The LORD commands Ezekiel to prophesy to the bones, communicating the LORD's intention to restore their bodies—sinew, flesh and skin—and then to put his breath into them that they might live again.

Here, one is perhaps reminded of the creation of Adam where, like a sculptor, the LORD fashioned a man out of the dry dust of the ground and then breathed into his nostrils the breath of life and "the man became a living being" (Gen 2:7).

37:7–10. Ezekiel prophesies as commanded, and everything comes about in two dramatic stages. In the first stage, the bones are reconnected and reformed into fully physical human bodies, yet the breath of life has not yet entered them. Then, at the LORD's animated behest, Ezekiel prophesies a second time, and a breath from the four winds sweeps through the valley and fills these bodies with life. When all is complete, the reconstituted and reanimated bodies stand forming as "a vast multitude" (37:10).

37:11–14. After this occurs, the LORD then explains to Ezekiel the meaning and significance of this vision. The exiles are in despair, believing that the LORD has abandoned them forever. They lament, "Our bones are dried up, and our hope is lost; we are cut off completely" (37:11). In response, the LORD gives Ezekiel this vision so that he might give the people hope by announcing that the end of exile is near. Yet the end of exile entails not only the physical return of Israel to the land, but also the spiritual transformation of the people (36:24–28, EastVig). For the breath that Ezekiel prophesies to is the very Spirit of God, who will give the people new life by enabling them to live faithfully and obediently in their covenant partnership with the LORD their God.

Suggestions for Lectors

Ezekiel's visionary experience easily lends itself to a dramatic reading, so your preparation will involve making sure that your reading is not overly dramatic. Of course, you still want to read it with feeling and intensity, but you may find it necessary to reign these in a bit in order to allow the text to have a more active role.

Begin 37:1 in your normal narrating voice until you come to *it was full of bones*, which you will want to read slowly and with a hint of surprised curiosity in your voice. Also, pause for a full second before you deliver this line. Then, as you read 37:2–3, imagine the silence, as the prophet wanders through this spectacle, stricken mute with wonder. Let your voice be hushed, intense, and filled with awe.

In 37:4–6, the story gathers momentum, as the Lord GOD utters the life-giving words of prophecy. In 37:9, when the Lord GOD says, *Prophesy to the breath, prophesy, mortal*, one gets the impression that God himself is eager to see these bones live again, perhaps even a bit impatient like an enthusiastic child; so add some excitement into your voice as you say these words.

Ezekiel 37:7–10 demands your greatest effort as the vision surges into action. Read 37:10 slowly, phrase by phrase, as the miracle happens. In 37:11–14, when the meaning of the vision is finally revealed—the restoration of the exiled nation by its God—speak more quietly, but with intensity, to the end.

Pronunciation Guide

Note the difference in pronunciation between the verbs, prophesy and prophesied, and the noun, prophecy: *prophesy* (vb., PRAH-fuh-sī), *prophesied* (vb., PRAH-fuh-sīd), *prophecy* (n., PRAH-fuh-see), *Ezekiel* (ee-ZEE-kee-uhl; ee-ZEE-kyuhl)

✠ JOEL 2:28–32

Commentary

The book of Joel belongs to a collection of OT writings known as the Book of the Twelve, which comprises the twelve Minor Prophets from Hosea to Malachi. Beyond the fact that Joel was a prophet and the son of Pethuel (Joel 1:1), we know nothing about him. Swarming throughout the first two chapters of Joel is the prophet's vivid description of the land devastated by a plague of locusts. The prophet interprets this devastation as a sign that the great and terrible Day of the LORD is drawing near; that is, the LORD is about to come and judge his people for their idolatry. Yet knowing that the LORD is a God who is "gracious and merciful, slow to anger, and abounding in steadfast love" and who "relents from punishing" (2:12–13, Ash), the prophet calls the people and their leaders to rend their hearts and return to their God. Who knows, the LORD may very well relent from his planned judgment and instead "leave a blessing behind him" when he comes (2:14). In 2:18ff, this is precisely what happens and today's reading paints a picture of the Day of the LORD's coming to his people no longer as a day of judgment but as a new day of forgiveness and restoration.

In the verses leading up to today's reading, the LORD says repeatedly, "my people shall never again be put to shame" for they will know not only that the LORD is their God but also that there are no other gods except the LORD (2:26–27). In other words, the LORD pledges that his people will never experience shame because they will remain faithful.

2:28–29. But how will the LORD bring this about? How can the LORD guarantee that his people will not forsake him and so be put to shame? Very simply, the LORD will pour out his Spirit on human beings. Here the sentiment being expressed is the same as that expressed by the prophet in Jeremiah 31:31–34 (Lent 5).

2:30–32. This will take place on the Day of the LORD, which will be a day attended by great signs in the heavens. And yet, ironically that "great and terrible day" (2:31) will be a day of *salvation* for *all* people "for everyone who calls upon the name of the LORD shall be saved." This is how Luke interprets Joel's prophecy in his narrative about the coming of the Holy Spirit on the day of Pentecost (Acts 2:14–21).

Suggestions for Lectors

As you read today, imagine that you are the prophet Joel announcing to your listeners the good news of God's plans for their restoration and well-being. Begin reading with a tone of rejoicing lightness that befits the good news you are proclaiming. Proceed in this manner until you come to 2:30. At this point, gradually introduce a heaviness and a sense of foreboding into your voice that will peak as you say *before the great and terrible day of the LORD comes* (2:31). Then, pause for a full second before proceeding with *Then, everyone who calls upon the name of the LORD shall be saved* (2:32a), which should be read as though the sun were breaking through the dark clouds following a particularly dreadful storm.

Pronunciation Guide

Joel (JOH-uhl; JOHL)

✠ ACTS 2:1–11

Commentary

Jesus' death, resurrection, and ascension are not the end of the gospel Story, just the end of the beginning of that Story. For along with the New Covenant instituted by Jesus comes the Spirit in a new way to create and equip a new people of God. Before his ascension, Jesus instructed his disciples "not to leave Jerusalem, but to wait there for the promise of the Father. 'This,' he said, 'is what you have heard from me; for John baptized with water, but you will be baptized with the Holy Spirit not many days from now'" (Acts 1:4–5, Asc). Today's reading opens with Jesus' disciples doing just that, waiting in Jerusalem.

2:1–4. The Holy Spirit comes on the day of Pentecost, also known as the Jewish Feast of Weeks (or First Fruits). Pentecost was one of three annual pilgrimage festivals celebrated at the temple in Jerusalem; the others were the Feast of Unleavened Bread (a.k.a., Passover) and the Feast of Tabernacles. The Feast of Weeks concluded a seven-week period that began with the presentation of the first barley sheaf during Passover; this is reflected in its Greek name, Pentecost, which simply means *fiftieth*. The Feast of Weeks was originally an agricultural festival marking the end of the grain harvest, but by the time of Jesus, it had become associated with the covenant and the giving of the Law at Mount Sinai, which included the Ten Commandments.

So, on the day of Pentecost, all of Jesus' disciples (not just the eleven apostles) are gathered together in a house in Jerusalem, when they hear the sound of a rushing wind. They also see what appear to be tongues of fire coming to rest upon each of them, at which point they all are filled with the Holy Spirit, who grants them the ability to speak in various foreign languages.

2:5–11. Because the Feast of Weeks was a pilgrimage festival, there were devout Jews from every nation who had made the journey to Jerusalem. The sound of the rushing wind drew their attention and to their bewilderment, when they heard the voices of Jesus' disciples, they heard them speaking in their own native tongues. Their amazement turns to astonishment when they discover that those speaking are Galileans, uneducated folk from the backwaters of Jewish society whose life experiences would not have put them in a position to learn or use these foreign languages.

The author lists just some of the languages that were heard, and here it is important to emphasize the fact that all of those present are Jews or Gentile-converts to Judaism who live in the Diaspora, that is, in Jewish communities outside Palestine. At this stage in Acts, the gospel is only being proclaimed to Jews; it will not be until Acts 10 that Gentiles are presented with the gospel and receive the Holy Spirit.

Suggestions for Lectors

The scene in today's reading is established quickly, in one brief sentence. As you read verses 2:2–4, do whatever you can to dramatize this moment. Raise your voice; speak with something of the intensity and wonder you might use when telling a story to young people. Let your every word convey the excitement of this wondrous happening.

Beginning in 2:5, let your intensity slow somewhat as you build toward a second climax, the listing of all the different nationalities of people who heard Jesus' followers proclaiming the gospel in their native language. To assist in this buildup, replace every comma in 2:9–11a with a period; that is, pause for each comma as though it were a period, or at least a semicolon. In addition, as you work your way through this list, read with slightly increasing amounts of awe and wonder in your voice to convey the people's astonishment, climaxing with *Cretans and Arabs* (2:11a). Then, after a pause and glance up at your listeners, conclude by reading, *in our own languages we hear them speaking about God's deeds of power* (2:11b), in a strong voice still tinged with amazement and excitement.

Pronunciation Guide

Arabs (AIR-uhbz), *Asia* (AY-zhuh), *Cappadocia* (kap'-uh-DOH-shuh), *Cretans* (KREET-uhnz), *Cyrene* (sī-REE-nee; *not* sī-REEN), *Egypt* (EE-jipt), *Elamites* (EE-luh-mīts), *Galileans* (gal'-uh-LEE-uhnz), *Judea* (joo-DEE-uh; -DAY-), *Libya* (LIB-ee-uh; LIB-yuh), *Medes* (MEEDZ), *Mesopotamia* (mes'-oh-puh-TAY-mee-uh), *Pamphylia* (pam-FIL-ee-uh), *Parthians* (PAHR-thee-uhnz), *Pentecost* (PEN-tuh-kost), *Phrygia* (FRIHJ-ee-uh), *Pontus* (PON-tuhs), *proselytes* (PRAH-suh-līts)

✠ ROMANS 8:14–17, 22–27

Notes

Suggested Reading. Romans 8:14–27

Commentary

For Paul, salvation is not simply a matter of having our sins forgiven, for we were not just sinners in need of forgiveness but dead people in need of life. Consequently, salvation was about a whole new kind of life, one guided, directed, and empowered by God's Spirit, who is given to all who place their trust in God's Son, Jesus.

8:14–17. In today's reading, Paul tells the Roman Christians that they are children of God by virtue of their having received God's very own Spirit. God's Spirit dwells within them and always reminds them who they are and to whom they belong. They belong to God as his adopted children, and so fully have they been brought into God's family that they can call upon God as their "Abba, Father" and also share Jesus' inheritance as God's Son.

8:18–21. In the second half of the reading, Paul reflects upon what the future holds for God's children, noting that the suffering we experience now is nothing compared to the glory that we will one day inherit as children of God. Moreover, all of creation stands on pins and needles until that day when God's children will come into their own, for that day will signal the beginning of the New Creation, when all of creation will experience redemption, that is, freedom from the vicious cycles of death and decay brought about by sin.

8:22–27. We too await that day when our adoption will be consummated. We have already received a new Spirit, but one day we will also receive new bodies, and our salvation will be complete. In the meantime, God's indwelling Spirit helps us in our weakness, even helping us in our prayers to God.

Suggestions for Lectors
Today's reading can be read in three sections: 14–17, 22–25 (or 18–25), and 26–27, so make sure to pause for a full second between each of these sections, perhaps a longer pause between the first two sections than between the last two. As you deliver this message to your listeners, be aware of the intensity of expression Paul invests in his words. Paul is trying to convey to his audience matters that he considers to be fundamental and central to Christian life and faith, so invest your voice with fervency, intensity, and confidence as the content and the context dictates.

Paul's sentences and reasoning can be both complex and compact, so when reading from one of Paul's writings, attend closely to the punctuation that has been provided, and do not be afraid to include additional pauses as well.

Pronunciation Guide
Abba (AH-buh)

✠ JOHN 7:37–39A

Notes
Suggested Reading. John 7:37–39

Commentary
In the Gospel according to John, Jesus describes himself using seven different *I am* statements:

> I am the bread of life (6:35, 48, Prop 14),
>   or, I am the living bread (6:51, Prop 15)
> I am the light of the world (8:12; 9:5)
> I am the gate for the sheep (10:7, 9)
> I am the good shepherd (10:11, 14, Epi 4)
> I am the resurrection and the life (11:25)
> I am the way, and the truth, and the life (14:6)
> I am the true vine (15:1, 5, Epi 5)

Yet, there is a statement that one might have expected Jesus to have used, which is not found in John, namely, *I am the water of life*, or *I am the living water.* For example, when Jesus converses with the Samaritan woman beside the well of Jacob, he says, "If you knew the gift of God, and who it is that is saying to you, 'Give me a drink,' you would have asked him, and he would have given you living water" (4:10). Why does Jesus not refer to himself as the living water, merely that he can give living water? Today's reading provides the answer.

7:37–39. In John 7:2, the Jewish Festival of Booths draws near (a.k.a., the Festival of Tabernacles), and Jesus' brothers sarcastically suggest that he go to the festival and reveal himself to the world (7:3–5). Jesus replies that his time has not yet arrived (7:6), yet after his brothers leave for the festival, Jesus himself goes, though in secret (7:10). On the climactic seventh day of the Festival of Booths, a festival in which a daily procession ended with the priests pouring libations of water over the altar, Jesus stands up and invites anyone who is thirsty to come to him to get their thirst satisfied for out of the heart of the one who believes in him will come "rivers of living water" (7:38). The narrator then explains to the reader that Jesus is speaking of the Holy Spirit, whom believers were to receive but had not yet received. This was because Jesus had not yet been glorified, that is, he had not yet been killed, raised, and ascended to his Father. As Jesus tells his disciples later at the Last Supper, when he goes away, he will not leave them as orphans (14:18). Instead, when he leaves, the Holy Spirit will be sent to them (14:17, 26). So while Jesus is not himself the living water, it is through Jesus that the living water comes; it is through Jesus that the eternal kind of life in the power of the indwelling Holy Spirit is made available.

Suggestions for Lectors
Today's reading is quite brief, but luckily it comes with its own introduction in 7:37, which sets up Jesus' proclamation quite nicely. Instead of just passing Jesus' words onto your listeners, proclaim them to your listeners as Jesus did to his, with an elevated, welcoming voice. In 7:39, drop your voice as the narrator introduces important background information.

DAY OF PENTECOST

If the passage from Ezekiel is chosen for the first reading, the passage from Acts is used as the second reading.

Acts 2:1–21	Ezekiel 37:1–14
Psalm 104:24–34, 35b (= 104:25–35, 37 BCP)	
Romans 8:22–27	Acts 2:1–21
John 15:26–27; 16:4b–15	

Acts 2:1–21

Notes
Sequence. 8 of 8

Commentary
Jesus' death, resurrection, and ascension are not the end of the gospel Story, just the end of the beginning of that Story. For along with the New Covenant instituted by Jesus comes the Spirit in a new way to create and equip a new people of God. Before his ascension, Jesus instructed his disciples "not to leave Jerusalem, but to wait there for the promise of the Father. 'This,' he said, 'is what you have heard from me; for John baptized with water, but you will be baptized with the Holy Spirit not many days from now'" (Acts 1:4–5, Asc). Today's reading opens with Jesus' disciples doing just that, waiting in Jerusalem.

2:1–4. The Holy Spirit comes on the day of Pentecost, also known as the Jewish Feast of Weeks (or First Fruits). Pentecost was one of three annual pilgrimage festivals celebrated at the temple in Jerusalem; the others were the Feast of Unleavened Bread (a.k.a., Passover) and the Feast of Tabernacles. The Feast of Weeks concluded a seven-week period that began with the presentation of the first barley sheaf during

Passover; this is reflected in its Greek name, Pentecost, which simply means *fiftieth*. The Feast of Weeks was originally an agricultural festival marking the end of the grain harvest, but by the time of Jesus, it had become associated with the covenant and the giving of the Law, which included the Ten Commandments.

So, on the day of Pentecost, all of Jesus' disciples (not just the eleven apostles) are gathered together in a house in Jerusalem when they hear the sound of a rushing wind. They also see what appear to be tongues of fire coming to rest upon each of them, at which point they all are filled with the Holy Spirit, who grants them the ability to speak in various foreign languages.

2:5–11. Because the Feast of Weeks was a pilgrimage festival, there were devout Jews from every nation who had made the journey to Jerusalem. The sound of the rushing wind drew their attention and to their bewilderment, when they heard the voices of Jesus' disciples, they heard them speaking in their own native tongues. Their amazement turns to astonishment when they discover that those speaking are Galileans, uneducated folk from the backwaters of Jewish society whose life experiences would not have put them in a position to learn or use these foreign languages.

The author lists just some of the languages that were heard, and here it is important to emphasize the fact that all of those present are Jews or Gentile-converts to Judaism who live in the Diaspora, that is, in Jewish communities outside Palestine. So at this stage in Acts, the gospel is being proclaimed only to Jews; it will not be until Acts 10 that Gentiles are presented with the gospel and receive the Holy Spirit.

2:12–16. Of course, such an amazing and incomprehensible occurrence begs some sort of explanation. In response to those who derisively dismiss it as due to excessive drinking, Peter stands up and addresses the crowd in an attempt to explain the meaning of what has happened, which he does by appealing to a prophecy found in Joel 2:28–32a (✠ PentVig).

2:17–21. In Joel, the prophet speaks of the coming of the great and terrible Day of the LORD, which will be a day of judgment because of the people's idolatry. At the same time, Joel recognizes that the LORD is also a God who is gracious, merciful, and ready to forgive. So, while the Day of the LORD may dawn in judgment, it will end in salvation for on this day God will pour out his Spirit on all flesh, regardless of age, gender, and social class so that all people can come to know God. Thus, anyone and everyone who calls upon the name of the Lord will be saved, and they will be given the Holy Spirit that they might receive God's life and be equipped to do God's will in the world.

Suggestions for Lectors

The scene in today's reading is established quickly, in one brief sentence. As you read verses 2:2–4, do whatever you can to dramatize this moment. Raise your voice; speak with something of the intensity and wonder you might use when telling a story to young people. Let your every word convey the excitement of this wondrous happening.

Beginning in 2:5, let your intensity slow somewhat as you build toward a second climax, the listing of all the different nationalities of people who heard Jesus' followers proclaiming the gospel in their native language. To assist in this buildup, replace every comma in 2:9–11a with a period; that is, pause for each comma as though it were a period, or at least a semicolon. In addition, as you work your way through this list, read with slightly increasing amounts of awe and wonder in your voice to convey the people's astonishment, climaxing with *Cretans and Arabs* (2:11a). Then, after a pause and glance up at your listeners, conclude by reading, *in our own languages we hear them speaking about God's deeds of power* (2:11b), in a strong voice still tinged with amazement and excitement.

Pause for a full second or two before 2:14 to mark the transition from the preceding narrative to Peter's speech. Peter is speaking to a large crowd of people, so without shouting, raise your voice as you proclaim his words. As always, do not think of yourself as merely conveying what Peter once said, imagine that you are Peter and proclaim these words to your listeners.

As you proclaim Joel's prophecy (2:17–21), read with a tone of rejoicing lightness as is befitting of the good news that you are proclaiming; proceed in this manner until you come to 2:19. At this point, introduce a heaviness and a sense of foreboding into your voice that climaxes with *before the coming of the Lord's great and glorious day* (2:20b). Then, pause for a full second before proceeding with *Then, everyone who calls upon the name of the* LORD *shall be saved* (2:21), which should be read as though the sun were breaking through the clouds after a particularly dark and gloomy day.

Pronunciation Guide

Arabs (AIR-uhbz), *Asia* (AY-zhuh), *Cappadocia* (kap'-uh-DOH-shuh), *Cretans* (KREET-uhnz), *Cyrene* (sī-REE-nee; *not* sī-REEN), *Egypt* (EE-jipt), *Elamites* (EE-luh-mīts), *Galileans* (gal'-uh-LEE-uhnz), *Joel* (JOH-uhl; JOHL), *Judea* (joo-DEE-uh; -DAY-), *Libya* (LIB-ee-uh; LIB-yuh), *Medes* (MEEDZ), *Mesopotamia* (mes'-oh-puh-TAY-mee-uh), *Pamphylia* (pam-FIL-ee-uh), *Parthians* (PAHR-thee-uhnz), *Pentecost* (PEN-tuh-kost), *Phrygia* (FRIHJ-ee-uh), *Pontus* (PON-tuhs), *proselytes* (PRAH-suh-līts), *prophesy* (vb., PRAH-fuh-sī) [*not* prophecy]

EZEKIEL 37:1–14

Commentary

In 598 B.C., the Babylonian empire under the leadership of King Nebuchadnezzar (a.k.a., Nebuchadrezzar) moved against Jerusalem and quashed a rebellion led by King Jehoiakim of Judah (2 Kgs 24:1–7). A few months later, in 597 B.C., the Babylonians returned to ransack the palace and temple, taking everything of value back to Babylon. In addition, in what is known as the First Deportation, a select group of Jerusalem's leading officials and citizens were taken as exiles to Babylon (2 Kgs 24:8–17). Among this group of Judean exiles was a young priest by the name of Ezekiel who, in the fifth year of the exile (Ezek 1:1–3), received a heavenly vision of God enthroned on a chariot-like throne (1:4–28). In this vision, Ezekiel is commissioned as a prophet and called to speak the word of the LORD to God's people (2:4; 3:11, 27), to those who live as exiles in Babylon and to those who still reside back in Judah. Like Isaiah and Jeremiah, Ezekiel's message was initially one of imminent judgment and exile, but after these came to pass, his message became one of forgiveness and restoration. A summary of Ezekiel's double message can be found in 39:23–29.

In today's reading, Ezekiel is granted a vision of the restoration of the exiled people of God, depicted as resurrection from the dead. Some ninety-five times, the LORD addresses the prophet as *Son of Man*, which is rendered *Mortal* in the NRSV.

37:1–6. The reading begins with the Spirit of the LORD transporting the prophet to a valley filled with dry bones. As the LORD guides Ezekiel around the valley, he asks him whether he thinks these dry dusty bones can live again, to which Ezekiel replies, "O Lord GOD, you know" (37:3). The LORD commands Ezekiel to prophesy to the bones, communicating the LORD's intention to restore their bodies—sinew, flesh and skin—and then to put his breath into them that they might live again. Here, one is perhaps reminded of the creation of Adam where, like a sculptor, the LORD fashioned a man out of the dry dust of the ground and then breathed into his nostrils the breath of life and "the man became a living being" (Gen 2:7).

37:7–10. Ezekiel prophesies as commanded, and everything comes about in two dramatic stages. In the first stage, the bones are reconnected and reformed into fully physical human bodies, yet the breath of life has not yet entered them. Then, at the LORD's animated behest, Ezekiel prophesies a second time, and a breath from the four winds sweeps through the valley and fills these bodies with life. When all is complete, the reconstituted and reanimated bodies stand forming as "a vast multitude" (37:10).

37:11–14. After this occurs, the LORD then explains to Ezekiel the meaning and significance of this vision. The exiles are in despair, believing that the LORD has abandoned them forever. They lament, "Our bones are dried up, and our hope is lost; we are cut off completely" (37:11). In response, the LORD gives Ezekiel this vision so that he might give the people hope by announcing that the end of exile is near. Yet the end of exile entails not only the physical return of Israel to the land, but also the spiritual transformation of the people (36:24–28, EastVig). For the breath that Ezekiel prophesies to is the very Spirit of God, who will give the people new life by enabling them to live faithfully and obediently in their covenant partnership with the LORD their God.

Suggestions for Lectors

Ezekiel's visionary experience easily lends itself to a dramatic reading, so your preparation will involve making sure that your reading is not overly dramatic. Of course, you still want to read it with feeling and intensity, but you may find it necessary to reign these in a bit in order to allow the text to have a more active role.

Begin 37:1 in your normal narrating voice until you come to *it was full of bones*, which you will want to read slowly and with a hint of surprised curiosity in your voice. Also, pause for a full second before you deliver this line. Then, as you read 37:2–3, imagine the silence, as the prophet wanders through this spectacle, stricken mute with wonder. Let your voice be hushed, intense, and filled with awe.

In 37:4–6, the story gathers momentum, as the Lord GOD utters the life-giving words of prophecy. In 37:9, when the Lord GOD says, *Prophesy to the breath, prophesy, mortal*, one gets the impression that God himself is eager to see these bones live again, perhaps even a bit impatient like an enthusiastic child; so add some excitement into your voice as you say these words.

Ezekiel 37:7–10 demands your greatest effort as the vision surges into action. Read 37:10 slowly, phrase by phrase, as the miracle happens. In 37:11–14, when the meaning of the vision is finally revealed—the restoration of the exiled nation by its God—speak more quietly, but with intensity, to the end.

Pronunciation Guide

Note the difference in pronunciation between the verbs, prophesy and prophesied, and the noun, prophecy: *prophesy* (vb., PRAH-fuh-sī), *prophesied* (vb., PRAH-fuh-sīd), *prophecy* (n., PRAH-fuh-see), *Ezekiel* (ee-ZEE-kee-uhl; ee-ZEE-kyuhl)

ROMANS 8:22–27

Notes

Sequence. 1 of 2

Commentary

Human beings were created in the image of God so that they might serve as the image-bearers of God in creation, as those who would reflect the character and the glory of God throughout creation. This is humanity's calling; this is our vocation. Yet our ability to fulfill our vocation was seriously undermined when, through disobedience, we introduced shame, sin, violence, and death into the created order (Gen 3). Instead of scrapping the whole project, God began a salvage operation whereby all of creation would be restored to its former glory. Since it was the fall of humanity that led to creation's downfall, God's rescue operation has been focused upon restoring human beings to their former glory so that they might once again serve as God's image-bearers in creation. This is what Paul is talking about in today's reading.

8:22–25. Creation is eagerly longing for the children of God to be revealed in all their glory so that it too might be set free from the corrosive, entropic forces of sin and death. Creation is waiting for the blessed hope, the resurrection of the dead. Christians too are also longing for that day. For while we have already begun to participate in the new creation by virtue of the indwelling Holy Spirit, our physical bodies, which belong to the created order, long to be set free from their subjugation to sickness, death, and decay. Though we know this will happen, we do not know exactly when it will happen, and so we wait patiently.

8:26–27. Of course, this practice of hopeful patience and patient hopefulness is not always easy. As we await our final redemption, we find ourselves not knowing even how to pray. Fortunately, when we find ourselves in this position, we have an Advocate. The Spirit of God who dwells in us, who reminds us that we are beloved of God (Rom 8:15–16; Tri), also prays for us and intercedes on our behalf. We do not even have to come up with words, for the Spirit prays with sighs that are deeper and truer than any word or series of words could ever be.

Suggestions for Lectors

As you deliver this message to your listeners, be aware of the intensity of expression Paul invests in his words. Paul is trying to convey to his audience matters that he considers fundamental and central to Christian life and faith, so read with energy, emotion, and conviction as the content and the context dictates.

As you make your preparations, pray and see if God might be leading you to emphasize something in today's reading.

John 15:26–27; 16:4b–15

Notes

Sequence. 5 of 6

Commentary

On the eve of his execution, Jesus announces to his friends and disciples that he is going away and that they cannot come along. This news is met with anxiety, and Jesus responds, "Do not let your hearts be troubled. Believe in God, believe also in me" (14:1) He informs them that he is returning to his Father in order to prepare a place for them. When everything is ready, he will come back and get them so that they can be with him wherever he is (14:2–3). In the meantime, he does not intend to abandon them. When he departs, he will ask his Father to grant the Spirit to be with them. The Spirit will guide and protect them and teach them just as he has done (14:15–17, 25–26). In today's reading, Jesus goes into more detail regarding the role the Spirit will play in the world and in the lives of Jesus' followers.

15:26–27. In John, the Spirit is sometimes designated "the Advocate" (variously translated as Helper or Counselor) (14:16, 26; 15:26; 16:7). The basic idea is that the Spirit will come alongside the disciples in order to support and equip them as they carry out their vocation to serve as Jesus' witnesses in the world.

16:4b–11. Once again, Jesus seeks to alleviate his disciples' anxiety over his departure. He claims that the disciples will benefit more from his going way because then he will be able to send the Advocate. The Advocate will support them in their mission by exposing the depth of the world's darkness and by convicting the world with regard to the matters of sin, righteousness, and judgment.

In John, unbelief is the fundamental sin, and so the Spirit will first convict the world regarding its failure to believe in Jesus, which is ironic since the world owes its very existence to him (1:10). Second, the Spirit will testify to the fact that the world was wrong in its assessment of Jesus. The world judged Jesus to be unrighteous, and so he was executed. Yet, God vindicated Jesus when he raised him from the dead. The fact that Jesus returns to the Father proves that the world got it wrong. Finally, the world is shown to be wrong because its ruler has been condemned and driven out (12:31). In short, the world does not have a leg to stand on. It has no moral ground, and the Spirit will make that abundantly clear.

16:12–15. There is still much that Jesus would like to communicate, but there is simply not enough time. And in any case, the disciples would not be able to handle it in their present state of sorrow. Instead, Jesus will assign the Spirit the responsibility of continuing his followers' education and guiding them into all truth.

Here, it is important to see that the Spirit plays a conservative role within the Christian community. The Spirit does not create new truth or speak on its own, but only passes on what it has received and heard from Jesus. Like the disciples, the Spirit's calling is to serve as a witness to Jesus. Consequently, any truth the disciples receive from the Spirit should be consistent with the truth that they have already seen and heard from Jesus. Understanding the Spirit's role as witness is critical. If it is not recognized or acknowledged, then Christian communities could easily be led astray by those who falsely or mistakenly claim to have received a new word or a new truth from the Spirit.

Of course, to say that the Spirit plays a conservative role does not mean that the Spirit never challenges our cherished beliefs and practices or that the Spirit never leads us into new, uncharted waters of what it means to be Christian in the world. It simply means that the Spirit's work is an extension of Jesus' work and so must always be consistent with it.

Suggestions for Lectors

As you prepare, it would be helpful to read John 15:26–16:15 inclusive because 16:1–4a talks about the persecution the disciples can expect to encounter as Jesus' followers. These verses provide the information necessary for understanding what Jesus is referring to when he says, *I did not say these things to you from the beginning, because I was with you* (16:4b). It would be even more helpful to begin your background reading with John 15:18.

We are perhaps used to Jesus chastising his disciples, but in today's reading, he seeks to encourage them. He knows that his departure will challenge his disciples' faith and sense of purpose. But he wants them to know, as he said before, that he is not abandoning or leaving them orphaned (cf. 14:18). He wants them to be encouraged by the knowledge that, in his absence, the Spirit will be their constant companion and advocate as they seek to fulfill their vocation as Jesus' witnesses in the world. So, as you speak to your listeners in the voice of Jesus, convey his compassion, understanding, and empathy.

SEASON AFTER PENTECOST

ORDINARY TIME

TRINITY SUNDAY

Isaiah 6:1–8
Psalm 29 *or* ✠ Canticle 2 *or* 13
Romans 8:12–17
John 3:1–17

ISAIAH 6:1–8

Commentary

Throughout the book of Isaiah, the Lord GOD is described as the Holy One and, much more frequently, as the Holy One of Israel (e.g., 12:6; 17:7; 48:17; 54:5). In today's reading, the prophet Isaiah has a vision in which he sees the Holy One of Israel enthroned in all of his holy glory. The prophet Ezekiel had a similar visionary experience (Ezek 1:4–28) as did John the seer (Rev 5).

As the opening verse of the book indicates, Isaiah served as a prophet during the reigns of four kings who ruled over the southern kingdom of Judah, beginning with Uzziah. During King Uzziah's reign, Judah experienced a period of relative peace and prosperity. Yet, this stability was seriously threatened in the years following Uzziah's death with the rise of the powerful Assyrian empire, which in 722 B.C. conquered the northern kingdom of Israel. Consequently, when Isaiah associates his vision with the death of King Uzziah, he is not simply providing a convenient way of dating his vision. Instead, he intends to communicate to the people of Judah that, while they may be experiencing anxiety within the current political climate, the LORD their God is still upon his throne.

6:1–3. Isaiah says that, in his vision, he "saw the Lord sitting on a throne, high and lofty; and the hem of his robe filled the temple" (6:1). What Isaiah sees, then, is God seated upon his throne in the heavens while his feet rest upon the earth in his temple. This corresponds to what Isaiah says later: "Thus says the LORD: Heaven is my throne and the earth is my footstool; what is the house that you would build for me, and what is my resting place?" (66:1; cf. Matt 5:35; Acts 7:49). In other words, though the temple is often referred to as the house of the LORD, it is clearly not a house that contains God as other ancient temples were often thought to do. Interestingly, in other biblical texts, it is the temple itself or the ark of the covenant within the temple's Holy of Holies that is described as God's footstool. So in Psalm 132:7, the psalmist declares, "Let us go to his dwelling place; *let us worship at his footstool.*" Similarly, when King David announces that the LORD has not selected him but rather has selected his son Solomon to build the temple, he says, "I had planned to build a house of rest for the ark of the covenant of the LORD, *for the footstool of our God*" (1 Chr 28:2).

In addition, Isaiah sees six-winged seraphs, or flaming serpents, serving as royal attendants and calling out, "Holy, holy, holy is the LORD of hosts; the whole earth is full of his glory" (6:3; cf. Rev 4:8). In other words, it is not just heaven that is filled with God's glory but all of creation, if only people had the eyes to see it.

6:4–8. As the house fills with smoke from the altar, Isaiah is suddenly overcome by his own sinfulness. In the presence of the Holy One of Israel, Isaiah becomes acutely aware of his own impurity and that of his people. He becomes overwhelmed with the same intense sense of shame that Adam and Eve experienced following their disobedience in the garden (Gen 3:7–8), and he cries out, "Woe is me! I am lost, for I am a man of unclean lips, and I live among a people of unclean lips; yet my eyes have seen the King, the LORD of hosts!" (6:5). But, the Holy One of Israel is a merciful and gracious God. Just as he provided garments for Adam and Eve (Gen 3:21), so now, with a live coal from the altar, the LORD cleanses Isaiah from all his sin thus delivering him from his debilitating sense of shame and unworthiness. With his *lips* having been cleansed, Isaiah is then able to answer the call to serve as a prophet who will *speak* the word of the LORD.

Suggestions for Lectors

As you read, remember that you are the prophet Isaiah telling your listeners about a heavenly vision you experienced while worshipping at the temple one day. You are filled with awe and wonder as you try to convey the immensity and indescribable glory of the LORD and the strangeness of his heavenly attendants. In 6:4, your awe becomes mixed with fear as the thresholds shake, and in 6:5 you become overwhelmed with a sense of your own shame and unworthiness. Pause for a full second before continuing with 6:6, which should communicate your relief as your shame dissolves and is replaced by a sense of peace and wholeness.

In 6:8, you might imagine that you are off in a corner listening, perhaps being overlooked, as the LORD wonders aloud to the divine council, *Whom shall I send…?* Then, imagine stepping forward out of the shadows and volunteering yourself. With appropriate humility and eagerness announce, *Here I am; send me!*

Throughout the reading, make sure to introduce pauses to signal the various changes of speaker. Do not deliver the seraphs' line in 5:3b, *Holy, holy, holy,…*, with somberness but with a joyful, perhaps even ecstatic, reverence.

Pronunciation Guide

Isaiah (Ī-ZAY-ah), *seraphs* (SAIR-afs, -uhfs),
terebinth (TAIR-uh-binth), *Uzziah* (u-ZĪ-ah; *not* yoo-ZĪ-ah)

Romans 8:12–17

Notes
Sequence. 2 of 2

Commentary
Paul defines a Christian as one in whom the Holy Spirit dwells by virtue of their having put their trust in Jesus. Leading into today's reading, Paul writes, "You are in the Spirit, since the Spirit of God dwells in you. Anyone who does not have the Spirit of Christ does not belong to him" (8:9b–10). Paul continues by talking about what it means to live a spiritual life, a life indwelt and guided by God's Spirit.

8:12–14. According to Paul, when the Spirit enters a person, everything changes (cf. 2 Cor 5:17, Prop 6). The new life in the Spirit sets us free from the law (6:15) and from the power of sin and death (8:2). Before the Spirit came, we were enslaved by our own passions and desires. But now, we have a new master, and we do not owe our old fallen nature anything. And yet, even though everything has changed, there is still work to be done. We have been given a new life, but we still must live it. While we do not earn our salvation, it does require effort on our part. Salvation is not so much about getting us into heaven as it is about getting heaven into us. It involves the transformation of the whole person into Christlikeness, into someone who can love God with all that they are and have and who can love their neighbors, even their enemies, as themselves. Such transformation does not come by osmosis, rather it requires our active participation. We have been set free from our old way of life, but it still calls to us. Therefore, Paul bids us to be intentional about relying upon and being guided by the Spirit.

8:15–17. When a child is adopted by a family, everything is different. Although they are a full member of the family by virtue of their adoption, they become even more a part of the family as they themselves adopt the family's values and way of life. As a child grows up in their adopted family, they increasingly acquire the family resemblance. In short, they become more of who they already are. So it is with followers of Jesus. When we put our trust in Jesus, we become full members of the family of God. As we become intentional about living our new life, we find ourselves being shaped by God's values and character, and we begin to bear the resemblance of our new family as we become more of who we are. In our efforts to adopt our adopted family's way of life, we will find that we are not alone. For when we were adopted, we were given the Spirit of adoption who continues to remind us who we are, namely, the beloved children of God who are free to address God, "Abba! Father!" (8:15). Moreover, as children of God we are due an inheritance. Though Jesus is God's Son by nature and we are only God's children by grace, we are joint heirs with Christ and so will receive the same inheritance that he received. As the Son of God, Jesus was raised from the dead and received a new glorified body; likewise, as the children of God, we are destined to receive new bodies in the resurrection in order that we might live in the new creation as the image-bearers of God's glory.

Suggestions for Lectors

Today's reading is intimate and personal. Paul addresses his readers as *brothers and sisters*, and he uses first and second person pronouns throughout (*we, our, you*). As you read, stand in Paul's place and deliver his words to your listeners as though they were written for them, for in a way, they were. Read with vigor and conviction and with an elevated voice. Highlight 8:14 in particular for it is the main point in 8:12–17. Devote some time in your preparations to 8:15b–17, which forms a single, complex sentence. Read these verses slowly, closely attending to the punctuation.

Pronunciation Guide

Abba (AH-buh)

JOHN 3:1–17

Notes

Sequence. 6 of 6

Commentary

All four gospels include an account of Jesus' demonstration in the temple where he drives out all who are buying and selling and overturns the tables of the money-changers (Matt 21:12–17; Mark 11:15–18; Luke 19:45–48; John 2:13–22, Lent 3). In the Synoptic gospels (Matthew, Mark, Luke), this episode is located at the end of Jesus' ministry during the last week of his life. In fact, in the Synoptics, it is the temple demonstration that galvanizes Jesus' Jewish opposition and ultimately leads to his arrest and crucifixion. In John, however, Jesus' demonstration in the temple is located at the beginning of his ministry, and it is the raising of Lazarus, not the demonstration in the temple, that persuades Jesus' opponents to plot his death (12:45–53).

In John, Jesus engages in a number of one-on-one conversations with individuals: a Samaritan woman (4:7–26), a woman caught in adultery (8:1–11), a blind man (9:1–41), Martha (11:17–27), Pilate (18:33–38, Prop 29), Mary (20:11–18, East), Thomas (20:19–29, East 2), and Peter (21:15–23). In today's reading, Jesus has a conversation with a Pharisee named Nicodemus.

3:1–10. The Pharisees were one of three primary Jewish sects in the first-century, the Sadducees and the Essenes being the other two. Unlike the Sadducees who were composed of priests from the aristocracy, the Pharisees were lay people. The Pharisees did not possess official authority unless, like Nicodemus, they also happened to be members of the Sanhedrin, the Jewish high ruling council. In John, Nicodemus is an exceptional Pharisee for he is not automatically predisposed against Jesus. Though this clandestine visit was likely prompted by Jesus' temple demonstration, Nicodemus is genuinely seeking answers. His questions are not designed to trap Jesus (cf. Mark 12:13). In fact, later he defends Jesus' right to a fair hearing (7:51), and in the end, he even supplies the spices for Jesus' burial (19:39).

In John, Jesus' interactions with people follow a predictable pattern. Jesus will make an ambiguous statement, which is clearly misunderstood by his listeners. This misunderstanding affords Jesus the opportunity to offer additional instruction that clarifies his original statement. The conversation between Nicodemus and Jesus is no exception. Jesus says, "Very truly, I tell you, no one can see the kingdom of God without being born from above" (3:3). Here, the Greek word translated *from above* can also mean *anew* or *again*. This explains why Nicodemus wonders aloud about the possibility of someone who is old going through birth a second time. Of course, Jesus is not speaking of a second physical birth but of a spiritual rebirth. And it could very well be that Nicodemus understands this. That is, Nicodemus might also be speaking metaphorically. He may not be questioning the possibility of someone reentering their mother's womb to be born again. Instead he may be questioning the possibility of someone being willing and able to submit their cherished beliefs, habits, and way of life to the sort of radical scrutiny and transformation that spiritual rebirth would require.

If so, Nicodemus' questions are reminiscent of the question asked by the disciples when Jesus announced that "it is easier for a camel to go through the eye of a needle than for someone who is rich to enter the kingdom of God" (Mark 10:25, Prop 23). Upon hearing this, the disciples ask, "Then who can be saved?," to which Jesus replies, "For mortals it is impossible, but not for God; for God all things are possible" (10:26–27). Likewise, Jesus replies to Nicodemus, "What is born of the flesh is flesh, and what is born of the Spirit is spirit" (John 3:6). In other words, being born from above is not something human beings can aspire to on their own; spiritual rebirth is accomplished solely by God's Spirit. Spiritual transformation requires divine, not human, authority and power; "the flesh is useless;" "it is the Spirit that gives life" (6:63, Prop 16). As the eternal Word and Son of God, Jesus is able to grant people *the power* to become the children of God (1:12). This power comes through the gift of the indwelling Holy Spirit given to those who believe in Jesus (7:37, Pent).

In 3:5, "being born of water" may refer to baptism. On the other hand, it might refer to physical birth with the water denoting amniotic fluid. If so, then "being born of water and Spirit" could be shorthand for both physical birth and spiritual rebirth.

3:11–17. The Holy Spirit, however, will only come after Jesus completes the work that his Father gave him to do (17:4), work that finds its climax in his death on the cross (19:30). This is why Jesus' discussion about being born of the Spirit shifts to a discussion about his death. "Just as Moses lifted up the serpent in the wilderness, so must the Son of Man be lifted up, that whoever believes in him may have eternal life" (3:14–15).

Here, Jesus recalls an incident that took place during Israel's sojourn in the wilderness following the Exodus (Num 21:4–9, Lent 4). Tired of trekking through the wilderness with little water and only manna to eat, the Israelites grumble against God and Moses. God responds by unleashing poisonous serpents upon the people, which results in many deaths. When the people repent, the LORD instructs Moses to make a bronze serpent and attach it to a pole so that it is visible. Whenever a fiery serpent bit someone, they would look at the bronze serpent on the pole and live. Thus, in the same way that Moses lifted up the serpent in the wilderness, so God intends to lift up his one and only Son on a cross so that all who look to him might live. Such is God's love for the world. After all, God's desire is not for the world's destruction, but for its transformation and renewal.

Suggestions for Lectors

Nicodemus comes to Jesus under the cloak of night, so begin the reading in something of a conspiratorial, clandestine tone, until Jesus makes his first statement in 3:3. In order to bring out the interaction between Jesus and Nicodemus, adopt a different voice, tone, and tempo for each.

John 3:16 is one of the most recognized and quoted verses in all of Scripture. Most of us, however, are not used to hearing this verse in context; we generally only hear it by itself. One of your goals, then, will be to deliver the second half of the reading (3:11–17) so that 3:16 is heard within its larger context. As was hinted at in the Commentary, *For God so loved the world* connects God's giving of his Son with Moses' lifting up of the serpent. The *so* points not simply to how much God loves us, but to the way in which God loves us. A translation that brings this out is, "For God loved the world *in this way* that he…," which points back to the lifting up of the Son of Man in 3:15. So when you read 3:16, do not pause beforehand; proceed from 3:15 to 3:16 smoothly so that the relationship between the two verses is maintained. Also, deliver both verses in the same manner; do not emphasize 3:16. Its familiarity will provide it with all the emphasis it needs. Instead, emphasize 3:17 as you draw your reading to a close. Elevate your voice, and then slow down and read the final clause deliberately: *but in order that the world might be saved through him* (3:17b).

Pronunciation Guide

Nicodemus (nik'-uh-DEE-muhs)
Pharisee (FAIR-uh-see)
Rabbi (RAB-bī)

PROPER 1 (= EPIPHANY 6)

May 8–14 (if after Trinity Sunday)

2 Kings 5:1–14
Psalm 30
1 Corinthians 9:24–27
Mark 1:40–45

Notes

The readings for Proper 1 are the same as the readings for the Sixth Sunday after the Epiphany, so go to Epiphany 6 on page 88 for the Commentary and Suggestions for Lectors for today's readings.

PROPER 2 (= EPIPHANY 7)

May 15–21 (if after Trinity Sunday)

Isaiah 43:18–25
Psalm 41
2 Corinthians 1:18–22
Mark 2:1–12

Notes

The readings for Proper 2 are the same as the readings for the Seventh Sunday after the Epiphany, so go to Epiphany 7 on page 93 for the Commentary and Suggestions for Lectors for today's readings.

PROPER 3 (= EPIPHANY 8)

May 22–28 (if after Trinity Sunday)

Hosea 2:14–20
Psalm 103:1–13, 22
2 Corinthians 3:1–6
Mark 2:13–22

Notes

The readings for Proper 3 are the same as the readings for the Eighth Sunday after the Epiphany, so go to Epiphany 8 on page 99 for the Commentary and Suggestions for Lectors for today's readings.

PROPER 4 (≈ EPIPHANY 9)

May 29 – June 4 (if after Trinity Sunday)

1 Samuel 3:1–10, (11–20)
Psalm 139:1–6, 13–18 (= 139:1–5, 12–17 BCP)
2 Corinthians 4:5–12
Mark 2:23–3:6

Deuteronomy 5:12–15
Psalm 81:1–10
2 Corinthians 4:5–12
Mark 2:23–3:6

1 Samuel 3:1–10, (11–20)

Notes

Sequence. 1 of 4

Commentary

Samuel is the beloved firstborn son of Hannah. In 1 Samuel 1:1–20 (Prop 28), we learn that Hannah lives with the disgrace of barrenness. On one of her annual pilgrimages to the central sanctuary in Shiloh, she pleads with the LORD for a child. If only the LORD would but look upon her and grant her a male child, she would return the LORD's favor by devoting that child to the LORD's service. The LORD did indeed look upon Hannah, and she kept her promise. When Samuel was weaned, Hannah brought him to Shiloh and left him to be raised at the sanctuary by the priest Eli (1:27–28). Once a year, Hannah would return to visit her son and provide him with a new robe. Thus, the boy Samuel "ministered to the LORD, in the presence of the priest Eli" (2:11). And it became said of him that as he "grew up in the presence of the LORD" (2:21), he grew "both in statue and in favor with the LORD and with the people" (2:26; compare this with what is said of Jesus in Luke 2:40, 52).

These descriptions of Samuel's character stand in sharp relief to those of Eli's own sons, Hophni and Phinehas, who are portrayed as scoundrels (2:11). In fact, just prior to today's reading, an unnamed man of God comes to Shiloh and announces judgment upon the house of Eli. So, in today's reading, the LORD's calling of Samuel serves simultaneously as the LORD's rejection of Eli and his line.

3:1. Today's episode begins with the words: "the word of the LORD was rare in those days; visions were not widespread" (3:1). This statement serves two purposes. First, it is a sign that things have become corrupt in Israel. The LORD has stopped speaking and appearing because there are precious few with eyes willing to see and ears willing to hear. Second, it helps explain why Samuel thinks the voice he hears is that of Eli and why Eli does not pick up on the fact that the LORD is calling the boy.

3:2–10. The lamp of God was lit from evening to morning (Lev 24:2), so the LORD calls to Samuel in the middle of the night, perhaps in early morning hours just before dawn. The text is ambiguous, but it appears that Samuel does not merely sleep in the temple but in the inner sanctuary where the ark of the covenant is housed. If so, then this is quite extraordinary since the inner sanctuary was off limits to everyone except the high priest. It reveals Samuel's purity and innocence and his devotion to the LORD.

3:11–18. The LORD informs Samuel of the judgment that will befall Eli and his sons. Though Eli seems to have been a good priest, he was not a good father for he allowed his sons to act shamefully in their priestly duties. How hard it must have been for Samuel to disclose the LORD's plans to this man who had been like a father to him! Eli, however, tries to lighten Samuel's burden by saying, "It is the LORD, let him do what seems good to him" (3:18).

3:19–20. Samuel is singularly devoted to the LORD, and everything that Samuel says comes to pass for "the LORD was with him and let none of his words fall to the ground" (3:20). For your information, Dan and Beer-sheba were the traditional northern and southern limits of Israel.

Suggestions for Lectors

Today's reading comes with its own introduction, so read 3:1 and then pause for a full second before continuing on. Also, introduce full-second pauses prior to verses 10, 15, and 19 as these are the beginning of new paragraphs.

The whole narrative is driven by dialogue, which tends to be the most challenging type of a narrative for the lector. Focus your preparations on the dialogues, practicing the speaking parts until you are comfortable and pleased with your delivery. In today's reading, three characters speak: the LORD, Samuel, and Eli.

On two occasions, the LORD repeats Samuel's name when he calls him: *Samuel! Samuel!* (3:4, 3:10). Instead of saying both names the same way, increase the volume on the second one as though you are trying to get his attention.

Samuel is clearly a devoted and obedient boy. Even though he is awakened three different times, every time he comes to Eli with the same simple words: *Here I am, for you called me* (3:4, 6, 8). In other words, there is no suggestion that Samuel is even the slightest bit annoyed. So deliver all three responses in the exact same way, with a respectful innocence. Then, use this same tone of voice when Samuel answers the LORD in 3:10, only increase your volume and deliver the line slowly for this is the high point of the story: *Speak, for your servant is listening.* One other line that deserves emphasis is Eli's response to Samuel's vision (3:18). Deliver this line without any bitterness, but with a sense of understanding and resignation: *It is the LORD; let him do what seems good to him* (3:18).

Between the second and third calls, the narrator stops the story to offer the reader some information to help explain why Samuel does not know that it is the LORD who is calling him. So lower your voice when reading 3:7, using the same voice you would use for a parenthetical expression. Also, it would be appropriate to make eye contact with your listeners as you begin your explanation.

The tone of the whole narrative drastically changes in 3:11 as the LORD reveals his intentions to punish the house of Eli. Let your voice be strong and determined, and invest it with hints of anger and especially disappointment.

Pronunciation Guide

Beer-sheba (beer'-SHEE-buh; bihr'-), *Dan* (DAN), *Eli* (EE-lī),
Israel (IZ-ree-uhl; -ray-), *Samuel* (SAM-yoo-uhl; SAM-yuhl)

DEUTERONOMY 5:12–15

Commentary

Deuteronomy is the fifth book of the Bible and the last of the Five Books of Moses (a.k.a., the Pentateuch or the Torah). Deuteronomy is presented as a speech that Moses delivers to the Israelites just prior to his death and just prior to Israel's entrance into the Promised Land of Canaan under the leadership of Joshua (Josh 3:1–17). In this speech (Deut 1:6–30:20), Moses reviews Israel's forty-year sojourn in the wilderness and instructs the people in the laws of the covenant that are to govern their personal and corporate lives once they are settled in Canaan. One might regard Deuteronomy, then, as a prolonged exposition on the Ten Commandments, a detailing of the many varied and specific ways one goes about loving the LORD with all of one's life and possessions and loving one's neighbor as oneself.

The Ten Commandments first appear in Exodus 20 (Lent 3) and then reappear in Deuteronomy 5 as Moses recounts the story of the giving of the law at Mt. Sinai. Today's reading focuses upon the fourth commandment regarding the sabbath.

5:12–14a. In the Bible, *holy* is a term generally used to denote someone or something that is set apart for special use. In this usage, the opposite of holy is not sinful or bad but *common* and *ordinary*. For example, we might say that a set of fine china is holy because it is only brought out and used on special occasions. In contrast, our common, everyday dishes are not bad, simply ordinary.

According to the fourth commandment, the seventh day of the week is to be set apart for special purposes. Whereas the people of God have been provided six good, ordinary days on which to do all their work, the seventh day is to be a sabbath, a day of rest. The seventh day is distinguished from all the other days because no ordinary work is done on this day. Sabbath observance is rooted in the created order itself. God completed his work of creation in six days. On the seventh day, God rested from all the work he had done in creation. In so doing, God blessed the sabbath and made it holy so that it could in turn be a blessing (Gen 2:2–3). As Jesus says in today's gospel, the sabbath was made for human beings (Mark 2:27).

For the Israelites, observing the sabbath day and keeping it holy was an exercise in trust. After all, in the subsistent economies of nomadic and agrarian societies, one did not eat if one did not work. By abstaining from work every seventh day, the Israelites were putting their faith in God's goodness and trusting that God would provide for them. Moreover, observing the sabbath can foster faith. If a person abstains from work on the sabbath and then finds that they still have everything they need, their trust in God is justified and their faith increases.

5:14b–15. Keeping the sabbath not only affects our relationship with God, it also affects our relationships with other people and even with creation itself. Not only are the Israelites not to do any work, but their children, their household slaves, and even their domesticated animals are not allowed to do any work. Even resident aliens are not allowed to do any work on the sabbath. The sabbath is not only a day of rest, it is a day of remembrance. In particular, it is a day to remember what their lives were like when they lived as slaves in Egypt and to remember how God rescued them. They in turn should treat their slaves and workers with the same regard and respect. Thus, sabbath observance is not only a matter of personal spirituality, it is also a matter of social justice.

Suggestions for Lectors

In today's reading, remember that you are Moses speaking to the Israelites, a people that you have led these past forty years. Like a father speaking to his adult children, let your voice be earnest, affectionate, and firm.

Moses begins by issuing the commandment to keep the sabbath holy; then, he devotes the rest of the reading to explaining the commandment and explicating its implications. This means that the opening verse is the most important and, therefore, should receive the most emphasis. So before you begin reading, make sure that your listeners are settled in, attentive, and ready. Then, deliver the opening line with a strong, firm voice, reading the first half of the verse at a slightly slower pace with a few additional pauses. For example, *Observe the sabbath day… and keep it… holy* (5:12). In 5:12, emphasize the imperatives, *observe* and *keep* as well as the imperative, *remember* in 5:15. In 5:13–14, emphasize *six days* and *seventh day* to bring out the contrast.

2 CORINTHIANS 4:5–12

Notes

Sequence. 3 of 8

Commentary

In the intervening time between the writing of 1 and 2 Corinthians, false apostles had infiltrated the church in Corinth. These "super-apostles," as Paul calls them pejoratively (11:5; 12:11), spend much of their time in self-aggrandizement as they seek to discredit Paul's apostolic authority and credentials. Paul must defend himself and his ministry so that the gospel might not be undermined. He hates doing it, not only because it gives the impression that he is engaging in a campaign of self-promotion just like the super-apostles, but more importantly because it takes the focus off of Christ.

4:5–6. And so, today's reading begins with a reminder from Paul that he and his coworkers do not proclaim themselves, they proclaim the gospel, the good news that Jesus Christ is Lord of all. Paul may be an apostle, but he does not regard his apostleship to be a position of privilege. Compared to Jesus, Paul is just a slave, serving the Corinthians for the sake of Jesus. Paul did not choose to be an apostle; he simply responded to God's call. The God who began creation with the words, "Let there be light," is the same God who revealed Jesus to Paul so that Paul might reveal Jesus as the face of God to the world.

4:7–12. Paul has suffered many hardships in his work as an apostle. In 2 Corinthians 11, he speaks of imprisonments, floggings and beatings, shipwrecks, hunger and thirst, sleepless nights, and all manner of other dangers. For Paul, these hardships constitute his apostolic credentials; they demonstrate that he and his coworkers are not in it for the money. "For we are not peddlers of God's word like so many; but in Christ we speak as persons of sincerity, as persons sent from God and standing in his presence" (2:17). And yet, Paul's opponents point to these same hardships as evidence that he is not a true apostle and that his gospel is defective.

Paul argues, however, that despite appearances, they have been entrusted with a treasure, the gospel concerning Jesus Christ who is the image-bearer and face of God (4:4, 6). Unlike the false apostles, Paul and his coworkers do not carry this treasure around in an ornate treasure chest. Instead, they keep it, as it were, in simple clay jars so that nothing might take away from the glory of the treasure itself. If Paul were eloquent, charismatic, and untouched by the shame of persecution, then those who came to believe through his preaching might mistakenly attribute the power they experience through the gospel to Paul and not to God.

For many, Jesus' crucifixion was a clear indication that he was not the Messiah. Yet, just as Paul is not ashamed of the cross of Christ (1 Cor 2:2), so he is not ashamed of his own persecutions. Christ's painful and humiliating death was the clay vessel that housed the glory of God. Likewise, the glory of the gospel is transported in the humiliations and hardships of its messengers. Far from disqualifying him as an apostle, Paul's persecutions are a sign that he is following in the way of his Lord.

Suggestions for Lectors

The first part of the reading contains a lengthy verse (4:6). As always, it is important to practice reading and rereading long verses until your timing, breathing, and intonation have been worked out. Verse 6 is complicated by the fact that it ends with a string of five prepositional phrases. Group the first three into one intonational unit, and the last two into a unit. An intonational unit is a phrase or clause that should be read in one breath without any internal pauses. The following shows the intonational units in verse 6:

1 For it is the God who said, ...
2 "Let light shine out of darkness, ...
3 who has shone in our hearts. .
4 to give the light of the knowledge of the glory of God. .
5 in the face of Jesus Christ.

Pause longer at the end of units 1 and 2 and more briefly at the end of units 3 and 4.

In 4:8–9, Paul repeats a grammatical structure four times. Whenever you are confronted by a repeated element or feature that occurs more than three times, it is important to vary your delivery so that the repetition becomes dynamic instead of monotonous. Read the first two lines in the same way; read them at a normal pace, with longer pauses after the commas and semicolons. Then, read lines 3 and 4 more quickly, almost as though they are a single line. Afterwards, return to your normal tempo.

1 We are afflicted in every way,... but not crushed;...
2 perplexed, ... but not driven to despair;...
3 persecuted, but not forsaken;
4 struck down, but not destroyed;

In the last three verses, emphasize the words *life* and *live*; there are four occurrences. In the final verse, slow down and read more deliberately. Emphasize *death* as well as *life* to bring out the contrast (4:12).

Pronunciation Guide

Corinthians (kuh-RIN-thee-uhnz)

MARK 2:23–3:6

Notes

Sequence. 4 of 11

Commentary

Prior to Mark 2:1, the response to Jesus' message about the kingdom and to his deeds of power has been overwhelmingly positive. But in 2:1, the first signs of opposition begin to surface. From 2:1 to 3:6, Jesus participates in a series of five public debates with the scribes and the Pharisees over matters related to Jewish law and practice. These debates are energized by the underlying, unanswered question of Jesus' identity and authority. Who is Jesus? Where does his power to do such amazing deeds come from? From God, or from Satan? Of course, the reader has known the answer to these questions since the opening line of the gospel; Jesus is "the Messiah, the Son of the God" (1:1, Adv 2). However, the characters in the gospel are not given this information in such a straightforward, unambiguous manner. They must weigh the evidence and decide for themselves who this Jesus is. The seriousness of these questions is reflected in the fact that following the last debate, two groups combine forces to bring about Jesus' death.

As God's anointed Messiah, Jesus has been called and equipped to inaugurate the kingdom of God by word and by deed. Jesus' *modus operandi* is to make an authoritative pronouncement about the kingdom and then to perform a miracle that demonstrates the truth of the pronouncement. So, Jesus proclaims, "Repent, for the kingdom of God has come near" (cf. 1:15), and then he performs an exorcism (1:21–28, Epi 4). The exorcism not only proves that God's kingdom is overthrowing Satan's, it is also the means by which God's kingdom is being established.

Likewise, in the first public debate, Jesus tells a paralytic, "Son, your sins are forgiven" (2:5, Epi 7). When Jesus is questioned about this pronouncement, he heals the paralytic with a word. According to Jesus, his ability to set a person free from a debilitating physical condition is proof that he has been granted the authority by God to set a person free from the debt and power of sin. As he says to the scribes, "'So that you may know that the Son of Man has authority on earth to forgive sins'—he said to the paralytic—'I say to you, stand up, take your mat and go to your home'" (2:10). The same pattern is present in today's episodes. Jesus proclaims himself lord of the sabbath, and then he performs a healing on the sabbath to substantiate his claim.

2:23–28. The Pharisees were a lay renewal movement that promoted strict observance of the law of Moses and the tradition of the elders, especially with regard to matters of Jewish identity (circumcision, the reading of Torah, kosher regulations, sabbath observance, etc.). In this scene, the Pharisees object to the disciples plucking grain on the sabbath, likely because they regard it as a form of work, which is not permitted on the sabbath (see today's OT reading). Instead of questioning the disciples about their actions, the Pharisees question Jesus, even though he himself was not plucking grain. This suggests that the real question being asked of Jesus is not, "Why are *they* doing what is not lawful on the sabbath?" but "Why are *you* allowing *your* disciples to do what is not lawful on the sabbath?" In short, the Pharisees are once again questioning Jesus' authority, his prerogative in sanctioning such actions on the sabbath. Jesus responds accordingly.

Jesus recalls an incident from the life of David, Israel's most celebrated king (1 Sam 21:1–9). He appeals to David's actions not only to defend his disciples' behavior but also to defend his authorizing their behavior. In short, Jesus' appeal to David serves two purposes. First, Jesus notes that David's *eating* of the loaves of the Presence was motivated by hunger and need. With this, Jesus is justifying his disciples' sabbath transgression on the presumption that they too were hungry and in need. This answers the Pharisees' *stated* question, "Why are *they* doing what is not lawful on the sabbath?" And it also provides justification for Jesus' first pronouncement: "The sabbath was made for humankind, and not humankind for the sabbath" (2:27).

In their attempt to honor the sabbath and keep it holy, the Pharisees have obscured the original intent and purpose of the sabbath. Second, by highlighting David's *giving* of the loaves to his companions, Jesus defends his own authority to authorize his disciples' actions. This answers the Pharisees' *unstated* question, "Why are *you* allowing *your* disciples to do what is not lawful on the sabbath?" Moreover, it also provides justification for Jesus' second pronouncement: "the Son of Man is lord even of the sabbath." (2:28).

"Son of Man" is how Jesus refers to himself, especially when he is talking about matters related to his authority and vocation as the Messiah (cf. 2:10; 8:31; 13:26; 14:62). As Lord of the sabbath, Jesus claims the authority—the same authority as God—to make pronouncements about what is and is not lawful on the sabbath. In the next scene, Jesus justifies this provocative claim by healing a man on the sabbath.

3:1–6. Presumably, the Pharisees regarded healing as a form of work, and therefore, something that was not permitted on the sabbath. We have evidence for such a belief in Luke. In Luke 13, the leader of a synagogue became indignant when Jesus healed a woman on the sabbath. He kept saying to the crowd, "There are six days on which work ought to be done; come on those days and be cured, and not on the sabbath day" (13:14).

Jesus is aware of those who are seeking to entrap him, and so he behaves very shrewdly. Instead of asking a question about whether healing on the sabbath constitutes work, Jesus asks a broader question, one that gets at the heart of the matter and one that exposes the hard-heartedness of his opponents: "Is it lawful to do good or to do harm on the sabbath, to save life or to kill?" (3:4). The answer is obvious, yet the Pharisees refuse to respond because they know what the next question will be, something along the lines of, "Is not healing the equivalent of doing good and saving a life?" Their failure to respond discloses their unwillingness to open themselves and their views to criticism or debate. Their stubborn silence shows them to be fundamentally opposed to Jesus and his kingdom-of-God mission. Though the kingdom of God is right there in front of them, they refuse to repent and believe in the good news. Grieved at their hardness of heart, Jesus heals the man anyway. In turn, the Pharisees begin to conspire with the Herodians against Jesus (cf. 12:13). The Herodians were political supporters of Herod Antipas, the tetrarch of Galilee who himself had arrested and killed Jesus' forerunner, John the Baptist, (6:14–29, Prop 10). From this point on, Jesus is a marked man.

Suggestions for Lectors

Today's episode comprises two related, yet distinct scenes (2:23–28; 3:1–6), so pause for a few seconds between the scenes.

By this point in the gospel, the Pharisees have already been in a few debates with Jesus, and by the end of the second scene, they are ready to kill him. Tensions are running high, so in the first scene, ask the Pharisees' question in a challenging, versus merely inquiring, tone of voice (2:24). Jesus is becoming frustrated with these debates as well, so respond with hints of exasperation and irritation in your voice. Intensify your voice as you read Jesus' final declaration. Emphasize *not*, *even*, and the first *humankind*, and pause briefly after *lord*, as in: *The sabbath was made for humankind, and not humankind for the sabbath; so the Son of Man is lord… even of the sabbath* (2:28).

In the second scene (3:1–6), return to your normal narrating voice until Jesus begins speaking in 3:4. Given the history between Jesus and the Pharisees, Jesus' question is already laced with frustration and anger, so convey this by intensifying your voice. When you ask Jesus' question, emphasize the positive options as though Jesus is helping the Pharisees by giving them clues to the correct answers. *Is it lawful to do good or to do harm on the sabbath, to save life or to kill?* (3:4). To emphasize their stubborn silence, pause for a second after the question, then read the next statement very slowly and deliberately with a slight pause after *they* and/or *were*, as in: *But they… were… silent* (3:4b). Pause again for a full second afterwards as Jesus looks around and his anger boils. You might even choose this moment to look up at your listeners. The narrator says that Jesus was both angry and grieved at their hardness of heart. So when you say to the man, *Stretch out your hand* (3:5), try to convey a sense of grief, resignation, and tiredness, knowing that even the restoration of the man's hand will not prompt a change of heart.

Pronunciation Guide
Abiathar (uh-BĪ-uh-thahr; ab-i-AY-thahr; *not* uh-BEE-), *David* (DAY-vid), *Herodians* (hih-ROH-dee-uhnz), *Pharisees* (FAIR-uh-seez), *sabbath* (SAB-uhth)

PROPER 5

June 5–11 (if after Trinity Sunday)

1 Samuel 8:4–11, (12–15), 16–20, (11:14–15)	Genesis 3:8–15
Psalm 138	Psalm 130
2 Corinthians 4:13–5:1	2 Corinthians 4:13–5:1
Mark 3:20–35	Mark 3:20–35

1 Samuel 8:4–11, (12–15), 16–20, (11:14–15)

Notes
Sequence. 2 of 4

Commentary
In last week's OT reading from 1 Samuel, we read of how the LORD called Samuel as a young boy and how Samuel accepted that call. Over the years, Samuel served God's people in a variety of capacities—as priest, prophet, judge, and military leader. In all that time, he remained singularly devoted to the LORD. He was the voice who called the people back to the LORD when they went after other gods, and he led the Israelites against their enemies, most notably, the Philistines.

In today's reading, the people of God stand at a crossroads. Samuel is getting old, and there is no one to take his place. Like his predecessor and surrogate father Eli, Samuel has two sons. And just like Eli's sons, Samuel's sons have not followed in their father's footsteps. Instead of serving faithfully as judges over Israel, "they took bribes and perverted justice" (1 Sam 8:3). So, the question becomes, "Who will guide Israel after Samuel is gone?"

8:4–9. The elders of the Twelve Tribes of Israel come to Samuel with an answer. They want Samuel to appoint a king over Israel so that they can be governed just like the other nations around them. Samuel is distraught by the suggestion not least because Israel was not called to be like other nations. They were God's special chosen people. Israel was to have no human king because the LORD God alone was their king. The LORD, however, is not surprised by the request. He has lived with his people long enough to know their ways. Over the years, they have forsaken the only true and living God for gods that do not exist, so it is not particularly surprising that they now are seeking to replace their divine King with a human one. What is surprising is that the LORD acquiesces. He does not punish his people for breaking faith with him but grants their wish. After all, having a king will be its own form of punishment.

8:10–18. Samuel informs the elders that the LORD has approved their request, but he wants them to understand the costs of the choice they are making. Kings are expensive. Kings will take the people's money, their lands, their livestock, their slaves, their sons and daughters, and their freedom. Moreover, if the people choose this course of action, they cannot expect the LORD to step in and rescue them when these things come to pass.

8:19–20. Despite Samuel's warnings, the people remain firm; they are determined to have a king. They want to be like other nations. They want a king who will go out before them and fight their battles. Clearly, they are blind to the fact that when the king goes out to fight their battles, he will be using their sons and their horses as his weapons of war.

11:14–15. The most surprising thing in this story is that, even after all his stern warnings, the LORD himself selects Israel's first king, a man by the name of Saul. In 1 Samuel 10, Samuel anoints Saul as king over Israel (10:1) and introduces him to the people (10:17–27). Not everyone, however, was convinced that Saul would be able to protect the people (10:27). In 1 Samuel 11, Saul answers his detractors by leading Israel in a successful campaign against the Ammonites. So today's reading ends with the people (re)affirming Saul's kingship.

Suggestions for Lectors

Today's reading requires your skill as a storyteller. Pay attention to the interactions between the characters, and adjust the tone of your voice according to the dictates of the action and dialogue.

In 8:11–18, Samuel lays outs for the people what they are getting themselves into. Read his speech on the ways of kings with energy and conviction. As you make your way through it, become increasingly animated. Read with increasing intensity and tempo until you reach a crescendo with *And in that day you will cry out because of your king, whom you have chosen for yourselves; but…* (3:18b). Then introduce a sudden pause after *but.* Once you have your listeners' undivided attention, conclude the verse in quieter voice, enunciating each word precisely with judiciously placed pauses, for example, *the LORD. . will not answer you. . in. . . that. . . day*. In 8:19b–20, convey the people's stubbornness with a hint of harshness in your voice.

Pronunciation Guide
Israel (IZ-ree-uhl; -ray-), *Israelites* (IZ-ree-līts), *Egypt* (EE-jipt), *Gilgal* (GIL-gal), *Samuel* (SAM-yoo-uhl; -yuhl), *Saul* (SAWL; rhymes with Paul), *Ramah* (RAY-muh)

GENESIS 3:8–15

Commentary
The Bible opens with two related, yet distinct accounts of the beginning of creation. These accounts are placed alongside one another in the opening chapters of Genesis (1:1–2:4a; 2:5–25). Each in its own way affirms the original goodness of creation. In Genesis 1, this affirmation comes in the observation that "God saw everything that he had made, and indeed, *it was very good*" (1:31). In Genesis 2, creation's goodness is affirmed through a comment about the original state of its leading citizens: "And the man and his wife were both naked, and *were not ashamed*" (2:25). But, whereas the first creation account concludes on the high note of creation's goodness, the second account continues on and offers a narrative analysis of what went wrong with God's good creation.

In Genesis 2, when the LORD places the man into the garden of Eden, he issues two commands. The first is a blessing, and the second a warning: "You may freely eat of every tree of the garden, but of the tree of the knowledge of good and evil you shall not eat, for in the day that you eat of it you shall die" (2:16–17). In other words, human beings were granted *free and unlimited access* to the tree of life. Nevertheless, in Genesis 3:1–7 and at the serpent's bidding, the first man and the first woman forsake the tree of life by partaking of the forbidden tree of knowledge.

Immediately, the LORD's warning comes to pass, albeit in an unexpected manner. The knowledge they receive is more than they can bear. Their eyes are opened to their own nakedness, and this awareness produces an overwhelming sense of shame. So profound is their shame that they cannot abide one another's presence. They must hide from one another, and they do so by fashioning loincloths to cover their nakedness. Contrary to what the serpent claimed, eating from the tree of the knowledge of good and evil did indeed bring about their deaths, not the death of their bodies, but the death of their ability to relate to one another, which is essential to what it means to be a human being in God's good creation.

3:8–15. Even more tragic is the fact that their shame prohibits them from enjoying the presence of God. In the very next scene, which begins today's reading, the LORD comes "walking into the garden at the time of the evening breeze" (3:8). The man and woman cannot abide God's presence even when their nakedness is covered. Instead of greeting the LORD with open arms, they can only run away and hide in fear; their shame becomes unbearable in the presence of their Creator. In short, their shame has had the effect of turning the blessing of God's presence into a curse. Relationship with God is now impossible; this is the tragedy of original shame.

From this point forward, Scripture tells the story of how God's gracious love and forgiveness seeks to overcome humanity's shame and shame's children, sin and death. In the world, our Creator is at work to restore humanity and all of creation so that one day God will be able to dwell among us such that we will no longer experience his presence as a curse but as a source of blessing, comfort, and joy. This is the picture of the end of all things that the book of Revelation paints (see 21:1–7).

Suggestions for Lectors

Today's episode is driven by dialogue, so in your preparations pay particular attention to what the characters are thinking and feeling at each moment in the story. Be expressive in your delivery. One technique that will help with this is to adopt facial expressions that match the mood and tone of what we are reading. What we do with our face affects what we are able to do with our voice. For example, it is very hard to convey excitement through our reading when our face is stern or emotionless.

In 3:10, when the man responds to the LORD's question, he is afraid, so deliver this line with hesitancy in your voice. This can be achieved by speaking slowly and by pausing slightly longer than you normally would at the punctuation marks. In 3:12, the man's hesitancy has given way to defensiveness. In fact, the man adopts an accusatory tone when he says to God, "The woman whom *you* gave me." In 3:13, the woman's line should be delivered in a defensive tone. When the LORD turns his attention to the serpent, speak with a firm intensity. Speak slowly and deliberately as though you want to make doubly sure that you have the serpent's undivided attention.

Finally, it has become common for lectors to emphasize words like *said* or *saying* when introducing direct speech, but this often puts the emphasis in the wrong place. The emphasis should be on the speech itself. So, drop your voice and glide through such words and phrases as if they were not there. (In the examples below, a smaller font has been used to represent this visually.) Then, *emphasize* a word at or near the beginning of the quotation. Also, pause only briefly for commas preceding the quotation.

9 …called to the man, and said to him, "*Where* are you?"
10 He said, "*I* heard the sound of you…"
11 He said, "*Who* told you…?"
12 The man said, "The *woman* whom you…"
13 The LORD God said to the woman, "*What* is this…?"
The woman said, "The *serpent* tricked me…"
14 The LORD God said to the serpent, "*Because* you…"

2 CORINTHIANS 4:13–5:1

Notes

Sequence. 4 of 8

Commentary

In last week's reading from 2 Corinthians, Paul writes: "we have this treasure in clay jars, so that it may be made clear that this extraordinary power belongs to God and does not come from us" (4:7). The "we" refers to Paul and his gospel coworkers—Timothy and Silvanus (cf. 1:19); the "treasure" is the gospel message about Jesus Christ; and the "clay jars" are the hardships and persecutions that they have endured for the sake of the gospel. The reading ends with Paul saying, "So death is at work in us, but life in you" (4:12). In other words, despite all the humiliation and pain they have suffered, Paul and his coworkers have continued to proclaim the gospel so that the Corinthians might receive the life it promises. In today's reading, Paul continues this line of thought as he talks about how the promise of future glory helps him endure present sufferings.

4:13–15. Paul writes that he and his coworkers possess the same confidence and faith as the psalmist who wrote: "I believed and so I spoke" (4:13; Ps 116:10).[7] This citation is from Psalm 116, a psalm of thanksgiving in which the psalmist celebrates God, who saved him from dying. Though those who proclaim the gospel are persecuted at every turn, Paul knows that suffering and death will not be the final word. For he is convinced that God will give them new life just as God gave Jesus new life by raising him from the dead. On that day, when the faithful Corinthian Christians are resurrected, they will know that the humiliations and hardships Paul endured were all for the Corinthians' benefit and not something to be ashamed of (as they are now). Instead, because Paul and his coworkers are willing to suffer, the gospel is spreading to more and more people, which means that more and more people are experiencing God's grace and God is receiving more thanksgiving.

4:16–5:1. Hope in the resurrection is what makes hardships tolerable. For Paul, belief in the resurrection—both the resurrection of Jesus and the resurrection of all believers—puts everything into perspective. It helps us look beyond the material aspects of human existence, which are temporary, so that we might see and experience by faith the unseen, yet eternal realities that await us in the age to come.

Suggestions for Lectors

In today's reading, Paul seeks to encourage his readers, to give them a sense of hope, so read with feeling and conviction as you attempt to forward this hope to your listeners. Normally, when delivering a quotation from the OT, we elevate our voice, but in today's reading, Paul's citation of Psalm 116:10 functions more like a parenthetical expression. Drop your voice, then, when reading, *"I believed, and so I spoke"* (4:13), as though it is interrupting the flow of thought.

---

[7] Paul cites a Greek version of Psalm 116, which differs slightly from the Hebrew version that our English translations are based upon. "I believed, therefore I have spoken: but I was greatly afflicted" (Greek). "I kept my faith, even when I said, 'I am greatly afflicted'" (Hebrew).

In the second half of the reading (4:16–5:1), Paul presents a series of contrasts. Bring out the contrasts by emphasizing the words that refer to the *positive* elements.

4:16	outer nature vs.	*inner nature*
4:17	slight momentary affliction vs.	*eternal weight of glory*
4:18a	what can be seen vs.	*what cannot be seen*
4:18b	temporary vs.	*eternal*
5:1	earthly tent vs.	*building from God, eternal in the heavens*

Pronunciation Guide
Corinthians (kuh-RIN-thee-uhnz)

Mark 3:20–35

Notes
Sequence. 5 of 11

Commentary
The first narrative movement in Mark extends from 1:9 to 3:35. It could be called, "A Tale of Two Kingdoms," for it tells the story of how the kingdom of God, through the ministry of Jesus, is establishing itself and overthrowing the kingdom of Satan. This first movement could also be called, "A Tale of Two Spirits." The movement begins with Jesus' baptism where he is anointed and equipped for ministry by the *Holy Spirit* (1:9–11, Epi 1, Lent 3). But then, in today's reading, it concludes with Jesus being accused of being possessed by *an unclean spirit.*

Today's episode fits the pattern of a Markan sandwich. In literary terms, a *sandwich* is a story-telling technique in which one story frames (or is interrupted by) another story, and so exhibits an A-B-A pattern. In today's episode, a story about Jesus' family (3:20–21, 31–35) frames a controversy between Jesus and the scribes (3:22–30). As a rhetorical strategy, the sandwich technique draws together two seemingly-unrelated episodes so as to render them mutually interpretive. Generally, the B-story provides the interpretive key for understanding the whole composite sandwich. In today's episode, both stories are concerned with the question of Jesus' identity and authority. More particularly, the question is: What is the power behind Jesus' exorcisms? Who is animating Jesus? Is it God, or is it Satan?

3:20–21. Jesus' Family, Part I. At his baptism, Jesus heard the voice of his heavenly Father saying to him, "You are my Son, the Beloved; with you I am well-pleased" (1:11). Yet, Jesus' earthly family has a different view of him. They have heard the reports about everything he has been doing, and they have also heard the rumors that he is crazy. So, they have come to restrain him, to prohibit him from continuing his mission. Their actions—however well intentioned—are akin to charging Jesus with demon possession.

3:22–27. Charged with Possession. Jesus has been performing exorcisms from the outset of his ministry. In fact, in his first public appearance, Jesus exorcises an unclean spirit (1:21–28, Epi 4). Since then, Jesus has traveled throughout Galilee, "proclaiming the message [of the kingdom] in their synagogues and casting out demons" (1:39, Epi 5). Thus, exorcisms are part and parcel of Jesus' kingdom mission. They demonstrate, like nothing else, the reality that the kingdom of God is taking over a world that has been under Satan's control.

Up to this point in the narrative, Jesus' exorcisms have not been questioned. Yet, in Mark 2:1, Jesus begins doing and saying things that put the religious establishment on high alert. From the perspective of his opponents, Jesus commits blasphemy by presuming to forgive sins (2:1–12, Prop 2); he shamelessly eats with tax-collectors and sinners (2:15–17, Prop 8); he allows his disciples to break the sabbath (2:23–28, Prop 4), and then he himself breaks the sabbath (3:1–6, Prop 4). Given all of these purported transgressions, Jesus' exorcisms take on a different look and feel. Scribes have come down from Jerusalem to observe him. According to their logic, if Jesus is transgressing the law of Moses and the tradition of the elders, then his exorcisms cannot be of God. Instead, they conclude that Jesus' ability to cast out demons must derive from Beelzebul, the ruler of demons.

Jesus responds to their charges, as he responds to all his opponents, with parables and other figures of speech that are designed to break through the hardness of heart that inspires and supports their flawed logic. According to Jesus, it is ludicrous to claim that his authority to exorcise demons comes from Beelzebul. That would be like saying that Satan is casting out Satan, and as everybody knows, a kingdom divided against itself cannot stand. Clearly, Satan is not casting out himself. Yet, even if he were, the scribes ought to rejoice because that would mean Satan's end has come.

According to Jesus, Satan's end *has* come, but it is not Satan's own doing; another explanation is called for. If a strong man's house is being plundered, then you can be assured that the strong man has been tied up. Otherwise, he would not allow someone to carry off his property. So it is with Jesus' exorcisms. His ability to exorcise so many demons and unclean spirits so easily indicates that Satan himself has been tied up, and only God is strong enough to bind Satan. The scribes, therefore, ought to realize that Jesus' exorcisms are a sign that the kingdom of God is at hand and that Jesus is God's anointed agent. In short, Jesus' authority and power to exorcise demons comes from God. Thus, Jesus is being animated by the Holy Spirit and not some unclean, demonic spirit. This would be obvious if only his opponents were willing to open their eyes.

3:28–30. Blasphemy against the Holy Spirit. But so far the scribes are refusing to open their eyes to the possibility that Jesus is of God. This puts them in danger of committing the one and only unforgiveable sin, blasphemy against the Holy Spirit. Many Christians have been traumatized by the fear that they have committed the unforgiveable sin, so it is important to recognize what it is and is not. Too many forgivable sins have been treated as though they were the unforgiveable sin. If a person is afraid that they have committed this eternal sin, then they probably haven't. Blasphemy against the Holy Spirit is "the sort of total, malignant opposition to Jesus that twists all the evidence of his life-giving power into evidence that he is demonically possessed; those guilty of such blasphemy would not be overly concerned about having committed it."[8]

It is important to see that Jesus' comments regarding blasphemy against the Holy Spirit are triggered by scribes' claim that he is possessed by an unclean spirit. Jesus is possessed by the Holy Spirit, so to claim that he is possessed by Beelzebul is to attribute the work of God to Satan. "From Mark's point of view, to refuse to believe in this good news [of the kingdom] is bad enough, but to pervert it into its opposite, and consider it the work of Satan rather than the work of God, is the ultimate human evil, the rejection of God's definitive last word."[9]

Now, we should not let this discussion of the unforgiveable sin cause us to overlook the positive pronouncement that Jesus begins with: "Truly I tell you, people will be forgiven for *all* their sins and *whatever* blasphemies they utter" (3:28).[10] In 2:10, Jesus claimed to have authority to forgive sins, and now he is saying that *all* sins will be forgiven, save one. In other words, there is not a list of a hundred, or ten, or even five unforgivable sins, just one. All other sins and blasphemies will be forgiven. This is a stunning pronouncement, not least because the sacrifices of the OT only ever covered unintentional sins (Lev 4; Num 15; Heb 9:7). No doubt this pronouncement rankled Jesus' already rankled opponents.

3:31–35. Jesus' Family, Part II. The narrative now returns to Jesus' family who has been waiting outside during the Beelzebul proceedings. When word reaches Jesus that his family is asking for him, he takes the opportunity to redefine family. The only father Jesus acknowledges is his heavenly Father; thus, the members of Jesus' family are not those to whom he is related but those who do the will of God. The arrival of God's kingdom has changed everything. The kingdom of God takes precedence over all other loyalties, be it family, friends, or country. It restructures all of our relationships. In the kingdom of God, blood is not the tie that binds but rather the Spirit is. In God's family, the Spirit is thicker than blood.

Suggestions for Lectors

Today's episode is driven by dialogue, so focus your preparations on delivering the lines of the different characters.

When Jesus speaks, raise your voice as though you are talking to a large crowd. Deliver his lines with energy and conviction. Make his speeches dynamic by adjusting your tempo and by emphasizing certain words and phrases. For example, emphasize the first *Satan* in 3:23, *that kingdom* and *that house* in 3:24–25, and *Satan* in 3:26 Also, as you make your way through 3:24–26, slowly increase your tempo and become increasingly more animated, then pause at the end of 3:26. When you resume with 3:27, return to a normal tempo and read more deliberately. Pause again after 3:27 before continuing.

---

[8] Joel Marcus, *Mark 1–8* (Anchor Bible 27a; New York: Doubleday, 2000), 284.

[9] M. Eugene Boring, *Mark* (New Testament Library; Louisville, Ky.: John Knox, 2006), 109.

[10] The NRSV does not have *all*, but the *all* is present in the underlying Greek text, as one can see by consulting other major English translations. For example, "I tell you the truth, people will be forgiven for all sins, even all the blasphemies they utter" (NET).

In 3:28, emphasize the good news that *whatever blasphemies they utter* will be forgiven. Then adopt a serious tone of voice as you deliver the climactic verse 29 in dramatic fashion. Emphasize *Holy Spirit*, *never*, *guilty*, and *eternal*, and introduce slight pauses after *Spirit* and *guilty*, as in: *but whoever blasphemes against the Holy Spirit... can never have forgiveness,... but is guilty... of an eternal sin.* In 3:30, the narrator interrupts the story to offer the reader an explanation of Jesus' harsh words, so drop your voice as you deliver this narrative aside.

For 3:31–35, return to your normal narrating voice. Slow down for the concluding verse, and emphasize the familial terms: *brother*, *sister*, and *mother*.

Pronunciation Guide
Beelzebul (bee-EL-zih-buhl; -zuh-), *Satan* (SAY-tuhn)

PROPER 6

June 12–18 (if after Trinity Sunday)

1 Samuel 15:34–16:13	Ezekiel 17:22–24
Psalm 20	Psalm 92:1–4, 12–15 (= 92:1–4, 11–14 BCP)
2 Corinthians 5:6–10, (11–13), 14–17	2 Corinthians 5:6–10, (11–13), 14–17
Mark 4:26–34	Mark 4:26–34

1 SAMUEL 15:34–16:13

Notes
Sequence. 3 of 4

Commentary
David was without question the most celebrated king in Israel's history, the king against whom all subsequent kings were measured. David was singularly devoted to the LORD, and he is described as a man after God's own heart (1 Sam 13:14). Under David's leadership, Israel becomes united politically and spiritually. Israel's archenemies, the Philistines, cease to be a threat. And the idolatry and apostasy that has so plagued Israel since their arrival in the Promised Land is replaced by a new, unparalleled devotion and commitment to the LORD. At the height of David's reign, the LORD establishes a covenant with David, making him the head of a dynasty of kings who will rule over Israel forever. With David, God's promises to Abraham and Sarah reach a new stage in their fulfillment. Their descendants have become a great nation (Gen 12:2); they are numerous (15:5), and they reside in the Promised Land (15:7). And now, they have a king (17:6, 17).

Yet, it had not been part of the LORD's original design for Israel to have a human king, for the LORD alone was to be their king (1 Sam 8:7). But when the people clamor for a king that they might be like other nations (8:5), the LORD consents to their wishes, all the while forewarning them about the ways of kings, with their conscripted labor and taxes. The people dismiss the warnings (8:19–20), so the LORD commissions the prophet Samuel to anoint Saul as king over Israel (9:15–10:24). On more than one occasion, Saul does not follow the LORD's instructions, and so the LORD regrets choosing Saul (15:11) and seeks a man after his own heart to shepherd his people (13:14). That man is David, and in today's lesson, we read of his anointing by Samuel.

15:34–35. Today's reading begins with Samuel and Saul going their own separate ways. Here and elsewhere, Samuel's grief over Saul reveals how committed he is to Saul and to God's people. Yet Samuel removes himself from Saul's life as a sign that the LORD has withdrawn his presence from Saul.

16:1–5. Today's reading continues with the LORD instructing Samuel to travel to the town of Bethlehem in search of a man named Jesse; for the LORD has selected a new king for Israel from among his sons. Jesse was the son of Boaz and Ruth, whose story is recorded in the OT book of Ruth. Samuel is apprehensive about this new assignment. Saul is still king and anointing his replacement would be viewed as an act of treason, punishable by death. To aid Samuel, the LORD devises a cover story whereby Samuel travels to Bethlehem under the pretense of offering a sacrifice.

16:6–13. Jesse and his sons are invited to the sacrifice. As the sons of Jesse pass by Samuel one by one, the prophet attempts to discern which son has been chosen by the LORD. When Samuel sees Eliab, the firstborn, he looks upon his appearance and concludes that this must be the LORD's anointed, but he is mistaken. As the LORD says,

> Do not look on his appearance or on the height of his stature, because I have rejected him; for the LORD does not see as mortals see; they look on the outward appearance, but the LORD looks on the heart (16:7).

This is an interesting statement, not least because Saul, before he was anointed, was described as "a handsome young man" who "stood head and shoulders above everyone else" (1 Sam 9:2).

Seven sons of Jesse pass by Samuel, and none of the seven is the LORD's chosen. Samuel inquires and discovers that Jesse has an eighth son, who had not been summoned, for he was but a youth and he was out tending the flock. When this eighth son arrives, the LORD identifies him as the one. Samuel anoints David and immediately the Spirit of the LORD comes upon David as a sign of his anointing and to equip him for his new vocation as king over Israel. David has been a shepherd of sheep, and now he will become a shepherd of God's people.

We do not know how old David was when he was anointed by Samuel, but it was some years before he was officially recognized as king. We do know that David was thirty years old when he ascended to the throne and that he ruled for a total of forty years (c. 1000–961 B.C.).

Suggestions for Lectors

In the biblical narrative, 1 Samuel 15:34–35 is not actually the beginning of an episode but the end of one. In today's reading, it serves to set the scene of David's anointing, which is a changing of the guard from Saul to David. Read it slowly and deliberately, decreasing your tempo through to the end of 15:35. You may even wish to read with a hint of mourning and regret in your voice. At the end of 15:35, pause for two or three seconds to allow your listeners the chance to experience the depth of the LORD's sadness and sorrow.

The rest of the reading occurs in two movements (16:1–5; 16:6–13), so pause for a full second or two between verses 5 and 6. The second movement is filled with dramatic tension as one by one Jesse's sons are brought before Samuel. Spend some time envisioning how you are going to create and sustain that suspense with your voice. One way would be to slowly increase the intensity of your voice until it climaxes with Samuel's anointing of David.

To add some dynamics to your reading, adopt a different voice for Samuel and for the LORD. In addition, when Samuel and the LORD are carrying on a private conversation, as in 16:6–7, drop your voice a bit. As you read, imagine you are having an internal dialogue with God that you are allowing your audience to listen in on.

You may wish to set David's entrance apart by pausing for a second after *He sent and brought him in* (16:12a) and then by reading at a slower, more deliberate pace through to the end of David's anointing. If any part stands out above the rest, it is the coming of the Spirit upon David. Read *from that day forward* (16:13b) by enunciating each word clearly with slight pauses between the words. Then return to your normal narrative voice as you conclude the reading with *Samuel then set out and went to Ramah* (16:13c).

Pronunciation Guide

Abinadab (uh-BIN-uh-dab), *Bethlehem* (BETH-luh-hem'), *Bethlehemite* (BETH-lih-hem-īt; -heh-mīt), *Eliab* (ee-LĪ-uhb), *Gibeah* (GIB-ee-uh), *Israel* (IZ-ree-uhl; -ray-), *Jesse* (JES-ee), *Ramah* (RAY-muh), *Saul* (SAWL; rhymes with Paul), *Samuel* (SAM-yoo-uhl; SAM-yuhl), *Shammah* (SHAM-uh)

EZEKIEL 17:22–24

Commentary

Prior to today's reading, the prophet Ezekiel presents a riddle in which there are two eagles, a cedar tree, and a vine (17:1–10). The riddle turns out to be an allegorical account of the events leading up to the Babylonian exile (17:11–21). The narrative account of these same events can be found in 2 Kings 24–25, 2 Chronicles 36, and Jeremiah 37 and 52. In Ezekiel's allegory, the two eagles represent the kings of Babylon and of Egypt. The cedar is the royal line of the Davidic monarchy, and "its topmost shoot" is King Jehoiakim of the southern kingdom of Judah. The vine is Jehoiakim's successor, King Zedekiah.

In 598 B.C., King Nebuchadnezzar of Babylon moved against Jerusalem and suppressed a rebellion led by Jehoiakim. A few months later, in 597 B.C., the Babylonians returned to ransack the palace and temple, taking everything of value back to Babylon. In addition, a select group of Jerusalem's leading officials and citizens were taken as exiles to Babylon; this is known as the First Deportation. Jehoiakim was among this first group of exiles; in Ezekiel's riddle, he is the topmost shoot of the cedar that is broken off and carried to a land of trade (17:4). In his place, Nebuchadnezzar installs Zedekiah as a puppet king in Judah. Like Jehoiakim, King Zedekiah is a descendant of David; in the riddle, he is the seed that is planted and sprouts into a vine (17:6).

Initially, the vine grows towards the first eagle (Babylon), but then it turns away and stretches forth toward the second eagle (Egypt) (17:7). This refers to events that take place a decade later when Zedekiah seeks Egypt's support in a failed attempt to break free of Babylonian control. In 587–586 B.C., the Babylonians return to deal with Zedekiah's treachery. They besiege Jerusalem, destroy the Temple, raze the city, and take a second deportation of exiles back to Babylon, including Zedekiah.

This brings us to today's reading. Ezekiel is a priest who was taken to Babylon in the First Deportation. While in Babylon, he receives a heavenly vision (1:1–28) in which he is commissioned as a prophet to speak God's word to God's people (2:1–7, Prop 9). In today's reading, Ezekiel's allegory is designed to give the exiles hope for the future.

17:22–24. When David first became king, the LORD made an eternal covenant with him. The LORD promised David that one of his descendants would always occupy the throne. The cedar tree, therefore, represents this eternal covenant, this promised line of kings descended from David. So, when the LORD says that he will take a sprig from the lofty top of a cedar and that he will break off a tender twig and plant it on a high and lofty mountain, he is saying that there will once again be a king sitting on David's throne and ruling over God's people from Jerusalem, which is situated on high and lofty Mt. Zion.

Once again, the kingdom of God's people will grow and flourish. This kingdom will become so grand, so glorious, and so noble that people from every nation will be drawn to it. These are the birds of every kind that will come to nest and live in the branches of this noble cedar. In the end, Israel will have fulfilled its vocation to be a light to the world, for all the nations ("all the trees of the field") shall come to know the only true and living God, the Creator of the heavens and the earth.

So has the LORD said, so will the LORD do.

Suggestions for Lectors

Today's reading comes with its own introduction, *Thus says the Lord GOD*, so pause for after *GOD* before continuing. Throughout the reading, the LORD announces the actions that he himself will perform to bring about his purposes and to make himself known; so accent each of the first person pronouns: *I* and *I myself.* That being said, do not emphasize them to the exclusion of everything else.

Punctuation is much more important in reading poetry than in reading prose. This whole passage is poetic, so pay particular attention to the punctuation, pausing slightly after commas, a bit longer after semicolons, and longer after periods. However, even as you attend to the punctuation, work to make sure that your reading remains smooth and does not become choppy. There are a few techniques that will help you produce a smoother reading. First, do not pause at the end of a poetic line if it does not end with any punctuation; simply continue on as if the line break were not there. For example, in the NRSV, 17:22 is formatted as follows:

I myself will take a sprig
    from the lofty top of a cedar;
    I will set it out.
I will break off a tender one
    from the topmost of its young twigs;
I myself will plant it
    on a high and lofty mountain.

But read it as follows:

I myself will take a sprig from the lofty top of a cedar;
    I will set it out.
I will break off a tender one from the topmost of its young twigs;
    I myself will plant it on a high and lofty mountain.

Second, pay attention to the poetic parallelism. Notice when the second line of a poetic couplet repeats or extends the meaning of first line. Consider the following.

a I bring low the high tree,
a' I make high the low tree.

b I dry up the green tree
b' and make the dry tree flourish.

c I the Lord have spoken;
c' I will accomplish it.

As you read, use the intonation of your voice to draw together the poetic lines of a couplet.

Overall, there is a difference between 17:22–23 and 17:24. The poetic lines of 17:24 are shorter than those of 17:22–23, which gives 17:24 more of a staccato feel. As you read 17:24, read more deliberately and pause slightly longer at the periods. In this way, you will reproduce the character and flavor of these lines. Read the last couplet (c-c') with firmness, and do not slow down as you normally would at the end of a reading. Instead, read *I will accomplish it* with the same tempo as you read *I the Lord have spoken*, then stop immediately and let this last line hang in the air. Pause for at least three seconds before you conclude with *The Word of the Lord* (or with whatever closing your church uses).

Pronunciation Guide
Ezekiel (ee-ZEE-kee-uhl; ee-ZEE-kyuhl)

2 CORINTHIANS 5:6–10, (11–13), 14–17

Notes
Sequence. 5 of 8

Commentary
Before Paul became a Christian, he belonged to the sect of the Pharisees. Like all good Pharisees, Paul believed in the resurrection of the dead: the belief that, at the end of the present evil age, all the faithful people of God would be re-embodied as physical human beings so that they could participate in the new creation in the age to come. Thus, for Paul and other first-century Jews, resurrection was not a belief about what would happen to a *single* individual in the *middle* of history but about what would happen to *many* people at the *end* of history. The resurrection of Jesus changed all that.

For early Christians, the resurrection of Jesus was a clear sign that the kingdom of God had arrived, despite the fact that nothing in the world seemed to have changed. The new age had come but not in any way that people had expected. The resurrection had occurred but, again, in a totally unexpected way. Jesus had been raised from the dead, but no one else had. What did this mean? When Paul encountered the risen Jesus on the road to Damascus, he was forced to rethink his understanding of the resurrection of the dead. Paul still regarded the resurrection as a single, eschatological event, but now he saw it as occurring in two stages (1 Cor 15:20–24):

> Christ has been raised from the dead, the *first fruits* of those who have died. For since death came through a human being, the resurrection of the dead has also come through a human being; for as all die in Adam, so all will be made alive in Christ. But each in his own order: *Christ the first fruits, then at his coming those who belong to Christ.* Then comes the end, when he hands over the kingdom to God the Father, after he has destroyed every ruler and every authority and power.

As the first fruits of the dead, the resurrection of Jesus signaled the dawning of the new age, but the new age would not arrive in all its fullness until Christ returned. At that time, all the dead who belonged to Christ would be raised to a new embodied life in the new creation. For Paul, then, Christians lived between the times, at the crossroads of the present evil age and the age to come. In today's reading, Paul describes our experience of being caught between the ages.

5:6–10. In 5:1–5, Paul speaks of how we long to trade in our present bodies for resurrection bodies "so that what is mortal might be swallowed up by life" (5:4). Despite his present sufferings, Paul is convinced that God will resurrect us. Not only did God raise Jesus from the dead, which is a sign of our future resurrection, but God also gave the Spirit to us "as a guarantee" (5:5). That is, the indwelling Holy Spirit serves as a down payment for the life we shall one day receive from God in all its eternal fullness. Until that day, we must walk by faith and not by sight; and yet, we do not walk alone. The Holy Spirit is always with us, to guide us, to comfort us, and to remind us of the glory that awaits us. This is why Paul is so confident even in the midst of all the hardships he experiences.

Of course, such confidence should not lead to spiritual complacency. We should, at all times and in everything we do, aim to please God, because in the end, we will be judged for how we have conducted ourselves in this life. In short, we should avoid taking God for granted but cultivate a healthy, reverential fear of the Lord.

5:11–13. It is this fear that motivates Paul to persuade others regarding the truth of the gospel. Paul knows that the gospel has the power to make people pleasing to God and to make them able to please God. Paul knows that the person who trusts in Christ will be transformed into the likeness of Christ so that when they stand before the judgment seat of Christ, as they must, they will be commended for all the good they accomplished by the grace and power of the Holy Spirit.

5:14–15. Paul is also motivated by the extent of Christ's love for humanity. Christ did not just die for those who would believe; he died for everyone. He died *for* every human being and *in the place of* every human being. In his life and in his death, Jesus represented the whole human race. This is why Paul can state logically, "one has died for all; therefore all have died" (5:14). Since Jesus did not simply die *for* us but died *in our place as our representative*, then his death really is everybody's death. So we are left with this paradox of grace: we no longer have to die because we have already died. But why did Jesus do this for us? So that we, having been set free from sin and death and our own self-interest, might live our lives for him.

5:16–17. When we put our trust in Christ, our worldview is transformed, and we no longer view anyone, including Jesus, from our old, human point of view. Moreover, we discover that not only has our worldview changed but *the world itself has changed.* Despite appearances, with the eyes of resurrection faith, we see that the old world has passed away and everything has become new. In short, in Christ, we are already participating in the new creation.

Suggestions for Lectors

Today's reading is straightforward; there are just a few points of emphasis. At the beginning of the reading, highlight 5:7 by increasing your volume and decreasing your tempo. Emphasize *faith* and then pause for a second afterward: *for we walk by <u>faith</u>,… not by sight.*

Likewise, the final verse should be emphasized. Raise your voice, and read it at a slower tempo, carefully enunciating each of the words, especially those in the final clause. Be generous with pauses, and stress *everything* and *new*, as in: *So… if anyone is in Christ, there is a new creation:… everything old has passed away;… see,… <u>everything</u>… has become <u>new</u>!* (5:17).

Note the potential pitfall in 5:16. Verse 16 is made up of two sentences separated by a semicolon. Although the semicolon signals a full stop, the second sentence begins with *even though*, and so it sounds as if it goes with what precedes it, as though the sentence were, "we regard no one from a human point of view, even though we once knew Christ from a human point of view." If it is helpful, imagine that the semicolon is a period and that *Even* is capitalized. This way, you will be sure to read it with what follows.

Mark 4:26–34

Notes

Sequence. 6 of 11

Commentary

In Mark 4, Jesus gets into a boat and begins to teach a large crowd gathered along the shores of the Sea of Galilee. Instead of speaking plainly to the crowds (cf. John 16:29), Jesus teaches them in parables, which are designed to reveal something about the nature of God's kingdom. In today's reading, we are treated to two such parables of the kingdom, both of which have to do with seeds and growth.

4:26–29. In the first parable, the kingdom of God is compared to a seed that grows on its own. The farmer does two things; he sows, and he reaps. He does not cause the seed to sprout and grow; in fact, he does not even know how it does these things. He simply goes about his normal daily routine until harvest time arrives. So it is with God's kingdom.

Those who oppose Jesus question his claim that the kingdom of God has arrived for—apart from the miraculous deeds he is performing, which may in fact be the work of Satan—the world does not look any different. Jesus offers this parable in response to such objections. Despite evidence to the contrary, the good news of the kingdom will sprout, take root, grow, and produce a harvest. Human beings are involved in the work of the kingdom, but its growth is beyond their control. Here, one is reminded of Paul's words to the church in Corinth: "I planted, Apollos watered, but God gave the growth" (1 Cor 3:6). Like the seed growing secretly, how the kingdom grows is a mystery, yet the fact that it will mature and bear fruit is assured.

4:30–32. Comparing the kingdom of God to a mustard seed is not the image one would naturally expect to be used to describe God's worldwide reign, but this is because God's empire does not operate according to the same principles and methodologies as the other empires of the world. The parable of the mustard seed is a parable of growth, offering a contrast between small beginnings and large endings. While Jesus has clearly caused a stir with his authoritative teaching and powerful deeds, the kingdom of God has not arrived in the earth-shattering way that people were expecting. The kingdom has not taken over everything all at once. While the kingdom may appear to be inconsequential, eventually it will take over the field. After all, once mustard gets into a field it is nigh impossible to get it out.

4:33–34. We often assume that Jesus' parables served as illustrations, so we treat them as though they were designed to make difficult concepts easy to understand. In actuality, the opposite is much closer to the truth. In Mark especially, Jesus' parables *cloak* truths about the kingdom of God that are easy to understand, *but* difficult to accept. This is why Jesus has to explain the meanings of parables to his disciples.

By concealing the truth and mystery of God's kingdom within a presumably innocuous story, Jesus is able to smuggle them past his opponents' defenses, thus giving them a better chance to take root in the hearts and minds of his detractors (and us), which in turn leads to repentance and faith. This explains why Jesus so often responds to opponents with parables.

A perfect example of the power and function of parables can be found in 2 Samuel 12, where the prophet Nathan confronts king David regarding his adultery with Bathsheba. Nathan sets a trap for David by telling him a parabolic story about a rich man who stole a poor man's only lamb. Upon hearing of such injustice, David becomes incensed and pronounces a death sentence upon the rich man. Then, very simply, Nathan says to David, "You are the man!" (12:7). Thus caught, David repents. Now, had Nathan confronted David directly with accusations, David's defenses would have been aroused, almost guaranteeing that he would never acknowledge his guilt, let alone experience any genuine remorse or repentance, as his energies would be devoted to his own self-defense and self-preservation.

Jesus' parables serve a very similar function to Nathan's story. For Jesus, telling a parable is like planting a seed, or even like planting a landmine in the minds and hearts of people, such that when the mine is triggered the mystery of God's kingdom explodes and transforms values, worldviews, and reality itself.

Suggestions for Lectors

Today, you get to play the role of a storyteller, specifically, a teller of parables. In the first parable (4:26–29), there is nothing that requires emphasis. Instead, watch out for the first sentence; it is somewhat lengthy and cumbersome. There is potential to run out of breath and lose intonation before you reach the end, so make sure to practice reading it over and over again until it becomes smooth and natural. In the NRSV, the last clause, *he does not know how*, sort of hangs there. In keeping with other translations, add the word *though* at the beginning, as in: *though he does not know how*. In the second parable (4:30–32), emphasize *mustard seed*, *smallest*, and *greatest.*

PROPER 7

June 19–25 (if after Trinity Sunday)

1 Samuel 17:(1a, 4–11, 19–23), 32–49 *or* 1 Samuel 17:57–18:5, 10–16	Job 38:1–11
Psalm 9:9–20 *or* Psalm 133	Psalm 107:1–3, 23–32
2 Corinthians 6:1–13	2 Corinthians 6:1–13
Mark 4:35–41	Mark 4:35–41

1 Samuel 17:(1a, 4–11, 19–23), 32–49

Notes

Sequence. 4 of 4

Commentary

In last week's reading from 1 Samuel, the prophet Samuel is sent to the tiny village of Bethlehem to find the man whom the LORD had chosen to replace Saul as king over Israel. As it turns out, the man is a boy named David, the eighth and youngest son of Jesse. He is chosen because the LORD sees in David "a man after his own heart" (1 Sam 13:14), someone who will be singularly devoted to the LORD and will carry out his commands, unlike Saul. In today's reading, we get our first glimpse of David's fierce loyalty as he confronts the Philistine giant, Goliath.

17:1a, 4–11, 19–23. The optional portion of today's reading details the circumstances leading up to David's encounter with Goliath. The Philistines were Israel's archenemies and had been ever since the Israelites entered the Promised Land. Goliath was their champion. He was a giant of a man, over nine feet tall, and heavily armored. In fact, it appears that the only exposed part of his body was his face and forehead. In contrast, David arrives on the scene in whatever he would have worn to tend his father's flock.

17:32–40. David is appalled when he witnesses the fear-filled immobility of the Israelite army in response to Goliath's boastings and blasphemies. David makes his way to king Saul and offers to defend the LORD's honor by facing this uncircumcised Philistine. Saul is initially wary but is moved by David's account of how the LORD has delivered him from lions and bears. Saul offers his armor to David, but David is unable to maneuver in it. So David goes out to face Goliath without any armor, with a staff instead of a sword, and armed with only a sling and five stones.

Back in 1 Samuel 8, when the elders of Israel clamor for a king, Samuel tries to warn them against such a course of action. But they insist, saying, "No! but we are determined to have a king over us, so that we also may be like other nations, and that our king may govern us and go out before us and fight our battles" (8:21, Prop 5). How ironic that king Saul sits back and waits in fear while their future king David fearlessly goes out to meet Goliath!

17:41–49. When David approaches the battle line, he matches Goliath's disdain with the conviction that the LORD will protect him and deliver Goliath and all the Philistines into his hands. For David, the victory he confidently anticipates will serve two purposes. First, it will demonstrate to the whole world that "there is a God in Israel" (17:46); after all, how else might one explain how this rustic shepherd boy could defeat a trained warrior like Goliath. Second, this victory will demonstrate to all Israel that it is the LORD who protects them. In other words, Israel need not amass weapons and an army; Israel need only trust in the LORD. For it is the LORD, and not any human king, who governs Israel and goes out before Israel and fights Israel's battles.

17:48–49. The battle is over almost before it begins. David has five smooth stones, but it only takes one to bring Goliath down.

Suggestions for Lectors

Today's reading is lengthy, especially if the alternative verses are included, but do not be tempted to rush. Lengthy readings allow your listeners to settle in and really enjoy the Scriptures. As always give yourself plenty of time to prepare and practice, and utilize your skill as a storyteller.

The most important part of today's reading is David's speech to Goliath (17:45–47). As you deliver these words, speak with great confidence and conviction, as one who is fully convinced of God's presence and ability to protect and save. Emphasize the following lines: *but I come to you in the name of the LORD of hosts, the God of the armies of Israel* (17:45); *so that all the earth may know that there is a God in Israel,* (17:46); and *that all this assembly may know that the* LORD *does not save by sword and spear* (17:47).

Pronunciation Guide
cubit (KYOO-buht), *David* (DAY-vid), *Elah* (EE-luh), *Gath* (GATH), *Goliath* (guh-LĪ-uhth; goh-), *Israel* (IZ-ree-uhl; -ray-), *Jesse* (JES-ee), *Philistines* (FIL-ih-steenz), *Saul* (SAWL; rhymes with Paul), *shekels* (SHEK-uhlz)

1 SAMUEL 17:57–18:5, 10–16

Notes
Sequence. 4 of 4
Suggested Reading. 1 Samuel 17:57–18:16

Commentary
In the first reading (see above), David's victory over the Philistine giant, Goliath, is recounted The story continues in this reading, and we are afforded some insight into the relationships between David and Saul and between David and Saul's son Jonathan.

17:57–58. Abner is the commander of the Israelite army. When David is making his way out to face Goliath, Saul turns to Abner and asks him whose son David is, but Abner does not know (17:55–56). Then, after Goliath is beheaded and the Philistine army is routed, Abner brings David before Saul, and David informs his king that he is the son of Jesse who lives in Bethlehem.

18:1–5. Jonathan is drawn to David, so much so that he enters into a covenant of friendship with David. As Saul's eldest son, Jonathan is heir to the throne. Therefore, his dramatic act of stripping off his robe and giving it to David along with his armor and weapons may imply a symbolic transfer of his claim to the throne to David. Furthermore, David is a successful warrior so Saul puts him in charge of the army.

18:6–9. David finds success in leading Israel's armies against their enemies, too much success as it turns out. David's popularity among the people, and even perhaps his popularity with Jonathan and the servants of Saul, triggers Saul's jealousy, and he begins to regard David as a potential political threat.

18:10–16. When Saul was first anointed as king of Israel, the LORD put his spirit upon him (1 Sam 10:6, 10; 11:6). Yet, after the LORD rejected Saul and chose David to take his place, "the spirit of the LORD departed Saul" (16:14), and he began to be afflicted by *evil* spirits. In the final scene of today's episode, Saul's jealousy and fear render him vulnerable to demonic attack. In the past, when evil spirits afflicted Saul, David would sooth him by playing of the lyre (16:14–23), but that is no longer effective. David has become too much of a political threat. Moreover, Saul recognizes that David now possesses the LORD's spirit, which had once resided in himself. To rid himself of David, Saul promotes him as commander of a thousand. Not only will this get David out of the palace, it might get him killed on the battlefield. Unfortunately for Saul, his plan backfires. David finds even more success than before. Saul's grip on the throne becomes tenuous, and David becomes the beloved of all the tribes of Israel and Judah.

Suggestions for Lectors

The suggested reading includes 18:6–9 because these verses speak of Saul's jealousy of David, a jealousy which is then exploited by an evil spirit. If these verses are not included in your reading, at least read them as part of your preparation.

Begin the reading in your normal narrating voice. When you come to the second scene (18:1–5), slow down and read with evident emotion in order to convey the tone and tenor of the interaction between Jonathan and David.

In the third scene (18:6–9), increase your tempo in order to reflect the excitement and celebration of the crowds. Highlight Saul's rage by delivering his lines with a jealous intensity in your voice. At the end of this scene, pause for a second before continuing into the third scene (18:10–12), which should be read energetically.

The final scene (18:13–16) summarizes the ongoing relationship between Saul and David, so return to your normal narrating voice to conclude the reading.

Pronunciation Guide

Abner (AB-ner), *Bethlehemite* (BETH-lih-hem-īt; -heh-mīt), *Israel* (IZ-ree-uhl; -ray-), *Jesse* (JES-ee), *Jonathan* (JAHN-uh-thuhn; JON-), *Judah* (JOO-duh), *lyre* (LĪ-uhr), *Philistine* (FIL-ih-steen), *Saul* (SAWL; rhymes with Paul)

Job 38:1–11

Commentary

In the first two chapters of the book, Job suffers the devastating loss of his livestock, his livelihood, his family, and his health. Then, over the next thirty-five chapters, Job must endure the "support" of his friends, who try to convince Job that, if he would only acknowledge his sin, his sufferings would be at an end. In their moral universe, only punishment for sin could account for such misfortune. But most of all, Job must contend with the despair and terror brought on by the complete silence and presumed absence of God.

As Job contends with his friends, he repeatedly expresses his desire to present his case before the LORD, before whom he expects a fair hearing and from whom he expects vindication.

> Oh, that I knew where I might find him,
>   that I might come even to his dwelling!
> I would lay my case before him,
>   and fill my mouth with arguments.
> I would learn what he would answer me,
>   and understand what he would say to me.
> Would he contend with me in the greatness of his power?
>   No; but he would give heed to me.
> There an upright person could reason with him,
>   and I should be acquitted forever by my judge (23:4–7, Prop 23).

In today's reading, Job finally gets his chance. The LORD appears, but things do not quite go as Job planned. Instead of getting to present his case before the LORD, the LORD presents his case to Job. It is a lengthy argument (38:1–39:30; 40:6–41:34), much of which consists of a series of rhetorical questions. This litany of questions demonstrates the LORD's incomparable wisdom and greatness, and they serve to put everything into its proper perspective.

38:1–3. Job has had plenty of opportunity to question God, and now it is God's turn. Out of the mighty whirlwind, the LORD addresses Job, "Get ready mortal because *I* will question *you*, and *you* shall answer *me*" (38:3). God begins by questioning Job about the beginnings of creation.

38:4–7, The earth. Where was Job when God constructed the universe? Was Job there when God laid the earth's foundations? Does Job even know what the foundations rest upon, or who laid the cornerstone?

38:8–11, The sea. In Genesis 1 (EastVig), the primordial deep and the impenetrable darkness represent the forces of chaos that threaten God's good creation. When the LORD began his work of creation, he did not get rid of the forces of chaos. Instead he limited their influence and reach by prescribing boundaries within which they could operate. Does Job know who shut the sea in when it threatened to destroy everything?

In the end, all the questions the LORD poses produce the desired effect—Job gains the perspective he needs to carry on despite his great misfortune and suffering. Instead of feeling compelled to make his case, Job is left almost speechless. In reverence and humility, Job declares: "I have uttered what I did not understand, things too wonderful for me, which I did not know" (42:3b, Prop 25).

Suggestions for Lectors

In today's reading, you are playing the part of the LORD, who asks question upon question in order to overwhelm Job. As you make your way through this whirlwind of questions, slowly increase your intensity and tempo. Never rush, but by the end of the reading, you want to be reading discernibly quicker than you were at the beginning. In a way, you are not wanting to give Job—that is, your listeners—a chance to catch their breath. You want to leave them with a sense of awe regarding the power and majesty of God.

At the beginning of the reading, highlight the only statement the LORD makes by reading it slowly and deliberately and by emphasizing the pronouns: *Gird up your loins like a man,… I will question you, and you declare to me* (38:3).

Pronunciation Guide

Job (JOHB; *not* JAWB)

2 CORINTHIANS 6:1–13

Notes

Sequence. 6 of 8

Commentary

False apostles have infiltrated the Corinthian church. These "super-apostles," as Paul pejoratively refers to them (11:5; 12:11), spend much of their time commending themselves and seeking to undermine and discredit Paul's apostolic authority. The hardships Paul suffers are offered as evidence of his weakness and inferiority. These and other arguments against Paul have gained some traction among the Corinthians, even though it was Paul who founded the church in Corinth. Paul must, therefore, defend himself so that the gospel he preaches will not be undermined. Yet, in defending himself, Paul will not deny his hardships. The super-apostles come with letters of recommendation that list their apostolic credentials, but Paul will not play that game. He will let his life speak for itself. He will not deny the hardships that he and Timothy have experienced because the things they have suffered they have suffered for the sake of the gospel *and* for the sake of the Corinthians. To deny their hardships would be to deny the gospel for, after all, Jesus suffered for the sake of others.

6:1–3. Leading up today's reading, Paul says that he and Timothy have been entrusted with the message of reconciliation, which concerns the life, death, and resurrection of Jesus Christ. In Christ, God "was reconciling the world to himself, not counting their sins against them" (5:19). God has removed any barriers or obstacles between the world and himself, and God has appointed people like Paul and Timothy to announce to the world what God has done for humanity through Christ. Paul writes, "So we are ambassadors for Christ, since God is making his appeal through us; we entreat you on behalf of Christ, *be reconciled to God*" (5:20). This is what Paul is referring to in today's reading when he says, "we urge you also not to accept the grace of God in vain" (6:1). For Paul, there is no time like the present to be reconciled to God; "now is the day of salvation!" (6:2). Moreover, through Christ, God has already accomplished everything that was needed to bring about reconciliation. The only thing that is required is for persons to accept their acceptance by faith. Unlike the false apostles who claim that the Corinthians must also adhere to the Jewish law, Paul is not putting any such obstacle in the Corinthians' way.

6:4–10. In 5:21, Paul wrote, "For our sake [God] made [Jesus] to be sin who knew no sin, so that in him we might become the righteousness of God." In other words, Christ suffered the pain and humiliation of crucifixion so that others might experience right-relationship with God. So Paul recounts the pain and humiliation that he and Timothy have suffered as ministers of the gospel; for the hardships they have endured not only serve as a witness of their love for Christ, they are also a testimony of the love they have for the Corinthians.

6:11–13. Paul is not shy; he speaks his mind to the Corinthians. He loves them with all his heart, but at present, his love is not being reciprocated. As their spiritual father, Paul calls upon them to open their hearts fully to him, even as his heart is fully open to them.

Suggestions for Lectors

In today's reading, Paul is pleading with the Corinthians, so read with a pleading tone of voice, not a whiny tone, but a strong pleading tone.

After the quotation from Isaiah, read its implications in an elevated, animated voice. In each clause, pause after *see* and emphasize *now*, as in: *See,… <u>now</u> is the accepta-*

ble time; see,... now is the day of salvation! (6:2b). Then, pause for a second before continuing.

Reading lists, like the one contained in 6:4b–7a, can be a tricky business. One wants to avoid the extremes of monotonous recitation, on the one hand, and "punching" or over-emphasizing each item, on the other hand. To avoid these extremes, group the individual items of a list into intonational units, or phrases. These phrases should be of varying lengths, ranging from one to three, or even four items each. Do not group an entire list into phrases of the same length because this can produce a cadence with a sing-song quality. The following is just one example of how the items in today's reading could be grouped; you may wish to adopt different groupings:

> through great endurance,... in afflictions, hardships, calamities,...
> beatings, imprisonments,... riots, labors, sleepless nights,... hunger;...
> by purity, knowledge, patience, kindness,... holiness of spirit,...
> genuine love, truthful speech,... and the power of God;

Verses 7b–10 possess a rhetorically-rich repetitiveness that can be quite a joy to read aloud. Pay attention to the punctuation and vary your intonation to bring out the contrasts. Again, you do not want to fall into a sing-song cadence, so vary your tempo as you make your way through these verses. Conclude the reading in a voice that is more personal, intimate, and affectionate (6:11–13).

Pronunciation Guide
Corinthians (kuh-RIN-thee-uhnz)

MARK 4:35–41

Notes
Sequence. 7 of 11

Commentary
There are five narrative movements in the Gospel of Mark. In the second movement, the Sea Crossing movement (4:1–8:30), Jesus and his disciples cross the Sea of Galilee no less than six times. Three of the six sea crossings are uneventful. Nothing happens on these voyages; they merely consist of a statement or two that provide the itinerary of Jesus and his disciples as they move about using the boat as a means of conveyance (5:18, 21; 6:32, 34; 8:10). The other three sea crossings are eventful; something takes place during the crossings themselves. During the first eventful sea crossing, Jesus stills a storm (5:35–41); during the second, Jesus walks upon the sea (6:45–52); and during the third, Jesus and his disciples have a discussion about the loaves (8:13–21). Today's episode recounts the first of these eventful sea crossings where Jesus' stills a storm at sea in exorcistic fashion.

4:35–36. "On that day" refers to the day that Jesus spoke to the crowds in parables (4:1–34). In 4:1, Jesus begins teaching beside the Sea of Galilee, but the crowd becomes so large that he climbs into a boat and teaches them while seated in the boat upon the sea. When evening comes, his disciples join him in the boat, and they set out for the other side of the sea, which is Gentile territory.

4:37–41. During the crossing, a great windstorm arises that threatens to capsize their boat. This storm at sea is reminiscent of the storm that threatened to break up Jonah's ship. Like Jonah, who was asleep in the hold of the ship (Jonah 1:5), Jesus is asleep in the stern of the boat when he is awakened by his frantic disciples. Yet, unlike Jonah, the calming of the sea will not require Jesus' being tossed overboard.

This storm has a demonic quality, as reflected in Jesus' rebuke and in the disciples concluding response. In Mark, the first mighty deed Jesus performs is the exorcism of an unclean spirit (1:21–28, Epi 4). When he encounters a demon-possessed man in the Capernaum synagogue, he *rebukes* the spirit, saying, "*Be silent*, and come out of him!" (1:25). In the exact same way, Jesus *rebukes* the wind and the sea, saying, "Peace! *Be silent!*" (4:39).[11] In addition, the disciples' response to the calming of the sea closely aligns with the people's response to Jesus' exorcism. Those in the synagogue "were all amazed, and they kept on asking one another, '*What is this?* A new teaching—with authority! *He commands even the unclean spirits, and they obey him*'" (1:27). Here, the disciples "were filled with great awe[12] and said to one another, 'Who then is this, that even the wind and the sea obey him?'" (4:41). Once again, Jesus acts with unprecedented authority, and it raises the question of his identity.

In the end, the stilling of the storm, as it is generally called, is really a large-scale exorcism, and it paves the way for the large-scale exorcism Jesus performs once they arrive on the other side of the sea. In the region of the Gerasenes, Jesus encounters a Gentile who is possessed by a legion of unclean spirits (5:1–20), who are cast into the very sea that Jesus has demonstrated his authority over.

The Sea of Galilee in Mark. The following comments belong to a larger study of Mark and are not based solely on today's episode. However, they do offer some insight into how this first sea crossing functions within its larger narrative context. In Mark, the Sea of Galilee separates Jewish and Gentile territories, but it is much more than a topographical feature. The Sea of Galilee represents the social, ethnic, and cultural barriers that define and so distinguish Jews and Gentiles. Consequently, the stormy sea symbolizes the demonic forces that oppose Jesus' kingdom mission. More specifically, the stormy Markan sea represents opposition to a Gentile mission. Yet, for all of its chaotic force and power, the sea presents no real obstacle for Jesus. With a word, Jesus can calm the sea securing safe passage to Gentile shores. Even when it rages, Jesus can walk upon the sea as though he were walking upon dry land (6:45–52). Thus, in Mark's Sea Crossing movement, Jesus is revealed as one who exercises divine prerogatives, as one who possesses divine authority over the demonic forces. This, in turn, provides divine justification for Jesus' inclusion of Gentiles within his proclamation of the good news of God's kingdom.

Yet, in today's episode, the disciples only see Jesus as a miracle worker and not as the one who secures passage to Gentiles by overcoming the barriers that separate

---

[11] Here, the NRSV translates Jesus' rebuke as, "Peace! Be still!," but the Greek word translated as "Be still!" in 4:49 is the same word the NRSV translates as, "Be silent!," in 1:25.

[12] In the Greek text, the disciples literally "feared a great fear," which offers another interesting parallel to the Jonah story. After Jonah is thrown overboard and the sea calms down, in the Hebrew text, the sailors are said to "fear a great fear" (Jon 1:16).

Jews from Gentiles. The fear that they exhibit amidst the storm symbolizes their resistance to Gentile mission, which resurfaces throughout the Sea Crossing movement and which was a major issue in the early church.

Suggestions for Lectors

Today's episode comes with its own introduction (4:35–36), so pause for a second or two at the end of 4:36 before you introduce the storm in 4:37. Pause again after 4:39, following the statement, *and there was a dead calm.*

When you describe the storm and the disciples' reaction to the storm and to its calming, read with increased energy and at a slightly faster pace. In contrast, relay Jesus' actions and words with a firm calmness in order to convey his authority and faith. In the final line, emphasize *Who* and *even.*

PROPER 8

June 26–July 2

2 Samuel 1:1, 17–27

Psalm 130

2 Corinthians 8:7–15

Mark 5:21–43

Wisdom of Solomon 1:13–15; 2:23–24
or Lamentations 3:22–33

Psalm 30

2 Corinthians 8:7–15

Mark 5:21–43

The Episcopal Church

Wisdom of Solomon 1:13–15; 2:23–24

✠ Lamentations 3:21–33[13] *or* Psalm 30

2 Corinthians 8:7–15

Mark 5:21–43

2 SAMUEL 1:1, 17–27

Notes

Sequence. 1 of 7

Commentary

When the Israelites entered the Promised Land after their exodus from Egypt and after their forty-year sojourn in the wilderness, they did not enter as a single nation but more as a confederacy of Twelve Tribes. They existed as the Twelve Tribes of Israel through the books of Joshua and Judges, but the books of 1 and 2 Samuel tell the story of their transition from a tribal confederacy to a monarchy.

---

[13] In its adaptation of the RCL, the Episcopal Church has made two modifications to the Lamentations reading. First, it no longer serves as an option for the OT reading. Instead, it has been transformed into a canticle and serves as one of the options for the response. Second, the reading begins with v. 21 instead of v. 22.

First Samuel concludes on a somber note with the deaths of Israel's first king, Saul, and his son Jonathan. In today's reading, 2 Samuel begins with David, who is soon to be Israel's second and most celebrated king, mourning their loss.

1:1. In 1 Samuel 30, while Saul and Jonathan are fighting the Philistines, David is pursuing a raiding party of Amalekites who had razed the Judean city of Ziklag and made off with his wives. After successfully dealing with the Amalekites, David returns to Ziklag only to be informed of the deaths of Saul and Jonathan.

1:17–18. To express his own grief and to help the nation express its grief, David composes a song of lamentation for Saul and Jonathan entitled, The Song of the Bow. The song is said to have been written down in the Book of Jashar, of which we have no record.

1:19–27. The glory of which David speaks is of course Saul and Jonathan (1:19). Though Saul made David's life miserable, David never forgot that Saul had been the LORD's anointed and, therefore, worthy of respect. Consequently, news of their deaths is not to be announced in Gath and Ashkelon, two of five Philistine city-states, for it would only result in Israel's enemies rejoicing. Furthermore, Saul and Jonathan perished on Mount Gilboa, so those mountains should mourn their deaths by becoming desolate.

When David and Jonathan first met, they regarded one another as kindred spirits and so entered into a covenant of friendship (1 Sam 18:3–4, Prop 7). In the next-to-last stanza, David stops talking *about* Jonathan and instead addresses his beloved friend directly.

Suggestions for Lectors

As you read, imagine that you are delivering a eulogy at a memorial service or a funeral. Read with evident emotion as you conduct your listeners on a journey of celebrating the lives and mourning the loss of their beloved king and prince. As you prepare, note where David rejoices over the lives of Saul and Jonathan and where he grieves over their deaths, and read accordingly. Also notice that David addresses different persons and entities: the nation of Israel (17:19); the mountains of Gilboa (17:21); the daughters of Israel (17:24); and finally, Jonathan himself (17:26).

Emphasize the thrice-repeated refrain, *How the mighty have fallen…* (17:19, 25, 27). Each time, read it with a raised voice and in a tone of grief and anguish.

Pronunciation Guide

Amalekites (uh-MAL-uh-kīts), *Ashkelon* (ASH-kuh-lon), *David* (DAY-vid), *Gath* (GATH), *Gilboa* (gil-BOH-uh), *Israel* (IZ-ree-uhl; -ray-), *Jashar* (JAY-shuhr), *Jonathan* (JAHN-uh-thuhn; JON-), *Judah* (JOO-duh), *Philistines* (FIL-ih-steenz), *Saul* (SAWL; rhymes with Paul), *Ziklag* (ZIK-lag)

Wisdom of Solomon 1:13–15; 2:23–24

Commentary

The Wisdom of Solomon (or just Wisdom) belongs to a collection of books known within Protestant traditions as the Apocrypha and within Roman Catholicism as Deuterocanonical (that is, Second Canon). In Eastern Orthodoxy, Wisdom is simply a part of the OT scriptures. Although King Solomon is not mentioned by name within the book, it presents itself as having come from Israel's celebrated king. For example, the first-person prayer in Wisdom 9 is an expansion of Solomon's prayer for wisdom at the beginning of his reign (1 Kings 3:6–9, Prop 15). Nevertheless, current consensus regards the Wisdom of Solomon as being the work of an anonymous Jew living during the Greco-Roman period, late first century B.C. or the early first century A.D., and possibly residing in Alexandria, Egypt.

In the opening chapters of Wisdom, the sage contrasts the lots of the righteous and the unrighteous. Those who love righteousness will receive wisdom and life, but those who love unrighteousness are courting death. Leading up to today's reading, the sage has warned his readers against practicing lawless deeds and unrighteous speech—grumbling, slander, and lying—because such things will not go unnoticed or unpunished by the Lord. So, he pleads with his readers: "Do not invite death by the error of your life, or bring on destruction by the works of your hands" (1:12).

1:13–15. But lest the reader think that God enjoys punishing sinners, the sage continues by arguing that God is not a God of death. When God created the world, he did not make death. In fact, the dominion of death, Hades, is not even located on earth; it is not part of God's creation.

2:23–24. Instead, death entered into God's good creation through the envy of the devil (2:24). This was not part of God's design. Originally, human beings were created in God's image; we were created to share in God's immortal, incorruptible, and eternal nature. To seek after righteousness is to participate in God's nature, "for righteousness is immortal." But those who keep company with the devil are inviting trouble and will inherit death.

Suggestions for Lectors

In today's reading, the sage seeks to convince his readers to adopt a different way of living, one that leads to life not death. He is trying to convince them of God's goodness and of God's good intentions for humanity. Therefore, when you read, imagine that you are trying to convince your own listeners of God's goodness and concern for them. Read with energy and conviction.

Pronunciation Guide

Hades (HAY-deez)
Solomon (SAH-luh-muhn; SOL-)

LAMENTATIONS 3:22–33

Commentary

The book of Lamentations consists of five psalms, poetic prayers in which the psalmist laments, mourns, and grieves over the destruction of Jerusalem and its temple by the Babylonians in 586 B.C. Lamentations has been attributed to the prophet Jeremiah, which is why it follows the book of Jeremiah in the Old Testament, but Jeremiac authorship remains uncertain. Regardless, Lamentations offers a graphic portrayal of suffering and death, destruction, and cruel conditions, suggesting for many that these poems draw upon the witness of those who experienced these events firsthand.

Today's reading is taken from the central section of the third psalm. In the first portion (3:1–18), the psalmist outlines his state of destitution. He presents a litany of the ways in which God is punishing him. He is on the brink of despair as he writes:

> The thought of my affliction and my homelessness
>   is wormwood and gall!
> My soul continually thinks of it
>   and is bowed down within me (3:19–20).

Suddenly, he shifts gears and exclaims:

> But this I call to mind,
>   and therefore I have hope:

The "this" he calls to mind is what follows in today's reading.

3:22–24. In spite of his unimaginable suffering, the psalmist still maintains that, despite appearances, the LORD will never fully and finally abandon his people; for his steadfast love, his covenant faithfulness and mercy will never come to an end. The LORD is the psalmist's only lot in life, and so he will put his hope in the LORD.

3:25–30. Hope, however, is not just wishful thinking; it is not just cognitive but involves action. So the psalmist continues by identifying specific and concrete ways in which hope is exercised. First and foremost, hope involves waiting. Hope does not consist of taking matters into our own hands in a desperate attempt to bring about a new state of affairs by our own efforts alone. Instead, hope is a matter of waiting patiently for the LORD to act in his own good time.

That being said, hope is not a passive sort of waiting but an active waiting. To silently endure the yoke of discipline without complaint is to wait actively. Instead of trying to escape punishment, the one who waits in hope submits to the LORD's discipline, which is what it means "to give one's cheek to the smiter and be filled with insults" (3:30). "To put one's mouth to the dust" is to adopt the posture of submission, and again is an expression of active waiting (3:29).

3:31–33. The psalmist advocates such hope-filled waiting because he knows the LORD to be good and loving and out to do us good. While the LORD's discipline may be hard to bear at times, it is not arbitrary, and it does not last forever. Moreover, the LORD's discipline pales in comparison to the abundance of his faithful love and compassion.

Suggestions for Lectors

As reflected in the Commentary, today's reading contains three stanzas (22–24, 25–30, 31–33), each of which begins with a positive pronouncement of the LORD's character and ways.

> 22 The steadfast love of the LORD never ceases,
>   his mercies never come to an end;

> 25 The LORD is good to those who wait for him,
>   to the soul that seeks him.

31 For the Lord will not reject forever.

These statements should receive the most emphasis in your reading. Deliver the opening line in a stronger, more elevated voice. Then, return to your normal reading voice as you complete each stanza.

Normally, one would pause for a second at the beginning of each stanza of a poetic text, but in today's reading, the third stanza stands as an exception to this general rule. In the second stanza, the psalmist encourages his listeners to endure the LORD's discipline with patience. The third stanza gives the rationale for this posture: *For the Lord will not reject forever* (3:31). A full-second pause before this line is not warranted, and in fact, would disrupt the flow of thought.

In any case, the text itself provides its own transition between these two stanzas. Notice that 3:31 is a single sentence; it is short and sweet. This stands in marked contrast to the previous sentence, which continues for four verses (3:27–30). Consequently, the tempo changes of its own accord at the beginning of the third stanza, and sets the third stanza apart without breaking its logical connection with the second stanza.

Pronunciation Guide

Lamentations (lam'-uhn-TAY-shuhnz)

2 CORINTHIANS 8:7–15

Notes

Sequence. 7 of 8

Commentary

In 2 Corinthians 8–9, Paul's attention turns to a relief effort that he has been organizing to collect funds from his Gentile churches for the Jewish-Christians in Jerusalem. References to the Jerusalem Collection are found in Acts 24:17 (cf. Acts 11:27–30) and throughout the letters of Paul (Rom 15:25–29; Gal 2:10; 1 Cor 16:1–4; 2 Cor 8–9). In 1 Corinthians, Paul offers guidance on how the church should organize its collection efforts. He instructs each of the Corinthians to set aside money at the beginning of each week. That way, the funds will have already been collected by the time he arrives. In 2 Corinthians, Paul returns to this matter, not least because relations between him and the church in Corinth have become strained (see Prop 2).

In 2 Corinthians 8:1–6, Paul lifts up the generosity of the Macedonian churches, which would include the churches in Thessalonica and Philippi. Even though the Macedonian Christians were experiencing their own hardships, they voluntarily contributed funds beyond their needs. In fact, they begged Paul for the privilege of "sharing in this ministry to the saints" in Jerusalem (8:4).

8:7. Paul wants the Corinthians to follow the example of the Macedonians. The Corinthians excel in all sorts of areas; now Paul wants them to excel in generosity by participating in the Jerusalem Collection eagerly and joyously.

8:8–9. At this point, Paul treads very carefully. He does not want his prodding to come across as though he were issuing a command. He does not want the Corinthians to give reluctantly or under compulsion for, as he says later, "God loves a cheerful giver" (9:7). Moreover, when we give freely, we are manifesting the same generosity of spirit that Jesus manifested when he became poor for our sakes. Here, we are reminded of what Paul writes in Philippians 2:5–7:

> Let the same mind be in you that was in Christ Jesus,
> who, though he was in the form of God,
> did not regard equality with God as something to be exploited,
> but emptied himself, taking the form of a slave,
> being born in human likeness.

Jesus, who possesses the glory of God, did not simply give of his wealth, he became poor that we might become rich.

8:10–15. Now Paul is not asking the Corinthians to go quite this far; he is not asking them to become destitute by giving away everything they have. But he wants them to follow through with the commitments that they made in the previous year. Most of all, he wants them to give eagerly. For Paul, the most important thing is not *how much* they give but simply *how* they give. "For if the eagerness is there, the gift is acceptable according to what one has—not according to what one does not have" (8:12). If the Corinthians will but trust God and give generously and willingly, they will discover that, if they ever find themselves in need in the future, God will provide for them through the generosity of others. It is just like the manna that fell in the wilderness: "The one who had much did not have too much, and the one who had little did not have too little" (8:15; cf. Exod 16:16–18).

Suggestions for Lectors
Although Paul is challenging the Corinthians to follow through with their commitments, he does so with praise and encouragement (8:7). He is neither harsh nor punitive, instead he explains his position and reasons with his readers. Let all of these positive qualities come through in your voice.

Read 8:9 slowly and with an elevated voice, especially the latter half: *though he was rich, yet for <u>your</u> sakes he became poor, so that by his poverty <u>you</u>… might become rich.* Emphasize *your* and *you*, and pause briefly after *you.*

The final verse, which is a poetic quotation from the OT, also deserves special treatment. Since you are drawing the reading to a close, read the first line at a slightly slower tempo and the second line even slower than the first. Emphasize *much* and *too much* as well as *little* and *too little*, and pause after the first of these in each line, as in:

> *The one who had <u>much</u>… did not have <u>too much,</u>*
> *and the one who had <u>little</u>… did not have <u>too little.</u>*

Pronunciation Guide
Corinthians (kuh-RIN-thee-uhnz)

MARK 5:21–43

Notes
Sequence. 8 of 11

Commentary

In today's reading, we are treated to a traditional Markan sandwich. In literary terms, a *sandwich* is a story-telling technique in which one story frames (or is interrupted by) another story, and so follows an A-B-A pattern. The narrator of Mark regularly employs this technique, thus the name Markan sandwich (3:20–35; 4:1–20; 5:21–43; 6:7–30; 11:12–21; 14:1–11; 14:17–31; 14:53–72; 15:40–16:8). As a rhetorical strategy, the Markan sandwich draws together two seemingly-unrelated stories in such a way as to render them mutually interpretive. Generally though, the B-story provides the interpretive key for understanding the whole composite sandwich. In today's reading, the story of Jairus and his daughter (5:21–24, 35–43) is interrupted by the story of an unnamed woman (5:25–34), and the purpose is to explore the nature of faith in Jesus.

The contrast between these two minor Markan characters is striking. Jairus is a man, and the woman is, of course, a woman. Jairus is named; the woman unnamed. As one of the leaders of the synagogue, Jairus is an upright and respected member of the Jewish community. The woman, however, has suffered from menstrual bleeding for twelve years, meaning that she has lived in a perpetual state of ritual impurity all that time. Such chronic impurity would have excluded her from participating in the synagogue and severely restricted her contact with all other members of her community. In short, this woman is a marginalized member of Jewish society. She and Jairus do share one thing in common, however. Both exhibit faith. Both seek out Jesus, firmly believing that he has the power and authority to transform their respective situations.

The two stories also have some noteworthy parallels. The characters that receive healing are both female and both unnamed. The woman has suffered from a *twelve-year old* flow of blood, and the little girl is *twelve years old.* Finally, according to Jewish purity laws, physical contact with either would have rendered Jesus ritually unclean.

5:21–24. Jairus, Part I. Once again Jesus is beside the Sea of Galilee surrounded by a large crowd (cf. 2:13; 3:7; 4:1). Jairus boldly makes his way through the crowd to Jesus. Such is his desperation and such is his faith that Jairus disregards social propriety for a man of his standing. He falls down at Jesus' feet and repeatedly begs him to come and touch his mortally-ill daughter. Jesus agrees, and they start off immediately for Jairus' house.

5:25–34. The Unnamed Woman. The crowd follows along, and within this sea of people is an unknown woman who has heard about Jesus. She is convinced that one touch of his clothes would do for her what all her money and all the physicians have failed to do. Such is her faith. Because the woman is in a state of ritual impurity, anybody she comes into contact with, whether she touches them or they touch her, would be rendered ritually impure until they perform the appropriate rituals. Disregarding these purity regulations, she makes her way through the jostling crowd, and reaches out and touches Jesus' clothes. Such is her desperation; such is her boldness. Immediately, her bleeding stops, and she knows she has been healed. No doubt, this anonymous woman had hoped to melt back into the crowd unnoticed, but the attention shifts to her when Jesus turns around and asks, "Who touched my clothes?" (5:30). The fact is, everybody had been touching Jesus' clothes, but only this woman was healed. Like Jairus, the woman comes and falls down before Jesus in a posture of humility. After she recounts her story, Jesus responds with gentle compassion, "Daughter, your *faith* has made you well; go in peace, and be healed of your disease" (5:34). These words have the effect of completing her healing. Her ritual impurity had cut her off from society, but Jesus' words welcome and draw her back into community, with God and with others. In the end, she received much more than she had been looking for.

Of course, it was the power of the Holy Spirit that went forth from Jesus and healed her; nevertheless, her faith activated that power. Had she not believed in Jesus, had her faith not given her the boldness to approach him, she would never have been healed.[14] As such, this woman's faith is the meat of this Markan sandwich. Jairus is about to receive news that could destroy his faith. Yet, if his daughter is to get well, he will need to exhibit the same faith that this woman has shown. Her faith also serves as a positive contrast to the lack of faith of Jesus' own disciples. The last time *faith* appeared in the narrative was in the first sea crossing from last week's reading. After Jesus calms the sea, he chastises his disciples: "Why are you afraid? Have you still no *faith*?" (4:40). In Mark, it is common for minor characters to serve as foils for the disciples by exhibiting the qualities of faith and understanding that the disciples fail to exhibit.

5:35–43. Jairus, Part II. In addition to providing the interpretive key to the whole episode, the story of the unnamed woman also injects drama and suspense into the story. Her interruption works to Jairus' disadvantage. While Jesus is conversing with the woman, Jairus receives the dreaded news that his daughter is dead. Had Jesus not stopped, perhaps his little girl would not have died. According to Jairus' friends, there really is no reason to bother Jesus anymore. Jesus, however, says to Jairus: "Do not fear, only *believe*" (5:36). Jairus does believe for he proceeds with Jesus as originally planned. Had he not continued to walk by faith, his little girl would have remained dead. As it is, Jesus brings her back to life. So, in the end, Jairus' faith also serves as a model of faith and a foil for the disciples' lack of faith.

Suggestions for Lectors

As noted in the Commentary, today's reading is a Markan sandwich and so contains three movements (5:21–24, 25–34, 35–43). Pause for a second between the first two movements and for two seconds between the second and third movements.

As lectors, it is important for us to become intimately acquainted with our assigned reading, and meditating on the reading is one of the best ways to do this. As you spend time with today's reading, put yourself in the emotional shoes of Jairus and of the hemorrhaging woman. What is driving them to act as they do? What are they feeling at each moment in the story?

What is Jairus feeling when he begs Jesus to come and lay his hands on his daughter—*desperation? fear?* What is he feeling when Jesus agrees to go with him—*relief? joy?* What is he feeling when Jesus stops to find out who touched him—*anxiety? anger?*

---

[14] For a discussion on the connection between faith and healing in the Gospel of Mark, see the Commentary for Mark 2:1–12 (Epi 7).

What is he feeling when he receives news that his daughter is dead—*grief? anger? frustration?* What is he feeling when Jesus turns to him and says, "Do not fear, only believe?" (5:36)—*doubt? relief? confusion?* And, what is he feeling when his little girl opens her eyes and begins to walk about—*joy? amazement? thankfulness?*

What is the hemorrhaging woman feeling as she comes up behind Jesus—*fear? anxiety? desperation?* What is she feeling when she knows that she has been healed—*relief? joy? peace?* What happens to these feelings when Jesus turns around and says, "Who touched my clothes?" What is she feeling as she approaches Jesus and tells him her story—*fear? anxiety?* And, what does she feel when Jesus addresses her as "Daughter" and tells her to go in peace—*relief? joy? exuberance? hope?*

In 5:28, the woman is carrying on an internal dialog, so drop your voice as she says, *If I but touch his clothes, I will be made well.* When Jesus asks, *Who touched my clothes?*, he is not angry, only curious (5:30). When Jesus addresses the woman, read slowly with warmth and compassion in your voice and with a smile on your face.

Then, after a significant pause, let the smile fade from your face as you relay the bad news in a depressed tone, *Your daughter his dead. Why trouble the teacher any further?* (5:35). Then, in a compassionate and confident tone, turn to Jairus and say, *Do not fear,... only believe* (5:36). When Jesus arrives at Jairus' house, elevate your voice as Jesus pronounces the girl asleep. Finally, using the same compassionate voice that Jesus used with the woman, say to Jairus' daughter, *Talitha cum.* Do it in a quiet (though not too quiet) voice as though you are waking her up from a long nap.

Pronunciation Guide
Jairus (JĪ-ruhs; JAY-uh-ruhs), *Talitha cum* (TAL-ih-thuh KOOM)

PROPER 9

July 2–9

2 Samuel 5:1–5, 9–10
Psalm 48
2 Corinthians 12:2–10
Mark 6:1–13

Ezekiel 2:1–5
Psalm 123
2 Corinthians 12:2–10
Mark 6:1–13

2 SAMUEL 5:1–5, 9–10

Notes
Sequence. 2 of 7

Commentary
In 1 Samuel 15, the LORD speaks to the prophet Samuel about Israel's first king. "I regret that I made Saul king, for he has turned back from following me, and has not carried out my commands" (15:11). Then, in 1 Samuel 16, Samuel is instructed to fill his horn with oil and to set out for the house of Jesse in the village of Bethlehem for, as the LORD says, "I have provided for myself a king among his sons." Samuel sets

out and eventually anoints David, a shepherd boy, the youngest of Jesse's sons. And from that day forward, "the spirit of the LORD came mightily upon David" (16:13, Prop 6).

Yet, that is just the beginning of the story. Although the LORD has rejected Saul and anointed David as his replacement, the journey of David's ascension to the throne will be a long and arduous one. In fact, it is only after Saul's death, many years later, that the people anoint David as their king. Even then, David is only recognized as king over the southern tribe of Judah (2 Sam 2:1–11). The rest of Israel recognizes Ishbaal, one of Saul's remaining sons, as their king.

5:1–3. When David first became king over Judah, he chose the city of Hebron as his capital (2 Sam 2:3), which is why representatives from the northern tribes of Israel meet David in Hebron. They have come to offer him their allegiance because their own king, Ishbaal, has been assassinated. At the same time, they recognize that even when Saul was reigning as king, it was really David who acted as a king, for it was David who "led out Israel and brought it in" (2 Sam 5:2; cf. 1 Sam 8:20, Prop 5). They also recognize that the LORD is with David and it is his will that David be the shepherd over all of God's people. So David makes a covenant with the northern tribes and becomes king over all Israel and Judah.

5:4–5. At this point, the narrator steps in to offer a brief summary of David's reign. David began ruling over Judah when he was thirty years old. He ruled Judah from Hebron for over seven years. When he was anointed as king over all Israel and Judah, he chose Jerusalem as his new capital and ruled for an additional thirty-three years. All in all, David's reign lasted just over forty years; it was a good, long reign.

5:9–10. In the final portion of today's reading, we return to the narrative. In 2 Samuel 5:6, David marches with his men to the Jebusite city of Jerusalem, a stronghold situated on Mt. Zion. David wrests control of Jerusalem from the Jebusites and establishes Jerusalem as the capital of the new United Kingdom of God's people.

Suggestions for Lectors

Today's reading is fairly straightforward. It is not long so make sure your listeners are settled in and attentive before you begin.

When the elders of the northern tribes of Israel come to David, they are anxious. After all, when Saul and Jonathan died, they did not select David as their king, but instead chose Saul's son Ishbaal. Then, when Ishbaal was assassinated, David executed his assassins. Thus, the elders do not quite know where they stand with David. Will David receive them or reject them? So the elders approach him tentatively as they seek to placate David's potential wrath and to convince him of their allegiance. Therefore, adopt a tentative and submissive tone, even perhaps an ingratiating tone, as you deliver their lines.

In 5:4–5, the narrator steps away from the story to offer his listeners an informative summary of David's reign. Read these verses with a lower voice, the voice you would use when delivering a narrative aside. Then return to your normal narrating voice for the conclusion of the episode.

Read the last verse slowly and with greater intensity, especially the final clause, *for the* LORD,*... the God of hosts,... was with him* (5:10). Pause longer than usual at the commas.

Pronunciation Guide
Hebron (HEE-bruhn; HEE-bron), *Israel* (IZ-ree-uhl; -ray-), *Judah* (JOO-duh), *Jerusalem* (juh-ROO-suh-luhm), *Millo* (MIL-oh), *Saul* (SAWL; rhymes with Paul)

EZEKIEL 2:1–5

Commentary
In 598 B.C., the Babylonian empire under the leadership of King Nebuchadnezzar (a.k.a., Nebuchadrezzar) moved against Jerusalem and quashed a rebellion led by King Jehoiakim of Judah (2 Kgs 24:1–7). A few months later, in 597 B.C., the Babylonians returned to ransack the palace and temple, taking everything of value back to Babylon. Then, in what is known as the First Deportation, a select group of Jerusalem's leading officials and citizens were taken as exiles to Babylon (2 Kgs 24:8–17). Among this group of Judean exiles was a young priest by the name of Ezekiel who, in the fifth year of the exile (Ezek 1:1–3), received a heavenly vision of God seated on a chariot-like throne (1:4–28).

In this vision, Ezekiel beholds the glory of the LORD, and he is so overwhelmed that he falls facedown upon the floor. From this position, he hears the voice of God speaking and calling him to serve as a prophet among God's exiled people. This call is the topic of today's reading.

2:1–5. First and foremost, a prophet is someone who speaks the word of the LORD. That word may be a word about the future, but more often it is a word about the failure of God's people to keep the covenant. Either the people and their leaders have failed to worship the LORD alone, or they have failed to act justly towards their neighbor. Often, both of these are the case. At this point, the LORD does not reveal to Ezekiel the particular message or messages that he will be asked to deliver. Ezekiel simply knows that when the LORD calls upon him to speak, he must speak without regard to the content of the message and certainly without regard to how that message is received. Like Isaiah and Jeremiah, Ezekiel speaks words of judgment and exile as well as words of forgiveness and restoration. A summary of Ezekiel's double message can be found in 39:23–29.

Suggestions for Lectors
In the NRSV, today's reading begins with, *He said to me.* The pronoun, *He,* clearly denotes the LORD, so begin instead with *The* LORD *said to me.* (If you are reading from a lectionary, this change will already have been made.) Then, pause for a second or two before continuing.

The LORD is not happy with his people, so adopt a strong, firm, and unwavering voice. In 2:4, emphasize the statement, *Thus says the Lord God,* by slowing down and increasing the intensity of your voice. Once again, pause for a second or two before continuing.

In the final verse, drop your voice as you read the parenthetical aside, *for they are a rebellious house.* Then, return to your firm voice as you draw the reading to a close. Emphasize *know* and then reduce your tempo as you enunciate each of the words in the concluding clause *that there has been a prophet among them.*

Pronunciation Guide
Ezekiel (ee-ZEE-kee-uhl; ee-ZEE-kyuhl)

2 Corinthians 12:2–10

Notes
Sequence. 8 of 8

Commentary
In 2 Corinthians 10–12, Paul returns to defending his apostolic vocation and ministry. Some in Corinth do not think Paul has the proper credentials to be an apostle, and some do not think he is a strong enough leader, at least not in person. They argue, "His letters are weighty and strong, but his bodily presence is weak, and his speech contemptible" (10:10). These criticisms are the product of a situation that has been brewing within the Corinthian church. Recently, other apostles with letters of recommendation have made their way to Corinth. These "super-apostles," as Paul calls them (11:5; 12:11), claim to possess a greater apostolic authority than Paul, and they have been proclaiming a different gospel than the one Paul proclaims.

Paul must mount a defense, not only of the gospel but of himself as well. He regrets doing this because it gives the impression that he is boasting and commending himself, something these false apostles do, which he despises. Yet, Paul recognizes that the truth of the gospel is intimately intertwined with his apostolic commission. Paul has been entrusted with the good news that Gentiles are now welcomed into the family of God solely on the basis of faith in Jesus and not by following the law (Eph 3:5; Rom 16:25). This revelation was given to Paul when the Lord Jesus Christ called and commissioned him to be an apostle (Gal 1:12; 2:2). That is why Paul describes himself as an apostle to the Gentiles (Rom 11:13; Gal 2:8), even though he proclaims the gospel to Jews as well. To discredit Paul is to invalidate the gospel, and vice-versa. So, while Paul thinks this practice of boasting and of commending oneself is a foolish game, he deigns to play it for the sake of the gospel.

He writes, "I repeat, let no one think that I am a fool; but if you do, then accept me as a fool, so that I too may boast a little. What I am saying in regard to this boastful confidence, I am saying not with the Lord's authority, but as a fool; since many boast according to human standards, I will also boast" (2 Cor 11:16–18). Paul then begins to enumerate his apostolic credentials, which mostly have to do with the innumerable injustices he has suffered on account of the gospel (11:21–29). This is an interesting approach because all of Paul's beatings and imprisonments have been interpreted by some as a clear indication that he is weak and has *not* been called by God. But, as Paul says, "If I must boast, I will boast of the things that show my weakness" (11:30). This brings us to today's reading.

12:2–7a. In 12:1, Paul writes, "It is necessary to boast; nothing is to be gained by it, but I will go on to visions and revelations of the Lord." Paul then begins to describe a mystical vision that someone he knows experienced. As the passage develops, it becomes clear that Paul is relaying his own experience, but for humility's sake he describes it in third person.

12:7b–10. In his vision, Paul heard things that most people are not permitted to hear. Such an experience could inflate anyone's sense of self-importance. To keep this from happening, Paul received a "thorn in the flesh." Over the centuries, scholars and lay persons alike have speculated as to what this thorn was, but Paul never says. All that we know is that, on three separate occasions, Paul asked God to take the thorn away only to be told, "My grace is sufficient for you, for power is made perfect in weakness" (12:9). So Paul has learned to boast in his weaknesses and to be content with his troubles because it is in the midst of these that he meets Christ.

Suggestions for Lectors

Today's reading is interesting because it begins with Paul relating a personal experience in third person (12:2–5). So as you read, imagine that you are telling a story about yourself, but telling it as though it happened to someone else. Then, in 12:6, change your tone as you begin speaking in first person. In verses 2 and 3, drop your voice as you read the statements that begin with *whether.*

In 12:7a–9a, slow your pace and increase your intensity as you talk about the thorn in the flesh. Read 12:8 with a hint of desperation in your voice, emphasizing the number of times you entreated the Lord: *Three times I appealed to the Lord about this, that it would leave me.* Read the Lord's response in a firm, yet compassionate voice. In the first half, slow down and emphasize *My grace*: *My grace is sufficient for you.* Slow down even more for the second half. To bring out the alliteration, emphasize *power* and *perfect*, and pause slightly after each, as in: *for power… is made perfect… in weakness* (12:9a).

Pause again after the Lord's response, then continue in a more positive, upbeat fashion throughout the remainder of the reading (12:9b–10) as Paul speaks about boasting in his weakness with gladness. Finally, as you draw the reading to a close, emphasize Paul's concluding statement: *for whenever I am weak, then I am strong* (12:10b).

Pronunciation Guide

Corinthians (kuh-RIN-thee-uhnz), *Paradise* (PAIR-uh-dīs), *Satan* (SAY-tuhn)

Mark 6:1–13

Notes

Sequence. 9 of 11

Commentary

The reader of Mark was first introduced to Jesus at his baptism. "In those days Jesus came *from Nazareth* of Galilee and was baptized by John in the Jordan" (1:9). The Spirit then drives Jesus into the wilderness where he is tested by Satan for a period of forty days. When Jesus finally emerges from his wilderness experience, he does not return to Nazareth. Instead, he relocates to Capernaum, which becomes the hub for his itinerate ministry of announcing the arrival of God's kingdom. In today's reading, after having traveled throughout Galilee and after having even spent some time in a foreign land, Jesus finally returns home to Nazareth where he and his message receive a less than enthusiastic reception.

6:1–6a. When Jesus traveled about Galilee, he proclaimed his message in their synagogues (1:39). So when he arrives in Nazareth, he enters his hometown synagogue on the sabbath and teaches. As the reader has come to expect, the people are amazed by his teaching, and they offer a multitude of responses. It is hard to catch the tone of these responses. They all appear to be overwhelmingly positive until the narrator steps in with, "And they took offense at him" (6:3). What exactly occasions their offense is hard to discern from the text. Perhaps this is a classic case of familiarity breeding contempt. Perhaps they think Jesus should be using his hands for honest work, for carpentry instead of for exorcisms. Perhaps they think Jesus is trying to raise himself above his working class upbringing by trying to be a rabbi. Perhaps they think Jesus has abandoned his family responsibilities as the eldest son.

Whatever the case, Jesus picks up on their negative tone. He says, "Prophets are not without honor, except in their hometown, and among their own kin, and in their own house" (6:4). These references to "kin" and "house" recall the time when his mother and brothers traveled to Capernaum in order to bring Jesus back home due to fears that he had gone out of his mind (3:21, 31, Prop 5).

The people are amazed at his teaching. Jesus, however, is amazed at their unbelief. When Jesus proclaims the kingdom, he says, "Repent and *believe*" (1:15). And, in last week's episode, he told the hemorrhaging woman, "Daughter your *faith* has made you well" (5:34). Faith is how we experience and participate in the kingdom of God. Unclean spirits and sickness do not pose any obstacles to the kingdom, but unbelief does. His hometown's lack of faith limits his abilities. Thus, Jesus is unable to perform any exorcisms. The most he can manage is to cure a few sick people.[15]

6:6b–13. When Jesus began his pubic ministry, the first thing he did was call disciples (1:16–20, Epi 3). As he conducted his ministry, more and more people began to follow him (2:15). Then, in 3:13–19, Jesus appointed twelve of his disciples to be apostles, a term that means "one who is sent out." While disciples follow and learn from their master, apostles are sent out to conduct their master's business. When Jesus appointed the Twelve, he was calling them "to be with him, and to be sent out to proclaim the message, and to have authority to cast out demons" (3:14–15).

In today's reading, the Twelve are sent out on their first missionary tour, and Jesus gives them very detailed instructions on how they are to outfit and conduct themselves. The Twelve are expected to rely upon the hospitality of others, so they must travel light. The prohibition against taking any bread, money, or a provision bag means that the disciples must depend upon others for food. Two tunics might be needed to keep warm if sleeping out of doors. If so, the prohibition against wearing two tunics implies that the disciples are to depend upon others for their shelter,

---

[15] For a discussion on the connection between faith and healing in the Gospel of Mark, see the Commentary for Mark 2:1–12 (Epi 7).

which may be related to the command to remain as houseguests in whatever house they find themselves in. Thus, when the Twelve are engaged in their apostolic vocation, they must rely upon those to whom they are sent for both food and shelter, which really means that they are being called to trust God to provide for their needs.

Their Galilean mission is quite successful. Just like Jesus, they proclaim that everybody should repent because the kingdom of God has arrived. And just like Jesus, they perform exorcisms and other healings that demonstrate the presence of the kingdom. So successful is their mission that, when they return in 6:30–32, they are inundated with crowds of people, which eventually turns into a crowd of five thousand that Jesus feeds with a few loaves and fish (6:33–44).

Suggestions for Lectors

In the opening scene of today's episode (6:1–6a), the people respond to Jesus' teaching with a variety of comments (6:2b–3a). Only after the comments are made is the reader informed that the people are offended by Jesus. So make sure to present their questions and comments in a negative way, with hints of sarcasm and disbelief in your voice. Also, since the quotation represents the responses of more than one person (at least four and possibly five persons), pause at the end of each, and deliver each response in a slightly different manner through adjustments in tone, volume, and tempo.

Person 1: Where did this man get all this?…
Person 2: What is this wisdom that has been given to him?…
Person 3: What deeds of power are being done by his hands!…
Person 4: Is not this the carpenter, the son of Mary and brother of James and Joses and Judas and Simon,…
Person 5: and are not his sisters here with us?

When delivering Jesus' words, raise your voice and with a hint of frustration emphasize all of the descriptors of those who are offended by him. *Prophets are not without honor, except in <u>their hometown</u>, and among their <u>own kin</u>, and in their <u>own house</u>.* Draw the first scene to a close by slowing down and reading the last line more deliberately: *And he was <u>amazed</u> at their unbelief* (6:6a).

The second scene is much more straightforward (6:6b–13). There is nothing that stands out, so there is nothing that requires special emphasis, except perhaps the final verse that relates their success.

Pronunciation Guide

James (JAYMZ), *Joses* (JOH-seez; JOH-zehz), *Judas* (JOO-duhs), *Simon* (SĪ-muhn)

PROPER 10

July 10–16

2 Samuel 6:1–5, 12b–19
Psalm 24
Ephesians 1:3–14
Mark 6:14–29

Amos 7:7–15
Psalm 85:8–13
Ephesians 1:3–14
Mark 6:14–29

2 Samuel 6:1–5, 12b–19

Notes

Sequence. 3 of 7

Commentary

In last week's reading from 2 Samuel, after many years of struggle, David finally ascends to the throne and is anointed king over all Israel and Judah. His first act is to establish Jerusalem as his new capital. Having established Jerusalem as the political center of the nation, David now seeks to establish it as the religious center as well. So, in today's reading, David brings the ark of the covenant into Jerusalem.

The ark of the covenant contained the stone tablets on which were written the Ten Commandments, and its rightful place was in the inner sanctuary of the tabernacle, also known as the tent of meeting. At the beginning of 1 Samuel, the ark was located at the sanctuary in Shiloh, where Eli and then Samuel served as priests. The ark served as the sign of God's presence and power among his people, so sometimes the ark was taken into battle. If the LORD was Israel's king and if a king's job was to go out before his people and fight their battles, then it made sense that the ark would lead the way. Unfortunately, the Israelites tended to forget what the ark represented. They treated it like a talisman or a magic wand instead of as the holy presence of the one true and living God. This happened back in 1 Samuel 4, with the result that the ark was captured by Israel's archenemies, the Philistines. Eventually, the ark was returned to Israel where it was placed in the house and under the care of Abinadab. There it remained for twenty years without mention (1 Sam 7:2), save one reference in 1 Samuel 14:18.

6:1–5. Twenty years later, David remembers the ark of God, and he attempts to relocate it to its new home in Jerusalem. David retrieves the ark from the house of Abinadab and begins to transport it to Jerusalem in a grand procession replete with liturgical singing, dancing, and music.

6:6–12a. Unfortunately, David does not take the proper precautions for transporting the ark. Since the ark represented the holy presence of God, it was never to be touched by human hands. Instead, the ark was designed to be carried by priests using poles set in rings that were attached to the ark (Exod 25:12–14). The lid for the ark (sometimes called the mercy seat) was designed to look like an ancient throne. It was made of gold, and golden cherubim were located on either side of the lid. As the LORD said, "There I will meet with you, and from above the mercy seat, from between the two cherubim that are on the ark of the covenant, I will deliver to you all my commands for the Israelites" (25:22; cf. Isaiah 37:16). When the ark of the covenant is being transported on poles by the priests, the picture we are to have is of an ancient ruler being transported on a litter, or palanquin. Transporting the ark of God using a cart pulled by oxen does not show proper respect, and it places those responsible for transporting it in danger. As it turns out, one of the attendants, Uzzah, reaches out his hand to steady the ark and is struck dead. At this point, David becomes afraid and is unwilling to bring the ark into Jerusalem. Instead, he leaves it in the care of a certain Obed-edom. Three months later, David is informed that the LORD has blessed the household of Obed-edom, and so he makes another attempt at bringing the ark into Jerusalem.

6:12b–19. On his second attempt, David gets it right. He does not take the presence of the LORD for granted. He shows proper respect by employing bearers for the ark and by offering sacrifices all along the way. Moreover, King David is girded with a linen ephod, the liturgical garb worn by priests (Exod 28:4; cf. 1 Sam 2:18). When the ark reaches Jerusalem, it is installed in a specially-constructed tent, and there David offers the appropriate sacrifices. Afterwards, he blesses the people and offers everyone portions of the sacrificial food, thereby transforming the procession into a sacred meal between the LORD and his people.

Suggestions for Lectors

Today's episode is filled with ceremony and celebration, except for 6:16, which reveals Michal's displeasure, so read with great energy and with a smile on your face.

Today's reading is also filled with unfamiliar names, so practice training your ear and tongue until you are able to pronounce the names with ease and confidence. Repeat the names over and over on their own, but also practice reading and rereading them in context. Most of the names appear in 6:1–5, so read these verses at a slightly slower pace.

Pronunciation Guide

Abinadab (uh-BIN-uh-dab), *Ahio* (uh-HĪ-oh), *Baale-judah* (bayl-uh-JOO-duh),
cherubim (CHEHR-uh-bim'; -oo-), *ephod* (EE-fod), *Israel* (IZ-ree-uhl; -ray-),
lyre (LĪ-uhr), *Michal* (MĪ-kuhl; MEE-kal), *Obed-edom* (OH-bid-EE-duhm),
Saul (SAWL; rhymes with Paul), *Uzzah* (UZ-uh)

AMOS 7:7–15

Commentary

The book of Amos belongs to a collection of OT writings called the Book of the Twelve, comprising the twelve Minor Prophets from Hosea to Malachi. Though a native of the southern kingdom of Judah, Amos was called to carry out a prophetic ministry in the northern kingdom of Israel in the first half of the eighth century B.C. This was a generation or two before Israel was taken into exile by the Assyrian empire in 722 B.C. At this time, with Israel's enemies no longer a threat, the development of international trade had resulted in a high level of economic prosperity, at least for some. As is so often the case, with great wealth came great greed. Social inequality and injustice escalated as the economic divide between the rich and the poor increased. Yet, because many regarded Israel's economic prosperity as a blessing from the LORD, a sign of God's favor, the social injustice went unchecked. It was to this situation that Amos was called to deliver the word of the LORD, a word of impending judgment and exile for Israel.

7:1–9. Today's reading begins with three visions of judgment that the LORD presents to Amos: a plague of locusts, a shower of fire, and a wall built with a plumb line. The first two visions follow the same pattern. Amos sees the land devastated by locusts and fire, and he intercedes on Israel's behalf.[16] Each time, the LORD relents, declaring that what Amos has seen will not come to pass.

In the third vision, Amos sees the LORD standing beside a wall built with a plumb line, a device used for determining whether a door frame or a wall is in line with the vertical. With this image, the LORD indicates that Israel's religious, political, and social institutions have been tested and do not measure up; they are out of line with God's values, ways, and laws. Consequently, Israel will experience judgment. "The high places of Isaac," which are altars dedicated to other gods, will be destroyed as will Israel's sanctuaries. In addition, the LORD will put an end to the reign and dynasty of King Jeroboam. This will come about through an enemy invasion.

7:10–13. Not surprisingly, the prophet's message was not well-received in the northern kingdom. Amaziah, the high priest in charge of the royal sanctuary in Bethel, sends word to King Jeroboam that something must be done about Amos. Amos is threatening the king's authority, and the people cannot bear his doom and gloom predictions of impending exile (7:10). Amaziah confronts Amos and orders him to return to Judah where he belongs and to make his living prophesying there. He is not welcome in Israel, especially not in Bethel.

7:14–15. Amos responds by saying, "I am no prophet, nor the son of a prophet." That is to say, Amos is not a professional prophet who earns his living by prophesying. Nor is he a member of a prophetic guild, whose members were known as "the sons of the prophets" (cf. 2 Kgs 2:3). Instead, Amos makes his living herding sheep (7:1, 14) and dressing sycamore trees, a type of fig tree that required someone to slit the fruits with a knife to induce ripening. Amos is only prophesying in Israel because the LORD called and sent him.

Suggestions for Lectors

Begin your reading imagining that you are Amos describing for your listeners a vision you received from the LORD. As always, raise your voice when the LORD speaks, in this case in 7:8b–9.

Pause and perhaps look at your listeners between 7:9 and 7:10, which will register a change in scene and characters. Adopt an offended and frustrated tone as you become Amaziah and take your complaint to the king (7:10b–11). Then, let your voice become stern and scornful as you turn to Amos and dismiss him with a command (7:12–13).

---

[16] In verses 2 and 4, Israel is referred to as Jacob.

In 7:14–15, you can imagine that Amos finds Amaziah's frustration and rage slightly amusing. So instead of adopting a defensive tone for Amos, speak in a calm, innocent, and slightly bemused voice as though you are not quite sure why all of this hostility is being directed at you. In effect, Amos' response to Amaziah amounts to, "If you want to be mad at someone, then be mad at God; take it up with him. After all, he is the one who made me give up my peaceful life; he is the one who tells me what to say."

Pronunciation Guide
Amaziah (am'-uh-ZĪ-ah), *Amos* (AY-muhs), *Bethel* (BETH-uhl),
Jeroboam (jair'-uh-BOH-uhm), *prophesy* (vb., PRAH-fuh-sī) [*not* prophecy]

EPHESIANS 1:3–14

Notes
Sequence. 1 of 7

Commentary
Throughout his Letter to the Ephesians, Paul celebrates the grace of God, bestowed upon us in the Lord Jesus Christ, the Beloved, and made effective through the promised Holy Spirit. In today's reading, Paul's letter begins with a veritable litany of praises and thanksgivings for the salvation and spiritual blessings that have been made available through the gospel of Christ.

1:3–6. Paul begins by blessing "the God and Father of our Lord Jesus Christ" for all of the blessings of salvation that were wrought for us through the life, death, resurrection, and ascension of Jesus. Even before the world was created, God's plan was to adopt us as his children, not on the basis of who we are and what we do, but on the basis of who Jesus is and what he would do. In short, our salvation in Christ is a gift freely given, a manifestation of God's grace. In the three sections that follow, Paul identifies the spiritual blessings that are found *in the Beloved* (1:6). Note how each section begins with a reference to the Beloved: "*In him* we have…" (1:7); "*In Christ* we have also…" (1:11); and "*In him* you also…" (1:13).

1:7–10. First, we have been redeemed by the blood of Christ. That is, through Christ's death, our trespasses have been forgiven, and we have been set free from the power of sin that enslaves us. All of this contributes to God's vision of reconciling all things to himself in Christ, as Paul says, "to gather up all things in him [that is, Christ], things in heaven and things on earth" (1:10). As Paul says elsewhere:

> So if anyone is in Christ, there is a new creation: everything old has passed away; see, everything has become new! All this is from God, who reconciled us to himself through Christ;… that is, in Christ God was reconciling the world to himself, not counting their trespasses against them (2 Cor 5:17–19a, Prop 6).

1:11–12. Second, having become God's adopted children in Christ, it stands to reason that we have also been granted an inheritance. Though Paul does not explicitly state it here, the inheritance to which he refers likely concerns the future hope of resurrection from the dead. For example, when Paul speaks of the future resurrection of the dead in 1 Corinthians 15, he uses the language of inheritance (15:50ff.). Moreover, the word *hope*, which occurs in 1:12, is often used by Paul as shorthand for resurrection from the dead (Rom 8:19–24, ✠ PentVig; 1 Cor 15:19; Col 1:27). Thus, when Paul speaks of "we, who were the first to set our *hope* on Christ," he is referring to those who first believed in Jesus and so first received the promised inheritance of eternal life, which Paul always understood to be a resurrected, embodied life in a restored creation (1 Cor 15:12–58).

Paul believes that, through Christ, God was not only rescuing humanity but was rescuing *the whole* of the created order from its subjugation to the chaotic, corrupting forces of sin and death. Consider the following from Romans 8:19–25 (✠ PentVig):

> For the creation waits with eager longing for the revealing of the children of God; for the creation was subjected to futility, not of its own will but by the will of the one who subjected it, in hope that the creation itself will be set free from its bondage to decay and will obtain the freedom of the glory of the children of God. We know that the whole creation has been groaning in labor pains until now; and not only the creation, but we ourselves, who have the first fruits of the Spirit, groan inwardly *while we wait for adoption, the redemption of our bodies. For in hope we were saved.* Now hope that is seen is not hope. For who hopes for what is seen? But if we hope for what we do not see, we wait for it with patience.

So, for Paul, the inheritance that awaits us as God's children is eternal life in God's restored creation, and the means by which we will come into our inheritance is through the restoration of our bodies, that is, through resurrection from the dead.

1:13–14. Of course, all of this is a future hope, a hope that we do not yet see, so we must be patient until God brings it about. Yet thankfully, God has left us with a guarantee that the inheritance of which Paul speaks really does await those of us who believe. When we come to faith in Christ Jesus, we are graciously granted the indwelling of the Holy Spirit. The Holy Spirit serves as God's pledge that one day we will in fact receive our inheritance, resurrection from the dead into God's new world. Furthermore, the Holy Spirit marks us as Christ's own forever and seals us to preserve and protect us until the time when we come into our inheritance (2 Cor 1:22, Epi 7).

Suggestions for Lectors

Read this passage so as to convey some measure of Paul's excitement and gratitude for the salvation that has been so graciously wrought for us in Christ.

This passage is filled with one theological truth after another, so it is important not to rush. Pay particular attention to the punctuation, and in keeping with the structure outlined above in the Commentary, pause for full a second prior to verses 7, 11, and 13.

Pronunciation Guide

Beloved (n., buh-LUV-uhd), *Ephesians* (eh-FEE-zhuhnz; ih-),

blessed in 1:3a (adj., two syllables; BLES-id),
blessed in 1:3b (vb., one syllable; BLEST)

Mark 6:14–29

Notes
Sequence. 10 of 11

Commentary
John the Baptist was a forerunner to Jesus in more than one way. Not only did his baptizing with water pave the way for Jesus' baptizing with the Holy Spirit, his arrest and execution foreshadowed Jesus' own fate. Following his baptism in the Jordan river, Jesus was driven into the wilderness to be tested by Satan. By the time he reemerged forty days later, John had been arrested (1:14). In today's retrospective account, we finally learn the circumstances surrounding the Baptist's arrest and subsequent death.

6:14–16. In last week's reading, Jesus sent the Twelve out on their first apostolic tour of duty (6:7–13). They traveled throughout Galilee proclaiming the good news of the kingdom and performing exorcisms and healings, exactly as Jesus had been doing. Jesus' own work had made his name known, but the mission of the Twelve caused his name to become even more widely known throughout Galilee. People began to speculate about his true identity. Was he Elijah, or perhaps one of the other ancient prophets? Even Herod Antipas had an opinion. He held the superstitious belief that John the Baptist had come back to life, which explained the powers that were at work in Jesus.

6:17–28. Antipas had John arrested because John had publicly condemned his marriage to Herodias. According to the first-century Jewish historian Josephus, Herodias divorced Antipas' half-brother, Herod Philip, in order to marry Antipas. As it so happened, Herodias was also Philip and Antipas' half-niece.

In Mark's account, Antipas is motivated by fear instead of by his own convictions. He arrests John because he was being pressured by Herodias, yet he keeps John alive because he himself is afraid of John. Then, Antipas has John beheaded because he fears breaking the oath he made before his courtiers and officials. Though Herod believed John to be a righteous and holy man, he succumbed to pressure and executed him to satisfy the wishes of others.

This is just one further example of John's role as the forerunner to Jesus. At the end of the gospel, when Jesus is brought before Pilate, Pilate does not think that Jesus has done anything to warrant the death penalty. Nevertheless, in order to satisfy the wishes of the people, Pilate he hands Jesus over to be crucified (15:15).

6:29. When John's disciples receive word of their master's death, they retrieve his headless body from Antipas and lay it in a tomb. Their courage and faithfulness stands in marked contrast to that of Jesus' disciples. Having abandoned their master at his arrest, Jesus' disciples are in hiding when it is time to bury him. In the end, it is not one of the Twelve, but Joseph of Arimathea who secures Jesus' body from Pilate, takes it down from the cross, and places it in his own tomb (15:42–47).

Suggestions for Lectors

In the opening verses (6:14–16), read the people's speculations in an animated, high-pitched voice to convey the sense of excitement over who this Jesus might be. In contrast, read Herod's conclusion in a calm, lower-pitched voice, as though he is the voice of reason.

The remainder of the reading is one of those dramatic, well-told biblical stories (6:17–29), so employ the skills of a storyteller in order to convey the intrigue of this bloody, aristocratic tale. In particular, this story would benefit from some well-placed pauses and changes in tempo. For example, Herod issues an oath in 6:22 that he re-asserts in 6:23. Read the first oath at a slightly quickened pace, but the second oath at a slightly slower pace with longer pauses at the commas. This reduction in tempo not only conveys the earnestness of Herod's oath but it increases the dramatic tension. This same technique can be used in the subsequent exchange between mother and daughter. When the daughter approaches her mother, ask her question in a somewhat hurried manner, as though she is excited and a bit out of breath: *What should I ask for?* (6:24). Then, in a cold, calculated, even triumphant voice, deliver her mother's slow reply: *The head… of John… the baptizer* (6:25). Emphasize *head* and introduce slight pauses after *head* and *John*.

Pronunciation Guide

Elijah (ee-LĪ-juh; ih-), *Galilee* (GAL-uh-lee), *Herod* (HAIR-uhd),
Herodias (hih-ROH-dee-uhs; hehr-oh-DĪ-uhs), *Philip* (FIL-ip)

PROPER 11

July 17–23

2 Samuel 7:1–14a	Jeremiah 23:1–6
Psalm 89:20–37	Psalm 23
Ephesians 2:11–22	Ephesians 2:11–22
Mark 6:30–34, 53–56	Mark 6:30–34, 53–56

2 Samuel 7:1–14a

Notes

Sequence. 4 of 7

Commentary

In last week's reading from 2 Samuel, we read the story of how David brought the ark of the covenant into his new capital, Jerusalem. When the ark was first constructed in the wilderness years, it was housed in the tabernacle, which was a portable shrine. So, when David brings the ark into Jerusalem, it seems entirely appropriate that he should install it in a tent.

7:1–3. Yet, when things have settled down and the kingdom is at peace, David begins to wonder about the disparity between his own palace of cedar and the LORD's tent. His prophetic advisor Nathan does not need a special word from the LORD. He has seen how the LORD has been with David and how he has blessed everything David has put his hand to, so he simply encourages David to do as he sees fit.

7:4–7. Still the LORD does have an opinion on the matter; after all it is his house they are talking about. The LORD sends a message to David through Nathan. He begins by stating that in all the time he has been with his people, he has never once asked anyone to construct a permanent place of residence for him. In any case, it would be impossible, for he is not a god made of wood or stone but the Creator of all that is, seen and unseen. As he says in Isaiah, "Heaven is my throne and the earth is my footstool; what is the house that you would build for me, and what is my resting place?" (Isa 66:1). In short, the LORD is content with what he has; he is not interested in a new house.

7:8–14a. What the LORD *is* interested in are his people and those whom he calls to shepherd them. The LORD has not forgotten his promise to Abraham and Sarah to make them into a great nation so that they may become the means by which God's blessing comes to all peoples (Gen 12:3). The LORD intends to protect and preserve his chosen people. He intends to shape them with his character so that they may live out their priestly vocation to mediate the presence, knowledge, and forgiveness of God to all peoples everywhere.

God's people need good leaders if they are going to live out their vocation as God's people. One way the LORD will accomplish this purpose is by making a house for David. Despite David's many faults, the LORD sees in him a faithful follower, a man after his own heart (1 Sam 13:14). The LORD will not only bless David, he will bless David's offspring as well. David's very own son will be raised up to take his father's place as king over Israel, and it shall be he who will build a house for God. Moreover, the LORD will establish his house forever. In other words, the LORD is committing himself to the Davidic line and establishing a royal dynasty. From now on, someone of David's line will rule over Israel, beginning with David's son Solomon. Solomon and those who inherit the throne will be treated like sons. Says the LORD, "I will be a father to him, and he shall be a son to me" (7:14a).

7:14b–16. The implications of this are spelled out in the verses following today's reading. The LORD will be fiercely devoted to David's offspring for better or for worse. Not only will the LORD bless them, he will correct them as well. If they step out of line, they will be disciplined, even severely disciplined. Yet, the LORD will *never* forsake them. He will not abandon them as he did Saul. Come what may, the LORD is committed to David and his descendants… forever.

Suggestions for Lectors

Read the opening verses in your normal narrating voice (7:1–3). Then, at the beginning of 7:4, drop your voice slightly and read with a different overall tone as you deliver the LORD's words to David through Nathan.

In 7:4–7, the LORD asks two rhetorical questions, both of which expect a negative response: *Are you the one to build me a house to live in?* (7:4) and *did I ever speak a word…?* (7:7). Increase the pitch of your voice when asking these questions.

The most important part of today's reading is the covenant that the LORD establishes with David and his offspring, so do what you can to highlight it. This can be done in a number of ways. For example, when you reach 7:12, you could reduce your speed and speak more deliberately, as though you are stating something so important that you do not want a syllable missed or misunderstood. When you reach 7:14a, slow down even more, and intensify your voice as you say, *I will be a father to him, and he shall be a son to me.*

Alternatively, since the covenant the LORD is making with David is a unilateral covenant, one established and maintained by the LORD himself, you could choose to highlight the commitments the LORD is making, by emphasizing each of the *I will*'s, again reaching a climax in 7:14a:

7:9 *I will make…*
7:10 *I will appoint…*
7:11 *I will give…*
7:12 *I will raise…*
7:12 *I will establish…*
7:13 *I will establish…*
7:14 *I will be…*

Pronunciation Guide

David (DAY-vid), *Egypt* (EE-jipt), *Israel* (IZ-ree-uhl; -ray-), *Nathan* (NAY-thuhn)

JEREMIAH 23:1–6

Commentary

According to the prophets of the OT, the nations of Israel and Judah were sent into exile on account of their ongoing failure to love God with singular devotion and to love their neighbors as themselves. According to Jeremiah, one of the principal factors that contributed to these sins of idolatry and injustice was poor leadership. In 23:9–40, Jeremiah criticizes the royal prophets who were enamored with their own prophetic experiences and spoke their own words and not the word of the LORD, thus deceiving and leading the people astray. Likewise, Jeremiah criticizes Judah's kings in 22:1–23:6. In today's reading, the prophet declares the LORD's plans to restore his exiled people and to raise up for them a shepherd king who will lead them in the way of justice and righteousness.

23:1–2. The LORD accuses Israel's and Judah's kings of not attending to his people as a shepherd tends his flock. Though the LORD brought about the judgment that led to the people being exiled, the kings are those who are truly responsible. The LORD says, "It is you who have scattered my flock, and have driven them away, and you have not attended to them. So I will attend to you for your evil doings" (23:2). These kings did not seek the word of the LORD or commit themselves to the way of the LORD. Instead, they committed idolatry and practiced injustice, serving as a bad examples that the people followed.

23:3–4. Consequently, when the LORD has mercy on Israel and Judah and restores their fortunes (30:3; 33:26), the LORD will also raise up shepherds over his people who will actually shepherd them. The people will thus be safe and secure and have no need to be afraid or dismayed.

23:5–6. More to the point, a day is envisioned when a particular king will be raised up who "shall execute justice and righteousness in the land" (23:5). In other words, this king will be completely devoted to the LORD and so will serve as a model for those who would love the LORD their God with all of their heart, soul, and strength (Deut 6:5, Prop 26). Likewise, this king will support justice and righteousness, thereby serving as a model for those called to love their neighbors as themselves (Lev 19:18).

In 2 Samuel, the LORD makes a covenant with king David, in which he promises that one of David's descendants would always occupy the throne (2 Sam 7:11b–16, Adv 4, Prop 11; 1 Kgs 8:25, Prop 16). Consequently, the king to be appointed will be a descendant of David, here described as a righteous Branch. This same imagery is found in Isaiah who envisions the coming of this king: "A shoot shall come out from the stump of Jesse [David's father], and a branch shall grow out of his roots" (11:1). Because of their judgment and exile, Israel's and Judah's kings are no more. David's dynasty is like a mighty tree that has been felled; only the stump and the roots remain. Yet, when the LORD restores his people, he will also remember his covenant with David and raise up a king who will inaugurate an age of peace and prosperity throughout the land and the whole world (Isa 11:1–10), and he will be known by the name, "The LORD is our righteousness" (23:6; cf. 33:16).

Suggestions for Lectors

This passage consists entirely of the words of the LORD, so that it becomes rather a proclamation, to be read as such, in a raised voice. Pause for a full second before verses 3 and 5, which will serve to divide the reading into three movements: 1–2, 3–4, and 5–6.

The first movement begins with *Woe* and is of such a nature that it should be read with some intensity and force of voice in order to convey the LORD's judgment. As you conclude the movement, emphasize the last sentence, by slowing down and enunciating each word clearly: *So I will attend to you for your evil doings, says the LORD* (23:2b). In keeping with older translations, you may wish to add a *thus* before *says*, so that you conclude with *thus says the LORD*, which sounds even more authoritative.

In the second movement, the LORD turns his wrathful gaze away from Israel's corrupt leadership and looks with mercy upon his exiled people. So read with a gentleness in your voice, but do not lose any of the strength in your voice. As before, slow down as you end the movement, concluding with another *thus says the LORD*.

The final movement is also to be read in this same gentle, yet strong manner. Once again, emphasize the last sentence through a reduced tempo and increased enunciation: *The LORD is our righteousness* (23:6b).

Pronunciation Guide

Jeremiah (jair'-uh-MĪ-uh)

EPHESIANS 2:11–22

Notes

Sequence. 2 of 7

Commentary

Within the first-century Jewish worldview, all of humanity was divided into just two groups: Jews and Gentiles—that is, Jews and everybody else. The earliest Christians were all Jews, but within a relatively short time, as the Christian movement spread throughout the Roman world, Gentiles started believing in and following Jesus as well. For Paul, the salvation that has been achieved by Christ not only brings about reconciliation between human beings and God, it also brings about reconciliation between one group of human beings and another. In particular, in Christ, God has dissolved the millennia-old division between Jews and Gentiles.

2:11–12. In today's reading, Paul addresses Gentile Christians. He reminds them that it is only by the grace of God that they belong to the people of God. After all, there was a time in the not-too-distant past when they were without God and without the hope of salvation and future resurrection, a time when they belonged neither to Israel nor to Christ.

2:13–18. But now things have changed. Jesus' death brought an end to the law. While the law contained general ethical instructions like "Do not murder" and "Do not steal" (Exod 20:13, 15, Lent 3), it also contained commandments and regulations specific to Jewish identity (laws governing dietary matters, circumcision, sabbath observance, etc.). In part, the law was designed to set Israel apart from the other nations. God's intent was to fashion a people who would acquire his character and values in order that they might serve as the light to the world. Israel's vocation was to draw all people into the knowledge and worship of the one, true, and living God.

Unfortunately, by the time of Jesus, the law had become an obstacle to mission instead of a vehicle for mission. Because of human sin, the law had become a wall that separated and, therefore, created hostility between Jews and Gentiles. In other NT passages, Christ's death is interpreted as the means by which human beings are reconciled to God; here, it is also understood as the means by which human beings are reconciled to one another. Jesus' death established peace between Jews and Gentiles by bringing an end to a socio-religious institution that had kept them strangers and enemies. Instead of two humanities, now there is only one humanity. Instead of many ways to God, there is just one, Jesus Christ, whose death draws all people into a relationship with God and with one another.

2:19–22. Now that the wall separating Jews and Gentiles has come down, a new structure is needed that reflects the peace inaugurated by Christ. Where once there stood a wall that divided humanity into two groups, there now stands a building that envelops and holds humanity together as one group. And, this building is not just any building; it is a temple, a place where God is worshipped and prayers are offered. This means that humanity is united when its common worship and prayer are directed to the one true God made known through his Son, Jesus. The foundation of this new spiritual temple is not the law but the proclamation of the apostles and prophets, and they proclaim the good news about *Jesus Christ.* Therefore, Jesus is the cornerstone of this new living temple in which the Holy Spirit resides.

Suggestions for Lectors

In today's passage, Paul speaks directly to his readers, so be intentional about directing the words you read to your listeners. Take on the persona of Paul as you remind your listeners about what Christ has done to establish peaceful relations between them and God, and between them and their neighbors. Speak with sincerity and conviction.

Paul seems to enjoy conveying his thoughts by means of long, complex sentences, and today's passage is filled with them. As you prepare, work out where you are going to pause, where you will take breaths, and how you are going to adjust and maintain the intonation of your voice. You do not want to start a sentence and run out of breath or have your intonation drop away. So make sure to practice reading aloud until your delivery is natural and smooth.

Pronunciation Guide

Ephesians (eh-FEE-zhuhnz; ih-), *Gentiles* (JEN-tīlz), *Israel* (IZ-ree-uhl; -ray-)

MARK 6:30–34, 53–56

Notes

Sequence. 11 of 11

Commentary

The editors of the Revised Common Lectionary chose not to include Mark's accounts of the feeding of the five thousand and Jesus' walking upon the sea. Instead, they chose John's accounts of these episodes, which appear in next week's reading. In today's reading, we once again witness Jesus, the authoritative teacher and healer, with a crowd of people around him.

In 6:7–13, Jesus sent the Twelve out on their first missionary tour of duty. They went forth in pairs, "proclaiming that all should repent. They cast out many demons, and anointed with oil many who were sick and cured them" (6:12–13, Prop 9). In short, the Twelve exercised the same authority to teach and heal that Jesus himself had been exercising.

6:30–34. Then, at the outset of today's reading, the Twelve return. So successful was their mission that crowds of people were coming and going, so many people that they did not have the time to eat. Jesus suggests they get away to recuperate. They withdraw in a boat, but unfortunately "they" are recognized; that is, not only do the people recognize Jesus, they now recognize *the Twelve.*[17] When Jesus and his disciples arrive at their destination, they are met by another large crowd. Jesus has compassion upon them and begins to teach them because they are "like sheep without a shepherd" (6:34),.

---

[17] Contrast with Mark 6:54 where only Jesus is recognized.

This expression first appears in Numbers. When the LORD informs Moses that he will not be permitted to lead Israel into the Promised Land (Num 27:13–14, cf. 20:12), Moses responds by saying:

> Let the LORD, the God of the spirits of all flesh, appoint someone over the congregation who shall go out before them and come in before them, who shall lead them out and bring them in, so that the congregation of the LORD may not be *like sheep without a shepherd* (27:16–17).

Moses' immediate successor was Joshua, the son of Nun (27:18), but his ultimate successor is another Joshua—Jesus of Nazareth.[18] Jesus shepherds the flock of God's people by proclaiming the good news of the kingdom in both word and deed.

6:53–56. Following the feeding of the five thousand (6:35–44) and Jesus' walking upon the sea (6:45–52), the disciples and Jesus cross the Sea of Galilee and disembark at Gennesaret on the western shore. Once again, people recognize Jesus and begin to bring the sick to him, and everyone is healed by Jesus, even those who merely touch the fringe of his cloak (cf. 5:28, Prop 8).

Suggestions for Lectors

Today's reading comprise two distinct scenes. In each scene, the emphasis comes at the end. In the first scene (6:30–34), Jesus is tired and in need of refreshment; nevertheless, he is not too tired to serve as a gracious teacher and host. Read 6:34b in a caring, concerned voice, stressing the word *compassion* and the phrase *sheep without a shepherd.*

Begin the second scene (6:53–56) at a slightly faster pace as people recognize Jesus and rush about to bring the sick to him. Then, read the final line slowly and deliberately, stressing *all* and pausing slightly after *it*, as in: *and <u>all</u> who touched it... were healed* (6:56b).

Pronunciation Guide

Gennesaret (gih-NEH-suh-ret')

PROPER 12

July 24–30

2 Samuel 11:1–15	2 Kings 4:42–44
Psalm 14	Psalm 145:10–18 (= 145:10–19 BCP)
Ephesians 3:14–21	Ephesians 3:14–21
John 6:1–21	John 6:1–21

[18] Joshua (that is, *Yeshua* or *Yehoshua*) was Jesus' name in Hebrew. The English name, Jesus, derives from the Latin, *Iesus*, which comes from the Greek, *Iēsous*, which translates the Hebrew, *Yeshua.*

2 SAMUEL 11:1–15

Notes

Sequence. 5 of 7

Commentary

Today's reading presents us with the well-known story of David and Bathsheba. Sometimes this story is retold or presented as an affair, but there is no hint of romance in the biblical account. Instead, this is the story of a powerful king taking the wife of one of his subjects.

11:1. When the Israelites first clamored for a king, they refused to heed Samuel's warnings about the danger of a monarchy. They said, "We are determined to have a king over us, so that we also may be like other nations, and that our king may govern us and *go out before us and fight our battles*" (1 Sam 8:19–20). Years later when the northern tribes pledged their allegiance to David, they said, "Look, we are your bone and flesh. For some time, while Saul was king over us, *it was you who led out Israel and brought it in*" (2 Sam 5:1–2a). Thus, in the people's eyes, a king's primary responsibility was to lead the nation into battle and fight on their behalf. So, when today's reading begins with David in Jerusalem while his commander, his officers, and all Israel are out on the battlefield, the reader is to detect a hint of foreshadowing. David is not where he is supposed to be; something bad is about to happen. And so it does.

11:2–5. The Adultery. David is lounging about with nothing to do when he finds himself not only watching a woman taking a bath but going a step further and making inquiries about her. When he discovers that she is the daughter of Eliam and the wife of Uriah, he sends for her and sleeps with her. Is that because he knows that Eliam and Uriah are away fighting the Ammonites?

In a parenthetical aside, the narrator informs the reader that, at the time, Uriah's wife "was purifying herself after her period" (11:4). In other words, conception is likely, and there is no possibility that the child is Uriah's. Sometime later, the woman informs David that she is pregnant. Thus, the cover-up begins.

11:6–15. The Murder. David sends for Uriah in hopes that he will come home, sleep with his wife, and return to the front none the wiser. Uriah, however, frustrates David's cover-up. Not only does he not sleep with his wife;[19] he does not even go to his house. When David asks why, he responds:

> The ark and Israel and Judah remain in booths; and my lord Joab and the servants of my lord are camping in the open field; shall I then go to my house, to eat and to drink, and to lie with my wife? As you live, and as your soul lives, I will not do such a thing (11:11).

Not only does Uriah's integrity spoil David's plans, it further demonstrates just how shameful and disgraceful David's actions have been. Out of a sense of duty, Uriah refuses to engage in behavior that he has every right to engage in; he refuses to go

[19] In the OT, washing one's feet is sometimes a euphemism for sexual relations.

home, eat and drink, and sleep with his wife. But David has remained at home, eaten and drunk his fill, and slept with another man's wife. How ironic!

In the end, David resorts to murder to cover up his adultery; Uriah is sacrificed to cover up his own shame. But as we shall see in next week's reading, the LORD does not allow David to get away with it; everything he has done is brought to light. Moreover, even though the LORD forgives David, his life is never the same again. His family becomes so dysfunctional that it becomes a constant source of pain and strife until the day he dies. David's son Amnon rapes his half-sister Tamar (2 Sam 13:1–22), and Tamar's brother Absalom avenges her shame by killing Amnon (12:23–36). Absalom usurps his father's throne (15:1–12), and in an exceedingly shameful act, he sleeps with his father's concubines within the sight of the people of Israel (16:20–23). The words that David intoned at the funeral of Saul and Jonathan apply to him as well, "How the mighty have fallen!" (2 Sam 1:19, Prop 8).

Suggestions for Lectors

Today's episode consists of an introduction (11:1) followed by three scenes (11:2–5, 6–13, 14–15). Pause for a full second between each of these sections. The whole episode is dramatic, so read with energy, dramatic pauses, and changes in tempo and tone of voice. In short, employ all the techniques of a good storyteller.

In the introduction, the last sentence should be emphasized because the trouble David gets himself into is a direct result of his having *remained at Jerusalem.*

In the first scene, the parenthetical expression is not just a bit of inconsequential trivia (7:4b); instead, it serves an important rhetorical function. It foreshadows Bathsheba's pregnancy, while at the same time, it removes any doubts that the child to be conceived is David's. By interrupting the narrative flow to offer this information, the narrator draws the reader deeper into the story. In effect, the narrator is establishing a relationship with his audience by inviting them into his confidence. So when you come to the parenthetical aside, drop your voice and read it in a conspiratorial tone, as though you are letting your listeners in on a secret. Just like in the first scene, the last sentence of the second scene should be emphasized: *I am pregnant* (11:5). Pause before embarking on the third scene.

In the third scene, David's duplicity and dishonesty stand in marked contrast to the innocence and integrity of Uriah. When David talks to Uriah, he is feigning curiosity and interest, whereas Uriah's responses are straightforward and honest. Bring each of these qualities out by modifying your tone of voice. As the scene progresses and David's attempts to cover up his actions are thwarted, his fear and agitation increase. Again, bring this out in your reading.

In the final scene, Uriah is ignorant regarding the contents of the letter he is being asked to carry. So when you read David's message to Joab, do so in a quiet voice as though you are sharing something that is private and not to be shared with others.

Pronunciation Guide

Ammonites (AM-uhn-īts), *Bathsheba* (bath-SHEE-buh), *Eliam* (ee-LĪ-uhm), *Hittite* (HIH-tīt), *Israel* (IZ-ree-uhl; -ray-), *Jerusalem* (juh-ROO-suh-luhm), *Joab* (JOH-ab), *Judah* (JOO-duh), *Rabbah* (RAB-uh), *Uriah* (yoo-RĪ-ah)

2 KINGS 4:42–44

Commentary

Elisha son of Shaphat was a prophet who was active in the northern kingdom of Israel in the mid- to late-ninth century B.C. Elisha's name means *my God is salvation*, and his stories are found in 1 Kings 19:19–21 and 2 Kings 2–9, 13:14–21. Elisha and his predecessor, Elijah, are sometimes referred to as *signs* prophets since they are remembered primarily for the signs and wonders they perform, in contrast to the *writing* prophets—figures like Isaiah, Jeremiah, Micah, Amos, etc.—who are primarily remembered for their words. In today's brief episode, Elisha performs a miracle on par with Jesus' feeding of the five thousand, which is the only one of Jesus's miracles that is recorded in all four gospels (Matt 14:13–21; Mark 6:30–44; Luke 9:10–17; John 6:1–14, Prop 12).

Today's miraculous multiplication of barley ears and loaves follows on the heels of another food-related miracle. In 2 Kings 4:38, a famine has descended upon the land, and food is scarce. Elisha and the guild of prophets make a startling discovery. The stew they have made has been accidentally contaminated by poisonous gourds. To throw the stew out would be to go hungry, but to eat the stew would be death. Elisha salvages the situation by miraculously purifying the stew with a handful of flour.

4:42–44. In today's reading, food continues to be scarce. Fortunately, a unnamed man brings his offering of first fruits to Elisha and his disciples. This is unusual because the first fruits of one's harvest belonged to God, and they were to be taken to the temple and consumed by the priests (Lev 23:20; Num 18:13; Deut 18:4–5). This is one of the ways in which the Levitical priests were provided for. The fact that this man brings his first fruits to Elisha indicates that he regards the temple in Israel to be corrupt and that he considers Elisha to be a genuine man of God. Unfortunately, because of the famine, the first fruits he has to offer are not enough to feed Elisha and all those under his care. Nevertheless, Elisha instructs his servant to place the offering before everyone, and the word of the LORD comes to pass. Not only did everyone have their fill, there was also some left over.

Suggestions for Lectors

Today's episode is quite brief, so make sure your listeners are settled in before you begin. In fact, after you introduce the reading, you may want to pause for a bit longer than normal.

This brief episode has three sections: background (4:42a), dialogue (4:42b–43), and conclusion (4:44). The introduction concludes with *in his sack*. Pause for a full second between each of these sections; this will help lengthen the reading. In the dialogue, use two different tones of voice for Elisha and his servant. Elisha has complete confidence in the Lord's ability to provide, so his words can be spoken in a straightforward, matter-of-fact, yet firm manner.

The final verse deserves special treatment since it climactically narrates the fulfillment of Elijah's extraordinary pronouncement. Instead of reading the three actions—*set*, *ate*, and *had some left*, as though they are three separate items in a sequence, transform the last two into a single phrase by removing the comma before *and*. Then, introduce a pause after *them* and before *according to*. These changes are illustrated as follows: *He set it before them,… they ate and had some left,… according to the word of the Lord.* As you read the concluding phrase, drop your voice and slow your tempo.

Pronunciation Guide
Baal-shalishah (bayl-SHAL-i-shuh), *Elisha* (ee-LĪ-shuh; ih-)

EPHESIANS 3:14–21

Notes
Sequence. 3 of 7

Commentary
In last week's reading, Paul reminded the Gentile Christians in Ephesus about what God has done for them through the life and death of his Son. Because of Jesus, the dividing wall of hostility that separated Jews and Gentiles has been torn down. By God's grace, Gentiles have been drawn into relationship with God and God's people by faith alone and not by the works of the law. Since the beginning of creation, God's vision for humanity has been for it to grow into a diverse, yet united, people of God, populated with persons "from every tribe and language and people and nation" (Rev 5:9). This vision, however, has remained a mystery; that is, it has remained undisclosed until the time of Christ. As Paul writes:

> In former generations this mystery was not made known to humankind, as it has now been revealed to his holy apostles and prophets by the Spirit: that is, the Gentiles have become fellow heirs, members of the same body, and sharers in the promise in Christ Jesus through the gospel (Eph 3:5–6, Epi).

For Paul, this mystery offers just a glimpse into how incomprehensible and immeasurable the grace and love of God is. In today's reading, Paul is so overcome by God's vision for humanity, both Jew and Gentile, that he moves into prayer and worship.

3:14–19. When Paul writes that every family in heaven and on earth takes its name from the Father, he is saying that all the people and people groups of the world—not just Israel—derive their existence and identity from the God and Father of Jesus Christ. In short, Paul wants Gentile Christians to know that they are not second-class citizens in the kingdom of God; they are God's beloved children just as much as their Jewish brothers and sisters in Christ. Paul's prayer for them and for all Christians is that they may come to experience and rely upon the power of the indwelling Holy Spirit who roots and grounds them in the rich soil of the love that God has for them. Paul also prays that they may be granted the ability to plumb the depths of God's love, to comprehend all the dimensions of God's love, "the breadth and length and height and depth" (3:18b).

3:20–21. Enraptured by the beauty, grandeur, and scope of God's love and salvation, Paul concludes with a doxology. In it, he reminds his readers that God's power, which is at work within us through the Holy Spirit, is able to accomplish far greater things than anything we might ask for, let alone imagine. All that is left is for us to worship, praise, and give thanks to God.

Suggestions for Lectors
Today's reading is a prayer, so it should be prayed, not simply read. The best way to deliver a communal prayer is to make it a personal prayer, and the best way to make a prayer personal is to pray it over and over again. So as you prepare, do not simply practice reading today's passage, pray it until it becomes your prayer, for you, for your church, and for the world. Pick out those elements, those words and phrases, that you feel called to emphasize, and pray with reverence, gratitude, and conviction.

Pronunciation Guide
Ephesians (eh-FEE-zhuhnz; ih-)

John 6:1–21

Notes
Sequence. 1 of 5

Commentary
The only miracle of Jesus recorded in all four gospels is his feeding of the five thousand. In John, this feeding becomes the background and context for Jesus' Bread of Life discourse, which extends from 6:22–71 and from which we will read for the next four Sundays. In John, the feeding of the five thousand does not just demonstrate Jesus' miraculous abilities, it is also a sign that points to Jesus as the one who is able to give life to the world.

6:1–4. The first episode opens with Jesus and his disciples retreating to the other side of the Sea of Galilee, that is, to the eastern side of the sea opposite Galilee. Jesus is trying to get away from the crowds for a brief period of rest and refreshment. Unfortunately, the crowds are persistent, and they follow him.

6:5–9. When Jesus sees the crowd approaching, he poses the problem of food to Philip, who happens to be the first disciple Jesus ever recruited (1:43, Epi 2). Here, and in contrast to the Synoptic accounts (cf. Mark 6:35–37), Jesus' question is presented as a test, for he already knows how he intends to rectify the situation. Two of his disciples respond. Philip emphasizes the level of need, "Six months' wages would not buy enough bread for each of them to get a little" (6:7), while Peter emphasizes the scarcity of their resources, "There is a boy here who has five barley loaves and two fish. But what are they among so many people?" (6:9). Though they have seen Jesus do some amazing things, neither can conceive of how their meager resources could be stretched to meet so great a demand.

6:10–13. The abundance of green grass foreshadows the abundance of food that Jesus is about to produce. It also resonates with the opening lines of Psalm 23:

> The LORD is my shepherd, I shall not want.
> He makes me lie down in *green pastures* (23:1–2).

Jesus takes the five barley loaves and the two fish, and after giving thanks for what they have, he shares the loaves and fish with the crowd. Miraculously, not only is there enough food for everyone, but there is enough food for everyone to get their fill. This is not just a meal; it is a banquet. Later on in the gospel, at his arrest, Jesus says, "I did not lose a single one of those whom you gave me" (18:9). Here, he insists that the leftover fragments be gathered up "so that nothing may be lost" (6:12). God may be extravagant, but he is not wasteful.

6:14–15. The episode concludes with the crowd's reaction to what has just taken place. This banquet of bread has afforded them a glimpse into who Jesus is. They exclaim, "This indeed is the prophet who is to come into the world" (6:14; cf. 7:40). In the first century, one of the expectations regarding the messiah was that he would be a prophet like Moses, Israel's first great liberator. As Moses said before the Israelites entered the Promised Land, "The LORD your God will raise up for you a prophet like me from among your own people; you shall heed such a prophet" (Deut 18:15). This Moses-like prophet would usher in the messianic age, and one of the signs that was to signal its arrival was a recurrence of manna from heaven. In fact, in next week's reading, the crowd asks Jesus for a sign, saying, "Our ancestors ate the manna in the wilderness; as it is written, 'He gave them bread from heaven to eat'" (6:30). Yet, in their excitement and zeal, the crowd seeks to make Jesus king by force, and so he withdraws by himself.

6:16–21. That evening, after the people have dispersed, the disciples set out in a boat to make the return journey to Capernaum on the western shore. Rough weather and sea conditions hinder their progress. In the middle of the night and in the middle of the sea, they become startled when they behold a figure coming toward them walking on the sea. It is Jesus, and as he nears the boat, he attempts to calm their fears by declaring, "It is I; do not be afraid" (6:20). Apparently, this does the trick, for the disciples want to take him in the boat. When they do, they find that the boat has suddenly and quite miraculously arrived at its intended destination.

This scene has all the hallmarks of an OT theophany. Walking upon the sea is a divine prerogative and is only ever predicated of God. Moreover, Jesus' declaration, "It is I," could also be translated, "I am," which recalls the incident of the burning bush when God reveals himself and his name to Moses. "God said to Moses, 'I AM WHO I AM.'… Thus you shall say to the Israelites, 'I AM has sent me to you'" (Exod 3:14). While the crowds believe that Jesus is the prophet like Moses, Jesus reveals himself to his disciples, not as Moses, but as the LORD—the God who made himself known to Moses.

Suggestions for Lectors

Feeding the Five Thousand, 6:1–15. The Feeding of the Five Thousand is one of the most familiar stories in the Bible; it is the only miracle that is recorded in all four gospels. It could be read as a straightforward narrative with no particular emphasis; but imagine that you are telling this story to an audience who has never heard it before and, like the disciples, has no idea what Jesus intends to do. How might this affect your telling of the story? Where would the drama be, and how would you present it?

These are just a few of the questions to consider when you are assigned such a familiar narrative.

If you have never heard this story before, the real drama begins when Jesus tells the disciples, *Make the people sit down* (6:10). Up to this point, you can read using your normal tempo and expressiveness as a narrator. Once the crowd is seated, the tone of the story changes. Things become quiet and time slows down as the crowds and the disciples, and even your listeners, wait with bated breath to see what is going to happen next. At this point, drop your voice, and read slowly and deliberately as you describe each movement Jesus makes: *took*, *had given thanks*, and *distributed* (6:11). Do not let your reading drag, but convey a sense of mystery and anticipation. Pause for a second after *so also the fish*, and then slowly but with emphasis read *as <u>much</u> as they wanted* (6:11). Pause again afterwards before continuing.

One of the recurrent motifs in John's gospel concerns Jesus not losing those who belong to God. Later in John 6, Jesus says, "This is the will of him who sent me, that I should *lose* nothing of all that he has given me, but raise it up on the last day" (6:39). Then, later in the gospel, Jesus prays, "I protected them in your name that you have given me. I guarded them, and not one of them was *lost* except the one destined to be lost" (17:12). Given this "lostness" motif, Jesus' instructions in 6:12 deserve to be emphasized, *Gather up the fragments left over, so that nothing may be <u>lost</u>.* Afterwards return to your normal narrating voice to finish off the feeding episode. Stress the number of baskets of leftovers they collected, *twelve* (6:13). Then, read the people's declaration with amazement and excitement. Pause for a second or two after 6:15, before proceeding with the walking-on-the-sea episode.

Walking Upon the Sea, 6:16–21. In John, the account of Jesus' walking upon the sea is not as long or as dramatic as the parallel accounts in Matthew and Mark; nevertheless, it is still dramatic.

Begin the episode in your normal narrative style. Become slightly animated as you read, *It was now dark* (6:17) and slightly more animated when you read, *the sea became rough…* (6:18). Then, in the middle of 6:19, drop your voice, slow your tempo, and convey a sense of confusion and fear as you read, *they saw Jesus walking on the sea and coming near the boat.* Then, with a raised voice proclaim, *It is I, do not be afraid* (1:20). Pause for a second or two afterwards to let these words sink in, then conclude the reading in your normal narrating voice.

Pronunciation Guide

Capernaum (kuh-PER-nay-uhm, -nuh-)
Galilee (GAL-uh-lee)
Tiberias (tī-BIHR-ee-uhs)

PROPER 13

July 31–August 6

2 Samuel 11:26–12:13a	Exodus 16:2–4, 9–15
Psalm 51:1–12 (= 51:1–13 BCP)	Psalm 78:23–29
Ephesians 4:1–16	Ephesians 4:1–16
John 6:24–35	John 6:24–35

2 Samuel 11:26–12:13a

Notes

Sequence. 6 of 7

Commentary

Today's reading presents one of the most well-known, dramatic episodes in all of biblical literature, as the prophet Nathan confronts King David regarding his adultery with Bathsheba and his murder of her husband Uriah. On display are Nathan's wisdom as well as his love for David as is evidenced by the fact that he does not accuse David directly. Had Nathan taken this approach, David's defenses would surely have been aroused, making it much less likely that he would have acknowledged his guilt and expressed any genuine remorse.

11:26–27. Last week's reading from 2 Samuel 11 recounted the story of David's adultery and his attempts to cover it up, which culminate in Uriah's death. Today's reading begins with one final intrigue as he ushers Bathsheba into his house and marries her in an attempt to hide the fact that his child was conceived illegitimately. David's cover-up might have been successful had it not been for the fact that "the thing that David had done displeased the LORD" (11:27b).

12:1–6. The LORD sends the prophet Nathan to confront David with his sin. Instead of accusing David, Nathan lays a trap by telling a story and asking David, in his role as king, to adjudicate the matter. As expected, David's anger and righteous indignation are aroused by such obvious injustice. David deems the rich man worthy of death and declares that he make a fourfold restitution.

12:7–12. Nathan's next words are succinct and to the point, "You are the man!" (12:7), and with these words David's world comes crashing down. Nathan lays out the LORD's case against David along with the severe consequences that will follow, not least that David's family will become so dysfunctional as to be a constant source of pain and strife until the day he dies. The following chapters begin to bear this out as David's son Amnon rapes his half-sister Tamar (13:1–22), and Tamar's brother Absalom avenges her shame by killing Amnon (12:23–36). Eventually, Absalom usurps his father's throne (15:1–12), and in an exceedingly shameful act, he sleeps with his father's concubines within the sight of the people of Israel (16:20–23). This brings to fulfillment the LORD's pronouncements in 12:11–12, which conclude with, "For you did it secretly; but I will do this thing before all Israel."

12:13a. In the end, David acknowledges his sin in what appears to be genuine remorse. Following today's reading, Nathan assures David that David himself will not die, though his unborn child will. This demonstrates that the forgiveness of sins does not necessarily preclude the consequences of sin. Here one is reminded of Exodus 34:7, where the LORD is described as "forgiving iniquity and transgression and sin, yet by no means clearing the guilty, but visiting the iniquity of the parents upon the children and the children's children."

Suggestions for Lectors

2 Samuel 11:26–27a provides the background for the story that follows so read it with your normal narrating voice, pausing after *and bore him a son* as a prelude to announcing the LORD's displeasure at David's behavior. In 12:1b–4, the prophet Nathan is setting a trap for David. He masks his intentions by relating this matter to David as though he were simply seeking the king's sage advice. Consequently, you may wish to tell this story in a decidedly calm, unemotional, and straightforward manner. Then, as you say, *As the LORD lives* (12:5b–6), convey David's sense of righteous indignation by intensifying and strengthening your voice.

Though your listeners probably know what is coming next, take care not spring the trap too soon; so, pause briefly after *he had no pity* (12:6b) and then introduce a fuller pause before Nathan announces to David loudly and clearly, *You are the man!* (12:7a). You may also wish to pause and look up at your listeners before proceeding with Nathan's judgment. At this point, Nathan is speaking to David on behalf of the LORD, but read as though you are the LORD and speaking directly to David. Imagine that David is a person after your own heart (1 Sam 13:14) or that David is your own son (2 Sam 7:14), and then try to convey your mixed emotions, ranging from love to disappointment, frustration and grief to anger. After Nathan concludes with *and before the sun* (12:12), pause for a second or two and look up at your audience, giving David (and your listeners) time to let it all sink in.

In 12:13, David's repentance is genuine, as Nathan's immediate absolution indicates; so speak these words with the appropriate hint of sorrow and remorse, not as someone who is attempting to avoid punishment but as someone who suddenly sees their sin and accepts full responsibility for their actions. Nathan's statement, *The LORD has put away your sin; you shall not die,* could be conveyed with a mixture of compassion and sadness, as it must be followed with the announcement that David's sin will, nevertheless, not go unpunished. Pause again briefly before 12:15.

Pronunciation Guide

Ammonites (AM-uhn-īts), *Hittite* (HIH-tīt), *Nathan* (NAY-thuhn),
Saul (SAWL; rhymes with Paul), *Uriah* (yoo-RĪ-ah)

EXODUS 16:2–4, 9–15

Commentary

At a critical juncture in their exodus from Egypt, the Israelites found themselves backed up against the Red Sea, hemmed in by Pharaoh's army with no obvious means of escape. In fear, they cried out to the LORD, saying to Moses:

> Was it because there were no graves in Egypt that you have taken us away to die in the wilderness? What have you done to us, bringing us out of Egypt? Is this not the very thing we told you in Egypt, "Let us alone and let us serve the Egyptians"? For it would have been better for us to serve the Egyptians than to die in the wilderness (Exod 14:11–12, EastVig).

Moses told them not to fear, that the LORD would deliver them from the Egyptians, which he did by leading them to safety through the parted waters of the Red Sea.

Given their miraculous escape from Egypt, one might assume that the Israelites would never complain again. It soon becomes clear, however, that grumbling and complaining are to be their way of life for the next forty years until they reach the Promised Land. In today's reading, God's people complain of hunger.

16:2–3. It has been one full month since the Israelites left Egypt (16:1; cf. 12:6, 17–18). They have been traveling through the wilderness in stages, making their way to Mount Sinai where the LORD first encountered Moses in the burning bush (Exod 3). In today's reading, hunger pangs prevent the people from appreciating their newfound freedom. They complain to Moses and Aaron, arguing that death in Egypt would have been preferable to dying of hunger in the wilderness. Though they were slaves in Egypt, at least they had their fill of meat and bread.

16:4. Their memory about life in Egypt is selective and exaggerated. Nevertheless, the LORD informs Moses of his plans to satisfy his people's hunger.

16:9–15. Though mention is made of meat in the evening and bread in the morning, the emphasis in the narrative is upon the bread from heaven for two reasons. First, the quail flown in for the evening meal only happens twice, once in today's reading and again later when the people are fed up with eating manna (Num 11). Second, the bread from heaven will fall six days a week for the next forty years. Thus, the manna will become the one constant in their lives, a daily reminder that the LORD provides what they need.

Centuries later, when Jesus teaches his disciples to pray, "Give us this day our daily bread" (Matt 6:11), he is alluding to this daily provision of manna that sustained God's people throughout their entire wilderness sojourn.

Suggestions for Lectors

Today's reading is primarily driven by direct speech in which the speakers and audiences are constantly changing: the Israelites complain to Moses and Aaron (16:3); the LORD speaks to Moses and Aaron (16:4); Moses speaks to Aaron (16:9); the LORD speaks to Moses (16:12); the Israelites ask a question, and Moses answers it (16:15). As you read, keep in mind who is speaking and to whom and be aware of the emotions the speakers are feeling and adjust your voice accordingly.

For example, when the people lodge their complaints with Moses and Aaron, elevate your voice. Similarly, when Moses and Aaron respond to the people, speak with an elevated voice, not only to convey their frustration, but also to convey the fact that they are speaking to a large crowd. Of course as lectors, we would not shout these words, but elevating our voice conveys to our listeners what is going on in the scene. Conversely, when the LORD speaks to Moses and Aaron, drop your voice back down to its normal volume and pitch since this is a private, one-on-one conversation.

When you come to the final line of the reading, *It is the bread that the LORD has given you to eat* (16:15), imagine that this statement was written expressly for your listeners. Pause for a second before *It is*, look up at your listeners, and then deliver these words slowly and deliberately. Emphasize *bread* and *the LORD* and perhaps *you.*

Pronunciation Guide
Aaron (AIR-uhn), *Egypt* (EE-jipt), *Israelites* (IZ-ree-līts), *Moses* (MOH-zuhs)

EPHESIANS 4:1–16

Notes
Sequence. 4 of 7

Commentary
In the last two readings from Ephesians (Prop 11–12), Paul has focused upon what God has done to restore fallen humanity. Through the life, death, and resurrection of his beloved Son, God has not only reconciled humanity to himself, he has also cleared the ground for reconciliation between diverse members of the human race, turning enemies and strangers into brothers and sisters "in the household of God" (2:19). In particular, Paul has shown how God has torn down the wall of hostility between Jews and Gentiles, thereby creating "one new humanity in place of the two" (2:15).

This is the mystery that was revealed to Paul when the Lord commissioned him to be the apostle to the Gentiles (3:1–3).

> In former generations this mystery was not made known to humankind, as it has now been revealed to his holy apostles and prophets by the Spirit: that is, the Gentiles have become fellow heirs, members of the same body, and sharers in the promise in Christ Jesus through the gospel (3:5–6, Epi).

Having argued that Jews and Gentiles are now members of the same household, Paul now turns his attention to how that household is to function, in all its unity and all its diversity.

4:1–6. The Ephesian church is made up of both Jewish Christians and Gentile Christians, and so it stands as a living monument to what God has done to reconcile human beings to one another. Paul enjoins the Ephesians to work to maintain the unity and peace that God has already established through the Son and the Spirit.

There is not a gospel for Jews and a gospel for Gentiles, any more than there is one god for the Jews and another god for the Gentiles. Instead, there is just one God and one gospel. The one God is the Father and Lord of *all* people, Jew and Gentile alike. Likewise, there is one faith by which all people are saved. Throughout his letters, Paul insists upon Christian unity because, for Paul, the body of Christ is to be a reflection and an embodiment of the oneness of God and of the salvation offered through the gospel.

4:7–13. That being said, Christ's body also exhibits an important measure of diversity. In Christ, we are all one, but we are not all the same. The different members of God's household have different roles and responsibilities because God has equipped his children for different ministries. As Paul writes in first Corinthians,

> Just as the body is one and has many members, and all the members of the body, though many, are one body, so it is with Christ. For in the one Spirit we were all baptized into one body—Jews or Greeks, slaves or free—and we were all made to drink of one Spirit (1 Cor 12:12–13).

In 1 Corinthians 12, Paul lists the varieties of spiritual gifts. Yet here in Ephesians, he is content with identifying those who are called to equip others to carry out the work of ministry. For Paul, apostles, prophets, evangelists, pastors, and teachers are not the only persons called and equipped for ministry; *every* Christian is called to participate actively in what God is doing in the world. That is why *every* Christian receives the Holy Spirit and spiritual gifts. Those singled out here have been given the particular task of helping the church reach Christian unity and maturity so that it is able to carry out its mission as Christ's body in the world.

4:14–16. One of the marks of a mature Christian is stability in the faith. Mature Christians are so grounded in the truth about God and Christ that they are not taken in by fashionable teachings or by false teachers. Instead, they guard and live out what they have learned from the apostles, prophets, evangelists, pastors, and teachers. Of course, being grounded in the Christian faith is not simply about believing the right things (though it certainly includes that!). It is also about growing as the community of faith; it is about working together in ministry and service in such a way that that the body grows and matures in the seedbed of truth and love.

Suggestions for Lectors

As reflected in the Commentary, today's reading can be divided into three sections: 1–6, 7–13, 14–16. Pause for a second or two between sections.

In the first section (4:1–6), Paul *begs* his readers to live into their calling, so read with a sense of urgency and fervency in your voice. In 4:4–6a, emphasize the repeated use of *one*, and in 4:6b, emphasize the prepositions: *above*, *through*, and *in*.

In the middle of the second section (4:7–13), verses 9 and 10 constitute a digression so read them in a lower voice. In 4:11, emphasize the repeated use of *some*, and in 4:12, emphasize *equip* and *building up*.

In the third section (4:14–16), emphasize the phrases that contain the word *love*: *speaking the truth <u>in love</u>* (4:15) and *in building itself up <u>in love</u>* (4:16).

Pronunciation Guide

Ephesians (eh-FEE-zhuhnz; ih-)

JOHN 6:24–35

Notes

Sequence. 2 of 5

Commentary

In last week's gospel reading, Jesus fed a crowd of thousands with just a handful of loaves and a couple of fish. The crowd interprets this miraculous banquet as a sign, and they intend to take Jesus by force and make him king. Jesus prevents this from happening by withdrawing by himself. Later that night, Jesus and his disciples make their escape and return to the western shore of the Sea of Galilee. The disciples go by boat, but Jesus walks upon the sea. In today's reading, the crowd goes looking for Jesus.

6:24–29. When they eventually find him in Capernaum, they ask him about how and when he arrived, for they know that he had not departed with his disciples in the boat (6:22). Instead of answering their question, Jesus questions their motivations. The feeding of the five thousand was not just a miracle, it was a sign that pointed to who Jesus really was. The crowd, however, seems to be motivated more by the miracle and the desire to eat their fill again. Jesus warns them about focusing all their energies upon things that are transitory in nature. Instead of working for food that spoils, they should work for food that lasts forever. The crowd then asks what this involves. What sort of work does this entail? Very simply, the work that God requires is to believe in the one whom God has sent.

6:30–35. If that is true, then the crowd wants some evidence, some confirmation that Jesus is in fact the one whom God has sent. So they ask him to perform a sign. Not only that, they already have a specific sign in mind, one that fits their preconceived notions of what the messiah would be and do. As was discussed in last week's Commentary, Jewish expectations regarding the messiah included the view that the messiah would be a prophet like Moses (Deut 18:15–18), who would liberate God's people and usher in God's kingdom. One of the signs that the messiah would perform was to cause manna to rain down from heaven once again. If Jesus did that, then they would certainly believe in him.

Jesus, however, corrects them. In truth, it was not Moses who fed the Israelites in the wilderness but God. Moreover, the bread that God now offers is far superior to the manna that fell from heaven because this bread is able to give life to the world.

Here, Jesus' description of the bread from heaven parallels his earlier description of the living water. In his conversation with the Samaritan woman, Jesus says, "Those who drink of the water that I will give them will never be thirsty. The water that I will give will become in them a spring of water gushing up to eternal life" (4:14). In reply, the woman says, "Sir, give me this water, so that I may never be thirsty or have to keep coming here to draw water" (4:15). In today's reading, the people make a similar request: "Sir, give us this bread always" (6:34). Today's reading concludes with a declaration that draws these two metaphors together: "I am the bread of life. Whoever comes to me will never be hungry, and whoever believes in me will never be thirsty" (6:35). As we shall see in next week's reading, the living bread that Jesus has to give is his life (6:51). The living water is the Holy Spirit (7:37–39, ✠ PentVig).

Suggestions for Lectors

Today's reading is driven by the back and forth exchange between the crowds and Jesus. Adopt a different manner of speech for each character. For the crowds, raise the pitch of your voice and speak with energy and intensity. For Jesus, lower the pitch of your voice, but still speak with energy and intensity. You might also deliver the crowd's lines at a faster pace, and Jesus' at a normal or slower pace. Emphasize the statements Jesus makes in 6:29 and 6:33.

In the concluding verse, you have an option. On the one hand, you can emphasize Jesus' being the bread of life by stressing the first person pronouns, as in: *I am the bread of life. Whoever comes to me will never be hungry, and whoever believes in me will never be thirsty* (6:35). On the other hand, you can emphasize who Jesus is and what needs he satisfies, as in: *I am the bread of life. Whoever comes to me will never be hungry, and whoever believes in me will never be thirsty*. With each option, you might also emphasize the two *nevers*.

Pronunciation Guide

Capernaum (kuh-PER-nay-uhm, -nuh-)

PROPER 14

August 7–13

2 Samuel 18:5–9, 15, 31–33	1 Kings 19:4–8
Psalm 130	Psalm 34:1–8
Ephesians 4:25–5:2	Ephesians 4:25–5:2
John 6:35, 41–51	John 6:35, 41–51

2 Samuel 18:5–9, 15, 31–33

Notes

Sequence. 7 of 7

Commentary

David had no idea of the whirlwind he would reap as a result of sleeping with Bathsheba and then having her husband killed. His acts of adultery and murder were like opening Pandora's box. In last week's reading, the prophet Nathan confronted David and delivered this word from the LORD:

> The sword shall never depart from your house.... I will raise up trouble against you from within your own house; and I will take your wives before your eyes, and give them to your neighbor, and he shall lie with your wives in the sight of this very sun. For you did it secretly; but I will do this thing before all Israel, and before the sun (2 Sam 12:10–12).

And so it comes to pass. David's son Amnon rapes his half-sister Tamar (13:1–22), and Tamar's brother Absalom avenges her shame by killing his half-brother Amnon (12:23–36). Then, as background to today's reading, Absalom instigates a rebellion in an attempt to wrest the kingdom from his father David. Absalom garners support and has himself declared king in Hebron, where David first reigned as king (2 Sam 2:1–11). Eventually, Absalom has David on the run, and he takes control of Jerusalem. Then, in an exceedingly shameful act, Absalom sleeps with his father's concubines within the sight of the people (16:20–23), thereby fulfilling the word of the LORD.

18:5–9, 15. In today's reading, King David and his men are preparing for battle with Absalom and the Israelites who are loyal to him. Before David sends his three commanders into battle, he implores them, "Deal gently for my sake with the young man Absalom" (18:5). Everybody hears the command, but nobody listens. For when Joab and his armor-bearers come upon a helpless and defenseless Absalom stuck in a tree, they slaughter him.

18:31–33. A Cushite runner brings good news to David; the rebellion has been suppressed. But when David receives the news of Absalom's fate, he can only grieve. He is a broken, broken man.

Suggestions for Lectors

Today, you are a storyteller, and the story you have to tell is tragic. Although today's episode recounts the death of Absalom, it is really about his father. David only appears on the fringes of the story, nevertheless he is the focal point. He is distraught and beside himself over Absalom, but no one shares his concerns. He remains alone in his anxiety and alone in his grief. So while David only appears in the opening and closing scenes, read the whole episode from his perspective. Read it as if you were David recounting the death of his son, Absalom.

For the lector, the most challenging part of today's reading comes at the very end when David expresses the depth of his anguish and grief. As lectors, we want to express emotion, but it is not always easy to convey great depth of feeling. So practice these lines until you are comfortable with your delivery. Increase the volume and intensity of your voice, but do not shout. Instead, convey David's depth of feeling by adjusting the speed; slow down and pause longer for the commas than you normally might.

Pronunciation Guide

Abishai (AB-uh-shī; uh-BĪ-shī), *Absalom* (AB-suh-lahm; -luhm), *Cushite* (KUSH-īt), *Ephraim* (EE-free-uhm), *Israel* (IZ-ree-uhl; -ray-), *Ittai* (IT-ī), *Joab* (JOH-ab)

1 KINGS 19:4–8

Commentary

In 1 Kings 18:20–46, Elijah wins a contest against the prophets of Baal on Mt. Carmel in the northern kingdom of Israel. Elijah demonstrates that it is the LORD (i.e., Yahweh) who is truly God and not Baal. Afterwards, all four hundred and fifty of the prophets of Baal are seized and executed. These defeated prophets were in the royal service of Queen Jezebel—the wife of King Ahab, the king of Israel. So, when

Jezebel learns of their fate, she puts out a contract on Elijah's life. She sends word to Elijah, saying, "So may the gods to do me, and more also, if I do not make your life like the life of one of them by this time tomorrow" (19:2). When Elijah receives Jezebel's murderous threats, he fears for his life, and he leaves the northern kingdom of Israel and makes his way to Beersheba, in the southern kingdom of Judah.

19:4–8. Leaving his servant behind, Elijah makes a day's journey alone into the wilderness where he collapses from stress and exhaustion and begs the LORD to take his life away. Instead of granting his request, the angel of the LORD provides Elijah with nourishment. On the strength of his second meal, he travels for forty days and forty nights until he arrives at Mt. Horeb (a.k.a., Mt. Sinai), the mountain of God. This is the same mountain around which Israel camped following the Exodus from Egypt and the same mountain on which the LORD revealed himself to Moses through the burning bush (Exod 3:1–6).

It is here, following today's reading, that Elijah will encounter the LORD, not in the wind, nor in the earthquake, nor in the fire, but in the sound of sheer silence, in the sound of a still small voice (1 Kings 19:12).

Suggestions for Lectors

In today's reading, the confident Elijah of 1 Kings 18 has been replaced by a fearful, distraught Elijah. His successful contest with the prophets of Baal has taken all of his energy and strength. He is now so mentally, emotionally, and physically exhausted that he is experiencing a severe let down in his faith. When Elijah cries out, *O LORD, take away my life* (19:4), he is not being overdramatic; he is genuinely depressed and afraid, so reflect this in your delivery. In contrast, as the angel of the LORD, let your voice possess a calming and rejuvenating quality.

Pronunciation Guide

Elijah (ee-LĪ-juh; ih-), *Horeb* (HOR-uhb, HOH-reb)

EPHESIANS 4:25–5:2

Notes

Sequence. 5 of 7

Commentary

In Paul's letters, theology precedes and prepares for ethics. That is, before Paul instructs his readers on how they should live their lives, he first instructs them in the fundamentals of Christian theology. He writes about who God is, what God has done, and who we are because of who God is and what God has done. For example in Romans 6, Paul spends the first ten verses of the chapter talking about our identity as those who have died and been raised with Christ in baptism. Only then does Paul offer instructions on how live lives of righteousness (6:12–15). This pattern of theology followed by ethics is not accidental. It reflects the shape and sequence of the gospel where God's gracious acts of deliverance precede and motivate our faithful response.

Up to this point in Ephesians, Paul has been describing the salvation that God brought about through the life, death, and resurrection of his Son. In particular, he has talked about the new community of God's people that has been called into being. This new community is constituted of people from many different backgrounds, people who, in many cases, do not share the same culture, values, or economic status—differences that present a challenge as Christians attempt to acquire the values of the kingdom of God and learn to live in community with one another. Having argued that God reconciled Jews and Gentiles into one body by tearing down the dividing wall of hostility between them (2:13–16, Prop 11), Paul now instructs them on how to live together in peace. Leading into today's reading, Paul writes:

> You were taught to put away your former way of life, your old self, corrupt and deluded by its lusts, and to be renewed in the spirit of your minds, and to clothe yourselves with the new self, created according to the likeness of God in true righteousness and holiness (4:21–24).

4:25–32. Paul continues in today's reading by offering specifics regarding Christian behavior. Some of his directives, like "putting away falsehood" and "give up stealing" derive from the Ten Commandments, while others are designed to promote peace and unity. For example, while anger is not sinful in and of itself, it can easily lead to a breakdown of community. Unresolved anger offers the devil an opportunity to introduce a divisive spirit into the community. Consequently, Paul instructs his readers not to let the sun go down on their anger. In short, anger between Christians should be dealt with immediately.

The Holy Spirit's role is to establish and preserve unity within Christian communities. Thus, in last week's reading, Paul called upon his readers to make "every effort to maintain the unity of the Spirit in the bond of peace" (4:3). In this context, then, "to grieve the Holy Spirit" likely refers to acting in ways that promote discord and disharmony within the body of Christ.

5:1–2. All of Paul's instructions on how to and how not to behave can be reduced to a single command, "be imitators of God" (5:1). In Christ, God has loved and forgiven us unconditionally; therefore, we ought to relate to others in the same way. To lead lives of unconditional love and forgiveness is to present ourselves as "a fragrant offering and sacrifice to God" (5:2).

Suggestions for Lectors

In today's reading, Paul offers a variety of commands and instructions. Each sentence (not each verse) can stand on its own, so do not move quickly from one sentence to the next. Instead, pause for a second or two longer than you normally would at each period; this will help signal the change in topic for your listeners.

When you come to the concluding, summative commands in 5:1–2, increase the volume and pitch of your voice, and read with more feeling and emotion.

Pronunciation Guide

Ephesians (eh-FEE-zhuhnz; ih-)

JOHN 6:35, 41–51

Notes

Sequence. 3 of 5

Commentary

Today's reading begins the exact same way that last week's reading ended, with Jesus declaring: "I am the bread of life. Whoever comes to me will never be hungry, and whoever believes in me will never be thirsty" (6:35). Here two images that have been presented in the gospel are brought together. In his encounter with the Samaritan woman, Jesus spoke of living water (4:7–15). Later, we learn that the living water is the Holy Spirit (7:37–39, ✠ PentVig). In last week's reading, Jesus spoke about the bread that comes down from heaven and gives life to the world (6:33). Today, we learn that this living bread is Jesus' very own life that he will lay down so that the world might live.

6:35, 41–42. Once Jesus identifies *himself* as the bread of life, controversy erupts. Like the Israelites who grumbled in the wilderness about not having food or about only having manna to eat (Exod 16:2; Num 11:4–6), so here "the Jews" grumble about Jesus claiming to have come down from heaven. After all, they know who this Jesus is; they know his family and where he comes from.

Who are "the Jews"? At this point, it would be prudent to offer some clarification regarding the use of the designation, *the Jews*, in the Gospel of John. In John, *the Jews* is very often used in a specialized sense to designate Jesus' opponents. In other words, *the Jews* does not generally refer to the Jewish people as a whole. Jesus is Jewish, his disciples are Jewish, and almost every character in the gospel is Jewish. Nevertheless, the author of John uses *the Jews* in a more restricted sense to refer to those who challenge and oppose Jesus. If we fail to recognize this specialized use of *the Jews*, then we can come away from John's gospel with a very distorted picture of both the Jewish people and the gospel.

6:43–46. When the Israelites grumbled against Moses and Aaron, Moses redirected their attention to God. "Your complaining is not against us but against *the LORD*" (Exod 16:8). Jesus employs the same strategy here. If Jesus' detractors wish to challenge his extraordinary claims, then they must take the matter up with the Father, who sent him. According to Jesus, if they wish to be taught by God, they must entertain the possibility that he is not only the son of Joseph, but the very Son of God. As the incarnate Son of God, Jesus is the only person who has ever seen the Father, and, therefore, he is the only person who can make the Father known.

6:47–51. Those who put their trust in Jesus will partake of the bread he has to offer. This bread is far superior to the manna that appeared day after day for forty years in the wilderness. As miraculous as that manna was, the people who consumed it are long dead. Yet, those who eat the living bread that has come down from heaven will live forever. Having said all this, Jesus gets even more specific. The bread that he has to offer is his *flesh*, by which he means his death. Of course, his listeners do not comprehend his meaning. Jesus' declaration offends their sensibilities and sets off a second controversy, which is presented in next week's reading.

Suggestions for Lectors

You have an option of how to deliver the opening verse. On the one hand, you can emphasize Jesus' being the bread of life by stressing the first person pronouns, as in: *I am the bread of life. Whoever comes to me will never be hungry, and whoever believes in me will never be thirsty* (6:35). On the other hand, you can emphasize who Jesus is and what needs he satisfies, as in: *I am the bread of life. Whoever comes to me will never be hungry, and whoever believes in me will never be thirsty*. With each option, you might also emphasize the two *nevers*.

In 6:41–42, drop your voice as though this is a private conversation, as though the Jews are discussing Jesus' outrageous claims amongst themselves. Then raise your voice as Jesus interrupts their deliberations and begins to speak. As you deliver Jesus' words, do so with energy and conviction; argue your point, and make your case. Emphasize the two *I am* statements: *I am the bread of life* (6:48) and *I am the living bread that came down from heaven* (6:51). Read these statements slowly and deliberately. As before, you can choose to emphasize the subject in each statement (*I*), or the predicate noun (*the bread of life, the living bread*).

When you come to the final verse, read the first half at your regular tempo. Then, slow down, and deliver the second half in a voice that sounds like you are letting your listeners in on a great secret. Pause after *world*, and accent flesh, as in: *and the bread that I will give for the life of the world… is my flesh* (6:51b).

PROPER 15

August 14–20

1 Kings 2:10–12; 3:3–14	Proverbs 9:1–6
Psalm 111	Psalm 34:9–14
Ephesians 5:15–20	Ephesians 5:15–20
John 6:51–58	John 6:51–58

1 KINGS 2:10–12; 3:3–14

Notes

Sequence. 1 of 2

Commentary

David was the most celebrated king in Israel's history, the king against whom all subsequent kings were measured. David was singularly devoted to the LORD, and under his leadership Israel became united politically and spiritually. Israel's enemies ceased to be a threat, and the idolatry and apostasy that had so plagued Israel was replaced by a new, unparalleled devotion and commitment to the LORD. At the height of his reign, the LORD established a covenant with David.

> When your days are fulfilled and you lie down with your ancestors,
> I will raise up your offspring after you, who shall come forth from

> your body, and I will establish his kingdom. He shall build a house for my name, and I will establish the throne of his kingdom forever. I will be a father to him, and he shall be a son to me. When he commits iniquity, I will punish him with a rod such as mortals use, with blows inflicted by human beings. But I will not take my steadfast love from him, as I took it from Saul, whom I put away from before you. Your house and your kingdom shall be made sure forever before me; your throne shall be established forever (2 Sam 7:12–16, Adv 4).

2:10–12. The first of David's children to ascend to the throne is his son, Solomon, whose mother is Bathsheba. Amidst rival claims to the throne, Solomon is anointed by the priest Zadok and the prophet Nathan (1 Kgs 1:28–53). When David dies, Solomon consolidates his reign, and "the kingdom is established in [his] hand" (2:46).

As a king, Solomon was known for his wisdom both within and outside the borders of Israel. The OT books of Proverbs, Ecclesiastes, and the Song of Songs are attributed to Solomon as is the Wisdom of Solomon in the Apocrypha. The following episode takes place at the onset of Solomon's reign, and in it we read of how Solomon acquired his renowned wisdom.

3:3–4. This episode opens with Solomon sacrificing at Gibeon, which is described as the principal high place, or shrine. In the OT, a high place was a sacred site where worship and sacrifices were offered to a particular god or gods. Most likely, a high place consisted of a multi-room structure, housing an altar and other cultic furniture and including rooms within which priests and worshippers could eat sacred meals. Although its name suggests some remote hill or mountaintop location, high places were often located in or around urban centers, as is the case in today's reading, where the high place is identified with the town of Gibeon. High places were notorious as centers of pagan worship and idolatry, but on this occasion that does not seem to be the case for the LORD appears to Solomon at Gibeon and does not question his offering of sacrifices there. Moreover, the temple in Jerusalem has not yet been built, so there is not a single, dedicated center of worship in Israel.

3:5–9. The LORD appears to Solomon in a dream and says, "Ask what I should give you" (3:6). Solomon begins his response by expressing his gratitude at having been granted the privilege of ascending to the throne of his father David. Solomon also expresses his anxiety over being so young and yet responsible for the welfare of an entire nation. In the end, he asks the LORD for the gift of wisdom that he might successfully lead the people of God.

3:10–14. The LORD is impressed with Solomon's request, which is a testimony to the wisdom and maturity Solomon already possesses. The LORD is more than pleased to grant his request and gives Solomon "a wise and discerning mind" (3:12), the likes of which no one has ever seen or ever will. In addition, the LORD grants Solomon what he did not ask for, namely, wealth and honor. If Solomon walks in the ways of the LORD, he will find himself enjoying a good long life.

Suggestions for Lectors

After a narrative introduction (2:10–12; 3:3–4), today's episode consists of dialogue: Solomon requesting wisdom and the LORD responding. Focus your preparation on conveying the feelings and emotions that are being expressed by the two speakers.

As earlier episodes demonstrate, Solomon has not led a sheltered life. Though he is young, he knows how the world works. He knows how to spot and participate in royal intrigue; so he is not helpless. Yet, Solomon recognizes that he does not have what it takes to lead God's people. His request for wisdom, therefore, is not an attempt to ingratiate himself to the LORD by asking for wisdom instead of wealth. Instead, his request is genuine and sincere, so convey this in your delivery.

As for the LORD, he is quite pleased with Solomon's request, like a parent who beams with pride when their child shows signs of maturity and selflessness. So as you read the LORD's response, have a smile on your face and allow your voice to be tinged with joy and pride.

Pronunciation Guide

David (DAY-vid), *Gibeon* (GIB-ee-uhn), *Hebron* (HEE-bruhn; -bron), *Israel* (IZ-ree-uhl; -ray-), *Solomon* (SAH-luh-muhn; SOL-uh-muhn)

PROVERBS 9:1–6

Commentary

When Solomon succeeded his father David as king over Israel and Judah, the LORD asked him in a dream, "Ask what I should give you" (1 Kgs 3:5, Prop 15). Solomon asked for understanding in order to govern God's people wisely (3:9). God was so pleased with Solomon's request that he gave him such a wise and discerning a mind (3:12) that he became famous and his wisdom legendary (4:29–34). The book of Proverbs is just one testament to that wisdom. Proverbs bears the superscription, "The proverbs of Solomon son of David, king of Israel" (1:1). This should not be read as indicating that Solomon himself composed all of the proverbs in the book. Proverbs contains much traditional wisdom known from elsewhere in the Ancient Near East, and it attributes proverbs to other sources (1:6; 22:17; 24:23; 30:1; 31:1). Therefore, the book of Proverbs is better understood as an anthology of wisdom sayings, containing proverbs Solomon composed, as well as those he and others collected.

In the book of Proverbs, God's Wisdom (or understanding, prudence, intelligence, etc.) is personified as a woman; as in: "Does not wisdom call, and does not understanding raise *her* voice" (8:1, EastVig). In today's reading, personified Wisdom hosts a feast to which the simple are invited.

9:1–6. Wisdom builds her house, butchers the meat, prepares the wine, and sets the table. Then, when everything is ready, Wisdom sends her servant-girls with an invitation to all and sundry, "You that are simple, turn in here!... Come, eat of my bread and drink of the wine I have mixed" (9:4a, 5). Those who accept the invitation to lay aside their foolishness and immaturity and to feast at the house of Wisdom will find life.

The house of Lady Wisdom stands in stark contrast to the house of Lady Folly, who also takes to the streets and calls, "You that are simple, turn in here!" (9:16). Folly says, "Stolen water is sweeter, and bread eaten in secret is pleasant" (9:17). But those who partake of Folly's feast only find death for "they do not know that the dead are there, that her guests are in the depths of Sheol" (9:18).

Suggestions for Lectors

Today's reading is relatively short so make sure that your listeners are attentive and ready before you begin. The first three verses convey a sense of excitement and anticipation as they describe the various preparations that have been made for the feast. So read these verses with mounting energy and enthusiasm until you come to the first announcement in 9:4.

In 9:4a, 5–6, increase the volume and pitch of your voice as you deliver Wisdom's invitation with joy in your voice and with a smile on your face.

EPHESIANS 5:15–20

Notes

Sequence. 6 of 7

Commentary

In last week's reading (Eph 4:25–5:2), Paul instructs the Ephesian Christians in matters of Christian behavior, especially behavior that promotes unity among believers. Then, in 5:3–14, Paul discusses matters of sexual immorality and calls the Ephesians to live into their identity as children of light in a world of deep darkness. In today's reading, Paul continues his ethical instruction by characterizing the life of the Spirit as a life of wisdom.

5:15–20. Paul issues three prohibitions: do not live as unwise people; do not be foolish; and do not get drunk. The last prohibition seems out of place until it is recognized that drunkenness is linked with folly in biblical literature (Prov 20:1). Paul counterbalances these three prohibitions with three exhortations: live wisely by making the most of the time that has been given to you; seek to understand God's will; and be filled with the Spirit. This last command is not so much the last command in a sequence of three as it is the one command that undergirds the first two, for persons who are filled with the Spirit are the embodiment of wisdom itself.

Moreover, to be filled with the Spirit is to know how truly to worship God in song and in thanksgiving. As Jesus once said to the Samaritan woman, "But the hour is coming, and is now here, when the true worshipers will worship the Father in spirit and truth, for the Father seeks such as these to worship him. God is spirit, and those who worship him must worship in spirit and truth" (John 4:23–24).

Suggestions for Lectors

In today's reading, Paul's instructions and commands occur in pairs, and each pair contains both a negative and a positive component. For example, Paul says to live *not as unwise people* (negative) *but as wise* (positive). As you work your way through these, stress the positive in each pair: *Be careful, wise* (15); *making* (16); *understand* (17); *be filled with the Spirit* (18); *singing and making melody* (19); and *giving thanks* (20).

Pronunciation Guide
Ephesians (eh-FEE-zhuhnz; ih-)

JOHN 6:51–58

Notes
Sequence. 4 of 5

Commentary
In last week's reading, Jesus' listeners were shocked by his claim that he was the bread that came down from heaven. In this week's reading, Jesus shocks them once again with an even bolder claim: "Whoever eats of this bread will live forever; and the bread that I will give for the life of the world is my *flesh*" (6:51).

6:51–58. When his opponents scoff at this cannibalistic idea of consuming his flesh, Jesus takes the imagery one step further. "Very truly, I tell you, unless you *eat the flesh* of the Son of Man and *drink his blood*, you have no life in you" (6:53). Clearly, Jesus is speaking figuratively here, but what exactly is he trying to convey? How does one go about consuming his flesh and imbibing his blood?

First, all of this talk of flesh and blood concerns Jesus' death. Ironically, Jesus will impart life to others through dying. As he will say later in the gospel, "Very truly, I tell you, unless a grain of wheat falls into the earth and dies, it remains just a single grain; but if it dies, it bears much fruit" (12:24, Lent 5). Likewise, if his life is going to become a life for others, it will have to be sacrificed. His body will have to be broken and his blood spilled for that is the only way in which these things can be distributed to others.

Given all of this, partaking of Jesus' flesh and blood is a graphic way of saying that we must participate in his death. When we do so, we receive the spiritual nourishment that his death affords. This, of course, raises the question, "How do we participate in his death?" First and foremost, the answer is believing in Jesus:

> This is the work of God, that you *believe* in him whom he has sent (6:29).
>
> Whoever comes to me will never be hungry,
> and whoever *believes* in me will never be thirsty (6:35).
>
> This is indeed the will of my Father, that all who see the Son and *believe* in him may have eternal life; and I will raise them up on the last day (6:40).

Of course, believing is not just thinking the right things, it is about trusting. It is about taking Jesus into ourselves, which is why the images of eating and drinking his flesh and blood are so apropos. All who entrust their lives to Jesus will experience, now and forever, the eternal kind of life that only Jesus has the power to give. They will abide in Jesus, and he will abide in them, and together they will abide with the living Father, who gives life through his Son.

Suggestions for Lectors

Today's reading starts quickly and begins with the most important statement of the passage, so make sure your listeners are ready before you begin. Because of the nature of this opening statement, begin the reading at a slower tempo than you normally would. As Jesus speaks, he focuses upon himself, so stress the *I* in *I am the bread of life* (6:51a). Likewise, stress *this bread* and *my flesh*.

The Jews take offense and debate Jesus' radical claim amongst themselves, so drop your voice in order to convey that this is a private discussion. Then, raise your voice as Jesus interrupts and begins to speak again. Deliver Jesus' words with an intensity born of conviction. In 6:55, emphasize both *trues*. As you draw the reading to a close, read the final verse very deliberately. Slow down for the concluding sentence, emphasizing *this bread* and *forever* and pausing after *bread* and *live*, as in: *But the one who eats this bread... will live... forever* (6:58).

PROPER 16

August 21–27

1 Kings 8:(1, 6, 10–11), 22–30, 41–43	Joshua 24:1–2a, 14–18
Psalm 84	Psalm 34:15–22
Ephesians 6:10–20	Ephesians 6:10–20
John 6:56–69	John 6:56–69

1 KINGS 8:(1, 6, 10–11), 22–30, 41–43

Notes

Sequence. 2 of 2

Commentary

When David finally ascended to the throne and was anointed king over all Israel and Judah, his first official act was to establish a new capital, which he did by taking over the Jebusite city of Jerusalem (2 Sam 5:6–10, Prop 9). David's second official act was to bring the ark of the covenant into a newly-constructed tent of meeting in Jerusalem (2 Sam 6:1–19, Prop 10). Sometime later, David conceived the idea of building a temple for the LORD, a permanent dwelling place for the ark of the covenant. The LORD, however, had other plans. It would not be David but his son (Solomon) who would build a house for the LORD's name (2 Sam 7, Adv 4, Prop 11). This same story is recounted by King Solomon in 1 Kings 8 as he presides over the dedication of the newly-constructed temple. Selections from Solomon's prayer of dedication form today's reading.

8:1, 6. The dedication of the temple is a national affair. The elders of the Twelve Tribes of Israel have assembled as have scores of priests and people from across the nation. In a grand procession, the ark of the covenant and all the other holy vessels from the tent of meeting are transferred to the temple. The temple, the basic design of which corresponded to the original tent of meeting, consisted of three spaces, each of increasing holiness: the forecourt (a.k.a., portico or vestibule), the Holy Place, and the inner sanctuary (a.k.a., Most Holy Place or Holy of Holies). The ark of the covenant was placed in the inner sanctuary.

8:10–11. Once the ark is in place, a thick cloud representing the glory and presence of the LORD fills the Holy Place, thereby signifying that the LORD has accepted the temple in Jerusalem as his new place of residence.

8:22–26. After describing the sequence of events that led to the temple's construction (8:14–21), Solomon turns his attention to the LORD and prays a prayer of dedication. Solomon begins by praising and thanking the LORD for his steadfast love and faithfulness. In particular, Solomon praises the LORD for making good on his promise to David that one of his offspring would sit on the throne of God's people forever.

8:27–30. In the ancient world, temples were often called houses because they were understood to be the place where the god or gods actually resided. This same language is employed in the Bible in reference to the temple in Jerusalem but always in a qualified sense. In a very real sense, the temple is indeed the LORD's house, the place where the LORD's name (that is, God's identity and character) will reside. Yet, this is not literally true, for how can the Creator be contained by anything within creation. As Solomon reminds the people, "But will God indeed dwell on the earth? Even heaven and the highest heaven cannot contain you, much less this house that I have built!" (8:30). Consequently, in his prayer of dedication, Solomon does not ask the LORD to dwell in this house so as to be contained by it. Instead he humbly asks that the LORD direct his gaze to the temple in Jerusalem, that the LORD be especially attentive to the prayers of God's people that are offered in the temple and also directed toward the temple.

8:41–43. In the remainder of his prayer of dedication, King Solomon expounds upon this last request by asking the LORD to answer particular types of petitions—petitions for justice, for mercy, for forgiveness, for deliverance, and so on. Then, in 8:41–43, Solomon makes a somewhat surprising request. He asks the LORD to answer the prayers of non-Israelites, the prayers of foreigners who have come to Jerusalem because they have heard of the LORD. In this request, one hears the words of Isaiah on the lips of Jesus, "My house shall be called a house of prayer for all the nations" (Isaiah 56:7; Mark 11:17). How interesting that Solomon recognizes that, while the LORD is Israel's God, the LORD is not Israel's God alone. In his prayer, Solomon recognizes the missionary identity of God's people. Israel is to become the light of the world so that all people might come to know and be blessed by the only true and living God. In part then, the temple serves as a reminder of that missionary identity.

Suggestions for Lectors

Today's reading has been pieced together from the account of the dedication of the temple that we find in 1 Kings 8. As you prepare for your reading, read the whole of chapter 8. This will give you a feel for everything that is going on with the dedication of the temple.

After reading the narrative introduction (8:1, 6, 10–11), turn your attention to God as you deliver King Solomon's prayer. That is, do not direct the prayer to your listeners, but imagine that you are Solomon praying to the LORD. As you pray, raise your voice and keep it raised throughout, remembering that you, as Solomon, are offering this prayer before a great assembly. Pray with energy and fervor, faith and conviction.

Pronunciation Guide
cherubim (CHEHR-uh-bim'; -oo-), *Israel* (IZ-ree-uhl; -ray-), *Israelites* (IZ-ree-līts), *Jerusalem* (juh-ROO-suh-luhm), *Solomon* (SAH-luh-muhn, SOL-uh-), *Zion* (ZĪ-uhn)

JOSHUA 24:1–2A, 14–18

Commentary
The book of Joshua narrates the story of the conquest of Canaan, which is the story of how the Israelites entered and took over the Promised Land. As reflected in the book's title, the main character is Joshua, the son of Nun. Moses led Israel throughout its forty-year sojourn in the wilderness, bringing the nation from Mount Sinai to the borders of Canaan. Then, upon his death, his assistant Joshua assumed leadership. Thus, it was Joshua who led the Israelites through the divided waters of the Jordan River into the land of Canaan (Josh 3). And, it was under Joshua's leadership that the Israelites successfully drove out the pagan inhabitants of Canaan, the land that the LORD swore to give to Abraham, Isaac, and Jacob as an inheritance (Gen 17:8).

In today's reading, we have come to the end of the book. The twelve tribes of Israel are gathered together to renew the covenant made with God at Mount Sinai and to reaffirm their singular allegiance to Yahweh, the LORD.

24:1–2a. Today's reading opens with the Twelve Tribes of Israel gathered together in the presence of Joshua. Addressing the whole assembly, Joshua begins to recount the old, old story, the story of when Israel was not yet a people, merely the LORD's promise of land and offspring to an unlikely, elderly couple—Abraham and Sarah.

24:2b–13. In this section of the narrative, which does not form part of today's reading, Joshua recounts the highlights of the LORD's dealings with Israel. He especially emphasizes how the LORD rescued Israel from its Egyptian taskmasters, how the LORD shepherded Israel through the wilderness for forty years, and how the LORD drove out the inhabitants of Canaan, thereby leading Israel to a place of prosperity and blessing.

24:14–15. Given all that the LORD has done for Israel and on Israel's behalf, Joshua calls upon the people to "revere the LORD, and serve him in sincerity and in faithfulness" (24:14). This is a call to worship the LORD with a singularity of devotion and an undivided heart. Israel is not offered the option of living with divided loyalties, of worshipping the LORD and offering devotion to the variety of other gods that are on the market. The Israelites are, therefore, faced with a choice, either worship Yahweh their God with all their heart, soul, and strength (Deut 6:4–5, Prop 26) or forsake Yahweh by serving other gods or by serving other gods in addition to

Yahweh. Joshua's allegiances are clear, "As for me and my household, we will serve the LORD" (24:15b).

24:16–18. The people readily acknowledge all that Yahweh has done for them and state unambiguously, "we also will serve the LORD, for he is our God" (24:18).

Suggestions for Lectors

Today's reading is carried along by the dialogue between Joshua and the people. As you read each of these speaking parts, do not think of yourself as a lector, but as the individual or the group who is speaking. When you are reading Joshua's parts, imagine that you are Joshua speaking to God's people, and deliver his words with energy and conviction. Likewise, when you are reading the people's parts, image that you are responding to your leader trying to convey the sincerity of the commitment you are making to follow the LORD.

Pronunciation Guide

Amorites (AM-or-īts)
Egypt (EE-jipt)
Shechem (SHEH-kem; SHEE-kuhm)

EPHESIANS 6:10–20

Notes

Sequence. 7 of 7

Commentary

In the first half of the Letter to the Ephesians (1:3–3:21), Paul describes what God has done in Christ to restore humanity and creation, "to gather up all things in him, things in heaven and things on earth" (1:10). Then, in the second half (4:1–6:20), Paul offers instructions on Christian living as our response to what God has done and is doing for us. Paul begins this section saying, "I… beg you to lead a life worthy of the calling to which you have been called" (4:1).

6:10–12. In today's reading, Paul draws his ethical instruction to a close by emphasizing the fact that the battle in which Christians are engaged is a spiritual one, cosmic in nature. While they may find themselves, like Paul, persecuted by human beings and human institutions, the real battle is with the demonic forces of evil. It is important to be properly prepared and equipped; a spiritual war requires spiritual armor and weaponry.

6:13–17. Moreover, because our enemies are so strong and powerful, it is necessary to go into the battle fully prepared, with the *full* armor of God. Paul identifies seven items with which Christians need to be outfitted—truth, righteousness, the gospel of peace, faith, salvation, the Spirit, and the word of God. Each of these receives treatment somewhere in the letter, especially in the opening chapter where Paul offers a summary of the gospel (1:3–14, Chr 2).

6:18–20. Finally, Paul instructs his readers to "pray in the Spirit at all times" (6:18a). Prayer could be considered an eighth weapon, one that supports and activates the rest of the armor of God.

Suggestions for Lectors

In today's reading, Paul uses repetition to great rhetorical effect. In 6:12, emphasize the objects of the repeated preposition *against*: *rulers*, *authorities*, *cosmic powers*, and *spiritual forces*. In 6:14–17, highlight the individual components of the armor of God: *the belt of truth*, *the breastplate of righteousness* (14); *shoes for your feet* (15); *the shield of faith* (16); *the helmet of salvation*, *the sword of the Spirit* (17). In 6:18–20, accent the entreaties: *Pray*, *keep alert*, *persevere* (18); *Pray* (19); and *Pray* (20).

Pronunciation Guide

Ephesians (eh-FEE-zhuhnz; ih-)

JOHN 6:56–69

Notes

Sequence. 5 of 5

Commentary

In the previous two gospel readings from John (Prop 14–15), Jesus makes claims for himself that cause his opponents to grumble and complain. "Is not this Jesus, the son of Joseph, whose father and mother we know? How can he now say, 'I have come down from heaven'?" (6:42). "How can this man give us his flesh to eat?" (6:52). In today's reading, we discover that even Jesus' own followers are having trouble with some of his claims.

6:56–59. When Jesus talks about flesh and blood, he is talking about his death. Eating his flesh and drinking his blood is, therefore, a graphic way of saying that we must participate in his death. We do this by believing in him (cf. 6:29, 35, 40). When we entrust our lives to Jesus, we feed on him in our hearts and receive the spiritual nourishment that his death affords. Of course, believing is not just thinking the right things, it is about trusting and abiding. It is about taking Jesus into ourselves, which is why the imagery of eating his flesh and drinking his blood is so apropos. All who entrust their lives to Jesus will experience, now and forever, the eternal kind of life that only Jesus has the power to give. They will abide in Jesus, and he will abide in them, and together they will abide with the living Father, who gives life through his Son.

6:60–65. Many of his disciples are disturbed by this cannibalistic discourse, and Jesus questions their reaction. Perhaps, they would like to see a sign that would satisfy their doubts. Jesus wonders aloud. Would they still be offended if they were to see him ascending to the Father from whence he came? He criticizes them for trying to understand spiritual matters from a human perspective. At the same time, he is not surprised because he has known from the beginning that not everyone who has been following him has actually been drawn to him by the Father.

6:66–69. In the end, Jesus' claims and demands are more than many of his followers are willing to commit to, and they stop following him. Jesus then offers his closest companions the opportunity to do the same. Will they remain, or would they like to go their own way as well? Speaking for the Twelve, Simon Peter professes their faith. They are convinced that the words Jesus speaks have the power to impart eternal life. Moreover, they have come to know and believe that Jesus is the

Holy One of God, that is, the one who has been set apart by God and has come down from God. At the beginning of John 6, Jesus fed five thousand people, who had followed him because of the signs he was performing (Prop 12). By the end of the chapter, that number appears to have dwindled to twelve, and then even one of those will eventually betray him (6:70–71).

Suggestions for Lectors

Last week's and this week's readings overlap. Last week's ended with 6:58, and this week's begins with 6:56. Yet, even though we are repeating some of the same words today, the emphasis is different. Last week, the focus was upon eating and drinking Jesus' flesh and blood. Those things certainly play a role in today's reading, but now the focus is upon abiding in Jesus. The reading opens with Jesus talking about abiding in him, and by the end, many of his disciples have chosen to part company. So, as you begin today's reading, really emphasize Jesus' opening statement: *Those who eat my flesh and drink my blood abide in me, and I in them* (6:56).

In 6:54b, the narrator interrupts the flow of the story to offer the reader some inside information about what Jesus is thinking. Drop your voice as you relay this information to your listeners.

Finally, when you come to Simon Peter's response, emphasize the references to Jesus: *Lord, to whom can we go? You have the words of eternal life. We have come to believe that you are the Holy One of God* (6:68). Read this last declaration slowly and deliberately as you draw the reading to a close.

Pronunciation Guide

Capernaum (kuh-PER-nay-uhm, -nuh-)

PROPER 17

August 28–September 3

Song of Solomon 2:8–13	Deuteronomy 4:1–2, 6–9
Psalm 45:1–2, 6–9 (= 45:1–2, 7–10 BCP)	Psalm 15
James 1:17–27	James 1:17–27
Mark 7:1–8, 14–15, 21–23	Mark 7:1–8, 14–15, 21–23

Song of Solomon 2:8–13

Commentary

The Song of Solomon (a.k.a., The Song of Songs) is a book of poetry, an anthology of love songs that celebrates the love between a man and a woman. The book opens with a superscription, which functions like a title page: "The Song of Songs, by Solomon" (1:1). The title, *The Song of Songs*, has a couple of possible meanings. Since the Song of Songs contains a number of different songs, the title could mean that what follows is one song composed of many songs. Or, like the superlative expression Holy of Holies, which designates the holiest space in the temple, the Song of Songs may be taken to mean that this song is the best song ever. At the Council of Jamnia in A.D. 90, Rabbi Akiba took this one step further:

> For in all the world there is nothing to equal the day on which the Song of Songs was given to Israel, for all the writings are Holy, but the Song of Songs is the Holy of Holies (Mishnah, *Yadaim* III, 5).

The phrase *by Solomon* is much harder to understand because the Hebrew preposition translated here as "by" could also mean *of*, *to*, or *concerning*. Thus, the Song of Songs could have been written *by* Solomon, *to* Solomon, or *about* Solomon, or even collected *by* Solomon. Fortunately, these differences do not affect the overall interpretation of the Song.

In Jewish bibles, the Song of Songs belongs to a collection of writings known as *Megillot*, or the Five Scrolls, which also includes Ruth, Lamentations, Ecclesiastes, and Esther. Each of these books is designated for reading on a major holy day of the Jewish liturgical year. The Song of Songs is read on the Sabbath of Passover because it is understood as a song about God's love for his people. In fact, for the better part of two thousand years, the Song of Songs has been interpreted allegorically. In Jewish tradition, the man's love for the woman represents God's love for Israel, while in Christian tradition, it represents Christ's love for the church and for individual Christians. Yet, over the past few centuries, the allegorical interpretations have largely been replaced with a more straightforward reading. Now the Song of Songs is widely understood as celebrating the covenant of love between a man and a woman in its spiritual, emotional, and especially physical dimensions.

In the beginning, God created humanity as male and female, and according to Genesis, sexual differentiation among human beings is a reflection of God's image. "So God created humankind in his image, in the image of God he created them; male and female he created them" (1:27). Then, God blesses their maleness and femaleness by calling them to be fruitful and multiply, that is, by calling them to sexual intimacy that will produce the fruit of the human race. Consequently, although God is never mentioned in the Song of Songs, by celebrating the sexual union between the man and the woman, the Song is celebrating and affirming God's original designs for creation and human beings.

In Eden, the first woman and man "were both naked, and were not ashamed" (Gen 2:25). In other words, they were spiritually, emotionally, and sexually intimate, and their intimacy was a source of blessing and life. Since the Fall, however, such intimacy between men and women has become distorted and is often a source of great pain and anguish. In this respect, the Song of Songs seeks to redeem human sexuality and intimacy in all its spiritual, emotional, and physical expressions.

In today's reading, the woman is enraptured by the coming of her beloved. Spring has arrived, and new life and love are in evidence all around.

2:8–9. The poem opens with the woman hearing the voice of her beloved. She looks up and sees him running to her from afar.

2:10–13. When he arrives, he speaks to her and says, "Arise, my love, my fair one and come away" (2:10). He has come for her because winter is over, and the signs of spring are all around. The flowers are blooming, the birds are singing, the fig trees are "figging," and the vineyard is blossoming. It is the perfect day for enjoying one another.

Suggestions for Lectors

Deliver the first portion of today's reading with excitement and energy, but without haste. Attend to the punctuation, pausing at all commas but not at the ends of lines that do not contain any punctuation (see 2:9). Without being overly dramatic, convey to your listeners the exhilaration you are feeling as you witness the arrival of your beloved.

Then, in 2:10–13, as you report your beloved's words, adopt a different tone of voice and proceed at a slightly slower pace so that you might relish his words. If anything deserves emphasis, it is the repeated line: *Arise, my love, my fair one, and come away* (2:10b, 13b).

Pronunciation Guide

beloved (n., buh-LUV-uhd)
Solomon (SAH-luh-muhn, SOL-uh-)

DEUTERONOMY 4:1–2, 6–9

Commentary

Deuteronomy is the fifth book of the Bible and the last of the Five Books of Moses (a.k.a., the Pentateuch or the Torah). Deuteronomy is presented as a speech that Moses delivers to the Israelites just prior to his death and just prior to Israel's entrance into the Promised Land of Canaan under the leadership of Joshua (Josh 3:1–17). In this speech (Deut 1:6–30:20), Moses reviews Israel's forty-year sojourn in the wilderness and instructs the people in the laws of the covenant that are to govern their personal and corporate lives once they are settled in Canaan. One might regard Deuteronomy, then, as a prolonged exposition of the Ten Commandments, a detailing of all the various and specific ways one goes about loving the LORD with all of one's life and possessions and loving one's neighbor as oneself.

4:1–2. In today's reading, Moses begins by stressing the importance of putting into practice everything that he is telling them. Their obedience to the LORD will ensure that they will enter and live good lives in the Promised Land.

4:6–8. Moreover, their obedience will perform an evangelistic function; it will serve as a witness to the world that there is no other God like the LORD. When the people of God live lives of reverence and obedience to the covenant, then they are fulfilling their vocation to be the light of the world that draws all people everywhere into a covenant relationship with the only true and living God.

4:9. The lives of God's people are to be lives of remembrance. We are to remember everything that the LORD has commanded us and everything that the LORD has done for us. One of the best ways of doing this is to make all these things known to our children and grandchildren.

Suggestions for Lectors

In today's reading, take on the persona of Moses as you deliver these instructions to your listeners. Remember that Moses is speaking to a people he has been leading for forty years. While at times they have been a stubborn and stiff-necked people, they are still God's people and Moses cares for them. He is like a father saying a final farewell and offering some parting advice to his adult children.

Let your voice be both firm, affectionate, and earnest. When reading the two questions in 11:7–8, raise your voice slightly and add a measure of intensity. Then, in 11:9, return to your normal voice as you conclude the reading. Slow down for the final command, *make them…*, enunciating each word clearly and emphasizing the first *children* and *children's*.

Pronunciation Guide

Deuteronomy (doo'-tuh-RON-uh-mee)
Israel (IZ-ree-uhl; -ray-)

JAMES 1:17–27

Notes

Sequence. 1 of 5

Commentary

Ancient letters began in a stereotypical fashion, with a salutation that identified the letter's author and recipients followed by a greeting and sometimes a prayer of thanksgiving. The Letter of James begins with the first three of these four elements. The author introduces himself as "James, a servant of God and of the Lord Jesus Christ" (1:1a). Traditionally, the author of James has been understood to be James, the brother of Jesus (Mark 6:2–3, Prop 9; Gal 1:19), a Jewish-Christian who was the leader of the Jerusalem church (Acts 12:17; 15:13; 21:18; 1 Cor 15:7; Gal 2:9, 12). He is not to be confused with the Apostle James—the son of Zebedee and the brother of John—who was martyred in Acts 12:2. Unlike most of the letters of Paul, which are addressed to a particular church or individual, the Letter of James is addressed more broadly "to the twelve tribes in the Dispersion (or Diaspora)" (1:1b). Originally, "the Dispersion" referred to Jews who lived outside Palestine, but here it more specifically refers to Jewish Christians who lived in the wider Roman world outside the Promised Land. The author might even have all Christians in view, both Jewish and Gentile, in which case "the twelve tribes of Israel" is being used symbolically to designate the new, ethnically-diverse people of God. Certainly, everything James says applies to all believers, regardless of their ethnic, religious, and cultural heritages.

With all this being said, James lacks many other formal features of ancient letters. Instead, James has much more in common with the moral and wisdom literature of the ancient world, within both Jewish and Greco-Roman traditions. Thus, James is replete with rhetorical devices, aphorisms, moral exhortations, diatribes, and mini treatises and essays. According to one scholar, "The rhetorical genre of the Hellenistic world that James most resembles… is the protreptic discourse, which sought to exhort those holding a profession to behavior consonant with their ideal."[20] In this case, the profession in view is that of being Christian, and James writes to exhort his colleagues—his brothers and sisters in Christ—to practice the profession of Christian, not by hearing alone, but by hearing and doing (1:22).

Today's reading is taken from the first chapter, which moves quickly from topic to topic, touching on a variety of issues that are treated more fully in subsequent chapters. For example, in 1:26, James issues a single-sentence warning about the dangers of an unbridled tongue, which anticipates and prepares his readers for his treatise on the tongue in 3:1–12. Yet, despite these changes in topic, there is a thread that runs the length of today's reading, which concerns the word of truth.

1:17–18, The Word as Gift. Immediately prior to today's reading, James wrote about the importance of enduring and overcoming temptations. Temptations, James argues, do not come from God but from within us. If we allow ourselves to be enticed by our own desires, then we will find our desires conceiving and giving birth to sin, which will eventually grow up and give birth to death.

God never tempts us because he is the Father of lights, that is, the source of all light. In the beginning, God could speak into the darkness and say, "Let there be light," precisely because "God *is* light and in him there is no darkness at all" (1 John 1:5). In short, God begets light and life, not darkness and death.

Moreover, God's light is constant and reliable. Unlike the sun, God's light does not change with the seasons nor does it vary throughout the day. Therefore, we can trust in God and the goodness of God, from whom comes every perfect gift. In the beginning, God spoke creation into being; so creation can be said to have come into being through the word of God. Likewise, Christians come into being through God's word. Like a mother, God gives birth to us by means of the word of truth, which is the good news about the salvation that has been made possible by Jesus Christ. As Paul writes, "In him you also, when you had heard *the word of truth*, the gospel of your salvation, and had believed in him, were marked with the seal of the promised Holy Spirit" (Eph 1:13).

1:19–21, The Implanted Word. The word of truth has not merely been spoken *to us*, it has been implanted *in us*; which means that it must be cultivated *by us*. We do this by receiving the word with meekness and by clearing out all the weeds of wickedness that spring up and attempt to choke out the word. In particular, we must weed out anger because anger inhibits the word from growing and maturing and producing a harvest of righteousness. As James writes later, "a harvest of righteousness is sown in peace for those who make peace" (3:18).

But, how does one root out anger? Fortunately, James offers his readers some practical, albeit pithy, advice. "Let everyone be quick to listen, slow to speak, slow to anger" (1:19). There is much wisdom to be mined from these three exhortations. Like his brother Jesus, James does not command the impossible. He does not say, "Do not be angry," but, "Be slow to anger" (cf. Matt 5:21–26). But, how does one become slow to anger? Very simply, by cultivating quickness of ear and slowness of

[20] Luke Timothy Johnson, *Brother of Jesus, Friend of God: Studies in the Letter of James* (Grand Rapids, Mich.: Eerdmans, 2004), 26.

tongue. When we are quick to speak and slow to listen, we become disconnected from others, and we allow our judgments of others to take the lead. When this happens, our natural capacity for empathy and compassion is blocked and replaced by anger. Thus, one of the best ways to slow our anger is to develop the habits of being quick to listen and slow to speak, which are two sides of the same coin.

1:22–25, Hearing and Doing the Word, Part I. Had the word of truth only been spoken, then hearing it might be sufficient. But as we have seen, God's word has been implanted in us and requires our active engagement if it is to sprout, grow, and mature. Jesus said that everyone who hears his words and acts on them is like a wise man who built his house on rock (Matt 7:24). James says that the one who becomes a hearer *and* doer of the word is like a person who looks at themselves in the mirror and remembers who they are when they walk away. Hearers of the word may forget to whom they belong, but doers of the word always remember that they are Christ's.

In James, "the law of liberty" is the OT law, which embodies God's will and intentions for his people. James calls it the law of *liberty* because when we live out the law, especially through loving our neighbors as ourselves (cf. 2:8), then we experience freedom. After all, faith is only living and life-giving when it is fulfilling the law, that is, when it is loving and serving others in concrete ways (cf. 2:14–17).

1:26–27, Hearing and Doing the Word, Part II. If we are to become doers of the word, where do we begin? James offers a few of suggestions. First, he emphasizes the need to control one's tongue for, as he says later, the person who is able to bridle their tongue is able to guide and direct their whole body (3:2, Prop 19). Second, James defines a pure and undefiled life before God as a life of sacrifice, a life that is devoted to serving those who do not have a place in this world, like orphans and widows. This refrain is repeated throughout the OT (Deut 10:18; Isa 1:17). In other words, a blameless life involves loving God by loving one's neighbor. This will not happen if a person is motivated by the world and its values because the world is not concerned with widows and orphans and the least of these. Consequently, a Christian must also cultivate a detachment from the world so that they can minister in the world while remaining unstained by it.

Suggestions for Lectors

Although there is a progression of thought in today's reading, the author moves from topic to topic. So, pause for a second or two between each of the sections (1:17–18, 19–21, 22–25, 26–27).

In the second section (1:19–21), highlight the aphorism in the opening sentence. Read slowly and deliberately with long pauses after each instruction, and accent each of the verbs, as in: *let everyone be <u>quick</u> to listen,… <u>slow</u> to speak,… <u>slow</u> to anger….* You might even choose to decelerate your tempo as you move from command to command so that *slow to anger* takes longer to say than *quick to listen.*

In the third section (1:22–25), the opening sentence should be emphasized. Again, deliver it slowly and deliberately, emphasizing *doers* and *hearers*, as in: *But be <u>doers</u> of the word,… and not merely <u>hearers</u> who deceive themselves* (1:22).

Finally, in the final section (1:26–27), the last line should be emphasized: *<u>to care</u> for orphans and widows in their distress,… and to keep oneself… <u>unstained</u> by the world* (1:27b).

Mark 7:1–8, 14–15, 21–23

Notes

Sequence. 1 of 12

Commentary

It has been a number of chapters since the scribes and Pharisees have appeared in the narrative. The last time we encountered the Pharisees, they were conspiring with the Herodians over how to destroy Jesus (3:6, Prop 4). And the last time we saw the scribes, they were accusing Jesus of being in league with Satan, and Jesus in turn was warning them that they were in danger of passing the point of no return by committing blasphemy against the Holy Spirit (3:22–30, Prop 5). Consequently, when the scribes and Pharisees reappear in today's reading and begin questioning Jesus about his disciples' behavior, tensions are running high.

7:1–8. In today's reading, the Pharisees seem to be concerned about a very inconsequential matter, the failure of some of Jesus' disciples to wash their hands before they eat. Yet, it is important to understand that the Pharisees' question is not concerned with personal hygiene but spiritual cleanliness. The Pharisees were a first-century Jewish sect that promoted the spiritual renewal of the Jewish nation. In their program of renewal, they attempted to live their *daily* lives with the same level of ritual purity that priests observed when carrying out their priestly duties in the temple. As much as possible, they avoided situations that might render them ritually impure, and they were hyper-vigilant when it came to dietary matters. What you ate, how you prepared your food, and the company you kept were all matters of utmost importance. So, when the Pharisees question the disciples' failure to maintain the tradition of the elders by eating with ritually defiled hands, they are questioning the disciples' spiritual commitment, in the same way that a person's patriotism might be called into questioned if they do not stand for the Pledge of Allegiance.

Jesus objects to their question and begins to criticize his opponents. Drawing upon Isaiah 29:13, he argues that all their religious observance amounts to nothing because it promotes outward appearance to the exclusion of inward transformation. In everything they do, they elevate the tradition of the elders over the commandments of God, thereby making the word of God null and void (cf. 7:13).

7:14–15. Turning to the crowd, Jesus declares that nothing external to a person can render them unclean. Only the things that originate within persons and then come out are able to defile them. In short, impurity is an inside-out matter, not an outside-in matter. This is the fundamental difference between Jesus' program of renewal and that of the Pharisees. The Pharisees focus their energy on external matters, while Jesus redirects people's energy to internal matters.

7:21–23. Following his authoritative pronouncement, Jesus meets with his disciples privately where he offers additional explanation. Eating certain foods cannot defile anyone because food simply passes through a person's physical body; it does not affect their heart. The things that truly defile people are all the evil intentions that originate within the human heart. These are the things that require our attention because these are the things that keep our hearts far from God. Instead of spending so much time performing unnecessary rituals—like washing our hands and washing our "cups, pots, and bronze kettles" (7:4)—a person should devote their time and energy to cleansing their hearts.

Opening the Way for Gentile Mission. Jesus' pronouncement in 7:15 is extraordinary. If "there is nothing outside a person that going in can defile [them]" (7:15), then that would seem to suggest that there is no longer any need to maintain Jewish kosher regulations and practices. And in fact, this is the very conclusion that the narrator draws: "Thus he declared all foods clean" (7:19). The implications are astounding. By rendering all foods clean, Jesus has torn down a thick barrier that has existed between Jews and Gentiles for centuries. If Jews no longer had to worry about what they ate and how it was prepared, then they would have the freedom to sit at table and share a meal with Gentiles (which was one of the major issues the early church struggled with).

In terms of expanding the kingdom, declaring all foods clean opened the way for a Jewish mission to Gentiles. When Jesus sent the Twelve out on their first mission, they were not allowed to pack any food or take along any money to buy food. Instead, they were to trust God and rely upon the hospitality of those to whom they were sent (6:8–10, Prop 9). This means that an observant Jew could not proclaim the good news to Gentiles because kosher laws would have prohibited them from accepting Gentile hospitality. By declaring all foods clean, Jesus removes this major obstacle to Gentile mission. Thus, it is not a coincidence that, as soon as this episode ends, Jesus embarks on a missionary tour within Gentile territories (7:24–8:10). There he casts out a demon from the daughter of a Syrophoenician woman, he heals a Gentile man who is both deaf and mute, and he feeds a crowd of four thousand Gentiles in the same miraculous manner as when he fed five thousand Jews.

Thus, Jesus' purity debate with the scribes and Pharisees is not simply a matter of personal spirituality, but it stands at the heart of his mission. Following the tradition of the elders not only keeps people's hearts away from God, it also prohibits the expansion of God's kingdom to all those whom God wishes to reach.

Suggestions for Lectors

As you prepare for today's reading, it would be beneficial to read the whole debate between Jesus and the Pharisees (7:1–23). This will give you a better understanding of the issues and the overall tenor of the passage.

Begin reading in your normal narrating voice. When you come to the Pharisees' question in 7:5, ask it in an accusatory manner. After all, the Pharisees are not merely being curious, they are challenging Jesus' ministry and authority. When Jesus responds, raise your voice and speak with great fervor and conviction, especially as you deliver the final line. Highlight the contrast by emphasizing *God* and *human*, as in: *You abandon the commandment of <u>God</u> and hold to <u>human</u> tradition* (7:8).

Do not pause between 7:14–15 and 7:21–23. Although in the gospel itself, 7:14–15 is directed at the crowds and 7:21–23 is directed at the disciples, read these verses as though they belong to a single address.

Reading lists can be a bit tricky. As lectors, we want to avoid the extremes of monotonous recitation, on the one hand, and "punching" or over-emphasizing each item, on the other hand. To avoid these extremes, group the individual items of a list into intonational units, or phrases. These phrases should be of varying lengths, ranging from one to three, or even four, items each. Do not group an entire list into phrases of the same length because this can produce a cadence with a sing-song quality. The following are just a couple examples of how the vices in 7:21–22 could be grouped into intonational units; you may wish to adopt different groupings:

> fornication,… theft,… murder,… adultery, avarice, wickedness,…
> deceit,… licentiousness,… envy, slander, pride,… folly.

> fornication,… theft, murder, adultery,… avarice, wickedness,…
> deceit, licentiousness,… envy, slander, pride,… folly.

Pronunciation Guide
Isaiah (ī-ZAY-uh), *Jerusalem* (juh-ROO-suh-luhm), *Pharisees* (FAIR-uh-seez)

PROPER 18

September 4–10

Proverbs 22:1–2, 8–9, 22–23	Isaiah 35:4–7a
Psalm 125	Psalm 146
James 2:1–10, (11–13), 14–17	James 2:1–10, (11–13), 14–17
Mark 7:24–37	Mark 7:24–37

PROVERBS 22:1–2, 8–9, 22–23

Notes
Sequence. 1 of 3

Commentary
When Solomon succeeded his father David as king over Israel and Judah, the LORD told him in a dream, "Ask what I should give you" (1 Kgs 3:5, Prop 15). Solomon asked for understanding in order to govern God's people wisely (3:9). God was so pleased with Solomon's request that he gave him such a wise and discerning a mind (3:12) that he became famous and his wisdom legendary (4:29–34). The book of Proverbs is just one testament to that wisdom. Proverbs bears the superscription, "The proverbs of Solomon son of David, king of Israel" (1:1). This should not be read as indicating that Solomon himself composed all of the proverbs in the book; for not only does Proverbs contain much traditional wisdom known from elsewhere in the Ancient Near East, but the book itself attributes proverbs to other sources (1:6; 22:17; 24:23; 30:1; 31:1). Therefore, the book of Proverbs is better understood as an anthology of wisdom sayings, containing proverbs Solomon composed as well as those he and others collected.

Although the book is entitled Proverbs, it contains more than simple, short aphoristic sayings. For example, in the first third of the book (chs. 1–9), we find repeated encouragements and admonitions to seek Wisdom, which is personified as a woman (cf. 8:1). These chapters generally consist of lengthy poems and developed images. In contrast, Proverbs 10–22:16 offers a miscellany of independent sayings, riddles, and aphorisms that come under the heading, The Proverbs of Solomon (10:1). The first four proverbs in today's reading come from this collection. The last proverb of the day is the first in a collection entitled, The Words of the Wise, which is found in Proverbs 22:17–24:22.

22:1. A good reputation is worthy more than material security.

22:2. To judge people on the basis of their economic and social status is to overlook the fact that all people belong to the same family by virtue of their having been created by the LORD.

22:8. Like the material universe, the moral universe operates on principles of cause and effect. As Paul says in his letter to the Galatians: "Do not be deceived; God is not mocked, for you reap whatever you sow. If you sow to your own flesh, you will reap corruption from the flesh; but if you sow to the Spirit, you will reap eternal life from the Spirit" (Gal 6:7–8).

22:9. This proverb has the feel of one of Jesus' beatitudes.

22:22–23. In the Ancient Near East, the city gates were the places where legal matters were heard and settled. In this context, robbing the poor or crushing the afflicted at the gates characterizes an unjust judicial system, one in which the rich receive preferential treatment. The wise advise against such legalized social injustice because the LORD is the public defendant of the poor and afflicted, and a person does not want find themselves in opposition to the LORD.

Suggestions for Lectors

Today's reading is a bit unusual because it consists of a sequence of five different proverbs. While all of the proverbs that have been selected have something to say about wealth and justice, each of them stands on its own. Therefore, after each proverb, pause for a full two to three seconds so that your listeners have a chance to let the message sink in before you move on. Proclaim each of the proverbs with a strong, clear voice.

ISAIAH 35:4–7A

Notes

Sequence. 1 of 2

Commentary

In Isaiah 1–39, the prophet announces the LORD's judgment upon the people of Judah and Jerusalem for their centuries of idolatry and injustice. Isaiah 39 ends ominously as the predicted destruction and exile by the Babylonian empire becomes imminent. Isaiah 35 is interesting because, in the midst of these chapters of judgment, it offers a glimpse of the future restoration of God's people following the Babylonian captivity. It is as though the LORD did not want his people to go into exile without knowing that one day they would experience God's forgiveness, experienced concretely through the ending of the exile and a return to their homeland. Much of the description in Isaiah 35 can be found later in Isaiah 40–55.

35:4. The prophet is to encourage the exiles and give them hope by announcing the advent of their God who will come to rescue them. Even though the LORD employed foreign nations to execute his judgment upon his chosen people, a day is coming when the LORD will judge the nations according to how they have treated God's chosen people (14:1–2; 34:1–17). As the LORD said when he first called Abraham and Sarah:

> I will make of you a great nation, and I will bless you, and make your name great, so that you will be a blessing. I will bless those who bless you, and *the one who curses you I will curse*; and in you all the families of the earth shall be blessed (Gen 12:2–3).

Thus, the day of vengeance for the nations will be a day of salvation for the people of God (34:8; 61:2; 63:4). That being said, there are many passages in Isaiah where foreigners are invited to become part of God's people (cf. 56:1–8), which fits Israel's vocation to be a blessing and a light to the nations (42:6; 49:6).

35:5–7a. A vast, rugged wilderness stands between Babylon and Jerusalem, and it will be transformed. Water will flow, and vegetation will flourish. In addition, a highway will be constructed in the wilderness to facilitate the exiles return home. This highway through the wilderness is reminiscent of the way through the sea during Israel's exodus from Egypt. This route will be safe; it will be so well-marked and straight that even fools could never get lost on it. The highway will be called the Holy Way because no one who is unclean will be permitted to travel on it (35:8–10).

From an ancient Jewish perspective, the unclean includes all Gentiles as well as those within Israel's own ranks who are blemished in some way, for example, the blind, the deaf, the mute, and the lame as identified in 35:5–6. The unclean within Israel will also not travel the Holy Way but for quite a different reason than the Gentiles. They will be healed of their infirmities and so made clean. The deaf will hear, the blind will see, the mute will talk, and the lame will leap. Israel's disabled population will be unclean no more, and so they will travel on the Holy Way along with the rest of God's holy people.

Suggestions for Lectors

Today's reading is filled with good news, so let your voice be filled with excitement and enthusiasm as you paint a picture of the renewed creation. The reading occurs in two movements, or stanzas (4, 5–7a). Pausing and looking up prior to the beginning of a new stanza is a nice way to signal transitions.

Pay particular attention to the punctuation and to how the poetic lines are related to one another. Biblical poetry is rife with repetition and parallelism, and cultivating an awareness of and an appreciation for these elements will help you develop a rhythm and intonation for reading biblical poetry.

For example, verse 5 is composed of two poetic lines where the second line (a') reinforces the thought of the first (a) through synonymous parallelism.

a Then the eyes of the blind shall be opened,
a' and the ears of the deaf unstopped;

This same synonymous parallelism is repeated throughout 35:6–7a.

JAMES 2:1–10, (11–13), 14–17

Notes

Sequence. 2 of 5

Commentary

Jesus summed up the whole law in two commandments—love of God and love of neighbor (Mark 12:29–31); his brother James reduced it to one. In today's reading, James writes, "You do well if you really fulfill the royal law[21] according to the scripture, 'You shall love your neighbor as yourself'" (2:8). Here, James finds an affinity with Paul, who writes in Galatians, "The whole law is summed up in a single commandment, 'You shall love your neighbor as yourself'" (Gal 5:14). Of course, James and Paul are not in conflict with Jesus. They too know the primacy of loving God, but practically speaking, the principal way in which we love God with everything we are and have is by loving our neighbor as ourselves in concrete ways.

The second greatest commandment did not originate with Jesus but is found, of all places, in the OT book of Leviticus. In Leviticus 19, the LORD says to his people, "You shall be holy, for I the Lord your God am holy" (Lev 19:2). But what exactly does it mean to be holy as the LORD is holy? What does a life of holiness look like? The remainder of Leviticus 19 offers answers in the form of commands and instructions. Some of these are reminiscent of the Ten Commandments as in "you shall not steal" and "you shall not swear falsely by my name" (19:11–12). Others, however, go beyond the Ten Commandments in both content and specificity, as in "You shall not strip your vineyard bare, or gather the fallen grapes of your vineyard; you shall leave them for the poor and the alien" (19:10). Although these commandments cover a wide range of situations and circumstances, all of them fall under a single rubric, namely, "You shall love your neighbor as yourself" (19:18). Thus, according to Leviticus, a life of holiness consists in love of neighbor, for it is in loving our neighbors that we embody God's character and fulfill our vocation to be God's holy people.

One area addressed by Leviticus 19 concerns the treatment of people from different socio-economic classes. "You shall not render an unjust judgment; *you shall not be partial to the poor or defer to the great*: with justice you shall judge your neighbor" (19:15). In short, the people of God are not to show partiality, which is the very issue that James addresses in today's reading.

2:1–7. James begins by issuing a prohibition against discriminatory practices: "My brothers and sisters, do not show prejudice if you possess faith in our glorious Lord Jesus Christ" (2:1 NET).[22] Rich Christians were receiving preferential treatment in

[21] Literally, the law of the kingdom.

[22] The NRSV is one of a very few English versions that translate 2:1 as a question: "My brothers and sisters, do you with your acts of favoritism really believe in our glorious Lord Jesus Christ?"

Christian assemblies. Yet making distinctions and showing favoritism is incompatible with faith in the Lord Jesus Christ. Not only has God raised up the poor and lowly to be rich in faith (cf. 1:9), but the rich do not deserve special treatment simply because they are rich. After all, it is the rich who oppress others and sue them in court. Faith and favoritism don't mix.

2:8–9. Instead of adopting the perspectives and practices of the wider culture, which discriminates on the basis of social class, we are called to treat *everyone* with the same respect, love, and concern as we treat ourselves. When we do this, we are fulfilling the royal law—that is, the law of Moses—for the command to love one's neighbor as oneself stands at the heart of God's will for all people. Yet, when a person treats others with partiality, they are transgressing the law and betraying the faith of Jesus.

2:10–13. Some might think that favoritism is not as serious as committing adultery and murder. Yet, the same law that prohibits murder and adultery also prohibits discrimination against the poor. Breaking one part of the law is still breaking the law. Failing to love our neighbor in just one aspect is still failing to love our neighbor as ourselves. For James, then, treating the poor with contempt is equivalent to adultery or murder. Therefore, Christians ought to live as though they will be judged by the law. If they judge people by making distinctions between the rich and the poor, then they can expect judgment (cf. Matt 7:2). But "mercy triumphs over judgment" (2:13); therefore, the one who treats the poor with mercy will find themselves being treated with mercy, by their neighbors and by God (cf. Matt 6:14–15).

2:14–17. Some might argue, however, that we are not going to be judged by the law, that we are not saved by the works of the law but by faith. Yet, James questions whether faith is really faith if there are no works of faith. Faith does not exempt us from loving our neighbor, for faith finds its proper fulfillment in the love of neighbor. Once again, James returns to his concern for the poor. What kind of faith wishes our poor brothers and sisters well, and yet does not act to provide for their needs? Can that sort of faith save us? Only a living faith can save us, for "faith by itself, if it has no works, is dead" (2:17; cf. 2:26). Once again, James finds an affinity with Paul who writes "the only thing that counts is faith working through love" (Gal 5:6).

Suggestions for Lectors

In today's reading, James challenges and criticizes his readers, but he is not punitive or unforgiving. He speaks frankly, but he does not distance himself from his readers. For example, in one breath he can say, "Have you not made distinctions among yourselves, and become judges with evil thoughts?" (2:4). While in the very next breath he can address them as his "beloved brothers and sisters" (2:5). Communicate both of these aspects through your tone of voice and manner of presentation. Read with great conviction and with righteous indignation over injustice, but balance this with moments of tenderness and compassion.

James uses rhetorical questions to great effect. These questions are good places to inject energy into your reading. For example, in 2:6–7, James asks three questions in a row, all of which begin, *Is it not.* As you read, increase your tempo and pitch incrementally with each succeeding question. Emphasize *It is not* plus the subject, as in:

> *Is it not the rich* who oppress you?
> *Is it not they* who drag you into court?
> *Is it not they* who blaspheme the excellent name that was invoked over you?

There are a lot of other phrases and statements that could be emphasized in today's reading, but we cannot emphasize everything. So in your preparation, find those things that speak to you, and highlight them in your delivery.

MARK 7:24–37

Notes

Sequence. 2 of 12

Commentary

In last week's reading, Jesus engaged in a debate with the scribes and Pharisees over the matter of ritual purity. In the middle of that debate, Jesus turns to the crowd and says, "there is nothing outside a person that going in can defile [them]" (7:15). This is a remarkable pronouncement because it would seem to suggest that there is no longer any need to maintain Jewish kosher regulations and practices. This is the very conclusion that the narrator draws: "Thus [Jesus] declared all foods clean" (7:19). The implications are astounding. By rendering all foods clean, Jesus has effectively torn down a wall that has existed between Jews and Gentiles for centuries. If Jews no longer have to worry about what they ate and how it was prepared, then they would have the freedom to sit at table and share a meal with Gentiles. This was one of the issues the early church struggled with (Acts 11:1–18; Gal 2:11–14).

In terms of expanding the kingdom, declaring all foods clean opens the way for a Jewish mission to Gentiles. When Jesus sent the Twelve out on their first mission, they were not allowed to pack any food or take along any money to buy food. Instead, they were to trust God and rely upon the hospitality of those to whom they were sent (6:8–10, Prop 9). If these directives were followed, an observant Jew could not proclaim the gospel to Gentiles because kosher laws would have prohibited them from accepting Gentile hospitality. By declaring all foods clean, Jesus removes this major obstacle to Gentile mission. Thus, it is not a coincidence that, as soon as the purity debate is over, Jesus embarks on a mission in Gentile territories (7:24–8:10). This mission included the exorcism of a Gentile woman's daughter, the healing of a Gentile man who is deaf and mute, and the miraculous feeding of four thousand Gentiles, which parallels the earlier feeding of five thousand Jews (6:34–44; 8:1–9). In today's reading, we are treated to the first two of these Gentile episodes.

7:24–30. Jesus cannot escape notice in the Gentile region of Tyre even though he has never been there before. Earlier in the gospel, a crowd of people came out to see Jesus, some of whom came from as far away as Tyre and Sidon. Presumably, they brought news of Jesus back with them when they returned home. In any case, when a certain Syrophoenician Gentile woman hears about Jesus, she seeks him out.

Like Jairus, this woman bows down before Jesus and begs him to heal her daughter (cf. 5:23–24). But instead of going with her as he did with Jairus, Jesus responds by saying, "Let the children be fed first, for it is not fair to take the children's loaf and throw it to the dogs" (7:27). Much has been made of this response. Is Jesus refusing to heal this woman's daughter? And if so, is it because she is a Gentile? What exactly is going on?

Up to this point in the narrative, Jesus has never refused to heal anyone who asks for help, and he has already healed at least one Gentile, the Gerasene demoniac (5:1–20). Jesus' response seems so completely out of character and so contrary to what the reader has come to expect; the surprise, the shock, and the questions it occasions are the first indications that more is going on than meets the eye. Here, a bit of background is needed.

In Mark's second narrative movement (4:1–8:30), the disciples go from bad to good to worse. In the first sea crossing, Jesus chastises them for their ongoing lack of faith, "Why are you afraid? Have you *still* no faith?" (4:41, Prop 7). Later though, the disciples carry out a very successful Galilean mission (6:6–13, 30, Prop 9). But then things start to go bad. Following the feeding of the five thousand, Jesus forces his disciples to cross over by boat to Bethsaida, which in Mark is understood to be Gentile territory (6:45). The only other time Jesus has sent the disciples off on their own was when he sent them on their Jewish mission. This suggests that Jesus is now sending them on another mission, this time to Gentiles, but the disciples fail to reach Bethsaida. As they are crossing the sea, a strong wind inhibits their progress, so much so that Jesus comes to them walking on the sea. Yet, even after Jesus enters the boat and the wind calms down, they do not continue on to Bethsaida as originally planned but return to the western Jewish shore.

In Mark, this failed sea crossing symbolizes the disciples resistance to Gentile mission. This helps explain why they cease being described as merely lacking faith and begin to be characterized as hardhearted. At the end of the second sea crossing, the narrator injects his interpretation of their failure: "for they did not understand about the loaves because their hearts were hardened" (6:52). This cryptic explanation links the disciples failure with the feeding of the five thousand. At the end of this miraculous feeding, the disciples gathered up twelve baskets of leftovers from the five loaves that Jesus began with, which demonstrated the magnitude of the miracle. Not only were five thousand people fed with just five loaves and two fish, but there was an abundance of leftovers. Yet, the disciples fail to understand the deeper significance of these leftovers, namely, that the leftover loaves—which stand for the abundant blessings of God's kingdom—are for the Gentiles. That is why Jesus sends the disciples into Gentile territory right after this Jewish feeding. But the disciples are fundamentally opposed to sharing Israel's blessings with Gentiles, which is why the narrator in 6:52, and then Jesus in 8:17, calls them hardhearted.

One of Mark's more intriguing rhetorical strategies is his use of minor characters. In Mark, minor characters often exhibit the faith and understanding that Jesus' own disciples lack, and so they serve as foils for the disciples. For example, in the first sea crossing, Jesus chastises the disciples for their *lack of faith* (4:41). But then, a few episodes later, an unnamed woman seeking healing is praised for her *faith* (5:34). In the second crossing, the disciples are described as *lacking understanding*, but then, a few episodes later in today's reading, another unnamed woman seeking healing is praised for her *understanding*. In fact, as we shall see shortly, this woman is praised for understanding the very thing that the disciples have failed to understand.

Returning to our episode: when Jesus responds as he does to the Syrophoenician woman's request, he is not refusing to heal her daughter. Instead, he is presenting her with a parable, a riddle to be solved. In Mark, Jesus speaks in parables to outsiders (4:11), but then he explains the parables to his disciples in private (4:34). On this occasion, however, the supposed "outsider" is the one who explains Jesus' riddle, and she does so by responding to Jesus with her own riddle.

In Jesus' riddle, *the children* represent the Jews, *the dogs* represent the Gentiles, and *the children's loaf* represents God's promises and blessings to Israel. When the woman requests healing for her daughter, Jesus does not say that God's blessings are not for Gentiles, only that the children must be fed *first*. In her parabolic reply, the woman acknowledges and accepts the priority of the children. She is not asking for the children's loaf, but only for the leftover crumbs that fall from the table. Moreover, she knows that the dogs are already consuming the crumbs. Although the crowd that gathered around Jesus in Galilee was primarily Jewish, it did include some Gentiles (3:7–12). Thus, she is only asking that she might also get a crumb. Through this exchange, it becomes clear that the Syrophoenician woman understands about the loaves. In marked contrast to Jesus' Jewish disciples, this Gentile woman understands that the leftover loaves—the overflow of God's blessings to Israel—are for the Gentiles. Moreover, she understands that Gentiles will receive and benefit from those blessings even before all of the Jews do. Her understanding about the loaves is confirmed by Jesus. She has answered wisely, and her daughter is healed.

One final word: The Gospel of Mark is replete with irony, and today's episode is no exception. Jesus' initial response to the woman's request was not only parabolic, it was also highly ironic because the content of the riddle does not represent Jesus' own views. As one scholar has observed:

> To read only what lies "on the surface of it" is to misread it. It is instead to be read as a bit of tongue-in-cheek. This is irony of a special kind.... it is peirastic irony.... a form of verbal challenge intended to test the other's response. It may in fact declare *the opposite of the speaker's actual intention*.[23]

So when Jesus says, "Let the children be fed first, for it is not fair to take the children's loaf and throw it to the dogs" (7:27), I would submit that Jesus is actually voicing one of the disciples' unstated objections to Gentile mission. In the early church, Jewish Christians struggled with the fact that so many of their fellow Jews were rejecting the gospel while at the same time so many Gentiles were coming into the faith. In Romans, Paul explains this mystery: "I want you to understand this mystery:

---

[23] Jerry Camery-Hoggatt, *Irony in Mark's Gospel: Text and Subtext* (SNTSMS 72; Cambridge: Cambridge University Press, 1992), 150 (emphasis added).

a hardening has come upon part of Israel, until the full number of the Gentiles has come in" (11:25). It would appear that the Syrophoenician woman beat Paul to it.

7:31–37. The second episode is not as complicated as the first, but it does have its own intriguing elements. After leaving the region of Tyre, Jesus continues his sojourn in Gentile territory and eventually comes into the region of the Decapolis. A deaf man, who understandably also has a speech impediment, is brought before Jesus. Generally, Jesus heals people simply by touching them and or by issuing a command. Yet, on this occasion, Jesus also employs spittle. This is quite unusual. The only other time Jesus uses spittle is in his healing of a blind man, who also happens to be a Gentile (8:22–26). Immediately, the deaf man is able to hear and to speak clearly. Those who witness this extraordinary event are utterly astounded. "He has done everything well; he even makes the deaf to hear and the mute to speak" (7:37). This statement connects with today's OT reading from Isaiah:

> Then the eyes of the blind shall be opened,
>   and *the ears of the deaf unstopped*;
> then the lame shall leap like a deer,
>   and *the tongue of the speechless sing for joy* (35:5–6).

As is so often the case, Jesus enjoins silence, but he is completely ignored (cf. 1:44–45). The more he tries to quiet the witnesses, the more they proclaim what he has done. They simply cannot help it. After all, as Jesus himself said earlier:

> Is a lamp brought in to be put under the bushel basket, or under the bed, and not on the lampstand? For there is nothing hidden, except to be disclosed; nor is anything secret, except to come to light. Let anyone with ears to hear listen! (4:21–23).

Their inability to remain quiet may account for the fact that in the very next episode a crowd of four thousand people has descended upon Jesus (8:1–9).

Suggestions for Lectors

7:24–30. Begin reading in your normal narrating voice. In the first half of 1:26, the narrator interrupts the story to insert information regarding the woman's ethnic background. This functions like a parenthetical expression, so drop your voice as you read it. Then, return to your normal narrating voice for *She begged....*

In the Commentary, it was suggested that Jesus' response to the woman's request is not a refusal to heal, but a riddle to be solved. In other words, Jesus' is not closing down communication but opening it up, which makes a significant difference in how Jesus' statement is to be delivered. Use a tone of voice that invites a response. One way this can be achieved is by reading the final phrase, *to the dogs*, with an upward inflection instead of a downward inflection, almost as though the statement has been transformed into a question at the end—almost, but not quite. Then, without any hint of desperation or fear, deliver the woman's rejoinder in a strong, firm, yet respectful manner.

7:31–38. After pausing for a couple of seconds between episodes, begin reading the second episode in your normal tone and tempo. In 7:33–35, Jesus takes the deaf man away from the crowd in order to heal him in private. So for these verses drop your voice ever so slightly and read slowly, as though you are trying to keep the healing a secret. Then, in 7:36–37, increase the pitch, speed, and volume of your voice as Jesus tries without success to suppress the crowd's excitement. Generally, one slows down when delivering the last line of an episode, but that is not necessary on this occasion. We do not want anything to diminish the crowd's astonishment.

Pronunciation Guide
Decapolis (dih-KAP-uh-lis; dee-), *Ephphatha* (EF-uh-thuh; ef-AH-thuh), *Galilee* (GAL-uh-lee), *Gentile* (JEN-tīl), *Sidon* (SĪ-duhn), *Tyre* (TĪR), *Syrophoenician* (sī-roh-fuh-NEE'-shuhn; sī-roh-fuh-NISH'-uhn)

PROPER 19

September 11–17

Proverbs 1:20–33	Isaiah 50:4–9a
Psalm 19 *or* Wisdom of Solomon 7:26–8:1	Psalm 116:1–9 (= 116:1–8 BCP)
James 3:1–12	James 3:1–12
Mark 8:27–38	Mark 8:27–38

Proverbs 1:20–33

Notes
Sequence. 2 of 3

Commentary
Although the book of Proverbs bears the superscription, "The proverbs of Solomon son of David, king of Israel" (1:1), Solomon did not compose all of the proverbs contained in the book. Not only does Proverbs contain much traditional wisdom known from elsewhere in the Ancient Near East, but the book itself attributes proverbs to other sources. Thus, Proverbs is best understood as an anthology of wisdom sayings, consisting of proverbs Solomon himself composed (10:1; 25:1) as well as proverbs that he and others collected (1:6; 22:17; 24:23; 30:1; 31:1).

In Proverbs, the Wisdom of God—that is, his understanding, prudence, intelligence—is personified as a woman. In fact, the first third of the book is given over, not to individual aphorisms, but to an extended treatise on the character of Lady Wisdom (1:20–9:18). More often than not, Wisdom speaks in first person and extols her own virtues, as in today's reading.

1:20–23. Wisdom does not simply make herself known to the wealthy, the powerful, or the privileged. She makes herself available to anyone who will listen. This is why Wisdom's voice can be heard in the streets, in market squares, on busy corners, and at the entrances to walled-in cities. If people will just listen, then Wisdom will give of herself and make them wise.

1:24–33. Despite her proactive approach, Wisdom finds that few people are interested in accepting what she has to offer. By and large, her counsel is ignored and her reprimands and warnings dismissed. And so, Wisdom will sit back and watch people suffer the consequences of their own folly. When those who have ignored Wisdom finally call upon her in their panicked distress, they will find that Wisdom is not available. Wisdom only responds to those who seek after her, to those who know that a life of reverence and fear of the LORD is the beginning of Wisdom (cf. 1:7; 9:10). And with Wisdom comes security.

Suggestions for Lectors

In today's reading, you will need two voices: one for the sage who introduces Wisdom (1:20–21) and one for Wisdom herself (1:22–33). Also, make sure to pause for a full second before 1:22 to signal the change in speakers. Wisdom is not shy; she is bold and outspoken, so read with great energy and conviction. As always, deliver these words as though you yourself are Wisdom, as though you are saying to your listeners, *Give heed to my reproof* (1:23a).

As you prepare for reading, pay attention to the poetic structure of these verses, the medium through which their meaning is conveyed. In most cases, you will find pairs of lines that reinforce, parallel, or relate to one another in some fashion. For example, in the following, notice how each line expresses the same thought with different words.

1:23 I will pour out my thoughts to you;
I will make my words known to you.

Often poetic lines are divided into two parts (a, b). In 1:28, notice how each part in the first poetic line has a partner in the second line. This rhetorical feature is called parallelism. In this instance, the parallelism forms an a-b-a'-b' pattern.

		a	b
1:28	Then	they will call upon me,	but I will not answer;
		a'	b'
		they will seek me diligently,	but will not find me.

In 1:20, the parallelism occurs in a different sequence. It follows an a-b-b'-a' pattern, which is a common rhetorical feature called a chiasm.

	a	b
1:20	Wisdom cries out	in the street;
	b'	a'
	in the squares	she raises her voice.

In short, have fun exploring and playing around with the rhetorical structures and features of biblical poetry. The more you cultivate an awareness, appreciation, and enjoyment of these features, the more you will be able to communicate the meaning of poetic texts to your listeners.

Isaiah 50:4–9a

Notes

Sequence. 2 of 2

Commentary

Through its rich poetry and prose, the book of Isaiah narrates a dramatic story of rebellion and judgment that gives way to forgiveness and redemption. The plot begins with God's chosen people, but then broadens to encompass all the nations of the world and even creation itself. In Isaiah 1–39, the drama focuses upon rebellion as humanity serves the gods of its own making and orders society through unjust practices and power structures. The prophet Isaiah is sent to announce the various judgments that will be executed by the LORD, the Holy One of Israel and the creator of the heavens and the earth. Judgment begins with the LORD's own people who have forsaken the covenant (Isa 1–12, 28–35) through their willful and persistent failure to love God with their whole heart (Deut 6:5, Prop 26; Exod 20:1–7, Lent 3) and to love their neighbors as themselves (Lev 19:18; Exod 20:8–17). Judgment then extends to the nations and empires of the world who oppose the sovereign rule of the LORD through their prideful and unjust exercise of power (Isa 13–23). Even the forces of chaos and evil that threaten God's good creation will be judged, not least death itself (25:7–8, East).

Yet beginning in Isaiah 40, the ominous tone of judgment gives way to a joyful note of hope as the prophet announces a *new thing* that the LORD is about to do (42:9; 43:19; 48:6). This new thing, which will eventually result in the restoration of all creation, will begin with the LORD forgiving and redeeming his chosen people. Through his chosen people, God will bring about the redemption and reconciliation of all peoples everywhere, in keeping with his covenant promises to Abraham and Sarah (Gen 12:2–3; Gen 17:16; 22:17–18, EastVig). Within this redemptive drama of Isaiah 40–55, we find four passages concerning an unidentified servant of the LORD (42:1–4; 49:1–6; 50:4–9; 52:13–53:12, GFri). These passages are often referred to as the Servant Songs. The servant appears sometimes as a corporate personality and sometimes as a single individual. There is a broad, general movement from the servant as *Israel* to the servant as *a single Israelite* who takes on Israel's vocation to be both the restorer of God's chosen people and the light to the nations (cf. 49:5–6).

Early Christians saw many similarities between Jesus and Isaiah's servant, especially with regard to Jesus' suffering and death. Their understanding of what God had done through Jesus' suffering and death was informed by the description of what the LORD did through the suffering of the servant in Isaiah, and vice versa. The importance of Isaiah's servant for understanding Jesus is reflected in the fact that each of the Servant Songs is read during Holy Week. In today's reading of the third Servant Song, we see that the servant's living out of his vocation was not without significant personal risk.

50:4–6. The servant begins by noting that the LORD has equipped him for his prophetic vocation by giving him "the tongue of a teacher, that I may know how to sustain the weary with a word" (50:4). In this context, the weary are those of God's chosen people who are living in Babylon waiting for the LORD to lead them back to the Promised Land, as the prophet announced God was about to do (cf. 40:1–11, Adv 2). Yet, the words that the servant has been given to speak are not welcomed by everyone. Perhaps the Babylonian authorities fear that the servant is inciting rebellion among the exiles. Much more likely, however, is the possibility that the servant is opposed by his own people. Among the exiles were those who had made good lives for themselves in Babylon; they were not disposed to re-immigrate to Judah and Jerusalem. They were not ready to take up their vocation as God's chosen people, a vocation that they found oppressive. Whatever the cause, the servant suffers humiliation and abuse as a direct result of his being obedient to his calling to be the servant of the LORD. The servant does not back down in the face of such persecution; he neither retaliates violently nor passively submits.

50:7–9a. Moreover, despite such persecution, the servant does not abandon his trust in God. The servant faithfully lives out his calling with firm resolve, knowing that in the end no one will be able to question the legitimacy of what he has done. Here, one is reminded of Jesus' predictions of his own suffering and death and his conviction that God would vindicate him by raising him from the dead (Mark 8:31–33, Lent 2; 9:30–32, Prop 20; 10:32–34).

Suggestions for Lectors

As a lector, it is helpful to break a reading up into smaller sections that are easier for aural consumption. Today's reading falls naturally into three sections, each of which begins with *The Lord GOD* (50:4, 5–6, 7–9a). Alternatively, since the reading is relatively short and the first two sections fit well together, you could think in terms of two sections (50:4–6; 50:7–9a). Whatever option you choose, pause for a full second before proceeding with each section, and slow your tempo as you conclude each section. Raise your voice in 50:7, as the servant uses courtroom terminology to state his case and express his hope. The reading ends firmly on this positive note.

Pronunciation Guide

Isaiah (ī-ZAY-uh)

JAMES 3:1–12

Notes

Sequence. 3 of 5

Commentary

In the opening chapter of James, the author moves quickly from topic to topic, engaging in brief discussions or offering pithy aphorisms that he will develop later in the letter. In 1:26 (Prop 17), James writes, "If any think they are religious, and do not bridle their tongues but deceive their hearts, their religion is worthless." In today's reading, James returns to discuss the tongue, the most powerful, and potentially the most destructive, organ in the whole human body.

3:1–2a. In the ancient Mediterranean world, teachers were accorded special honor, but James discourages people from becoming teachers because teachers will be held to a higher standard. Teaching involves speaking, and we all make a lot of mistakes when we speak, making it even harder to live up to the high standard by which teachers will be judged.

3:2b–5a. James then makes a stunning claim: "Anyone who makes no mistakes in speaking is perfect, able to keep the whole body in check with a bridle" (3:2b). But how can human perfection be reduced to a matter of speech, particularly when James has insisted that true religion is a matter of putting our faith into action and caring for others (1:27; 2:14–17, Prop 18)? Because the tongue is able to control the whole human person, to guide and direct what a person thinks, feels, and does, for good or for ill. The tongue is like a horse's bit and a ship's rudder. Though small, these are able to control things much bigger than themselves. In short, the tongue is a very powerful member of the body, which is both a blessing and a curse.

3:5b–9. The tongue can set a whole community on fire just as easily as a spark can set a forest ablaze. And, with our modern advancements in communication (email, text messaging, and twitter), the tongue can now destroy relationships and infect communities more quickly and thoroughly than at any other time in human history.

3:10–12. The human tongue must be tamed; it must be redeemed. The tongue must become sacred and only used for holy purposes, like blessing God and blessing our neighbor. To bless God and then to curse God's image-bearers is contradictory. One thing cannot produce two contradictory effects. A spring cannot produce both fresh water and salt water; it is either one or the other. Moreover, something cannot produce something else that is not in keeping with its own nature. A fig tree cannot produce olives.

The tongues of Christians must serve Christian ends. If Christians were to exercise appropriate control over their tongues, then according to the logic of James, they would fulfill the whole law because, through their speech, they would be able to direct and guide their actions and those of Christ's community toward loving their neighbors as themselves (2:8, Prop 18).

Suggestions for Lectors

In today's reading, a change takes place in the middle of 3:5. Up to this point, James is instructing his readers in a fairly straightforward manner, teaching them about the power of the human tongue and how perfection lies in one's ability to control their speech. James then concludes with, *the tongue is a small member, yet it boasts of great exploits* (3:5a).

Once this statement is made, James becomes more impassioned. He uses this statement as a springboard to launch into a treatise on the destructive power of the tongue. He becomes more energetic and animated, and you will want to reflect this in your delivery. At this point, read with greater energy and intensity by increasing the pitch of your voice and the tempo with which you read.

In 3:9, highlight the point being made by emphasizing the words *bless* and *curse.* With incredulity read, *From the same mouth come blessing and cursing* (3:10a). Then, with a sense of urgent pleading, declare, *My brothers and sisters, this ought not to be so* (3:10b).

MARK 8:27–38

Notes
Sequence. 3 of 12

Commentary
In today's reading, Jesus and his disciples travel north, deep into Gentile territory to Caesarea Philippi for what will be a major turning point in the gospel. In the villages of Caesarea Philippi, Peter declares that Jesus is the Messiah, at which point Jesus begins telling his disciples that a cross awaits him in Jerusalem.

Leading into today's reading, Mark narrates a most extraordinary event. In 8:22, a blind man is brought to Jesus for healing. Jesus generally heals people by touching them and or by issuing a command. On this occasion, however, Jesus does not say anything, instead he touches the man and spits in his eyes. This is unusual; the only other time Jesus used spittle was in last week's healing of a man who was deaf and mute (7:33). Yet, what is so extraordinary is that the blind man is not fully healed, at least not initially. Jesus asks him, "Can you see anything?," and he replies, "I can see people, but they look like trees, walking" (8:24). Jesus touches the blind man a second time, and finally the man's sight is restored completely, and "he can see everything clearly" (8:25). This has never happened before with one of Jesus' miracles. As we shall see, this unprecedented two-stage healing is symbolic and serves a rhetorical function in Mark's gospel.

8:27–30. Ever since Jesus began his public ministry, questions about his identity and the nature of his authority have followed him. After his first miracle, an exorcism, the amazed witnesses exclaimed, "*What is this?* A new teaching—with authority! He commands even the unclean spirits, and they obey him" (1:27, Epi 4). Then, after his exorcistic stilling of the storm, his own awe-filled disciples ask, "*Who then is this*, that even the wind and the sea obey him?" (4:41, Prop 7). These rhetorical questions remain unanswered throughout the first half of Mark's gospel. They lurk behind everything that transpires in the narrative and only receive an adequate answer in today's climactic recognition scene.

As they make their way to the villages of Caesarea Philippi, Jesus asks his disciples, "Who do people say that I am?" The responses they give are the same speculations encountered earlier in the gospel (6:14–16, Prop 10). Jesus is John the Baptist or Elijah *redivinus*, or one of the prophets. But when Jesus asks them, "But who do you say that I am?," Peter, speaking for the disciples, declares: "You are the Messiah" (8:29). This is a climactic moment as Peter is the first and only character in Mark's gospel to recognize Jesus as God's Anointed. The reader, of course, has known this from the very beginning (1:1), but none of the other human characters in the gospel ever declare Jesus to be the Messiah. Jesus responds in typical Markan fashion by enjoining silence regarding his true identity (cf. 1:34; 3:11–12).

8:31–33. Peter's confession is a watershed moment. The exorcisms, healings, and mighty deeds that are so prominent in the first half of the gospel all but come to an end in the second half. In their place, Jesus begins to prepare his disciples for the fate that awaits him in Jerusalem. Now that his disciples know he is the Messiah, Jesus begins to reveal what his messianic vocation entails. "He began to teach them that the Son of Man must undergo great suffering, and be rejected by the elders, the chief priests, and the scribes, and be killed, and after three days rise again" (8:31). Here, we see that Jesus is no longer speaking in metaphor and in parable; rather, he is speaking quite openly and unambiguously about his death.

Jesus predicts his suffering, death, and resurrection three times in Mark (8:31; 9:30–32; 10:32–34), and each of these passion predictions follows the same pattern. After each prediction, the disciples do or say something that indicates they have not fully understood the implications of what Jesus has told them. In today's episode, Peter plays this part. He rebukes Jesus for talking about suffering and death, and he thereby exposes a deficiency in his and the other disciples' understanding of who Jesus is. Just a few moments previous, Peter correctly identified Jesus as the Messiah, but clearly he does not understand what messiahship entails.

Peter is like the blind man after Jesus' first touch. He sees who Jesus is, but his vision is blurred. The disciples have seen Jesus say and do some powerful and amazing things, and on this basis, they rightly recognize that Jesus is the Messiah. Yet, again their sight is only partial. If they (and we as Mark's readers) are to gain full sight of who Jesus is as Messiah and Son of God, a second touch is required.

In Mark, second touch that brings full sight is the crucifixion itself, which constitutes a second climactic recognition scene. When the Gentile centurion sees the way in which Jesus dies, he declares, "Truly this man was God's Son!" (15:39, Palm). The centurion is the only human character in Mark to recognize Jesus as the Son of God. Demons know it (1:24, 34; 3:11; 5:7), and God declares it (1:11; 9:7), but again, the centurion is the only *human* character to recognize and acknowledge Jesus as God's Son. Ironically, it is not one of Jesus' miracles, but rather his death that generates the centurion's insight. Jesus' death on the cross is not only a sacrifice for sins (cf. 10:45; 14:24), it is also the means by which his divine identity is fully and finally made known. In short, the crucifixion is an act of divine revelation.

The authoritative words and deeds of Jesus reveal him to be the Messiah (the first touch), but it is only his suffering and death that reveal him to be the divine Son of God (the second touch). Together, these two confessions—Messiah and Son of God—paint the full picture of who Jesus is (cf. 1:1). In today's episode, the disciples are halfway there. From Jesus' exorcisms and healings, they have rightly discerned that he is the Messiah who has come to usher in the kingdom of God. But, only when the disciples are finally able to incorporate suffering and death into their understanding of who Jesus is as the Messiah will they have full insight, not only into who Jesus is, but also into who they are as his followers.

Unfortunately, the disciples never come to full recognition of who Jesus is, at least not within the narrative of Mark's gospel. In the end, they abandon Jesus to his fate, and he dies alone, forsaken by his closest companions and seemingly forsaken by God. Thus, it is up to a Gentile centurion—a non-Jew and a non-disciple—to receive the revelation of who Jesus is as the suffering Son of God.

8:34–38. If the way of the Messiah entails suffering and death, then the way of the Messiah's disciples will also entail suffering and death. Paradoxically, only those who give up their lives for Jesus and the gospel will save their lives. When Jesus says, "Those who are ashamed of me and my words…" (8:38), Peter's rebuke of Jesus is in the background. In this context, to be ashamed of the Messiah is to reject the way of the Messiah and so refuse to walk the way of the cross. Those who are ashamed of Jesus will find that he is ashamed of them when he appears in all his kingly glory. Persons cannot share in Jesus' messianic glory unless they are also willing to share in his messianic suffering.

Without diminishing the severity of these words or the importance of taking up one's cross, it is of some comfort to recall that every one of Jesus' disciples abandoned him, yet he did not abandon them. On the eve of his crucifixion, Jesus predicts that his disciples will all desert him, yet he promises to meet them again in Galilee after his resurrection (14:27–28). Peter denies Jesus, and the rest run away, but Jesus still forgives them. Anyone who wants to follow Jesus must travel the way of suffering and death; there are no exceptions. Fortunately, however, there are signposts and rest stops of grace all along the way.

Suggestions for Lectors

Begin today's reading in your normal narrating voice. Do not emphasize Jesus' first question; it is the second question that warrants emphasis. Instead, ask the first question as though Jesus were merely curious, as though his question were not leading up to anything. The disciples' response contains three different speculations. Pause for a second between each to give the impression that more than one disciple is answering Jesus' question. In the second question, emphasize *you*: *But who do <u>you</u> say that I am?* (8:29). Slow down as you present Peter's response. Speak with seriousness, enunciating each word with care and emphasizing *Messiah*: *You are <u>the Messiah</u>* (8:30).

After a dramatic pause, continue with the second half of the reading. Although Jesus speaks in the third person (the Son of Man), he is talking about his own fate, so read with evident emotion in your voice. Read slowly and adopt a tone of voice that conveys the gravity of what Jesus is trying to communicate to his disciples. Raise and harden your voice when rebuking Peter. Emphasize *Satan*, *not*, *divine*, and *human*, and also introduce slight pauses after *mind* and *things*, as in: *Get behind me, <u>Satan</u>! For you are setting your mind… <u>not</u> on <u>divine</u> things… but on <u>human</u> things* (8:33).

Pause for a full second as the scene shifts from the disciples to the crowds. Then, raise your voice and proclaim Jesus' words to your listeners as though they are meant for them—which, of course, they are. Highlight Jesus' first two statements by reading them slowly and deliberately. In the first statement, emphasize all of the imperatives: *deny*, *take up*, and *follow* (8:34). In the second statement, emphasize *save* and *lose*, both of which occur twice (8:35). In 8:36–37, shift to a slightly higher tempo, then reduce the tempo for 8:38. In this final declaration, emphasize both occurrences of *ashamed* (8:38).

Pronunciation Guide

Caesarea (ses'-uh-REE-uh, sez'-, seez'-),
Elijah (ee-LĪ-juh; ih-), *Messiah* (muh-SĪ-uh),
Philippi (FIL-uh-pī; fih-LIP-ī), *Satan* (SAY-tuhn)

PROPER 20

September 18–24

Proverbs 31:10–31	Wisdom of Solomon 1:16–2:1, 12–22
	or Jeremiah 11:18–20
Psalm 1	Psalm 54
James 3:13–4:3, 7–8a	James 3:13–4:3, 7–8a
Mark 9:30–37	Mark 9:30–37

PROVERBS 31:10–31

Notes

Sequence. 3 of 3

Commentary

In the book of Proverbs, Wisdom and Folly are both personified as women, and the life that Lady Wisdom offers (cf. 9:1–6, Prop 15) is contrasted with the death afforded by Dame Folly (9:13–18). Similarly, Proverbs contains a number of aphorisms extolling the blessings of a wise and virtuous wife (18:22; 19:14) over against the grief and turmoil that an adulterous or contentious wife can bring (6:24–26; 21:9; 25:24; 27:15–16). For example, "A good wife is the crown of her husband, but she who brings shame is like rottenness in his bones" (12:4).

In last week's reading from the first chapter of Proverbs, we heard Wisdom call all and sundry to heed her words. In this week's reading, the whole book of Proverbs concludes with an ode to a capable Wife, described as one who embodies the virtues and bears the fruit of Lady Wisdom. That being said, a question still remains: How does this hymn function in Proverbs, and how should it be read?

Is it providing a description of the ideal wife, one that husbands can measure their own wives against and one that wives are expected to emulate? If so, then this seems like a strange way to conclude a collection of wisdom sayings. Instead, it is more likely that this hymn is another portrait of Wisdom personified, not simply as a woman but as a wife. If so, then the message seems to be, look what happens when one seeks out and marries Wisdom. With Wisdom as one's Spouse and with this Spouse guiding all of one's affairs, all of life becomes blessed, abundant, and right. Thus, Proverbs concludes with a hymn that revels in the manifold blessings and virtues of Wife Wisdom.

31:10–31. Wife Wisdom is the most treasured possession in all the earth (31:10; cf. 8:11). The husband who trusts her will find "no lack of gain" (31:11), and his life will be full and satisfying (31:12). With Wisdom by his side, his reputation will grow until he takes his seat among the wise elders of the community, who hear and settle disputes, which are presented at the city gates (31:23).

Wife Wisdom provides food (31:14–16), clothing (31:13, 19, 22), and the means for making a living (31:18, 24). Wisdom is generous to all. It is not the rich alone who benefit from Wisdom for she "opens her hand to the poor, and reaches out her hands to the needy" (31:20). In the end, Wisdom receives honor and praise from her husband and her children and all her works (31:28, 31).

Suggestions for Lectors

If there is a verse in today's reading that warrants special emphasis, it is the first one. *A capable wife who can find? She is far more precious than jewels* (31:10). Read it with a raised voice and at a slower tempo, then pause for a second before continuing with the remainder of the reading.

In poetry, it is common for the word order to be different from what is common in prose texts or in normal speech. For example, in regular speech, we would expect the question to be, "Who can find a capable wife?" But, in 31:10, the direct object has been brought forward for emphasis. Consequently, this is a question that starts out more like a statement, so pause for a second after *wife*, as in: *A capable wife… who can find?*

Each verse describes some quality of Wife Wisdom. While some verses can be read together—for example, 1:11–12 and 1:28–29—most are able to stand on their own. Instead of presenting us with a sustained argument or treatise on Wife Wisdom, today's reading serves as a litany of praise. Therefore, do not feel compelled to create smooth transitions between verses; after all, this is a book of proverbs. Instead, it would be appropriate to treat each verse as an individual proverb, by pausing for longer than normal between verses (except, of course, with 1:11–12, 1:28–29).

Some verses share a catchword, so they could be read together. For example, while verses 19 and 20 highlight two completely different qualities, both repeat the word *hand(s)*, which has a unifying effect:

> 19 She puts her *hands* to the distaff,
> and her *hands* hold the spindle.
> 20 She opens her *hand* to the poor,
> and reaches out her *hands* to the needy.

So, these verses could be read without a break between them. Similarly, verses 24 and 25 share some common imagery. Verse 24 speaks of *linen garments* and *sashes*, while verse 25 speaks of *clothing*. So, you may wish to read these verses together, or you could treat them as individual proverbs. It is entirely up to you. The important thing is to attend to the text, to become familiar with it and make conscious decisions on how best to present it to your listeners.

Pronunciation Guide

distaff (DIS-taf; DIS-tahf)

WISDOM OF SOLOMON 1:16–2:1, 12–22

Commentary

The Wisdom of Solomon (or just Wisdom) belongs to a collection of books known within Protestant traditions as the Apocrypha and within Roman Catholicism as Deuterocanonical (that is, Second Canon). In Eastern Orthodoxy, Wisdom is simply a part of the OT scriptures. Although King Solomon is not mentioned by name, the book presents itself as having come from Israel's celebrated king. For example, the first-person prayer in Wisdom 9 is an expansion of Solomon's prayer for wisdom at the beginning of his reign (1 Kings 3:6–9, Prop 15). Nevertheless, current consensus regards the Wisdom of Solomon as being the work of an anonymous Jew living during the Greco-Roman period, late first century B.C. or the early first century A.D., and possibly residing in Alexandria, Egypt.

In the opening chapters of Wisdom, the sage contrasts the lots of the righteous and the unrighteous. Those who love righteousness receive wisdom and life, but those who practice unrighteousness are courting death. In today's reading, the sage reveals how the ungodly think about life and how their perspectives on life, or rather their perspectives on death, inform and shape their behavior.

1:16. The problem with sin is that it is an invitation to death. Practicing sin, be it with our words or our actions, is akin to making a covenant with death; it is inviting Death to be our best friend. But why would anybody want to do that?

2:1. According to the author of Wisdom, the problem lies in how the ungodly think about life. They mistakenly assume that death is a natural part of creation, as though God made death (contrast with 1:13, Prop 8). They assume that because everyone's life ends in death, that there is no recovery from death and that nothing exists beyond death. For them, death is all there is to this ill-fated human life. For the ungodly, human life is, in the words of Thomas Hobbes, "solitary, poor, nasty, brutish, and short." Given such an outlook, it is no wonder that the unrighteous not only happen to sin, but they make plans to sin.

2:12–20. For example, the unrighteous lie in wait to waylay the righteous because the latter oppose and disapprove of their ungodly behavior. Even the existence of a righteous person presents a challenge to the unrighteous because it pricks their conscience: "the very sight of him is a burden to us" (2:15). Yet, instead of listening to their conscience, they conspire to persecute, destroy, and kill the righteousness. They are like a person who, instead of attending to the raging fire, disconnects the ringing smoke alarm because it is too annoying and bothersome.

In addition, the ungodly justify their persecution of the righteous. They reason, "If the righteous are really of God, if they are really the children of God, then God will deliver and protect them from their adversaries, that is, from us."

2:21–22. The author of Wisdom hopes that the inherent flaws in this reasoning are obvious. The sin and wickedness of the ungodly renders them incapable of discerning the purposes of God because the wisdom that comes from God will not "enter a deceitful soul, or dwell in a body enslaved to sin" (1:4). They are caught up in a vicious cycle of their own making. They act as though death has the final say in life, and ironically, for them, it does. Their self-inflicted blindness keeps them from seeing that there is a reward for a holy and blameless life, namely, eternal life. As the sage says following today's reading, "God created us for incorruption, and made us in the image of his own eternity" (2:23, Prop 8). In other words, God destined us to live forever with him, and so righteousness will carry us beyond death into immortality (1:15).

Suggestions for Lectors

Begin the reading in your normal narrating voice until 2:1b when you start quoting the words, thoughts, and reasonings of the ungodly. Then, adjust the tone of your voice to match what is being conveyed by the ungodly.

In 2:1, the ungodly are presenting their view of life, so you can deliver these lines in a fairly straightforward manner. But beginning in 2:12, the ungodly go on the attack as they plot, *Let us lie in wait for the righteous man*.... At this point, harden your voice and invest it with traces of anger, disgust, and contempt. In 2:17, the opposition of the ungodly to the righteous has reached a fevered pitch, so increase your intensity and your tempo through the end of the reading. Emphasize each *Let us*, which occurs four times.

Pronunciation Guide

Solomon (SAH-luh-muhn, SOL-uh-)

JEREMIAH 11:18–20

Commentary

In today's gospel reading, Jesus speaks to his disciples about the suffering and death that awaits him in Jerusalem. In today's OT reading, the prophet Jeremiah is informed about a plot against his life, and the conspirators are citizens of Anathoth (Jer 11:21), Jeremiah's hometown (1:1). But why have members of Jeremiah's own community, some of whom were likely his kinsfolk and relatives, conspired against him? The text does not say, but most likely, they opposed Jeremiah's message of impending judgment against the nation of Judah and the inhabitants of Jerusalem (11:2, 6, 9 12, 13). Not only was Jeremiah's message unpopular, some probably considered it blasphemous for not only did Jeremiah announce the destruction of the nation, but he also announced the destruction of the temple, the LORD's own house. In fact, later on, when Jeremiah engages in a prophetic demonstration in the temple precincts, he is arrested and put in the stocks (20:2).

Today's reading belongs to a group of passages in the book of Jeremiah that are variously referred to as the Lamentations, the Complaints, or the Confessions of Jeremiah (11:18–23; 12:1–6; 15:10–12; 17:14–18; 18:18–23). In these passages, the prophet takes a break from speaking the word of the LORD and instead directs his own words to the LORD. In these heartfelt and rather blunt prayers, Jeremiah rails against the LORD and against his own prophetic calling. He complains about the situations the LORD has forced him into, and he demands deliverance.

11:18–20. In today's reading, Jeremiah notes that it was the LORD himself who opened his eyes to the plot against his life. Before that revelation, Jeremiah was like a lamb being led to the slaughter, he was unknowingly walking into mortal danger. Jeremiah knows that he is innocent, so he asks the LORD to judge the situation, knowing that the LORD will correctly identify and punish the guilty, that is, Jeremiah's enemies.

Suggestions for Lectors

Today's reading is relatively brief, so pause for a few seconds between introducing the reading and beginning. This will ensure that your listeners are attuned and ready to listen. In your preparation and in your delivery, do not think of yourself as simply passing on somebody else's words, imagine that *you* are Jeremiah and that you are telling *your* story.

Begin the reading at a normal volume and pace. Then, at the beginning of 11:19, soften your voice ever so slightly as you read, *But I was like a gentle lamb*.... Then, increase your volume, tempo, and intensity, as you read the schemes of Jeremiah's enemies, *Let us destroy... remembered!* (11:19b). Pause for a second at the end of 11:19, but retain the same intensity as you deliver Jeremiah's response in 11:20, as you ask God to judge your enemies. Finally, as you draw the reading to a close, reduce the intensity of your voice and deliver the final poetic line with a tone of quiet confidence, *for to you I have committed my cause.*

Pronunciation Guide

Jeremiah (jair'-uh-MĪ-uh)

JAMES 3:13–4:3, 7–8A

Notes

Sequence. 4 of 5

Commentary

The Letter of James has much in common with the wisdom literature of the Bible,[24] both in form and in content. In biblical wisdom literature, the sages speak of the two ways (or the two paths)—the way of wisdom and the way of folly. In today's reading, James follows in this tradition when he writes about the two wisdoms—wisdom from above and wisdom from below. Wisdom from above is the fruit of friendship with God, while wisdom from below results from friendship with the world.

3:13–18. Earlier in the letter, James talks about being "doers of the word, and not merely hearers who deceive themselves" (1:22, Prop 17). So, it is not surprising that when he talks about wisdom, he does so by talking about good works. While wisdom involves thought and intentionality, wisdom is only wisdom when it finds embodiment in concrete actions, just as faith is only alive when it expresses itself through love and care for others (cf. 2:8, 14–17, Prop 18).

Wisdom from below is born of envy and selfish ambition, which leads to disorder and all varieties of wickedness (3:16) and to conflicts, disputes, and murder (4:1–2). On the other hand, the seven qualities of wisdom from above engender harmony, unity, and community.

One of the recurrent themes in wisdom literature is that we reap what we sow. Here in James, it is not only *what* we sow but *how* we sow it that is important. In 3:13, James writes, "show by your good life that your works are done *with gentleness* born

---

[24] This includes the Old Testament books of Job, Proverbs, and Ecclesiastes as well as Sirach and the Wisdom of Solomon in the Apocrypha.

of wisdom." Then, in 3:18, he writes that a harvest of righteousness is produced when peacemakers sow *in peace*, that is, when they sow in a gentle, merciful, willing-to-yield manner.

4:1–3. In the first chapter, James writes that, if we allow ourselves to be enticed by our own desires, they will give birth to sin, which will grow and mature and eventually give birth to death (1:14–15). James returns to this topic and talks about how our desires and cravings can lead to covetousness and murder, to the destruction of individuals and communities. Our desires even corrupt and twist our prayers so that we do not receive what we ask for because we are being motivated by self-interest.

4:7–8a. The solution to this problem is to break off our friendship with the world (4:4–6) and submit ourselves to God. This involves two movements, resisting the devil and drawing near to God. Both of these movements should occur at the same time, and both of them should become habitual. In other words, we do not wait to resist the devil and draw near to God when temptation is already upon us.

According to James, if we refuse to give into our temptations, if we resist the devil, he will flee from us. This was Jesus' experience in the wilderness. More importantly, James says that, if we draw near to God, then God will graciously draw near to us. All too often, when we are tormented by temptation, we think that our only relief, our only way out is to give into the temptation. In these moments of anguish, Satan feels too powerful, and God feels too absent. But neither of these things is true. This is not reality but a false reality created by our own cravings and desires. If, *by faith*, we resist Satan and draw near to God, then we will find the resources to overcome our temptations and live in freedom.

Suggestions for Lectors

James is a very energetic writer, full of insight and conviction. Therefore, deliver his words with great energy, confidence, and conviction. Speak to your listeners as you imagine James would. As you prepare, it would be helpful to read James 3:13–4:10; this will fill in some of the gaps and give you a better feel for today's reading.

Reading silently to ourselves is not the same as reading aloud to others. For example, written punctuation may work for the visual consumption of a text, but not always for its oral presentation. This is why as lectors, we use the punctuation as a guide, but we do not become its slaves. Sometimes we ignore the punctuation; sometimes we add our own. For example, we do not pause at every comma, and sometimes we pause when no comma is present.

With today's reading, however, the punctuation is an excellent oral guide, so pay attention to it. Notice when the punctuation is present, and when it is not. For example, in 4:2a, James writes, "You want something and do not have it; so you commit murder." There is not a comma after *something*, as we might have expected, so do not pause here. Conversely, in 4:3a, there is a comma after *because* though it is not necessary: "You do not have, because you do not ask." The presence or absence of a comma does not affect the meaning of this statement, but pausing after *have* has a greater rhetorical impact on the listener.

Finally, portions of today's reading have a poetic, lyrical quality to them, which is achieved through the repetition of grammar, syntax, and words. Consider the following examples:

> You want something and do not have it;
>   so you commit murder.
> And you covet something and cannot obtain it;
>   so you engage in disputes and conflicts.
> You do not have,
>   because you do not ask.
> You ask and do not receive,
>   because you ask wrongly,
>   in order to spend what you get on your pleasures (4:2–3).

> Resist the devil,
>   and he will flee from you.
> Draw near to God,
>   and he will draw near to you (4:7b–8a).

Read the repetitive parts in the same basic way. For example, *Resist the devil* and *Draw near to God* should be read in the same tone of voice, tempo, and intonation. As you attend to the poetic dimensions of this text, your voice will naturally fall into a cadence and a rhythm that will have a greater rhetorical impact on your listeners.

Mark 9:30–37

Notes

Sequence. 4 of 12

Commentary

There are five narrative movements in the Gospel of Mark. In the third movement, The Way movement (8:27–10:52), Jesus teaches his disciples what it means to follow one who has been called to a vocation of faithful witness unto death. In this movement, Jesus predicts his suffering, death, and resurrection three times (8:31; 9:30–32; 10:32–34). Each of these predictions begins a new cycle of material that follows the same general pattern. After a prediction, the disciples say or do something that indicates they have not understood the implications of what Jesus has said. Jesus then teaches his disciples what it means to follow him on the way of the cross.

Each cycle includes a paradoxical statement that encapsulates the essence of Christian discipleship. After the first passion prediction, Jesus says, "those who want to save their life will lose it, and those who lose their life for my sake, and for the sake of the gospel, will save it" (8:35, Prop 19). After the third and final prediction, Jesus says, "whoever wishes to become great among you must be your servant, and whoever wishes to be first among you must be slave of all" (10:43–44).

9:30–32. Today's reading begins with Jesus' second passion prediction. Each of the predictions becomes increasingly more detailed. In the first, Jesus says he will suffer, be rejected and killed, and then rise on the third day. Here, in the second prediction, Jesus adds that he will be betrayed.

9:33–35. Jesus and his disciples have been traveling south through Galilee from Caesarea Philippi (8:27; 9:30). They finally arrive back home in Capernaum, and Jesus knowingly asks them what they had been arguing about on the way. The disciples, like most of their contemporaries in the first-century Mediterranean world, were discussing status and honor; they were arguing about who among them was the greatest. While they were in Caesarea Philippi, Jesus had said, "If any want to become my followers, they must deny themselves and take up their cross and follow me" (8:34). Clearly the twelve do not understand the implications of this pronouncement. To take up one's cross is to die. Everybody who follows Jesus is a dead man, and dead men have no social standing. If a disciple truly wishes to be first among their number, then that disciple must paradoxically become the servant of all the others. This is how status and honor work in the kingdom of God.

9:36–37. Jesus then places a child in their midst as an enacted parable. In the Mediterranean world of Jesus' day, children were not primarily symbols of innocence. Instead, they symbolized those who lacked legal rights and social standing. That is why on this occasion, Jesus does not talk about *becoming* like a child but about *welcoming* a child, that is, welcoming those who lack social standing. When Jesus said earlier, "Whoever wants to be first must be last of *all* and servant of *all*" (9:35), he meant *all*, not just those with a higher social standing, but those with a lower social standing as well. The kingdom of God is introducing a completely different set of social values and expectations than those currently offered in the wider Mediterranean world with its honor and shame culture. Jesus' disciples are being called to adopt, acquire, and embody those new values.

Suggestions for Lectors

In the first half of today's story, highlight Jesus' prediction of his upcoming fate by emphasizing the three verbs: *betrayed*, *kill*, and *rise.*

In the second half, it is hard to tell whether Jesus is frustrated when he asks his disciples, *What were you arguing about on the way?* (9:33). As you work with this text, if you conclude that he is frustrated, convey frustration through your tone of voice.

The most important element in today's reading is Jesus' paradoxical statement about becoming a servant. Emphasize *first*, *last*, and *servant*, and pause briefly after *first*, as in: *Whoever wants to be first... must be last of all and servant of all* (9:35).

As you draw the reading to a close, read the last line at a slower tempo: *but the one who sent me* (9:37).

Pronunciation Guide

Capernaum (kuh-PER-nay-uhm, -nuh-)
Galilee (GAL-uh-lee)

PROPER 21

September 25–October 1

Esther 7:1–6, 9–10; 9:20–22
Psalm 124
James 5:13–20
Mark 9:38–50

Numbers 11:4–6, 10–16, 24–29
Psalm 19:7–14
James 5:13–20
Mark 9:38–50

ESTHER 7:1–6, 9–10; 9:20–22

Commentary

The story of the book of Esther is set during the time of the Persian Empire (539–333 B.C.). As in the narratives concerning Joseph in Egypt (Gen 37–50) and Daniel in Babylon (Dan 1–6), one of the principal themes in Esther is "the challenge of living a faithful life in an unfaithful culture."[25] In all of these stories, the central figure belongs to the Jewish (or Israelite) minority within a larger pagan society, and the central question is, "How does one faithfully navigate life in such a situation?" That is, when and to what extent does one *adapt* to the larger culture, *oppose* the larger culture, or *withdraw* from the larger culture? These questions can be explored by reading Esther.

The story of Esther is a dramatic one. It begins with the ruler of the Persian empire, King Ahasuerus, dismissing his queen, Queen Vashti, for insubordination. Eventually, a young virgin by the name of Esther is chosen as Vashti's replacement. But unknown to the king and the rest of his court is the fact that Esther is actually a Jew whose Hebrew name is Hadassah and who is the adopted daughter of a Jew named Mordecai.

One day, Mordecai refuses to bow down to Haman, the king's second in command. In response to this slight, Haman convinces King Ahasuerus to issue a decree calling for the annihilation of all the Jews through the empire. When news of the decree reaches Esther, she is dismayed. But initially, she refuses to act on behalf of her people. As she tells her father, if she were to approach the king without first being summoned, she could be put to death. Mordecai responds by saying:

> Do not think that in the king's palace you will escape any more than all the other Jews. For if you keep silence at such a time as this, relief and deliverance will rise for the Jews from another quarter, but you and your father's family will perish. Who knows? Perhaps you have come to royal dignity *for just such a time as this* (4:13b–14).

Esther responds to her father, "I will go to the king, though it is against the law; and if I perish, I perish" (4:16b).

When she approaches King Ahasuerus, Esther finds favor in his sight. So much so, that instead of decreeing her death, the king offers to give her whatever she asks.

---

[25] Carol M. Bechtel, *Esther* (Interpretation. Louisville, Ky.: John Knox, 2002), 10.

"What is it, Queen Esther? What is your request? It shall be given you, even to the half of my kingdom" (5:3). Esther asks that the king and Haman come to a banquet, and she will make her request known then. The king agrees, and in today's reading, we hear her request.

7:1–6. Esther's request is simple; she just wants her life and the life of her people spared. Her request is wisely and subtly worded. At no point does she explicitly identify herself or her people as Jews. Moreover, she appeals to what the king will lose if this happens. Esther's request springs like a trap upon its prey unawares. Before Haman has even the slightest clue as to what is going on, he has been caught.

7:9–10. Ironically, Haman is hung on the very gallows he had constructed on which to hang Mordecai the Jew (5:9–15).

9:20–22. Epilogue. The rest of the story is as follows. In the original edict, a specific day was appointed on which the pogrom against the Jews was to be carried out, the thirteenth day of the twelfth month, Adar 13th. Haman arrived at this date by casting a lot, known as Pur (3:7). After Haman is executed, a new edict is sent out, giving Jews throughout the empire permission to assemble, to take up arms, and to defend themselves on the allotted day (8:11–12). The tables are turned, and those who would destroy the Jews are themselves destroyed. The next day, Adar 14th, the Jews rest. Yet, in the city of Susa where the drama of Esther takes place, Jews are allowed to take up arms on Adar 14th as well; so they do not rest until Adar 15th.

Our reading concludes with a new edict, establishing Adar 14th and 15th as a Jewish holiday to be celebrated throughout the empire annually. This holiday becomes known as the festival of Purim (plural of Pur), and is still celebrated by Jews today.

Suggestions for Lectors

Esther is the length of a short story and does not take long to read, so take this opportunity to read the whole book. This will give you a better understanding of the story and a much better feel for the significance of today's dramatic episode.

Notice that the reading contains a number of long, complex sentences. As you practice, work out where you are going to pause, where you will take breaths, and how you are going to adjust and maintain the intonation of your voice. You do not want to start a sentence, then run out of breath or have your intonation drop away. So make sure to practice reading aloud until your delivery is natural and smooth.

Queen Esther is not only bold and courageous, she is also clever and wise. Notice that she does not presume to think for the king or to tell the king what to do. Instead, she makes her request with deference and diplomacy. She only raises her voice in 7:6 when she responds to the king's angry question. So read 7:3–4 in a calm, deferential tone.

Her brief speech is rhetorically powerful; the first half has a poetic quality:

> If I have won your favor, O king,
>   and if it pleases the king,
> let my life be given me
>   —that is my petition—

and the lives of my people
    —that is my request.
For we have been sold,
    I and my people,
to be destroyed, to be killed, and to be annihilated.

The last line should receive emphasis because this is what inspires the king to act, *but no enemy can compensate for this damage to the king* (7:4b).

Esther's speech has its intended effect; it has aroused the king's anger. So deliver his questions with a measured intensity, emphasizing the two interrogative pronouns: *Who is he, and where is he, who has presumed to do this?* Note that the final clause, *who has…*, is not a third question but a relative clause expanding upon *he*. This is why the last *who* is not emphasized. So drop you voice a bit when reading this clause. Also, you may ignore the comma after *where is he* so that the question is: *where is he who has presumed to do this?*

In 7:6, introduce a dramatic pause after *enemy*, and then raise your voice as you identify the enemy: *A foe and enemy,… THIS WICKED HAMAN!*

In today's reading, 9:20–22 functions like an epilogue. So, pause for a second or two before concluding with these verses. Then, read them in the same tone of voice you would use for an epilogue.

Pronunciation Guide
Adar (AY-dahr; ah-DAHR), *Ahasuerus* (uh-hazh-yoo-EHR-uhs),
cubit (KYOO-buht), *Esther* (ES-tuhr), *eunuch* (YOO-nuhk; YOO-nik),
Haman (HAY-muhn), *Harbona* (hahr-BOH-nuh), *Mordecai* (MOR-duh-kī)

NUMBERS 11:4–6, 10–16, 24–29

Commentary
Numbers is the fourth book of the Bible and the fourth book of the Pentateuch (a.k.a., The Five Books of Moses). Its English title, Numbers, is a translation of its title in ancient Greek editions, *Arithmoi*. These titles emphasize the two military censuses that take place in chapters 1 and 26. However, its Hebrew title offers a more accurate description of the book's contents. In Hebrew, the book is called *Bemidbar*, that is, *In the Wilderness*, because it recounts the story of Israel's forty-year sojourn in the wilderness as they make their way from Mt. Sinai to the borders of the Promised Land on the plains of Moab.

As today's reading illustrates, an even more accurate title might be *Grumblings in the Wilderness*. The reason it took Israel forty whole years to enter Canaan is that the people grumbled at every turn instead of trusting in the word and provision of the LORD. In Numbers 13–14, the LORD instructs Israel to take over and occupy the Promised Land, but the people refuse. They fear the land's pagan inhabitants and so make plans to return to Egypt (14:1–4). The LORD becomes angry at this latest lack of faith, but his anger abates when Moses intercedes on behalf of the people. Nevertheless, the LORD declares that no one from the Exodus generation will enter the Promised Land.

> The LORD said, "I do forgive, just as you have asked; nevertheless —as I live, and as all the earth shall be filled with the glory of the LORD—none of the people who have seen my glory and the signs that I did in Egypt and in the wilderness, and yet have tested me these ten times and have not obeyed my voice, shall see the land that I swore to give to their ancestors; none of those who despised me shall see it." (14:20–23)

One of these "ten times" is recorded in today's reading.

11:4–6. Back in the book of Exodus, the Israelites were excited to leave Egypt until hunger and thirst set in. When they complained, the LORD provided them with bread and water. The bread came in the form of manna that fell daily during the whole of Israel's forty-year journey in the wilderness (Exod 16). So by the time of today's story in Numbers, the Israelites have been eating manna for years, and they are tired of it; tired of eating it, and tired of looking at it. So they grumble.

11:10–16. For his part, Moses is tired of bearing the weight of the people's constant grumbling, so he lifts up his own grumblings and complaints to the LORD. For the moment, the LORD disregards the people's request for meat, and instead focuses upon the needs of his servant Moses. The LORD instructs Moses to gather seventy of the elders of Israel at the tent of meeting, for he says:

> I will come down and talk with you there; and I will take some of the spirit that is on you and put it on them; and they shall bear the burden of the people along with you so that you will not bear it all by yourself (11:17).

11:24–25. Moses does as instructed, and he places the seventy elders around the tent of meeting. The tent of meeting (a.k.a., the tabernacle) housed the ark of the covenant and was the place where Moses met and spoke with the LORD. As promised, the LORD spoke with the elders and took some of the spirit that was upon Moses and distributed it to the others.

11:26–29. At this point, we are informed that two of the seventy did not make it to the tent of meeting as instructed. Oddly enough, the LORD is not angry, for Eldad and Medad receive the spirit like all the rest. Neither is Moses angry, for when he receives a report about what has happened, he says, "Are you jealous for my sake? Would that all the LORD's people were prophets, and that the LORD would put his spirit on them!" (11:29).

Moses' words foreshadow the days of the New Covenant, when the LORD will pour out his spirit "on all flesh" (Joel 2:28, ✠ PentVig; Acts 2:17, Pent). These words also express a sentiment found in today's gospel reading. When the disciples tell Jesus that they stopped a man from casting out demons in Jesus' name because he was not one of them, Jesus instructs them to leave him alone. "Whoever is not against us is for us" (Mark 9:40).

Suggestions for Lectors

In today's reading, the speaking parts are the most important components in the episode, so focus your preparation on the speaking parts, especially those of the people and Moses, which have the most energy and feeling.

When reading the people's grumblings in 11:4b–6, begin with an intense anger as you exclaim, *If only we had meat to eat!* (11:4b). Then, without losing your intensity, replace the anger with a sense of nostalgia as you reminisce about the food you once ate back in Egypt (11:5). Finally, lace your voice with despair and frustration as you express your revulsion and anger over having to eat manna day after day.

When reading a list of more than three items, it is important to give it some dynamics by introducing and taking away pauses and by adjusting your tempo. Consider the following: *the cucumbers,… the melons, the leeks,… the onions and the garlic.* Here, longer pauses have been introduced after *cucumbers* and *leeks,* while the comma after onions has been removed.

Moses is tired of the people's constant grumbling and he is at his wits end, so he directs his anger, frustration, and exhaustion at the LORD. In 11:11–15, read with increasing intensity and feeling that climaxes with the three questions: *Did I conceive all this people? Did I give birth to them…? Where am I to get meat…?* (11:12). In 11:14, begin backing off on the intensity, and then deliver 11:15 in a fed up, somewhat pleading tone.

The most important line in today's reading is the concluding line, delivered by Moses: "Would that *all* the LORD's people were prophets, and that the LORD would put his spirit on them!" (11:29). Deliver these lines at a reduced pace and with a magnanimous, hopeful voice, emphasizing the word *all.* Moses is not chastising Joshua so much as he is articulating a glorious hope and vision.

Pronunciation Guide

Egypt (EE-jipt), *Eldad* (EL-dad), *Israel* (IZ-ree-uhl; -ray-),
Israelites (IZ-ree-līts), *Joshua* (JOSH-yoo-uh), *manna* (MAN-uh),
Medad (MEE-dad), *Moses* (MOH-zuhs), *Nun* (NUN)

JAMES 5:13–20

Notes

Sequence. 5 of 5

Commentary

The Letter of James is written to Christians who are experiencing hardship, although the exact nature of these hardships is difficult to determine from the letter itself. Are the recipients being targeted and persecuted because they are Christian? Or, are they simply struggling to live the Christian life within a world whose culture and values are so different and antithetical to those of the gospel. Whatever the nature of their trials and hardships, James writes to support them in their faith by encouraging them to persevere with patience and prayer.

At the beginning of the letter, James writes, "My brothers and sisters, whenever you face trials of any kind, consider it nothing but joy, because you know that the testing of your faith produces endurance; and let endurance have its full effect, so that you may be mature and complete, lacking in nothing" (1:2–4). James then talks about the importance of prayer, of asking God for wisdom and trusting in God's generosity and willingness to grant wisdom (1:5–8).

James concludes the letter in much the same way, by urging his readers to be patient and by highlighting the importance of prayer. James tells his readers to be patient in the midst of their suffering because the coming of the Lord is near. He writes, "As an example of suffering and patience, beloved, take the prophets who spoke in the name of the Lord. Indeed we call blessed those who showed endurance" (5:10–11). But what exactly does patience look like? As we see in today's reading, patience is the fruit of prayer and community, of prayer in community.

5:13–18. According to James, prayer is appropriate in every season of the Christian life. In sickness and in health, in suffering and in joy, prayer—which includes praise—is to be our constant practice. Here, one is reminded of Paul's words in 1 Thessalonians, "Rejoice always, *pray without ceasing*, give thanks in all circumstances; for this is the will of God in Christ Jesus for you" (5:16–18).

Prayer is not just a private practice, but also a communal practice. Prayer not only connects us with God, it also connects us with one another. When we are physically sick, James encourages us to call the elders together for prayer and anointing with oil because "the prayer of faith will save the sick" (5:15). When we are spiritually sick with sin, James encourages us to confess our sins to one another and to pray for one another. This leads to healing because "the prayer of the righteous is powerful and effective" (5:16). If anyone doubts the power of prayer, they need only consider Elijah, who accomplished great things through prayer although he was just a human being like us.

5:19–20. James recognizes that it is not easy to persevere and remain patient in the midst of trials and hardships. Therefore, there will be those who wander away from the truth. When this happens, the faithful might be tempted to become angry and judgmental. Lest this should happen, James tells his readers that those who bring sinners back into the fold will cover a multitude of sins and save them from death. In other words, compassion, love, and prayer are called for, not anger and judgment. As James wrote earlier, "anger does not produce God's righteousness" (1:20, Prop 17), and "mercy triumphs over judgment" (2:13, Prop 18).

Suggestions for Lectors

Today's reading concludes the letter, and constitutes the author's parting remarks to his addressees. The reading begins with a series of questions that James asks and then answers himself (5:13–14). Work through these questions slowly and deliberately. Pause for a second after each question and for two seconds after each answer. Emphasize the final word in each question: *suffering*, *cheerful*, and *sick*.

Beginning in 5:15, return to your normal reading style and tempo, and continue in this manner until you come to the end of the reading. Emphasize the two statements about prayer: *The prayer of faith will save the sick* (5:15a), and *The prayer of the righteous is powerful and effective* (5:16b).

Pronunciation Guide
Elijah (ee-LĪ-juh; ih-)

MARK 9:38–50

Notes
Sequence. 5 of 12

Commentary
In last week's reading, Jesus chastised his disciples for arguing about who among them was the greatest. The disciples were operating with the wrong set of social values and expectations, so Jesus said, "Whoever wants to be first must be last of *all* and servant of *all*" (9:35). By *all*, Jesus meant *all*, not just those with a higher social standing and not just other Christians, but everyone they met regardless of their place within society. To make his point, Jesus placed a child in their midst, not as a symbol of innocence but to represent those who lacked legal rights or social standing in the wider culture. On this occasion, Jesus did not talk about *becoming* like a child but about *welcoming* those who, like children, lacked social standing. In today's reading, Jesus continues on the theme of Christian hospitality.

9:38–41. The moment Jesus finishes emphasizing the need to serve and welcome everyone, the apostle John recounts an incident in which the apostles tried to stop an exorcist from exorcizing demons in Jesus' name because he was not one of them. How ironic! Just a few episodes earlier the apostles themselves were unable to cast out a demon in Jesus' name (9:14–29). Now they have tried to stop a successful exorcist from exorcising in Jesus' name simply because he was not one of the Twelve to whom Jesus gave the authority to cast out demons (3:15).

The Twelve are operating with the same flawed logic that the scribes employed when they concluded that Jesus was casting out demons by the power of Beelzebul (3:22). Jesus pointed out how ludicrous it was to think that Satan was casting out Satan. In today's episode, the disciples are treating the exorcist as though he were an opponent. Yet, if a person is casting out demons in Jesus' name, how can that person be an enemy? It is impossible for a person to exorcise a demon in *Jesus'* name, and in the next breath curse *Jesus*. The Twelve need to learn to be more welcoming, inviting, and hospitable because, as Jesus says, "Whoever is not against us is for us" (9:40). And whoever shows the Twelve hospitality will receive a reward.

Jesus' attitude is similar to that of Moses in today's reading from Numbers. Seventy elders were appointed to receive some of Moses' spirit at the tent of meeting. Two of the seventy did not make it to the tent; nevertheless, they received the spirit just like the others. When Moses was informed about the situation, he showed no anger. Rather he said, "Are you jealous for my sake? Would that all the LORD's people were prophets, and that the LORD would put his spirit on them!" (Num 11:29). Jesus could very well have said, "Would that everybody have the power to cast out demons in my name!"

Thus, we see one of the pitfalls of being preoccupied with one's own status. As Eugene LaVerdiere writes, "The disciples' concern with being the greatest (9:34) easily leads to preventing others from doing good (9:38)."[26]

9:42–48. Moreover, preoccupation with who is the greatest "could also escalate to causing others to sin," that is, to stumble.[27] Consequently, the Twelve should make every effort not to do anything that might cause somebody else to stumble in their faith. And, if they find something in their lives that causes themselves to stumble, they should make every effort to get rid of it, even if it is painful. After all, being severely handicapped in the kingdom of God is still far better than being physically whole in hell.

9:49–50. Instead of arguing about who is the greatest, the Twelve should work to be at peace with one another. That is what it means to have salt in oneself.

Suggestions for Lectors

When John informs Jesus that the disciples tried to prohibit an exorcist from exorcising demons in Jesus' name, John is expecting to be commended, so read his part with a bit of zeal. The energy of Jesus' response in 9:39–41 is harder to establish from the text. He might be in a teaching mode, in which case you will want to adopt an informative tone of voice. Or more likely, Jesus might be expressing his frustration and anger at his disciples' ongoing failure to understand the nature of his mission, in which case you will want to adopt a more severe tone. Either way, emphasize the statement, *Whoever is not against us… is <u>for</u> us* (9:40b).

In 9:42–48, increase the intensity and severity of your tone as you deliver the dire warnings Jesus issues. In each of the three illustrations Jesus uses, emphasize the command by pausing both before and after the command and by slowing down: *cut it off* (9:43); *cut it off* (9:45); and *tear it out* (9:47). Also, emphasize the results of the commands: *maimed* (9:43); *lame* (9:45); and *one eye* (9:47). In 9:48, stress both of the *nevers.*

Finally, in 9:49–50, wind down the reading by reducing your intensity. Read the last sentence in a slow, deliberate manner. Direct these words to your listeners, as you once again emphasize the commands: *<u>Have salt</u> in yourselves, and <u>be at peace</u> with one another* (9:50). Consider memorizing this line so that you can look at your listeners as you deliver it.

---

[26] Eugene A. LaVerdiere, *The Beginning of the Gospel: Introducing the Gospel according to Mark* (2 vols.; Collegeville, Minn.: Liturgical Press, 1999), 2:59.

[27] Ibid.

PROPER 22

October 2–8

Job 1:1; 2:1–10
Psalm 26
Hebrews 1:1–4; 2:5–12
Mark 10:2–16

Genesis 2:18–24
Psalm 8
Hebrews 1:1–4; 2:5–12
Mark 10:2–16

Job 1:1; 2:1–10

Notes
Sequence. 1 of 4

Commentary
It is often assumed that the book of Job is primarily concerned with suffering and with the question of, "Why do the innocent suffer?" While suffering plays a critical role in Job, another question is more central. When the LORD boasts to the Satan[28] that there is no one as upright and blameless as his servant Job, the Satan replies, "Does Job fear God for nothing?" (1:9). In other words, is Job's faith genuine, or does he serve God merely out of self-interest? Does he not worship God simply because God blesses and protects him? In this respect, suffering is not so much the subject of Job as it is the crisis that provides the setting in which to test whether there is such a thing as disinterested faith, faithfulness that is not motivated by the expectation of blessing or reward.

The book begins with a prose prologue that introduces the reader to the person and character of Job. The prologue also relates the events that stand behind Job's misfortunes and suffering. This information gives the story its dramatic quality, for the reader knows things about Job's situation that *none* of the characters are privy to, even Job. Thus, the reader is in a better position to evaluate the speeches and statements of Job, his friends, and eventually God.

1:1. The story begins by describing Job as one who is blameless and upright, as a man who fears God and turns away from evil. So scrupulous is Job that he will arise early on a morning and offer sacrifices to God on behalf of his children just on the off chance that they committed a transgression the night before (1:4–5). This initial sketch of Job's virtuous character must be kept in mind throughout the book. For example, when Job repeatedly maintains his innocence and integrity, the reader knows that he is not being arrogant, simply honest. Moreover, when Job's friends insist that he must have sinned, the reader knows that they have absolutely no idea what they are talking about. As we shall see in today's reading, Job's misfortunes have nothing to do with him, but with a wager between the LORD and the Satan.

28 Here, this figure is designated as *the* Satan, instead of simply Satan, because in the Hebrew text of Job, Satan is not a proper name but a title. "The Accuser" or "the Prosecutor" might even be a better translation.

The opening scene of today's reading is the second exchange between the LORD and the Satan. In the first exchange (1:6–12), the divine council of heavenly beings convenes in heaven, and the figure of the Satan is among them. In Job, while the Satan is an antagonist, he is not the evil, demonic character we find in the NT. Here, he plays more the role of a prosecuting attorney, or the Devil's advocate. Interestingly and most importantly, the Satan is not the first to speak; the LORD is. The LORD asks him, "In your travels to and fro upon the earth, 'have you considered my servant Job? There is no one like him on the earth, a blameless and upright man who fears God and turns away from evil'" (1:8). In reply, the Satan does not question Job's righteousness, only his motivation. "Does Job fear God for nothing?" (1:9). Who wouldn't be righteous if they had been blessed with everything that the LORD has blessed Job with? The LORD implicitly enters into an wager with the Satan. He grants him leave to do whatever he would like with Job, the only caveat being that he must not lay a finger on Job himself (1:12). The Satan obliges, and in a single day all of Job's livestock, all of his servants, and all of his children have been taken or killed (1:13–19). Job is overcome by grief and enters into mourning, but as the narrator says, "In all this Job did not sin or charge God with wrongdoing" (1:22).

2:1–6. Today's reading picks up at this point. When the divine council reconvenes, the LORD once again boasts about the upright character of Job even in the face of such misfortune. The Satan suggests that the test of Job's faith did not go far enough because people will give anything to save their own skins. So the LORD grants the Satan permission to do with Job whatever he would like, short of killing him.

2:7–8. Job's health is taken away as he contracts a chronic skin disease over the whole of his body. The disease leaves him alive, yet in agony without any comfort.

2:9–10. In light of all that has happened, Job's wife is convinced that he must have done something to merit all this misfortune and suffering. Her council is that he should give up this pretense of being righteous. "Just be done with it. 'Curse God, and die'" (2:9). Job, however, refuses to take the easy way out. He would rather endure unbearable pain, suffering, and disgrace, than admit to transgressions that he has not committed, which would itself be a transgression. Moreover, he asks, "Shall we receive the good at the hand of God, and not receive the bad?" (2:10a). Once again, the narrator offers this assessment: "In all this Job did not sin with his lips" (2:10b). With that, the LORD's position is vindicated. The Satan loses, and he is not heard from again. This, however, is only the beginning of the story.

Suggestions for Lectors

Today's reading comes with its own introduction, *There was once a man…* (1:1). After reading 1:1, pause for a second before continuing.

As suggested in the Commentary, while the Satan is the story's antagonist, he is not a demonic character; he is not trying to perpetuate evil. He simply thinks that the LORD has over-estimated Job, so he contests what he believes to be the LORD's unfounded assertions regarding Job's motivations and integrity. Therefore, when you read the Satan's responses to the LORD, read them as though you consider yourself to be the voice of reason.

Two lines deserve special treatment. The first is the Satan's claim, *All that people have they will give to save their lives* (2:4), and the second is Job's response to his wife, *Shall we receive the good at the hand of God, and not receive the bad?* (2:9). Read both lines slowly and deliberately and with greater intensity than the lines that are around them.

Pronunciation Guide
Job (JOHB; *not* JAWB), *potsherd* (POT-sherd), *Satan* (SAY-tuhn), *Uz* (UZ)

Genesis 2:18–24

Notes
Suggested Reading. Genesis 2:18–25

Commentary
The book of Genesis begins with two accounts of the beginnings of creation (1:1–2:4a and 2:4b–25). These accounts are quite different from one another in many of their particulars (for example, their structure, their imagery, their chronology, etc.), yet they have something very similar to say about the nature and role of human beings. In the first account, human beings are created in the image of God as male and female (1:27, EastVig). Thus, it is in our maleness and femaleness, in our relationships with one another, that we human beings are able to rule and serve as the image-bearers of God in creation. Human beings are the last of God's creation, and once they are in place, God offers a final self-assessment of his six days of work. "God saw everything that he had made, and indeed, it was *very good*" (1:31).

2:18–20. It is striking then that, in the second account, after God has fashioned the man, breathed life into him, and placed him in Eden that God should declare, "It is *not good* that the man should be alone" (2:18a). God attempts to rectify the situation by fashioning other living creatures from the ground, from the same stuff from which the man was formed (cf. 2:7). Each of the animals is brought before the man, and he names them all. Yet, none of these other earth creatures are suitable partners for the man in his vocation to till and keep the garden (cf. 2:15).

2:21–24. God then fashions another creature to bring before the man. Unlike the others God brought before the man, this one is not formed from the ground but from the man himself. When he awakens from his sleep-induced state following his surgery, the Man beholds this newest of God's creatures and recognizes that the one who shall be called Woman is "bone of my bones and flesh of flesh" (2:23). Finally, a suitable partner has been found for the man; humanity is now complete. The Man and the Woman commit themselves to one another. They become united in purpose and vocation; in other words, they become one flesh.

It is instructive that the Woman was taken from the Man's *side* and not from his head or his heal. This suggests that the Woman was "made to stand alongside him rather than to rule him or be ruled by him."[29] Hierarchy in the relationship between

[29] John Goldingay. *Old Testament Theology: Israel's Gospel* (Downers Grove, Ill.: InterVarsity Press, 2003), 109.

the Man and the Woman does not come into play until after sin and death are introduced into creation by their disobedience (3:16).

2:25. As in the first creation account, humanity is not complete until there is both male and female. Only as male and female together can humanity fulfill its vocation to be the caretakers of creation. At this point in the first creation account, God declared that everything *was very good.* That same assessment is expressed at the end of the second account with the declaration that the man and the woman, "were both naked, and were not ashamed" (2:25). To be naked and not ashamed implies right relationship with one another and with God.

Unfortunately, this state of affairs will be short-lived. In the very next episode in Genesis, the Man and the Woman find themselves naked and ashamed, so ashamed that they can no longer stand to be in one another's presence, let alone in God's presence (3:7–11).

Suggestions for Lectors

As lectors, we must continually remind ourselves that we are not simply readers; we are narrators and storytellers. So, pay attention to how today's story is told. Who are the characters? What are they trying to accomplish, and what are their motives? What are the conflicts or problems in the story, and how do these get resolved? Allow the answers to these and other questions to inform and shape your retelling of the story.

The opening speech in 2:18 should be emphasized because it identifies the problem that is addressed in the rest of the narrative. Pause before *It is* and after *partner*, and read the statement firmly and deliberately. The Man's speech in 1:23 should also be emphasized. As you deliver it, elevate your voice and invest it with a measure of excitement. Remember, thus far in the story, the man is the only one of his kind, and none of the effort that he and God have expended has rectified his lonely state. Read the rest of the narrative in your normal storytelling voice.

HEBREWS 1:1–4; 2:5–12

Notes

Sequence. 1 of 7

Commentary

The Letter to the Hebrews begins with a description of Jesus as the one uniquely identified with God and, therefore, uniquely qualified to reveal God and to implement God's purposes for humanity and all of creation.

1:1–4. Throughout Hebrews, the author highlights the superiority of Jesus and his vocation over all of God's other servants, past, present and future. In the opening lines, these later themes are anticipated. In the past, God communicated God's purposes through the prophets whom God called and equipped to speak his word. But now, in these climactic days, God speaks to us through one who knows God intimately—God's very own Son. Jesus does not simply *tell* us about God, he actually *reveals* God, which goes well beyond what any prophet could do. Jesus is able to do this because, as God's Son, he bears the family resemblance, or as Hebrews says, "He is the reflection of God's glory and the exact imprint of God's very being" (1:3).

This description of Jesus' unique, divine identity is consistent with what we find elsewhere in the New Testament (cf. John 1:1, 18, 14:9; Col 1:15) and is expressed in the Nicene Creed ("Light of Light, very God of very God,… of one substance with the Father"). Consequently, Jesus exercises God's authority and power. He has been appointed as God's heir over all things. All things were created through him, and everything is sustained by his word.

Moreover, Jesus not only revealed God to us, he made *us* presentable to God by cleansing us from all our sins (1:3). Unlike other high priests who had to offer sacrifices year after year because their sacrifices were provisional at best (10:11), as our Great High Priest (4:14–5:10, GFri), Jesus purified us once and for all through his single, once-for-all-time sacrifice of himself (10:10, 12). Jesus then sat down at the right hand of God because his work was complete (1:3; 10:12). This demonstrates that his name and his ministry are far superior, even to that of the angels.

2:5–8a. Although angels are divine beings, God did not place creation under their authority and control. Neither does God intend to give them dominion over the new creation. Instead, God created human beings to be the lords and stewards of everything in creation. This truth is what inspired the psalmist to compose Psalm 8, which the author of Hebrews cites here.

2:8b–9. Of course, when one looks around at this fallen world, there is little if any evidence that human beings are in control, except when we look at Jesus. The Son of God became the human being Jesus of Nazareth, and now this Jesus has been exalted to the right hand of God (10:12; 12:2), which means that he exercises authority over angels and over all creation. Thus, the resurrected and ascended Jesus offers us a glimpse of what humanity will become in the new creation. Moreover, Jesus was crowned with this glory and honor because he sacrificed his life. In other words, he was crowned not because he wielded power but because he suffered for the sake of others.

2:10–12. To the author of Hebrews, this seems most fitting. Even though the worlds came into being through him and even though he possesses God's divine nature, Jesus made himself our equal; he became our brother by sharing our human condition and even our suffering. Through this act of solidarity with humanity, Jesus has drawn us into his family. His Father has become our Father, and Jesus is not ashamed to introduce us as his brothers and sisters. Here again, the author of Hebrews appeals to the psalms to illustrate his point, in this case Psalm 22:22.

Suggestions for Lectors

Today's reading begins in a story-like fashion with the words *Long ago*, so adopt a narrating voice for the first two verses. Pause before verse 3, and then read 1:3–4 in a more explanatory manner with a hint of proclamation in your voice. Continue in this same manner for the second portion of the reading (2:5–12).

When reading the quotations from the OT (2:6b–8, 12), raise your voice, and read them slowly and deliberately. Both quotations are from the psalms so pay attention to their poetic structure. In 2:12, notice the synonymous parallelism between the two lines. *I will proclaim your name* is parallel to *I will praise you*; and *to my brothers and sis-*

ters finds a parallel in *in the midst of the congregation.* The order of the a and b elements are reversed in the second line, forming a chiastic a-b-b'-a' pattern.

> I will proclaim your name to my brothers and sisters,
> in the midst of the congregation I will praise you.

MARK 10:2–16

Notes

Sequence. 6 of 12

Commentary

In Deuteronomy 24:1–4, Moses describes a situation in which a husband who has found something objectionable about his wife writes her a certificate of divorce and sends her away. According to the law, if she becomes another man's wife and he divorces her or dies, the first husband is not allowed to remarry her. Writing a certificate of divorce is not commanded here, but is simply part of the hypothetical situation Moses discusses. However, by the time of the first century, certificates of divorce had become required for divorce. A husband could not simply turn his wife out of his house, he must make the divorce official by giving her a written certificate of divorce. In a patriarchal society, this certificate was essential to the woman's survival. Without it, she would not be allowed to return to her father's house or remarry and so would be left to provide for herself.

In first-century Jewish society, divorce was an accepted yet undesirable practice. So the question that rabbis debated did not have to do with divorce per se, but with the legal grounds for it. In Deuteronomy 24, the husband divorces the woman "because he finds something objectionable about her," but what exactly constitutes *objectionable*? This is the question that the Pharisees ask Jesus in Matthew: "Is it lawful for a man to divorce his wife *for any cause*?" (Matt 19:3). The conservative rabbinic school of Shammai argued that divorce was only permitted in cases of sexual immorality; while the liberal school of Hillel argued that a man could divorce his wife for the most trivial of offenses, including burning his toast. On this occasion, Jesus sides with the conservative school of Shammai: "I say to you, whoever divorces his wife, *except for unchastity*, and marries another commits adultery" (Matt 19:9).

In Mark's account, the Pharisees' question does not include the qualifying phrase "for any cause." Neither does Jesus' response in Mark offer any exceptions. This means that Jesus' stated position on divorce is more radical and absolute in Mark than it is in Matthew.

10:2–9. Mark interprets the Pharisees' question on divorce as a test, and it is a very dangerous test as it turns out. Ever since 3:6 (Prop 4), the Pharisees have been conspiring with the Herodians to bring about Jesus' death. The Herodians were the political supporters of Herod Antipas, the tetrarch of Galilee. And it was Antipas who had John the Baptist arrested and imprisoned because John had been challenging the lawfulness of Antipas' marriage to Herodias, who divorced Antipas' brother Philip to marry Antipas (6:18, Prop 10). John was later beheaded on Antipas' orders. It is possible, then, that the Pharisees are trying to trick Jesus into making a public pronouncement condemning divorce. If so, then Antipas might have the political willpower to imprison and execute Jesus. So, while the question about divorce is primarily a religious matter, in this context, it also possesses political undertones. This may help explain why Jesus never states unambiguously in public what he declares privately to his disciples.

Jesus responds to the Pharisees' question with a question of his own. He wants to know how they are parsing the Scriptures. They point out that Moses allowed a husband to dismiss his wife with a certificate of divorce. Jesus counters by arguing that Moses was making a concession because of human sinfulness. Moses' concession does not constitute an argument for divorce because it does not represent God's intentions for marriage as they are encoded in creation itself, which predates the Mosaic legislation. Citing Genesis 1:27 and 2:24, Jesus argues that the very fact that human beings were created male and female indicates that we were created for relationship with one another. When a husband and wife come together, they become so united that they are no longer to be accounted as two but as one flesh. This union has been established by God, therefore no human—not even Moses—can dissolve that union. Jesus concludes with his own authoritative pronouncement, "What God has joined together, let no one separate" (10:9).

10:10–12. Throughout Mark, Jesus has taken a liberal position on matters like fasting, sabbath keeping, ritual purity, and Jewish dietary laws, but his stance on divorce and remarriage seems to be more conservative than any of his contemporaries. This becomes even more apparent when Jesus explains his views privately to his disciples. According to Jesus, the whole business of divorce and remarriage involves people in adultery. If there are any exceptions, they are not offered in Mark.

In Mark, Jesus announces the good news that the kingdom of God has come. The kingdom of God is part of God's plan to redeem, renew, and restore humanity and all of creation. Restoring humanity involves reconciling human beings to one another. It also involves redeeming the various types of relationships that exist between human beings, not least marriage, which is built into the created order itself. Through his life, death, and resurrection, Jesus is transforming all of creation and returning it to its original intentions. When the world is fully restored, there will be no divorce and remarriage because people will not die and relationships will not die.

To be sure, this is a hard text, and our views of marriage, divorce, and remarriage cannot be based on only one text of Scripture. Yet, we must resist the temptation to pass over or dismiss this word. If we are too quick in trying to find any possible exceptions, concessions, or loopholes to what the Markan Jesus has to say to us, then we may miss an important part of God's vision for the new world. Let us not be like the rich man in next week's reading who walks away the moment he receives a hard word from Jesus (10:22). Instead, let us be like the distraught father who acknowledges his own struggles, and asks Jesus for help: "I believe; help my unbelief!" (9:24). Perhaps, if we took the time to think and act as though divorce were not an option, then we might work to re-envision and restructure our world, our institutions, and our relationships so that marriages need never end in divorce.

10:13–16. In an earlier reading, Jesus spoke about *welcoming* children (9:36–37, Prop 20). Today, he calls on us to become *like* children. In the ancient Mediterranean world of Jesus' day, children were not symbols of purity and innocence.

> [In 9:36–37], Jesus used the example of a child as a way of teaching about the service to others, especially those who seemed to be social nobodies. There the emphasis was on the child's *lack of social status and legal rights.* [In today's reading], children are presented as symbolizing *powerlessness, dependence, and receptivity.*[30]

When Jesus says that the kingdom of God belongs to those who are like children, he is not saying that it belongs to the pure and innocent. Instead, the kingdom of God is for those who have nothing to contribute. We have no claim on God or his blessings, so we must allow ourselves to be vulnerable enough to accept God's love and blessings as the gift that they are. Moreover, we must not prohibit others from receiving the gift of God's blessing simply because we do not consider them qualified. That was the disciples' failure.

Suggestions for Lectors

Today's reading comprises two different episodes that can be treated independently of one another.

10:2–9. The Pharisees are testing Jesus, trying to trap him by getting him to say something inflammatory or blasphemous. Their question is not sincere but is part of a hidden agenda. Convey this by adopting a tone of feigned interest or innocence when reading their question. Jesus, of course, is well aware of their schemes. By this point, Jesus is fed up with their hypocrisy and legalism, and his response is cutting as he criticizes their *hardness of heart* (10:5). Raise your voice as you deliver Jesus' views on divorce. In particular, draw attention to his concluding injunction in 10:9 by reading it slowly and by emphasizing the contrasts. Either stress *God* and *no one*, or stress *joined together* and *separate*. Likewise, read Jesus' explanation to the disciples in the same slow, deliberate manner, emphasizing *whoever* and the two *shes* (10:11–12). Afterwards, pause for a few seconds, and take the opportunity to look up at your listeners before proceeding onto the second episode.

10:10–13. In the second episode, let Jesus' indignation be evident as he chastises the disciples in a raised voice. When you come to the last verse, set aside your righteous indignation and read the last line with a smile on your face, as Jesus takes the children into his arms and blesses them.

Pronunciation Guide

Moses (MOH-zuhs)
Pharisee (FAIR-uh-see)

---

[30] John R. Donahue and Daniel J. Harrington. *The Gospel of Mark* (Sacra Pagina 2. Collegeville, Minn.: Liturgical Press, 2002), 301.

PROPER 23

October 9–15

Job 23:1–9, 16–17	Amos 5:6–7, 10–15
Psalm 22:1–15	Psalm 90:12–17
Hebrews 4:12–16	Hebrews 4:12–16
Mark 10:17–31	Mark 10:17–31

JOB 23:1–9, 16–17

Notes

Sequence. 2 of 4

Commentary

In last week's reading from Job, we witnessed a debate between the LORD and the figure of the Satan[31] on the question of the existence of a genuine, disinterested faith. That is, is there such a thing as human faithfulness that is not motivated by the prospects of receiving a blessing or reward? The LORD offers up his servant Job as an exemplar of disinterested faith, but the Satan demurs. He argues that Job is so scrupulously religious because it pays to be so, for the LORD blesses everything Job puts his hand to. He wagers that if Job were to lose everything—his wealth, his health, and his family—then he would curse the LORD to his face (2:5). The Satan is granted permission to conduct this experiment in disinterested faith. Yet, when Job loses everything, though he suffers greatly, his integrity remains intact. As he says to his wife, "Shall we receive the good at the hand of God, and not receive the bad?" (2:10). Job's response to adversity upholds the LORD's position. The Satan loses the friendly wager, and he is not heard from again. Yet, this is only the beginning of the story.

Though Job's faith persists, he himself has been reduced to a man of great sorrow, anguish, and suffering. When his three friends—Eliphaz, Bildad, and Zophar—hear of his misfortune, they come to offer him their "comfort" and "support." They do this by trying to convince Job to repent of his obvious sin. They believe that God's moral universe operates according to predictable laws of cause and effect: upright behavior produces prosperity while sinful behavior results in suffering. Job remains unpersuaded by their arguments for he has seen the wicked prosper. Though he does not think of himself as never having sinned, he is convinced that nothing he has done remotely merits the level of suffering and misfortune he has endured.

The central portion of the book is given over to three cycles of dialogue between Job and his friends (chs. 4–14; 15–21; 22–27). In these cycles, each of Job's friends speak, and then Job responds to each in turn. Today's reading comes from the last

---

[31] Here, this figure is designated as *the* Satan, instead of simply Satan, because in the Hebrew text of Job, Satan is not a proper name but a title. "The Accuser" or "the Prosecutor" might even be a better translation.

cycle. In it, Job refutes Eliphaz's insistence that his wickedness must be great and his iniquities endless (22:5).

23:1–7. Job begins by expressing his deep, deep desire to be given the opportunity to speak with God face to face. His friends have not lifted the burden of his suffering; they have only made it worse. They speak the conventional wisdom of the day, but it does not match reality as Job sees it. If he could just have his day in court, if he could present his case before God himself, then he knows he would get a fair hearing, which is certainly not what he has received from his friends who are more concerned about Job's orthodoxy than his pain and suffering.

23:8–9. As it is, Job has not been able to get a response from God. No matter what direction he turns, Job cannot catch a glimpse of God. It is as though God were completely absent.

23:16–17. His sense of being utterly alone and on his own has terrified him. He would rather disappear and die than live in such fear.

Suggestions for Lectors

As reflected in the Commentary, today's reading occurs in three movements. The last two movements have a different tone from the first. In the first movement (23:1–7), Job is frustrated and bitter, yet remains confident. If he could but find God, he knows God would listen to him and decide in his favor. Read these verses in a strong, confident, and elevated voice.

In the second movement (23:8–9), the mood changes drastically. Job has been unable to find God, so he is without hope. This same mood continues into the third movement (23:16–17) so read both of them with a voice touched by anguish and despair. Increase your sense of despair as you deliver the final line: *If only I could vanish in darkness, and thick darkness would cover my face!* (23:17).

When preparing to read a poetic passage, it is always helpful to take the time to notice how the poetry is structured. One of the most common characteristics of biblical poetry is the use of repetition, especially parallelism. In the following examples, notice how the second poetic line of a strophe reinforces the first line by restating it in different words.

a Oh, that I knew where I might find him,
a' that I might come even to his dwelling!

b I would lay my case before him,
b' and fill my mouth with arguments.

Sometimes, the second line restates the first while also maintaining the same or a similar grammatical structure as the first.

c	I would	<u>learn</u>	<u>what he would answer me</u>,
c'	and	<u>understand</u>	<u>what he would say to me</u>.
d		<u>God</u>	<u>has made my heart faint</u>;
d'		<u>the Almighty</u>	<u>has terrified me</u>;

By attending to the structure of poetic texts, your voice will fall into a cadence and an intonation that is well-suited for reading poetic texts. This will help your listeners to better experience, appreciate, and understand the reading.

Pronunciation Guide
Job (JOHB; *not* JAWB)

AMOS 5:6–7, 10–15

Commentary
The book of Amos belongs to a collection of OT writings called the Book of the Twelve, which comprises the twelve Minor Prophets from Hosea to Malachi. Though a native of the southern kingdom of Judah, Amos was called by God to carry out a prophetic ministry in the northern kingdom of Israel in the first half of the eighth century B.C. This was a generation or two before Israel was taken into exile by the Assyrian empire in 722 B.C.

In Amos's day, Israel's enemies no longer posed a threat. This political freedom fostered the development of international trade, which resulted in a high level of economic prosperity… at least for some. As is so often the case, with great wealth comes great greed. Social inequality and injustice escalated as the economic divide between the rich and the poor increased. Because many regarded Israel's economic prosperity as a blessing from the LORD, a sign of God's favor, these social inequalities and injustices went unchecked. Into this situation Amos was sent to deliver the word of the LORD, a word of impending judgment and exile for Israel.

Being the people of God is not only a great privilege but also a great responsibility. Belonging to the people of God opens one up to both blessing and discipline. As the LORD declares to Israel: "You only have I known of all the families of the earth; therefore I will punish you for all your iniquities" (Amos 3:2). In Amos 4, the LORD recites a litany of the chastisements and punishments that he has administered to his chosen people. These were designed to inspire repentance but to no avail. Whether it was drought, famine, blight, pestilence, or invasion, the people's response to the LORD's disciplinary actions was the same. As the LORD repeats a full five times, I did such and such, "yet you did not return to me" (4:6, 8, 9, 10, 11).

5:6–7. In Amos 5, the LORD, speaking through the prophet, repeatedly pleads with his people to seek that which genuinely leads to life: "Seek me and live" (5:4); "Seek good and not evil, that you may live" (5:14); and, as today's reading begins, "Seek the LORD and live" (5:6).

In poetic literature, Ephraim is often used to designate the northern kingdom of Israel (cf. Hos 5:3, 5; Ezek 37:16–20). In today's reading, the name of Ephraim's father, Joseph, serves in this capacity. Bethel, which means "House of God," was an important city on the southern border of Israel. In Amos' day, an Israelite sanctuary was in operation at Bethel, having been established in the late tenth century B.C. by King Jeroboam, the first king of the northern kingdom of Israel (1 Kgs 12:25–33).

5:10–15. But what does it mean to seek the LORD? For Amos, it means establishing and maintaining a system in which there is equal justice for all, the rich and the poor, the politically connected and the marginalized. In 5:15, Amos speaks of "establishing justice in the gate." In the ancient world, the gates of a city not only served as an important part of a city's defense, the gates were where merchants conducted business and where kings and other city officials settled disputes and administered justice. Thus, the city gates belonged to the economic and judicial spheres of public life. In today's reading, the judicial dimension of the gates is under scrutiny.

In Amos' day, the judicial system was thoroughly corrupt. Justice went to the highest bidder, and any who stood up for the truth and challenged the moral authority of the law courts was hated and despised. So corrupt was the legal system, so far beyond repair, that Amos did not think there was much point in confronting it. As he says, in these evil times, "the prudent will keep silent" (5:13). Nevertheless, Amos calls upon Israel to seek good, to love good, and to work to establish justice in the legal system. This is part and parcel of what it means to seek the LORD. And who knows, the LORD may yet relent and restore those of his people who remain (5:15; cf. Jonah 3:9).

Suggestions for Lectors

As you begin today's reading, adopt a harsh, severe tone of voice, for you are warning your listeners about the judgments and calamities that will befall them if they do not change their ways. Maintain this tone through 5:13.

Emphasize the commands that Amos issues:

> 6 *Seek* the LORD and live, …
>
> 14 *Seek* good and not evil, …
>
> 15 *Hate* evil and *love* good,
> and *establish* justice in the gate; …

When you come to 5:14–15, replace your harshness and severity with a tone of voice that conveys a sense of compassionate pleading. There is still time for the people to change and for God to relent. So plead passionately and compassionately with your listeners that they might take your warnings and instructions to heart.

Like most biblical prophets, Amos delivers the word of the LORD through verse. As lectors, then, one of the keys to learning to read the prophets aloud is to develop an awareness of and an appreciation for how biblical poetry works. The most prominent and pervasive characteristic of biblical poetry is repetition, especially the repetition that occurs between two or more poetic lines, which we call parallelism.

For example, in today's reading, 5:12a is composed of two poetic lines where the second line reinforces the first by restating it in different words. This is called synonymous parallelism.

> a For I know how many are your transgressions,
> a' and how great are your sins

Not only can parallelism exist between two lines, it can also exist between two strophes. (A strophe is made up of two or three poetic lines.) Consider the following. In

5:11, a construction image is presented in the first strophe (a-a') and an agricultural image is employed in the second (b-b').

a you have built houses of hewn stone,
a' but you shall not live in them;

b you have planted pleasant vineyards,
b' but you shall not drink their wine.

Though different images are employed, the grammatical structure for each strophe is the same; line a parallels b, and line a' parallels b'. Moreover, the meaning is the same for each strophe, namely, the people will not enjoy the fruit of their labors. As lectors, these insights inform and shape our reading. So, in 5:11, a and b ought to be delivered in the same manner as a' and b'.

Pronunciation Guide
Amos (AY-muhs), *Bethel* (BETH-uhl), *Joseph* (JOH-sif; -suhf)

HEBREWS 4:12–16

Notes
Sequence. 2 of 7

Commentary
In the gospels, Jesus of Nazareth is portrayed primarily as a prophet. Even Jesus refers to himself as a prophet (Mark 6:4, Prop 9; Luke 4:24; 13:33–34) and compares himself to other prophets (Luke 4:25–27; 11:32; Matt 12:41). Acts 3:22–23 also describes Jesus as a prophet. Then, near the end of his earthly life, Jesus begins to be characterized as a king (Matt 21:5; John 18:37, Prop 29), and he is even crucified as "The King of the Jews" (Mark 15:26). Throughout the rest of the NT, Jesus' kingship is expressed through designations like Messiah, Christ, and Lord. In addition to prophet and king, Jesus is also depicted as a high priest, especially in the Letter to the Hebrews. In today's reading, we discover that our great high priest is able to sympathize with our weaknesses as human beings because he himself endured suffering as a human being.

4:12–13. Today's reading begins by describing the word of God as "living and active, sharper than any two-edged sword" (4:12). Like a surgeon's scalpel, God's word is able to define and separate things that are close together, even intertwined. The word that God sends forth is able to navigate all our pretenses and justifications, to get behind them and open us up to God by exposing our hearts true thoughts and intentions. Here, the word of God seems cold and uncompromising, but this unsettling image is balanced by the warmth and compassion of our great high priest, whom the author introduces next.

4:14–16. The Letter of Hebrews opens with a creed-like description of Jesus' exalted status as the Son of God:

> He is the reflection of God's glory and the exact imprint of God's very being, and he sustains all things by his powerful word. When he

> had made purification for sins, he sat down at the right hand of the Majesty on high, having become as much superior to angels as the name he has inherited is more excellent than theirs (1:3–4, Chr III).

In today's reading, this same Jesus, who has passed into the heavens as our great high priest, is also able to sympathize with our human predicament. Although Jesus committed no sin, as a human being, he experienced every category of temptation and test known to humankind. Consequently, he is able to sympathize with us in our struggles, and we are able to approach his throne with boldness knowing that he will receive us with mercy. On the other hand, precisely because he remained without sin, despite being tested in every respect as we are, we are able to approach him with confidence knowing that he will supply us with the grace—that is, the power and strength—to remain obedient in our time of need.

Suggestions for Lectors

Today's reading is short and starts quickly, so begin with a clear, strong voice. The reading falls into two sections so pause for a full second between verses 13 and 14 to indicate this break. In 4:14–16, the author employs first person plural pronouns (*we, us, our*), so adopt a tone and a manner of expression that indicates you belong to and identify with the people to whom you are speaking. In 1:15, pause for a second after *as we are*, before you add the exception *yet… without sin.* The final verse should receive the most emphasis. Read it more deliberately, and emphasize *boldness*, *mercy*, and the second use of *grace.*

MARK 10:17–31

Notes

Sequence. 7 of 12

Commentary

In Mark 4:3–9, Jesus tells a parable about a sower who sows his seed by broadcasting it such that his seed is sown in four different types of soil of varying fertility. Three of the soils fail to produce a harvest, while the good soil produces three different yields of harvest. As Jesus' explanation to the disciples reveals, the parable is allegorical (4:13–20). The four different soils represent four possible responses to Jesus and his message of the kingdom.

In Mark, we encounter characters who represent each of these soils. Jesus' opponents are represented by the seed sown on the path where birds take the seed away before it even has a chance to sprout. The seeds sown on rocky ground spring up quickly but have no root and so fall away the moment trouble or persecution arises. Somewhat surprisingly, Jesus' own disciples share many of these characteristics. When Jesus called the four fishermen—Simon and Andrew, James and John—they immediately abandoned their livelihoods to follow Jesus (1:16–20, Epi 3). Yet, in the end, they all desert Jesus when he is being arrested. Interestingly enough, it is the minor characters in the gospel who most often exhibit the characteristics of the good soil. Characters like Jairus, the hemorrhaging woman, the Syrophoenician woman, and Bartimaeus are models of faith and understanding and so produce the fruit of the kingdom.

In today's reading, we encounter a man who fits the description of the third soil. "Others are those sown among the thorns: these are the ones who hear the word, but the cares of the world, and the lure of wealth, and the desire for other things come in and choke the word, and it yields nothing" (4:18–19).

10:17–22. The NRSV reads, "As [Jesus] was setting out on a journey" (10:17a). But a better translation would be, "As [Jesus] was setting out *on the way*," because Jesus is not setting out on just any journey, he is *on the way* to Jerusalem, that is, *on the way* to the cross. As he is on the way, a man catches up with Jesus in order to ask him what it takes to receive eternal life. Here, one might expect Jesus to say, "Repent, and believe in the good news" (1:15), but instead he draws the man's attention to the Ten Commandments (Exod 20:1–17, Lent 3). The first four commandments lay out what it means to love God, while the last six what it means to love our neighbors as ourselves. Jesus lists the commandments in this last category with one notable omission. He does not mention the prohibition against coveting, and this is not accidental.

When the man replies that he has kept all these commandments, Jesus says that there is just one thing the man lacks. If he wants to inherit eternal life, then he needs to let go of his earthly treasures. He should sell everything, give the proceeds to the poor, and then follow Jesus *on the way*. Here, it is important to recognize that Jesus is not trying to make the man earn his salvation nor is he trying to punish him, for the text expressly states that Jesus is motivated by his love for this man. Clearly, the man is possessed by his possessions, and unfortunately exorcisms do not work with this type of possession. Jesus wishes to free the man from that which enslaves him, so he offers him a concrete, albeit difficult, solution to help him overcome his earthly attachments. It is not that selling his possessions will earn him the right to enter the kingdom of God, but that selling his possessions will free him so that he can experience the fullness of life that the kingdom of God has to offer. It's the same type of advice one might offer an alcoholic. If you want freedom from alcohol, stop drinking and never touch the stuff again. For this man, selling his possessions will give him the eternal life he seeks.

10:23–27. After the man departs, Jesus turns to his disciples and graphically expresses how difficult it is for someone of wealth to enter the kingdom of God. "It is easier for a camel to go through the eye of a needle than for someone who is rich to enter the kingdom of God" (10:25). The disciples (along with Mark's readers) are stunned by this statement. After all, wealth is and was often viewed as a sign of God's blessing. If those who are blessed by God cannot enter the kingdom of God, then who can? Jesus replies, "For mortals it is impossible, but not for God; for God all things are possible" (10:27).

Here one is perhaps reminded of the distraught father who brought his demon-possessed son to Jesus begging him saying, "if you are able to do anything, have pity on us and help us." Jesus responds with, "If you are able!—All things can be done for the one who believes," and the man replies, "I believe, *help my unbelief!*" (9:22b–24). In the end, Jesus does help him, so the reader suspects that, had the rich man asked, Jesus would have been more than willing to help him find a way to let go of his attachment to his possessions. After all, Jesus has the power to exorcise more than unclean spirits.

10:28–31. Peter is quick to point out that he and the other apostles have left everything to follow Jesus. Here, one might expect Jesus to chastise them for such self-interested concern, but he does not. Instead, he affirms that they will receive back far more than what they have given up, not only in the age to come but even in the present age. When a person gives up everything to follow Jesus, they become a member of the kingdom-of-God family where resources are shared and people take care of one another, not because they are related by blood or marriage but because they belong to Christ (cf. 3:33–35, Prop 5). Of course, this does not exempt Jesus' followers from hardship; in the present age, all rewards will be accompanied by persecutions. Those who are last in the eyes of the world—like the disciples—will find themselves first in the kingdom; while those who are first in the eyes of the world—like the rich man—will find themselves last in the kingdom.

Suggestions for Lectors

The man poses his question to Jesus from a kneeling position, so invest your voice with respect and humility as you ask, *Good Teacher, what must I do to inherit eternal life?* (10:17). Use this same tone of voice in 10:20 when the man replies to Jesus with all sincerity, *Teacher, I have kept all these since my youth.*

Jesus responds in a challenging, almost chastising tone of voice, *Why do you call me good?* (10:18), but his tone softens as he begins naming the commandments. Jesus begins by saying, *You know the commandments*, so read through the commandments in the tone of voice you would use when reminding someone of something (versus the tone of voice you would use if you were introducing the commandments for the first time). You are looking for a relaxed, understated tone. After all, at this point in the exchange, Jesus is just clearing the ground. For it is not the six commandments that Jesus identifies that are most important, but rather the *one* commandment that he intentionally leaves out and will introduce momentarily that is the most important.

The first part of 10:21 is worth lingering over. Read it slowly with generous pauses at the commas and after *him*, as in: *Jesus,... looking at him,... loved him....* Then, deliver Jesus' instructions with compassion and concern in your voice. Remember, Jesus loves him. He is not trying to punish the man for being rich; he is simply trying to set him free so that he might get what he came for, namely, eternal life.

Retain this same compassion and concern as Jesus relates how hard it is for the rich to enter the kingdom of God (10:23–27). Jesus repeats himself in 10:24, so up the intensity at this point. Highlight Jesus' concluding declaration in 10:27. In the first half of the verse, emphasize *mortals* and *God*, or *impossible* and *not.* Read the second half of the verse slowly, deliberately, and with great conviction: *for God... all things are possible.*

In 10:29–31, Jesus reassures his disciples that the sacrifices they have made in following him will not go unrewarded. So employ a reassuring tone of voice in this section, even for the concluding statement about the first and the last because in this particular context, it is not offered as a challenge but as a promise.

PROPER 24

October 16–22

Job 38:1–7, (34–41)	Isaiah 53:4–12
Psalm 104:1–9, 24, 35c (= 104:1–9, 25, 37b BCP)	Psalm 91:9–16
Hebrews 5:1–10	Hebrews 5:1–10
Mark 10:35–45	Mark 10:35–45

JOB 38:1–7, (34–41)

Notes

Sequence. 3 of 4

Commentary

In the first two chapters of the book, Job suffers the devastating loss of his livestock, his livelihood, his family, and his health. Then, over the next thirty-five chapters of the story, Job must endure the "support" of his friends, who try to convince Job that, if he would only acknowledge his sin, his sufferings would be at an end. In their moral universe, only punishment for sin could account for such misfortune. But most of all, Job has to contend with the despair and terror brought on by the complete silence and absence of God.

In last week's reading, Job is worn out from defending himself to his friends. He expresses his desire to present his case before the LORD himself, before whom he expects a fair hearing and from whom he expects vindication.

> Oh, that I knew where I might find him,
> that I might come even to his dwelling!
> I would lay my case before him,
> and fill my mouth with arguments.
> I would learn what he would answer me,
> and understand what he would say to me.
> Would he contend with me in the greatness of his power?
> No; but he would give heed to me.
> There an upright person could reason with him,
> and I should be acquitted forever by my judge (23:4–7, Prop 23).

In this week's reading, Job finally gets his chance. The LORD appears, but things do not go as Job had envisioned. Instead of presenting his case to the LORD, the LORD presents his case to Job. It is a lengthy case (38:1–39:30; 40:6–41:34), much of which consists of a series of rhetorical questions. This litany of questions demonstrates the LORD's incomparable wisdom and greatness and serves to put everything into its proper perspective.

38:1–3. Job has had plenty of opportunity to question God, and now it is God's turn. Out of the mighty whirlwind, the LORD addresses Job, "Get ready mortal because *I* will question *you*, and *you* shall answer *me*" (38:3).

38:4–7. God begins by questioning Job about the beginnings of creation. Where was Job when God was constructing the universe? Was Job there when God laid the earth's foundations? Does Job even know what the foundations rest upon, or who laid the cornerstone?

38:34–38. The next set of questions highlight God's authority. Can Job command the forces of nature? Can he make it rain? Can he produce thunder with his voice or trigger lightening? And who, other than God is the source of wisdom? Who, other than God, can give the gift of understanding?

38:39–41. Finally, who other than God provides for all his creatures under the heavens? Does Job track down the food that lions and their cubs feed upon? What about the food for the birds and their offspring?

In the end, all the questions the LORD poses produce the desired effect—Job gains the perspective he needs to carry on despite his great misfortune and suffering. Instead of feeling compelled to make his case, Job is left almost speechless. In reverence and humility, Job declares: "I have uttered what I did not understand, things too wonderful for me, which I did not know" (42:3b, Prop 25).

Suggestions for Lectors

In today's reading, you are playing the part of the LORD, who asks question upon question in order to overwhelm Job. As you make your way through this whirlwind of questions, slowly increase your intensity and tempo. Never rush, but by the end of the reading, you want to be reading discernibly quicker than you were at the beginning. In a way, you are not wanting to give Job—that is, your listeners—a chance to catch their breath. You want to leave them with a sense of awe regarding the power and majesty of God.

At the beginning of the reading, highlight the only statement the LORD makes by reading it slowly and deliberately and by emphasizing the pronouns: *Gird up your loins like a man,… I will question you, and you declare to me* (38:3).

Pronunciation Guide

Job (JOHB; *not* JAWB)

ISAIAH 53:4–12

Commentary

Through its rich poetry and prose, the book of Isaiah narrates a dramatic story of rebellion and judgment that gives way to forgiveness and redemption. The plot begins with God's chosen people, but then broadens to encompass all the nations of the world and even creation itself. In Isaiah 1–39, the drama focuses upon rebellion as humanity serves the gods of its own making and orders society through unjust practices and power structures. The prophet Isaiah is sent to announce the various judgments that will be executed by the LORD, the Holy One of Israel and the creator of the heavens and the earth. Judgment begins with the LORD's own people who have forsaken the covenant (Isa 1–12, 28–35) through their willful and persistent failure to love God with their whole heart (Deut 6:5, Prop 26; Exod 20:1–7, Lent 3) and to love their neighbors as themselves (Lev 19:18; Exod 20:8–17). Judgment then extends to the nations and empires of the world who oppose the sovereign rule of the LORD through their prideful and unjust exercise of power (Isa 13–23). Even the forces of chaos and evil that threaten God's good creation will be judged, not least death itself (25:7–8, East).

Yet beginning in Isaiah 40, the ominous tone of judgment gives way to a joyful note of hope as the prophet announces a *new thing* that the LORD is about to do (42:9; 43:19; 48:6). This new thing, which will eventually result in the restoration of all creation, will begin with the LORD forgiving and redeeming his chosen people. Through his chosen people, God will bring about the redemption and reconciliation of all peoples everywhere in keeping with his covenant promises to Abraham and Sarah (Gen 12:2–3; 17:16; 22:17–18).

Within this redemptive drama of Isaiah 40–55 are four passages concerning an unidentified servant of the LORD (42:1–4; 49:1–6; 50:4–9, Palm; 52:13–53:12). These passages are called the Servant Songs. The servant appears sometimes as a corporate personality and sometimes as a single individual. There is a broad, general movement from the servant as *Israel* to the servant as *a single Israelite* who takes on Israel's vocation to be both the restorer of God's chosen people and the light to the nations (cf. 49:5–6).

In today's reading of the fourth and final Servant Song, we see an intensification of the abuse and humiliation that the servant underwent in the third Servant Song (50:4–9a). The fourth Servant Song goes beyond the third, seeing the servant's death and vindication as the means by which the LORD enacts the forgiveness, healing, and restoration of his chosen people and all the peoples of the world.

53:4–6. In today's reading, the first-person plural pronouns (*we*, *us*, *our*) indicate that the people as a collective whole are speaking. Here, God's chosen people make a public confession of sin. They bear witness to the unspeakable things that the servant endured as a direct result of their own rebellion and disobedience. They are responsible for the servant's suffering and death. The people acknowledge that when the servant was alive, they completely disregarded him because he was "despised and rejected by others" (53:3). Like Job's friends, they assumed that his chronic sickness and suffering were a sure sign that the LORD had forsaken him, so they too took no account of him. But now they recognize that they were completely mistaken about the servant and that they themselves are to blame. They see that the servant bore the humiliation and abuse that they should have borne had they not abandoned their vocation as God's chosen people.

53:7–11a. The people continue by bearing witness to the fact that the servant was innocent of any wrongdoing and that he endured the unjust abuse, humiliation, and death willingly. Moreover, they have come to see that the servant's life of suffering, far from being a sign of God-forsakenness, actually served God's purposes, for the LORD vindicated his servant by accepting and making "his life an offering for [the people's] sin" (53:10a).

53:11b–12. In the last section, the speaker is the LORD, and he bears witness to the life and accomplishments of "my servant" (53:11b). The servant's life, though cut short (53:8), was not without significance. Because the servant remained obedient to God and carried out his calling faithfully even unto death, the LORD will raise him up and "allot him a portion with the great" (53:12), for he gave his life for others less righteous than he.

Suggestions for Lectors

Today's reading comprises three stanzas of three verses each: 4–6, 7–9, 10–12. Pause for a full second between stanzas, and conclude each by slowing down for the last line of the stanza.

Of paramount importance is the tone of voice you adopt. To convey the mood of these somber enumerations of suffering, you must read slower than usual. Frequent pauses, at least after every sentence, will help set the scene and will serve to accent, by isolation, the importance of each trial the Servant endures. Though the whole passage possesses a somber tone, a few rays of light break through in the last stanza (53:10–12) as the prophet speaks of the servant's vindication and the community's gratitude for what the servant has endured on account of its sins.

Pronunciation Guide

Isaiah (ī-ZAY-uh)

HEBREWS 5:1–10

Notes

Sequence. 3 of 7

Commentary

In Jewish tradition, the high priest was responsible for what took place in the temple. While the other priests carried out their priestly duties in the inner court (a.k.a., the Holy Place), only the high priest was allowed to enter the Most Holy Place (a.k.a., the Holy of Holies), the inner sanctuary where the ark of the covenant resided. Even then, the high priest only entered the Holy of Holies once a year on the Day of Atonement (a.k.a., Yom Kippur; Lev 16; Heb 9:3–7).

In last week's reading, Jesus was described as our great high priest who is able to relate to us in our weaknesses because he himself suffered as all human beings do (4:14). In today's reading, the author of Hebrews presents Jesus' qualifications for the office of high priest—humility and suffering.

5:1–6. The primary responsibility of the high priest was to offer sacrifices for sin. Because high priests were fallible, sinful human beings like everybody else, they were in a position to treat others with understanding and mercy. (Whether or not they did this is another matter). Since high priests were not without sin, the sacrifices they offered were not only for the sins of others but for their own sins as well.

Given their own foibles and sinful proclivities, high priests were to exercise humility and not take it upon themselves to become high priests. Instead, this honor was reserved for those whom God had chosen and called. This is how it was when God appointed Moses' brother Aaron to be the first high priest (Num 16:5; 17:5; 18:1–7). Even Jesus, who was "without sin" (4:15, Prop 23), did not presume to take this honor. Instead, he was appointed by God as the psalms testify: "You are my

Son, today I have begotten you" (Ps 2:7), and "You are a priest forever, according to the order of Melchizedek" (110:4). And so, the first qualification for being high priest is humility.

5:7–10. One might naturally assume that a high priest is too important and too holy to suffer, but suffering is what qualified Jesus to be our great high priest. One might also assume that because Jesus was the Son of God obedience was automatic for him. Yet, the author of Hebrews writes that, "Although he was a Son, he *learned* obedience through what he suffered" (5:8). Jesus achieved perfection by living a life of obedience even in the midst of suffering. Therefore, Jesus became the source of eternal life and salvation for any who would follow after him and live a life of humble obedience even in the face of suffering and death.

Generally speaking, in the OT, priests were taken from the tribe of Levi, and they made up the Levitical priesthood (Num 3:5–10). Moses' brother, Aaron, was a Levite and a priest. He and his sons were appointed by God to be responsible for the priestly duties that took place in relation to the tabernacle (Exod 28). In addition, Aaron was anointed as the first high priest, and all other high priests were to be descendants of Aaron. So within the Levitical priesthood, there was the Aaronic priesthood, which included the office of high priest. As a descendant of Judah (vs. Levi), Jesus belonged to neither of these priestly orders. Instead, in keeping with Psalm 110, the author of Hebrews sees Jesus as belonging to the priestly order of Melchizedek (5:6, 10; 6:20; 7:11, 17). Melchizedek is a mysterious figure who briefly appears in Genesis, where he is identified as the *king* of Salem and the *priest* of God Most High (14:18–20; Heb 7:1–10). These twin roles make Melchizedek—whose name means *king of righteousness*—the ideal candidate to prefigure the coming of the kingly high priest, Jesus.

Because Jesus is alive forevermore, he will remain in the office of high priest indefinitely and will be able to offer a salvation that never ends. As we read next week, Jesus "holds his priesthood permanently, because he continues forever. Consequently he is able for all time to save those who approach God through him, since he always lives to make intercession for them" (Heb 7:24–25).

Suggestions for Lectors

In today's reading, the author of Hebrews is like a professor lecturing on the topic of high priests in ancient Judaism, focusing on the services they performed and how they were appointed to office. So deliver this reading as though you are giving a lecture, not a dry, boring lecture, but a stimulating one. Speak with enthusiasm and evident interest in your subject.

When you read the quotations from the OT, raise your voice, and emphasize the first line of each: *You are my Son* (5:5), and *You are a priest forever* (5:6).

Beginning in 5:7, become more animated as you speak about the suffering Jesus endured. Emphasize 5:8 by reading it slowly and deliberately. Read it in three intonational phrases by stressing the concluding words of each unit—*Son*, *obedience*, and *suffered*—and by pausing after each unit, as in: *Although he was a Son,... he learned obedience... through what he suffered;...* (5:8). Read the last phrase slower than the first two. After 5:8, return to your normal pace and tempo as you conclude your talk.

Pronunciation Guide
Aaron (AIR-uhn), *Hebrews* (HEE-brooz), *Melchizedek* (mel-KIZ-uh-dek)

Mark 10:35–45

Notes
Sequence. 8 of 12

Commentary
In Mark's third narrative movement (8:27–10:52), Jesus prepares his disciples for the fate that awaits him in Jerusalem. In 8:29, Peter declares, "You are the Messiah," and immediately Jesus begins "to teach them that [he] must undergo great suffering, and be rejected by the elders, the chief priests, and the scribes, and be killed, and after three days rise again" (8:31). Thus, the moment the disciples recognize that Jesus is the Messiah, Jesus begins to reveal to them what being the messiah will entail, both for himself *and* for any who would follow after him. His vocation as the Messiah is not just about working miracles; it is about transforming a sinful, violent world God's way, which often means that Jesus' followers will be on the receiving end of the world's violence and sin.

In this movement, Jesus predicts his suffering, death, and resurrection no less than three times (8:31; 9:30–32; 10:32–34). Each time Jesus issues a passion prediction, his disciples do or say something that indicates they have not grasped the implications of what Jesus has been telling them. Jesus then takes the opportunity to teach them what it means to follow him on the way of the cross.

10:35–40. Immediately prior to today's reading, Jesus issues his third and final passion prediction (10:32–34). Afterwards, James and John approach Jesus with a bold request. When Jesus has come into his own, when he has established God's kingdom and is reigning over it, James and John want to be his first and second in command, his right- and left-hand men. Jesus remarks that they have no idea what they are asking, and then asks them whether they think they are up to the task. The road of glory is the way of the cross. Can they drink the bitter cup of suffering that he is about to drink? Can they be cleansed by the painful and humiliating death that awaits him? To their credit, James and John do not shy away but confirm that they are able. Here, one is reminded of Peter's response to Jesus' prediction that everyone will desert him: "Even though all become deserters, I will not" (14:29). At this point, James and John are probably expecting Jesus to say something like, "Well, if you are really able to drink my cup and be baptized with my baptism, then the seats are yours." Instead, Jesus confirms that they will indeed suffer as he does, but he quickly adds that they cannot have the places of honor because those places have already been assigned. There is great irony in this exchange. James and John endure the cost of discipleship, but they will not get the reward they so covet.

10:41–45. When the other disciples find out about the request, they are incensed, so Jesus calls them all together. In the kingdom of God, true honor is not to be found in holding positions of honor. True glory comes from serving others, not ruling over them. Thus, Jesus does not dissuade the disciples from seeking greatness, but he does redefine it, and here he offers another of his paradoxical statements: "whoever wishes to become great among you must be your servant, and whoever wishes to be first among you must be slave of all" (10:43–44). After all, Jesus himself, who is their lord and master, did not come to be served but to serve and give his life for others. Moreover, one suspects that even when Jesus comes into his glory, he will still be serving those who worship him because service is a core kingdom value and God's nature is self-emptying love.

Suggestions for Lectors

Today's episode is simple and straightforward and requires nothing more than the basic skills of a narrator. There are, however, places that would benefit from some minor emphasis. In 10:39, emphasize *you will drink* and *you will be baptized*, leaning on the twice-repeated *will*. At the beginning of 10:43, emphasize *But* and pause briefly afterwards. In 10:43–44, emphasize the contrasting words, *great* and *servant* and then *first* and *slave*.

Conclude the reading by delivering the final verse in a more deliberate manner. Slow down, and enunciate each of the words clearly and precisely. Emphasize *not*, *serve*, and *ransom*, and introduce slight pauses after *not*, *served*, and *life*, as in: *For the Son of Man came not... to be served... but to serve, and to give his life... a ransom for many.*

Alternatively, one might emphasize *served*, *serve*, and *give* and pause slightly after *served* and *life* while ignoring the comma after *serve*, as in: *For the Son of Man came not to be served... but to serve and to give his life... a ransom for many.* In this way, *serve* and *give* are joined together as one action not two, which creates a smoother reading.

If you think it would sound better, instead of pausing after *life*, you could insert the word *as*, as in: *to serve and to give his life [as] a ransom for many*. This corresponds to a number of other English translations of Mark 10:45.

Pronunciation Guide

Gentiles (JEN-tīlz)
Zebedee (ZEB-uh-dee)

PROPER 25

October 23–29

Job 42:1–6, 10–17	Jeremiah 31:7–9
Psalm 34:1–8, (19–22)	Psalm 126
Hebrews 7:23–28	Hebrews 7:23–28
Mark 10:46–52	Mark 10:46–52

Job 42:1–6, 10–17

Notes

Sequence. 4 of 4

Commentary

Today's reading from Job is the last of four sequential readings. Two weeks ago, Job was worn out, not only by his suffering but also by the counsel of his friends. Job's suffering challenged the predictability of their moral universe, a universe that operated according to laws of cause and effect. In their universe, upright behavior produced prosperity while sinful behavior resulted in suffering. So unsettled were they by Job's suffering that they could not offer him empathy and understanding; rather, the only "comfort" they could offer their friend was argument and advice. Thus, Job longs to present his case before the LORD himself. "Oh, that I knew where I might find him,... I would lay my case before him, and fill my mouth with arguments.... and I should be acquitted forever by my judge" (23:3–4, 7b, Prop 23).

Last week, Job finally got his chance. The LORD appeared, but things did not go as anticipated. Instead of presenting his case to the LORD, the LORD presented his case to Job. Through a litany of questions and accomplishments, the LORD demonstrated his incomparable wisdom and greatness. Today, we read of Job's response.

42:1–6. The LORD's words have left Job almost speechless. Instead of filling his mouth with arguments, as he said he would do, Job's words are reverent, humble, and few. He has been given the gift of realizing just how much he does not know. "I have uttered what I did not understand, things too wonderful for me, which I did not know" (42:3b). The LORD has put things into perspective for Job, and Job no longer feels compelled to make his case. Instead he is satisfied with repenting in dust and ashes, the stuff out of which he has been made.

Of course, Job's friends have been insisting all along that he repent of the sin he must have committed, but this is not why Job repents. Job repents because he is no longer relying upon hearsay (42:5a); he has seen God, and he has heard truth from the LORD's own mouth (42:5b). Consequently, Job no longer feels the need to defend himself against the attacks and advice of friends whose understanding is limited and self-serving. In the presence of Almighty God, who knows everything and judges rightly, Job can let go of the need to defend his innocence. Thus, Job repents of insisting on his own righteousness.

In the NRSV and in some other translations, the question in 42:3a and the statement in 42:4 are placed in single quotation marks because these are not Job's words, but rather the LORD's words that Job is citing from 38:2–3 (see last week's reading).

42:7–9. In the portion of the story that has been left out of today's reading, an interesting turn of events takes place. The moment Job repents, the LORD declares that Job has been right all along. The LORD says to Eliphaz, "My wrath is kindled against you and against your two friends; for you have not spoken of me what is right, *as my servant Job has*" (42:7). So, the LORD acquits Job after all, just as Job had predicted (23:7).

The LORD then directs his three friends to offer a burnt offering for themselves, though Job should be the one to make the intercession. These actions serve two purposes. First, by offering a sacrifice, the friends are acknowledging their own guilt in this affair. Second, in having Job pray for them, the LORD is helping the four friends walk down the road of forgiveness and reconciliation.

42:10–17. As soon as this occurs, Job's fortunes are reversed. Everything that he lost in the beginning is returned two-fold (cf. 1:3), and Job once again finds himself in the midst of the community.

Like before, Job is granted seven sons and three daughters (cf. 1:2). Interestingly, only the three daughters are named and described. Even more interesting is the fact that they receive a share of the inheritance like their brothers. Normally, daughters only received an inheritance when there were no surviving sons. This is just one more indication that the latter days of Job were more blessed than those in the beginning.

Suggestions for Lectors

Today's reading begins in poetry (42:1–6) but ends in prose (42:7–17). The poetic portion is the most challenging to deliver because it alternates between Job's own words and the words of the LORD quoted by Job. This is easy to represent visually, but much harder to convey orally. The italicized portions are the LORD's words.

2 "I know that you can do all things,
  and that no purpose of yours can be thwarted.

3 *'Who is this that hides counsel without knowledge?'*
Therefore I have uttered what I did not understand,
  things too wonderful for me, which I did not know.

4 *'Hear, and I will speak;*
  I will question you, and you declare to me.'
5 I had heard of you by the hearing of the ear,
  but now my eye sees you;
6 therefore I despise myself,
  and repent in dust and ashes."

No matter what you do to distinguish Job's words from the LORD's, your listeners will not be able to tell that Job quoting someone else in verses 3a and 4a (unless perhaps they are following along in a printed text or this is pointed out to them beforehand). Nevertheless, you still want to deliver their words in a different manner from one another. One suggestion would be to read Job's words at your normal volume in an apologetic tone with hints of regret and sorrow. Before 3a and 4a, pause for a second; then read the LORD'S words with a stronger voice, with more volume and intensity and with an accusatory tone.

The prose portion is much more straightforward. Read it with a sense of joy and satisfaction as if everything is now good and right with the world. When you come to the final line, slow down and read more deliberately with liberal pauses: *And Job died,… old… and full of days* (42:17). Read this line with joy and satisfaction as well. Although it tells of Job's *death*, it is intended to celebrate the fact that, despite all his suffering, in the end, Job had a good, long *life.*

Pronunciation Guide

Jemimah (juh-MĪ-muh), *Job* (JOHB; *not* JAWB),
Keren-happuch (kehr'-uhn-HAP-uk), *Keziah* (kuh-ZĪ-uh; kih-ZĪ-uh)

JEREMIAH 31:7–9

Commentary

When Jeremiah was called to be a "prophet to the nations" (Jer 1:5), his prophetic vocation was described with six actions: "See, today I appoint you over nations and over kingdoms, to pluck up and to pull down, to destroy and to overthrow, to build and to plant" (1:10). The first four actions denote judgment, and it is with the judgment and exile of Judah that the first twenty-nine chapters of Jeremiah is concerned. Yet, in Jeremiah 30–33, the actions *to build* and *to plant* hold precedence. These chapters are often designated *The Book of Consolation*, for in them the LORD speaks to his exiled people and promises to restore them (30:2–3; cf. 33:26):

> Thus says the LORD, the God of Israel: Write in a book all the words that I have spoken to you. For the days are surely coming, says the LORD, when I will restore the fortunes of my people, Israel and Judah, says the LORD, and I will bring them back to the land that I gave to their ancestors and they shall take possession of it.

In today's reading, the prophet paints a picture of reconciliation between the LORD and his people. This reconciliation is manifest in the ending of the exile, the gathering of the exiles, and their return to the Promised Land.

31:7–9. In 722 B.C., the northern kingdom of Israel was defeated by the Assyrian empire and its citizens dispersed throughout the world. Then, in 597 and 586 B.C., the southern kingdom of Judah was twice defeated by the Babylonian empire and its citizens exiled to Babylon. These are the exiles the LORD intends to bring "from the land of the north, and gather… from the farthest parts of the earth" (31:8a). That exiles from both kingdoms are in view is confirmed later in the chapter when the LORD declares, "The days are surely coming… when I will sow the house of *Israel* and the house of *Judah* with the seed of humans and the seed of animals" (31:27).

More significantly, the LORD will not just bring back the unblemished and the able-bodied, for among the returning exiles will be "the blind and the lame, those with child and those in labor, together; a great company, they shall return here" (31:8b). The return journey may be a long one, but it will not be difficult, for like a good shepherd, the LORD will lead them back along "brooks of water" and guide them along "a straight path in which they shall not stumble" (31:9a). In other words, this will not be like Israel's forty-year sojourn in the wilderness in which water was not plentiful and the route was not straight.

Suggestions for Lectors

In today's reading, there are no mood changes and no verses that require special attention or emphasis. Read with your voice raised in gladness as though you are leading the company of returning exiles as they march through the wilderness toward the Holy City (31:8).

Your principal effort will be to keep a positive, happy tone throughout. Pay attention to the various groups of people you are addressing: the blind, the lame, and the pregnant. Accent each group as they are named for, as Jeremiah repeatedly insists, this good news is for all the people.

Pronunciation Guide
Ephraim (EE-free-uhm)
Jeremiah (jair'-uh-MĪ-uh)

Hebrews 7:23–28

Notes
Sequence. 4 of 7

Commentary
In first-century Judaism, the high priest was responsible for what took place in the temple in Jerusalem. While the other Levitical priests carried out their duties in the inner court (a.k.a., the Holy Place), only the high priest was allowed to enter the Most Holy Place (a.k.a., the Holy of Holies), the inner sanctuary where the ark of the covenant resided. Even then, the high priest only entered the Holy of Holies once a year on the Day of Atonement (a.k.a., Yom Kippur) to offer sacrifices for the sins of the whole nation (Lev 16; Heb 9:3–7).

In Hebrews, Jesus is presented as our great high priest (2:17; 3:1; 4:14; 5:10; 6:20) who sacrificed himself for our sins (9:26, Prop 27) and learned obedience through what he suffered (5:8, Prop 24). In today's reading, the author contrasts Jesus' *eternal* priesthood with the *transient* priesthoods of all previous high priests and distinguishes between the old, *transitory* covenant, which is disappearing (8:13), and the new, *eternal* covenant (13:20).

7:23–25. The new covenant is better than the old covenant, primarily because the high priest of the new covenant will live forever. The old covenant had a succession of high priests because each high priest was subject to death and could not continue in office indefinitely. But our great high priest, Jesus, possesses "an indestructible life" as demonstrated by his resurrection from the dead (7:16). Therefore, his ministry of offering intercession for us will never end, which in turn means that the salvation we receive under the new covenant will never end; it is eternal (cf. 5:9, Prop 24). This is why the author argues that Jesus has "become the guarantee of a better covenant" (7:22), "has obtained a more excellent ministry" (8:6a), and is "the mediator of a better covenant" (8:6b).

7:26–28. Unlike the priests and high priests who served under the old covenant, the great high priest of the new covenant is holy and blameless, without blemish and without sin (cf. 4:15). In other words, he is the perfect sacrifice for sin.

From this, two conclusions can be drawn. First, unlike all previous high priests, Jesus did not have to offer up sacrifices for his own sins before he could offer sacrifices for the sins of others. His perfectly obedient life qualified him to offer sacrifices on behalf of others. This dimension of his ministry is explored in more detail in the reading from Hebrews 9:24–28 in two weeks' time (Prop 27). Second, because Jesus was the perfect sacrificial victim, his death serves as a once-for-all-time sacrifice for sin. His self-sacrifice did not just cover sin temporarily; it completely and permanently removed sin. While his ministry of intercession continues, his ministry of sacrifice is over and done. In short, his death was completely and fully effective.

Once again, this demonstrates that the superiority of the new covenant to the old is rooted in the fact that the high priest of the new covenant is far superior to all of the high priests of the old covenant combined.

Suggestions for Lectors

In last week's reading, it was suggested that the author of Hebrews could be compared to a university professor lecturing on the role and function of high priests in ancient Judaism. The same holds true for today's reading, so deliver your reading as though you are giving a lecture, not a dry, boring lecture, but a stimulating one. Speak with energy and enthusiasm, as one who is interested and deeply invested in their subject.

In your preparation, decide which phrases or ideas you would like to emphasize. Suggestions for emphasis are: *he is able for all time to save those who approach God through him* (7:25) and *this he did once for all when he offered himself* (7:27).

In the final verse, do what you can to highlight and bring out the contrast between *the law* and *the word of oath*, and between *high priests* and *a Son*. Then, read the final clause slowly and deliberately, emphasizing and pausing after *perfect*, as in: *who has been made perfect... forever.*

MARK 10:46–52

Notes

Sequence. 9 of 12

Commentary

There are five narrative movements in the Gospel of Mark. In the third movement, The Way movement (8:27–10:52), the disciples' blindness is on full display. At the beginning of the movement, Peter declared that Jesus was the Messiah, but ever since then, the disciples have struggled to come to terms with the cruciform shape Jesus' messiahship will take. Jesus has repeatedly revealed to them what will take place when they arrive in Jerusalem, namely, that he is going to suffer and die (8:31; 9:30–32; 10:32–34). Yet, on each and every occasion, the disciples do or say something that demonstrates their fundamental failure to understand the implications of what Jesus is telling them. They may recognize that Jesus is the Messiah, but they are blind to what being the messiah entails, for Jesus *and* for those who follow him.

Just last week, James and John asked Jesus to grant them positions of honor when he comes into his kingdom (10:35). Their request for honor and glory stands in stark contrast to the blind beggar's request for mercy in today's reading. Jesus' healing of blind Bartimaeus holds out hope that the disciples' blindness might eventually be cured.

10:46–52. In 10:17, Jesus and his disciples set out for Jerusalem. Today, they pass through Jericho, the last major stop before Jerusalem. As they are leaving Jericho, a blind beggar calls out to Jesus, "Jesus, Son of David, have mercy on me!" (10:47). In the first century, one of the popular expectations regarding the Messiah was that he would be a descendent of king David, and thus a king himself. Of course, Solomon was the son of David par excellence, and by Jesus' day, Solomon had gained the reputation of being a powerful exorcist and healer. So, when Bartimaeus addresses Jesus as Son of David, he is not only honoring him as Israel's king, he is also seeing Jesus as one who has the authority and power to restore his sight.

When James and John first approached Jesus, they said, "Teacher, we want you to do for us *whatever* we ask of you." Jesus responds, "What is it you want me to do for you?" (10:35–36). Bartimaeus cries out for mercy, and Jesus asks him the same question, "What do you want me to do for you?" (11:51). Unlike James and John, this blind beggar does not presume to ask the Son of David for a seat of honor; instead, he simply wants to see again. Of course, this makes perfect sense. Who would choose a position of honor over sight? Bartimaeus knows that he is blind, but James and John and the other disciples do not know that they too are blind. If they did, then they would not argue about who is the greatest (9:34) or jockey for positions of honor (10:37). Instead, they would ask Jesus to have mercy on them and beg him to heal them of their spiritual blindness.

Earlier Jesus rejected the request of James and John, but he grants Bartimaeus' request. Jesus tells him the same thing he told the hemorrhaging woman: "Go; your faith has made you well" (10:52; cf. 5:34). Yet, Bartimaeus does not *go*, instead he *follows*. In other words, he is not just a recipient of Jesus' mercy, he has become his disciple. More importantly, he follows Jesus "on the way," which has two levels of meaning. First, Bartimaeus is following Jesus *on the way* to Jerusalem to celebrate Passover. Having been cured of his blindness, Bartimaeus is now ritually clean and, therefore, able to enter the temple and participate fully in the Passover festivities. Second, Bartimaeus is following Jesus *on the way* to the cross. By following Jesus on the way to Jerusalem where Jesus will suffer and die, Bartimaeus is fulfilling his vocation as a disciple.

At the beginning of The Way movement, Jesus said, "If any want to become my followers, let them deny themselves and take up their cross and follow me" (8:34). Now, in the last episode of the movement, Bartimaeus serves as a model disciple, for he follows Jesus on the way of suffering and death. Once again, a minor character in Mark exhibits the qualities of discipleship that Jesus' own disciples fail to exhibit.

Suggestions for Lectors

It has become common for lectors to emphasize words like *said* or *saying* when introducing direct speech, but this often puts the emphasis in the wrong place. The emphasis should be on the speech itself. So, drop your voice and glide through such words and phrases as if they were not there. (In the examples below, a smaller font has been used to represent this visually.) Then, *emphasize* a word at or near the beginning of the quotation. Also, only pause briefly for commas preceding the quotation.

47 he began to shout out and say, "*Jesus*, Son of David,…"
49 Jesus stood still and said, "*Call* him here."
50 they called the blind man, saying to him, "Take *heart*;…"

51 Then Jesus said to him, "*What* do you want..."
The blind man said to him, "My *teacher*,..."
52 Jesus said to him, "*Go*; your faith..."

In 10:47, raise your voice as Bartimaeus tries to get Jesus' attention. Deliver his entreaty in three parts as though the text were punctuated with exclamation points, as in: *Jesus!... Son of David!... Have mercy on me!* In 10:48, raise your voice even higher as you cry out with Bartimaeus, *Son of David!... Have mercy on me!* In contrast, have Jesus summon Bartimaeus in a calmer voice.

In 10:50, read in a more energetic tone and at a slightly quicker pace to convey Bartimaeus' excitement as he casts off his cloak and springs to his feet as though he were already healed. When Jesus asks Bartimaeus what he would like him to do for him, respond in an excited, almost breathless voice, *My teacher, let me see again!* (10:51). After pausing, deliver Jesus' final line in the tone of a blessing. Read it slowly and intently with compassion in your voice and a smile on your face. Imagine that you are looking into Bartimaeus' dead eyes, knowing that they are about to come alive and transform this beggar's life. As you conclude the reading, emphasize the final phrase, *on the way*.

Pronunciation Guide

Bartimaeus (bahr-tuh-MEE-uhs, -MAY-), *Jericho* (JAIR-ih-koh; JAIR-uh-koh), *Nazareth* (NAZ-uh-reth; *not* -rus), *Timaeus* (tih-MEE-uhs; -MAY-)

PROPER 26

October 30–November 5

Ruth 1:1–18
Psalm 146
Hebrews 9:11–14
Mark 12:28–34

Deuteronomy 6:1–9
Psalm 119:1–8
Hebrews 9:11–14
Mark 12:28–34

RUTH 1:1–18

Notes

Sequence. 1 of 2

Commentary

The book of Ruth is one of just two biblical books that bear the name of a woman; the other is the book of Esther. In Jewish bibles, the books of Ruth and Esther belong to a collection of writings known as *Megillot*, or the Five Scrolls, which also includes the Song of Songs, Lamentations, and Ecclesiastes. Each book is designated for reading on a major holy day of the Jewish liturgical year. Ruth is read during the Festival of Weeks (or Pentecost), which originally celebrated the end of the barley harvest. This time for reading Ruth is appropriate since the principal plot in this story takes place during the barley harvest.

In Christian bibles, Ruth is located in its proper chronological sequence between the books of Judges and 1 Samuel. Judges tells the story of Israel in the Promised Land when it still existed as a loose confederacy of Twelve Tribes, while 1 Samuel tells the story of the rise of monarchy in Israel. In this respect, Ruth serves as a transitional narrative. On the one hand, the story takes place "in the days when the judges ruled" (Ruth 1:1). On the other hand, two of the main characters, Ruth and Boaz, turn out to be the great-grandparents of king David (4:17), Israel's second and most celebrated king. In today's reading, we are introduced to the Israelite, Naomi, and her Moabite daughter-in-law, Ruth. The story is both dramatic and touching.

1:1–5. The biblical narrative is filled with stories of people being displaced due to famine. In today's reading, a famine induces Naomi's husband to move the family from their ancestral home in Bethlehem of Judah and to settle in Moab, where they remain for many years. During their ten-year sojourn, tragedy strikes three times. First, Naomi loses her husband; then she loses both her sons. In any society, the loss of one's spouse and children would be devastating, but in a patriarchal society such as this, the situation is even more dire. Without any male relatives to support her, Naomi's life is destined for destitution.

1:6–14. Even with the good news that the Promised Land is flourishing again, Naomi has no guaranteed means of support for herself, let alone her daughters-in-law. As she makes her way back to Judah, she encourages them to return to their own people in the hope that they might find security with new husbands. Her blessing reminds one of Tevye and Golde's "Sabbath Prayer" in *Fiddler on the Roof*:

> May God bless you and grant you long lives.
> May He send you husbands who will care for you.

In response to Naomi's entreaties, Orpah tears herself away from her mother-in-law and departs with a tearful kiss. Ruth, however, can only cling to Naomi.

1:15–18. Once again, Naomi instructs her daughter-in-law to seek a better life with her own people, but Ruth refuses. Then, in a very moving declaration, she binds herself to Naomi and to Naomi's fate. In so doing, Ruth goes far beyond what would have been required or even expected of her in this situation.

Suggestions for Lectors

The first five verses introduce and provide the background for today's story. Your goal is to read the introduction as smoothly as possible, which is complicated by the fact that it contains many names that you and your listeners may not be familiar with. So, give yourself plenty of time to work on pronunciation. Repeat the names on their own, then practice reading and rereading them in context until your reading becomes smooth, natural, and confident. One of the pitfalls when reading a passage containing so many unfamiliar names is that, even when we pronounce the names correctly, we might place so much emphasis upon the names themselves that the larger meaning of the text becomes lost. Preparation will help you avoid this pitfall. It might also be helpful to read these introductory verses at a slightly slower pace, affording you a better opportunity to pronounce the names with ease and clarity while still putting the emphasis where it needs to be.

The remainder of the episode is filled with strong emotion and is quite dramatic. When faced with such a dramatic narrative, we as lectors must remind ourselves that we are more than readers, we are storytellers. Pay attention to how the story is told. Who are the characters? What are their motives, and what are they feeling at each point in the story? What is the nature of the conflict, and how does it get resolved? Meditate upon these questions, and let your answers inform and shape your retelling of this wonderfully touching and powerful story.

Ruth's speech forms the climax of today's story (1:15–17). If you consult a Bible (versus a lectionary), you will notice that Ruth's speech is formatted as poetry instead of prose. Notice that the poetic lines occur in pairs, that they parallel one another in meaning and sometimes in syntax.

1a Do not press me to leave you
1b   or to turn back from following you!

2a Where you go, I will go;
2b   where you lodge, I will lodge;
2c your people shall be my people,
2d   and your God my God.

3a Where you die, I will die—
3b   there will I be buried.

4a May the LORD do thus and so to me,
4b   and more as well,
4c if even death parts me from you!

In your preparations, attend to the variations in punctuation—to the commas, semicolons, and periods—which represent different lengths of pause. This will help you establish a suitable pace and tempo. For example, looking at lines 2a–2d, both 2a and 2b have an internal comma and a concluding semicolon while 2c and 2d have just a single comma at the end of 2c. This means that you should deliver 2a and 2b at a slower, somewhat halting pace, whereas you will want to accelerate through 2c and 2d. Note, however, that accelerating does not mean reading fast, it simply means slowly increasing the pace and tempo as one reads.

Pronunciation Guide

Bethlehem (BETH-luh-hem'), *Chilion* (KIL-ee-uhn; -on), *Elimelech* (ee-LIM-uh-lek; ih-), *Ephrathites* (EF-ruh-thīts; EF-rath-īts), *Judah* (JOO-duh), *Mahlon* (MAH-lohn; -luhn), *Moab* (MOH-ab), *Moabite* (MOH-uh-bīt), *Naomi* (NAY-oh-mee; nay-OH-mee), *Orpha* (OR-puh; *not* OH-pruh), *Ruth* (ROOTH)

DEUTERONOMY 6:1–9

Commentary

Deuteronomy is the fifth book of the Bible and the last of the Five Books of Moses (a.k.a., the Pentateuch or the Torah). Deuteronomy is presented as a speech that Moses delivers to the Israelites just prior to his death and just prior to Israel's entrance into the Promised Land of Canaan under the leadership of Joshua (Josh 3:1–17). In this speech (Deut 1:6–30:20), Moses reviews Israel's forty-year sojourn in the wilderness and instructs the people in the laws of the covenant that are to govern their personal and corporate lives once they are settled in Canaan. One might regard Deuteronomy, then, as a prolonged exposition on the Ten Commandments, a detailing of the many varied and specific ways one goes about loving the LORD with all of one's life and possessions and loving one's neighbor as oneself.

In today's gospel, a scribe asks Jesus, "Which commandment is the first of all?" (Mark 12:28). Jesus responds by quoting the Shema (shuh-MAH), which is found in today's reading from Deuteronomy.

6:1–3. In Deuteronomy 5, Moses retells the story of the giving of the Law at Mt. Sinai, and he recites the Ten Commandments from Exodus 20 (Lent 3). Moses then emphasizes the importance of following these commandments and all the others that the LORD has conveyed through Moses. He anticipates the temptations the Israelites will face once they enter Canaan and encounter the vast array of pagan gods, idols, and places of worship. He knows that the key to the Israelites living long, productive, and blessed lives in the Promised Land depends upon their remaining faithful to the LORD and to the covenant.

6:4–5, The Shema. While the books of Exodus, Numbers, Leviticus, and Deuteronomy contain a near-comprehensive list of commandments, statutes, ordinances, and decrees that seem to address every dimension of life, yet there is one commandment that stands above them all, the Shema. *Shema* is the Hebrew word for *listen*, and it is this word that introduces the first and greatest commandment. The Shema has two parts, and the first can be translated in a variety of ways:

> "Hear, O Israel: The LORD is our God, the LORD alone."
> "Hear, O Israel: The LORD our God, the LORD is one."
> "Hear, O Israel: The LORD is our God, the LORD is one."

In English editions of the Bible, *the LORD* (when written in SMALL CAPS) is a translation of the name, Yahweh, which is the name that God revealed to Moses from the burning bush (Exod 3:15). Thus, the Shema begins with the declaration that Yahweh and Yahweh alone is Israel's God. This echoes the first of the Ten Commandments. "I am the LORD (Yahweh) your God, who brought you out of the land of Egypt, out of the house of slavery; you shall have no other gods before me" (Exod 20:2–3; Deut 5:6–7).

If the LORD is the only God, then it logically follows that the people of God owe the LORD their complete allegiance. This is why the Shema concludes with, "You shall love Yahweh your God with *all* your heart, and with *all* your soul, and with *all* your might" (6:5). In other words, there is no room for divided loyalties. We cannot pledge our allegiance to anyone or anything else. Everything we are, have, and ever hope to be is to be given over entirely to the LORD. As the LORD says, "I the Lord your God am a jealous God" (Exod 20:5; Deut 5:9).

6:6–9. Everything else that the LORD commands follows from this one great commandment. So Moses reiterates his insistence that the people of God put into practice everything that the LORD has commanded. They are to keep these words in their hearts because that is where our will resides. In the biblical worldview, the heart is not the place of emotions but the very center of the human person and personality. The heart guides and directs everything we think, feel, and do. Consequently, a heart that is informed and shaped by the Great Commandment—the love of God—is a heart that fulfills the entire Law.

Moses does not simply tell us to keep this commandment in our hearts, he gives us specific, practical advice on how to do so. Recite these words to your children in all places and in all times. Write these words down, and put them up where you can see them throughout the day. In fact, find a way to attach them to your person. In short, find ways to eat, drink, and breath the love of God.

Suggestions for Lectors

In today's reading, adopt the voice and persona of Moses as you deliver what Jesus will call the first and greatest commandment. The first three verses comprise two very long sentences. Practice these sentences until you can read them smoothly with the proper intonation, never running out of breath and never straining your voice.

In 6:6–9, emphasize all the imperatives: *keep* (6:6); *recite* and *talk* (6:7); *bind* (6:8); and *write* (6:9). In 6:7, notice how the four *when* clauses are punctuated—how the first two and the last two are to be read together, with only a pause after *away*:

> when you are at home and when you are away,…
> when you lie down and when you rise.

With respect to intonation, drop your voice slightly for *home* and *down*, and raise it up for *away* and *rise*.

Of course, the most important part of today's reading is the Shema itself (6:4–5). In order to set it apart, pause for a second or two both before 6:4 and after 6:5. Deliver *Hear, O Israel!* in a firm, strong voice. As you do so, look up and scan your audience. Pause again after *Israel* before continuing.

You might be tempted to introduce a longer-than-normal pause between 6:4 and 6:5 so that each verse gets its due. Yet, as reflected in the Commentary, these verses are logically connected and need to be drawn together in your reading. Without rushing from 6:4 to 6:5, take only the slightest of pauses at the end of 6:4. Alternatively, you might insert a logical connector like *and* or *so* or even *therefore* at the beginning of 6:5, as in: *The LORD is our God, the LORD alone. [And/So/Therefore], you shall love the LORD your God with <u>all</u> your heart, and with <u>all</u> your soul, and with <u>all</u> your might* (6:4–5).[32] In addition, emphasize each of the *alls*.

Pronunciation Guide

Deuteronomy (doo'-tuh-RON-uh-mee)

---

[32] The King James Version uses *And* while the New American Bible uses *Therefore* at the beginning of 6:5

Hebrews 9:11–14

Notes
Sequence. 5 of 7

Commentary
Throughout the Letter to the Hebrews, the author seeks to establish the superiority of Jesus Christ. As the Son of God, Jesus is superior to the angels (Heb 1:5–2:18), to Moses (3:1–19), and to Joshua (4:1–13). As our great high priest, Jesus is superior to all the priests and high priests who served under the Old Covenant (4:14–7:28). Because Jesus led a life of "reverent submission" (5:7), he obtained "a more excellent ministry" than theirs, and he is "the mediator of a better covenant" (8:6)—a new, eternal covenant that has dealt with sin once and for all (8:1–10:18). In today's reading, the author contrasts Jesus' self-sacrifice that inaugurated the New Covenant with the animal sacrifices offered by priests under the Old Covenant.

Leading up to today's reading, the author briefly describes the earthly sanctuary, the portable tabernacle that God instructed Moses to build and which eventually served as the model for the construction of the temple in Jerusalem (9:1–10). The earthly sanctuary had two principal spaces, what the author calls tents. The first tent was the Holy Place where *priests* carried out their *daily* duties, and the second tent was the Holy of Holies where only the *high priest* served and then only *once a year* on the Day of Atonement (a.k.a., Yom Kippur). A curtain hung at the entrance to the Holy Place and a second curtain separated it from the Holy of Holies. According to Hebrews, this earthly sanctuary is merely a copy, just "a sketch and shadow" of the real sanctuary in heaven (8:5). Consequently, the sacrifices offered by the priests and high priests in the earthly sanctuary cannot compare to the self-sacrifice offered by the great high priest in the heavenly sanctuary.

9:11–12. In 4:14, the author speaks of Jesus passing through the heavens. In today's reading, this same action is described in terms of Jesus having come through "the greater and perfect tent" (9:11). With these images, the author paints a picture of Jesus carrying out his high priestly duties. By his death, resurrection, and ascension, Jesus makes his way through the various spaces of the heavenly sanctuary. The reader is to imagine him passing through the first curtain, then through the Holy Place, and then finally beyond the second curtain into the Holy of Holies, where God sits enthroned and is attended by angels. Just like the high priest on Yom Kippur, Jesus makes atonement for sin by bringing blood into the Holy of Holies.[33]

9:13–14. Yet, unlike other high priests, Jesus brings his own blood, whose cleansing properties are far superior to the blood of goats and bulls and to the ashes of the red heifer (Num 19). These sacrifices that were offered under the Old Covenant did not address the problem of human sin and defilement at its deepest level. They only offered a superficial cleansing; they purified a person's outer nature (their flesh) but

---

[33] Here, rendered "the Holy Place" in the NRSV. Hebrews uses *the Holy Place* to designate two different spaces in the sanctuary, which can be confusing for the reader. In 9:2, *the Holy Place* refers to the first tent where ordinary priests served. But here in 9:12 and later in 9:25, *the Holy Place* actually refers to the Holy of Holies where only the high priest operated.

not their inner nature (their conscience). Under the Old Covenant, persons had to offer sacrifices that only brought partial and temporary relief from the shame and guilt of sin (cf. 10:1). Instead of being able to worship God in freedom, their lives were given over to performing these dead works over and over again. Thankfully, Jesus' sacrifice of his blameless self has the power to cleanse the consciences of those who seek to worship God (9:9, 14; 10:22; 13:8). Instead of wasting our time and energy in futile attempts to manage our own sin by engaging in rituals that do not impart life, we are free to draw near and worship the living God because Jesus has dealt with sin once and for all.

Suggestions for Lectors

In your preparations, it would be helpful to read Hebrews 9:1–10. This will provide some background and give you a better feel for your passage, assisting you in your practice and delivery. Throughout the reading, use inflection and intonation to bring out the contrasts the author is presenting.

In 9:11, drop your voice for the parenthetical expression. Do the same for the lengthy relative clause in 9:14, *who… to God,* which interrupts the sentence. In contrast, read the first and last portions of 9:14 at a higher volume and pitch so that your listeners will connect these parts and thereby hear the complete thought, which is: *how much more will the <u>blood</u> of Christ,… purify our conscience from dead works to worship the living God!*

Mark 12:28–34

Notes

Sequence. 10 of 12

Commentary

In Mark 11:1–11 (Palm), Jesus enters Jerusalem at the beginning of what will turn out to be the last week of his life. He rides in on a colt amid shouts of "Hosanna! Blessed is the one who comes in the name of the Lord!" (11:9b; Ps 118:25–26). The next day he returns to Jerusalem to perform another symbolic action. He enters the temple precincts and disrupts all commerce by driving out the sellers and buyers and by overturning the tables of the money changers (11:15–19). On the third day, Jesus returns to the temple yet again, where he engages in a series of public debates with detractors who demand that Jesus offer justification for engaging in these disruptive, disrespectful prophetic demonstrations (11:27–28).

First, the chief priests, scribes, and elders question his authority. In typical fashion, Jesus responds with criticisms of his own, veiled in parables (11:27–12:12). Next, the Pharisees try to entrap him with a question about taxes (12:13–17), and the Sadducees try to confound him with a question about resurrection (12:18–27). Then, in today's reading, one of the scribes approaches Jesus with a question about the law. Of all of the debates, this one is the most positive.

12:28. In Mark, the scribes are almost always characterized as hostile toward Jesus. They are offended by his presumption to pronounce absolution (2:6, Epi 7); they question his practice of dining with tax-collectors and other sinners (2:16, Epi 8);

and they even accuse him of being possessed by Beelzebul (3:22, Prop 5). Moreover, the scribes are one of the groups who conspire to bring about Jesus' death (8:31; 10:33; 11:18; 14:43, 53; 15:1, 31). But in this scene, the scribe who approaches Jesus does not appear to be an enemy. Although Matthew presents the scribe's question as a test (22:35), there is no hint of ulterior motives in Mark's account. After all, Jesus normally responds to challenges from opponents with a parable, but in this case, Jesus provides an open, unambiguous response.

Scribes were experts in the Jewish law—the written law of Moses as well as the body of oral tradition that sought to offer an authoritative interpretation of Mosaic legislation. Faced with the whole volume of laws, statutes, and regulations in the law of Moses and in the tradition of the elders, teachers of the law sought to define and articulate the heart or essence of Jewish law. Thus, the question that the scribe asks is one that was widely discussed in the first century. In posing this question to Jesus, the scribe is treating him and honoring him as a colleague.

12:29–31. Jesus' summary of the law is thoroughly traditional. He begins with what, in Jewish tradition, is called the *Shema*, which is Hebrew for *Hear!*. The Shema is taken from Deuteronomy 6:4–5 (see today's OT reading), and it was recited daily by observant Jews. The first commandment, Jesus says, is "Hear, O Israel: the Lord our God, the Lord is one; you shall love the Lord your God with all your heart, and with all your soul, and with all your mind, and with all your strength" (12:30). Then, without taking a breath, Jesus quickly adds a second commandment, which comes from Leviticus 19:18: "You shall love your neighbor as yourself" (12:31).

According to Jesus, these are the two greatest commandments; everything else in the law must derive from and support the love of God and the love of neighbor. The scribe had asked for the first commandment, and Jesus gives him the second as well. For, while the love of God takes precedence over everything else, no one can love God with all they are and have without loving their neighbors as themselves. To love others in this way is what it means to love God. In next week's reading, Jesus condemns the scribes for failing to love God through failing to act with justice and compassion toward their neighbors, namely, widows.

12:32–34. The scribe agrees with Jesus as his paraphrase of Jesus' response indicates. In turn, Jesus remarks that the scribe is not far from the kingdom. So saying, Jesus' critics are silenced, and he is never again openly challenged in public. Instead, his opponents will go underground to plot his arrest and execution (14:1–2).

Suggestions for Lectors

As was mentioned in the Commentary, today's scribe poses an honest question. There is no hint of trickery, so ask his question as though he is genuinely interested in what Jesus has to say regarding the heart of the Jewish law.

Clearly, the author of Mark wants to highlight the double-love commandment, which is why the speeches of Jesus and the scribe contain the same basic content. If Mark simply wanted to show that the scribe agreed with Jesus' interpretation of the law, he could have done so in a single sentence: *You are right, Teacher* (12:32). By repeating the double-love commandment, Mark hopes to have a greater rhetorical impact upon his readers. At the same time, he does not want to bore his readers with monotonous repetition, so the scribe's response includes some variations. That is, he does not quote Jesus verbatim. Repetition with variation is a powerful rhetorical technique, and one that Mark uses to great effect. As lectors, we would do well to recreate this repetition with variation by delivering the speeches of Jesus and the scribe in a different manner.

When Jesus responds to the scribe's inquiry, he does so by addressing the crowd that has been listening to him. He treats this as a teachable moment so proclaim Jesus' words to your listeners with a raised voice.

In contrast, the scribe directs his comments to Jesus, so a raised voice is not necessary. Moreover, the scribe is inspired and encouraged by Jesus' views. He has found in Jesus a kindred spirit. So read his reaction with energy and enthusiasm. This energy can be conveyed by increasing the pitch of your voice and by reading at a slightly faster pace.

PROPER 27

November 6–12

Ruth 3:1–5; 4:13–17
Psalm 127
Hebrews 9:24–28
Mark 12:38–44

1 Kings 17:8–16
Psalm 146
Hebrews 9:24–28
Mark 12:38–44

RUTH 3:1–5; 4:13–17

Notes
Sequence. 2 of 2

Commentary
Last week, we were introduced to two remarkable women: the Israelite, Naomi, and her Moabite daughter-in-law, Ruth. When a severe famine overtakes the Promised Land, Naomi's family relocates. They leave Bethlehem in Judah, and resettle in the foreign land of Moab. During the next decade, tragedy strikes. First, Naomi's husband dies, then her two sons die, leaving her destitute. Naomi has no means of supporting herself, let alone her two Moabite daughters-in-law. When she receives word that the famine is over, she makes plans to return to Bethlehem. She insists that her daughters-in-law seek a better future for themselves among their own people. Orpah leaves, but Ruth clings to Naomi, begging to be allowed to remain with her:

> Do not press me to leave you or to turn back from following you!
> Where you go, I will go; where you lodge, I will lodge;
> your people shall be my people, and your God my God.
> Where you die, I will die—there will I be buried.
> May the LORD do thus and so to me, and more as well,
> if even death parts me from you! (Ruth 1:16–17)

And so, come what may, Ruth commits the rest of her life to Naomi, going far beyond what would have been required or even expected of her in this situation.

When they arrive in Bethlehem, Ruth takes it upon herself to work long hours in the barley fields during harvest. She gleans from the leftover sheaves, which the poor were permitted to do. The field she happens to choose belongs to a prominent rich man, named Boaz, who, as it turns out, is a relative of Naomi's husband. Boaz looks with favor upon Ruth, not least because he has heard of her remarkable loyalty to her mother-in-law (2:11). Boaz lets Naomi eat her fill along with his hired hands, and he lets her glean from sheaves that have not yet been harvested. In this way, Boaz is revealed to possess a character similar to that of Ruth—strong, loyal, and selfless—for he too goes beyond what is required or expected in order to help another.

Back in chapter one, when Naomi had first insisted that her daughters-in-law return to their own people, it was in the hopes that they might find new husbands who would be able to provide them with a secure future (1:9). She said, "Turn back, my daughters, why will you go with me? Do I still have sons in my womb that they may become your husbands?" (1:11). Such was the reality in a patriarchal society.

3:1–5. In today's reading, Naomi is still seeking to secure Ruth's future by finding a husband for her. Naomi plays matchmaker, and her plan is a bold and daring one. Ruth is to make herself up and then to visit Boaz at the threshing floor, yet only after he has eaten and drunk and lain down for the night. She needs to take note of exactly where Boaz lies down because it will be dark when Ruth approaches him, and a mistake would spell disaster. Naomi's instructions are very suggestive, and the reader wonders what exactly Naomi is asking her daughter-in-law to do. Remarkably, Ruth agrees, without question, to follow her mother-in-law's instructions to the letter.

3:6–13. Naomi's plan bears fruit. Ruth does as instructed, and at midnight, Boaz is startled to find himself partially uncovered and a woman lying at his feet. If these women had supposed that Boaz would knowingly or unknowingly take advantage of Ruth in such a compromising situation, then things did not turn out as expected. Instead of telling Ruth what to do, Boaz asks what he might do for her: "And now, my daughter, do not be afraid, I will do for you all that you ask" (3:11).

4:13–17. There is a bit more drama that plays out between 3:13 and 4:13, but in the end, Boaz takes Ruth as his wife, and she bears a son. Thus, with a husband and a male child, the future of Ruth and that of her mother-in-law is secure.

The story concludes with a surprising revelation as the identity of Ruth's son is revealed. His name is Obed, and he is the great-grandfather of David, the son of Jesse. Thus, King David—who is Israel's most celebrated king and the progenitor of Israel's most celebrated dynasty—has Moabite ancestry.

Suggestions for Lectors

Understanding the text is the first and most important task for the lector. One of the best ways to understand any text is to read it within its larger context. This is especially important when preparing for today's reading, where one and a half chapters of intervening material have been left out of the reading. The lector would do well to read whole book of Ruth; after all, it is just four chapters long. At a minimum, chapters 3 and 4 ought to be read. This will help fill in the large gap between 3:1–5 and 4:13–17, especially for the lector who is not already familiar with the story of Ruth and Boaz. By reading Ruth, you will gain not only an understanding of the story but a real feel for it, which you can draw upon as you retell it in your reading.

In 3:1–4, Naomi offers Ruth a detailed set of instructions, so use an instructional tone for this part of the story. Use a different tone of voice for Ruth's response; she is obedient, yet not submissive.

In 4:13–17, read what the women say to Naomi with joy and excitement in your voice and a smile on your face. Yet, when reading 4:16, which concerns Naomi becoming the child's wet nurse, tone down the excitement, not because Naomi feels any less joy but because it is a deeper, quieter, more peaceful joy, one that matches the quiet peacefulness of a child nursing at the breast.

Pronunciation Guide

Boaz (BOH-az), *David* (DAY-vid), *Israel* (IZ-ree-uhl; -ray-), *Jesse* (JES-ee), *Naomi* (NAY-oh-mee; nay-OH-mee), *Obed* (OH-bid), *Ruth* (ROOTH)

1 Kings 17:8–16

Commentary

Elijah the Tishbite was a prophet who was active in the northern kingdom of Israel in the mid-ninth century B.C. during the reign of Ahab. His stories are found in 1 Kings 17–19, 21 and 2 Kings 1–2. Elijah and his successor, Elisha, are sometimes referred to as *signs* prophets since they are remembered primarily for the signs and wonders they perform, in contrast to the *writing* prophets—figures like Isaiah, Jeremiah, Micah, Amos, etc.—who are primarily remembered for their words. Elijah's name means *the LORD is my God*, that is, *Yahweh is my God.*

Immediately preceding today's reading, Elijah is sent to King Ahab to notify him about a coming drought: "As the LORD the God of Israel lives, before whom I stand, there shall be neither dew nor rain these years, except by my word" (17:1). This drought was the LORD's response to Ahab's idolatry, to his colluding with his wife Jezebel in promoting the worship of the Canaanite deities, Baal and Asherah, alongside the worship of Yahweh. This drought, which lasts many years, results in a severe famine that extends well beyond Israel's borders. In today's reading, Elijah is sent to the Gentile region of Sidon to minister to the needs of a poor, widowed, non-Israelite woman.

17:8–16. Elijah is sent far north to a widow in Zarephath so that his needs might be taken care of during the time of the drought and famine. When he encounters the widow at the entrance to the town, he asks for a bit of water. Providing hospitality to strangers was an important virtue in the Ancient Near East. So, even though she has been gathering kindling for what she believes to be her and her son's last meal, she immediately sets out to fetch him some water. As she is going, Elijah also asks for a bit of bread, at which point she reveals how desperate her situation in life is. What is particularly noteworthy is that she prefaces her response with, "As Yahweh your God lives," thus indicating that this non-Israelite woman knows about and seems to honor Elijah's God (17:12). Elijah reciprocates by responding with a word from "Yahweh the God of Israel" (17:14). If she will go and make him a small cake with what meal and oil she has left, then the LORD will make sure that neither she nor her son will go hungry, for "The jar of meal will not be emptied and the jug of oil will not fail until the day that the LORD sends rain on the earth" (17:14). Demonstrating her faith, she follows Elijah's instructions, and the LORD keeps his word.

Suggestions for Lectors

In today's reading, the land was in its third year of drought, which accounts for the poverty of the widow as well as her belief that this would be her last meal. But notice, and bring it out in the tone of your voice, that her hospitality to a stranger is willing and immediate. The widow's despair is expressed in 17:12 and is followed by the immediate contrast of Elijah's strong and reassuring words in 17:13. In 17:14, Elijah speaks the word of the LORD, so proclaim these words in an elevated tone. Then return to your normal storytelling voice for the concluding verses, in which your listeners learn that the events promised by Elijah came to pass.

Pronunciation Guide

Elijah (ee-LĪ-juh; ih-)
Sidon (SĪ-duhn)
Zarephath (ZAIR-uh-fath)

HEBREWS 9:24–28

Notes

Sequence. 6 of 7

Commentary

Throughout the Letter to the Hebrews, the author seeks to demonstrate the superiority of Jesus and the covenant that he established through his life of reverence, obedience, suffering, and death. In Hebrews 9, the differences between the Old and New Covenants are explored by contrasting the type and quality of worship that each system affords. Each covenant has its own regulations, its own sanctuary, and its own personnel for performing priestly duties. Under the Old Covenant, there was a successions of priests and high priests who offered an endless stream of animal sacrifices within an earthly sanctuary. Under the New Covenant, there is just one high priest, who sacrificed himself and brought his own blood into the heavenly sanctuary. This is the topic of today's reading.

9:24–26. When Hebrews speaks of Jesus entering the heavenly sanctuary, cultic language is being used metaphorically to illuminate the significance of Jesus' death. While animal sacrifices might be appropriate for an earthly sanctuary that is merely a copy—"a sketch and shadow" (8:5)—of the true sanctuary in heaven, the heavenly sanctuary itself requires "better sacrifices than these" (9:23).

Once a year on the Day of Atonement (a.k.a., Yom Kippur), the high priest would enter the earthly Holy of Holies with the blood of bulls and goats that was simply unable to take away sins (cf. 10:1–4). Jesus, however, entered the heavenly Holy of

Holies[34] with his own blood, which was so powerful and efficacious that sin was removed once and forevermore. Thus, by his single act of self-sacrifice, Jesus accomplished what centuries of animal sacrifice under the Old Covenant had never accomplished nor ever could. The lives of unblemished animals just do not compare to the unblemished life of the obedient Son of God.

9:27–28. Jesus Christ has changed the way the world works. Prior to his death, people died and then faced judgment. But now that he has completely removed sin, salvation instead of judgment awaits those who have given their lives to him.

On the Day of Atonement, the people of God waited expectantly for the high priest to emerge from the Holy of Holies, signifying that the sacrifice for the nation's sins had been accepted by God. How much more eagerly do we await the emergence of our great high priest from the heavenly Holy of Holies, for that will be the day when we shall receive our inheritance, eternal salvation (1:14).

Suggestions for Lectors

Today's reading is filled with contrasts, so emphasize those words and expressions that will highlight those contrasts for your listeners. For example, the first contrast concerns the sanctuary Christ entered as our great high priest. He did not enter *a mere copy* but *heaven* itself (9:24).

Unlike other high priests, Christ did not enter the Holy of Holies *again and again* and *year after year* (9:25) because that would mean that he would have to have suffered *again and again* (9:26a). Instead, he appeared *once for all* at the end of the age to remove sin through the sacrifice of himself (9:26b).

Finally, Christ appeared *once* to deal with sin, but he will appear a *second time* to rescue those who are waiting for him.

Mark 12:38–44

Notes

Sequence. 11 of 12

Commentary

In Mark 11:1–11 (Palm), Jesus enters Jerusalem at the beginning of what will turn out to be the last week of his life. He rides in on a colt amid shouts of "Hosanna! Blessed is the one who comes in the name of the Lord!" (11:9b; Ps 118:25–26). The next day he returns to Jerusalem to perform another symbolic action. He enters the temple precincts and disrupts all commerce by driving out the sellers and buyers and by overturning the tables of the money changers (11:15–19). On the third day, Jesus returns to the temple yet again, where he engages in a series of public debates with detractors who question his authority for engaging in these disruptive prophetic demonstrations (11:27–28). First, he debates the chief priests, scribes, and elders (11:27–12:12); then the Pharisees (12:13–17); then the Sadducees (12:18–27); and

---

[34] Here, rendered "the Holy Place" in the NRSV. Hebrews uses *the Holy Place* to designate two different spaces in the sanctuary, which can be confusing for the reader. In 9:2, *the Holy Place* refers to the first tent where ordinary priests served. But here in 9:25 and earlier in 9:12, *the Holy Place* actually refers to the Holy of Holies where only the high priest operated.

then a solitary scribe, which we encountered in last week's reading (12:28–34, Prop 26). Finally, Jesus goes on the offensive, and he begins to challenge his opponents, in particular, the scribes (12:35–40). Why he singles out the scribes is unclear, but perhaps it is because they have been challenging him from the beginning (2:6, 16; 3:22; 7:1).

12:38–40. Jesus denounces the scribes for being motivated and obsessed with honor and status. They put on a pious show with their long prayers, but they fail show mercy and act with justice. In the OT, taking care of orphans and widows is the true hallmark of piety. In Psalm 68, God is described as a "Father of orphans and protector of widows" who "gives the desolate a home to live in" (68:5–6), but the scribes devour widows' houses. In short, they do not manifest the values of the kingdom of God in their lives.

12:41–44. Speaking of widows, Jesus witnesses a widow who puts to shame the scribes and all those who have been blessed with wealth. Though this poor widow has nothing, she commits what she does have to God. By placing everything she has into the temple treasury, she reveals that she loves the Lord God with everything she is and has and that she trusts in God's abundant provision for her.

Suggestions for Lectors

In the first half of today's reading (12:38–40), Jesus is speaking to the crowds in the temple, so raise your voice as you denounce the scribes. Become increasingly animated as you make your way through this brief diatribe. Then, when you come to the final sentence, pause for a second and drop your voice as you read, *They will receive the greater condemnation* (12:40b).

Deliver the second half of the reading in your normal narrating voice (12:38–40). When Jesus speaks, he is only addressing his small group of disciples, so there is no need to raise your voice. Instead, invest it with more feeling and expression especially for the final verse. Stress the contrasting words, *abundance* and *poverty*, as well as the words that reveal the extent of the widow's sacrifice, *everything* and *all* (12:44).

PROPER 28

November 13–19

1 Samuel 1:4–20	Daniel 12:1–3
1 Samuel 2:1–10	Psalm 16
Hebrews 10:11–14, (15–18), 19–25	Hebrews 10:11–14, (15–18), 19–25
Mark 13:1–8	Mark 13:1–8

1 Samuel 1:4–20

Notes

Suggested Reading. 1 Samuel 1:1–20

Commentary

The book of Joshua tells the story of Israel's conquest of Canaan, of how the Israelites, after having spent forty years wandering in the wilderness, entered the Promised Land and drove out its inhabitants. The book of Judges continues this story by offering vignettes of what life was like for the people of God in the Promised Land. The land was indeed "a good and broad land, a land flowing with milk and honey" (Exod 3:8), just as the LORD had promised; but it was also a land of temptation. It is one thing to be singularly devoted to the LORD when you are being miraculously fed through the daily provision of manna, yet quite another thing entirely to remain faithful when the land produces abundantly. As the LORD will say later through Hosea, Israel "did not know that it was I who gave her the grain, the wine, and the oil, and who lavished upon her silver and gold that they used for (the fertility god) Baal" (Hos 2:8).

Despite the LORD's unfailing faithfulness, Israel struggles to live as the faithful people of God. One might characterize this struggle as a conflict between God's vision of what Israel should be and Israel's vision of what God should be. Though they repeatedly demonstrate themselves to be a stubborn and stiff-necked people, God never abandons them. Over the first few centuries in the land, the LORD raises up certain individuals to lead Israel against her enemies and to call the people back to the LORD when they stray. These leaders are called judges; some are priests, some are prophets, but none are kings, for the LORD is Israel's king. The last of these judges is the priest and prophet Samuel, the story of whose birth is recounted in today's reading.

The Bible is filled with stories of how God blesses barren women with children. The first of these is Sarah who gives birth to her first child, Isaac, in her ninetieth year. The last of these is the aging Elizabeth who bears John the Baptizer (Luke 1:5–25, 57–67). Yet, the situation in today's reading is more akin to that of Jacob's wives, Rachel and Leah, who at various times cry out to God (Gen 29:31–30:24).

1:1–3. The first three verses of 1 Samuel are replete with the names of people and places that are unfamiliar and so make the lector's task more challenging. Presumably, this is why the editors of the RCL chose to begin the reading at verse 4. Yet, 1:1–3 introduces the characters and sets the stage for the drama that plays out in today's story. So, we suggest beginning today's reading at 1:1, or at least with something like the following:

> There was a certain man from the hill country of Ephraim, whose name was Elkanah. He had two wives; the name of the one was Hannah, and the name of the other Peninnah. Peninnah had children, but Hannah had no children.
>
> Now this man used to go up year by year from his town to worship and to sacrifice to the LORD of hosts at Shiloh.

1:4–8. During this period, the tabernacle which housed the ark of the covenant was located in Shiloh, about twenty miles north of Jerusalem. Since the LORD God was one LORD, sacrifices were to be offered at one central sanctuary. So Elkanah made his annual pilgrimage to Shiloh to worship and offer sacrifices. Some of the prescribed sacrifices involved the worshipper partaking of the sacrificial meat, which symbolized fellowship and communion with the LORD. Some have suggested that the festival being celebrated here was the Feast of Tabernacles, which among other things celebrated the end of the harvest season. If so, then this annual celebration of the land's fertility was an annual reminder of Hannah's own infertility.

1:9–11. In her frustration and grief, Hannah does not participate in the festivities and eventually makes her way to the sanctuary, where she pours out her heart to the LORD. She asks the LORD to *look upon* her misery, which is the same language Leah used when she gave birth to her first child, Reuben: "the Lord has *looked upon* my affliction" (Gen 29:32). Hannah is so desperate for a child that, should the LORD grant her the honor of conceiving and bearing a male child, she promises to devote him entirely to the LORD; this is the sacrifice she will bring (cf. 1:28).

1:12–18. With all of the celebrating going on in Shiloh, Eli mistakenly thinks Hannah is intoxicated. When he chastises her for her seemingly shameful behavior, Hannah turns from pouring her heart out to God and begins to pour it to this man of God. Acknowledging his mistake, Eli blesses her.

1:19–20. Immediately, Hannah's grief departs. With this blessing, she returns to celebrate with the others. In due time, she conceives and gives birth to Samuel, whose name means something like *asked of God*, *heard of God*, or *name of God*.

Suggestions for Lectors

As reflected in the Commentary, today's reading occurs in four or five movements, depending upon whether one starts with 1:1 or 1:4. Pause for a full second between each of these movements.

Whether beginning at 1:1 or 1:4, the reading contains a number of people and place names that may be unfamiliar, so give yourself plenty of time to work on pronunciation. As you prepare, repeat the names individually and then read and reread them in context until your reading becomes smooth, natural, and confident.

In the first two movements (1:1–3, 1:4–8), there is nothing that requires special attention. Simply read with your normal narrating voice and follow the dictates of this wonderfully written narrative. Continue in this manner in the third movement (1:9–11). When you reach Hannah's prayer, drop your voice as though you were talking to yourself. Of course, make sure your listeners can still hear and understand what you are saying. As you deliver Hannah's prayer, do not just read it; make it your own and pray it.

In the fourth movement (1:12–18), return to your normal narrating voice as you relate the interaction between Eli and Hannah. Invest your voice with hints of the characters' feelings. For example, Eli's first statement to Hannah should convey his disgust, while Hanna's response should have a hint of pleading in it.

In the fifth and final movement (1:19–20), the tempo should be slightly upbeat in an effort to convey Hannah's hope for a new future. As you draw the reading to a close, read the last sentence slowly and with slightly longer pauses at the commas: *She named him <u>Samuel</u>,… for she said,… "I have asked him of the LORD"* (1:20b). Also, emphasize the name *Samuel.*

Pronunciation Guide
Eli (EE-lī), *Elihu* (ee-LĪ-hoo; ih-LĪ-hoo), *Elkanah* (el-KAY-nuh), *Ephraimite* (EE-fra-ihm-īt), *Hannah* (HAN-uh), *Hophni* (HOF-nī; HOF-nee), *Israel* (IZ-ree-uhl; -ray-), *Jeroham* (juh-ROH-huhm), *nazarite* (NAZ-uh-rīt), *Peninnah* (pih-NIN-uh; -ah), *Phinehas* (FIN-ee-uhs; -huhs), *Ramah* (RAY-muh), *Ramathaim* (ray-muh-THAY-uhm), *Samuel* (SAM-yoo-uhl; SAM-yuhl), *Shiloh* (SHĪ-loh), *Tohu* (TOH-hoo), *Zuph* (ZOOF), *Zuphite* (ZOOF-īt)

DANIEL 12:1–3

Notes
Sequence. 1 of 2

Commentary
The book of Daniel is set in Babylon during the period of the Babylonian exile. In 598 B.C., the Babylonian empire under the leadership of King Nebuchadnezzar moves against Jerusalem and quashes a rebellion led by King Jehoiakim of Judah (2 Kgs 24:1–7). A few months later, in 597 B.C., the Babylonians return to ransack the palace and temple, taking everything of value back to Babylon. In addition, a select group of Jerusalem's leading officials and citizens are taken to Babylon (2 Kgs 24:8–17). Among this group of Judean exiles is a young nobleman by the name of Daniel.

The book of Daniel can be divided into two parts (1–6; 7–12). Much like the stories of Joseph in Egypt (Gen), the first part of the book tells how Daniel and his friends rose to prominence within the Babylonian administration. Here we find the well-known stories of Shadrach, Meshach, and Abednego in the fiery furnace (Dan 3) and Daniel in the lions' den (Dan 6). The second part of the book contains reports of three visions that Daniel receives, which are concerned with world politics and the coming of God's empire. Today's reading comes from the last of these visions (10:1–12:13).

By the time of Daniel's final revelation, the Persian empire has overthrown the Babylonian empire (539 B.C.). In this vision, an angelic messenger appears to Daniel saying, "I have come to help you understand what is to happen to your people at the end of days" (10:14). The angel then proceeds to tell a tale of the rise and fall of kings and empires. Caught in the middle of this international intrigue are the Jewish people, who are persecuted and killed (11:29–35).

12:1–3. Michael, the great prince, is one of the archangels, and it is he who has been charged with protecting the Jewish nation (10:13, 21). When history starts to wind down and reach its climax, Michael will arise to defend God's people against the angelic princes who fight for God's enemies. This will be a time of great suffering, but in the end, all of God's people will be delivered. Some will live through the tribulation, and they will witness the arrival of God's empire. Yet, even those who have died will not miss out. For all who have been found in the book of life, though they rest in the dust of the earth, will be raised by God that they might enjoy the new, eternal world of God's making.

Suggestions for Lectors

In today's reading, an angelic messenger is speaking to Daniel. As the lector, you are the angelic messenger, and your listeners are Daniel, so deliver these words to your listeners as though they were intended for them—which, of course, they are.

The messenger began addressing Daniel back in 10:11, and the address reaches its climax in 12:1–3, so read the whole of today's reading with intensity. The messenger's news is good and glorious, so it would be appropriate to deliver it with a smile on your face and a hint of joy in your voice.

As you read the final verse, decrease your tempo even as you increase your intensity. In addition to the punctuation provided in the text, pause slightly after *shine* and after *stars*. Conclude your reading by saying *forever and ever* slowly and deliberately with a sense of wonder.

Pronunciation Guide

Daniel (DAN-yuhl), *Michael* (MĪ-kuhl)

HEBREWS 10:11–14, (15–18), 19–25

Notes

Sequence. 7 of 7

Commentary

In the Letter to the Hebrews, Jesus is portrayed as a high priest (4:14). Within Jewish tradition, the high priest was responsible for what took place in the temple. In particular, the high priest was the only person allowed to enter the Holy of Holies where the ark of the covenant resided, and then only once a year on the Day of Atonement in order to offer sacrifices that would atone for the sins of the nation (Lev 16; Heb 9:3–7). According to Hebrews, Jesus served as our great high priest by removing our sin by sacrificing *himself* (9:26, Prop 27), by taking his *own blood*, not the blood of bulls and goats (9:12, Prop 26), into the *heavenly sanctuary*, not the earthly sanctuary (9:24).

10:11–14. Jesus' death accomplished what all other sacrifices had never accomplished, the complete removal of sin (10:12, Prop 28). The blood of animals might *cover* sins, thereby offering worshippers temporary respite from their consciences, yet such sacrifices could never *take away* sins (10:4). Otherwise, asks the author, "would they not have ceased being offered since the worshippers, cleansed once for all [time], would no longer have any consciousness of sin?" (10:2). When Christ came, his self-sacrifice served as a single, once-for-all-time removal of sins that "perfected for all time those who are sanctified" (10:1). Thus, Jesus stands in marked contrast to all those who served as high priests up until the time of Jesus. These priests never ran out of work; so they stood performing their high priestly duties day after day and year after year, "offering again and again the same sacrifices that [could] never take away sins" (10:11). Jesus, however, did sit down because his work was finished.

10:15–18. All of this is a fulfillment of the new covenant described in Jeremiah 31:31–34, which the LORD intended to establish with the houses of Israel and Judah after they had served their time in exile (Lent 5). Earlier in Hebrews 8:8–12, the author cited Jeremiah's new covenant prophecy in its entirety to demonstrate that a new and better covenant had already been envisioned in the OT. Here, the author returns to Jeremiah in order to highlight two features of the new covenant that Jesus as high priest fulfilled through his sacrificial death.

First, under the new covenant, the LORD says, "I will put my laws in their hearts, and I will write them on their minds" (10:16; Jer 31:33). Through his death, Jesus has "made perfect those who approach" to worship God (10:1; cf. 10:14), by cleansing them so thoroughly that they "no longer have any consciousness of sin" (10:2). With no consciousness of sin, they can worship God with their whole heart, which is the essence of the whole law. Thus, to have the law of God written on one's heart and mind corresponds to having one's heart emptied of any consciousness of sin.

Second, under the new covenant, the LORD says, "I will remember their sins and their lawless deeds no more" (10:17; Jer 31:34). This suggests a complete removal of sin, which as we have already seen, was accomplished through Christ's once-for-all-time, self-sacrifice. Thus, the author concludes, "Where there is forgiveness of these, there is no longer any offering for sin" (10:18).

10:19–25. The implications of our sins having been completely forgiven and of our consciences thoroughly cleansed of sin is that now there is nothing standing between us and God. We can now approach God without fear and with "a true heart in full assurance of faith" (10:22), confident of the fact that the death of our great high priest, Jesus, has opened for us a "new and living way" into the heavenly Holy of Holies where God and Jesus sit enthroned. When we have confidence in what Jesus has accomplished on our behalf, we no longer have to be preoccupied with the business of making ourselves right before God. Instead, we can focus our life and energies on loving and serving others, provoking "one another to love and good deeds,… meeting together,… and encouraging one another" (10:24–25).

Suggestions for Lectors

Just like last week's reading, the first part of today's reading offers a series of contrasts, so emphasize those words and expressions in order to highlight those contrasts for your listeners. For example, other priests perform their duties *day after day* and *again and again* because their sacrifices only offer temporary relief from sin (10:11). In contrast, Christ's sacrifice offered a permanent solution to the problem of human sin; all that was needed was a *single*, once *for all time* sacrifice for sin (10:12). Likewise, whereas other priests always *stand* because their duties are never ending, Christ *sat down* next to God because his work was finished.

If you are not reading 10:15–18, when you come to 10:14, slow down and read it more deliberately as you draw the first half of today's passage to a close. If 10:15–18 is to be read, then wait until 10:18 to slow down. In either case, pause for a full second afterwards before proceeding with 10:19–25, which has a different focus and tenor.

The second half is filled with first person pronouns (*we, us, our*), so adopt a tone of voice and a manner of expression that indicates that you belong to and identify with the people to whom you are speaking. Soften your voice a bit and read with more feeling; after all, you address your listeners as *my friends.*

Watch out for the two lengthy sentences (10:19–22, 24–25). Using well-placed pauses and variations in intonation, practice reading these sentences until you are able to hold each together and present each as a single thought to your listeners.

MARK 13:1–8

Notes
Sequence. 12 of 12

Commentary
In the late seventh or early sixth century B.C., prior to the Babylonian exile, the prophet Jeremiah purchased an earthenware jug from a local potter. Then, taking along some of the elders of the people and some of the senior priests, he took the jug into the temple courts and smashed it to pieces in their presence. This symbolic act dramatically foreshadowed the destruction that God had decreed for Jerusalem and the temple (Jer 19).

In Mark, Jesus also engages in a prophetic symbolic action in the temple. Following his triumphal entry into Jerusalem, Jesus enters the temple precincts and begins driving out the sellers and buyers and overturning the tables of the money changers (11:15–19). Citing the prophets, Jesus argues that the temple, which God intended to be "a house of prayer for all the nations" (Isa 56:7), has been turned into "a den of robbers" (Jer 7:11). By temporarily disrupting temple operations, Jesus dramatizes the fact that one day temple operations will cease altogether. In short, Jesus is predicting the temple's destruction. This interpretation is reinforced by the fact that prior to his demonstration in the temple, Jesus had cursed a fig tree because it was not bearing any fruit. After the demonstration, the disciples discover that the fig tree has withered; it will never produce fruit again. The message is simple. The temple is no longer serving its intended purpose; it is not bearing any fruit, and so it shall wither and die. Like Jeremiah's shattered jug, Jesus' symbolic actions foreshadow the destruction of the temple. In today's reading, Jesus speaks more plainly about the temple's destruction and the events that will signal the end of the present evil age and the arrival of the age to come.

13:1–3. As Jesus leaves the temple for the last time, his disciples express amazement about the grandeur of the temple complex with its massive stones and buildings. Jesus is not impressed. Since the temple is not fulfilling its God-ordained purpose, it will be destroyed. Its destruction will be thorough for "not one stone will be left hereupon another, all will be thrown down" (13:2). Within a generation, his predictions come true. In A.D. 70, the armies of Rome raze the Jerusalem temple as punishment for the First Jewish Revolt in A.D. 66.

13:4–8. Jesus' disciples ask him about when this destruction will take place and what signs will anticipate the arrival of the end of the age. Their question assumes that the destruction of the temple will coincide with the end of the age.

Jesus says that the signs will be numerous, yet ambiguous. People will falsely claim to be the Messiah. There will be news of wars and insurrections, yet these themselves are not the end. There will be political upheavals as nations and kingdoms rise up against one another. Even creation itself will experience upheaval in the form of earthquakes and famines. Yet again, these are not the end, merely the initial labor pains of the new age. As Jesus says later, "About that day or hour no one knows, neither the angels in heaven, nor the Son, but only the Father" (13:32). His counsel then is to "keep alert; for you do not know when the time will come" (13:33).

Suggestions for Lectors

When the disciples point out the magnificence and grandeur of the temple complex, they are filled with the exuberance and wonder of little children. Convey their excitement with your voice; smile and speak more quickly. Jesus, however, does not share their exuberance. He remains grieved and frustrated by the temple's failure to fulfill its vocation as a house of prayer for all nations. Moreover, he knows that the temple's days are numbered and that when destruction comes it will be total. Therefore, his words should be read in a grave tone of voice. Emphasize *one* and *all*, with a slight pause after *all*, as in: *Not one stone will be left upon another; all... will be thrown down* (13:2b).

Return to this grave tone of voice when Jesus describes the sorts of things that will take place as the end draws near. Emphasize Jesus' two commands: *Beware that no one leads you astray* (10:5) and *do not be alarmed* (10:7). Also, highlight the two statements that imply the need for patience and endurance: *but the end is still to come* (13:7) and *This is but the beginning of birth pangs* (13:8).

PROPER 29 — CHRIST THE KING

November 20–26

2 Samuel 23:1–7	Daniel 7:9–10, 13–14
Psalm 132:1–12, (13–18) (= 132:1–13, (14–19) BCP)	Psalm 93
Revelation 1:4b–8	Revelation 1:4b–8
John 18:33–37	John 18:33–37

2 SAMUEL 23:1–7

Commentary

King David was the most celebrated king within ancient Israel, the king by which all other kings were measured. In today's reading, we are treated to the last words of this great king. These last words are described as an oracle, a prophetic utterance from God. And like most oracles, it is lyrical in form.

23:1. The reading begins by describing who David is. David is not only identified by his patronymic, "son of Jesse," he is also identified as one who has been exalted, anointed, and favored by God. God himself is also variously identified as "God," "the God of Jacob," and "the Strong One of Israel". This last descriptor, *the Strong One of Israel,* reminds God's people who Israel's champion really is. David may have been the king who led Israel into battle, yet it was God who delivered his people from their enemies.

23:2–4. Thus, the oracle begins with David's recognition that it is the spirit of the LORD who speaks through him and works through him. Here we are reminded of the time when the prophet Samuel sought out this youngest son of Jesse and anointed him as king over Israel. "Then Samuel took the horn of oil, and anointed him in the presence of his brothers; and the spirit of the LORD came mightily upon David from that day forward" (1 Sam 16:13a, Prop 6).

The spirit of the LORD does not simply empower Israel's kings to defeat their enemies but equips them to rule over God's people justly, to establish and maintain a just and righteous society by exercising royal authority on behalf of the poor, the weak, the powerless, the marginalized, and the afflicted. As the psalmist prays in Psalm 72:1–4:

> Give the king your justice, O God,
>   and your righteousness to a king's son.
> May he judge your people with righteousness,
>   and your poor with justice.
> May the mountains yield prosperity for the people,
>   and the hills, in righteousness.
> May he defend the cause of the poor of the people,
>   give deliverance to the needy, and crush the oppressor.

When a leader truly rules as God's agent, then the glory of the LORD is shown forth in all of creation. It can be likened to the glory of the glistening dew on a bright and clear morning.

23:5–7. The oracle concludes with David reminding us of the commitment that God has made, a commitment that is designed to give God's people a sense of security. Not only did the LORD make David king, the LORD also promised to make David's offspring kings after him… for forever (2 Sam 7:1–16, Adv 4, Prop 11). This is a great privilege but an even greater responsibility. The LORD's promise to David may be unconditional but it is not without its obligations. The king is expected to be singularly devoted to the LORD and to rule justly. If the Davidic kings act in godless ways, then they will be severely disciplined (2 Sam 7:14–15).

Suggestions for Lectors

Today's reading comes with its own introduction (23:1). Read the four descriptions of David as though you are listing his accomplishments. Let each one stand on its own.

The most important line in the reading is the first line of the oracle: *The spirit of the LORD speaks through me, his word is upon my tongue* (23:2). Pause for a second before this line, then deliver it slowly with great confidence and conviction. Remember, as a lector, you are not simply passing on David's words; instead, you are David himself, and you are delivering your own oracle.

In 23:5, increase the intensity and pitch of your voice as David asks rhetorical questions and announces the covenant that God made with him. Then, drop your voice for 23:6–7 in order to provide a contrast between David and the godless.

Pronunciation Guide
David (DAY-vid), *Israel* (IZ-ree-uhl; -ray-)
Jacob (JAY-kuhb), *Jesse* (JES-ee)

DANIEL 7:9–10, 13–14

Notes
Sequence. 2 of 2

Commentary
As was mentioned in the Commentary for last week's reading, Daniel was one of the Judean exiles transported to Babylon in 597 B.C. While there, Daniel rises to prominence in the Babylonian administration, in large part because he has the gift for interpreting dreams and visions. In the second half of the book (chapters 7–12), Daniel receives three visions, each of which is concerned with world politics and the coming of God's kingdom. Today's reading is taken from the first vision (7:1–28).

In this vision, Daniel sees four beasts arising out of the sea. The beasts are described in some detail, each seemingly more terrifying than the former, especially the fourth beast. Later, Daniel discovers that these beasts represent four kings (7:17) and four kingdoms (7:23). The fact that a beast represents a single individual and a kingdom at the same time demonstrates just how fluid the language and imagery of such visions can be. In coming out of the sea (vs. the land), the beasts are to be understood as representing *Gentile* kings and kingdoms.

7:9–10. In the midst of this beastly night vision, Daniel witnesses another scene, in which preparations for a trial are made. Thrones are put in place, and the first of these becomes occupied by the judge, the Lord God Almighty, described here as the Ancient One (a.k.a., the Ancient of Days).

7:13–14. Into this scene, Daniel sees one like a human being (literally, one like a son of man) coming with the clouds of heaven. Though this figure is not described as taking a throne, this seems to be implied. Not only is there at least one more throne available, but this figure is granted exclusive and absolute divine authority over all the peoples and nations of the world. Moreover, his kingship and the kingdom over which he rules is eternal, never to be destroyed.

The description of this solitary figure is so powerful and vivid that the reader might easily assume that he only represents a single individual, yet even here we see some fluidity in the language and imagery. Daniel is told afterward that "the holy *ones* of the Most High shall receive the kingdom and possess the kingdom forever—forever and ever" (7:17) and later that "the kingship and dominion and the greatness of the kingdoms under the whole heaven shall be given to the *people* of the holy *ones* of the Most High" (7:27). In the end, the son of man functions in the same manner as the four beasts, namely, he represents both the kingdom of God's people and the king that rules over them. The son of man is both *Israel* and the one *Israelite*—the Messiah—whom the LORD will send to rule over his people, to free them from their enemies, and to equip them to fulfill their vocation to be the light of the world, the image-bearers of God in creation.

Suggestions for Lectors

In today's reading, Daniel describes a scene that no other human being has witnessed. As the lector, imagine that you are Daniel, and seek to convey the wonder and mystery of what you have seen. Do not read quickly; instead read slowly and deliberately, relishing and reveling in the description of what his taking place. Construct the scene for your listeners piece by piece—first the thrones, then the Ancient One, then the thousand thousands, the court, and the books.

The reading falls into two sections (7:9–10; 7:13–14). Each section begins with the same three words, *As I watched.* Pause for a second or two between these sections. In the second section, after saying, *As I watched in the night visions*, you may wish to tilt your head to one side and briefly glance skyward, as you recall seeing the *one like a human being coming with the clouds of heaven.*

Midway through 7:14, beginning with *His dominion*, description is replaced by proclamation as Daniel declares the eternal nature of the kingdom that the one like a human being received. Alter the your tone of voice as you deliver these words to your listeners. Highlight *everlasting* and *never*, and pause after *never* as you draw the reading to a close.

REVELATION 1:4B–8

Commentary

As its name implies, the book of Revelation belongs to a genre of ancient literature that was intended to *reveal* something that had hitherto been unknown or undisclosed. Another name for Revelation is the Apocalypse of St. John. In Greek, an *apocalypse* is an uncovering, a disclosure, or a revelation. In this instance, Revelation discloses God's ultimate purposes for creation: the conversion of all nations to the worship of the one true God; God's final victory over evil, violence, and Satan; and the establishment of a new heavens and a new earth. Revelation also discloses *how* these purposes will be brought about by God and specifically highlights the role that Christians, as followers of the slaughtered Lamb, are expected to play. Consequently, Revelation takes the form of a first-century circular letter addressed to seven churches in the Roman province of Asia (1:4a, 11).

1:4b–8. John addresses the seven churches in Asia with a standard Christian greeting, "Grace to you and peace from…" (1:4b; cf. Rom 1:7b), which is then followed by a series of descriptions in which each person of the Trinity is mentioned (1:4b–5a). The attention then shifts to Jesus, what he accomplished in his first coming (4:5b–6), and the announcement of his second coming (4:7).

Suggestions for Lectors

Read today's passage as though you are John addressing the seven churches of Asia Minor, making your voice as solemn and profound as you can manage. John packs a lot of information and theology into this brief passage, so make sure to enunciate each phrase. Allow yourself frequent pauses, including full-second pauses after each *Amen*, which occurs at the end of verses 6 and 7.

When you come to 1:7, let your voice ring out in this poetic verse as you proclaim the return of Jesus. Then, in 1:8, intone the words of God slowly and with less expression and intensity as a fitting conclusion to the reading.

Pronunciation Guide
Alpha (AL-fuh), *Omega* (oh-MAY-guh),
Revelation (rev'-uh-LAY-shuhn; *not* Revelations)

JOHN 18:33–37

Commentary
When Jesus is arrested, he is brought before the Jewish authorities. In John, he is brought before Annas and Caiaphas, who are both identified as high priests. Technically, only one high priest served at a time, and Caiaphas was the high priest that year (11:49; 18:12). Yet, Annas was Caiaphas' father-in-law, and he had reigned as high priest from A.D. 6–15. Clearly, he still occupied a position of power and authority, for Jesus was brought to him first (18:12–14). Annas questions Jesus about his disciples and his teaching, but nothing incriminating surfaces (18:19–23). Annas then sends Jesus to his son-in-law (18:24), but John offers no account of what took place before Caiaphas. In the morning, Jesus is delivered to Pilate (18:28).

Pontius Pilate held the office of prefect (or governor) of the Roman province of Judaea from A.D. 26–36. Though his official headquarters were located in the coastal town of Caesarea, Pilate resided in Jerusalem during Passover in order to oversee security and maintain order as tens of thousands of Jewish pilgrims made their way to Jerusalem to celebrate their national day of independence.

18:33–37. Clearly, Pilate has been informed that Jesus is the leader of a revolutionary movement, for the first question Pilate puts to Jesus is, "Are you the King of the Jews?" (18:33). To answer in the affirmative would necessitate death by crucifixion, a form of Roman punishment reserved for runaway slaves and insurrectionists. While Jesus never answers Pilate's question, he does eventually claim to be a king, albeit one who rules a kingdom that is not of this world. His mission is not to disrupt Roman rule and order—at least not in the way that Pilate might be thinking. Instead, he has come into the world as a witness to the truth. At this point, Pilate interjects with a rhetorical question, "What is truth?" (18:38).

Clearly Pilate does not expect an answer, and one is not forthcoming in the narrative. Instead, the question invites a response from the reader. Readers who have been attentive up to this point in the gospel not only know the correct answer but, more importantly, they know the correct *question*. The question is not, "*What* is truth?," but rather, "*Who* is the truth?" The answer, of course, is Jesus. As he once taught his disciples, "I am the way, and *the truth*, and the life. No one comes to the Father except through me" (14:6).

Suggestions for Lectors
Today's reading is driven by dialogue, so focus your preparation on delivering the lines of each character. Although Pilate is interviewing Jesus, Jesus controls the conversation. So present Jesus as calm and collected, and Pilate as spirited.

The first question Pilate asks is straightforward, *Are you the King of the Jews?* (18:33). But as the dialogue progresses, Pilate's questions and responses become more animated as he expresses incredulity and even sarcasm. So when you deliver Pilate's lines, increase the pitch and volume of your voice.

Pronunciation Guide

Pilate (PĪ-luht)

SCRIPTURE INDEX

ABBREVIATIONS

Adv	*Advent*
Asc	*Ascension Day*
AshW	*Ash Wednesday*
Chr	*Christmas*
East	*Easter*
EastEv	*Easter Evening*
EastVig	*Easter Vigil*
Epi	*Epiphany*
GFri	*Good Friday*
Lent	*Lent*
MThu	*Maundy Thursday*
Name	*Holy Name of Jesus*
Palm	*Palm Sunday*
Pent	*Pentecost*
PentVig	*Pentecost Vigil*
Prop	*Proper*
Tri	*Trinity Sunday*

OLD TESTAMENT

APOCRYPHA

NEW TESTAMENT

PRONUNCIATION

PRONUNCIATION KEY

1. Syllables with a primary accent are CAPITALIZED.
2. Syllables with a secondary accent are followed by an accent mark: '
3. To save space, alternative pronunciations have not always been given in full. For example, the entry *Beer-sheba* (beer'-SHEE-buh; bihr'-) indicates that *Beer-sheba* can be pronounced either beer'-SHEE-buh or bihr'-SHEE-buh.

VOWELS

a	c**a**t (short ă)
ah	f**a**ther
ahr	y**ar**d
ai	**air**
aw	j**aw**
ay	d**ay** (long ā)
e, eh	b**e**d (short ĕ)
ee	b**ee**d (long ē)
er	h**er**
ī	s**i**de (long ī)
i, ih	t**i**p (short ĭ)
ihr	f**ear**
o	h**o**t (short ŏ)
oh	b**o**ne (long ō)
oo	b**oo**t (long ū)
or	f**or**
ow	h**ow**
oy	t**oy**
u	p**u**t (short ŭ)
uh	**a**lone (schwa)
x^{uh}	barely pronounced

CONSONANTS

b	**b**ug	p	**p**ack
ch	**ch**in	r	**r**un
d	**d**o	s	**s**it
f	**f**un	sh	**sh**y
g	**g**et	t	**t**ie
h	**h**at	th	**th**in
hw	**wh**en	th	**th**at
j	**j**oin	tw	**tw**in
k	**k**ite	v	**v**ow
kw	**qu**een	w	**w**e
l	**l**ove	x	ve**x**
m	**m**at	y	**y**ard
n	**n**o	z	**z**ipper
ng	si**ng**	zh	vi**s**ion

COMPREHENSIVE PRONUNCIATION GUIDE

When a lectionary reading contains names or words that are potentially unfamiliar or difficult to pronounce, phonetic pronunciations are provided in the Pronunciation Guide for each reading just after the Suggestions for Lectors. The following Comprehensive Pronunciation Guide contains pronunciations for *all* the names that occur in Year B readings and the names of all biblical books, regardless of their difficulty.

A

Aaron (AIR-uhn)
Abana (uh-BAY-nuh; AB-uh-nuh)
Abba (AH-buh)
Abiathar (uh-BĪ-uh-thahr; ab-i-AY-thahr; *not* uh-BEE-)
Abinadab (uh-BIN-uh-dab)
Abishai (AB-uh-shī; uh-BĪ-shī)
Abner (AB-ner)
Abraham (AY-bruh-ham)
Abram (AY-bruhm)
Absalom (AB-suh-lahm; -luhm)
Achor (AY-kohr)
Adar (AY-dahr; ah-DAHR)
Ahasuerus (uh-hazh-yoo-EHR-uhs)
Ahio (uh-HĪ-oh)
Alexander (al'-ig-ZAN-duhr; -ZAHN-)
Alpha (AL-fuh)
Alphaeus (al-FEE-uhs)
Amalekite (uh-MAL-uh-kīt)
Amaziah (am'-uh-ZĪ-ah)
Amen (AY-men'; ah-MEN)
Ammonite (AM-uhn-īt)
Amorite (AM-or-īt)
Amos (AY-muhs)
Andrew (AN-droo)
Anna (AN-uh)
Annas (AN-uhs)
Apollos (uh-POL-uhs; -ohs)
apostle (uh-PAH-s^uh^l)
Arab (AIR-uhb)
Aram (AIR-uhm)
Aramean (air'-uh-MEE-uhn)
Archelaus (ahr'-kuh-LAY-uhs)
Arimathea (air'-uh-muh-THEE-uh)
Asher (ASH-uhr)
Ashkelon (ASH-kuh-lon)
Asia (AY-zhuh)
Augustus (uh-GUHS-tuhs; aw-)
Azotus (uh-ZOH-tuhs)

B

Baal (BAY-uhl)
Baal-shalishah (bayl-SHAL-i-shuh)
Baale-judah (bayl-uh-JOO-duh)
Baals (BAY-uhlz)
Babel (BA-buhl; BAY-buhl)
Barabbas (bah-RA-buhs; bahr-AB-uhs)
Barsabbas (BAHR-suh-buhs; *not* bahr-SAB-buhs)
Bartimaeus (bahr-tuh-MEE-uhs)
Baruch (bah-ROOK)
Bathsheba (bath-SHEE-buh)
Beelzebul (bee-EL-zih-buhl; -zuh-)
Beer-sheba (beer'-SHEE-buh; bihr'-)
beloved (n., buh-LUV-uhd)
Bethany (BETH-uh-nee)
Bethel (BETH-uhl)
Bethlehem (BETH-luh-hem')
Bethlehemite (BETH-lih-hem-īt; BETH-lih-heh-mīt)
Bethphage (BETH-fuh-jee; BETH-fayj)
Bethsaida (beth-SAY-uh-duh)
bitumen (bih-TOO-muhn; -tyoo-)
blessed (adj., two syllables; BLES-id)
blessed (vb., one syllable; BLEST)
Boaz (BOH-az)
bulrush (BOOL-ruhsh)

C

Caesarea (ses'-uh-REE-uh; sez'-; seez'-)
Caiaphas (KĪ-uh-fuhs; KAY-uh-fuhs)
Canaan (KAY-nuhn)
Candace (KAN-duh-see; kan-DAY-see; *not* KAN-duhs)
Capernaum (kuh-PER-nay-uhm; -nuh-)
Cappadocia (kap'-uh-DOH-shuh)
centurion (sen-CHUR-ee-uhn)
Cephas (SEE-phus)
cherubim (CHEHR-uh-bim'; -oo-)
Chilion (KIL-ee-uhn; -on)
Christ (KRĪST)
Cleopas (KLEE-oh-puhs)
Clopas (KLOH-puhs)
cohort (KOH-hawrt)
Colossians (kuh-LOSH-uhnz)
Corinth (KOR-inth; KAHR-inth; *not* koh-RINTH)
Corinthians (kuh-RIN-thee-uhnz)
Cretan (KREET-uhn)
cubit (KYOO-buht)
Cushite (KUSH-īt)
Cyrene (sī-REE-nee; *not* sī-REEN)

D

Damascus (duh-MAS-kuhs)
Dan (DAN)
Daniel (DAN-yuhl)
David (DAY-vid)
Decapolis (dih-KAP-uh-lis; dee-)
Deuteronomy (doo'-tuh-RON-uh-mee)
distaff (DIS-taf; DIS-tahf)

E

Ecclesiastes (e-klee'-zee-AS-teez)
Eden (EE-d^{uh}n; EE-duhn)
Edom (EE-duhm)
Egypt (EE-jipt)
Egyptian (ih-JIP-shuhn; ee-JIP-shuhn)
Elah (EE-luh)
Elamite (EE-luh-mīt)
Eldad (EL-dad)
Eli (EE-lī)
Eliab (ee-LĪ-uhb)
Eliam (ee-LĪ-uhm)
Elihu (ee-LĪ-hoo; ih-LĪ-hoo)
Elijah (ee-LĪ-juh; ih-LĪ-juh)
Elimelech (ee-LIM-uh-lek; ih-)
Elisha (ee-LĪ-shuh; ih-LĪ-shuh)
Elkanah (el-KAY-nuh)
Eloi (EE-loi; ee-LOH-ī)
Emmaus (eh-MAY-uhs; ih-MAY-uhs)
Ephah (EE-fah)
Ephesians (eh-FEE-zhuhnz; ih-)
Ephesus (EF-uh-suhs; EH-fuh-suhs)
ephod (EE-fod)
Ephphatha (EF-uh-thuh; ef-AH-thuh)
Ephraim (EE-free-uhm)
Ephraimite (EE-fra-ihm-īt)
Ephrathite (EF-ruh-thīt; EF-rath-īt)
Esther (ES-tuhr)
Ethiopian (ee'-thee-OH-pee-uhn)
eunuch (YOO-nuhk; YOO-nik)
Exodus (EK-suh-duhs)
Ezekiel (ee-ZEE-kee-uhl; ee-ZEE-kyuhl)
Ezra (EZ-ruh)

F

frankincense (FRANG-kin-sens)

G

Gabbatha (GAB-uh-thuh)
Gabriel (GAY-bree-uhl; *not* GAB-ree-el')
Galatians (guh-LAY-shuhnz)
Galilean (gal'-uh-LEE-uhn)
Galilee (GAL-uh-lee)
Gath (GATH)
Gaza (GAH-zuh; GAY-zuh)
Genesis (JEN-uh-sis)
Gennesaret (gih-NEH-suh-ret')
Gentile (JEN-tīl)
Gethsemane (geth-SEM-uh-nee; geth-SEH-muh-nee)
Gibeah (GIB-ee-uh)
Gibeon (GIB-ee-uhn)

Gilboa (gil-BOH-uh)
Gilgal (GIL-gal)
Golgotha (GOL-guh-thuh; gol-GOTH-uh)
Goliath (guh-LĪ-uhth; goh-)
Greek (GREEK)

H

Habakkuk (huh-BAK-uhk)
Hades (HAY-deez)
Haggai (HAG-ī; HAG-ee-ī)
Ham (HAM)
Haman (HAY-muhn)
Hannah (HAN-uh)
Harbona (hahr-BOH-nuh)
Hebrews (HEE-brooz)
Hebron (HEE-bruhn; HEE-bron)
Herod (HAIR-uhd)
Herodian (hih-ROH-dee-uhn)
Herodias (hih-ROH-dee-uhs; hehr-oh-DĪ-uhs)
Hezekiah (hez'-uh-KĪ-ah)
Hittite (HIH-tīt)
Ho (HOH)
Hophni (HOF-nī; HOF-nee)
Hor (HOR)
Horeb (HOR-uhb; HOH-reb)
Hosanna (hoh-ZAN-nuh; -ZAHN-)
Hosea (hoh-ZAY-uh)

I

Isaac (Ī-zik)
Isaiah (Ī-ZAY-ah)
Iscariot (is-KAIR-ee-uht)
Israel (IZ-ree-uhl; -ray-)
Israelite (IZ-ree-līt)
Ittai (IT-ī)

J

Jacob (JAY-kuhb)
Jairus (JĪ-ruhs; JAY-uh-ruhs)
James (JAYMZ)
Japheth (JAY-fuhth)
Jashar (JAY-shuhr)
Jemimah (juh-MĪ-muh)
Jeremiah (jair'-uh-MĪ-uh)
Jericho (JAIR-ih-koh; JAIR-uh-koh)
Jeroboam (jair'-uh-BOH-uhm)
Jeroham (juh-ROH-huhm)
Jerusalem (juh-ROO-suh-luhm)
Jesse (JES-ee)
Jesus (JEE-zuhs)
Jew (JOO)
Jewish (JOO-ish)
Joab (JOH-ab)
Job (JOHB; *not* JAWB)
Joel (JOH-uhl; JOHL)
John (JAHN; JON)
Jonah (JOH-nuh)
Jonathan (JAHN-uh-thuhn; JON-)
Jordan (JOR-duhn)
Joseph (JOH-sif; JOH-suhf)
Joses (JOH-seez; JOH-zehz)
Joshua (JOSH-yoo-uh)
Judah (JOO-duh)
Judas (JOO-duhs)
Jude (JOOD)
Judea (joo-DEE-uh; joo-DAY-uh)
Judean (joo-DEE-uhn; joo-DAY-uhn)
Justus (JUS-tuhs)

K

Keren-happuch (kehr'-uhn-HAP-uk)
Keziah (kuh-ZĪ-uh; kih-ZĪ-uh)
Kidron (KID-rahn; KID-ruhn)

L

Lamentations (lam'-uhn-TAY-shuhnz)
lema (LAY-muh)
Levi (LEE-vī)
Levite (LEE-vīt)
Leviticus (luh-VIT-ih-kuhs)
Libya (LIB-ee-uh; LIB-yuh)
lintel (LIN-t^{uh}l)
Luke (LOOK)
lyre (LĪ-^{uh}r)

M

Magdalene (MAG-duh-leen; -lee-nuh)
Mahlon (MAH-lohn; -luhn)
Malachi (MAL-uh-kī)
Malchus (MAL-kuhs)
manna (MAN-uh)
Mark (MAHRK)
Mary (MAIR-ee)
Matthew (MATH-yoo)
Matthias (muh-THĪ-uhs)
Medad (MEE-dad)
Medes (MEEDZ)
Melchizedek (mel-KIZ-uh-dek)
Mesopotamia (mes'-oh-puh-TAY-mee-uh)
Messiah (muh-SĪ-uh)
Micah (MĪ-kuh)
Michael (MĪ-kuhl)
Michal (MĪ-kuhl; MEE-kal)
Midian (MID-ee-uhn)
Millo (MIL-oh)
Miriam (MIR-ee-uhm)
Moab (MOH-ab)
Moabite (MOH-uh-bīt)
Mordecai (MOR-duh-kī)
Moriah (moh-RĪ-uh)
Moses (MOH-zuhs)
myrrh (MER)

N

Naaman (NAY-uh-muhn)
Nahum (NAY-uhm)
Naomi (NAY-oh-mee; nay-OH-mee)
Nathan (NAY-thuhn)
Nazareth (NAZ-uh-reth; *not* -rus)
nazarite (NAZ-uh-rīt)
Nazorean (NAZ-or-ee-uhn)
Nehemiah (nee'-uh-MĪ-uh)
Nicodemus (nik'-uh-DEE-muhs)
Nineveh (NIN-uh-vuh)
Noah (NOH-uh)
Nun (NUN)

O

Obadiah (oh'-buh-DĪ-uh)
Obed (OH-bid)
Obed-edom (OH-bid-EE-duhm)
Olives (OL-ihvz)
Omega (oh-MAY-guh)
Orpha (OR-puh; *not* OH-pruh)

P

Pamphylia (pam-FIL-ee-uh)
Paradise (PAIR-uh-dīs)
Parthian (PAHR-thee-uhn)
paschal (PAS-kuhl)
Paul (PAWL)
Peninnah (pih-NIN-uh; -ah)
Pentecost (PEN-tuh-kost)
Peter (PEE-ter)
Phanuel (FAN-yoo-uhl; fuh-NOO-uhl)
Pharaoh (FAY-roh; FAIR-oh)
Pharisee (FAIR-uh-see)
Pharpar (FAHR-pahr)
Philemon (fī-LEE-muhn)
Philip (FIL-ip)
Philippi (FIL-uh-pī; fih-LIP-ī)
Philippians (fih-LIH-pee-uhnz)
Philistine (FIL-ih-steen)
Phinehas (FIN-ee-uhs; -huhs)
Phrygia (FRIHJ-ee-uh)
Pilate (PĪ-luht)
Pontus (PON-tuhs)
potsherd (POT-sherd)
prophecy (n., PRAH-fuh-see)
prophesy (vb., PRAH-fuh-sī)
proselyte (PRAH-suh-līt)
Proverbs (PRAH-verbz)
Psalms (SAHLMZ)

Q

Quirinius (kwih-RIN-ee-uhs; kwuh-)

R

Rabbah (RAB-uh)
rabbi (RAB-bī)
Rabbouni (rab-BOH-nī; -nee)
Rachel (RAY-chuhl)
Ramah (RAY-muh)
Ramathaim (ray-muh-THAY-uhm)
Rephidim (REF-uh-dim)
Revelation (rev'-uh-LAY-shuhn;
not Revelations)
Romans (ROH-muhnz)
Rufus (ROO-fuhs)
Ruth (ROOTH)

S

sabachthani (sah-bahk-TAH-nee;
suh-BAK-thuh-nī)
sabbath (SAB-uhth)
Salome (suh-LOH-mee)
Samaria (suh-MAIR-ee-uh)
Samuel (SAM-yoo-uhl; SAM-yuhl)
Sarah (SAIR-uh)
Sarai (SAIR-ī)
Satan (SAY-tuhn)
Saul (SAWL; rhymes with Paul)
seraph (SAIR-af; SAIR-uhf)
Shammah (SHAM-uh)
Sheba (SHE-buh)
Shechem (SHEH-kem; SHEE-kuhm)
shekel (SHEK-uhl)
Shem (SHEM)
Shiloh (SHĪ-loh)
Shinar (SHĪ-nahr)
Sidon (SĪ-duhn)
Silvanus (sil-VAY-nuhs)
Simeon (SIM-ee-uhn)
Simon (SĪ-muhn)
Sinai (SĪ-nī; SĪ-nee-ī)
Sirach (SĪ-rak)
Solomon (SAH-luh-muhn; SOL-)
Syria (SIHR-ee-uh)
Syrophoenician (sī-roh-fuh-NEE'-shuhn;
sī-roh-fuh-NISH'-uhn)

T

Talitha cum (TAL-ih-thuh KOOM)
terebinth (TAIR-uh-binth)
Theophilus (thee-OFF-ih-luhs)
Thessalonians (thes'-uh-LOH-nee-uhnz)
Tiberias (tī-BIHR-ee-uhs)
Timaeus (tih-MEE-uhs)
Timothy (TIM-uh-thee; -oh-)
Titus (TĪ-tuhs)
Tohu (TOH-hoo)
Tyre (TĪR)

U

Uriah (yoo-RĪ-ah)
Uz (UZ)
Uzzah (UZ-uh)
Uzziah (u-ZĪ-ah; *not* yoo-ZĪ-ah)

Z

Zarephath (ZAIR-uh-fath)
Zebedee (ZEB-uh-dee)
Zechariah (zek'-uh-RĪ-uh)
Zephaniah (zef'-uh-NĪ-uh)
Ziklag (ZIK-lag)
Zion (ZĪ-uhn)
Zuph (ZOOF)
Zuphite (ZOOF-īt)

Additional Praise

"Dr. Blakley provides an invaluable resource for the Church. With masterful brevity and just the right amount of scholarship, he locates the assigned text within its literary context, the biblical narrative, and the liturgical theme of the day. After identifying the salient thoughts, he prudently suggests where and how to bring the text alive for the Church. Finally the scholar, the liturgist, the rhetorician, the lector, and the pew sitter are united! All of our lectors will have a copy. Bless you, Ted, for you have blessed us."

Jim Clark
Rector, Saint Barnabas on the Desert Episcopal Parish; Scottsdale, Arizona
Author of *The Art of Engaging Holy Scripture Study Series*

"The Lector's Guide and Commentary is an amazing gift to those of us who preach, teach and read the Scriptures in worship. The most difficult task of the scholar is to be succinct yet thorough, and Dr. Blakley has done this. In the Introduction, he says his aim is 'to make the Bible accessible so that people might more easily enter into the biblical narrative and be encountered by the God of the Bible.' An ambitious goal, but one that the book accomplishes. In addition, the pronunciation guide is a great help to those of us who, even after years of study, struggle to say strange names and places correctly. This book is a blessing in so many ways."

James Bryan Smith
Assistant Professor of Theology, Friends University; Wichita, Kansas
Author of several books in Christian spirituality, including The Apprentice Series

Additional Praise

"It is a wonderful privilege to belong to a church that uses a lectionary rather than relying on a narrow range of scriptures chosen by the pastor, but the other side of the privilege is that we read all sorts of passages without being sure what they are about. It is a huge privilege to read scripture in church, and these introductions will help readers do so in a way that brings the passage home to the people. They will help preachers too."

John Goldingay
Professor of Old Testament, Fuller Theological Seminary; Pasadena, California
Author of *The Old Testament for Everyone* Commentary Series

"Why is it that when we proclaim THE WORD OF THE LORD following a scripture reading in worship, it sounds so implausible?

It is because the church—across denominations—has slipped into such bad habits for reading and presenting the scriptural text aloud, that it scarcely sounds like anything God would say. How could the Word of God be as boring as we make it out to be? What is needed are guides for reading that will help our lectors restore the life and meaning to the texts we read each Sunday.

J. Ted Blakley has given us another of his helpful lector guides. Readers will find material to understand each text in the commentary section and performance suggestions for reading the texts with understanding. This is an indispensable resource for congregations who follow the lectionary and desire to let people hear and understand THE WORD OF THE LORD."

Clayton J. Schmit
Professor of Preaching, Fuller Theological Seminary; Pasadena, California
Author of *Too Deep for Words: A Theology of Liturgical Expression*
and *Public Reading of Scripture: A Handbook*